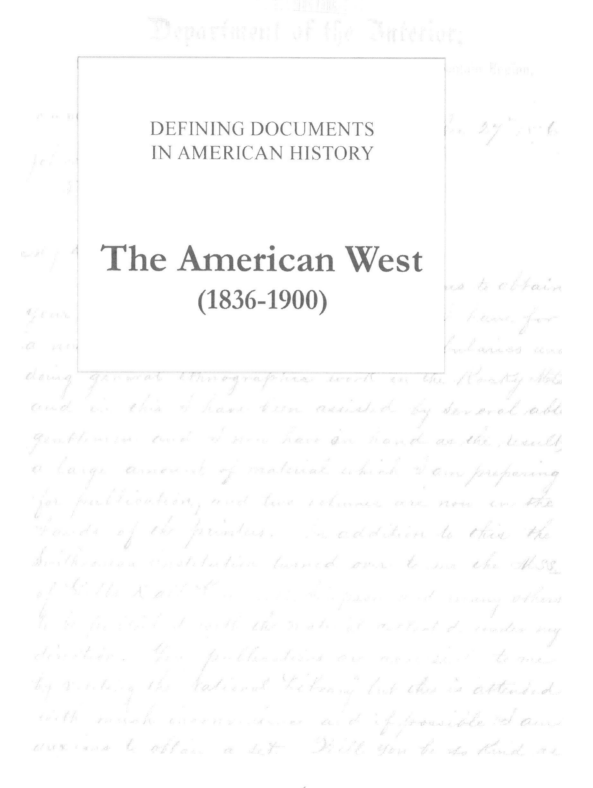

DEFINING DOCUMENTS
IN AMERICAN HISTORY

The American West
(1836-1900)

Library of Congress Cataloging-in-Publication Data

American West (1836-1900) / editor, Michael Shally-Jensen, PhD. -- [First edition].

    pages : illustrations ; cm. -- (Defining documents in American history)

    Includes bibliographical references and index.
    ISBN: 978-1-61925-533-3

    1. West (U.S.)--History--19th century--Sources. 2. United States—Territorial expansion--Sources. 3. Indians of North American--History--19th century--Sources. 4. Chinese Americans--West (U.S.)--History--19th century--Sources. 5. Frontier and pioneer life--West (U.S.)--History--19th century--Sources. 6. Nature conservation--West (U.S.)--History--19th century--Sources. I. Shally-Jensen, Michael. II. Series: Defining documents in American history (Salem Press)

F591 .A547 2015
978.02

FIRST PRINTING
PRINTED IN THE UNITED STATES OF AMERICA

Table of Contents

SHIFTING BORDERS

WESTWARD MOVEMENT

INDIAN WARS AND WOES

ASIAN AMERICAN AFFAIRS

COWBOYS AND OUTLAWS

ENVIRONMENTAL ACTIONS

BEYOND THE WEST

Appendixes

Publisher's Note

Defining Documents in American History series, produced by Salem Press, consists of a collection of essays on important historical documents by a diverse range of writers on a broad range of subjects in American history. *Defining Documents in American History: American West* surveys key documents produced from 1836-1900, organized under seven broad categories:

Shifting Borders
Westward Movement
Indian Wars and Woes
Asian American Affairs
Cowboys and Outlaws
Environmental Actions
Beyond the West

Historical documents provide a compelling view of this unique period of American history. Designed for high school and college students, the aim of the series is to advance historical document studies as an important activity in learning about history.

Essay Format

American West contains 45 primary source documents – many in their entirety. Each document is supported by a critical essay, written by historians and teachers, that includes a Summary Overview, Defining Moment, Author Biography, Document Analysis, and Essential Themes. Readers will appreciate the diversity of the collected texts, including journals, letters, speeches, political sermons, laws, government reports, and court cases, among other genres. An important feature of each essay is a close reading of the primary source that develops evidence of broader themes, such as author's rhetorical purpose, social or class position, point of view, and other relevant issues. In addition, essays are organized by section themes, listed above, highlighting major issues of the period, many of which extend across eras and continue to shape American life. Each section begins with a brief introduction that defines questions and problems underlying the subjects in the historical documents. A brief glossary included at the end of each document highlights keywords important in the study of the primary source. Each essay also includes a Bibliography and Additional Reading section for further research.

Several maps in the front matter of this work help visualize the western territories as they were created as well as Native American territory borders.

Appendixes

•**Chronological List** arranges all documents by year.

•**Web Resources** is an annotated list of web sites that offer valuable supplemental resources.

•**Bibliography** lists helpful articles and books for further study.

Contributors

Salem Press would like to extend its appreciation to all involved in the development and production of this work. The essays have been written and signed by scholars of history, humanities, and other disciplines related to the essay's topics. Without these expert contributions, a project of this nature would not be possible. A full list of contributor's names and affiliations appears in the front matter of this volume.

Editor's Introduction

The American West has a geography, history, and culture all its own. It has inspired legions of artists, writers, photographers, filmmakers, and historians to attempt to capture something of its essence and communicate the results to the wider world. The West has been the subject of the wildest speculations as to what it might hold for the future of the nation, just as it has been the site of some of the most devastating actions by commercial interests and government bodies. For every "amber wave of grain" rustling in the American consciousness, there has been, it seems, an equal and opposite unleasing of dark forces across the land.

The West, it might be argued, begins at the western edge of the Mississippi River Valley. That demarcation, however, would include much of what today is commonly understood to belong to the Midwestern United States (Missouri and Iowa, for example). Although, historically speaking, the Midwest was indeed once regarded as the West, for the period covered by the present volume (1836–1900) a different approach is needed. We identify the West as starting basically with the Great Plains region. More specifically, we point to the ninety-eighth meridian, which divides Texas, Oklahoma, Kansas, Nebraska, and the Dakotas into eastern and western portions. To the east lies a relatively moist section containing tall prairie grass, and to the west lies a relatively dry section containing short prairie grass. Rainfall in the western portion is generally below twenty inches per year, making regular crop production difficult or impossible. Past the Great Plains, we then encounter the vast expanse of the high plains and Rocky Mountains, followed by the Great Basin and Range area and, finally, the Pacific border states. All told, the West is comprised of seventeen states plus Alaska. During most of the period treated in this book, however, it consisted of just a few large "territories."

As for the human dimension, the West has long been a crossroads of cultures. A great many American Indian nations already inhabited the land when Spanish explorers and settlers first arrived from Mexico. Indeed, much of what is now the southwestern United States *was* Mexico at the time. From the East came people from European countries and, later, from the United States itself. From the Far East, or East Asia, came Chinese settlers to California, followed by Japanese. African Americans arrived in the West as soldiers and cowboys in the nineteenth century. In the Southwest, in particular, there was considerable blending of peoples and cultures. However, the encounters between racial and ethnic groups were not always peaceful; Indian wars, white hostility toward Hispanics and Asians, and other instances of racial violence attest to that. At the same time, ethnic diversity has profoundly shaped the West's social and cultural makeup and history.

Westward Movement

Between 1836 and 1900, the U.S. population surged westward in a series of migrational phases, each representing a more complex mixture of technology, economics, and social forces. Opportunity—or perceived opportunity—was the main draw that brought men and women from Europe and the eastern United States into the sparsely settled West. It was thought that nature's resources were so plentiful that settlers need only apply their muscles, smarts, and courage to improve themselves and their families' prospects. Opportunity was present in many different forms, and these accounted for the nature of the various migrational phases of settlement of the frontier region. In the earliest phase, there were trappers and fur traders who sought profit in the form of animal hides—from beaver pelts and deerskins to bear and buffalo hides. Close behind them came miners, searching the streams and mountain slopes for telltale signs of the presence of precious metals, especially gold and silver. Fortunes could be made at the prospecting trade, and many tried their hand at it. From the 1840s, as well, came caravans of covered wagons, filled with dreamers seeking fertile farmlands in distant Oregon and California. Although few in number, these travelers played critical roles in blazing trails and paving the way for later settlers.

The occupation of western lands might have proceeded at a relatively slow pace were it not for the discovery of gold in 1848 at a spot—Sutter's Mill—downstream from California's Sierra Nevada Mountains. Most of the tens of thousands of "forty-niners" who subsequently arrived on the scene failed to find riches there and so turned instead to farming or shopkeeping. They established a sufficient population base to allow California to win statehood in 1850. Others, not yet ready to give up prospecting, headed out of the state in search of wealth in Nevada, Arizona, Colorado, Wyoming, Idaho, Montana, and the Black Hills of South Dakota. Over the two decades after 1849, these remote mining camps bloomed into permanent settlements, as shops and services popped up, and farmers flocked in to buy supplies and food. The "boom towns" associated with gold mining could and did produce conditions of squalor. Yet, by the last quarter of the century, the geographically-scattered mining industry had come under the control of large capitalized companies that made use of heavy machinery and scores of employees, all connected to the industrialized East via the railroads.

Another significant environmental impact was made by the next group of settlers, the pioneer families who farmed the land. Impelled westward by a desire for economic improvement and the search for adventure, they viewed undeveloped spaces as the enemy of progress. To them, every rock or tree was a barrier between themselves and opportunity. Thus, they cut down the forests and broke up the prairie sod in order to build their cabins, raise their crops, and expand their holdings. When neighbors or social conflicts pressed in on them, they often chose to move on and begin the settlement process anew, selling their land to a second wave of farmers who came more fully equipped with capital and machinery. These latter, more permanent settlers would then complete the forest clearing and fence in their property, expand their homes, and build roads to connect their communities to the railroads and eastern markets. As commercial activity continued to grow, another group of frontier settlers appeared—the merchants, millers, blacksmiths, distillers, lawyers, and so on. Eventually, the presence of white settlers was evident throughout the backcountry.

About the same time as the miners and early settlers arrived, cattlemen came looking for fresh fields in which to fatten their expanding herds. The cattle industry in the West was based on the use of the open range as a pastureland. Concentrated between the years 1865 and 1890, ranching was also founded on the presence of the transcontinental railroad and its many feeder lines. From Texas, the main source of cattle production, herds were pushed north to the railroads over the Chisholm Trail and other paths. Decade by decade, though, the wire fences and plowed fields of the settler cut into the cattlemen's domain, driving the ranchers farther west and diminishing the open range. The ranchers fought back, generally unsuccessfully, using threats, guns, wire cutters, and lawsuits. Ultimately organized, the range cattle industry soon became big business, involving substantial capital investment and large corporate entities. The local slaughterhouse passed into history as large regional packinghouses arose to prepare and transport beef for the national market.

Indian Wars

The Indian Wars that took place in the West after the Civil War represented the end-phase of over 200 years of Indian-white conflict. They were carried out by the United States for three reasons: 1) to "pacify" a region in order to make it safe for whites; 2) to place Indians on reservations; and 3) to keep them there. The issue was largely economic, but also, in part, political. It was fueled by the encroachment of westward-migrating whites on traditional Indian lands, or hunting grounds, and by the unsavory conditions present on the reservations. The treaties of the 1860s, under which Native Americans were expected to reside on designated reservations while providing half of their food by hunting, were thoroughly undermined by the rapid pace at which the West was being developed. For virtually every promise written into a treaty, there was a new, contradictory fact on the ground: a gold find, a needed passage for whites, a tract of land ideal for railroad development, and so on. Most of the final Indian Wars unfolded in far-flung regions of the West: the Modoc War (1872–73), in northern California and southern Oregon; the Great Sioux War (1876–77), in the Black Hills; the Nez Perce War (1877), in northern Idaho and surrounding regions; the Bannock War (1878), in southern Idaho and northern Nevada; and the Apache Wars of the 1880s, in the Southwest. This is why the US campaign against Native peoples was also political; it was a means, simply, to clear the land of Indians and facilitate white possession of the continent, "from sea to shining sea." The last remaining Indian Territory (apart from the reservations) vanished in 1889, when the western half of what is now Oklahoma was declared available for land claims by incoming settlers.

Federal policy for addressing the "Indian question" had long included the goal of breaking up the tribes to speed the integration of Native Americans into general society. Not until passage of the Dawes Allotment Act (1887), however, was the legal status of "domestic dependent nation" with respect to Indian tribes abandoned in favor of allotting plots of reservation land to individual Indians. While, in practice, federal guardianship of American Indians remained in effect, by 1890 Indians came to be viewed quite differently by the American people. They were now their own agents, for better or for worse. Sales of lands quickened, and vast quantities passed into the hands of speculators and developers. The peopling of the "Last West," as the remaining western territories are sometimes called, brought several new states into the nation: North Dakota, South Dakota, Montana, and Washington in 1889; Idaho and Wyoming in 1890; Utah in 1896; Oklahoma in 1907; and New Mexico and Arizona in 1912. The railroads had much to do with this, as millions of acres of Indian lands were seized and sold cheaply to private interests.

As Roxanne Dunbar-Ortiz writes in her *Indigenous People's History of the United States*:

> Under the crust of that portion of Earth called the United States of America—"from California … to the Gulf Stream waters"—are interred the bones, villages, fields, and sacred objects of American Indians. They cry out for their stories to be heard through their descendants who carry the memories of how the country was founded and how it came to be as it is today.

Law and Order

From the mid-1860s, cattle ranching expanded dramatically across the western plains, and the cowboy reigned supreme. The cowboy was the rugged individualist par excellence, the American frontiersman on horseback. He was a trailblazer, a horse trader, a seat-of-the-pants naturalist, and a plainspoken follower of the cowboy code of ethics—which stated, among other things, that one must live each day with courage and that some things, such as one's reputation, are not for sale. The cowboy was, at the same time, a hard-living, hard-drinking, rather raw individual who occasionally skirted the law or took the law into his own hands.

Inevitably, the American West is described as a region of lawlessness and violence. Frontiersmen used guns for hunting and self-defense and made use of their fists, knives, and six-shooters to settle disputes. Settlers typically landed in the region before the hiring of officers of the peace or the creation of courts of law, and even when those two institutions of government were in place (along with a mayor) they could be sketchy affairs often prone to quid pro quo arrangements (i.e., money or favors in return for political deeds). Indian tribes, wary of white incursions into their homelands,

embarked on raids and acts of revenge at the edges of the settlements. Meanwhile, the settlers themselves practiced traditions of feuding, self-defense, and revenge—or what one could call vigilante law and order. With little structural pressure on the lawless minority of outlaws, criminals, and violent youths to conform, frontier violence was indeed inevitable.

Some settlers entered the western frontier with adequate experience in the eastern backwoods to enable them to adjust to almost any demand put upon them. Others came with virtually no preparation for the harsh conditions they encountered, and adjustment was hard or impossible. Thousands of migrants from eastern communities attempted to set themselves up directly in the Wild West only to experience all manner of frustration and heartbreak. Those who did last were often obliged to devise their own system of law and order, however faulty it may have been.

National Heritage

It is often remarked that the experience of the western frontier, over the two centuries during which it was an active frontier, left an indelible mark on the "American character." This has been the argument, at least since 1893, when historian Frederick Jackson Turner published his provocative paper "The Significance of the Frontier in American History." Since then, historians have sought to uphold or refute Turner's thesis. It is easy, of course, to see certain widely recognized national character traits, such as rugged individualism, self-sufficiency, and confidence in the face of the unknown as having their roots in the frontier experience. On the other hand, it should also be recognized that frontiersmen and -women could be provincial, barely literate, suspicious of outsiders, opinionated, possessive, and nationalistic. Turner seemed to recognize as much when he noted that Americans exemplify a kind of individualism that extends "beyond its proper bounds" and sometime show a "lack of highly developed civil spirit" in their actions. Still, Turner seems to have admired the "coarseness and strength" of the American character, claiming that it was the direct result of settlers having successfully conquered the frontier. That may be so, but today, we recognize many other influences as well.

—*Michael Shally-Jensen, PhD*

Bibliography and Additional Reading

Billington, Ray Allen. *Westward Expansion: A History of the American Frontier,* 5th ed. New York: Macmillan, 1982. Print.

Dunbar-Ortiz, Roxanne. *An Indigenous People's History of the United States*. Boston: Beacon Press, 2014. Print.

Lamar, Howard R., ed. *The New Encyclopedia of the American West*. New Haven: Yale UP, 1998. Print.

Tate, Michael L. *Indians and Immigrants: Encounters on the Overland Trails*. Norman: U of Oklahoma P, 2006. Print.

Wellman, Paul I. *A Dynasty of Western Outlaws*. Lincoln: U of Nebraska P, 1986. Print.

The West. Dir. Stephen Ives. PBS/WETA, 1996. Film.

Wooster, Robert. *The American Military Frontiers: The United States Army in the West, 1783–1900*. Albuquerque: U of New Mexico P, 2009. Print.

Contributors

Anna Accettola, MA
Stockton, CA

Michael P. Auerbach, MA
Marblehead ,MA

Steven L. Danver, PhD
Mesa Verde Publishing
Washougal, Washington

K.P. Dawes, MA
Chicago, IL

Jennifer L. Henderson Crane, PgDip
Fife, Scotland

Michael Shally-Jensen, PhD
Amherst, MA

Donald A. Watt, PhD
Middleton, ID

Maddie Weismann, MA
California State University, Los Angeles

Mark S. Joy, PhD
Jamestown University

Jennifer D. Henry. M.Ed.
Lancaster, PA

Wendy Rouse, PhD
San Jose State University

- Maps

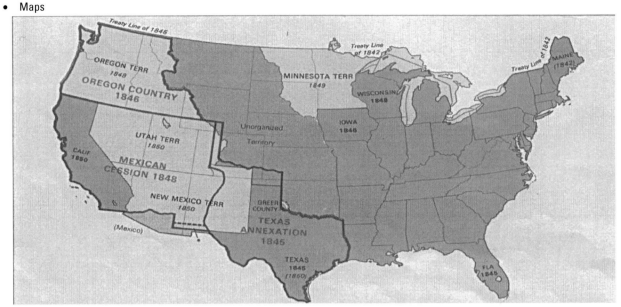

U.S. Territorial Growth Chart 1850: Courtesy of the University of Texas Libraries, The University of Texas at Austin.

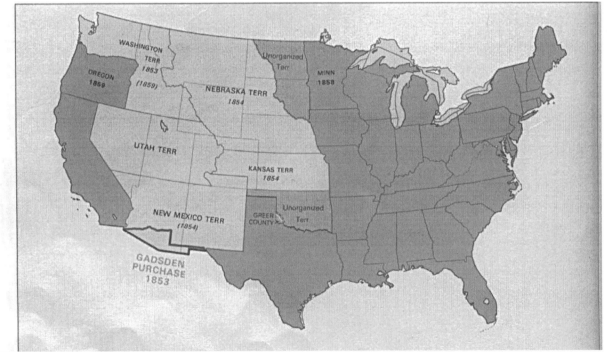

U.S. Territorial Growth Chart 1860: Courtesy of the University of Texas Libraries, The University of Texas at Austin.

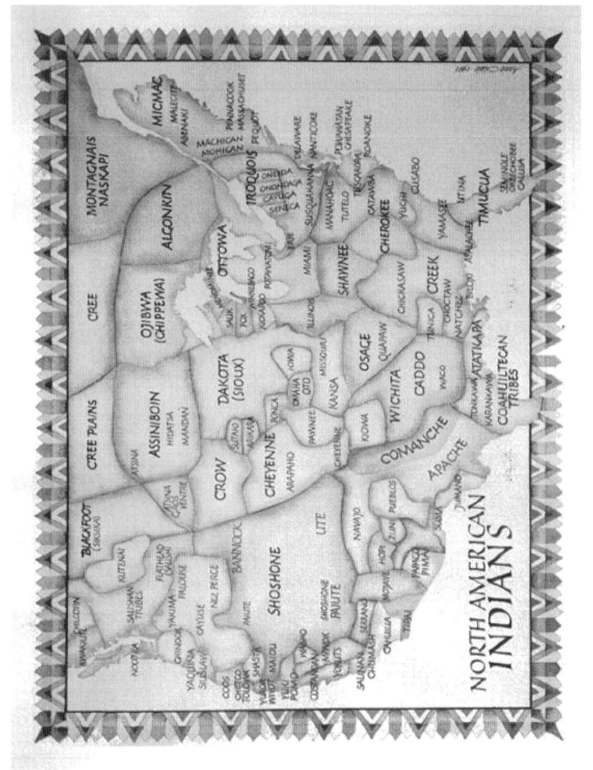

North American Indian Nations Map; Courtesy of Annie Cicale Graphic Design at www.cicaleletteringdesign.com

DEFINING DOCUMENTS
IN AMERICAN HISTORY

The American West
(1836-1900)

SHIFTING BORDERS

Before Texas was a state, or even a US territory, it was part of Mexico, the province of Coahuila Tejas. Mexico itself initially was a Spanish possession, New Spain, and after 1692 the Spanish Crown sent an army into the Rio Grande region and California to establish a buffer zone between New Spain and surrounding French, British, and Russian territories. Along with Catholic missions, the Spanish built forts there, including one in San Antonio (the Alamo) and one in San Francisco (the Presidio). By the early 1800s, however, the Spanish state was crumbling economically and politically, and Mexican nationalists, together with France, succeeded in ousting Spain and gaining independence (1821). A period of instability and internal conflict in Mexico ensued, during which Anglo settlers in Texas recruited more of their own with an eye toward setting up a free state, which they proclaimed in 1835. They established the independent Republic of Texas a year later, after a brief, but bloody, war with Mexico.

More white settlement in Texas followed. By the 1840s, Texas leaders were pressing for US statehood, and they achieved this through an act of Congress in 1845. However, the annexation of Texas riled Mexico, which—despite the interregnum of Texas's free-state status—still considered the province its own. War broke out between the United States and Mexico in 1846, lasting until 1848. The victor was the United States, which demanded additional territorial concessions from Mexico in the Treaty of Guadalupe Hidalgo (1848). With this treaty, not only Texas, but most of the rest of what is now the southwestern United States, including California, was ceded to the US government.

■ On Texas Independence

Date: March 7, 1836
Author: Stephen Austin
Genre: speech

Summary Overview

On March 7, 1836, Stephen F. Austin, the most successful empresario (one who recruited settlers) of Texan colonization, gave a speech in Louisville, Kentucky, imploring Americans to lend their support and assistance in Texas's quest for independence from Mexico. His speech was methodical, detailing the history of Mexican involvement with Texas, the desire to raise colonies of respectable citizens—to do so was a deterrent to invading Native American tribes such as the Comanche—and the escalating issues with the Mexican government, culminating in the denial of basic rights. On two occasions, Austin strategically reminds his audience of the similar feelings of oppression that drove their forefathers to revolt against Great Britain only sixty years before, thus recalling a central part of American history still within living memory. It is important to note that Austin was not asking for Texas to be admitted into the Union; rather, he was seeking the assistance of one nation for another in its quest for self-government.

Defining Moment

This speech of Stephen F. Austin's presents a powerful message, even to a modern reader. His words were written not in haste but with careful thought and preparation. There is much evidence to suggest he wished to represent Texas's pursuit for independence as thoroughly and honestly as possible; to this end, Austin was particular with dates and other details. Although not included below, found within the unabridged speech is a list of reasons Austin gave to prove that the Mexican government had failed in its federal duties to Texas and its people, principally the recent dissolution of the government by General Santa Anna. The following is an exceptionally emphatic example of Austin's message regarding this: "The people of Texas firmly adhered to the last moment, to the constitution which they and the whole nation had sworn to support. The government of Mexico have not—the party now in power have overturned the constitutional government and violated their oaths—they have separated from their obligations, from their duty and from the people of Texas; and, consequently, they are the true rebels." Although this section does not include a reference to the American Revolution, similarities may be drawn between the two conflicts. Governments have obligations to their constituents and, therefore, should be held responsible when they fail. For Austin, this particular failure could only be remedied by the secession of Texas.

The entirety of Austin's speech makes a number of references to the American Revolution; no doubt this was done specifically to generate sympathy for Texas's fight. Austin implored his listeners to recognize the justifiable reasons he and his people had for complete separation from Mexico, arguing that they, too, had been ill used by those in power and were no longer willing to endure it.

Author Biography

Stephen Fuller Austin, despite the many years that have passed since his death, is still fondly remembered and hallowed within the state of Texas, where he is popularly regarded as the father of the state. He was born in Virginia on November 3, 1793, to Moses and Maria Austin and was raised in Missouri. The career of Texan empresario was not the path Stephen chose for himself; rather, the vision of colonization throughout Texas was the dream of his father. Moses Austin, who originally dealt with the Spanish with regard to Texas, knew that Spain wished the land settled and had attempted to do so repeatedly in the past in order to "keep interlopers and Indians at bay and lend credibility to Spanish claims of possession" (Brands 21). Soon after permission for his colony was granted, Moses died, leaving his son Stephen in charge of carrying out his dream.

Settlement of Texas may not have been Stephen's life goal, but it was a promise to his father that he successfully fulfilled, despite tangles with the Mexican government after Mexico won its independence from Spain. In time, he came to hold his own vision for Texas, which included a capital city: "The Texas of his dreams was not a collection of isolated homesteads but a community of cooperating individuals and families" (Brands 91).

The last year of Austin's life—1836, the same year as his speech—saw the establishment of the Republic of Texas on March 2, followed the next month by the momentous victory against General Santa Anna at the Battle of San Jacinto. He passed away from pneumonia on December 27, 1836, at the age of forty-three. Sam Houston, a general of the Texan army and later the first president of the new republic, lamented, "The Father of Texas is no more! The first pioneer of the wilderness has departed!" (qtd. in Brands 478). Since his death, Stephen F. Austin has continued to be hailed throughout the land he led toward independence.

HISTORICAL DOCUMENT

It is with the most unfeigned and heartfelt gratitude that I appear before this enlightened audience, to thank the citizens of Louisville, as I do in the name of the people of Texas, for the kind and generous sympathy they have manifested in favor of the cause of that struggling country; and to make a plain statement of facts explanatory of the contest in which Texas is engaged with the Mexican Government.

The public has been informed, through the medium of the newspapers, that war exists between the people of Texas and the present government of Mexico. There are, however, many circumstances connected with this contest, its origin, its principles and objects which, perhaps, are not so generally known, and are indispensable to a full and proper elucidation of this subject.

When a people consider themselves compelled by circumstances or by oppression, to appeal to arms and resort to their natural rights, they necessarily submit their cause to the great tribunal of public opinion. The people of Texas, confident in the justice of their cause, fearlessly and cheerfully appeal to this tribunal. In doing this the first step is to show, as I trust I shall be able to do by a succinct statement of facts, that our cause is just, and is the cause of light and liberty:—the same holy cause for which our forefathers fought and bled:—the same that has an advocate in the bosom of every freeman, no matter in what country, or by what people it may be contended for.

But a few years back Texas was a wilderness, the home of the uncivilized and wandering Comanche and other tribes of Indians, who waged a constant warfare against the Spanish. These settlements at that time were limited to the small towns of Bexar, (commonly called San Antonio) and Goliad, situated on the western limits. The incursions of the Indians also extended beyond the Rio Bravo del Norta, and desolated that part of the country.

In order to restrain these savages and bring them into subjection, the government opened Texas for settlement. Foreign emigrants were invited and called to that country. American enterprise accepted the invitation and promptly responded to the call. The first colony of Americans or foreigners ever settled in Texas was by myself. It was commenced in 1821, under a permission to my father, Moses Austin, from the Spanish government previous to the Independence of Mexico, and has succeeded by surmounting those difficulties and dangers incident to all new and wilderness countries infested with hostile Indians. These difficulties were many and at times appalling, and can only be appreciated by the hardy pioneers of this western country, who have passed through similar scenes.

The question here naturally occurs, what inducements, what prospects, what hopes could have stimulated us, the pioneers and settlers of Texas, to remove from the midst of civilized society, to expatriate ourselves from this land of liberty, from this our native country, endeared to us as it was, and still is, and ever will be, by the ties of nativity, the reminiscences of childhood and youth and local attachments, of friendship and kindred? Can it for a moment be supposed that we severed all these ties—the ties of nature and of education, and went to Texas to grapple with the wilderness and with savage foes, merely from a spirit of wild and visionary adventure, without guarantees of protection for our persons and property and political rights? No, it cannot be believed. No American, no Englishman, no one of any nation who has a knowledge of the people of the United States, or of the prominent characteristics of the Anglo-Saxon race to which we belong—a race that in all ages and in all countries wherever it has appeared has been marked for a jealous and tenacious watchfulness of its liberties, and for a cautious and calculating view of the probable events of the future—no one who has a knowledge of this race can or will believe that we removed to Texas without such guarantees, as free born and enterprising men naturally expect and require.

The fact is, we had such guarantees; for, in the first place the government bound itself to protect us by the mere act of admitting us as citizens, on the general and long established principle, even in the dark ages, that protection and allegiance are reciprocal—a principle which in this enlightened age has been extended much further; for its received interpretation now is, that the object of government is the well being, security, and happiness of the governed, and that allegiance ceases whenever it is clear, evident, and palpable, that this object is in no respect effected.

But besides this general guarantee, we had others of a special, definite, and positive character—the colonization laws of 1823, '24, and '25, inviting emigrants generally to that country, especially guaranteed protection for person and property, and the right of citizenship.

When the federal system and constitution were adopted in 1824, and the former provinces became states, Texas, by her representative in the constituent congress, exercised the right which was claimed and exercised by all the provinces, of retaining within her own control, the rights and powers which appertained to her as one of the unities or distinct societies, which confederated together to form the federal republic of Mexico. But not possessing at that time sufficient population to become a state by herself, she was with her own consent, united provisionally with Coahuila, a neighbouring province or society, to form the state of COAHUILA AND TEXAS, "until Texas possessed the necessary elements to form a separate state of herself." I quote the words of the constitutional or organic act passed by the constituent congress of Mexico, on the 7th of May, 1824,

which establishes the state of Coahuila and Texas. This law, and the principles on which the Mexican federal compact was formed, gave to Texas a specific political existence, and vested in her inhabitants the special and well defined rights of self-government as a state of the Mexican confederation, so soon as she "possessed the necessary elements." Texas consented to the provisional union with Coahuila on the faith of this guarantee. It was therefore a solemn compact, which neither the state of Coahuila and Texas, nor the general government of Mexico, can change without the consent of the people of Texas.

In 1833 the people of Texas, after a full examination of their population and resources, and of the law and constitution, decided, in general convention elected for that purpose, that the period had arrived contemplated by said law and compact of 7th May, 1824, and that the country possessed the necessary elements to form a state separate from Coahuila. A respectful and humble petition was accordingly drawn up by this convention, addressed to the general congress of Mexico, praying for the admission of Texas into the Mexican confederation as a state. I had the honor of being appointed by the convention the commissioner or agent of Texas to take this petition to the city of Mexico, and present it to the government. I discharged this duty to the best of my feeble abilities, and, as I believed, in a respectful manner. Many months passed and nothing was done with the petition, except to refer it to a committee of congress, where it slept and was likely to sleep. I finally urged the just and constitutional claims of Texas to become a state in the most pressing manner, as I believed it to be my duty to do; representing also the necessity and good policy of this measure, owning to the almost total want of local government of any kind, the absolute want of a judiciary, the evident impossibility of being governed any longer by Coahuila, (for three fourths of the legislature were from there,) and the consequent anarchy and discontent that existed in Texas. It was my misfortune to offend the high authorities of the nation—my frank and honest exposition of the truth was construed into threats.

At this time (September and October, 1833,) a revolution was raging in many parts of the nation, and especially in the vicinity of the city of Mexico. I despaired of obtaining anything, and wrote to Texas, recommending to the people there to organize as a state de facto without waiting any longer. This letter may have been imprudent, as respects the injury it might do me personally, but how far it was criminal or treasonable, considering the revolutionary state of the whole nation, and the peculiar claims and necessities of Texas, impartial men must decide. It merely expressed an opinion. This letter found its way from San Antonio de Bexar, (where it was directed) to the government. I was arrested at Saltillo, two hundred leagues from Mexico, on my way home, taken back to that city and imprisoned one year, three months of the time in solitary confinement, without books or writing materials, in a dark dungeon of the former inquisition prison. At the close of the year I was released from confinement, but detained six months in the city on heavy bail. It was nine months after my arrest before I was officially informed of the charges against me, or furnished with a copy of them. The constitutional requisites were not observed, my constitutional rights as a citizen were violated, the people of Texas were outraged by this treatment of their commissioner, and their respectful, humble and just petition was disregarded.

These acts of the Mexican government, taken in connection with many others and with the general revolutionary situation of the interior of the republic, and the absolute want of local government in Texas, would have justified the people of Texas in organizing themselves as a State of the Mexican confederation, and if attacked for so doing in separating from Mexico. They would have been justifiable in doing this, because such acts were unjust, ruinous and oppressive, and because self-preservation required a local government in Texas suited to the situation and necessities of the country, and the character of its inhabitants. Our forefathers in '76 flew to arms for much less. They resisted a principle, "the theory of oppression," but in our case it was the reality—it was a denial of justice and of our guarantied rights—it was oppression itself.

Texas, however, even under these aggravated circumstances forbore and remained quiet. The constitution, although outraged and the sport of faction and revolution, still existed in name, and the people of Texas still looked to it with the hope that it would be sustained and executed, and the vested rights of Texas respected. I will now proceed to show how this hope was defeated by the total prostration of the constitution, the destruction of the federal system, and the dissolution of the federal compact.

It is well knows that Mexico has been in constant revolutions and confusion, with only a few short intervals, ever since its separation from Spain in 1821. This unfortunate state of things has been produced by the effects of the ecclesiastical and aristocratical party to oppose republicanism, overturn the federal system and constitution, and establish a monarchy, or a consolidated government of some kind.

In 1834, the President of the Republic, Gen. Santa Anna, who heretofore was the leader and champion of the republican party and system, became the head and leader of his former antagonists—the aristocratic and church party. With this accession of strength, this party triumphed. The constitutional general Congress of 1834, which was decidedly republican and federal, was dissolved in May of that year by a military order of the President before its constitutional term had expired. The council of government composed of half the Senate which, agreeably to the constitution, ought to have been installed the day after closing the session of Congress, was also dissolved; and a new, revolutionary, and unconstitutional Congress was convened by another military order of the President. This Congress met on the 1st of January, 1835. It was decidedly aristocratic, ecclesiastical and central in its politics. A number of petitions were presented to it from several towns and villages, praying that it would change the federal form of government and establish a central form. These petitions were all of a revolutionary character, and were called "pronunciamientos," or pronouncements for centralism. They were formed by partial and revolutionary meetings gotten up by the military and priests. Petitions in favour of the federal system and constitution, and protests against such revolutionary measures, were also sent in by the people and by some of the State Legislatures, who still retained firmness to express their opinions. The latter were disregarded and their authors persecuted and imprisoned. The former were considered sufficient to invest Congress with plenary powers. It accordingly, by a decree, deposed the constitutional Vice President, Gomez Farias, who was a leading federalist, without any impeachment or trial, or even the form of a trial, and elected another of their own party, Gen. Barragan, in his place. By another decree it united the Senate with the House of Representatives in one chamber, and thus constituted, it declared itself invested with full powers as a national convention. In accordance with these usurped powers, it proceeded to annul the federal constitution and system, and to establish a central or consolidated government.

How far it has progressed in the details of this new system is unknown to us. The decree of the 3d of October last, which fixes the outlines of the new government, is however sufficient to show that the federal system and compact is dissolved and centralism established. The States are converted into departments.

GLOSSARY

appertained: rightfully belonged

Bexar: short form of San Antonio's original name, San Antonio de Béxar

Gen. Barragan: Miguel Barragán (1789–1836), a Mexican general who also served as interim president

Gen. Santa Anna: Antonio López de Santa Anna (1794–1876), president of Mexico both before and after Barragán, best remembered for his infamous clash with the Texans at the Alamo

organic act: an act that institutes a fundamental aspect of government, such as establishing a territory

plenary: absolute and unchecked

Rio Bravo del Norta: the Mexican name for the Rio Grande, the river that forms the present-day border between Mexico and Texas

Document Analysis

Stephen F. Austin spoke before a crowd in Louisville, Kentucky, describing the plight of the newly declared Republic of Texas and making the case for its complete independence from Mexico. To him, the government of Mexico had no recourse to challenge the Texans' decision; in fact, the government's actions had precipitated the colonists' pursuit of freedom. The available resources make it difficult to determine who exactly made up the audience for this speech, but it is clear that Austin possessed a strong desire to set the record straight. He opened by saying, "The public has been informed, through the medium of the newspapers, that war exists between the people of Texas and the present government of Mexico"; although his speech then describes how this has been misconstrued, Texas was indeed at war with Mexico. A crucial event in Texan history had occurred the day before Austin gave this speech, though he made no references to it; it is unclear whether he had yet received news of the Battle of the Alamo.

The Alamo

The Alamo is an integral part of Texas, both its history and its culture. Originally a mission, the Alamo, also referred to as the Mission San Antonio de Valero, was for the Texan side a symbol of the battle lines in the ensuing conflicts with the Mexican army. For two of the three men most associated with its defense, there was mixed communication from the start as to what exactly to do with the old mission. James Bowie, under direction from General Sam Houston, was determined to destroy it before leaving, as he saw the Alamo as difficult to defend; however, his attitude soon changed. William Barret Travis wanted to defend the fort, but he, like Bowie before him, realized it held far too few men to do so. In a letter later echoed by pleas from Travis, Bowie wrote, "Our force is very small; the returns this day to the commandant is only hundred and twenty officers and men. . . . It would be a waste of men to put our brave little band against thousands" (qtd. in Brands 340). Bowie and Travis, who held joint leadership over those stationed at the Alamo, were severely outnumbered by Santa Anna and the Mexican army, which has been estimated at approximately five thousand troops.

In the end, the men defending the Alamo could not fend off the troops surrounding them. Historian Richard Flores details the scene at the old mission: "Upon arriving, Santa Anna orders the men in the Alamo to surrender. Unwilling to do so, Travis answers with a canon [sic] shot aimed at the Mexican forces" ("Alamo" 93). The men in the Alamo made their choice, and surrender was not an option. The final battle on March 6, 1836, saw the fall of approximately two hundred men, including Travis and Bowie, as well as the illustrious Davy Crockett. In his detailed account of Texas's fight against Mexico for freedom, historian H. W. Brands states that while Santa Anna proved his military might against the mission in San Antonio de Béxar that day, his success was a veneer, as it merely handed the Texans "a rallying cry that lifted their political struggle against Santa Anna to the moral realm. . . . Santa Anna's great blunder at Béxar was not to lose so many of his own men but to kill so many of the enemy (and after the battle to burn their bodies, which added to the sacrificial significance)" (378).

Texas from Wilderness to Colonization

Although hostilities with the Mexican army were known to Austin at the time of his speech, he chose instead to focus on what he and others had brought to the Mexican territory of Texas. He may have chosen this approach in order to present Texas's bid for independence as a measured decision, rather than as simply the result of provocation due to armed conflict. This approach lent more credibility to their cause, especially given Austin's past: he had led the first legal settlement within the territory; therefore, no one else possessed more authority to speak on the subject than he. In his speech, Austin said, "The government opened Texas for settlement. Foreign emigrants were invited and called to that country. American enterprise accepted the invitation and promptly responded to the call. The first colony of Americans or foreigners ever settled in Texas was by myself." Historian Sam W. Haynes writes that the Mexican government was highly interested and invested in empresarios bringing in settlers; each empresario was obligated to "bring at least one hundred families to settle the area within a six-year period," and to fulfill their mission, the empresarios were given vast land grants (57). In an effort to preserve heritage and cultural values, the government issued two stipulations that the settlers were to abide by and that, presumably, each individual empresario was required to enforce: they had to be Roman Catholics (or agree

to convert), and they had to become Mexican citizens. Given the generous endowments of land the Mexican government was offering in order to bring in a population, most were willing to adhere to these requirements. However, as time went on and more settlers began arriving, more and more of them proved resistant to the government's conditions. Haynes writes that Austin tried valiantly to carry out his obligations as an empresario, but "the challenge of turning [the settlers] into loyal Mexican citizens . . . proved more difficult. . . . Anglo-Texans possessed neither the resources nor the inclination to abide by the Mexican government's insistence on building Spanish-speaking schools and Catholic churches" (57).

Immigration from the United States into Texas came to a halt in April 1830, nearly a decade after Austin's first settlement. A Mexican official, Manuel de Mier y Terán, had made a visit to the territory two years before and was appalled by what he saw; there had been little attempt by the colonists to observe the precepts set down by the officials and particularly a lack of respect toward acculturation, inclining the colony dangerously toward what Mexico did not want to happen: the acquisition of Texas by the United States. Haynes closes his article by stating that the banning of new settlements in the territory, as well as the abolition of slavery—then a highly heated topic within the US government—led directly to the fight for Texan independence.

Texans vs. the Mexican Government: Who Was to Blame?

In Austin's speech, he averred that he had done much for the Mexican government, turning Texas from a "wilderness" to a civilized society where the people had no fear of Indian raids; his speech specifically named the Comanche tribe as one that caused problems. He also brought the settlers the Mexican government had requested, thereby creating a thriving population of fresh Mexican citizens. Mexico failed to uphold its end of the bargain by not providing a stable government: "The constitutional general Congress of 1834 . . . was dissolved in May of that year by a military order of the President before its constitutional term had expired. The council of government composed of half the Senate . . . was also dissolved." To Austin's way of thinking, what good would the colonies be if there was not a proper overall structure and legislation in place for the populace?

However, Stephen Austin's claim that Mexico was pushing Texas toward independence leaves out a critical detail. Austin, like his father before him, had assured Mexican officials that those signed on to move to the settlements either would already be professed Roman Catholics or would become so, and that they would become Mexican citizens, with the attendant adoption of associated cultural factors. As Mier y Terán had observed, these conditions had not been upheld. In this regard, whether due to the empresarios' reluctance to hold the new colonists to the rules requested by the government or the colonists' resistance to such regulations, Stephen Austin and the other empresarios had not fulfilled their part of the bargain.

Despite this, Austin's argument about being let down by officials holds the most sway. No society can adequately be provided for without the support of a stable government. The repeated actions of the Mexican officials left the settlers with little confidence in those in power, as the balance shifted again and again among a mix of faces and offices. As already mentioned, Mexico greatly feared the annexation of Texas by the United States, which would have cost the nation a great territory. However, given the lack of a consistent administration, the loss of Texas was perhaps not surprising.

Essential Themes

There are recurring references throughout Austin's speech to "our forefathers." His choice of words is clever: by using the word "our," he includes his audience in the Texans' plight. The audience, hearing the references to the revolution, may have held that parallel in their minds throughout his speech, ensuring empathy in the hearts of his listeners. Here was semiautonomous, English-speaking Texas being oppressed by Mexico, its parent country. The people of the United States, previously under the yoke of England, had risen up and broken away; such a nation would sympathize with the plight of Texas. At one point in his speech, Austin went further, suggesting that the Texans had a stronger case for independence: "Our forefathers in '76 flew to arms for much less. They resisted a principle, 'the theory of oppression,' but in our case it was the reality—it was a denial of justice and of our guaranteed rights—it was oppression itself." Although it is unknown how effective Austin's speech would have been if the tragedy at the Alamo had not occurred, or even what it lent to their cause overall along with the massacre, the Texans did find their support. The Republic of Texas was a separate entity in North America for nine years before being granted US statehood in 1845. The endeavors of Stephen Austin, William Travis, James Bowie, Davey Crockett, and Sam Houston have not been forgotten in the state. Their names have been enshrined in history, and Texans continue to hold them in the highest esteem.

—*Jennifer L. Henderson Crane*

Bibliography and Additional Reading

Austin, Stephen F. *"Address of the Honorable S. F. Austin, Delivered at Louisville, Kentucky, March 7, 1836."* PBS: New Perspectives on the West. West Film Proj. and WETA, 2001. Web. 13 Mar. 2013.

Barker, Eugene C. *"Austin, Stephen Fuller."* The Handbook of Texas Online. Texas State Hist. Assn., n.d. Web. 13 Mar. 2013.

The Biographical Encyclopedia of Texas. New York: Southern, 1880. The Portal to Texas History. Web. 13 Mar. 2013.

Brands, H. W. *Lone Star Nation: The Epic Story of the Battle for Texas Independence.* New York: Anchor, 2005. Print.

Flores, Richard R. "The Alamo: Myth, Public History, and the Politics of Inclusion." *Radical History Review* 77 (2000): 91–103. Print.

"Memory-Place, Meaning, and the Alamo." *American Literary History* 10.3 (1998): 428–45. Print.

Haynes, Sam W. "'To Colonize 500 Families . . . Catholics, and of Good Morals': *Stephen Austin and the Anglo-American Immigration to Texas,* June 4, 1825." OAH Magazine of History 19.6 (2005): 57. Print.

Sherrod, Rick. "The Road from Nacogdoches to Natchitoches: John Sprowl; the Failed Fredonian Rebellion." *East Texas Historical Journal* 48.2 (2010): 9–40. Print.

"Stephen F. Austin." San Jacinto Museum of History. San Jacinto Museum of Hist., n.d. Web. 13 Mar. 2013.

Barton, Betty. *"Stephen F. Austin's Arrest and Imprisonment in Mexico, 1834–1835."* Texana 11.1 (1973): 1–17. Print.

Davis, William C. *Three Roads to the Alamo: The Lives and Fortunes of David Crockett, James Bowie, and William Barret Travis.* New York: Harper, 1998. Print.

Donovan, James. *The Blood of Heroes: The 13-Day Struggle for the Alamo—and the Sacrifice That Forged a Nation.* New York: Little, 2012. Print.

Fehrenbach, T. R. *Lone Star: A History of Texas and the Texans.* Boulder: Da Capo, 2000. Print.

Jones, Robert, and Pauline H. Jones. "Stephen F. Austin in Arkansas." *Arkansas Historical Quarterly* 25.4 (1966): 336–53. Print.

"Stephen F. Austin in Missouri." Texana 3.1 (1965): 44–59. Print.

■ A Foreigner in My Own Land

Date: 1842
Author: Juan Nepomuceno Seguin
Genre: memoir; diary

Summary Overview

Seguín's memoir illustrates how a prominent figure in Texas history became denigrated and marginalized in the grand historical narrative; it exposes the shifting sociocultural and political milieu occurring in the Southwest as American foreign policy called for westward expansion during the nineteenth century. Authored by Juan Nepomuceno Seguín—a native and former mayor of San Antonio, Texas—this excerpt attempts to vindicate his purported betrayal of Texas through a detailed recounting of the events that occurred and the players responsible for the decline of his public image.

Once a reliable compatriot in the fight for Texan independence, Seguín quickly became viewed as a traitor and was forced out of Texas without due process. He alludes to the racial undertones of his treatment, which reflects the broader sociocultural trends occurring during this period of rapid expansion when white colonists clashed with natives on the North American continent. Several Tejanos (Mexican Texans) bravely fought for independence for Texas but were subsequently relegated to second-class status in the new Republic of Texas. The desire for white hegemony and an Anglo (i.e., Anglo-American) culture necessitated the removal of Tejanos like Seguín who possessed political clout. This excerpt alludes to Seguín's value to Texas during the revolution and insinuates that the cause of his downfall lay in his status as a Tejano who possessed power in a land the Anglos so desperately wanted. His detailed account of the events surrounding his abrupt transformation into a foreigner in his own land elucidates the shifting political, socioeconomic, and cultural structures wrought by Manifest Destiny and its detrimental effects on nonwhite citizens. Such structures left an enduring legacy on the land and illustrate the roots of a racial status quo that many feel has endured into the present day.

Defining Moment

During the nineteenth century, the United States experienced significant internal tensions brought about by a foreign policy of expansion and conquest, symbolized in the 1872 allegorical painting American Progress by artist John Gast.

The term "Manifest Destiny," first coined by John O'Sullivan in a 1845 newspaper article, is the belief that the United States was destined and divinely ordained to expand across the North American continent to cover the land from the Atlantic Ocean to the Pacific Ocean. This concept necessitated a reimagination of land as vacant despite the presence of peoples who had resided on it for centuries. Seguín's excerpt alludes to the adverse affects of westward movement and the thirst for land and power that resulted in heightened tensions between Anglos and native peoples.

Antagonism towards Seguín and his fellow Tejanos undergirded the complicated and contested image of Seguín as a traitor, despite his heroism and his role in the Texas Revolution. As the United States expanded westward, Texas had a unique political function, and the imminent battles over the territory provided a stage for Seguín to craft his identity in the minds of Texans and Mexicans.

The Texas Revolution of the 1830s and the events that followed serve to demonstrate American exceptionalism and the swiftly changing political, social, and cultural milieu occurring on the American frontier. The shifting conditions were caused primarily by heavy Anglo migration into Texas, which altered the balance of power and created a venue for white hegemony. Following the Texas Revolution (and after Seguín fled to Mexico), the remaining Tejanos who had fought for Texan independence at first enjoyed some political clout in the new republic. Before long, however, they suffered from arbitrary governmental seizures of their land, livestock, and food. They were treated as second-class citizens, and after Mexico twice invaded Texas during the 1840s, Tejanos—by virtue of their ethnicity—were viewed as aliens in their homeland. The new constitution codified this second-class citizenship by denying the protection of guaranteed rights and land grants to those who did not support the revolution. All Tejanos were categorized as traitors unless they could show clear proof they were not. Additionally, Tejanos who left Texas during the revolution were considered aliens upon their return.

The stipulations set forth in the constitution engendered violence against Tejanos, including lynchings and riots, that ultimately led to the reduction of the Tejano population in Texas. This serves as a microcosm for the changes wrought by Manifest Destiny and the chafing of clashing cultures. The acquisition of land became central to the ideology of Manifest Destiny, and land occupation produced serious sociocultural and political changes. After the annexation of Mexican territory at the conclusion of the Mexican-American War, an anti-Mexican sentiment permeated US society and stigmatized Mexican Americans as perpetual others within American culture. Such sentiments implied that Mexican culture was separate from American culture, thus creating tensions in a region Mexicans had once owned and were native to.

Author Biography

Juan Nepomuceno Seguín was born into a respected and wealthy Tejano family on October 27, 1806, in San Antonio, Texas, to Juan José Maria Erasmo Seguín and María Josefa Becerra during a time when Texas was important politically. Seguín's father and mother operated the post office in the city of Bexar. Juan was the oldest of three children: Tomas, a younger brother who died during infancy, and a younger sister who was born in 1809. Information regarding his early childhood remains scant due to a scarcity of records.

At a young age, Seguín became a provisional mayor, or alcade, of San Antonio, and after holding various political offices he played an active role in the Texas Revolution or War for Independence against Mexico. After banding together Tejanos sympathetic to the Anglo cause, Seguín led them against Mexican General Santa Anna in 1835 and participated in the siege of the Alamo the following year, narrowly escaping death. His engagement in the battle risked his family property and fortune, revealing his loyalty to Texas and its severing from Mexican control. Sympathetic to the Anglos in the wake of the revolution, Seguín campaigned for the controversial Texan senator and Anglo military general

Sam Houston, which fostered skepticism and feelings of betrayal in the eyes of some Tejanos; Houston ordered Seguín to protect the Mexican frontier from the encroaching Mexican army. Seguín and his Tejano legion contributed to the defeat of Santa Anna's army at the Battle of San Jacinto, which brought the Texan Revolution to an end. The residual effects of the revolution, however, greatly impacted Seguín's position and the place of other Tejanos within Anglo society and the new republic. Mexican armies continued to attempt invasions into Texas, which alienated the Tejanos living there and rendered them suspect as traitors or potential traitors in the eyes of the Anglo government. In 1842, Mexican General Ráfael Vásquez briefly seized control of San Antonio, of which Seguín was then mayor. Although Seguín led a force in pursuit of the retreating Vásquez, he was blamed for the attack and forced to flee to Mexico, dashing his dreams of securing freedom for all Texans, Tejano and Anglo alike. Such realities exasperated Seguín and prompted him to write about his intense feelings of betrayal by those he had perceived as loyal countrymen and comrades.

The Mexican government did not welcome Seguín when he arrived at Nuevo Laredo in 1842. Police officials arrested him and gave him an ultimatum: either he serve in the Mexican army or be sent away for a very long prison sentence. Choosing to join the army, Seguín fought in the Mexican-American War starting in 1846 against the United States. Despite switching sides, Seguín is hailed as a hero for his contributions during the Battle of the Alamo and at San Jacinto. At the conclusion of the war in 1848, Seguín moved back north to his hometown in Texas, but he returned to Mexico in 1867 after continued threats on his life. He then began authoring his Personal Memoirs of Juan N. Seguín in an attempt to rectify and rehabilitate his reputation in the eyes of Americans. Concurrently he voiced his aversion to the nebulous position and status of Tejanos in American society; he had become what ethnic studies professor Mae Ngai terms an "impossible subject," or an individual without a country. Unprotected by their US citizenship because of their race, Tejanos exercised minimal political clout and suffered from identity crises as a result of their culture and citizenship. Throughout much of his political and military career, Seguín battled being labeled a traitor by both Anglos and Tejanos. In 1890, Seguín died in Mexico near the Rio Grande and across from the land he had fought so hard to liberate.

HISTORICAL DOCUMENT

The tokens of esteem, arid evidences of trust and confidence, repeatedly bestowed upon me by the Supreme Magistrate, General Rusk, and other dignitaries of the Republic, could not fail to arouse against me much invidious and malignant feeling. The jealousy evinced against me by several officers of the companies recently arrived at San Antonio, from the United States, soon spread amongst the American straggling adventurers, who were already beginning to work their dark intrigues against the native families, whose only crime was, that they owned large tracts of land and desirable property.

John W. Smith, a bitter enemy of several of the richest families of San Antonio, by whom he had been covered with favors, joined the conspiracy which was organized to ruin me.

I will also point out the origin of another enmity which on several occasions, endangered my life. In those evil days, San Antonio was swarming with adventurers from every quarter of the globe. Many a noble heart grasped the sword in the defence of the liberty of Texas, cheerfully pouring out their blood for our cause, and to them everlasting public gratitude is due; but there were also many bad men, fugitives from their country, who found in this land an open field for their criminal designs.

San Antonio claimed then, as it claims now, to be the first city of Texas; it was also the receptacle of the scum of society. My political and social situation, brought me into continual contact with that class of people. At every hour of the day and night, my countrymen ran to me for protection against the assaults or exactions of those adventurers. Sometimes, by persuasion, I prevailed on them to desist; some times, also, force had to be resorted to. How could I have done other wise? Were, not the victims my own countrymen, friends and associates? Could; I leave them defenceless, exposed to the assaults of foreigners, who, on the pretext that they were Mexicans, treated them worse than brutes. Sound reason and the dictates, of humanity would, have precluded a different conduct on my part. . . .

1842.
After the retreat of the Mexican army under Santa Anna, until Vasquez invasion in 1842, the war between Texas and Mexico ceased to be carried on actively. Although open commercial intercourse did not exist, it was carried on by smuggling, at which the Mexican authorities used to wink, provided it was not carried on too openly, so as to oblige them to notice it, or so extensively as to arouse their avarice.

In the beginning of this year, I was elected Mayor of San Antonia. Two years previously a gunsmith, named Goodman, had taken possession of certain houses situated on the Military Plaza, which were the property of the city. He used to shoe the horses of the volunteers who passed, through San Antonio, and thus accumulated a debt against the Republic, for the payment of which he applied to the President to give him possession of the buildings referred to, which had always been known as city property.

The board of Aldermen passed a resolution to the effect, that Goodman should be compelled to leave the premises; Goodman resisted, alleging that the houses had been given to him by the President, in payment for public services. The Board could not, of course, acknowledge in the President any power to dispose of the city property, and consequently directed me to carry the resolution into effect. My compliance with the instructions of the Board caused Goodman to become my most bitter and inveterate enemy in the city.

The term for the mortgage that Messrs. Ogden and Howard held on my property, had run out. In order to raise money and comply with my engagements, I determined to go to Mexico for a drove of sheep. But fearful that this new trip would prove as fatal as the one already alluded to, I wrote to General Vasquez, who was then in command of the Mexican frontier, requesting him to give me a pass. The tenor of Vasquez' answer caused me to apprehend that an expedition was preparing against Texas, for the following month of March.

I called, a session of the Board of Aldermen, (of which the Hon. S. A. Maverick was a member,) and laid before them the communication of General Vasquez, stating, that according to my construction of the letter we might soon the approach of the Mexicans.

A few days afterwards, Don José Maria Garcia, of Laredo, came to San Antonio; his report was so circumstantial, as to preclude all possible doubts as to the near approach of Vasquez to San Antonio. Notice was immediately sent to the Government of the impending danger. In the various meetings held to devise means of defence, I expressed my candid opinion as to the impossibility of defending San Antonio. I observed, that for myself; I was going to the town of Seguin, and advised everyone to do the same.

On leaving the city, I passed through a street where some men were making breastworks; I stated to them that I was going to my ranch, and thence to Seguin, in case the Mexican forces should take possession of San Antonio.

From the Nueces river, Vasquez forwarded a proclamation by Arista, to the inhabitants of Texas. I received at my ranch, a bundle of those proclamations, which I transmitted at once to the Corporation of San Antonio.

As soon as Vasquez entered the city, those who had determined upon defending the place, withdrew to Seguin. Amongst them were Dunn and Chevallie, who had succeeded in escaping from the hands of the Mexicans, into which they had fallen while on a reconnoitering expedition on the Medina. The latter told me that Vasquez and his officers stated that I was in favor of the Mexicans; and Chevallie further added that, one day as he was talking with Vasquez, a man, named Sanchez, came within sight, whereupon the General observed: "You see that man! Well, Colonel Seguin sent him to me, when he was at Rio Grande. Seguin is with us." He then drew a letter from his pocket, stating that it was from me. Chevallie asked to be allowed to see it, as he knew my handwriting, but the General refused and cut short the interview.

On my return to San Antonio, several persona told me that the Mexican officers had declared that I was in their favor. This rumor, and some threats uttered against me by Goodman, left me but little doubt that my enemies would try to ruin me.

Some of the citizens of San Antonio had taken up arms in favor of the enemy. Judge Hemphill advised me to have them arrested and tried, but as I started out with the party who went in pursuit of the Mexicans, I could not follow his advice.

Having observed that Vasquez gained ground on us, we fell back on the Nueces river. When we came back,

to San Antonio, reports were widely spreading about my pretended treason. Captain Manuel Flores, Lieutenant Ambrosio Rodriguez, Matias Curbier, and five or six other Mexicans, dismounted with me to find out the origin of the imposture. I went out with several friends leaving Curbier in my house. I had reached the Main Plaza, when several persons came running to inform me, that some Americans were murdering Curbier. We ran back to the house, where we found poor Curbier covered with blood. On being asked who assaulted him, he answered, that the gunsmith. Goodman, in company with several Americans, had struck him with a rifle. A few minutes afterwards, Goodman returned to my house, with about thirty volunteers, but, observing that we were prepared to meet them, they did not attempt to attack us. We went out of the house and then to Mr. Guilbeau's, who offered me his protection. He went out into the street, pistol in hand, and succeeded in dispersing the mob, which had formed in front of my house. Mr. John Twohig offered me a shelter for that night; on the next morning, I went under disguise to Mr. Van Ness' house; Twohig, who recognised me in the street, warned me to "open my eyes." I remained one day at Mr. Van Ness'; next day General Burleson arrived at San Antonio, commanding a respectable force of volunteers. I presented myself to him, asking for a Court of Inquiry; he answered, that there were no grounds for such proceedings. In the evening I went to the camp, and jointly with Colonel Patton, received a commission to forage for provisions in the lower ranchos. I complied with this trust.

I remained, hiding from rancho to rancho, for over fifteen days. Every party, of volunteers en route to San Antonio declared, "they wanted to kill Seguin." I could no longer go from farm to farm, and determined to go to my own farm and raise fortifications.

Several of my relatives and friends joined me. Hardly a day elapsed without receiving notice that a party was preparing to attack me; we were constantly kept under arms. Several parties came in sight, but, probably seeing that we were prepared to receive them, refrained from attacking. On the 30th of April, a friend from San Antonio sent me word that Captain Scott, and his company were coming down by the river, burning the ranchos on their way. The inhabitants of the lower ranchos called on us for aid against Scott. With those in my house, and others to the number of about 100, I started to lend them aid. I proceeded, observing the movements of Scott, from the function of the Medina to Pajaritos. At that place we dispersed and I returned to my wretched life. In those days I could not go to San Antonio without peril of my life.

Matters being in this state, I saw that it was necessary to take some step which would place me in security, and save my family from constant wretchedness. I had to leave Texas, abandon all, for which I had fought and spent my fortune, to become a wanderer. The ingratitude of those, who had assumed to themselves the right of convicting me; their credulity in declaring me a traitor, on mere rumors, when I had to plead, in my favor the loyal patriotism with which I had always served Texas, wounded me deeply.

But, before leaving my country, perhaps for ever, I determined to consult with all those interested in my welfare. I held a family council. All were in favor of my removing for some time to the interior of Texas. But, to accomplish this, there were some unavoidable obstacles. I could not take one step from my ranch; towards the Brazos, without being exposed to the rifle of the first person who might meet me, for, through the whole country, credit had been given to the rumors against me. To emigrate with my family was impossible, as I was a ruined man, from the time of the invasion of Santa Anna and our flight to Nacogdoches, furthermore, the country of the Brazos was unhealthier than that of Nacogdoches, and what might, we not expect to suffer from disease in a new country, and without friends or means.

Seeing that all these plans were impracticable, I resolved to seek a refuge amongst my enemies, braving all dangers. But before taking this step, I sent in my resignation to the Corporation of San Antonio, as Mayor of the city, stating to them, that, unable any longer to suffer the persecutions of some ungrateful Americans, who strove to murder me, I had determined to free my family and friends from their continual misery on my account; and go and live peaceably in Mexico. That for these reasons I resigned my office, with all my privileges and honors as a Texan.

I left Bexar without any engagements towards Texas, my services paid by persecutions, exiled and deprived of my privileges as a Texan citizen, I was in this country a being out of the pale of society, and when she could not protect the rights of her citizens, they seek protection elsewhere. I had been tried by a rabble, condemned without a hearing, and consequently was at liberty to provide for my own safety.

GLOSSARY

breastwork: fortifications for defense against an impending attack

credulity: the quality of quickly trusting someone without good reason; the quality of being gullible

enmity: hatred, animosity, or ill will

evince: to show or make clear

inveterate: established, enduring, or persistent

invidious: causing resentment or jealousy

rabble: crowd of disorderly individuals; mob

reccoiter: to inspect in order to gather information for military purposes

Document Analysis

The contradictory image of Juan Nepomuceno Seguín as a traitor and a hero in Texas during the nineteenth century has been debated by historians up to the present day. Seguín's memoir regarding his controversial political and military career illustrates the changes that occurred during a time of expansion across the North American continent that resulted in shifting socioeconomic, political, and cultural structures. As the title suggests, land—Texas and Mexican territory—became crucial to the fulfillment of Manifest Destiny, or the idea that Americans are divinely ordained to expand across the North American continent. Such an ideology called for Anglo settlers to come into contact with native Mexicans, which led to mounting sociocultural tensions as a result of political and economic imperatives. Settlers, or "adventurers," carried with them notions of white hegemony over natives as the American political domain expanded. As a result, nonwhite individuals such as Seguín who possessed status, political clout, and land faced mounting opposition and contempt from their Anglo compatriots.

Around age thirty-five, Seguín was the mayor of San Antonio, a city that was integral to Anglo dreams of fulfilling their Manifest Destiny. Marked a traitor for the majority of his adult life, Seguín sought to clear his name through this deeply passionate memoir in which he elucidated not only the origin of his branding as a traitor but also conveyed his loyalty to his family as a reason for his perceived divided loyalties (which many other Tejanos conveyed and continue to demonstrate into the present day). He uses vivid language that sets up a binary between criminal and hero in order to rehabilitate his legacy as a hero of Texas and a Tejano leader. In this way he seeks to subvert the image of the angelic Anglo settler set against the criminal, brutish native Mexican.

Cultural artifacts produced during the nineteenth century articulated various political sentiments, racial stereotypes, and salient historical inquiries that permeated this period. John Gast's painting American Progress conveyed ubiquitous ideas that undergirded Manifest Destiny and Anglo relations with nonwhite natives; Seguín subtly alludes to such ideas in his vindication of his tarnished legacy. Gast's depiction conveys how social characteristics became inscribed on real and imagined space emanating from the notion of Manifest Destiny. He portrays the US nation-state in the symbol of a sexualized, angelic, and white mother figure whose aggressive movement westward conveys a protective posture; built into the construction of whiteness is the notion of purity. She holds books in her hands to demonstrate her knowledge as she moves into corners of the word depicted and racialized as dark and in need of enlightenment. The painting contrasts a progressive, cultured, and divine white race with the dark, backwards, savage, nonwhite, and uncivilized natives. Such attitudes regarding native Mexicans undergirded US treatment of them after the moment of contact and subsequent conquest. The ideology of Manifest Destiny spawned the increasingly tense interactions between westward moving Anglos and the natives residing in formerly Mexican territory in the Southwest as a result of occupied land and racial and cultural differences.

Seguín sets a binary of Anglo settlers as the true "criminals" against the sovereignty of native Tejanos as a way of elevating his heroic status and contesting his image as a traitor. Furthermore, he stressed his loyalty to Texas, to his fellow Tejanos, and to his family, despite constant questioning of his moral character; he left Texas not out of betrayal but to protect his family from the suffering they were enduring as a result of Anglo oppression. Seguín fervently believed in the idea that a Tejano could be proud of his or her national heritage while remaining a "loyal Tejano" (Montejano 26). He heroically fought for Texas during the Texas Revolution out of his loyalty to and love for his native land. However, many Anglo "adventurers" migrating into the land fought for the "liberty of Texas" as a part of their "criminal designs" to steal the land once independence was achieved; Tejano property and life were therefore not secure during this turbulent period. Seguín subverts the image of himself as a traitorous criminal by deflecting such a delineation onto encroaching Anglo settlers through his use of vivid and explicit diction. On the other hand, he also used his position in the government to protect his defenseless countrymen from the criminal activity of and the force used by Anglo adventurers. Seguín does so to emphasize a moral code based on the justice he lived by and acted on. Furthermore, he alludes to the racial undertones of the Anglos' perceived prerogatives in the region as depicted by Gast; Mexicans were viewed and treated as savage "brutes" who were not self-possessed or worthy of owning "desirable property." Additionally, Seguín articulates an image of himself as a victim of this Anglo hatred, brutish treatment, and oppression by top officials to garner sympathy; he left Texas not by choice but out of necessity, to save his family from "enemies trying to ruin" him, and it was he who warned city officials of the advancing Mexican army towards the city, thus constructing himself as a heroic figure.

As a prominent Tejano senator who sympathized with the Anglo government during the Texas Revolution, Seguín endured accusations of being traitor by his fellow Tejanos, while Anglo "dignitaries of the Republic" concurrently treated him with vigilant suspicion. His position as mayor of San Antonio gave him political clout to which Tejanos generally did not have access during this period of American expansion. Although his prominent political position fostered Anglo aversion toward him, most of his purported transgressions emanated out of his actions as a leader in the military. Such disdain and "jealousy" demonstrated by prominent Anglos within the army toward him and his fellow Tejanos for owning land that they felt was ordained for them fostered similar attitudes in the Anglo masses. Property and land formed the roots of his enemies' disdain toward him and other Tejanos, whose "only crime was that they owned large tracts of land and desirable property."

Seguín's work as a land speculator combined with the centrality of land to the ideology of Manifest Destiny also played a huge role in sullying his public image. As a land speculator, Seguín worked for several Anglo detractors who accused him of fraud in his selling land. Many alleged that he would not return money he had confiscated when residing in San Antonio. Seguín asserts that he dealt with land and property disputes according to Texas law and maintained compliance with the directions of the board. However, several of his decisions regarding the land of prominent Anglo families incurred him bitter enemies despite his adherence to legal standards. Following the Texas Revolution, Mexican families living along the Guadalupe and San Antonio rivers experienced high rates of expulsion and land seizures by the Texas government (Montejano 26); Mexicans who remained loyal to Texas rather than Mexico nonetheless endured random acts of violence, land and livestock seizures, and acts of humiliation by people who held anti-Mexican sentiments. By the 1840s, the majority of the prominent Mexican families with Spanish ties had left Texas, either by force or under threat of murder.

The role of land during US expansion with regard to American Indians further helps explain Anglo sentiments toward Seguín and the complicated image he inherited as a result of his social status and land ownership. The colonial relationship between American Indians and Anglo-Americans enabled the US government to strip American Indians of their tribal sovereignty through the dispossession of their culturally sacred, ancestral lands; to do so, a racialized public discourse helped to support various legal precepts that maintained the myth of American Indians as, increasingly, a "vanishing race." Bolstered by the ideological conceits of the myth, white sellers perceived natives as infantilized and impotent in order to refute indigenous land claims and justify European domination. For the United States to become a country ruled by the masculinized "Yankee spirit" of the Euro-American colonist required the extermination of indigenous people, both physically and culturally, from the American landscape. Ultimately, it was the unequal relationship established upon contact that provided the colonists the tools to wipe the American Indians off of their native landscape and ultimately from the American consciousness through reimagining space with regard to racial hierarchies (Espiritu 46). The reimagining of land and space within the United States thus reinforced the white hegemony over the natives' sociocultural systems of native groups and provided an impetus for the cultural genocide of American Indians.

Such processes began to take place upon Anglo advancement into Texan land and infusion into the existing socioeconomic and political systems. Rumors of Seguín's loyalty to the Mexicans destroyed his reputation in the eyes of Texans, both Anglo and Tejano. Seguín describes in anguish the severe danger he and his family faced as the Mexican army threatened to seize San Antonio and several of the surrounding cities. Such daily affliction and peril caused by "mere rumors" forced him to move his family and become "a wanderer" in the land he had served and fought for. His former friends and colleagues turned on him, forcing his family to flee to Mexico while he faced incarceration and forced military service against his former homeland during the Mexican-American War. Seguín invokes his military accolades in the service of Texas and his political accomplishments to emphasize his loyalty and garner more sympathy for his adverse treatment. A loyal and productive citizen, Seguín was betrayed and abandoned by the country he served, and his anguish resonates with the many other Mexican American families betrayed by a country they too served and inhabited for generations.

Throughout this excerpt from Seguín's memoir, it is clear that the sociocultural and political landscapes were drastically shifting as a result of US expansion westward. Mexican Americans became increasingly subordinated to the status of second-class citizens, and they saw their citizenship rights violated without due process. Land grants were violated frequently, and force was often used to seize desired land plots from Mexican families, leaving them no choice but to flee their native land. This process of arbitrarily rendering Mexican Americans stateless for Anglo gain exposes the salient racial antagonisms that characterized this period. A legacy of white supremacy and dispossession rather than one of liberty and justice as the foundation of America emerged out of this hotly contested time. Citizenship for nonwhite individuals—event prominent political figures such as Seguín—did not guarantee the protection of rights codified by the US constitution.

Essential Themes

Juan Nepomuceno Seguín was a Tejano who possessed unusual socioeconomic status and political clout. He lived a patriotic life fighting for Texas, his native land that he served ardently both in the military and in politics. Additionally, he combated an image of himself as a traitor both to his own Mexican heritage and to the land that he served. His conflicted life represents a microcosm of the Tejano experience in Texan regions to the present day, which has inspired cultural articulations of such struggles. In the face of Anglo-American colonization and hegemony in the American Southwest, author Americo Paredes's George Washington Gomez (1990) details the struggles of Mexicotexans, as he calls them, to preserve their culture and identity in the face of growing Anglo hegemony in the American Southwest in the early twentieth century.

With the development of railroads in Texas, Anglos migrated into borderland towns and displaced the Tejano power structure; as a result, this demographic shift led to drastic sociocultural and political changes. Paredes's novel centers around a young Mexican-American boy who struggles with his identity while living in Jonesville, a fictional, rural town on the border between Texas and the United States in which the Anglo migrants displaced the Tejanos (Mexicotexans) through settler-colonialism. The colonial processes that take place in Paredes's novel demonstrate that, while this novel typifies the American story between the 1910s and 1940s, the history of Mexicans living in the Southwest suffer-

ing violence at the hands of Anglo-Americans shaped an idiosyncratic narrative rooted in vicious oppression that is symbolic of the region and the rendering of native Mexicans as foreigners in their own land. Paredes's novel depicts the idiosyncrasies of life on the borderland caused by colonial structures as a result of Anglo migration and hegemony in a predominately rural region. Nonetheless, the themes and issues raised in George Washington Gómez—although set on the Texas borderlands—convey a typical American story by dramatizing the extent to which nativist sentiment undergirded US government policies between the 1910s and the 1940s; thus, Paredes portrays national sociocultural trends on a local level that took root during the period in which Seguín lived; his experiences represented the experiences of Tejanos living in a region in transition.

The violent history between Anglos and Mexicans in the American Southwest resulting in colonial social structures renders regional economic trends as exceptional in comparison to national trends. Paredes's depiction of race in the American Southwest implicates a social system structured by "internal colonialism" that discriminates against individuals of Mexican descent (Ngai). This colonial structure took in the antagonistic relationship between Mexico and the United States as a result of the US annexation of Mexican land following the Mexican-American War in 1848; Paredes's protagonist Feliciano expresses extreme rage over the "gringos" taking Mexican land by force (102). Settler-colonialism is the process by which a hegemonic population occupies space by forcibly removing an inhabiting population. Paredes implicates these colonial processes that structure life for Mexican Americans at the borderland when discussing the significance of chaparral (the shrubland of southern California) to Mexicotexans. Indigenous to the Southwest, chaparral represented the Mexicotexan's "guarantee of freedom" from "alien law" and allowed small farmers to work their own land independently (42). However, once the Americans annexed the Southwest, they developed the land by eradicating the chaparral, which did not benefit them economically; using Mexican labor and paying them barely enough money to subsist, American farmers replaced the chaparral with cotton and citrus orchards (42). American policies such as this suggest that they sought to integrate this region into the global economy both ethnically and economically, and to do so required an eradication of the traditional Mexican way of life. Paredes's projection of Mexicans as colonized individuals within

America renders them as an oppressed people in their native land and implicates their subjection to prejudice and violence. The notion that the Mexican family's standard of living was much lower than the Anglo's portrays Mexicans in the rural Southwest as an inferior stock of people compared with their Anglo oppressors (200).

This nativist sentiment experienced by Seguín in his transition into an "impossible subject" survived into the twentieth century and translated into gross civil rights violations during the 1930s and 1940s. Paredes dramatizes the dialogue between the police and a Mexican worker who did not have his documentation papers with him, resulting in his forced repatriation back to Mexico (197). Between five hundred thousand and one million Mexicans and Mexican Americans in California alone had their citizens' rights violated through forced repatriation during the 1930s as a result of job competition during the Great Depression. Economic uncertainties "inflamed racial hostility toward Mexicans," which prompted the deportation and repatriation of Mexicans regardless of citizenship status (Ngai 71). This legacy of nonwhite Americans arbitrarily becoming foreigners in their own land has persisted well into the twentieth and twenty-first centuries. Through his emotional memoirs, Seguín articulated the grief and anger over his tarnished image and second-class citizenship and expressed the experiences of many Tejanos and other nonwhite groups due to Anglo discrimination, which in some ways endures into the present day.

—*Maddie Weissman, MA*

Bibliography and Additional Reading

Espiritu, Yen Le. *Home Bound: Filipino American Lives across Cultures, Communities, and Countries.* Berkeley: U of California P, 2009. Print.

Galdeano, Daniel. *"Juan Seguín: A Paradox in the Annals of Texas History."* Seguín Family Historical Society. Seguín Family Historical Society, n.d. Web. 14 Mar. 2013.

Montejano, David. *Anglos and Mexicans in the Making of Texas, 1836–1986.* Austin: U of Texas P, 1994. Print.

Ngai, Mae M. *Impossible Subjects: Illegal Aliens and the Making of Modern America.* Princeton: Princeton UP, 2004. Print.

Paredes, Américo. *George Washington Gómez: A Mexicotexan Novel.* Houston: Arte Publico, 1990. Print.

Seguín, Juan N. "The Fate of the Tejanos, 1858." American History 135, Primary Documents. U. of South Alabama, 2009. Web. 14 Mar. 2013.

Chemerka, William R. *Juan Seguín: Tejano Leader.* Houston: Bright Sky, 2012. Print.

Henderson, Timothy J. *A Glorious Defeat: Mexico and Its War with the United States.* New York: Farrar, 2007. Print.

Weber, David J., ed. *Foreigners in Their Native Land: Historical Roots of the Mexican Americans.* Albuquerque: U of New Mexico P, 1973. Print.

Mexican Denunciations of the United States

Dates: June 4, 1845; March 18, 1846; and April 20, 1846
Authors: Jose Joaquin de Herrera; Francisco Mejia; Mariano Arista
Genre: legislation; speech

Summary Overview

As of early 1845, while Mexico had not formally acknowledged that Texas was independent, President John Tyler had begun the formal process to annex it. With the inauguration of James K. Polk as US president in March 1845—a politician who had run on a platform of westward expansion—Mexico faced the prospect of the loss of not only Texas but the rest of its northern territory. Thus, in 1845, Jose Joaquin de Herrera responded to the prospect that Texas would soon be part of the United States. As he states in the document included here, this was unacceptable to him (and to the other Mexican leaders). Even when it was part of Mexico, the exact western border of Texas had been an issue, so that with its annexation by the United States, the issue was now between the Americans and the Mexicans. It became apparent that this conflict would not be resolved peacefully, as both countries were recruiting soldiers and sending them to the disputed territory. The material by Mejia included here was a part of the Mexican call-to-arms for the conflict, which officially began on April 25, 1846. Arista's communiqué approaches the problem from the opposite side, appealing to the American soldiers to desert and, in return, to accept land grants from the Mexican government.

Defining Moment

With the close of the Mexican war for independence in 1821, the new nation inherited uncertain relations with its neighbor to the north. Although initially the United States had no plans for the annexation of any Mexican territory, sentiments changed over the succeeding twenty-five years. As early as 1822, American settlers were being invited into what is now Texas. In California, most Americans were hunters and trappers—until John Sutter was given a large land grant in the Central Valley, where he welcomed other emigrants from the United States. The growing populations of Americans in both areas resulted in pressure for independence from the weak Mexican government. Texas fought for and won its independence. The beginning of the process for Texas's annexation as a state, under the United States, brought the issue of Mexican sovereignty north of the Rio Grande to a head. Few doubted that war could be avoided. The Mexican congress passed a resolution warning the United States to stop the process of annexing Texas, which is the first of these historical documents. When that failed to occur, steps were taken on both sides to prepare for the oncoming war. The United States sent half of its small fleet to the Pacific to take control of California when the war started. Contingents from the army were sent to Texas, to establish a base in the disputed territory of west Texas. During that time, the speeches, represented by the second and third historical documents, were given to build support for the Mexican cause, to gain volunteers for the armed forces, and to try to weaken the American forces. They also served as a final warning to the United States that any further actions would result in war.

The documents reprinted here are representative of the nationalistic pride of the Mexican leaders and their unwillingness to ignore American encroachment into what they considered their own territory. While these views were heard by leaders in the United States, the Americans were just as firm in their belief that the United States should stretch from the Atlantic to the Pacific. They also held the belief that the United States would prevail in any conflict, so there was no need to compromise. Although several proposals were put forward by different parties which would have resulted in payment by the United States for the territory from west Texas to the Pacific, a variety of things (including the instability of the Mexican government) prevented these from being accepted. Thus, the Mexican leaders could only call upon their citizens to make preparations for what seemed to be an inevitable conflict.

Author Biography

Mariano Arista (1802–1855) was an officer in the Spanish Army who defected to the side of those seeking an independent Mexico. He remained in the military and fought against the Texans, who were seeking independence. He was the commander of the forces that attacked the American Army in west Texas, starting the Mexican-American War (1846–48). After the war, he was elected president of Mexico in 1851, serving until 1853.

José Joaquin de Herrera (1792–1854) was a career military officer, originally fighting on the side of Spain during the war for Mexican independence. However, he retired before the war ended and eventually joined those rebelling. After independence, he opposed several authoritarian leaders. He was elected president in 1845, but then deposed in 1846 by the army he had created. After the war was elected again, in 1848, serving until 1851.

Francisco Mejia (died 1852) was twice governor of the state of Coahuila in the early 1840s and a general in the Mexican Army. When he made the proclamation at Matamoros, he was the general in charge of the Army of the North, with his forces then on the south bank of the Rio Grande. Many believed this speech to his troops was a declaration of war against the United States.

HISTORICAL DOCUMENT

[José Joaquin de Herrera, June 4, 1845]

The minister of foreign affairs has communicated to me the following decree: José Joaquin de Herrera, general of division and president ad interim of the Mexican Republic, to the citizens thereof.

Be it known: That the general congress has decreed, and the executive sanctioned, the following:

The national congress of the Mexican Republic, considering:

That the congress of the United States of the North has, by a decree, which its executive sanctioned, resolved to incorporate the territory of Texas with the American union;

That this manner of appropriating to itself territories upon which other nations have rights, introduces a monstrous novelty, endangering the peace of the world, and violating the sovereignty of nations;

That this usurpation, now consummated to the prejudice of Mexico, has been in insidious preparation for a long time; at the same time that the most cordial friendship was proclaimed, and that on the part of this republic, the existing treaties between it and those states were respected scrupulously and legally;

That the said annexation of Texas to the U. States tramples on the conservative principles of society, attacks all the rights that Mexico has to that territory, is an insult to her dignity as a sovereign nation, and threatens her independence and political existence;

That the law of the United States, in reference to the annexation of Texas to the United States, does in nowise destroy the rights that Mexico has, and will enforce, upon that department;

That the United States, having trampled on the principles which served as a basis to the treaties of friendship, commerce and navigation, and more especially to those of boundaries fixed with precision, even previous to 1832, they are considered as inviolate by that nation.

And, finally, that the unjust spoliation of which they wish to make the Mexican nation the victim, gives her the clear right to use all her resources and power to resist, to the last moment, said annexation;

IT IS DECREED 1st. The Mexican nation calls upon all her children to the defence of her national independence, threatened by the usurpation of Texas, which is intended to be realized by the decree of annexation passed by the congress, and sanctioned by the president, of the United States of the north.

2d. In consequence, the government will call to arms all the forces of the army, according to the authority granted it by the existing laws; and for the preservation of public order, for the support of her institutions, and in case of necessity, to serve as the reserve to the army, the government, according to the powers given to it on the 9th December 1844, will raise the corps specified by said decree, under the name of "Defenders of the Independence and of the Laws."

MIGUEL ARTISTAN, President of the Deputies.
FRANCISCO CALDERON, President of the senate.

Approved, and ordered to be printed and published.
JOSÉ JOAQUIN DE HERRERA. A. D. LUIS G. CUEVAS
Palace of the National Government, City of Mexico, June 4, 1845.

* * *

[Francisco Mejia, March 18, 1846]

FELLOW-CITIZENS: The annexation of the department of Texas to the United States, projected and consummated by the tortuous policy of the cabinet of the Union, does not yet satisfy the ambitious desires of the degenerate sons of Washington. The civilized world has already recognized in that act all the marks of injustice, iniquity, and the most scandalous violation of the rights of nations. Indelible is the stain which will for ever darken the character for virtue falsely attributed to the people of the United States; and posterity will regard with horror their perfidious conduct, and the immorality of the means employed by them to carry into effect that most degrad-

ing depredation. The right of conquest has always been a crime against humanity; but nations jealous of their dignity and reputation have endeavoured at least to cover it by the splendour of arms and the prestige of victory. To the United States, it has been reserved to put in practice dissimulation, fraud, and the basest treachery, in order to obtain possession, in the midst of peace, of the territory of a friendly nation, which generously relied upon the faith of promises and the solemnity of treaties.

The cabinet of the United States does not, however, stop in its career of usurpation. Not only does it aspire to the possession of the department of Texas, but it covets also the regions on the left bank of the Rio Bravo. Its army, hitherto for some time stationed at Corpus Christi, is now advancing to take possession of a large part of Tamaulipas; and its vanguard has arrived at the Arroya Colorado, distant eighteen leagues from this place. What expectations, therefore, can the Mexican government have of treating with an enemy, who, whilst endeavouring to lull us into security, by opening diplomatic negotiations, proceeds to occupy a territory which never could have been the object of the pending discussion? The limits of Texas are certain and recognized; never have they extended beyond the river Nueces; notwithstanding which, the American army has crossed the line separating Tamaulipas from that department. Even though Mexico could forget that the United States urged and aided the rebellion of the former colonists, and that the principle, giving to an independent people the right to annex itself to another nation, is not applicable to the case, in which the latter has been the protector of the independence of the former, with the object of admitting it into its own bosom; even thought it could be accepted as an axiom of international law, that the violation of every rule of morality and justice might serve as a legitimate title for acquisition; nevertheless, the territory of Tamaulipas would still remain beyond the law of annexation, sanctioned by the American Congress; because that law comprises independent Texas, the ground occupied by the rebellious colony, and in no wise includes other departments, in which the Mexican government has uninterruptedly exercised its legitimate authority.

Fellow-countrymen: With an enemy which respects not its laws, which shamelessly derides the very principles invoked by it previously, in order to excuse its ambitious views, we have no other resource than arms. We are fortunately always prepared to take them up with glory, in defence of our country; little do we regard the blood in our veins, when we are called on to shed it in vindication of our honour, to assure our nationality and independence. If to the torrent of devastation which threatens us it be necessary to oppose a dike of steel, our swords will form it; and on their sharp points will the enemy receive the fruits of his anticipated conquest. If the banks of the Panuco have been immortalized by the defeat of an enemy, respectable and worthy of the valour of Mexico, those of the Bravo shall witness the ignominy of the proud sons of the north, and its deep waters shall serve as the sepulchre for those who dare to approach it. The flames of patriotism which burns in our hearts will receive new fuel from the odious presence of the conquerors; and the cry of Dolores and Iguala shall be re-echoed with harmony to our ears, when we take up our march to oppose our naked breasts to the rifles of the hunters of the Mississippi.

FRANCISCO MEJIA.
Matamoros, March 18, 1846

* * *

[General Mariano Arista, April 20, 1846]

Soldiers!—You have enlisted in time of peace to serve in that army for a specific term; but your obligation never implied that you were bound to violate the laws of God, and the most sacred rights of friends! The United States government, contrary to the wishes of a majority of all honest and honorable Americans, has ordered you to take forcible possession of the territory of a friendly neighbour, who has never given her consent to such occupation. In other words, while the treaty of peace and commerce between Mexico and the United States is in full force, the United States, presuming on her strength and prosperity, and on our supposed imbecility and cowardice, attempts to make you the blind instruments of her unholy and blind ambition, and force you to appear as the hateful robbers of our dear homes, and the unprovoked violators of our dearest feelings as men and patriots. Such a villainy and outrage, I know, is perfectly repugnant to the noble sentiments of any gentleman, and it is base and foul to rush you on to certain death, in order to aggrandize a few lawless individual, in defiance of the laws of God and man!

It is to no purpose if they tell you, that the law for the annexation of Texas justifies your occupation of the Rio Bravo del Norte; for by this act they rob us of a great part of Tamaulipas, Coahuila, Chihuahua, and new Mexico; it is barbarous to send a handful of men on such an errand against a powerful and warlike nation. Besides, the most of you are Europeans, and we are the declared friends of a majority of the nations of Europe. The North Americans are ambitious, overbearing, and insolent as a nation, and they will only make use of you as vile tools to carry out their abominable plans of pillage and rapine.

I warn you in the name of justice, honour, and your own interests and self-respect, to abandon their desperate and unholy cause, and become peaceful Mexican citizens. I guarantee you, in such case, a half section of land, or three hundred and twenty acres, to settle upon, gratis. Be wise, then, and just, and honourable, and take no part in murdering us who have no unkind feelings for you. Lands shall be given to officers, sergeants, and corporals, according to rank, privates receiving three hundred and twenty acres, as stated.

If, in time of action, you wish to espouse our cause, throw away your arms and run to us, and we will embrace you as true friends and Christians. It is not decent or prudent to say more. But should any of you render important service to Mexico, you shall be accordingly considered and preferred.

GLOSSARY

Dolores: the city where the Mexican war for independence began

Iguala: the city where the Mexican war for independence ended

Panuco, banks of: the area where Spanish forces invading Mexico, in 1829, were defeated

perfidious: treacherous

Document Analysis

These three documents represent the progression of the crisis between Mexico and the United States. Up until the last minute, President Herrera believed a negotiated settlement might be possible, and so he tries to approach the subject in a legalistic manner. General Mejia spoke only five weeks before the formal conflict commenced and, as such, was attempting to rally the forces of northern Mexico as well as to speak about the legitimacy of the Mexican position. Less than a week before the first skirmish between Mexican and American forces, General Arista tried to undercut the morale of the American soldiers and offered them incentives to desert. As should be expected of a nation's leaders, all three were trying to rally their country and weaken their rival.

Herrera and the Mexican congress issued the resolution in 1845, when there might have been a chance to stop the impending hostilities. Although the American president, James Polk, had been elected on the platform of America's Manifest Destiny, he was willing to purchase the land. However, Mexico demanded that their view of Texas as essentially Mexican first be recognized. Although the Mexican government was strongly opposed to the annexation of Texas, what riled them even more was that the United States did not recognize the "boundaries fixed with precision" for Texas. As a result of the Americans not recognizing Mexico's claim on Texas or its borders, Herrera called for a new army reserve to be created to be prepared to protect Mexico's interest. Stopping just short of declaring war, Herrera hoped to create a stronger incentive for negotiations by stating his position and by having a stronger army with which to defend Mexico's interests.

Having been recently appointed commander of the Army of the North, Mejia gathered his troops together to give them what was essentially a pep talk. He outlines the ways in which the United States had violated Mexican trust and international laws. Starting with the annexation of Texas, he depicts it as a "violation of the rights of nations," having obtained control of the territory by "treachery." In addition, the western border of Texas was, for Mexico, the Nueces River, while for the United States, it was the Rio Grande. Referring back to landmark victories in Mexico's struggle for independence, Mejia goes on to call for a forceful defense of all territory claimed by Mexico, including Texas.

Arista was in command of the forces in Matamoros when the American general, Zachery Taylor, built a small fort just across the Rio Grande. With many immigrants having joined the American Army, Arista hoped to have them desert and join the Mexican side. He depicts the American enlisted man as being "forced" to serve the "unholy and blind ambition" of the American leaders. He offers them free land and a warm welcome, if they crossed the river. He seems to especially try to have those from Catholic countries join the Mexicans, as this was what he meant by "Christians." Some American soldiers did accept his offer, crossing the river to Matamoros. This caused Taylor to order sentries to shoot anyone in the river, which they did. This stopped the flow of deserters and ended any effect this proclamation had.

Essential Themes

Although after being defeated at the Battle of San Jacinto and being captured, Santa Anna had signed a document granting Texas independence in 1836, with the border being set as the Rio Grande. However, the Mexican government never ratified this agreement, since Santa Anna signed it while a prisoner. Neither side lived up to the promises made in what came to be called by Americans the Treaty of Velasco. Thus, Mexico always claimed Texas was still a part of their nation. This is echoed forcefully in the documents from Herrera, Mejia, and Arista. For Mexico, annexation of Texas by the United States was an illegal land grab, no matter what boundaries were recognized. Thus, each, in their own way, pronounced the United States as treacherous, violated international law, and initiated hostilities. The desire by the United States to take Alta California (now the state of California) and territories to its east only accentuated America's "scandalous violation of the rights of nations." Thus, Mexico was prepared to defend its sovereignty and to finally seek to regain control of Texas.

While these points were clearly made, and with some justification, they essentially were ignored by most. The American government had recognized Texas as an independent country, and then it was annexed into statehood. No amount of complaining by the Mexican government would alter that fact. While it might have been possible to negotiate the sale of land west of Texas to the United States, since Mexico had very few citizens or economic interests even in Alta California, neither side was really listening to the other. Even in Mexico, the call to its defense resulted in only 6,000 men joining the new reserve force request by President Herrera.

Thus, while these documents reflect the views of the Mexican leaders, they did not reflect views for which most Mexicans were willing to lay down their lives. As a result, when the war did come, President Polk was able to achieve all of his goals.

—Donald A. Watt, PhD

Bibliography and Additional Reading

Brooks, N.C. *A Complete History of the Mexican War.* Philadelphia: Grigg, Elliot & Co., 1849. Internet Archive, 2009. Web. 17 Oct. 2014.

Henderson, Timothy J. *A Glorious Defeat: Mexico and Its War with the United States.* New York: Hill and Wang, 2008. Print.

"Prelude to War." The U.S.-Mexican War (1846-1848). PBS/KERA, 1995–2006. Web. 17 Oct. 20014.

Vazquel, Josefina Zoraida. *"War and Peace with the United States."* The Oxford History of Mexico. Eds. Michael C. Meyer & William H. Beezley. Oxford: Oxford UP, 2000. Print.

■ Treaty of Guadalupe Hidalgo

Date: February 2, 1848
Author: Nicholas Philip Trist
Genre: treaty

Summary Overview

In May 1846, the Mexican-American War officially began. Spain and the United States had signed a treaty regarding the boundaries between the Spanish colony of Mexico and the United States, which Mexican leaders honored when they gained independence. However, with Texas's annexation to the United States, there were issues regarding the western border of that state. President James Polk sought territorial expansion and pressed the issue, resulting in the beginning of hostilities. Although the United States forces had won all the major battles and virtually every confrontation when US diplomat Nicholas Trist arrived in mid-1847, the Mexican government refused to negotiate. However, toward the end of 1847, after another series of military defeats, including the American occupation of Mexico City, representatives of a new Mexican government accepted the invitation to negotiate and quickly reached an agreement to end the war. The treaty not only granted the United States' desire for all the territory west of Texas (known as the Mexican Cession), it set the framework for United States–Mexican relations for decades to come.

Defining Moment

The United States' granting of statehood to Texas in 1845 set the stage for the Mexican-American War. Mexico had never fully accepted the independence of the Republic of Texas, declared in 1836. Mexico asserted that the territory of Texas stopped at the Nueces River, while Texas claimed territory farther south and west with the Rio Grande as the border. During the process of the United States annexing Texas, Mexico broke off diplomatic relations but did not declare war. President Polk ordered troops into Texas and then subsequently into the territory between the Nueces and the Rio Grande. In April 1846, a month after the American forces arrived in the disputed territory, Mexican cavalry attacked a small American scouting party.

General Zachary Taylor then began to push south, forcing the Mexican troops out of the disputed area and, within five months, capturing Monterrey, a major city in northeastern Mexico. While Taylor, facing stiff opposition, continued to move slowly south, General Winfield Scott convinced Polk to order most of the forces to go with him and invade Mexico through Veracruz, with Mexico City as the ultimate goal. Because the American forces were split into two armies, Taylor's and Scott's troops were always outnumbered. However, in spite of this, both continued to be successful on the battlefield. The plan to capture Mexico City succeeded, and on September 14, 1847, just under six months after the campaign started in Veracruz, Scott was in the Mexican capital.

Appointed in April 1847 to negotiate a peace treaty with Mexico, Nicholas Trist traveled to Veracruz and accompanied General Scott's army. When the opportunity arose for discussions with Antonio López de Santa Anna, the Mexican president and general, Santa Anna would not grant major concessions. In October 1847, Santa Anna was deposed, and the new government was open to negotiations with Trist. That same month, Polk decided to recall Trist to Washington. In mid-November, Trist received the orders to return but refused to leave and instead continued negotiating. In January 1848, an agreement was reached, and the treaty was signed on February 2. While Polk was upset that Trist had not followed his orders, Polk did read the treaty and saw that it accomplished most of what he wanted (though the treaty gave the United States about 55 percent of Mexico, and Polk had desired more.) Polk was ready for the war to end, so he accepted the pact and sent it to the Senate for ratification. The treaty and the war established that the United States expected to hold the superior position in its relationship with Mexico. This was the case for many decades and, to a certain extent, is still reflected in American foreign policy.

Author Biography

Born in 1800, in Charlottesville, Virginia, Nicholas Philip Trist was the son of Hore Browse Trist and Mary Louisa Brown Trist. His father was given the post of customs agent in Natchez, Louisiana, by President Thomas Jefferson when Trist was quite young. After finishing his formal education at the College of Orleans, Trist traveled to Monticello, where he met his future wife, Jefferson's granddaughter Virginia Jefferson Randolph. Trist briefly attended West Point but left to seek sufficient resources to marry. In 1823, following his mother's death, he began formal law studies with Jefferson and, a year later, married Virginia, with whom he had three children. After assisting Jefferson as a private secretary until Jefferson's death, Trist used his connections to obtain a post in the State Department.

From 1828 to 1833, Trist was a clerk in the State Department, except for a short period when he was a private secretary to President Andrew Jackson. He was then posted to Havana, Cuba, for eight years. During this time, his work as US consul received mixed reviews due to his strong support of slavery and questions regarding whether he was forging documents for slave traders. Although he returned to Washington under a cloud, he continued work with the State Department. In 1845, President Polk appointed him chief clerk, which, at that time, was the State Department's second-highest position. He served as chief clerk until April 1847, when he was sent by Polk as his personal envoy to the Mexican government to negotiate a peace treaty. This was to be the high point of Trist's career. Traveling toward Mexico City from the Gulf Coast with General Scott, Trist and Scott were able to negotiate a temporary truce in late August when American forces were poised to capture Mexico City. Because the Mexican government would not make any serious concessions, that round of negotiations failed. Scott captured the city, and Trist was then able to enter into negotiations with a new Mexican government. Because the August negotiations were not successful, Trist was officially recalled to Washington by Polk. Trist refused to go, writing a sixty-one-page letter in response. Trist and the Mexican negotiators were able to draw up the Treaty of Guadalupe Hidalgo, which eventually was accepted by both governments, after some amendments by the United States Senate.

When Trist returned to Washington, Polk, who by then had formally fired Trist, refused to pay him for his expenses or for his last several months of work. Trist never recovered financially from this setback, but was able to obtain clerical work at a railroad. In 1871, he was finally paid back wages for his work negotiating the treaty and was appointed postmaster of Alexandria, Virginia, by President Ulysses S. Grant. Trist died on February 11, 1874.

HISTORICAL DOCUMENT

TREATY OF PEACE, FRIENDSHIP, LIMITS, AND SETTLEMENT BETWEEN THE UNITED STATES OF AMERICA AND THE UNITED MEXICAN STATES CONCLUDED AT GUADALUPE HIDALGO, FEBRUARY 2, 1848; RATIFICATION ADVISED BY SENATE, WITH AMENDMENTS, MARCH 10, 1848; RATIFIED BY PRESIDENT, MARCH 16, 1848; RATIFICATIONS EXCHANGED AT QUERETARO, MAY 30, 1848; PROCLAIMED, JULY 4, 1848.

IN THE NAME OF ALMIGHTY GOD

The United States of America and the United Mexican States animated by a sincere desire to put an end to the calamities of the war which unhappily exists between the two Republics and to establish Upon a solid basis relations of peace and friendship, which shall confer reciprocal benefits upon the citizens of both, and assure the concord, harmony, and mutual confidence wherein the two people should live, as good neighbors have for that purpose appointed their respective plenipotentiaries, that is to say: The President of the United States has appointed Nicholas P. Trist, a citizen of the United States, and the President of the Mexican Republic has appointed Don Luis Gonzaga Cuevas, Don Bernardo Couto, and Don Miguel Atristain, citizens of the said Republic; Who, after a reciprocal communication of their respective full powers, have, under the protection of Almighty God, the author of peace, arranged, agreed upon, and signed the following: Treaty of Peace, Friendship, Limits, and Settlement between the United States of America and the Mexican Republic.

ARTICLE I

There shall be firm and universal peace between the United States of America and the Mexican Republic, and between their respective countries, territories, cities, towns, and people, without exception of places or persons. . . .

ARTICLE V

The boundary line between the two Republics shall commence in the Gulf of Mexico, three leagues from land, opposite the mouth of the Rio Grande, otherwise called Rio Bravo del Norte, or Opposite the mouth of its deepest branch, if it should have more than one branch emptying directly into the sea; from thence up the middle of that river, following the deepest channel, where it has more than one, to the point where it strikes the southern boundary of New Mexico; thence, westwardly, along the whole southern boundary of New Mexico (which runs north of the town called Paso) to its western termination; thence, northward, along the western line of New Mexico, until it intersects the first branch of the river Gila; (or if it should not intersect any branch of that river, then to the point on the said line nearest to such branch, and thence in a direct line to the same); thence down the middle of the said branch and of the said river, until it empties into the Rio Colorado; thence across the Rio Colorado, following the division line between Upper and Lower California, to the Pacific Ocean.

The southern and western limits of New Mexico, mentioned in the article, are those laid down in the map entitled "Map of the United Mexican States, as organized and defined by various acts of the Congress of said republic, and constructed according to the best authorities. Revised edition. Published at New York, in 1847, by J. Disturnell," of which map a copy is added to this treaty, bearing the signatures and seals of the undersigned Plenipotentiaries. And, in order to preclude all difficulty in tracing upon the ground the limit separating Upper from Lower California, it is agreed that the said limit shall consist of a straight line drawn from the middle of the Rio Gila, where it unites with the Colorado, to a point on the coast of the Pacific Ocean, distant one marine league due south of the southernmost point of the port of San Diego, according to the plan of said port made in the year 1782 by Don Juan Pantoja, second sailing-master of the Spanish fleet, and published at Madrid in the year 1802, in the atlas to the voyage of the schooners Sutil and Mexicana; of which plan a copy is hereunto added, signed and sealed by the respective Plenipotentiaries.

In order to designate the boundary line with due precision, upon authoritative maps, and to establish upon the ground land-marks which shall show the limits of both republics, as described in the present article, the two Governments shall each appoint a commissioner and a surveyor, who, before the expiration of one year from the date of the exchange of ratifications of this treaty, shall meet at the port of San Diego, and proceed to run and mark the said boundary in its whole course to the mouth of the Rio Bravo del Norte. They shall keep journals and make out plans of their operations; and the result agreed upon by them shall be deemed a part of this treaty, and shall have the same force as if it were inserted therein. The two Governments will amicably agree regarding what may be necessary to these persons, and also as to their respective escorts, should such be necessary.

The boundary line established by this article shall be religiously respected by each of the two republics, and no change shall ever be made therein, except by the express and free consent of both nations, lawfully given by the General Government of each, in conformity with its own constitution. . . .

ARTICLE VII

The river Gila, and the part of the Rio Bravo del Norte lying below the southern boundary of New Mexico, being, agreeably to the fifth article, divided in the middle between the two republics, the navigation of the Gila and of the Bravo below said boundary shall be free and common to the vessels and citizens of both countries; and neither shall, without the consent of the other, construct any work that may impede or interrupt, in whole or in part, the exercise of this right; not even for the purpose of favoring new methods of navigation. Nor shall any tax or contribution, under any denomination or title, be levied upon vessels or persons navigating the same or upon merchandise or effects transported thereon, except in the case of landing upon one of their shores. If, for the purpose of making the said rivers navigable, or for maintaining them in such state, it should be necessary or advantageous to establish any tax or contribution, this shall not be done without the consent of both Governments.

The stipulations contained in the present article shall not impair the territorial rights of either republic within its established limits.

ARTICLE VIII

Mexicans now established in territories previously belonging to Mexico, and which remain for the future within the limits of the United States, as defined by the present treaty, shall be free to continue where they now reside, or to remove at any time to the Mexican Republic, retaining the property which they possess in the said territories, or disposing thereof, and removing the proceeds wherever they please, without their being subjected, on this account, to any contribution, tax, or charge whatever.

Those who shall prefer to remain in the said territories may either retain the title and rights of Mexican citizens, or acquire those of citizens of the United States. But they shall be under the obligation to make their election within one year from the date of the exchange of ratifications of this treaty; and those who shall remain in the said territories after the expiration of that year, without having declared their intention to retain the character of Mexicans, shall be considered to have elected to become citizens of the United States.

In the said territories, property of every kind, now belonging to Mexicans not established there, shall be inviolably respected. The present owners, the heirs of these, and all Mexicans who may hereafter acquire said property by contract, shall enjoy with respect to it guarantees equally ample as if the same belonged to citizens of the United States.

ARTICLE IX

The Mexicans who, in the territories aforesaid, shall not preserve the character of citizens of the Mexican Republic, conformably with what is stipulated in the preceding article, shall be incorporated into the Union of the United States. and be admitted at the proper time (to be judged of by the Congress of the United States) to the enjoyment of all the rights of citizens of the United States, according to the principles of the Constitution; and in the mean time, shall be maintained and protected in the free enjoyment of their liberty and property, and secured in the free exercise of their religion without restriction.

ARTICLE X

[Stricken out]

ARTICLE XI

Considering that a great part of the territories, which, by the present treaty, are to be comprehended for the future within the limits of the United States, is now occupied by savage tribes, who will hereafter be under the exclusive control of the Government of the United States, and whose incursions within the territory of Mexico would be prejudicial in the extreme, it is solemnly agreed that all such incursions shall be forcibly restrained by the Government of the United States whensoever this may be necessary; and that when they cannot be prevented, they shall be punished by the said Government, and satisfaction for the same shall be exacted all in the same way, and with equal diligence and energy, as if the same incursions were meditated or committed within its own territory, against its own citizens.

It shall not be lawful, under any pretext whatever, for any inhabitant of the United States to purchase or acquire any Mexican, or any foreigner residing in Mexico, who may have been captured by Indians inhabiting the territory of either of the two republics; nor to purchase or acquire horses, mules, cattle, or property of any kind, stolen within Mexican territory by such Indians.

And in the event of any person or persons, captured within Mexican territory by Indians, being carried into the territory of the United States, the Government of the latter engages and binds itself, in the most solemn manner, so soon as it shall know of such captives being within its territory, and shall be able so to do, through the faithful exercise of its influence and power, to rescue them and return them to their country, or deliver them to the agent or representative of the Mexican Government. The Mexican authorities will, as far as practicable, give to the Government of the United States notice of such captures; and its agents shall pay the expenses incurred in the maintenance and transmission of the rescued captives; who, in the mean time, shall be treated with the utmost hospitality by the American authorities at the place where they may be. But if the Government of the United States, before receiving such notice from Mexico, should obtain intelligence, through any other channel, of the existence of Mexican captives within its territory, it will proceed forthwith to effect their release and delivery to the Mexican agent, as above stipulated.

For the purpose of giving to these stipulations the fullest possible efficacy, thereby affording the security and redress demanded by their true spirit and intent, the Government of the United States will now and hereafter pass, without unnecessary delay, and always vigilantly enforce, such laws as the nature of the subject may require. And, finally, the sacredness of this obligation shall never be lost sight of by the said Government, when providing for the removal of the Indians from any portion of the said territories, or for its being settled by citizens of the United States; but, on the contrary, special care shall then be taken not to place its Indian occupants under the necessity of seeking new homes, by committing those invasions which the United States have solemnly obliged themselves to restrain.

ARTICLE X

All grants of land made by the Mexican government or by the competent authorities, in territories previously appertaining to Mexico, and remaining for the future within the limits of the United States, shall be respected as valid, to the same extent that the same grants would be valid, if the said territories had remained within the limits of Mexico. But the grantees of lands in Texas, put in possession thereof, who, by reason of the circumstances of the country since the beginning of the troubles between Texas and the Mexican Government, may have been prevented from fulfilling all the conditions of their grants, shall be under the obligation to fulfill the said conditions within the periods limited in the same respectively; such periods to be now counted from the date of the exchange of ratification's of this treaty: in default of which the said grants shall not be obligatory upon the State of Texas, in virtue of the stipulations contained in this Article.

The foregoing stipulation in regard to grantees of land in Texas, is extended to all grantees of land in the territories aforesaid, elsewhere than in Texas, put in possession under such grants; and, in default of the fulfillment of the conditions of any such grant, within the new period, which, as is above stipulated, begins with the day of the exchange of ratifications of this treaty, the same shall be null and void.

GLOSSARY

appertaining: belonging

character of Mexicans: citizenship of Mexico

Guadalupe Hidalgo: the name of the Basilica of Guadalupe in Villa Hidalgo, where the treaty was signed

plenipotentiaries: diplomats or government representatives with full authority to act on behalf of the leaders who sent them

prejudicial in the extreme: a polite way of stating the incursions to which this phrase applied would devastate the area and cost many Mexicans their lives

redress: remedy; compensation

savage tribes: refers to the Comanches and, to a lesser extent, Apaches and Navajos, whose numerous raids throughout northern Mexico had destroyed the local economy and killed thousands of people prior to the war

Document Analysis

The Treaty of Guadalupe Hidalgo was an exhaustive attempt to outline the steps that should be taken not only to end the Mexican-American War, but also to create a stronger peace in the future. Nicholas Trist and the three Mexican negotiators clearly understood the balance of power between the two nations. However, Trist limited American demands to the goals that had been outlined prior to the war, as well as giving the Mexicans some assistance in rebuilding after the war. The impact of a country's losing more than half its territory cannot be minimized. However, the fact that neither President Polk nor Nicholas Trist listened to Americans who desired to annex all of Mexico indicated that their understanding of Manifest Destiny did not include incorporating all of North America into the United States. Although the United States Senate felt free to make changes to the document, and some provisions of the treaty were not upheld for Mexicans who became American citizens, the main points of the intergovernmental relationship were met by both nations. The relationship reflected in this treaty made possible the Gadsden Purchase, a roughly 30,000-square-mile area occupying present-day southern Arizona and southwestern New Mexico, acquired from Mexico in late 1853.

Obviously, the initial paragraph in the extract above was not a part of the original treaty, since it contains information about the ratification process by the United States after the treaty was signed on February 2, 1848. The designation of this treaty as a "Treaty of Peace, Friendship, Limits, and Settlement" is an attempt to describe the full content and intent of the agreement. It is more than a statement that the war was finished. As with most treaties, this one is better known by the designation of where it was signed, Guadalupe Hidalgo. From the time it was signed, it took just over a month for the United States Senate to amend and ratify it. These changes were referred to the Mexican ambassador to the United States, and he tentatively approved them. The statement "ratified by president, March 16, 1848" indicates that President Polk had accepted the changes made by the Senate. While this was happening, Mexico was formally approving the treaty as well. The meeting with Mexican leaders in Querétaro was to fulfill article 23, which states that representatives of the two governments would meet to exchange formal copies of the ratified treaty. Since the United States had made unilateral changes to the treaty (even though they had

been provisionally accepted by the Mexican ambassador), a second agreement had to be drawn up to reflect these changes and to represent formal acceptance of them by the Mexican government. Thus, the Protocol of Querétaro was drawn up by representatives of the United States and the Mexican minister of foreign affairs. The points in the protocol each address one of the changes by the United States. The first is that the original article 9 (civil rights) was deleted and article 3 of the Treaty of Louisiana (Louisiana Purchase) was substituted. The protocol states that the United States "did not intend to diminish in any way what was agreed upon by the aforesaid article IX." Similarly, the United States claimed that in deleting article 10, it did not intend to take away the "grants of land made by Mexico." Finally, Mexico was assured that the deletion of the last part of article 12 did not change any rights Mexico had with regard to the money that the United States was going to pay. The formal acceptance of these three changes by the Mexican foreign minister made it possible for the agreement to go into effect immediately, without the Mexican government having to repeat its ratification process.

The preamble to the treaty identifies its goal, the nations that were party to the agreement, and who had been authorized to negotiate on behalf of the two nations. The United States of America and the United Mexican States (also called the Mexican Republic) had "a sincere desire to put an end to the calamities of the war which unhappily exists between the two Republics and to establish Upon a solid basis relations of peace and friendship." Thus, Trist and the Mexican representatives had authority from their two governments to make a formal agreement with the intention of creating an enduring peace. They sought to create a situation in which their countries could live together "as good neighbors."

Article 1 states the reason for the agreement: "firm and universal peace" between the two nations was the intent of both. Prior to the war, there had been military threats from both sides. Mexico had threatened war if the United States annexed Texas, which Mexico still claimed, and President Polk had put forward for the United States the idea of Manifest Destiny and began taking appropriate actions to ensure the fulfillment of this idea. Although Polk's campaign slogan of "Fifty-Four Forty or Fight" was directed toward the British, with whom he peacefully negotiated an agreement regarding Oregon territory, his campaign had made it clear that he had a similar goal of extending the United States to California. Because of the rebellion in Texas, there had not been a firm peace between the United States and Mexico for more than a decade.

The three articles not printed in this text (2, 3, and 4) all dealt with the disengagement of military forces, leaving Mexican military supplies and fortifications intact, reestablishing civilian rule, and a timely withdrawal of American troops from Mexico. While most of the moves were to be "at the earliest moment practicable," the withdrawal from Mexico City was to occur within a month from the time the military commander had been notified that the peace treaty had been ratified by both countries. Provisions for mutual support were a part of the treaty; for instance, if the American forces were not able to be withdrawn from the tropical ports on the Gulf of Mexico (Veracruz) by the "sickly season" (May through October), the forces would move inland away from the cities, as protection from the tropical diseases.

Article 5 outlined the new borders between the United States and Mexico. In many ways, this was the most important article in the treaty, as the lack of clarity regarding Texas's borders had initiated the war. It was clear from the descriptions of the new border that none of the negotiators had firsthand experience in that region. They did not even know if the Rio Grande had one or more channels where it entered the Gulf of Mexico or if the Gila River intersected the western border of New Mexico. In terms of the territory that had precipitated the war, the Texas border was set where the United States said it should be, at the Rio Grande. In places where there was uncertainty, reference maps were identified as authoritative for the treaty. In a region that had neither been formally surveyed nor mapped in detail, it was not easy to identify the border clearly. Thus, in the third paragraph of this article, provision is made for a joint surveying team to be appointed in order to identify and mark the boundary between the United States and Mexico. What the surveyors identified, following the directions in the first two paragraphs of this article, would stand as the border and be "religiously respected by each of the two republics." The surveyors did discover that the city of El Paso was actually about a hundred miles west of where the negotiators had assumed it was located, resulting in a dispute until the Gadsden Purchase was negotiated.

Article 6, not printed in this text, details the rights of American ships and boats to free transit through the Gulf of California and up the Colorado River to reach American territory. Prior to the damming of the Colorado and Gila Rivers, it was possible to navigate the sixty miles to what is now Yuma, although the city never developed into a seaport. Examining all possibilities, the treaty also states that if a road or railroad were built close to the Gila River by either country, it would be a cooperative venture to serve both nations. Similar considerations are contained in article 7, which states that rivers forming the boundary between the two nations would be open to navigation by both. However, as the land on each bank belonged to the respective nations, this freedom of movement did not apply to the "landing upon one of their shores." These articles were changed by the Gadsden Purchase's movement of the border further south.

Articles 8 and 9 refer to the rights given to Mexican citizens who would live in the United States as a result of the transfer of more than 525,000 square miles of territory west of the state of Texas. These articles of the treaty were the ones least observed by various jurisdictions in the United States, as the property of many former Mexican citizens was not respected. Article 8 gives Mexican citizens now in United States territory one year in which to decide whether they wanted to retain Mexican citizenship or accept American citizenship. The default was for them to become American citizens. If they chose to return to Mexico, they were free to dispose of their property and take "the proceeds wherever they please." This article also grants the right of property ownership in the United States to Mexican citizens "as if the same belonged to citizens of the United States." Article 9 was shortened by the US Senate, to bring it into greater conformity with the laws for all other territories. The shortened article 9 is a basic statement that the territory would become states in accordance with the laws governing this process, and in the meantime, the people would have "the free enjoyment of their liberty and property, and secured in the free exercise of their religion without restriction." The deleted text included a guarantee that they would keep any rights they had under Mexican law, rights matching those given to people in the former Louisiana or Florida territories; a guarantee regarding the freedom for religious officials "in the discharge of the offices of their ministry"; and a statement that Catholics in the new American territories would have free access to and unhindered communication with Catholic officials in Mexico.

Article 10 was deleted from the treaty but is printed

here at the end of the excerpt above. Even though the Protocol of Querétaro states that "suppressing" this section did not "annul the grants of lands made by Mexico in the ceded territories," this was actually the intent of many who supported this change. In California, the very large haciendas (estates) granted by the Spanish and Mexican governments were not respected by the American settlers. In addition, during the decade between Texas obtaining its independence and its annexation to the United States, land grants had been made in that territory by the Mexican government. This article would have mandated that Texas and the United States respect these grants, some of which would have conflicted with deeds issued by Texas. Thus, for logistical reasons in Texas and by the desires of Americans more generally, article 10 was stricken by the Senate. The Protocol of Querétaro was a simple way of getting the treaty wording accepted by the Mexican government. While the American negotiators may have believed that the protocol would be supported in Washington, it was never really implemented by the US government.

The last article printed in this text, article 11, had to do with the predominant American Indian tribes in the region acquired by the United States. The Comanche confederation and two Apache tribes had become major problems for Mexico. Spain had made peace with most of the tribes in the eighteenth century, but that was not seen as applying to Mexico. Thus, since the 1820s, thousands of people had been killed and the economic ventures of the Mexicans had suffered greatly. Because the American settlers were willing to trade for the cattle and horses the American Indians had taken in their raids, many Mexicans believed the Americans were encouraging the American Indians to continue their raids on Mexican settlements. Since the traditional homelands of the tribes would become part of the United States, they became the problem of the United States. As such, the United States promises that "all such incursions shall be forcibly restrained by the government of the United States." This was easier to put into a document than to carry out. Many historians believe that this was the only positive thing to come out of the war for Mexico. In the first few years after the war, almost three-quarters of the US Army was assigned to this task, with limited success. Mexico was demanding more protection and/or reparations. When the treaty for the Gadsden Purchase was being negotiated, the United States paid Mexico to accept the negation of article 11.

Not printed in this text, article 12 states that the American government would pay Mexico fifteen million dollars for the land being acquired and gives a schedule for the payments. (This was less than half the money that had been offered prior to the war.) In addition, article 13 states that the United States will assume payment to United States citizens for American court judgments that had been made against Mexico, a sum of no more than $3.25 million, according to article 15. Article 14 states that no further claims could be made, and article 15 clarifies the process for paying the claims.

Article 16 allows both countries to "fortify whatever point within its territory it may judge proper." The next article renews an 1831 commerce treaty. Article 18 clarifies that money or goods sent to Mexico to support American troops would not be subject to any Mexican taxes. On a related topic, article 19 describes how taxes should be applied to nonmilitary goods that came into areas of Mexico not occupied by American forces during the war, and article 20 deals with the importation of goods between the time the treaty is signed and is ratified. Article 21 promises that if any "disagreement shall hereafter arise between the Governments of the two republics," they would try to resolve their differences peacefully. Article 22 lists certain rules that would be followed if another war were to break out. The final article, article 23, deals with the ratification and notification process for the treaty.

Trist and his Mexican counterparts strove to make certain that all contingencies were covered in the treaty. It passed this test in that President Polk—who, when he received it, had already fired Trist and was looking for any flaws—accepted the treaty and sent it on to the Senate. The Mexican officials had very little choice in the major provisions of the treaty. The most important point was that the treaty did end the war, on terms desired by the United States, and allowed the United States and Mexico to enter into a more peaceful, if not always harmonious, relationship.

Essential Themes

The Mexican-American War had come about because both the United States and Mexico had pushed toward the brink, allowing one small skirmish to result in a full-blown war. President Polk had tried to negotiate for the desired territory, while constant turmoil in the Mexican government did not allow for any substantive negotiations. Once the war started, the United States forces pushed back the Mexican army until Mexico had no real choice but to negotiate. For the United States, the most important point in the treaty was Mexico giving up any claim to the land from the eastern border of Texas to the Pacific coast in California. This is outlined in article 5, and the ceded territory contained everything that Trist had been told to request, from the Rio Grande to San Diego. While ending the war as soon as possible was essential and peaceful relations with Mexico were important, the key point in the treaty was what is known as the Mexican Cession, the territory acquired by the United States. Manifest Destiny, as envisioned by American leaders, was not to be stopped for any reason. Other points in the treaty, such as the rights of Mexican citizens in the new territories and property and commercial rights, represented items similar to what had been outlined in previous annexation treaties. Although it is doubtful that the US government agreed to these provisions without intending to fulfill all its obligations, these were of substantially lower importance than the territory. Since the ratification of the Treaty of Guadalupe Hidalgo, the two nations have not only peacefully coexisted, but have developed closer cooperation across many areas of mutual concern.

—*Donald A. Watt, PhD*

Bibliography and Additional Reading

Griswold del Castillo, Richard. "Appendix 1: The Original Text of Articles IX and X of the Treaty of Guadalupe Hidalgo and the Protocol of Querétaro." *The Treaty of Guadalupe Hidalgo: A Legacy of Conflict.* Norman: U of Oklahoma P, 1990. 179–82. Print.

Ohrt, Wallace. *Defiant Peacemaker: Nicholas Trist in the Mexican War.* College Station: Texas A; M UP, 1997. Print.

"Treaty of Guadalupe Hidalgo; February 2, 1848." *Treaties and Conventions between the United States of America and Other Powers since July 4, 1776.* Washington: GPO, 1871. Avalon Project. Web. 15 Mar. 2013.

U.S.-Mexican War: 1846–1848. KERA, 14 Mar. 2006. Web. 15 Mar. 2013.

Bloom, John Porter, ed. *The Treaty of Guadalupe Hidalgo, 1848.* Las Cruces: Yucca Tree, 1999. Print.

Mahin, Dean B. *Olive Branch and Sword: the United States and Mexico, 1845–1848.* Jefferson: McFarland, 1997. Print.

Merry, Robert W. *A Country of Vast Designs: James K. Polk, the Mexican War, and the Conquest of the American Continent.* New York: Simon, 2009. Print.

"*Milestones: 1830–1860.*" Office of the Historian. Bureau of Public Affairs, United States Department of State, 2010. Web. 15 Mar. 2013.

Schroeder, John H. *Mr. Polk's War: American Opposition and Dissent, 1846–1848.* Madison: U of Wisconsin P, 1973. Print.

■ On Seizing Land from Native Californians

Date: April 1855
Author: Pablo de la Guerra
Genre: speech

Summary Overview

In his speech known as "On Seizing Land from Native Californians," Pablo de la Guerra—an influential nineteenth-century Mexican American politician in the California State Assembly—addresses the state Senate regarding a ratified bill known as the Land Law (1851), which allowed for the seizure of land by the US government if its Latino residents failed to provide official documentation of their land grants. Scant documentation of land rights existed during this era, leading to the unjust confiscation of land and, thus, an eradication of the rights codified by the Treaty of Guadalupe Hidalgo at the conclusion of the Mexican-American War (1846–48). As one of the only Mexican American citizens serving in the California State Assembly, de la Guerra used that political forum to voice his opposition to the blatant social injustice experienced by native Mexicans in the aftermath of the war. Although the Treaty of Guadalupe Hidalgo promised the protection of native land grants from American settlers migrating west, the US government ostensibly ignored the treaty with the onset of the California gold rush and allowed for the land to be claimed by settlers. De la Guerra subtly elucidates the racialization of Mexican Americans initiated by the treaty through poignant diction and language. During an epoch in which the ideology of Manifest Destiny guided US foreign policy, de la Guerra attempts to give a political voice to Mexican Americans by protecting their landholdings through legal means during an era of unequal representation in politics. He engages with ubiquitous tropes in the Latino counternarrative, dealing with issues surrounding race, citizenship, and multiculturalism in a country that claims its fundamental pillars to be liberty and democracy. De la Guerra's speech conveys a legacy of conflict and hardship wrought by the Treaty of Guadalupe Hidalgo and elucidates the origin of the Latino civil rights movement within the treaty itself and the social injustice that enabled the trend of land loss throughout annexed Mexican territory. The racial logic of white hegemony undergirded US foreign policy along with overt economic motives.

Defining Moment

The nineteenth century was an epoch of rapid westward US expansion as a result of "Manifest Destiny" and the reimagining of occupied land and space as available. Coined by John O'Sullivan, Manifest Destiny—the view that claimed God wanted the people of the United States to control all North American land from the Atlantic to the Pacific Oceans—became the central ideology for US foreign policy and expansion during the nineteenth century. The shifting frontier became associated with American identity of the "rugged individual" espoused by Frederick Jackson Turner, an American historian whose frontier thesis argued that up until the 1890s, the history of the United States had been characterized by territorial expansion, military conquest, and cultural amalgamation; westward expansion defined the United States and justified the divinely ordained American prerogative to seize control of the land despite the presence of native inhabitants whose claim to the land harked back centuries before the existence of the United States. De la Guerra's speech elucidates both how the myth of a vanishing frontier functioned and the material consequences it spawned: the illegal seizure of native Mexicans' land by the conquering United States in the aftermath of the Mexican-American War. The war centered on a dispute over land in the Rio Grande territory and resulted in US victory; the subsequent peace treaty shifted geopolitical borders of the United States and Mexico. Mexicans immediately became colonized persons within their homeland; this idea undergirded the Chicano movement during the twentieth century, as participants based their movement on the imagined homeland they called Aztlán, the American Southwest stolen from them at the conclusion of the Mexican-American War.

The colonization of the West and the expansion of

the American frontier into previously Mexican territory complicated both the definition of American citizenship and who received its full privileges. With the ratification of the Treaty of Guadalupe Hidalgo, US borders quickly changed, rendering Mexicans living in the region subject to US rule with little protection despite the treaty's promises. De la Guerra emerged as one of the sole advocates for Mexican American land claims and sought to defend them against racial violence. Born a Mexican citizen, de la Guerra sympathized with the natives when land-seizure bills continued to be put forth in the Senate. His speech addressing an unsympathetic Senate questioned the "liberal myth" of the United States as founded on democratic principles of equality and liberty by highlighting the injustice undergirding the land-seizure bills targeting Mexicans as conquered citizens of color. Annexed by the United States as a result of the Mexican-American War, the American Southwest complicated and redefined the meanings of nationality and citizenship. Mexicans were given an ascriptive form of citizenship that the government used to deflect the reality that Mexicans were a conquered people. The negotiation of Mexican land that de la Guerra discusses serves as a microcosm for the experience of persons of color in the United States as the definition of citizenship was contested and reformulated throughout the nineteenth and twentieth centuries.

Author Biography

Pablo de la Guerra was born on November 29, 1819, in Santa Barbara, California—then a viceroyalty of Spain—into a distinguished household. He was born in a Spanish colony, worked for the Mexican government in what became the Mexican state of California after Mexican independence, and died a US citizen after his homeland came under US hegemony following the Mexican-American War. His father, José de la Guerra, migrated from Spain to Mexico during the 1790s and married Antonia Carrillo, a member of a well-to-do family residing in California. Born a Mexican citizen, de la Guerra chose to naturalize as an American citizen under the terms of the 1848 Treaty of Guadalupe Hidalgo.

Because of his family's prestige within the community, de la Guerra became an active public servant, serving in local and statewide government legislative bodies, including California's constitutional convention in 1849. This convention formally granted Mexicans citizenship rights enjoyed by whites, hinting at the racial prerequisites of "whiteness" for American citizenship. Delegates

came to a consensus that "a small amount of Indian blood" was admissible for US citizenship, and Mexicans would be formally enfranchised while excluding both African Americans and American Indians. In 1850, California was officially recognized as a state, which conferred on de la Guerra US citizenship. During the 1860s, de la Guerra became the acting lieutenant governor of California and also served in the California state legislature. Legally defined as white, de la Guerra relished the privileges enjoyed by white citizens, especially in the political arena; his political clout—a rarity for individuals of Mexican descent during that era—gave him a forum for his advocacy of Mexican American rights. As a member of the California State Assembly and Senate, de la Guerra emerged as an advocate for Mexican American rights and was recognized as dependable by both Latinos and whites.

However, when de la Guerra was elected as a California state court judge in 1869, California filed a lawsuit that questioned his eligibility for the position based on his questionable citizenship because of the color of his skin. The prosecutor, M. M. Kimberly, argued that the California act of April 20, 1863, stipulated that only US citizens retained eligibility for the elected office of district judge. Invoking several articles of the Treaty of Guadalupe Hidalgo, Kimberly argued that de la Guerra was not a US citizen, because the treaty never granted the power to render Mexicans or Americans Indians citizens and because he was not white. De la Guerra rebutted that he was white and therefore was excluded from the racial laws in practice in California. Although the California Supreme Court sided with de la Guerra by classifying him as white, and therefore exempt from racial laws, the decision reaffirmed citizenship as race-based; as a white citizen, de la Guerra had the privileges of citizenship under constitutional law protected while nonwhite Mexicans did not. Thus, the US government retained the power to distribute political privileges to individuals on the basis of race.

Despite his legal battles, de la Guerra remained a staunch advocate for Mexican American rights and claims under the stipulations of the Treaty of Guadalupe Hidalgo. He fought every land-seizure bill that entered the Senate and ultimately set the foundation for the Hispanic American civil rights movement during the twentieth century. Eventually, mounting political pressure defeated his efforts as white settlers migrating to California vehemently demanded reclamation of the "vacant" land. De la Guerra died on February 5, 1874.

HISTORICAL DOCUMENT

I hope the Senate will allow me to offer a few remarks upon the merits of the bill, and to state why, upon the principles of reason and justice I consider that the bill should be indefinitely postponed. :

Well, sir, the war took place, and we, after doing our duty as citizens of Mexico, were sold like sheep abandoned by our nation, and as it were, awoke from a dream, strangers on the very soil on which we were native and to the manor born. We passed from the hands of Mexico to that of the United States, but we had the consolation of believing that the United States, as a nation, was more liberal than our own. We had the greatest respect for an American. Every American who came to our country was held in higher estimation than even one of our countrymen. And I call upon every American who visited us to bear testimony to this fact. And after being abandoned by our own country and annexed to the United States, we thought that we belonged to a nation the most civilized, the most humane-a nation that was the foremost in planting the banner of liberty on every portion of its dominions-a nation that was the most careful in protecting the just rights of its citizens. Well, sir, in 1849, a great many emigrated to California, not to settle upon the land or to cultivate the soil, but to work in the mines and go home; and from '49 to '52 they had no other object, but many finding that it was hard work in the mines, and being told that the land in the State had not been separated from the public domain, had no boundaries and being probably further misled by lawyers, or interested persons, who stated that the land in this condition would never be confirmed to the owners by the Supreme Court of the United States, came and settled upon our lands. And I ask, are we to suffer for that?

I believe that I speak advisedly, when I say that three-fourths of the settlers upon the lands, have been aware that someone had a prior claim; they knew it by common report, that such a one and such a one had a claim upon the land; but they thought that even if it was confirmed to the owners, that the use of the land until the confirmation, would be worth more than the improvements that they would make. Perhaps one-fourth went upon the land in good faith. I do not know that such was the case, but I am willing to grant it; but now, when they find

that it is probable that the Supreme Court of the United States will confirm these grants, and after deriving all the benefits for the use of the same, they apply to the Legislature, in order that a State Law may be set up as a bar against the action of the Court of the United States.

I say, sir, that already we have suffered deeply; our property has been sacrificed. The Bay of San Francisco alone, at one time, had more cattle than can now be found in the counties of Santa Clara, Monterey, Santa Cruz, San Luis Obispo, and Santa Barbara. Horses, at that time could be counted by the thousands; and I believe that many settlers have settled upon lands for the purposes of stealing the cattle and sending them to the San Francisco market for sale.

Now, sir, of the 113 members in this Legislature, I am the only native of this state; and the native population expect from me, and through me, that in my place in this Legislative Hall, that I shall call the attention of this body to the facts I have now stated, and to tell you that badly treated as they have been in every respect, they look around them and find no other aid except in the mercy of Heaven, and the justice of this Legislature; and now, in their name, I call upon you, Senators, to consider that if they are deprived of what is left to them, they have no other place to go to. They have been rejected by the Mexicans; they know no other country but California, and by depriving them of their rights, they will be compelled to be beggars in the streets; and in order to prevent this terrible calamity from overtaking them, they, through me, throw themselves upon your mercy and clemency; and they ask and expect from you protection that will justify before the eyes of the world the belief in justice of the American people. If the American settlers are deprived of what they have expended for their improvements, they can go home and meet the aid and sympathies of their friends and countrymen; but the Californian, what prospect has he before him, or where shall he go?

I wish to make one remark about the expression, "settled in good faith," and I am done. Sir, if this bill has effect, it will be from the countries of Santa Clara upward, because in the south we have no settlers; but in those counties I am now referring to, the settlers greatly outnumber the land claimants, and it is useless to say that juries are incorruptible. We know that such is not the case from our daily experience. And these juries will be formed by whom? Sir, they will consist of those very settlers. The Sheriff will summon such a jury as will suit their views. I have seen a good deal of juries in California. I have seen where proof, clear as noon day, would not alter the decision of a jury from their preconceived opinions.

And I will affirm that I believe that out of 100 cases tried between the settlers and the land owners that 99 will be given in favor of the settler.

And, sir, to conclude these remarks, permit me to assure you, upon my honor as a gentleman, that everything I have stated is true and as clear as conviction itself. I know that I am in the Senate chamber of California, where full liberty of speech is allowed, but if I were speaking to a barbarous people, I should still advocate the same sentiments, and even if I were killed for so doing, I should at least have the satisfaction of dying in a just cause, and should receive the reward from Him who has said, "Blessed are those who are persecuted, for righteousness sake, for of such is the kingdom of heaven."

GLOSSARY

calamity: catastrophe, disaster

clemency: forgiveness, mercifulness

consolation: comfort, solace

liberal: progressive, favorable to reform

the war: Refers to the Mexican-American War, in which the United States defeated Mexico and annexed the land that comprises the modern-day American Southwest (including California)

Document Analysis

De la Guerra's speech represents a defense of Mexican American civil rights and laid the foundation for the subsequent twentieth-century Chicano movement. The language he uses alludes to the racial undertones of US immigration and foreign policy during the nineteenth century; in a covert fashion, de la Guerra addresses and laments an American legal system supported by structural and institutional racism that denies persons of color the protections promised by US citizenship. Thus, his staunch defense of land rights highlights broader themes in US history regarding racial hegemony. Invoking a recurring theme of liberty, de la Guerra juxtaposes the actions of the US government with the rudimentary American value of liberty to elucidate the dissonance, and thus hypocrisy, of American values. Born a Mexican citizen into a well-to-do family, de la Guerra possessed political clout that he was willing to exercise in his fight for social justice for Mexican Americans. De la Guerra—the only California native serving in the state legislature—not only recognized the injustices occurring around him but also demonstrated the courage to stand up to a government comprising elite white men who possessed the salient racial attitudes that characterized the time period.

In the opening of his speech, de la Guerra describes native Mexicans as docile, compliant citizens despite their savage treatment at the hands of the US government during and after the Mexican-American War. Identifying himself at the outset with these native Mexicans despite his position in the California legislature, de la Guerra quickly establishes himself as an advocate for and defender of native rights despite his decision to naturalize as an American citizen. His goal in this speech is twofold: he seeks to subvert common knowledge in US public discourse and cultural attitudes toward Mexicans and subtly expose the fallacy of American values and character. He does so immediately by using specific diction associated with the mythos of the United States and its founding principles. The United States expanded westward by touting itself as a beacon of liberty, spreading democracy, equality, and freedom across the North American continent. Native Mexicans viewed the United States as a "humane . . .

nation" that would welcome, embrace, and protect inhabitants of Mexico as equal citizens. These expectations articulated by de la Guerra mirror the sentiments held by immigrants throughout American history who seek refuge in a country that promises a better life and equal, just treatment.

Such expectations of the United States expressed by de la Guerra on behalf of the Mexican Americans he served emanate from the mythos in public discourse and public consciousness; myths transcend stereotypes and become deeply embedded within the social consciousness. Through his subtle assertion of Mexicans as second-class citizens, de la Guerra realizes the fallacy of the myth of a United States "more liberal" than Mexico in its approach to immigration and assimilation, and he conveys such sentiments through his exasperated tone at the outset of his speech.

The promised protection of citizenship rights of Mexican Americans and the ensuing violation of them contribute to de la Guerra's postulate that US values had become the antithesis of what they claimed to be through founding documents such as the Constitution. Prior to and during the Mexican-American War, American settlers were considered aliens in Mexico whose presence was not welcomed by the native Mexicans. Following American victory, the United States annexed the territory known as the Mexican Cession. Arbitrary land laws passed by the US government at the state and national levels made the "calamity" of loss of land and citizenship possible and left Mexicans in the annexed territory vulnerable to attacks on their rights. Laws such as those for which de la Guerra expresses disapproval in his speech thereby arbitrarily constructed Mexicans as illegal, rendering them "strangers" on their native soil. Mexicans living within the territorial borders of the United States had no legal status; "abandoned" by Mexico and betrayed by the United States. As de la Guerra notes, without their rights protected vis-à-vis land grants, Mexicans would become "beggars" in the street hoping for law courts to uphold justice. Therefore, de la Guerra contends that the hypocritical actions of the US government make its representatives the true "barbarians," rather than the Mexicans whom they ostensibly sought to enlighten.

Anglo-Americans never fully accepted Mexicans as racial equals despite allowing those living in the ceded territories to acquire US citizenship. Manifest Destiny—the ideology that guided US expansion throughout the nineteenth century—glorified the white set-

tler. As historian Mae M. Ngai discusses, though US expansionists desired to control all of Mexico, racial suspicions led them to abandon such sentiments out of aversion to incorporating a nonwhite race into the United States. De la Guerra recognizes such racial attitudes and suspicions held by the US government in his speech and uses both metaphors and particular diction to convey the binary of civilized and uncivilized peoples, but he does so to subvert popular conceptions. Although viewed as barbarous, savage, and uncivilized, Mexicans, de la Guerra asserts, treated the United States and its citizens upon annexation with respect and fidelity. Conversely, however, rather than receive "humane" treatment, Mexicans had their land seized by the government and reclaimed by white settlers despite their knowledge of its rightful ownership. Furthermore, de la Guerra laments the institutional racism toward Mexican Americans underpinning the US legal system. Viewing juries comprising settlers as corruptible and possessing "preconceived opinions," de la Guerra critiques the inequities latent in law courts dealing with land-claim disputes. He thereby suggests that juries racialized Mexicans and rendered them second-class citizens because of their nationality and race; thus, Mexicans could never fully acculturate and become truly American. Therefore, Mexicans remained at the fringe of US citizenship because of their second-class treatment at the hands of a government that touted the values of equality and liberty for all.

The dissonance between the function of land in Mexican culture—a culture rooted in land as a sacred space to be protected and treasured—and its capitalistic role in American culture further explain the cruel actions of the American government that de le Guerra describes in his speech. De la Guerra outlines the emotional trauma of native Mexicans losing their land and having their property "sacrificed" and "stolen" for the economic gain of a conquering nation. Euro-American colonialism and expansion across the North American continent historically led to violent encounters between natives and the European colonists. The cultural divide between the natives and the colonists regarding the sanctity and importance of land within their respective worldviews catalyzed colonial antagonisms once the natives were uprooted from their sacred lands. The removal and dissociation of natives from their culturally sacred land—to which they had been tied both spatially and culturally for thousands of years—conveys how land lay at the heart of the violent colonial practices waged against indigenous communities in the American Southwest. Mexicans not only viewed land as the key to their survival but also as tied in to their spirituality and religious beliefs. De la Guerra laments how US capitalism led to the exploitation for the sake of profit of Mexican's once fertile lands. He thus highlights the primacy of capitalism—a profit-driven and amoral economic system—in the development of the United States. Capitalism required the alienation of native land claims by reimagining American land as unclaimed to enable white settlers to claim it as their own. Thus, de la Guerra implies, westward expansion was rooted in conquest, with latent political, economic, and cultural imperatives rather than the mere desire to "plant" and spread the "banner of liberty" in Mexican soil.

De la Guerra invokes religiosity to further highlight the hypocrisy of the government's actions in seizing native land. Rendered stateless and unprotected by a conquering US government that violated its own treaty, Mexican Americans became "beggars in the streets" whose livelihood depended on the mercy of a settler government who perceived Mexicans as lesser people. De la Guerra questions the moral basis of settlers occupying Mexican land "in good faith" by questioning the religious justification for stealing land. Such actions delineate the US government as "barbarous people" rather than the enlightened, righteous, and civilized individuals that they tout themselves to be. Thus, de la Guerra invokes the religious principles Americans claim fundamentally underpin the country's origin to expose the hypocrisy and irreligious behavior involved in stealing land and persecuting native Mexicans. Such sentiments subvert the images of the civilized Yankee and subhuman Mexican that dominated public attitudes and discourse during a turbulent epoch. The conquest and annexation of Mexican territory catalyzed a period of US foreign policy marked by colonialism and imperialism that had lasting consequences for the United States in terms of both its global relations and its internal structures.

Essential Themes

The US government continued to treat Mexicans as second-class citizens following the Treaty of Guadalupe Hidalgo; unequal political representation and the absence of protection for Mexican American citizenship rights through the seizure of land revealed such second-class treatment. Overtly racist stereotypes soon permeated public discourse, and anti-Mexican rhetoric resulted in a production of knowledge regarding the figure of the Mexican as dirty, incompetent, and subhuman. The emergence of scientific racism contributed to the degradation of Mexicans well into the twentieth century and underlay the efforts to restrict Mexican immigration during the 1920s despite the need for cheap labor in the agribusinesses of the Southwest. As Ngai notes, although racialized, Mexicans retained a legal status as white, although this category remained unstable because of their race. Their presence in regions once under Mexican control rendered them "racialized aliens" whose labor was needed but presence was resented because of the to the deep-seated antagonisms dating back to the Treaty of Guadalupe Hidalgo and subsequent land seizures.

De la Guerra delivered his speech on the seizure of native land prior to his legal debacle regarding his fitness for citizenship and service in California legislative bodies. Despite suffering from the injustice latent in government institutions toward citizens of Mexican descent, de la Guerra emerged as the sole advocate for native rights in the California Senate during a time when ideas connoted by Manifest Destiny permeated both elite circles and the public domain. Despite de la Guerra's efforts to advocate for and defend native rights, the system of white hegemony prevailed. Nonetheless, his efforts served as a foundation for a subsequent civil rights movement during the twentieth century known as the Chicano movement. This cultural movement during the 1960s sought to revive native Mexican culture and reclaim land that was rightfully theirs in the American Southwest. Members of the Chicano movement sought to reclaim their homeland of Aztlán, thereby aligning Mexican Americans with the American Indian cause. Furthermore, the psychological trauma of Mexican American loss of land led their descendants to negotiate a new identity for Mexican Americans that claimed indigeneity and resulted in the emergence of a nationalism based on culture rather than geopolitical borders and mythos.

—*Maddie Weissman, MA*

Bibliography and Additional Reading

Menchaca, Martha. *Recovering History, Constructing Race: The Indian, Black, and White Roots of Mexican Americans*. Austin: U of Texas P, 2001. Print.

Ngai, Mae M. *Impossible Subjects: Illegal Aliens and the Making of Modern America*. Princeton: Princeton

UP, 2004. Print.

Smith, Andrea. *Conquest: Sexual Violence and American Indian Genocide*. Cambridge, MA: South End, 2005.

Garcia y Griego, Manuel. "Persistence and Disintegration: New Mexico's Community Land Grants in Historical Perspective." *Natural Resources Journal* 48.4 (2008): 847–56. Academic Search Premier. Web. 12 Aug. 2012.

Hernández, Sonia. "The Legacy of the Treatyof GuadalupeHidalgo on Tejanos' Land." *Journal of Popular Culture* 35.2 (2001): 101. Print.

Johnson, Kevin R. *Immigration, Citizenship, and U.S./Mexico Relations*. Bilingual Review 25.1 (2000): 23–39. Print.

"Pablo de la Guerra Speaks Out against Injustice." *Santa Barbara Independent*. Santa Barbara Independent, 2 Aug. 2007. Web. 12 Aug. 2012.

■ Walt Whitman: The Spanish Element in Our Nationality

Date: July 20, 1883
Author: Walt Whitman
Genre: letter

Summary Overview

In the summer of 1883, the citizens of Santa Fe, New Mexico, celebrated the 333rd anniversary of the city's settlement (based on a presumed settlement date of 1550, although 1610 is now used as the accepted year). City leaders invited prominent American poet Walt Whitman to deliver a commemorative poem on the occasion. Whitman instead penned a letter—published in papers throughout the country—that criticized the popular notion of a predominantly Anglo-Saxon heritage in the United States and spoke of the need to take into consideration Hispanic contributions to American culture as the United States continued to develop its national identity.

Defining Moment

By the mid-nineteenth century, many Americans held strongly negative views of Hispanic Americans. Much of this sentiment stemmed from the Texas War of Independence against Mexico (1835–36) and the subsequent Mexican-American War (1846–48). The Treaty of Guadalupe Hidalgo, which brought an end to the Mexican-American War, established the Rio Grande as the border between the United States and Mexico, giving the United States ownership of California, Nevada, Utah, and large portions of present-day Arizona, New Mexico, Colorado, and Wyoming, which had formerly been under Mexican control. The approximately eighty-five thousand Mexican citizens living in these areas were given the option to move south of the new border or remain on their property for one year and become US citizens. The strong patriotic fervor stirred by the US victory over Mexico and the surge of American settlers into the newly conquered southwestern territories led to widespread discrimination against individuals of Hispanic descent.

As a result of this "Hispanophobia," many of the legal and social institutions established by Spain during the colonial years and by Mexico in the years following the country's independence in 1821 were replaced with white Anglo-Saxon practices by the mid- to late 1800s. Spanish names were removed from institutions and cities and replaced with anglicized versions. Mexicans living in the Southwest and in the Rio Grande Valley faced significant legal harassment, land seizures, and violence. It was in this context that Walt Whitman penned his letter to the people of Santa Fe on the occasion of the anniversary of the city's settlement. Whitman was unable to attend the celebrations, but instead published his letter in several national newspapers, so that people across the country could read his thoughts on the importance of Hispanic influences on American culture.

Author Biography

Walt Whitman was born on May 31, 1819, in West Hills, New York. He later moved with his family to Brooklyn. He received a basic education, but at the age of eleven, he began to educate himself on such topics as literature, history, and art. He became an apprentice at a local newspaper and developed a talent for typesetting, a practice that supported him throughout his career. As a young adult, Whitman began to travel throughout the United States, composing poetry based on inspiring scenes and individuals he saw. He also developed an interest in political issues; for example, one of his seminal works, *Leaves of Grass* (1855), includes a harsh indictment of slavery. Whitman had a successful career combining writing and publishing, and he is among the most influential American poets of all time. After volunteering as a nurse during the Civil War and working as a government clerk in Washington, DC, Whitman moved to Camden, New Jersey, where he continued to produce poetry, publishing several revised editions of *Leaves of Grass*, despite ailing from a stroke. Whitman died on March 26, 1892, at his home in Camden.

HISTORICAL DOCUMENT

CAMDEN, NEW JERSEY,

July 20, 1883.

To Messrs. Griffin, Martinez, Prince, and other Gentlemen at Santa Fé:

DEAR SIRS:—Your kind invitation to visit you and deliver a poem for the 333d Anniversary of founding Santa Fé has reach'd me so late that I have to decline, with sincere regret. But I will say a few words off hand.

We Americans have yet to really learn our own antecedents, and sort them, to unify them. They will be found ampler than has been supposed, and in widely different sources. Thus far, impress'd by New England writers and schoolmasters, we tacitly abandon ourselves to the notion that our United States have been fashion'd from the British Islands only, and essentially form a second England only—which is a very great mistake. Many leading traits for our future national personality, and some of the best ones, will certainly prove to have originated from other than British stock. As it is, the British and German, valuable as they are in the concrete, already threaten excess. Or rather, I should say, they have certainly reach'd that excess. To-day, something outside of them, and to counterbalance them, is seriously needed.

The seething materialistic and business vortices of the United States, in their present devouring relations, controlling and belittling everything else, are, in my opinion, but a vast and indispensable stage in the new world's development, and are certainly to be follow'd by something entirely different—at least by immense modifications. Character, literature, a society worthy the name, are yet to be establish'd, through a nationality of noblest spiritual, heroic and democratic attributes—not one of which at present definitely exists—entirely different from the past, though unerringly founded on it, and to justify it. To that composite American identity of the future, Spanish character will supply some of the most needed parts. No stock shows a grander historic retrospect—grander in religiousness and loyalty, or for patriotism, courage, decorum, gravity and honor. (It is time to dismiss utterly the illusion-compound, half raw-head-and-bloody-bones and half *Mysteries-of-Udolpho,* inherited from the English writers of the past 200 years. It is time to realize—for it is certainly true—that there will not be found any more cruelty, tyranny, superstition, &c., in the résumé of past Spanish history than in the corresponding résumé of Anglo-Norman history. Nay, I think there will not be found so much.)

Then another point, relating to American ethnology, past and to come, I will here touch upon at a venture. As to our aboriginal or Indian population—the Aztec in the South, and many a tribe in the North and West—I know it seems to be agreed that they must gradually dwindle as time rolls on, and in a few generations more leave only a reminiscence, a blank. But I am not at all clear about that. As America, from its many far-back sources and current supplies, develops, adapts, entwines, faithfully identifies its own—are we to see it cheerfully accepting and using all the contributions of foreign lands from the whole outside globe—and then rejecting the only ones distinctively its own—the autochthonic ones?

As to the Spanish stock of our Southwest, it is certain to me that we do not begin to appreciate the splendor and sterling value of its race element. Who knows but that element, like the course of some subterranean river, dipping invisibly for a hundred or two years, is now to emerge in broadest flow and permanent action?

If I might assume to do so, I would like to send you the most cordial, heartfelt congratulations of your American fellow-countrymen here. You have more friends in the Northern and Atlantic regions than you suppose, and they are deeply interested in the development of the great Southwestern interior, and in what your festival would arouse to public attention.

Very respectfully, &c.,
WALT WHITMAN.

GLOSSARY

autochthonic: indigenous; originating where found

Mysteries of Udolpho: a reference to a 1794 Gothic novel by Ann Radcliffe

Document Analysis

Whitman's comments, part of a congratulatory message to the people of Santa Fe, offer a reminder that US society is born of a much more complex ancestral tapestry than most Americans at the time were willing to acknowledge. Whitman opens his letter by noting that "we Americans have yet to really learn our own antecedents, and sort them, to unify them. They will be found ampler than has been supposed, and in widely different sources." Although Americans, particularly in the Northeast, were often led to believe that their cultural heritage was predominantly British in origin, Whitman suggests that Americans should take into account the Hispanic culture and traditions that have influenced the nation, particularly in the Southwest and West, in a deep and positive manner.

Whitman's first point is that Americans are largely blinded by a common misperception that Americans are descended from northern European stock. In particular, he argues, Americans are taught that their culture and way of life have been fashioned solely in the British manner. In essence, he suggests that Americans have been led to see their nation as a "second England," an idea that he derides as a "very great mistake." Rather, Whitman states that many of the outstanding traits that have helped to form the unique American national character have undoubtedly been derived from countries and cultures outside of the British Isles and territories.

This choice of words is significant, as he is suggesting that American society was still a work in progress. Even the trends that he finds most troubling—such as the United States' growing economic power, which he terms "the seething materialistic and business vortices of the United States"—are likely to change as the nation continues to develop its sense of self. He explains, "As it is, the British and German, valuable as they are in the concrete, already threaten excess. . . . To-day, something outside of them, and to counterbalance them, is seriously needed."

Hispanic influences, Whitman argues, can help supply some of the "most needed parts" to establishing a national identity, citing elements of the "Spanish character," such as religious piety, loyalty, courage, honor, and patriotism, that are worthy of emulation. He quickly dismisses prevailing notions of Spain as a bastion of aggression and tyranny—centuries-old beliefs that helped to fuel long-standing feuds between England and Spain prior to and throughout the colonization of the Americas. Whitman even suggests that Anglo-Saxon practices of the time could easily be compared to the tyranny and cruelty of Spain in the past. Whitman then turns his attention to the "Spanish stock of our Southwest," suggesting that Americans "do not begin to appreciate the splendor and sterling value of its race element." He suggests that appreciation of Hispanic culture comes in and out fashion, similar to the course of an underground river. He expresses hope that such appreciation "is now to emerge in broadest flow and permanent action."

Finally, Whitman also takes a moment to honor the indigenous peoples of North America and their unique cultural contributions. He states that many of these tribes are dwindling in number and threatening to disappear from the nation's memory. Whitman cautions that, if the United States is to look outside its borders for inspiration on how to define itself as a nation, it must not ignore the unique native influences that have long existed within its borders. He pointedly asks, "Are we to see [America] cheerfully accepting and using all the contributions of foreign lands from the whole outside globe—and then rejecting the only ones distinctively its own?"

Essential Themes

The United States, Whitman argued, was by the late nineteenth century still developing its own character and identity. In his letter, Whitman expresses his hope that many of the trends that he and others abhorred—such as the country's increasingly aggressive business practices—were likely to change over time once the country's national character was fully established. Whitman suggests that Americans were, therefore, standing on the threshold of an important turning point in their country's history.

In this vein, Whitman urges the American people to take note of the many non-British influences that helped to shape the unique national identity of the United States. It was time to discard old notions of Spanish tyranny, he argues, for that nation shared with the people of the United States many exceptional qualities, such as patriotism, loyalty, and religious dedication. Hispanic culture, emanating from Mexico and other Latin American countries, had already significantly influenced the American Southwest and California, and Whitman argues that such influences should not be ignored or replaced.

Furthermore, Whitman urges his fellow Americans to see the cultural contributions of American Indians as an essential component of American identity and culture. If Americans were to draw on Western European culture to develop their national character, Whitman argues, they should also look inward to the tribes of the Southwest and Midwest, whose cultural contributions to the United States are "the only ones distinctively its own." Whitman's letter also speaks to the idea of American exceptionalism, suggesting that, as the national identity of the United States developed, Americans had the option of drawing on the best influences of a number of different cultures and turning them into something distinctively American; Whitman's letter strongly cautions Americans against ignoring these positive cultural influences merely due to prejudice.

—*Michael P. Auerbach, MA*

Bibliography and Additional Reading

Blake, David Haven, & Michael Robertson. *Walt Whitman, Where the Future becomes Present*. Iowa City: U of Iowa P, 2008. Print.

Folsom, Ed, & Kenneth M. Price, eds. Walt Whitman Archive. Center for Digital Research in the Humanities at the University of Nebraska–Lincoln, 2014. Web. 20 Feb. 2014.

Jaksic, Ivan. *The Hispanic World and American Intellectual Life, 1820–1880*. Hampshire: Palgrave, 2012. Print.

Reynolds, David S. *Walt Whitman's America: A Cultural Biography*. London: Vintage, 1996. Print.

Weber, David J. *Spanish Frontier in North America*. New Haven: Yale UP, 2009. Print.

Whitman, Walt. *November Boughs*. Philadelphia: McKay, 1888. Print.

WESTWARD MOVEMENT

The Europeans who settled North America's Atlantic Coast were not content to remain there long, given the vastness of the continent before them. Although the new land was already inhabited, albeit sparsely, by Native peoples, the westward movement of white settlers proceeded throughout the eighteenth and nineteenth centuries. Pioneers entered the broad Mississippi Valley and quickly extended their reach along its rivers. When they came to the Great Plains in the 1840s, they did not at first settle there, for a want of resources, but instead continued westward on covered wagons to California and Oregon. The Great Plains were settled last, after decades of settlement elsewhere.

The "frontier," of course, is something of a moving target, shifting westward (and back) with each successive wave of human settlement. At the far edges of the frontier arrive, first, the explorers, hunters, and fur trappers, who seek pathways and access to readily exploitable resources. Then come the miners and, in the wooded areas, the lumbermen. These seekers are then succeeded, on the rangeland, by the cattlemen who want space and fodder for their herds. Along with the cattlemen come the pioneer farmers, looking to clear forestland and break soil in order to plant crops. In time, the early farmers come to welcome more neighbors as villages and small towns arise.

Along the way, many stories are written about the trials and travails of the trail or life on the frontier. A few of those stories are presented here.

■ The Fremont Expedition Across the Sierra Nevada Range

Date: February 1844
Author: John C. Fremont
Genre: journal

Summary Overview

Having previously led an expedition to document the geography of the Platte River, Second Lieutenant John C. Fremont had been given the task of mapping the western section of the Oregon Trail, an easier and more southerly route to the Columbia River than that taken by Lewis and Clark forty years earlier. Although a few groups of families had previously used the trail, thousands were making plans to move west to Oregon Territory. The nation was eager for information about the West, and when Fremont's journals were published they were a sensation. They accurately presented information about the geography in the area where his expedition had traveled, but they also contained the story of struggles and perseverance, against incredible odds, by Fremont and his men. This "bestseller" made Fremont a national hero, and his exploits increased the push for the United States to incorporate this western territory within its boundaries.

Defining Moment

During the 1840s, the westward push of the United States was in full force. Manifest Destiny, which most took to mean a divine right to spread the political and social system of the United States all the way to the Pacific Ocean, was at its peak. The British in the Northwest and the Mexicans in the Southwest were rivals opposing the American expansion. Settlers from the United States were ready to move into these areas, but for many, additional information about the land through which they would travel was needed. Thus, a series of expeditions were commissioned by the United States government to explore and record the areas west of what had been acquired through the Louisiana Purchase. The Lewis and Clark expedition in 1803 had been sent to the Pacific Ocean, even though it was clear that the territory that the United States had recently bought did not go that far. This, and other early expeditions, laid the groundwork for further expansion.

Within a decade, the Astor Pacific Fur Trading Company was active along the Columbia River, beginning a full scale competition with the British for the economic wealth of the region, as well as for the territory itself.

With the migration of farmers to the Willamette and Columbia River Valleys having started, John Charles Fremont was given the task of mapping the region west of where he had ventured on his previous expedition, to allow an even larger number of people to travel to Oregon. Because of Fremont's efforts, the Oregon Trail became an avenue, though dangerous and rough, to carry people to Oregon and for the policy of America's westward expansion to succeed in the Northwest. Within three years of his expedition, the number of Americans traveling to Oregon was sufficient to force the British to give up their claim. Joint control, provided for in an 1818 treaty, was changed to British control in the North (Canada) and American in the South.

Fremont's plans to return by a more southerly route, from which the excerpt included in this article is taken, was an intentional move into territory that was recognized as Mexican. Although the Republic of Texas had not yet been admitted as a state, discussions had been underway for several years, and when that happened, many talked about expanding into the Southwest, including California. Thus, when Fremont's journals were published in March 1845, not only was information about territory around the Oregon Trail made available, but so too was extensive information about what the interior areas of California had to offer. Fremont excited the imaginations of Americans and increased the political pressure on the government to take whatever steps were necessary to fulfill the dreams of Manifest Destiny.

Author Biography

John Fremont (1813–1890) was born in Georgia to unwed parents. His father, Charles Fremon (no "t") died when Fremont was five, leaving his mother, Anne Whiting Pryor, to raise him. In the 1830s, Fremont taught for several years and then, in 1838, was commissioned in the Corps of Topographical Engineers to help survey the West. In 1841, he married Jessie Benton, daughter of a powerful senator who helped his career in many ways. Fremont led four expeditions, with the second being the most ambitious. The journals of the first two made Fremont a popular hero.

In 1845, Fremont took a group of soldiers to California to agitate against the weak Mexican authorities and fought in California during the Mexican-American War. He was court-martialed for insubordination, but his sentence commuted by the president. He served as a senator from California and also acquired wealth from the gold fields. Fremont was nominated in 1856 as the first Republican candidate for president, but lost the election to James Buchanan. He served in the Army, without distinction, during the Civil War and later served as governor of the Arizona Territory. Retiring to Staten Island, New York, Fremont died in New York City in 1890.

HISTORICAL DOCUMENT

In the morning, I acquainted the men with my decision, and explained to them that necessity required us to make a great effort to clear the mountains. I reminded them of the beautiful valley of the Sacramento, with which they were familiar from the descriptions of [Kit] Carson, who had been there some fifteen years ago, and who, in our late privations, had delighted us in speaking of its rich pastures and abounding game, and drew a vivid contrast between its summer climate, less than a hundred miles distant, and the falling snow around us. I informed them (and long experience had given them confidence in my observations and good instruments) that almost directly west, and only about 70 miles distant, was the great farming establishment of Captain Sutter—a gentleman who had formerly lived in Missouri, and emigrating to this country, had become the possessor of a principality. I assured them that, from the heights of the mountain before us, we should doubtless see the valley of the Sacramento River, and with one effort place ourselves again in the midst of plenty. The people received this decision with the cheerful obedience that had always characterized them; and the day was immediately devoted to the preparations necessary to enable us to carry it into effect. Leggings, moccasins, clothing—all were put into the best state to resist the cold.

I have already said that our provisions were very low; we had neither tallow nor grease of any kind remaining, and the want of salt became one of our greatest privations. The poor dog which had been found in the Bear river valley, and which had been a compagnon de voyage ever since, had now become fat, and the mess to which it belonged requested permission to kill it. Leave was granted. Spread out on the snow, the meat looked very good; and it made a strengthening meal for the greater part of the camp. Indians brought in two or three rabbits during the day, which were purchased from them…

February 2—It had ceased snowing, and this morning the lower air was clear and frosty; and six or seven thousand feet above, the peaks of the Sierra now and then appeared among the rolling clouds, which were rapidly disappearing before the sun. Our Indian shook his head as he pointed to the icy pinnacles, shooting high up into the sky, and seeming almost immediately above us. Crossing the river on the ice, and leaving it immediately, we commenced the ascent of the mountain along the valley of a tributary stream. The people were unusually silent; for every man knew that our enterprise was hazardous, and the issue doubtful.

The snow deepened rapidly, and it soon became necessary to break a road. For this service, a party of ten was formed, mounted on the strongest horses; each man in succession opening the road on foot, or on horseback, until himself and his horse became fatigued, when he stepped aside; and the remaining number passing ahead, he took his station in the rear. Leaving this stream, and pursuing a very direct course, we passed over an intervening ridge to the river we had left. On the way we passed two low huts entirely covered with snow, which might very easily have escaped observation. A family was living in each; and the only trail I saw in the neighborhood was from the door hole to a nut-pine tree near, which supplied them with food and fuel. We found two similar huts on the creek where we next arrived; and, traveling a little higher up, encamped on its banks in about four feet depth of snow. Carson found near, an open hill side, where the wind and the sun had melted the snow, leaving exposed sufficient bunch grass for the animals to-night—

February 4—I went ahead early with two or three men, each with a led horse, to break the road. We were obliged to abandon the hollow entirely, and work along the mountain side, which was very steep and the snow covered with an icy crust. We cut a footing as we advanced, and trampled a road through for the animals; but occasionally one plunged outside the trail, and slided along the field to the bottom, a hundred yards below. Late in the day we reached another bench in the hollow, where in summer, the stream passed over a small precipice. Here was a short distance of dividing ground between the two ridges, and beyond an open basin, some ten miles across, whose bottom presented a field of snow. At the further or western side rose the middle crest of the mountain, a dark-looking ridge of volcanic rock.

The summit line presented a range of naked peaks, apparently destitute of snow and vegetation; but below, the face of the whole country was covered with timber of extraordinary size. Annexed (as a sketch in the book) you are presented with a view of this ridge from a camp on the western side of the basin.

Towards a pass which the guide indicated here, we attempted in the afternoon to force a road; but after a laborious plunging through two or three hundred yards, our best horses gave out, entirely refusing to make any further effort; and, the time, we were brought to a stand. The guide informed us that we were entering the deep snow, and here began the difficulties of the mountain; and to him, and almost to all our enterprise seemed hopeless…

Tonight we had no shelter, but we made a large fire around the trunk of one of the huge pines; and covering the snow with small boughs, on which we spread our blankets, soon made ourselves comfortable. The night was very bright and clear, though the thermometer was only at 10°. A strong wind, which sprang up at sundown, made it intensely cold; and this was one of the bitterest nights during the journey.

Two Indians joined our party here, and one of them, an old man, immediately began to harangue us, saying that ourselves and animals would perish in the snow; and that if we would go back he would show us another and a better way across the mountain. He spoke in a very loud voice, and there was a singular repetition of phrases and arrangement of words, which rendered his speech striking, and not unmusical.

We had now begun to understand some words, and, with the aid of signs, easily comprehended the old man's simple ideas. "Rock upon rock—rock upon rock—snow upon snow—snow upon snow," said he; "even if you get over the snow, you will not be able to get down from the mountains." He made us the sign of precipices, and showed us how the feet of the horses would slip, and throw them off from the narrow trails which led along their sides. Our Chinook, who comprehended even more readily than ourselves and believed our situation hopeless, covered his head with his blanket, and began to weep and lament. "I wanted to see the whites," said he; "I came away from my own people to see the whites, and I wouldn't care to die among them; but here"—and he looked around into the cold night and gloomy forest, and, drawing his blanket over his head, began again to lament.

Seated around the tree, the fire illuminating the rocks and the tall bolls of the pines round about, and the old Indian haranguing, we presented a group of very serious faces….

February 6—Accompanied by Mr. Fitzpartrick, I sat out to-day with a reconnoitering party, on snow shoes. We marched all in a single file tramping the snow as heavily as we could. Crossing the open basis, in a march of about ten miles we reached the top of one of the peaks, to the left of the pass indicated by our guide. Far below us, dimmed by the distance, was a large snowless valley, bounded on the western side at the distance of about a hundred miles, by a low range of mountains, which Carson recognised with delight as the mountains bordering the coast. "There," said he "is the little mountain—it is 15 years ago since I saw it; but I am just as sure as if I had seen it yesterday." Between us, then, and this low coast range, was the valley of the Sacramento; and no one who had not accompanied us through the incidents of our life for the last few months could realize the delight with which at last we looked down upon it.

It was late in the day when we turned towards the camp;

and it grew rapidly cold as it drew towards night. One of the men became fatigued, and his feet began to freeze, and building a fire in the trunk of a dry old cedar, Mr. Fitzpartrick remained with him until his clothes could be dried, and he was in a condition to come on. After a day's march of 20 miles, we straggled into camp, one after another, at night fall; the greater number excessively fatigued, only two of the party having ever traveled on snow shoes before….

February 10—The elevation of the camp, by the boiling point, is 8,050 feet. We are now 1,000 feet above the level of the South Pass in the Rocky mountains, and still we are not done ascending. The top of a flat ridge near was bare of snow, and very well sprinkled with bunch grass, sufficient to pasture the animals two or three days; and this was to be their main point of support. This ridge is composed of a compact trap, or basalt, of a columnar structure; over the surface are scattered large boulders of porous trap. The hills are in many placed entirely covered with small fragments of volcanic rock.

Putting on our snow shoes, we spent the afternoon in exploring a road ahead. The glare of the snow, combined with great fatigue, had rendered many of the people nearly blind; but we were fortunate in having some black silk handkerchiefs, which, worn as veils, very much relieved the eye…

February 13—We continued to labor on the road; and in the course of the day had the satisfaction to see the people working down the face of the opposite hill, about three miles distant. During the morning we had the pleasure of a visit from Mr. Fitzpartrick, with the information that all was going on well. A party of Indians had passed on snow shoes, who said they were going to the western side of the mountain after fish. This was an indication that the salmon were coming up the streams; and we could hardly restrain our impatience as we thought of them, and worked with increased vigor.

The meat train did not arrive this evening, and I gave Godey leave to kill our little dog, (Tlamath,) which he prepared in Indian fashion; scorching off the hair, and washing the skin with soap and snow, and then cutting it up into pieces, which were laid on the snow. Shortly afterwards, the sleigh arrived with a supply of horse meat, and we had to-night an extraordinary dinner—pea soup, mule, and dog.

February 14—With Mr. Preuss, I ascended today the highest peak to the right; from which we had a beautiful view of a mountain lake at our feet, about fifteen miles in length, and so entirely surrounded by mountains that we could not discover an outlet. (According to historian Francis P. Farquhar, the mountain that Fremont and Preuss ascended was Red Lake Peak. The lake they saw from the summit was Lake Tahoe). We had taken with us a glass; but, though we enjoyed an extended view, the valley was half hidden in mist, as when we had seen it before. Snow could be distinguished on the higher parts of the coast mountains; eastward, as far as the eye could extend, it ranged over a terrible mass of broken snowy mountains, fading off blue in the distance. The rock composing the summit consists of a very coarse dark volcanic conglomerate; the lower parts appeared to be of a slaty structure. The highest trees were a few scattering cedars and aspens. From the immediate foot of the peak, we were two hours in reaching the summit, and one hour and a quarter in descending. The day had been very bright, still, and clear, and spring seems to be advancing rapidly. While the sun is in the sky, the snow melts rapidly, and gushing springs over the face of the mountain in all the exposed places; but their surface freeze instantly with the disappearance of the sun….

February 16—We had succeeded in getting our animals safely to the first grassy hill; and this morning I started with Jacob on a reconnoitering expedition beyond the mountain. We travelled along the crests of narrow ridges, extending down from the mountain in the direction of the valley, from which the snow was fast melting away. On the open spots was tolerably good grass; and I judged we should succeed in getting the camp down by way of these. Towards sundown we discovered some icy spots in a deep hollow and, descending the mountain, we encamped on the head water of a little creek, where at last the water found its way to the Pacific.

The night was clear and very long. We heard the cries of some wild animals, which had been attracted by our fire, and flock of geese passed over during the night. Even these strange sounds had something pleasant to our senses in this region of silence and desolation.

We started again early in the morning. The creek acquired a regular breadth of about 20 feet, and we soon began to hear the rushing of the water below the ice surface, over which we travelled to avoid the snow; a few miles below we broke through, where the water was several feet deep, and halted to make a fire and dry our clothes. We continued a few miles father, walking being very laborious without snow shoes.

I was now perfectly satisfied that we had struck the stream on which Mr. Sutter lived; and , turning about, made a hard push, and reached the camp at dark. Here we had the pleasure to find all the remaining animals, 57 in number, safely arrived at the grassy hill near the camp; and here, also, we were agreeably surprised with the sight of an abundance of salt. Some of the horse guard had gone to a neighboring hut for pine nuts, and discovered unexpectedly a large cake of very white fine-grained salt, which the Indians told them they had brought from the other side of the mountain; they used it to eat with their pine nuts, and readily sold it for goods.

February 20—we encamped with the animals and all the materiel of the camp, on the summit of the Pass in the dividing ridge, 1,000 miles by our travelled road from the Dalles of the Columbia.

February 23—This was our most difficult day; we were forced off the ridges by the quantity of snow among the timber, and obliged to take to the mountain sides, where, occasionally, rocks and a southern exposure afforded us a chance to scramble along. But these were steep, and slippery with snow and ice; and the tough evergreens of the mountain impeded our way, tore our skins, and exhausted our patience. Some of us had the misfortune to wear moccasins with parfleche soles, so slippery that we could not keep our feet, and generally crawled across the snow beds. Axes and mauls were necessary to-day, to make a road through the snow. Going ahead with Carson to reconnoitre the road, we reached in the afternoon the river which made the outlet of the lake. Carson sprang over, clear across a place where the stream was compressed amount rocks, but the parfleche sole of my moccasin glanced from the icy rock, and precipitated me into the river. It was some few second before I could recover myself in the current, and Carson, thinking me hurt, jumped in after me, and we both had an icy bath. We tried to search a while for my gun, which had been lost in the fall, but the cold drove us out and we went back to meet the camp. We afterwards found that the gun had been slung under the ice which lined the banks of the creek.

Using our old plan of breaking the road with alternate horses, we reached the creek in the evening, and encamped on a dry open place in the ravine.

Another branch, which we had followed, here comes in on the left; and from this point the mountain wall, on which we had travelled to day, faces to the south along the right bank of the river, where the sun appears to have melted the snow; but the opposite ridge is entirely covered. Here, among the pines, the hill side produces but little grass— barely sufficient to keep life in the animals. We had the pleasure to be rained upon this afternoon; and grass was now our greatest solicitude. Many of the men looked badly, and some this evening were giving out.

GLOSSARY

Carson, Kit: mountain man/scout since 1825

Fitzpatrick, Thomas: a mountain man since 1823

nut-pine tree: the piñon pine

parfleche: dried, untanned rawhide

Preuss, Charles: a German cartographer

Sutter, Captain John: settler, owner of Sutter's Mill.

Document Analysis

Exploring is intended to be a round-trip journey. While Fremont and his expeditionary party were well prepared to travel west to the Oregon Territory, when Fremont decided to take an indirect route home, leaving the Columbia River on November 25, 1843, it was a much different story. The provisions included cattle and plenty of horses and mules, but Fremont underestimated the severity of the journey and weather along the east side of the Cascades and Sierra Nevada Mountains. However, his optimistic outlook on life and his confidence that it would all work out allowed him to continue when others might have changed course. The excerpts from his journal that are reproduced here demonstrate how even in the midst of great hardship Fremont was confident. Recognizing the problems that winter travel was causing for his expedition, he decides to head west to California. The most desperate days of the trip were those at the end of February, as they cross through what is now called Carson Pass in the Sierra Nevada range. However, by the end of the first week of March, they were at Captain Sutter's estate recuperating from their arduous journey, but still with a long way to go.

Opening with Fremont's decision to cross the mountains to the Central Valley of California, the optimist saw that there were only seventy miles to travel. However, that distance was the case only "as the crow flies," i.e., only if they could have flown directly. Going across the mountains, on the other hand, it took more than a month to travel a much greater distance to make it to the Central Valley. In retrospect, Fremont's decision not to winter in what is now Nevada could be called into question. The difficulty in moving forward, getting enough food, and the harsh weather are dramatically illustrated by Fremont in his journal. Even though many of the friendly Native Americans thought Fremont and his men crazy for trying to cross the mountains in winter, many helped by trading food. Others who were traveling themselves gave hope to the men that it was possible to make it across. Finding forage for their animals was, of course, as important as obtaining food for themselves.

Virtually every paragraph of this section of the journal contains a reference to snow, with the cold conditions referenced just as often. What might have seemed to be an obsession was actually Fremont facing the realities of the situation. The cold and snow were the party's unrelenting enemies as they strove to make it to California. Although none of the incidents mentioned was fatal, things easily could have turned out otherwise. Fremont's lack of accurate knowledge of the terrain through which they were passing could have led to an unfortunate end for all of them. However, the skills that the leaders had developed over the years allowed them to survive, although not comfortably.

The rain mentioned at the end of this excerpt indicated that they were finally getting to a lower elevation, where the warmer Pacific air might assist them in their survival. They still had some days to reach Sutter's estate, but at least the constant fear of freezing was gone. The warmer conditions also meant that game could be found in the forest, even if grass for their animals was not yet plentiful. The main struggle was over, and Fremont's seemingly endless hope had been justified.

Essential Themes

John Fremont, with the editorial assistance of his wife Jessie, helped open the West to Americans from all parts of the country. While relatively few would follow in his footsteps, the writings, maps, and illustrations gave them a picture of what lay in the region from the Rocky Mountains to the Pacific Ocean. His upbeat temperament and picturesque language gave a new vision to the people. Before the end of the decade, the United States would own all the territory through which Fremont had passed. His writings helped gain support for this expansion. The maps that he and Charles Preuss created were an essential item in the packs of travelers through this region for decades. While a few might have decided not to head west after reading his journals, for many others they created a vision of great possibility. For example, because of his description of the area around the Great Salt Lake, Mormon leaders began to consider moving to that part of the Great Basin.

The publication of his journals, with support by the government, helped clarify some mistaken beliefs that had arisen about the West. For example, although a few others had circled to the Great Salt Lake to verify that there was no outlet to the ocean, Fremont's travels and his journals finally put this belief to rest for the general public. By 1846, Preuss had printed several maps representing the full length of the Oregon Trail. The information that the expedition had acquired continued to have wider and wider distribution. Things mentioned in passing, such as viewing Lake Tahoe from the south, or in a previous passage, Pyramid Lake, allowed explorers, scholars, and the general public, to gain insights into this relatively unknown territory.

Fremont and his men were lucky that the weather was not severe for that time of year. As difficult as their journey across the mountains was, in many years it would have been impossible. For any who were considering a journey west, the journal served as a cautionary tale about getting through the mountains before winter and having the proper equipment to deal with the snow. However, his nearly miraculous journey, and his easily-read description of the events made Fremont a superstar of his time. For better or worse, Fremont's work also helped the United States further realize its goal of Manifest Destiny.

—Donald A. Watt, PhD

Bibliography and Additional Reading

Chaffin, Tom. *Pathfinder: John Charles Fremont and the Course of American Empire*. 2002. Norman: U of Oklahoma P, 2014. Print.

Fremont, John C., with Anne F. Hyde (introduction). *Fremont's First Impressions: The Original Report of his Exploring Expeditions of 1842–1844*. Lincoln: U of Nebraska P, 2012. Print.

Fremont, John C., Donald Jackson, & Mary Lee Spence, eds. *The Expeditions of John Charles Fremont*. Vol. 1 "Travels from 1838 to 1844." Urbana: U of Illinois P, 1970. Web. 13 Oct. 2014.

Roberts, David. A *New World: Kit Carson, John C. Fremont, and the Claiming of the American West*. New York: Simon & Schuster, 2001. Print.

Spence, Mary Lee. *"John Charles Fremont"* Utah History to Go. State of Utah, 2014. Web. 13 Oct. 2014.

■ Across the Plains in 1844

Date: 1844
Author: Catherine Pringle
Genre: autobiography; memoir

Summary Overview

The piece provided below is from the first chapter of the memoir of Catherine Sager Pringle, written around 1860, though it centers upon events in 1844. Pringle, along with her parents and six siblings, joined hundreds of other families in migrating across the plains in the early 1840s, headed for Oregon. Not yet a part of the United States (it would not achieve statehood until 1859), Oregon was presented as a healthful country with fertile fields. The Sager family, originally from Ohio, set off on their westward trek from St. Joseph, Missouri, a city along the Missouri River that was a popular jumping-off point for the trails toward Oregon and California.

Pringle's memories of the journey westward are highly visual, and they resonate with other journals of those who followed the Overland Trail, a more southern alternative to the Oregon Trail. Her words are even more intriguing given her age of nine years at the time of her family's travels. While her family endured tragedy and heartache, Pringle and three of her siblings did eventually succeed in their mother's hope that they would reach Oregon and a better life, though it was not in the way that Naomi Sager had envisioned.

Defining Moment

For Catherine Sager Pringle's father, Henry, the dream of the West held much promise, and he fully intended that he and his family would reach it and erect a family home that would endure for generations. The climate, advertised as good for one's health and well-being, would greatly improve his wife's strength, and his children would grow with vitality. As he possessed skills both in farming and as a blacksmith, Henry Sager could easily have slotted into a comfortable role within a new community; after all, Pringle wrote that her father "had a wide reputation for ingenuity." Sadly, like so many others who preceded them on the trail west, and the others that followed, Sager did not live to set foot upon Oregon, and neither did his wife. The Sagers planned well, travelling during the optimum time (late spring and summer), but, just like the weather, illness and accidents could not be foreseen.

Oregon Country, later a territory in 1846, was the land held aloft as fresh and open. The fields were lush with flora and fauna, a more picturesque area not to be found elsewhere. The alluring descriptions of Oregon were widespread through the 1830s and 1840s, and soon it reached such a crescendo, as historian Frank McLynn wrote, "that it almost seemed as that the laws of God's universe had been breached and that missionaries had found themselves back in the Garden of Eden" (33). Ginger Wadsworth, in her work Words West: Voices of Young Pioneers (2003), quotes Edward Lenox, who rode the Overland Trail with his father, as hearing that, "they do say that out in Oregon, the pigs are running about under the great acorn trees, round and fat, and already cooked, with knives and forks sticking in them" (44).

It is left to history what stories or hyperbole Henry Sager may have heard. Whatever prompted him to relocate his family from Missouri to Oregon, there is little doubt that he held only the best intentions for his family. However, as described by his daughter, the Sagers' overland trip was laden with accidents and tragedy. Knowing his end imminent as he lay dying of typhoid, or what his daughter terms "camp fever," he despaired, "Poor child! What will become of you?" The Sagers did not travel with any relatives, nor did any relatives live in Oregon or other reaches west. Pringle wrote, "His wife was ill, the children small, and one likely to be a cripple," in reference to an injury explained below. It would be left to the charity of strangers among the other travellers and those already in Oregon to care for Sager's seven children.

Author Biography

Catherine Sager Pringle, born on the fifteenth of April in 1835, holds a secure place in the history of American westward migration. Though she provides history with a rich recounting of her journey, she neglects or simply chooses not to include a narrative of her life before the family's decision to relocate. One of seven children (two sons, five daughters) born to Henry and Naomi Sager, Pringle survived the trek to Oregon, but at a severe price. Accidents were certainly common enough in everyday life, but even more so along the Overland Trail, especially for those unused to a nomadic life as part of a caravan. Parents were busy with a variety of duties—aside from driving the wagons and animals—to get their families through each day. On the first of August, roughly four months along the trail, Pringle leaped from the wagon while it was still in motion, but the hem of her dress "caught on an axe handle and the wagon wheels ran over her, crushing her legs" (McFlynn 208). Of the accident, Pringle wrote that her father "picked me up and saw the extent of the injury when the injured limb hung dangling in the air. In a broken voice he exclaimed, 'My dear child, your leg is broken all to pieces!'" Though the leg was set, Pringle had to ride inside the wagon for the duration of the trip. Within less than a month, worse occurrences followed.

Both parents died of typhoid within weeks of each other, leaving Pringle and her siblings orphans. Before Henry Sager's death, he spoke to the wagon train's captain, William Shaw, and begged that he bring his family to the mission run by Dr. Marcus Whitman and Narcissa Whitman in Oregon, which was established in the region of Waiilatpu. Following Naomi Sager's death in September of 1844, the Shaws installed themselves as temporary guardians of the seven orphans until they met with the Whitmans the following month. Sadly, the tragedy of the Sager orphans did not end with their adoption by the Whitmans. Three years later, in November 1847, the Whitman mission was attacked by a branch of the Cayuse Indian tribe. Both Dr. and Mrs. Whitman were among the dead, as were the two Sager boys, John and Francis. Louisa, still a young child, succumbed to disease, leaving Catherine, Elizabeth, Matilda, and Henrietta, the baby born on the trail. Catherine, along with Elizabeth and Matilda, lived to old age, passing away in 1910 in her mid-seventies.

HISTORICAL DOCUMENT

CHAPTER I: ON THE PLAINS IN 1844

My father was one of the restless ones who are not content to remain in one place long at a time. Late in the fall of 1838 we emigrated from Ohio to Missouri. Our first halting place was on Green River, but the next year we took a farm in Platte County. He engaged in farming and blacksmithing, and had a wide reputation for ingenuity. Anything they needed, made or mended, sought his shop. In 1843, Dr. Whitman came to Missouri. The healthful climate induced my mother to favor moving to Oregon. Immigration was the theme all winter, and we decided to start for Oregon. Late in 1843 father sold his property and moved near St. Joseph, and in April, 1844, we started across the plains. The first encampments were a great pleasure to us children. We were five girls and two boys, ranging from the girl baby to be born on the way to the oldest boy, hardly old enough to be any help.

STARTING ON THE PLAINS

We waited several days at the Missouri River. Many friends came that far to see the emigrants start on their long journey, and there was much sadness at the parting, and a sorrowful company crossed the Missouri that bright spring morning. The motion of the wagon made us all sick, and it was weeks before we got used to the seasick motion. Rain came down and required us to tie down the wagon covers, and so increased our sickness by confining the air we breathed.

Our cattle recrossed in the night and went back to their winter quarters. This caused delay in recovering them and a weary, forced march to rejoin the train. This was divided into companies, and we were in that commanded by William Shaw. Soon after starting Indians raided our camp one night and drove off a number of cattle. They were pursued, but never recovered.

Soon everything went smooth and our train made

steady headway. The weather was fine and we enjoyed the journey pleasantly. There were several musical instruments among the emigrants, and these sounded clearly on the evening air when camp was made and merry talk and laughter resounded from almost every camp-fire.

INCIDENTS OF TRAVEL

We had one wagon, two steady yoke of old cattle, and several of young and not well-broken ones. Father was no ox driver, and had trouble with these until one day he called on Captain Shaw for assistance. It was furnished by the good captain pelting the refractory steers with stones until they were glad to come to terms.

Reaching the buffalo country, our father would get someone to drive his team and start on the hunt, for he was enthusiastic in his love of such sport. He not only killed the great bison, but often brought home on his shoulder the timid antelope that had fallen at his unerring aim, and that are not often shot by ordinary marksmen. Soon after crossing South Platte the unwieldy oxen ran on a bank and overturned the wagon, greatly injuring our mother. She lay long insensible in the tent put up for the occasion.

August 1st we nooned in a beautiful grove on the north side of the Platte. We had by this time got used to climbing in and out of the wagon when in motion. When performing this feat that afternoon my dress caught on an axle helve and I was thrown under the wagon wheel, which passed over and badly crushed my limb before father could stop the team. He picked me up and saw the extent of the injury when the injured limb hung dangling in the air.

THE FATHER DYING ON THE PLAINS

In a broken voice he exclaimed: "My dear child, your leg is broken all to pieces!" The news soon spread along the train and a halt was called. A surgeon was found and the limb set; then we pushed on the same night to Laramie, where we arrived soon after dark. This accident confined me to the wagon the remainder of the long journey.

After Laramie we entered the great American desert, which was hard on the teams. Sickness became common. Father and the boys were all sick, and we were dependent for a driver on the Dutch doctor who set my leg. He offered his services and was employed, but though an excellent surgeon, he knew little about driving oxen. Some of them often had to rise from their sick beds to wade streams and get the oxen safely across. One day four buffalo ran between our wagon and the one behind. Though feeble, father seized his gun and gave chase to them. This imprudent act prostrated him again, and it soon became apparent that his days were numbered. He was fully conscious of the fact, but could not be reconciled to the thought of leaving his large and helpless family in such precarious circumstances. The evening before his death we crossed Green River and camped on the bank. Looking where I lay helpless, he said: "Poor child! What will become of you?" Captain Shaw found him weeping bitterly. He said his last hour had come, and his heart was filled with anguish for his family. His wife was ill, the children small, and one likely to be a cripple. They had no relatives near, and a long journey lay before them. In piteous tones he begged the Captain to take charge of them and see them through. This he stoutly promised. Father was buried the next day on the banks of Green River. His coffin was made of two troughs dug out of the body of a tree, but next year emigrants found his bleaching bones, as the Indians had disinterred the remains.

We hired a young man to drive, as mother was afraid to trust the doctor, but the kindhearted German would not leave her, and declared his intention to see her safe in the Willamette. At Fort Bridger the stream was full of fish, and we made nets of wagon sheets to catch them. That evening the new driver told mother he would hunt for game if she would let him use the gun. He took it, and we never saw him again. He made for the train in advance, where he had a sweetheart. We found the gun waiting our arrival at Whitman's. Then we got along as best we could with the doctor's help.

Mother planned to get to Whitman's and winter there, but she was rapidly failing under her sorrows. The nights and mornings were very cold, and she took cold from the exposure unavoidably. With camp fever and a sore mouth, she fought bravely against fate for the sake of her children, but she was taken delirious soon after reaching Fort Bridger, and was bed-fast. Travelling in this condition over a road clouded with dust, she suffered intensely. She talked of her husband, addressing him as though present, beseeching him in piteous tones to relieve her sufferings, until at last she became unconscious. Her babe was cared for by the women of the train. Those kind-hearted women would also come in at night and wash the dust from the mother's face and otherwise make her comfortable. We travelled a rough road the day she died, and she moaned fearfully all the time. At night one of the women came in as usual, but she made no reply to questions, so she thought her asleep, and washed her face, then took her hand and discovered the pulse was nearly gone. She lived but a few moments, and her last words were, "Oh, Henry! If you only knew how we have suffered." The tent was set up, the corpse laid out, and next morning we took the last look at our mother's face. The grave was near the road; willow brush was laid in the bottom and covered the body, the earth filled in—then the train moved on.

Her name was cut on a headboard, and that was all that could be done. So in twenty-six days we became orphans. Seven children of us, the oldest fourteen and the youngest a babe. A few days before her death, finding herself in possession of her faculties and fully aware of the coming end, she had taken an affectionate farewell of her children and charged the doctor to take care of us. She made the same request of Captain Shaw. The baby was taken by a woman in the train, and all were literally adopted by the company. No one there but was ready to do us any possible favor. This was especially true of Captain Shaw and his wife. Their kindness will ever be cherished in grateful remembrance by us all. Our parents could not have been more solicitous or careful. When our flour gave out they gave us bread as long as they had any, actually dividing their last loaf. To this day Uncle Billy and Aunt Sally, as we call them, regard us with the affection of parents. Blessings on his hoary head!

At Snake River they lay by to make our wagon into a cart, as our team was wearing out. Into this was loaded what was necessary. Some things were sold and some left on the plains. The last of September we arrived at Grande Ronde, where one of my sister's clothes caught fire, and she would have burned to death only that the German doctor, at the cost of burning his hands, saved her. One night the captain heard a child crying, and found my little sister had got out of the wagon and was perishing in the freezing air, for the nights were very cold. We had been out of flour and living on meat alone, so a few were sent in advance to get supplies from Dr. Whitman and return to us. Having so light a load we could travel faster than the other teams, and went on with Captain Shaw and the advance. Through the Blue Mountains cattle were giving out and left lying in the road. We made but a few miles a day. We were in the country of "Dr. Whitman's Indians," as they called themselves. They were returning from buffalo hunting and frequented our camps. They were loud in praise of the missionaries and anxious to assist us. Often they would drive up some beast that had been left behind as given out and return it to its owner.

One day when we were making a fire of wet wood Francis thought to help the matter by holding his powder-horn over a small blaze. Of course the powder-horn exploded, and the wonder was he was left alive. He ran to a creek nearby and bathed his hands and face, and came back destitute of winkers and eyebrows, and his face was blackened beyond recognition. Such were the incidents and dangerous and humorous features of the journey.

We reached Umatilla October 15th, and lay by while Captain Shaw went on to Whitman's station to see if the doctor would take care of us, if only until he could become located in the Willamette. We purchased of the Indians the first potatoes we had eaten since we started on our long and sad journey. October 17th we started for our destination, leaving the baby very sick, with doubts of its recovery. Mrs. Shaw took an affectionate leave of us all, and stood looking after us as long as we were in sight. Speaking of it in later years, she said she never saw a more pitiful sight than that cartful of orphans going to find a home among strangers.

We reached the station in the forenoon. For weeks this place had been a subject for our talk by day and formed our dreams at night. We expected to see log houses, occupied by Indians and such people as we had seen about the forts. Instead we saw a large white house surrounded with palisades. A short distance from the doctor's dwelling was another large adobe house, built by Mr. Gray, but now used by immigrants in the winter, and for a granary in the summer. It was situated near the mill pond, and the grist mill was not far from it. . . .

GLOSSARY

camp fever: typhoid, a disease common on the Overland Trail, and often fatal

Dutch doctor: Theophilos Dagen, the doctor who attended Catherine's injury

Grande Ronde: a valley in Oregon near the Blue Mountains; sometimes referred to as "La Grande Ronde"

Laramie: a fort on the North Platte River, today in Wyoming, that served as a stop on the trail

Snake River: a river that flows through the states of Idaho, Oregon, Washington, and Wyoming

South Platte: a river running through Colorado and Nebraska

St. Joseph: a city in Missouri found along the Missouri River, which functioned as a starting-off point

Umatilla: a river in Oregon

Whitman, Dr.: Marcus Whitman, who with his wife established a mission in the Oregon territory; Catherine's adopted parents

Willamette: a valley in northwest Oregon

William Shaw: captain of the wagon train of which the Sager family was a part

Document Analysis

When Henry and Naomi Sager set out on their journey in April of 1844 from St. Joseph, Missouri, they had with them their six children—John, Francis, Catherine, Elizabeth, Matilda, and Louisa—who ranged in age from three to thirteen years. Months into the trail, Naomi gave birth to a fifth daughter, Henrietta. This venture into the unknown eventually led to both Henry and Naomi's deaths from typhoid, termed by Pringle "camp fever," as well as a variety of accidents to Pringle and her siblings. With Henry's death in August of that year, Naomi—whose own demise closely followed his—and her seven children were left on the trail with the others in their caravan, trusting to charity for their support and maintenance. As they were so far along the trail, turning back was not possible, nor did the Sagers have any relatives joining them on the trek or ahead of them in Oregon.

Pringle's details, namely the tragedies and various accidents, including that of her leg being run over by a wagon wheel, reveal a forthright description of progress along the trail, yet there is a measure of detachment in her memoir. This may be read in a variety of ways, such as simply the passage of time. The events of 1844 occurred when Pringle was only nine years old, whereas she recorded her memories around the age of twenty-five.

Despite the eclipse of approximately sixteen years from the events to her writing of them, Pringle is very clear on particulars, such as the rivers she passed and the people she met. This would suggest, though the resources do not account for it, that she may have had help during the writing process, or, at some point after settling in Oregon, was moved to record her memories. Either way, her memoir provides modern readers with valuable insight into her experience and that of countless others.

Life on the Trail

A journey along the Overland Trail, despite the daily hard work, all the hours of travelling, and the consequent stresses, presented itself as a big adventure to the hundreds of children making their way across the plains with their parents. As the majority of those on the trail were of farming families, their children would not have been strangers to hard work; they would already have been used to heavy chores throughout their daily routines. Adapting such duties to the outdoor spectrum on the dusty plains took getting used to, especially for those involved in the family's cooking and washing. Here, men, women, and children performed their various chores while exposed to torrential rains and sweeping winds, excessive heat, and, if delayed, snow and hail storms.

Travelling westward required great fortitude and hardiness, and it came with a heavy price tag. The journey itself would take months, but the planning stages could take that or longer. Supplies had to be bought, gathered, or made, enough to sustain an entire family for the trek west. Posts and forts were located along the trail that sold various goods and supplies, but typically their prices were at a premium. Francis Parkman, a historian from Boston, Massachusetts, travelled the Oregon Trail in the 1840s—around the same time as the Pringle family—and was not impressed with the actions of storekeepers: "They [emigrants on the trail] were plundered and cheated without mercy. In one bargain, concluded in my presence, I calculated the profits that accrued to the fort, and found that at the lowest estimate they exceeded eighteen hundred percent" (McLynn 106). Planning and saving for the emigration to Oregon might have taken a while, but, as shown by Parkman, it was far better than running out of supplies and losing money at forts.

A rather large item of necessity, and the iconic image of the western pioneer, was the wagon. The wagon served a number of purposes: conveyance, storage, shelter, sickroom, and pantry. It had to be structurally sturdy to withstand the rigors of the trip, and yet not too heavy, as it still needed to be pulled easily along by animals. Frank McLynn cites oak, hickory, and maple as some of the more popular types of wood used in construction, with elm and ash also favored (53). The top cover—typically made of "a heavy rainproof canvas, caulked, oiled, and painted, usually linen, sailcloth, or oilcloth" (53)—provided shelter to the goods inside. The oxen or mules (both were popular for teams) did not have an easy time; wagons could carry anywhere from 1,000 to 2,500 pounds, though 1,600 pounds was the recommended weight limit. Generally, the wagon was not used to carry all members of the family, as the back of the wagon was mainly for storage. Excepting the ill and the very young, all others walked alongside the wagon; it was not merely an issue of space, but extra weight for the animals at the head. Pringle, due to her leg accident, could not walk, so was allocated a spot in the wagon for the remainder of the journey. Given that the wagon would not have been built with suspension, her ride inside would not have been very comfortable or enviable, and all the bumps along the trail may have aggravated her injury further.

Gathering supplies for an entire family for a months-long journey into the relatively unknown took up the bulk of the preparation time, and it did not merely include food. The wagon was to be a home in miniature. With that in mind, all essential items had to be brought: tools for fixing the wagon, candles, soap, kitchen utensils, medicine and various other medical items, clothes, bedding, sewing materials, guns and ammunition, and other things deemed essential. Ginger Wadsworth cites the memory of a thirteen-year-old girl, Kit Scott, who recorded her memories of her family's westward preparation of clothes and other goods:

[The] fingers of the women and girls all the winter, providing . . . bedding, blankets, of stockings and sunbonnets, of hickory shirts and gingham aprons . . . that the family might be outfitted for the trip. Ah! The tears that fell upon these garments, fashioned with trembling fingers by the flaring light of tallow [animal fat] candles; the heartaches that were stitched and knitted and woven into them, through the brief winter afternoons. (14)

While measures were taken for keeping warm and dry during the trip, many families spent much of their preparation time ensuring that their families would be well fed. Some practiced cooking over open fires so that they might be ready when the time came. Others put time into making what they could before the journey, such as the snack so often associated with Civil War soldiers, hardtack. John Roger James, cited by Wadsworth, remembered how he, his father, and his brothers spent much of their time in this occupation before setting out for Oregon:

Father fixed up a place to mix up a lot of dough and knead it with a lever fastened to the wall. He would put a pile of dough into a trough . . . and would have us boys spend the evening kneading the dough thoroughly, then roll it out and cut it into cracker shape about four inches square and then bake them hard and fill them into seamless grain sacks. There would be no lard or butter used, as there would be danger of them spoiling. (16)

Hardtack was not known for being an epicurean delight, but it was food and it satisfied hunger, if not taste, especially if there was nothing else available.

It is very probable that the extra chores performed before a family made their way westward also served as trials for the children for the work they would be expected to do along the trail. As deemed by their sex, older daughters were babysitters from the start, along with assisting their mothers with the cooking, mending, and doctoring. While the various duties of children may have differed from family to family according to their needs, there was one chore that all historians document, the same chore remembered by many who made the journey as children: the collection of buffalo chips. Wood for fuel was not always readily available along the plains. The pioneers took to using whatever was plentiful and available, and one that filled both these criteria was the dried dung of buffalos, known as buffalo chips. McLynn states that the chips, "when dry . . . resembled rotten wood and would make a clear hot fire" (103). Marion Russell, a child on the trail, remembered being on the prairie and collecting buffalo chips:

I would stand back and kick them, then reach down and gather them carefully, for under them lived spiders and centipedes. Sometimes scorpions ran from beneath them. I would fill my long full dress skirt with the evening's fuel and take it back to mother. (Wadsworth 84–85)

For others, the drudgery of chores held highlights, such as driving the teams pulling the wagons and cracking the whip. Taking part in such a grown-up activity, especially given the arduous life on the trail, must have indeed been a special treat.

Buffalo

Pringle's father, like many men, was anxious to score a buffalo (or bison) kill; according to Pringle, he did accomplish this, but there is no mention whether Mr. Sager made any use of the meat. Pringle wrote only that "he not only killed the great bison, but often brought home on his shoulder the timid antelope." Read at face value, Pringle presents her father as shooting for sport, rather than for the necessity of feeding his large family, particularly when faced with Pringle's comment that her father "was enthusiastic in his love of such sport." The buffalo, like the covered wagon an iconic image of the westward movement, roamed the plains in such large numbers so as to look like brown waves moving about the land. Although the assorted American Indian tribes were scrupulous in using every part of the animal, those on the trail were not so meticulous. Only a small portion of the buffalo was taken for food—the "tongues, hump meat, and marrow bones," the rest left to scavenger animals such as vultures and wolves, while the American

Indians could fashion clothing, shelter, and food from the buffalo (Wadsworth 80). Buffalo hunting for sport came into vogue during this time, driving the animals nearly to extinction. The sport continued through the late nineteenth century, attracting the likes of future president Theodore Roosevelt.

The Sagers, like countless other families striving to make a fresh start in Oregon, met with tragedies they never could have foreseen. Plagued by accidents and then the deaths of their parents, the Sager children experienced the thrill of the trail, but also the trail at its most harsh and brutal. It would be impossible to estimate the number of families that did not arrive in the West without losing someone they loved. Despite the sadness of her story, Catherine Sager Pringle left for history the testimony of her experience, an experience shared by more people than she could have realized.

Essential Themes

As evidenced in Pringle's excerpt, accidents along the trail could occur easily, as when Pringle jumped off the moving wagon. Simple accidents and infections, though, particularly in a time of limited medical knowledge—much less being situated along the plains far from a doctor—could spell certain death. For example, during the Civil War, twenty years after these events, more soldiers died from disease and infection than from gunshots. There were cases, such as those of Henry and Naomi Sager, in which even the presence of a doctor could not assuage bouts with typhoid. Typhoid and cholera, both prevalent along the plains (as well as in cities back East) could act swiftly, often with fatal results.

The Sagers' affliction with typhoid aside, accidents were what plagued the family the most. Before the mention of her own accident, Pringle recounts one of her mother. She states, "Soon after crossing South Platte the unwieldy oxen ran on a bank and overturned the wagon, greatly injuring our mother." This occurrence was also documented by McLynn; he states that in addition to injuring Naomi Sager, the overturning wagon also tore off Pringle's dress and that "Henry Sager's face was badly skinned" (209). The day did not end there for the Sager family, as "later, the girls went out for a midnight stroll and were nearly killed when a sentry shot at them, mistaking them for Indians" (209). Life on the trail, though filled with promise and excitement, was also filled with dread, as demonstrated by Pringle's memories.

—Jennifer L. Henderson Crane,

Bibliography and Additional Reading

Frizzell, Lodisa. *Across the Plains to California in 1852: Journal of Mrs. Lodisa Frizzell*. Ed. Victor Hugo Paltsits. 1915. Project Gutenberg, 2010. E-book. Web. 25 Mar. 2013.

Gwartney, Debra. "Plucked from the Grave: The First Female Missionary to Cross the Continental Divide Came to a Gruesome End Partly Caused by Her Own Zeal. What Can Learn from Her?" *American Scholar* 80.3 (2011), 71–81. Print.

Jones, Karen. "'My Winchester Spoke to Her': Crafting the Northern Rockies as a Hunter's Paradise, c.1870–1910." *American Nineteenth Century History* 11.2 (2010), p. 183–203. Print.

Keyes, Sarah. "'Like a Roaring Lion': The Overland Trail as a Sonic Conquest." *Journal of American History* 96.1 (2009), 19–43. Print.

McLynn, Frank. *Wagons West: The Epic Story of America's Overland Trails*. London: Cape, 2002. Print.

Menard, Andrew. "Down the Santa Fe Trail to the City upon a Hill." *Western American Literature* 45.2 (2010): 162–188. Print.

Pringle, Catherine Sager. *Across the Plains in 1844*. c.1860. Archives of the West. West Film Project and WETA (PBS), 2001. Web. 25 Mar. 2013.

Royce, Sarah. *Across the Plains: Sarah Royce's Western Narrative*. Ed. Jennifer Dawes Adkison. Tucson: U of Arizona P, 2009. Print.

Wadsworth, Ginger. *Words West: Voices of Young Pioneers*. New York: Clarion, 2003. Print.

Bagley, Will. *So Rugged and Mountainous: Blazing the Trails to Oregon and California, 1812–1848*. Norman: U of Oklahoma P, 2010. Print.

With Golden Visions Bright before Them: Trails to the Mining West, 1849–1852. Norman: U of Oklahoma P, 2012. Print.

"Diaries, Memoirs, Letters, and Reports along the Trails West." *The Overland Trail*. Elizabeth Larson, n.d. Web. 25 Mar. 2013.

Thompson, Erwin N. *Shallow Grave at Waiilatpu: The Sagers' West*. Portland: Western Imprints, 1985. Print.

Werner, Emmy E. *Pioneer Children on the Journey West*. Boulder: Westview P, 1995. Print.

■ Donner Party Diary

Date: 1847
Author: Patrick Breen
Genre: diary

Summary Overview

Of all the stories to come out of the American West, few have such morbid resonance as that of the Donner Party. Having set out in 1846 from Independence, Missouri, as part of the mad rush to settle the frontier, the Donner Party, a collection of several families spread out across dozens of wagons, became trapped in the snows of the Sierra Nevada after taking a shortcut through the mountain range. Faced with a brutal winter and few supplies, some of the immigrants resorted to cannibalism to survive. Nearly half the party perished, and as the details of the ordeal emerged—accounts both of heroism and moral failure—the story of the Donner Party became a cautionary tale against the hubris and folly of human greed in the face of nature. But the tragedy also touched people for another reason: beyond the lurid sensationalism, it forced Americans, fifteen years before the outbreak of the Civil War, to look in the mirror and consider how they may act when faced with impossible circumstances.

Defining Moment

Beginning in the 1840s, sparked by the promise of opportunity and driven by the drumbeat of Manifest Destiny, the singular belief that God himself had bequeathed the West to Americans, millions of pioneers set off on the wagon trails toward Oregon and California. Some, like Patrick Breen, went in search of religious freedom, while others, like George Donner and James F. Reed, set off simply to follow the enduring westward dream.

Traveling by wagon train, pioneers were made up primarily of whole families, banded together into companies to pool resources and assure mutual safety. Most pioneers set off from Independence, Missouri, following the Oregon Trail for up to six months to the Great Continental Divide, the spine of mountains that separated the furthermost western states from the rest of the nation, where wagon trains had a choice of several routes to their final destination. The most perilous part of the trip into California was the last 100 miles, where wagon trains had to go up and over the Sierra Nevada, one of the most treacherous mountain ranges in North America, characterized by jagged rock and heavy snowdrifts.

In 1842, Lansford Hastings, an ambitious young lawyer, originally from Ohio, travelled to California and concocted a plan to wrest the territory from Mexico, proclaim on it an independent republic and establish himself at its ruler. To hasten his plan, he encouraged immediate settlement by writing *The Emigrants' Guide to Oregon and California,* in which he proclaimed the territory a new Eden, and advertised a shortcut through the Sierra Nevada, which he himself had never actually traveled.

With a copy of Hastings' guide in hand, the Donner Party, a wagon train of some ninety people, including several children, led by James F. Reed and George Donner, set out in the spring of 1846. Suffering delays due to weather, the Donner Party was eager to make up time when they arrived at Hastings Cutoff, the untested shortcut into California. Despite many warning signs, including the wavering of Hastings himself, whom the party met along the trail, the wagon train headed further into the cutoff, fighting for every mile, sometimes forced to veer off, losing even more time before the onset of the first snows. As things became harder, tempers flared and James F. Reed was banished from the wagon train after killing another pioneer in a scuffle. By late October 1846 the party was splintered, and as snow began to fall, the battered settlers decided to make winter camp, one at Tuckee Lake and another at Alder Creek in the high Sierras.

Within weeks of setting camp, what rations the party had were gone. Soon, they began to consume hides and whatever else was edible, but after a short while, even this too was gone. By the start of the new year, several members of the party began to consume human flesh.

Author Biography

Born in 1806 in Ireland, Patrick Breen originally settled in Iowa before joining the Donner Party along with wife Margaret and their seven children. Throughout the winter of 1846, Breen was the only member of the party to keep a diary of the events, making his the only contemporary account of the ordeal. From those who set off from Missouri the previous spring, the Breens all survived to reach safety in California. Breen's account appeared in newspapers, but often without his name. Largely ignored and forgotten by the press, Patrick Breen died in 1868. His daughter Isabella, who had only been a baby at the time of the events, lived to be the last surviving member of the Donner Party, finally passing in 1935.

HISTORICAL DOCUMENT

"came to this place on the 31st of last month that it snowed we went on to the pass the snow so deep we were unable to find the road, when within 3 miles of the summit then turned back to this shanty on the Lake, Stanton came one day after we arriveed here we again took our teams & waggons & made another unsuccessful attempt to cross in company with Stanton we returned to the shanty it contiuneing to snow all the time we were here we now have killed most part of our cattle having to stay here untill next spring & live on poor beef without bread or salt"

— *November 20, 1846*

"still snowing now about 3 feet deep...killed my last oxen today will skin them tomorrow gave another yoke to Fosters hard to get wood"

— *November 29, 1846*

"... snow about 5 ½ feet or 6 deep difficult to get wood no gong from the house completely housed up looks as likely for snow as when it commenced, our cattle all killed but three or four them, the horses & Stantons mules gone & cattle suppose lost in the Snow no hopes of finding them alive"

— *December 1, 1846*

"... Milt. & Noah went to Donnos 8 days since not returned yet, thinks they got lost in the snow..."

— *December 17, 1846*

"... May we with Gods help spend the comeing year better than the past which we purpose to do if Almighty God will deliver us from our present dreadful situation..."

— *December 31, 1846*

"... Keyburg sent bill to get hides off his shanty & carry them home this morning, provisions scarce hides are the only article we depend on, we have a little meat yet, may God send us help"

— *January 17, 1847*

"... John Battice & Denton came this morning with Eliza she wont eat hides Mrs Reid sent her back to live or die on them Milt. Got his toes froze the donoghs are all well"

— *January 21, 1847*

"... those that went to Suitors not yet returned provisions getting very scant people getting weak liveing on short allowance of hides"

— *January 26, 1847*

"John & Edw went to Graves this morning the Graves Seize d on Mrs Reids goods until they would be paid also took the hides that she & family had to live on."

— January 30, 1847

"... Peggy very uneasy for fear we shall all perish with hunger we have but a little meat left & only part of 3 hides has to support Mrs. Reid she has nothing left but one hide..."

— February 5, 1847

"... J Denton trying to borrow meat for Graves had none to give they have nothing but hides all are entirely out of meat but a little we have our hides are nearly all eat up but with Gods help spring will soon smile upon us"

— February 10, 1847

"... Mrs Graves refused to give Mrs Reid any hides put Suitors pack hides on her shanty would not let her have them says if I say it will thaw it then will not, she is a case"

— February 15, 1847

"... shot Towser today & dressed his flesh Mrs Graves came here this morning to borrow meat dog or ox they think I have meat to spare but I know to the Contrary they have plenty hides I live principally on the same"

— February 23, 1847

"... The Donnos told the California folks that they commence to eat the dead people 4 days ago, if they did not succeed that day or the next in finding their cattle then under ten or twelve feet of snow..."

— February 26, 1847

"... there has 10 men arrived this morning from bear valley with provisions we are to start in two or three days & Cash our goods here there is amongst them some old they say the snow will be here untill June"
— March 1, 1847

GLOSSARY

shanty – a small, crudely built shack

yoke – a wooden crosspiece placed over the heads of two animals and attached to the plow or cart they are to pull

Document Analysis

Patrick Breen's diary is a short, simple document, recording one man's steady loss of hope, and a group's gradual breakdown, in the face of tragic events. Beginning as a simple account of the weather and the party's dwindling food stores, Breen starts to invoke religion more and more as the weeks pass, desperate for some sort of divine intervention, to the point of pleading to God. He records the growing desperation, how some people vanished attempting to find rescue, while others turned to eating first the hides they used for their shelters and then to the flesh of those who had died.

Breen's account reveals how a community slowly disintegrates as members of the Donner Party sit in their camps, hoping against hope for salvation, and slowly weakening from starvation and malnutrition. When rations first become scarce, several people in the party refuse to eat the hides, but as hunger persists, the hides become highly desired. At one point, hides are forcibly taken from others, and people are left to starve. The choices are stark, and compassion is lacking, both in action and in Breen's account. In fact, it is a little shocking how dispassionately he writes about unfolding events.

Beyond the document, through later testimony, we know that cannibalism became widely practiced in the weeks before rescue. In at least a couple of circumstances, members of the party were killed by others so they could be eaten. Interestingly, we see little indication of murder or cannibalism in Breen's account. His only mention of cannibalism comes at the very end, and only in reference to members of the Donner family. Although the diary is scant, it does bring up questions of deliberate omissions on the part of Patrick Breen.

Eventually, thanks to the efforts of James F. Reed, more than half of the Donner Party was saved. But rather than draw the survivors together, the tragedy created long-lasting resentments between them. While the choices of some resulted in the survival of others, a few of the party had made questionable, perhaps immoral choices. Ultimately, the Breens fared as well as they did by relying on one another to get through each day and often refusing help to others. Whether this was morally right or wrong is difficult to determine in such circumstances.

Essential Themes

The story of the Donner Party, seen through the lens of Patrick Breen's diary, is the story of impossible choices. A group of pioneers, filled with the hope for riches and freedom, spurred on by the promise of Manifest Destiny, and believing in the righteousness of their endeavor, trusted the wrong booster and were taught a terrible lesson by nature. Simple kindness and human empathy were stripped away in order to survive. Choices that meant the difference between life and death were made daily. Of the many tragedies that befell settlers rushing westward throughout the nineteenth century, that of the Donner Party is relatively insignificant in terms of lives lost and historical impact. However, few other events from the era struck the public with such force. In many ways, the story of the Donner Party is a story about the loss of innocence, a rebuke concerning the promise of divine protection, and a cautionary tale to proponents of American exceptionalism. But more fundamentally, it is the story about the terrible price that sometimes must be paid for desire. At this time in the nation's history, as Native peoples were being forcefully displaced and a large segment of the population was enslaved, the tale of the Donner Party forced the nation to reexamine its collective morals. The event, which did help slow migration into California until gold was discovered in 1849, moved people to question whether the price of a new life was too high. On a deeper level, it forced Americans to look inward. What would we do in such circumstances? What line would we cross? In the increasingly connected and complicated contemporary world, in which the United States plays a pivotal role, these are questions with which we still grapple. Unfortunately, the introspection spurred by the Donner Party's misfortune was short-lived. The drive west continued, and settlement only increased. And for most, the Donner Party became only a gruesome tale of horror in the American West.

—KP Dawes, MA

Bibliography and Additional Reading

"The Donner Party." American Experience. Dir. Ric Burns. PBS. 1992. Film.

McGlashan, C. F. *History of the Donner Party.* 1881. Palo Alto, California: Stanford UP, 1940. Print.

Murphy, Virginia Reed. *Across the Plains in the Donner Party.* Silverthorne, CO: Vistabooks, 1995. Print.

Rarick, Ethan. *Desperate Passage: The Donner Party's Perilous Journey West.* New York: Oxford UP, 2008. Print.

■ The Discovery of Gold in California

Date: November 1857
Author: John Sutter
Genre: article; memoir

Summary Overview

In Hutchings' California Magazine in 1857, John Augustus Sutter recounted the events surrounding the discovery of gold at his mill near Coloma, California, some nine years earlier. He explained how word of the discovery spread and how the discovery affected him personally. Sutter, a Swiss immigrant who became an early California landowner, could have become extremely wealthy as a result of the discovery of gold on his land, but it ran counter to his goals and eventually became the catalyst for a series of business failures that would characterize much of his later life. Within the context of American history, however, the discovery of gold in California helped to justify the country's belief in Manifest Destiny. It also set into motion large-scale and rapid immigration, and forced the nation to further address whether slavery would be allowed to expand westward.

Defining Moment

In January 1848, the United States was already preparing to expand its holdings in the Southwest. The war with Mexico was ending, and the goals of Manifest Destiny—the belief that the United States was destined by Providence to expand all the way across the North American continent—were becoming realities with the negotiation of the Treaty of Guadalupe Hidalgo, under which Mexico ceded to the United States all the land from Texas to the Pacific. This Mexican Cession, as it was called, included the territory of Alta California, or Upper California, a name the Americans shortened to California.

Prior to Mexican independence in 1821, Alta California was a Spanish colony, and the search to find wealth in the Southwest dates back to the earliest Spanish entradas, or explorations, in the 1530s and 1540s. Stories of riches such as the mythical Seven Cities of Cibola had fuelled the imagination of explorers like Francisco Vásquez de Coronado, but in truth, the Spanish colonies of Texas, New Mexico, and Alta California had been a drain on Spanish resources. The riches the Spanish had found in their other colonies, such as Peru and Mexico, seemed not to be in evidence in Spain's northern holdings. Therefore, relatively few Spaniards colonized Alta California, although a vibrant Hispanic culture, based around the large landholdings of a number of wealthy Californios (Spanish-speaking inhabitants of California) and the numerous Franciscan missions, was well established by the time the Americans arrived. Before US annexation, the future cities of San Diego, Los Angeles, and San Francisco (then called Yerba Buena) were nothing more than small towns in a region far from the corridors of Spanish, Mexican, or American power.

The events that John Sutter describes, however, would change everything. California would almost overnight go from a primitive expanse occupied by Mexican landowners to a bustling and wild frontier region dominated by mostly young, single men from the eastern United States, Europe, and China. Prior to the gold rush, Americans had gradually been moving across the continent. Afterward, as historian J. S. Holliday aptly put it, "the world rushed in." The gold that flowed out of California, which had remained hidden until just after the Americans took over, seemed to justify the American notion of Manifest Destiny and the country's preordained right to inhabit the continent.

Author Biography

Born in Baden, Germany, to Swiss parents in 1803, Johann August Sutter emigrated from Berne, Switzerland, to the United States in 1834 in order to avoid mounting debt, changing his first two names to John Augustus. He left his wife and family behind, though he hoped to bring them to the United States when his fortunes turned. He found his way to California in 1839, after stops in St. Louis, the Oregon Territory, and

Hawaii. Along the way, Sutter relied on inflated stories of his past and his considerable "gift of gab" to get him out of financial difficulties and convince merchants to extend him credit and government officials to view him as a valuable new member of the community. Even the nickname "Captain" was the result of exaggerating his time as an under lieutenant in the Bernese reserve corps into service as a commander in the famed Swiss Guard (Hurtado 19–20). He tried his hand at trading along the Santa Fe Trail, raising horses and cattle, and building a hotel before leaving for California in order to avoid being sued for default on his debts in Missouri.

Once in California, Sutter impressed both American traders and Mexican government officials with his stories and apparent wealth, claiming, for instance, that he owned a ship. He applied for and received Mexican citizenship and then received a grant of 50,000 acres near present-day Sacramento, where he hoped to raise horses, cattle, and sheep. Once he made peace with the local Nisenan and Miwok Indians, whom he employed as laborers and as his own personal military force, his compound, which he named Sutter's Fort, became the social, political, and commercial center for the entire inland region. Because the area was so isolated from the centers of Mexican power closer to the coast, Sutter became the de facto authority of the region. But the events that would change the history of California and the United States as a whole occurred on another part of Sutter's land grant, about forty-five miles away from Sutter's Fort at a sawmill he had commissioned in the Coloma Valley, named for a nearby Maidu Indian settlement.

HISTORICAL DOCUMENT

It was in the first part of January, 1848, when the gold was discovered at Coloma, where I was then building a saw-mill. The contractor and builder of this mill was James W. Marshall, from New Jersey. In the fall of 1847, after the mill seat had been located, I sent up to this place Mr. P. L. Wimmer with his family, and a number of laborers, from the disbanded Mormon Battalion; and a little later I engaged Mr. Bennet from Oregon to assist Mr. Marshall in the mechanical labors of the mill. Mr. Wimmer had the team in charge, assisted by his young sons, to do the necessary teaming, and Mrs. Wimmer did the cooking for all hands.

I was very much in need of a new saw-mill, to get lumber to finish my large flouring mill, of four run of stones, at Brighton, which was commenced at the same time, and was rapidly progressing; likewise for other buildings, fences, etc., for the small village of Yerba Buena, (now San Francisco.) In the City Hotel, (the only one) at the dinner table this enterprise was unkindly called "another folly of Sutter's," as my first settlement at the old fort near Sacramento City was called by a good many, "a folly of his," and they were about right in that, because I had the best chances to get some of the finest locations near the settlements; and even well stocked rancho's had been offered to me on the most reasonable conditions; but I refused all these good offers, and preferred to explore the wilderness, and select a territory on the banks of the Sacramento. It was a rainy afternoon when Mr. Marshall arrived at my office in the Fort, very wet. I was somewhat surprised to see him, as he was down a few days previous; and then, I sent up to Coloma a number of teams with provisions, mill irons, etc., etc. He told me then that he had some important and interesting news which he wished to communicate secretly to me, and wished me to go with him to a place where we should not be disturbed, and where no listeners could come and hear what we had to say. I went with him to my private rooms; he requested me to lock the door; I complied, but I told him at the same time that nobody was in the house except the clerk, who was in his office in a different part of the house; after requesting of me something which he wanted, which my servants brought and then left the room, I forgot to lock the doors, and it happened that the door was opened by the clerk just at the moment when Marshall took a rag from his pocket, showing me the yellow metal: he had about two ounces of it; but how quick Mr. M. put the yellow metal in his pocket again can hardly be described.

The clerk came to see me on business, and excused himself for interrupting me, and as soon as he had left I was told, "now lock the doors; didn't I tell you that we might have listeners?" I told him that he need fear nothing about that, as it was not the habit of this gentleman; but I could hardly convince him that he need not to be suspicious. Then Mr. M. began to show me this metal, which consisted of small pieces and specimens, some of them worth a few dollars; he told me that he had expressed his opinion to the laborers at the mill, that this might be gold; but some of them were laughing at him and called him a crazy man, and could not believe such a thing.

After having proved the metal with aqua fortis, which I found in my apothecary shop, likewise with other experiments, and read the long article "gold" in the Encyclopedia Americana, I declared this to be gold of the finest quality, of at least 23 carats. After this Mr. M. had no more rest nor patience, and wanted me to start with him immediately for Coloma; but I told him I could not leave as it was late in the evening and nearly supper time, and that it would be better for him to remain with me till the next morning, and I would travel with him, but this would not do: he asked me only "will you come tomorrow morning?" I told him yes, and off he started for Coloma in the heaviest rain, although already very wet, taking nothing to eat. I took this news very easy, like all other occurrences good or bad, but thought a great deal during the night about the consequences which might follow such a discovery. I gave all my necessary orders to my numerous laborers, and left the next morning at 7 o'clock, accompanied by an Indian soldier, and vaquero, in a heavy rain, for Coloma. About half way on the road I saw at a distance a human being crawling out from the brushwood.

I asked the Indian who it was: he told me "the same man who was with you last evening." When I came nearer I found it was Marshall, very wet; I told him that he would have done better to remain with me at the fort than to pass such an ugly night here but he told me that he went up to Coloma, (54 miles) took his other horse and came half way to meet me; then we rode up to the new Eldorado. In the afternoon the weather was clearing up, and we made a prospecting promenade. The next morning we went to the tail-race of the mill, through which the water was running during the night, to clean out the gravel which had been made loose, for the purpose of widening the race; and after the water was out of the race we went in to search for gold. This was done every morning: small pieces of gold could be seen remaining on the bottom of the clean washed bed rock. I went in the race and picked up several pieces of this gold, several of the laborers gave me some which they had picked up, and from Marshall I received a part. I told them that I would get a ring made of this gold as soon as it could be done in California; and I have had a heavy ring made, with my family's cost of arms engraved on the outside, and on the inside of the ring is engraved, "The first gold, discovered in January, 1848." Now if Mrs. Wimmer possesses a piece which has been found earlier than mine Mr. Marshall can tell, as it was probably received from him. I think Mr. Marshall could have hardly known himself which was exactly the first little piece, among the whole.

The next day I went with Mr. M. on a prospecting tour in the vicinity of Coloma, and the following morning I left for Sacramento. Before my departure I had a conversation with all hands: I told them that I would consider it as a great favor if they would keep this discovery secret only for six weeks, so that I could finish my large flour mill at Brighton, (with four run of stones,) which had cost me already about from 24 to 25,000 dollars—the people up there promised to keep it secret so long. On my way home, instead of feeling happy and contented, I was very unhappy, and could not see that it would benefit me much, and I was perfectly right in thinking so; as it came just precisely as I expected. I thought at the same time that it could hardly be kept secret for six weeks, and in this I was not mistaken, for about two weeks later, after my return, I sent up several teams in charge of a white man, as the teamsters were Indian boys. . . .

Mr. Brannan made a kind of claim on Mormon Island, and put a tolerably heavy tax on "The Latter Day Saints." I believe it was 30 per cent, which they paid for some time, until they got tired of it, (some of them told me that it was for the purpose of building a temple for the honor and glory of the Lord.)

So soon as the secret was out my laborers began to leave me, in small parties first, but then all left, from the clerk to the cook, and I was in great distress; only a few mechanics remained to finish some very necessary work which they had commenced, and about eight invalids, who continued slowly to work a few teams, to scrape out the mill race at Brighton. The Mormons did not like to leave my mill unfinished, but they got the gold fever like everybody else. After they had made their piles they left for the Great Salt Lake. So long as these people have been employed by me they have behaved very well, and were industrious and faithful laborers, and when settling their accounts there was not one of them who was not contented and satisfied.

Then the people commenced rushing up from San Francisco and other parts of California, in May, 1848: in the former village only five men were left to take care of the women and children. The single men locked their doors and left for "Sutter's Fort," and from there to the Eldorado. For some time the people in Monterey and farther south would not believe the news of the gold discovery, and said that it was only a 'Ruse de Guerre' of Sutter's, because he wanted to have neighbors in his wilderness. From this time on I got only too many neighbors, and some very bad ones among them.

What a great misfortune was this sudden gold discovery for me! It has just broken up and ruined my hard, restless, and industrious labors, connected with many dangers of life, as I had many narrow escapes before I became properly established. . . .

At the same time I was engaged in a mercantile firm in Coloma, which I left in January, 1849—likewise with many sacrifices. After this I would have nothing more to do with the gold affairs. At this time, the Fort was the great trading place where nearly all the business was transacted. I had no pleasure to remain there, and moved up to Hock Farm, with all my Indians, and who had been with me from the time they were children. The place was then in charge of a Major Domo.

It is very singular that the Indians never found a piece of gold and brought it to me, as they very often did other specimens found in the ravines. I requested them continually to bring me some curiosities from the mountains, for which I always recompensed them. I have received animals, birds, plants, young trees, wild fruits, pipe clay, stones, red ochre, etc., etc., but never a piece of gold. Mr. Dana of the scientific corps of the expedition under Com. Wilkes' Exploring Squadron, told me that he had the strongest proof and signs of gold in the vicinity of Shasta Mountain, and furthers south. A short time afterwards, Doctor Sandels, a very scientific traveler, visited me, and explored a part of the country in a great hurry, as time would not permit him to make a longer stay.

He told me likewise that he found sure signs of gold, and was very sorry that he could not explore the Sierra Nevada. He did not encourage me to attempt to work and open mines, as it was uncertain how it would pay and would probably be only for a government. So I thought it more prudent to stick to the plow, notwithstanding I did know that the country was rich in gold, and other minerals. An old attached Mexican servant who followed me here from the United States, as soon as he knew that I was here, and who understood a great deal about working in placers, told me he found sure signs of gold in the mountains on Bear Creek, and that we would go right to work after returning from our campaign in 1845, but he became a victim to his patriotism and fell into the hands of the enemy near my encampment, with dispatches for me from Gen. Micheltorena, and he was hung as a spy, for which I was very sorry.

By this sudden discovery of the gold, all my great plans were destroyed. Had I succeeded for a few years before the gold was discovered, I would have been the richest citizen on the Pacific shore; but it had to be different. Instead of being rich, I am ruined, and the cause of it is the long delay of the United States Land Commission of the United States Courts, through the great influence of the squatter lawyers. Before my case will be decided in Washington, another year may elapse, but I hope that justice will be done me by the last tribunal— the Supreme Court of the United States. By the Land Commission and the District Court it has been decided in my favor. The Common Council of the city of Sacramento, composed partly of squatters, paid Adelpheus Felch, (one of the late Land Commissioners, who was engaged by the squatters during his office), $5,000, from the fund of the city, against the will of the tax-payers, for which amount he has to try to defeat my just and old claim from the Mexican government, before the Supreme Court of the United States in Washington.

GLOSSARY

aqua fortis: a solution of nitric acid that dissolves most metals other than gold

Eldorado: an area of great wealth, based on the Spanish legend of El Dorado, a city of gold

major domo: an administrator who acts on behalf of an absent landowner or supervises an owner's business

Mormon Battalion: a military unit made up of members of the Church of Jesus Christ of Latter-Day Saints, which were then known as Mormons, that served during the Mexican-American War, many of whom settled in California

Document Analysis

John Sutter had an ambition that was certainly as big as the events that swept through his land grant starting in January 1848, and though he personally did not profit from the gold rush that followed, he was an integral member of the drama that played out in California, transforming the area from a sparsely populated Mexican backwater to one of the economic engines of the United States in a matter of less than five years.

One might think that someone with Sutter's ambitions who also had the good fortune to have gold discovered on his land would be well positioned to profit from the discovery. However, Sutter achieved all he had more by force of personality and slyness than business acumen, and this became readily apparent in the years following the discovery. By the time Sutter told his story to a popular journal—nearly a decade after the discovery—the gold rush was already well known across the nation. But the details Sutter revealed demonstrate much about who he was as a man as well as the importance of the California gold rush in the history of the state, the region, and the nation.

Sutter had chosen the then-remote area near the confluence of the American and Sacramento Rivers as his land grant some seven years earlier, despite having the chance to acquire land closer to the coast. However, being at a distance from the centers of power suited Sutter well, as he wished to have complete control over the development of his land grant as well as the people residing on it. In Sutter's vision, what was wilderness at the time would become a profitable operation, producing cowhides, beef, horses, and lumber for the slowly growing cities of Monterey and Yerba Buena on the coast. Development had been slower than Sutter anticipated, though, and Sutter's Fort was not yet self-sufficient. As a result, he was often seeking credit from suppliers on the coast to keep his operation functioning, something with which he had quite a bit of experience. Sutter had additional reasons for apprehension about what the future might bring in late 1847 and early 1848, as the United States was still at war with Mexico. Although California was still technically Mexican territory, it was by that time under the control of the United States, and a permanent change in government was almost inevitable. Sutter's authority in the region was largely based upon the fact that the Mexican government in Alta California was weak, and his grant was far enough from the Mexican territorial capitol at Monterey that he had unrestrained control over his land (Brands, 17–18).

In late 1847, Sutter had entered a partnership with James W. Marshall to build a sawmill on the South Fork of the American River. Marshall was a mechanic from New Jersey who, like Sutter, had gradually made his way west. Like Sutter, he had briefly settled in the Oregon Territory, but, disliking the weather, moved farther south into California. Men like Marshall who had extensive experience with tools and construction were in high demand in the West, and he had no problem finding work with Sutter. The main portion of Sutter's 50,000-acre land grant was near the present city of Sacramento, California, but he also had an additional grant in the Coloma Valley, which was in the foothills of the Sierra Nevada. Being close to the mountains and on a stream made a perfect location for a sawmill that would provide Sutter's Fort and the surrounding area with the wood needed for construction, and Sutter and Marshall had agreed to share equally in the lumber that the mill produced.

By January, the workers building the mill were digging out the millrace that was to bring the water from the river into the sawmill, turning the wheel that would power the operation. On January 24, 1848, as the water flowed through the millrace, Marshall noticed flakes of a gleaming yellow metal left behind. As the flowing water would have washed away any dirt or lighter minerals, it was clear to Marshall that the metal left behind was gold. Quickly, Marshall collected the flakes and, together with a number of his workers, performed several tests to verify the identity of the metal. Convinced that it was gold he possessed, four days later Marshall embarked on the forty-five mile trip to from Coloma to Sutter's Fort to discuss this development with his business partner.

As Sutter enters into his description of Marshall's arrival at Sutter's Fort, it is interesting that he veers into what others thought of his decision to settle on the Sacramento River rather than nearer to the coast. It appears that he is using the discovery of gold on his property to justify his decision and make his detractors look like fools, which is ironic considering the fact that Sutter profited very little from the discovery. In Sutter's account, when Marshall does arrive, he appears to have a full sense of the significance of the discovery, as he asked to discuss the matter in "a place where we should not be disturbed, and where no listeners could come and hear what we had to say." Marshall asks Sutter to lock the door, and Sutter portrays himself as somewhat incompetent when he forgets to lock the door and his clerk comes into the room just as Marshall is removing the gold from his pocket.

After Marshall shows Sutter the gold, Sutter does exactly what Marshall did at the mill, chemically testing the metal to ensure that it actually was gold and reading up on the material to determine its quality. Satisfied that this was, indeed, high-quality gold, Marshall returned to Coloma, and Sutter left to join him the next morning. Sutter, too, was well aware of the consequences of the discovery, and he became determined to keep the secret for as long as possible. Although Sutter asks the workers at the mill to keep the discovery secret, he states that he knew that it would be nearly impossible to prevent the workers from talking. After the visit, Sutter explained that "On my way home, instead of feeling happy and contented, I was very unhappy, and could not see that it would benefit me much, and I was perfectly right in thinking so; as it came just precisely as I expected." The workers at the mill were well acquainted with the workers at Sutter's Fort, so Sutter concludes that it was inevitable that word would escape. At the same time, Sutter takes great pride in describing the

ring that he had made with the first gold taken from the millrace, which he stated he did very soon after, so Sutter himself could have been responsible for spreading news of the discovery. Rather than seeking a way to profit from the discovery personally, Sutter laments the fact that he could see no way to profit, as it did not fit with his plans to build a flour mill and continue his other operations at Sutter's Fort. Rather than seizing the opportunity to profit from gold before the world rushed in, Sutter remains steadfast in his own operations, "as it was uncertain how it would pay and would probably be only for a government. So I thought it more prudent to stick to the plow, notwithstanding I did know that the country was rich in gold, and other minerals." In fact, finding no way to participate in the gold rush itself, Sutter's other operations suffered as his workers left his employ in droves, looking instead to enrich themselves by being among the first in the gold fields.

Interestingly, Sutter mentions in passing Sam Brannan of Mormon Island, who he said placed a tax on his people to mine there. What he does not mention is that Brannan was also a merchant who ran a store at Sutter's Fort. Perhaps if Sutter had possessed the business acumen of his hero John Jacob Astor, he might have followed Brannan's example. As soon as he learned of the discovery, Brannan bought up all of the mining supplies he could, took a trip to San Francisco, and did everything he could to spread the word of the gold strike. As a result, Brannan became the first millionaire in California, not through joining the rush to the gold fields, but by realizing that he was in the right place at the right time to profit from it. However, Sutter continues to complain about the discovery of gold ruining his dream of setting up his private kingdom: "What a great misfortune was this sudden gold discovery for me! It has just broken up and ruined my hard, restless, and industrious labors, connected with many dangers of life, as I had many narrow escapes before I became properly established." Narrow escapes certainly characterized Sutter's life, though his self-pity was meant to disguise the fact that the narrow escapes were too often from circumstances of his own making.

As the gold rush progressed, Sutter focused on keeping what he had. But the vast majority of those who worked for him, with the exception of American Indian workers who were largely chased away from the gold fields, led the throngs that would come to California from all over the United States and the rest of the world to seek their fortunes. Many of the early miners were successful, as there was a significant portion of gold that could be found in much the same way that Marshall had. Placer gold—gold that is on the surface of the earth rather than underground—was still relatively abundant, and miners quickly descended on the region's streams hoping to follow Marshall's example. Governmental jurisdiction of the land was lax because of the gold fields' distance from the coast and because the Treaty of Guadalupe Hidalgo did not go into effect until July 4, 1848. The absence of effective government restrictions meant that there were no rules and no taxes. Small impresarios like Sutter could no longer hold sway over their land grants, as the miners largely made up their own laws to govern themselves in the mining camps.

As much as Sutter had sought to delay the spreading of the news, those like Brannan, who saw opportunity in the influx of immigrants that was sure to follow, ensured that the word would get out. The first outsiders to seek their fortunes began to arrive during the summer of 1848. News had spread to the neighboring Oregon Territory, where many Americans had already migrated. By the end of the year, miners were appearing from Hawaii, Mexico, and South America, and the first settlers from the eastern United States were beginning to arrive. But those numbers would snowball during 1849, when tens of thousands flocked to the California territory. Most came on the overland route via the California Trail, although those with some means could purchase a ticket to come by ship and sail either around the cape at the southern tip of South America or by the Panama shortcut (the Panama Canal would not be built for another sixty-five years).

Mining became more difficult as the "forty-niners" arrived. Competition over claims in the gold fields was intense, and the prices that miners paid to merchants like Brannan for necessary supplies were often exorbitant. It was said that just to survive, a miner in 1849 or 1850 had to mine one ounce of gold every day. Although those who arrived came looking for easy wealth, mining whatever gold was available was extremely difficult work. Success could still be found during those first few years, but after 1853, the amount of placer gold that was mined began to decrease while the number of miners continued to increase.

It is impossible to separate the history of the gold rush from the story of the rapid population growth in California. Although many of the miners returned home disappointed and destitute, many others de-

cided to stay in the region, which became a state on September 9, 1850. Ironically, it was those very miners who saw the potential of the region as agricultural land who realized many of Sutter's dreams, albeit on a much smaller scale.

Like Sutter's own life, the fate of California was determined by a number of events that seemingly overwhelmed the area. The gold rush, clearly, brought huge numbers of people and made the dream of Manifest Destiny a reality. Only nine days after Marshall's discovery of gold, the Treaty of Guadalupe Hidalgo was signed, which, when ratified by the US Senate, would make California a US territory. The timing of the discovery of gold, combined with the transfer of California from Mexico to the United States, made the fate of the region a national issue, since Congress had been debating for decades whether new states and territories would be admitted into the union as slave or free. The rapid increase in the population of California meant that quick statehood would be a necessity. California was ultimately admitted as a free state, but only as a part of the Compromise of 1850, which allowed for a popular vote on slavery in other parts of the territory gained from Mexico, the continuation of slavery in Washington, DC, and, most importantly to Southerners, the passage of a new Fugitive Slave Act, which stated that Southern slave owners could cross into the non-slave states and territories to capture escaped slaves.

Sutter, however, remained focused not on the transformative impact that the discovery of gold on his land had on the region, but rather on his own personal misfortune that was caused by his poor business decisions. His concluding remarks continue his theme of feeling personally ruined by the discovery of gold. "By this sudden discovery of the gold, all my great plans were destroyed. Had I succeeded for a few years before the gold was discovered, I would have been the richest citizen on the Pacific shore; but it had to be different. Instead of being rich, I am ruined."

Essential Themes

The discovery of gold on John Sutter's land in 1848 had dramatic consequences for many different populations within California. For miners, the impact was felt economically, and for a few of them it was a time of incredible profit and good fortune. For others, it was a fool's errand, and they returned home destitute and in disgrace. Furthermore, for many of California's American Indians, Sutter's discovery was the beginning of the end of their culture. As happened in other regions where Euro-American settlers arrived in large numbers, disease spread rapidly, decimating many communities. The dependency some tribes had on Euro-American trade meant that with the increased prices of those trade goods, many Indians slipped into poverty or even died of starvation. The justice of the gold fields did not include justice for the Indians, who were sometimes killed for their land. Those who remained had their land and their cultures invaded by the flood of Euro-Americans.

The gold rush that resulted from the discovery also greatly diversified the California population. Mexicans and American Indians constituted the majority of native inhabitants in the region at the time of the discovery. That would quickly change, however, as immigrants from all over the world flooded in. The Chinese arrived in greater numbers than any other. By 1850, there were five hundred Chinese in California, and by 1855 the number of Chinese who had made the trip across the Pacific to the "Gold Mountain" reached twenty thousand, over twice the entire population of the region seven years earlier. San Francisco quickly became the center of Chinese American culture, and although many other cities in California developed Chinatowns, San Francisco's remained dominant and iconic. Chinese miners, like Indians, were persecuted and many had their claims stolen by Euro-American miners. However, the Chinese soon earned a reputation for making profitable claims that other miners had abandoned. After the gold rush, discrimination increased, and by 1882, the United States passed the Chinese Exclusion Act, which was the first immigration law restricting the entry of one particular group based on ethnicity.

Finally, the discovery had a dramatic impact on the landscape. Once the placer gold began to run out in 1853, more destructive means were employed to extract gold from beneath the surface. Hydraulic mining decimated entire hillsides by using torrents of water to find the gold hiding underneath. Chemicals such as arsenic, cyanide, and mercury—used to extract the gold from the materials in which it was embedded—poisoned the land and water. The burgeoning population cut down huge stands of timber to fuel the growth of their towns. In the end, the discovery of gold resulted in the creation of a new California, but—as Sutter would have pointed out—at the expense of destroying the old California.

—*Steven L. Danver, PhD*

Bibliography and Additional Reading

Brands, H. W. *The Age of Gold: The California Gold Rush and the New American Dream*. Rev. ed. New York: Random, 2002. Print.

Holliday, J. S. *The World Rushed In: The California Gold Rush Experience*. New York: Simon, 1981. Print.

Rush for Riches: Gold Fever and the Making of California. Berkeley: U of California P, 1999. Print.

Hurtado, Albert L. John Sutter: *A Life on the North American Frontier*. Norman: U of Oklahoma P, 2006. Print.

Osborne, Thomas J. *Pacific Eldorado: A History of Greater California*. New York: Wiley-Blackwell, 2013. Print.

Starr, Kevin. *Americans and the California Dream, 1850–1915*. New York: Oxford UP, 1986. Print.

Dillon, Richard. *Fool's Gold: The Decline and Fall of Captain John Sutter of California*. Sanger, CA: Write Thought, 2012. Print.

Owens, Kenneth N., ed. *John Sutter and a Wider West*. Rev. ed. Lincoln: U of Nebraska P, 2002. Print.

Riches for All: The California Gold Rush and the World. Lincoln: U of Nebraska P, 2002. Print.

Trafzer, Clifford E. and Joel R. Hyer, eds. *Exterminate Them! Written Accounts of the Murder, Rape, and Slavery of Native Americans during the California Gold Rush, 1848–1868*. East Lansing: Michigan State UP, 1999. Print.

Vaught, David. *After the Gold Rush: Tarnished Dreams in the Sacramento Valley*. Baltimore: Johns Hopkins UP, 2007. Print.

■ A Woman's Trip Across the Plains

Date: 1849
Author: Catherine Haun
Genre: memoir; autobiography

Summary Overview

Like countless other Americans, Catherine Haun heard the stories of ordinary people who struck it rich in California following the discovery of gold there in 1848. Compared by many to El Dorado, the legendary city of gold, California was viewed as a place where anyone capable of hard work could earn his or her rightful due. As part of a group of travelers, Haun and her husband journeyed west in 1849 in the hope of "'pick[ing] up' gold enough" to settle their debts. Despite the many hardships she faced, including rough travel, fear of attack by American Indians, and rampant disease, Haun persevered, ultimately arriving safely in California late in 1849. Her chronicle of her journey, "A Woman's Trip across the Plains," provides a detailed contemporary account of a pivotal time in the history of both California and the United States as a whole. Haun records even the smallest details, such as the foods the pioneers ate, the clothing they wore, and the geological formations they encountered, thus providing later readers with an in-depth understanding of the pioneer experience.

Defining Moment

On January 24, 1848, James W. Marshall discovered several small pieces of gold while supervising the construction of a sawmill in what is now Coloma, California. News of his discovery spread quickly, and so-called gold fever soon affected countless Americans who saw in California the promise of lucrative rewards in exchange for difficult but profitable labor. Thousands traveled to California, seeking to start new lives on the West Coast or to return home after becoming wealthy. Of these travelers, only a few wrote accounts of their journeys, and memoirs such as Haun's provide crucial details about the lives of those who traveled west in search of gold.

Those traveling along the trails to California faced many difficulties. Diseases such as cholera, smallpox, and typhoid were prevalent, and many travelers feared that they would be robbed, attacked, or killed by American Indians. Despite these hardships and the exhausting travel, many of those bound for California sought to take elements of their old lives with them. As Haun documents, the women of the trails held fast to their customs of socializing, swapping recipes and foods, knitting, and mending clothes. Such practices, Haun notes, "kept [the women] in practice of feminine occupations and diversions." The women adapted to the use of dried buffalo dung ("buffalo chips") as fuel in their cooking and cleaning and adjusted to the noise and openness all around them at night, but they would not part with the activities that nineteenth-century society expected of them as ladies. Performing these tasks—seemingly mundane chores—kept home traditions alive and ensured the survival of the travelers' way of life despite the sweeping wind and dust along the plains.

Author Biography

Little is known about Catherine Haun's life prior to her journey to California. She and her husband, a lawyer, lived near the town of Clinton, in eastern Iowa. Part of the French territory transferred to the United States in the 1803 Louisiana Purchase, Iowa achieved statehood only three years before the Hauns' departure for California and was renowned for its agriculture. Despite the state's fertile fields, at least some residents of the Iowa were struggling financially by the time of the gold rush. Haun refers to "a period of National hard times" and notes that she and her husband, "being financially involved in . . . business interests near Clinton," hoped to travel to California and find "gold enough with which to return and pay off [their] debts." It is possible that the "period of National hard times" to which she refers was the aftermath of the Panic of 1837, which set off a depression that enveloped the United States for nearly a decade. Although Haun does not specify the nature of her family's financial difficulties, it is possible that the

Hauns' "business interests" were affected by the economic upheaval of the period, prompting their move west in search of gold.

In early 1849, Haun and her husband began to plan their journey to California. They departed in April, accompanied by about twenty-five fellow Iowans. After enduring the many hardships and setbacks detailed in Haun's memoir, the majority of the travelers arrived safely in Sacramento, California, in early November. In January, the Hauns settled in the small town of Marysville, where Haun's husband established a law practice. Little is known about Haun's life after this point, and whether she and her husband ever searched for gold themselves or returned to Iowa remains unknown.

HISTORICAL DOCUMENT

Early in January of 1849 we first thought of emigrating to California. It was a period of National hard times and we being financially involved in our business interests near Clinton, Iowa, longed to go to the new El Dorado and "pick up" gold enough with which to return and pay off our debts. . . .

At that time the "gold fever" was contagious and few, old or young, escaped the malady. On the streets, in the fields, in the workshops and by the fireside, golden California was the chief topic of conversation. Who were going? How was best to "fix up" the "outfit"? What to take as food and clothing? Who would stay at home to care for the farm and womenfolks? Who would take wives and children along? Advice was handed out quite free of charge and often quite free of common sense. However, as two heads are better than one, all proffered ideas helped as a means to the end. The intended adventurers dilligently collected their belongings and after exchanging such articles as were not needed for others more suitable for the trip, begging, buying or borrowing what they could, with buoyant spirits started off. Some half dozen families of our neighborhood joined us and probably about twenty-five persons constituted our little band. . . .

It was more than three months before we were thoroughly equipped and on April 24th, 1849 we left our comparatively comfortable homes—and the uncomfortable creditorsfor the uncertain and dangerous trip, beyond which loomed up, in our mind's eye, castles of shining gold.

There was still snow upon the ground and the roads were bad, but in our eagerness to be off we ventured forth. This was a mistake as had we delayed for a couple of weeks the weather would have been more settled, the roads better and much of the discouragement and hardship of the first days of travel might have been avoided.

. . .

At the end of the month we reached Council Bluffs, having only travelled across the state of Iowa, a distance of about 350 miles every mile of which was beautifully green and well watered. . . .

As Council Bluffs was the last settlement on the route we made ready for the final plunge into the wilderness by looking over our wagons and disposing of whatever we could spare. . . .

The canvas covered schooners were supposed to be, as nearly as possible, constructed upon the principle of the "wonderful one-horse shay." It was very essential that the animals be sturdy, whether oxen, mules or horses. Oxen were preferred as they were less liable to stampede or be stolen by Indians and for long hauls held out better and though slower they were steady and in the long run performed the journey in an equally brief time. Besides, in an emergency they could be used as beef. When possible the provisions and ammunition were protected from water and dust by heavy canvas or rubber sheets.

Good health, and above all, not too large a proportion of women and children was also taken into consideration. The morning starts had to be made early—always before six o'clock—and it would be hard to get children ready by that hour. Later on experience taught the mothers that in order not to delay the trains it was best to allow the smaller children to sleep in the wagons until after several hours of travel when they were taken up for the day.

Our caravan had a good many women and children and although we were probably longer on the journey owing to their presence—they exerted a good influence, as the men did not take such risks with Indians and thereby avoided conflict;were more alert about the care of the teams and seldom had accidents; more attention was paid to cleanliness and sanitation and, lastly but not of less importance, the meals were more regular and better cooked thus preventing much sickness and there was less waste of food. . . .

After a sufficient number of wagons and people were collected at this rendezvous we proceeded to draw up and agree upon a code of general regulations for train government and mutual protection—a necessary precaution when so many were to travel together. Each family was to be independent yet a part of the grand unit and every man was expected to do his individual share of general work and picket duty.

John Brophy was selected as Colonel. He was particularly eligible having served in the Black Hawk War and as much of his life had been spent along the frontier his experience with Indians was quite exceptional.

Each week seven Captains were appointed to serve on "Grand Duty." They were to protect the camps and animals at night. One served each night and in case of danger gave the alarm.

When going into camp the "leader wagon" was turned from the road to the right, the next wagon turned to the left, the others following close after and always alternating to right and left. In this way a large circle, or corral, was formed within which the tents were pitched and the oxen herded. The horses were picketed near by until bed time when they were tethered to the tongues of the wagons.

While the stock and wagons were being cared for, the tents erected and camp fires started by the side of the wagons outside the corral, the cooks busied themselves preparing the evening meal for the hungry, tired, impatient travelers.

When the camp ground was desirable enough to warrant it we did not travel on the Sabbath.

Although the men were generally busy mending wagons, harness, yokes, shoeing the animals etc., and the women washed clothes, boiled a big mess of beans, to be warmed over for several meals, or perhaps mended clothes or did other household straightening up, all felt somewhat rested on Monday morning, for the change of occupation had been refreshing. . . .

During the entire trip Indians were a source of anxiety, we being never sure of their friendship. Secret dread and alert watchfulness seemed always necessary for after we left the prairies they were more treacherous and numerous being in the language of the pioneer trapper: "They wus the most onsartainest vermints alive."

One night after we had retired, some sleeping in blankets upon the ground, some in tents, a few under the wagons and others in the wagons, Colonel Brophy gave the men a practice drill. It was impromptu and a surprise. He called: "Indians, Indians!" We were thrown into great confusion and excitement but he was gratified at the promptness and courage with which the men responded. Each immediately seized his gun and made ready for the attack. The women had been instructed to seek shelter in the wagons at such times of danger, but some screamed, others fainted, a few crawled under the wagons and those sleeping in wagons generally followed their husbands out and all of us were nearly paralyzed with fear. Fortunately, we never had occasion to put into actual use this maneuver, but the drill was quite reassuring and certainly we womenfolk would have acted braver had the alarm ever again been sounded. . . .

Finally after a couple of weeks' travel the distant mountains of the west came into view.

This was the land of the buffalo. One day a herd came in our direction like a great black cloud, a threatening moving mountain, advancing towards us very swiftly and with wild snorts, noses almost to the ground and tails flying in midair. I haven't any idea how many there were but they seemed to be innumerable and made a deafening terrible noise. As is their habit, when stampeding, they did not turn out of their course for anything. Some of our wagons were within their line of advance and in consequence one was completely demolished and two were overturned. Several persons were hurt, one child's shoulder being dislocated, but fortunately no one was killed.

Two of these buffaloes were shot and the humps and tongues furnished us with fine fresh meat. They happened to be buffalo cows and, in consequence, the meat was particularly good flavor and tender. It is believed that the cow can run faster than the bull. The large bone of the hind leg, after being stripped of the flesh, was buried in coals of buffalo chips and in an hour the baked marrow was served. I have never tasted such a rich, delicious food! . . .

Buffalo chips, when dry, were very useful to us as

fuel. On the barren plains when we were without wood we carried empty bags and each pedestrian "picked up chips" as he, or she, walked along. Indeed we could have hardly got along without thus useful animal, were always appropriating either his hump, tongue, marrowbone, tallow, skin or chips! . . .

Trudging along within the sight of the Platte, whose waters were now almost useless to us on account of the Alkali, we one day found a post with a cross board pointing to a branch road which seemed better than the one we were on. . . . We decided to take it but before many miles suddenly found ourselves in a desolate, rough country that proved to be the edge of the "Bad Lands" I shudder yet at the thought of the ugliness and danger of the territory. . . .

We saw nothing living but Indians, lizards and snakes. Trying, indeed, to feminine nerves. Surely Inferno can be no more horrible in formation. The pelting sun's rays reflected from the parched ground seemed a furnace heat by day and our campfires, as well as those of the Indians cast grotesque glares and terrifying shadows by night. The demen needed only horns and cloven feet to complete the soul stirring picture!

To add to the horrors of the surroundings one man was bitten on the ankle by a venemous snake. Although every available remidy was tried upon the wound, his limb had to be amputated with the aid of a common handsaw. Fortunately, for him, he had a good, brave wife along who helped and cheered him into health and usefulness; for it was not long before he found much that he could do and was not considered a burden, although the woman had to do a man's work as they were alone. He was of a mechanical turn, and later on helped mend wagons, yokes and harness; and when the train was "on the move" sat in the wagon, gun by his side, and repaired boots and shoes. He was one of the most cheery members of the company and told good stories and sang at the campfire, putting to shame some of the able bodied who were given to complaining or selfishness. . . .

Finally after several days we got back onto the road and were entering the Black Hills Country. . . .

We had not traveled many miles in the Black Hills—the beginning of the Rocky Mountains—before we realized that our loads would have to be lightened as the animals were not able to draw the heavily laden wagons over the slippery steep roads. We were obliged to sacrifice most of our merchandise that was intended for our stock in trade in California and left it by the wayside; burying the barrels of alcohol least the Indians should drink it and frenzied thereby might follow and attack us. . . .

During the day we womenfolk visited from wagon to wagon or congenial friends spent an hour walking, ever westward, and talking over our home life back in "the states" telling of the loved ones left behind; voicing our hopes for the future in the far west and even whispering a little friendly gossip of emigrant life.

High teas were not popular but tatting, knitting, crocheting, exchanging recipes for cooking beans or dried apples or swapping food for the sake of variety kept us in practice of feminine occupations and diversions.

We did not keep late hours but when not too engrossed with fear of the red enemy or dread of impending danger we enjoyed the hour around the campfire. The menfolk lolling and smoking their pipes and guessing or maybe betting how many miles we had covered the day. We listened to readings, story telling, music and songs and the day often ended in laughter and merrymaking.

It was the fourth of July when we reached the beautiful Laramie River. Its sparkling, pure waters were full of myriads of fish that could be caught with scarcely an effort. It was necessary to build barges to cross the river and during the enforced delay our animals rested and we had one of our periodical "house cleanings." This general systematic re-adjustment always freshened up our wagon train very much, for after a few weeks of travel things got mixed up and untidy and often wagons had to be abandoned if too worn for repairs, and generally one or more animals had died or been stolen.

Cholera was prevalent on the plains at this time; the train preceding as well as the one following ours had one or more deaths, but fortunately we had not a single case of the disease. Often several graves together stood as silent proof of smallpox or cholera epidemic. The Indians spread the disease among themselves by digging up the bodies of the victims for the clothing. The majority of the Indians were badly pock-marked. . . .

It was with considerable apprehension that we started to traverse the treeless, alkali region of the Great Basin or Sink of the Humboldt. Our wagons were badly worn, the animals much the worse for wear, food and stock feed was getting low with no chance of replenishing the supply. During the month of transit we, like other trains, experienced the greatest privations of the whole trip. It was no unusual sight to see graves, carcasses of animals and abandoned wagons. In fact the latter furnished us with wood for the campfires as the sagebrush was scarce and unsatisfactory and buffalo chips were not as plentiful as on the plains east of the Rocky Mountains. . . .

Across this drear country I used to ride horseback several hours of the day which was a great relief from the continual jolting of even our spring wagon. I also walked a great deal and this lightened the wagon. One day I walked fourteen miles and was not very fatigued. . . . The men seemed more tired and hungry than were the women. Our only death on the journey occurred in this desert. The Canadian woman, Mrs. Lamore, suddenly sickened and died, leaving her two little girls and grief stricken husband. We halted a day to bury her and the infant that had lived but an hour, in this weird, lonely spot on God's footstool away apparently from everywhere and everybody. . . .

We reached Sacramento on November 4, 1849, just six months and ten days after leaving Clinton, Iowa, we were all in pretty good condition. . . . Although very tired of tent life many of us spent Thanksgiving and Christmas in our canvas houses. I do not remember ever having had happier holiday times. For Christmas dinner we had a grizzly bear steak for which we paid $2.50, one cabbage for $1.00 and—oh horrors—some more dried apples! And for a Christmas present the Sacramento river rose very high and flooded the whole town! . . . It was past the middle of January before we . . . reached Marysville— there were only a half dozen houses; all occupied at exorbitant prices. Some one was calling for the services of a lawyer to draw up a will and my husband offered to do it for which he charged $150.00.

This seemed a happy omen for success and he hung out his shingle, abandoning all thought of going to the mines. As we had lived in a tent and had been on the move for nine months, traveling 2400 miles we were glad to settle down and go housekeeping in a shed that was built in a day of lumber purchased with the first fee.

GLOSSARY

cholera: a commonly fatal illness caused by contaminated water

Council Bluffs: a town in Iowa that served as the beginning of the Mormon Trail

El Dorado: a legendary golden city

Laramie River: a tributary of the Platte River located in present-day Colorado and Wyoming

Sink of the Humboldt: a dry lake bed in Nevada; also known as Humboldt Sink

smallpox: a highly infectious and frequently fatal disease causing the appearance of pustules on the skin

Document Analysis

It is impossible to ascertain the thoughts that ran through Haun's mind as she and her husband set off for California in 1849. However, it is safe to presume that worries about the weather and disease and the rumors of American Indian attacks on wagon trains were at the forefront of her mind throughout the journey. In this, Haun was similar to the many other women traveling across the plains. But the journey was also an adventure that took her out of the home, away from the limited domestic sphere, and plunged her into a relatively un-known realm. Along with the other women in her group, Haun adapted to cooking, mending, cleaning, and living out in the open. Although she witnessed death and accidents en route, she also worked to preserve elements of her life in Iowa, balancing the unpredictability of life on the trails with the customs and practices then considered essential to civilized society. As a detailed chronicle of Haun's journey, "A Woman's Trip across the Plains" can teach twenty-first-century readers much about the long and arduous trek made by those seeking wealth and new opportunities in California.

In her memoir, Haun states that she and her husband began seriously thinking of making the long journey in January of 1849. They must have decided to move forward with their plan quickly, for Haun notes that their party, which was made up of "some half dozen families," was "thoroughly equipped" within a matter of months. "On April 24th, 1849," she writes, "we left our comparatively comfortable homes." Three months was a relatively short time in which to plan and prepare for such a journey, and the speed with which the travelers did so indicates that their area of Iowa was likely well stocked with the necessary provisions for the journey westward.

Careful preparation was crucial to the success of any such journey. In his work *Wagons West: The Epic Story of America's Overland Trails*, historian Frank McLynn notes that in 1843, each family migrating to the West Coast was recommended to bring "no less than two hundred pounds of flour and one hundred pounds of bacon for every family member, as well as other provisions—beans, rice, ship's biscuits and dried fruit being particularly recommended" (130). A wagon, which Haun calls a "schooner," was also required, as were spare parts and animals to pull the loaded vehicle. As trees were not always plentiful along the plains, lumber for repairs was also a necessity. McLynn estimates that fitting out a wagon and team cost between three hundred and six hundred dollars, a significant sum in the mid-nineteenth century.

The question of which animals were best suited to pulling the wagons was subject to debate. Although horses were used at times, the main choice was between oxen and mules, and there were arguments in favor of each. Mules, writes McLynn, "were tough and durable, moved faster, did not get sore feet as oxen did and could subsist on cottonwood bark and alkaline water" (56). Oxen, on the other hand, "were less likely to be stolen than mules . . . were better able to withstand fatigue, could exist on a wider variety of sparse vegetation, were less likely to stray from camp, were safer, more reliable and almost as fast" (56). Cost was also an important consideration, with a mule at times costing three times as much as a single ox. Haun touches on this debate in her memoir, writing, "It was very essential that the animals be sturdy, whether oxen, mules or horses. Oxen were preferred as they were less liable to stampede . . . and for long hauls held out better and though slower they were steady and in the long run performed the journey in an equally brief time." Ever practical, Haun additionally notes that "in an emergency [the oxen] could be used as beef."

Like a great number of those setting off for brighter futures on the West Coast, the members of the Hauns' wagon train began their journey with far more possessions than they needed, and many of these items, both practical and impractical, did not make it to California. In this, they were not alone. For those crossing the plains, trying to fit as many items as possible within the wagons was understandable, though certainly not practical. These small touches of home, or convenience, allowed families to feel connected with their old lives and the communities they left behind. As they moved west, however, the travelers were often forced to leave possessions behind to lighten the wagons' loads or make space for sick or injured individuals. The journey of Haun and the others in her wagon train was no different. She notes that after reaching Council Bluffs, a popular starting point for California-bound travelers located in western Iowa, she and her fellow travelers "made ready for the final plunge into the wilderness by looking over [their] wagons and disposing of whatever [they] could spare." Later, Haun's party was forced to leave behind more supplies in order to travel safely across mountainous terrain. Possessions left behind by earlier travelers became a common sight for those en route to California, and Haun adds that her party at times built campfires using wood from abandoned wagons.

Graves were another inevitable part of the scenery across the plains, as many travelers died along the way. Cholera, a commonly fatal disease caused by bacteria in contaminated water, took a number of lives along the trail. The disease was known to strike quickly and could kill a person in a day. Haun's wagon train was lucky, as none of the members fell ill, but Haun and her companions were all too aware of the disease's toll on their fellow travelers, seeing clusters of graves that "stood as silent proof of . . . cholera epidemic." Accidents were also firmly a part of the westward experience, one to which Haun was a witness. One man in her party was bitten by a poisonous snake, and although the wagons carried various medicines, both commercial and homemade, these remedies were ineffective. The man's leg was therefore amputated "with the aid of a common handsaw." Despite the dangers of performing such an operation in unsanitary conditions, however, Haun reports that the man survived and remained a productive member of the group.

The survival of wagon trains such as Haun's depended on a number of factors, perhaps most importantly food. The travelers had to be sure that they obtained supplies that would last the journey, and the women who went westward, Haun notes, tried their hardest to prepare good, though at times monotonous, meals. Haun even suggests that women were brought on the trails because their food was better than that made by men and therefore "prevent[ed] much sickness and . . . waste of food." Cooking on the trail was not an easy feat, and even the act of making coffee could be difficult for one not acquainted to cooking in the open. However, the travelers soon adapted to their surroundings, and in addition to the supplies they carried with them, they found another food source on the plains. Widely known as the buffalo, the American bison served as a source of fresh meat for travelers bound for the West Coast. Haun notes that after killing two buffalo, her group enjoyed a meal of meat and roasted bone marrow. In addition to the meat and marrow, Haun mentions that the party made use of the buffalo's hide; tallow, or fat; and chips, or dried dung.

After more than six months of grueling labor and unimaginably uncomfortable travel by wagon, foot, and horse, Haun's journey across the plains came to an end in November of 1849, when her wagon train arrived in Sacramento. She and her husband settled in nearby Marysville in January. Although the journey was difficult, Haun and her companions were lucky; they arrived in California safely, with only two fatalities. Given the prevalence of disease among other groups of travelers, this in itself was a remarkable feat. Although neither Haun's memoir nor the available historical sources reveal whether she and her husband achieved their goal of finding gold and settling their debts, they were successful in their journey, and Haun further succeeded in documenting it. By recording the details of her long voyage west, Haun provided a key resource for those interested in the lives of the many Americans who hoped to make their fortunes during the gold rush.

Essential Themes

Haun's memoir reflects the concerns of her time, particularly the fear the wagon trains traveling to California would be robbed or attacked by groups of American Indians. This fear was common, though the frequency with which such attacks actually occurred during the period of westward expansion is unknown. The amount of contact, friendly or otherwise, that California-bound travelers had with American Indians is also unclear. In the memoir Across the Plains, Sarah Royce, who similarly traveled to California in 1849, recalls encountering American Indians at Council Bluffs—the same spot at which Haun's party disposed of extra cargo. Royce writes, "From our first arrival at Council Bluffs we had been annoyed by begging and pilfering Indians" (34). Haun's description of Council Bluffs, however, includes no such mention of American Indians.

It is difficult to determine the extent to which Haun, or her wagon train in general, engaged with American Indians during the journey, as her comments are vague. Her train held a drill in which the men, at the prompting of the party's leader, gathered their weapons and stood in readiness, but this event seems to have been more a preparedness measure than a response to an expected threat. Haun did at one point come into visual contact with American Indians, as indicated by her statement that the party "saw nothing living but Indians, lizards and snakes." By mentioning American Indians alongside lizards and snakes, Haun suggests that she viewed them more as hazards of the western environment than as fellow human beings. She also notes that they were "a source of anxiety" throughout the journey, although she does not discuss the rumors she may have heard in depth. In her discussion of the diseases prevalent among travelers, Haun mentions that American Indians contracted cholera and smallpox as a result of grave robbing and that many Indians were greatly pockmarked. This would suggest that her wagon train had more contact with American Indians than Haun indicates, but Haun keeps the details of these interactions to herself.

—*Jennifer L. Henderson Crane*

Bibliography and Additional Reading

McLynn, Frank. *Wagons West: The Epic Story of America's Overland Trails*. London: Cape, 2002. Print.

Robinson, Forrest G. "Introduction: Rethinking California." *Rethinking History* 11.1 (2007): 1–9. Print.

Royce, Sarah. *Across the Plains: Sarah Royce's Western Narrative*. Ed. Jennifer Dawes Adkison. Tucson: U of Arizona P, 2009. Print.

Shetler, Douglas. "Monetary Aggregates Prior to the Civil War: A Closer Look." *Journal of Money, Credit; Banking* 5.4 (1973): 1000–1006. Print.

Vehik, Susan C. "Conflict, Trade, and Political Development on the Southern Plains." *American Antiquity* 67.1 (2002): 37–64. Print.

Wadsworth, Ginger. *Words West: Voices of Young Pioneers*.

New York: Clarion, 2003. Print.

Brown, Sharon. "Women on the Overland Trails—A Historical Perspective." *Overland Journal* 2.1 (1984): 35–39. Print.

Fryer, Judith. "The Anti-Mythical Journey: Westering Women's Diaries and Letters." *Old Northwest* 9.1 (1983): 77–90. Print.

Schlissel, Lillian. "Mothers and Daughters on the Western Frontier." *Frontiers: A Journal of Women Studies* 3.2 (1978): 29–33. Print.

Women's Diaries of the Westward Journey. New York: Schocken, 1992. Print.

Unruh, John David. *The Plains Across: Emigrants, Wagon Trains, and the American West.* London Pimlico, 1992. Print.

■ Observations Regarding the Transcontinental Railroad

Date: July 2, 1867; May 10, 1869 (published 1923)
Author: Editors of *Harper's Weekly*; Alexander Toponce
Genre: editorial; memoir

Summary Overview

Congress authorized the building of the first railroad across the western parts of the United States in the summer of 1862 with the passage of the Pacific Railroad Act. The two excerpts included here deal with the building of this railroad, the combined Union Pacific and Central Pacific. The editorial from *Harper's Weekly* was written almost two years before the railroad was completed, and speculates grandly about the impact that the railroad could be expected to have. It is typical of the kind of enthusiasm many Americans had for the project and the benefits they expected to flow from it. The second excerpt is from the reminiscences of Alexander Toponce, a Western businessman who supplied beef to the railroad's construction crews and was at Promontory Summit when the railroad was completed on May 10, 1869. He describes the celebratory spirit of that occasion, when a special ceremony was held to commemorate the driving of the "last spike."

Defining Moment

In the 1840s, the United States settled the controversy with Great Britain over the Pacific Northwest and also acquired most of the American Southwest as a result of the war with Mexico from 1846 to 1848. Almost immediately, speculation arose about the possibility of building a railroad across the western region. Before the Civil War, however, Congressional debates over the railroad invariably became entangled in the sectional controversy, as Northern and Southern interests each wanted the first line in their region. During the Civil War, when Southern congressmen were not present, the Republican-controlled Congress passed the Pacific Railroad Act, which was signed by President Abraham Lincoln on July 1, 1862. The bill gave a federal business charter to a new railroad corporation, the Union Pacific, to build westward from the Missouri River. It also gave a charter to the Central Pacific Railroad, an existing short line in California, to build eastward from

Sacramento, CA. In order to finance this massive construction venture, the government gave generous aid, including massive land grants and cash loans, to the two corporations. The land grants included ten square miles of government land for each mile of track built; this was later increased to twenty square miles per mile of track. The government also agreed to negotiate with the Indians to obtain title to the lands the railroads would cross. The railroads could sell their land to settlers to raise money for construction. However, since the settlers were not likely to come until the railroad was built, in practice the railroads had to borrow money through bond sales, hoping that later shipping revenues and land sales would generate the funds to repay these obligations. Together, the Union Pacific and Central Pacific received about 45,000,000 acres of federal land.

While the gold rush of the late 1840s had brought much settlement and development to California, the first transcontinental railroad was largely built through unsettled land, with few customers needing the transportation services the railroad would provide. In a sense, then, the railroads were built for future needs—creating the railroad would bring the farms, ranches, mines, lumbering companies, and other businesses that would need to ship their products and buy manufactured goods from the East. Economists describe this concept as "building ahead of demand." Because they had vast lands they needed to sell, all of the western railroads that received land grants were heavily involved in promotion of settlement and townsite development, often sending agents to Europe to attract immigrants to come and buy land from the railroads. Even if settlers bought land from the government, or got land free through homesteading, the railroads stood to benefit from the traffic that their economic activity would stimulate. These two excerpts ably illustrate the sense of expectancy and the hopes for the future that surrounded the building of the first transcontinental railroad.

Author Biography

The 1867 editorial from *Harper's Weekly* was an unsigned piece by the editorial staff. *Harper's Weekly* was one of the most prominent American journals of its day. It was founded in 1850 by the book publishers Harper and Brothers. Alexander Toponce (1839–1923), the author of the reminiscence about the "Golden Spike" ceremony, was an emigrant from France who had his hand in several different business ventures on the western frontier. Most of his later life was spent in Idaho, the southern parts of Montana, and northern Utah. He prospected for gold, ran freighting businesses with wagon trains, and when the transcontinental railroad was being built, he contracted with both the Central Pacific and Union Pacific to provide beef for their work camps. His *Reminiscences of Alexander Toponce*, from which this excerpt is taken, was published by his wife shortly after his death.

HISTORICAL DOCUMENT

[*Harper's Weekly* editorial on the transcontinental railroad, 1867]

We have … expressed the belief that the constantly changing wants and exigencies of a growing country like ours demand, and will compel, a radical change in our present railway system; that with the completion of the grand arterial road across the continent to the Pacific, all other roads must become tributary and subservient to it—the direction of railway traffic (freights) being traverse to the water communication that cuts the country from north to south. A consolidation of railroad interests will naturally result, as well as a change in the mode of operating and running. The future requirements are already foreseen and felt; the first movement toward the new order of things is the proposed combination of leading railroads to form a great Western route under one management. The parties to the combination are the New York Central, Lake Shore, Cleveland and Toledo, Michigan Southern, and those other roads that constitute the northernmost tier of transverse communication. Another rival organization is promised, to include a more southern route, and will embrace the Pennsylvania Central, Pittsburg, Fort Wayne and Chicago, etc. Their interests will not conflict; on the contrary, the commercial necessities of the country will on the course of time require one or two more routes still further south to convey the produce of the sea-board States to their western destination.

When the Pacific Railroad is completed in 1870, all these gigantic tributaries will converge toward the main stem, like the fingers of a hand. All the immense and richly productive districts of the Atlantic and the East will contribute to supply the vital fluid that courses through them. Even the vast domain of the "New Dominion" [i.e., Canada] … will be induced to furnish its quota of subsistence. But the seat of the vital principle will be in the city of New York. There will the mighty beat of its palpitation be heard. Already the commercial centre of America, it will then, by its geographical position, become the commercial centre of the world. We do not assume that the Pacific Railway will supersede vessels in the carrying trade, for that would be impossible; a dozen lines of railroad could not furnish the required transportation, even if it could carry as cheaply. But from its closer relations and proximity to other countries, New York could command the commerce. It would be as nearly united to Asia as it has been to Europe. The distance to China, now accomplished in forty-three to forty-five days, will be shortened to thirty days. A letter will reach Hong Kong by way of San Francisco much quicker than when it went by way of Liverpool, just as our enterprise had shortened the time of our communication with Brazil. The London banker would no longer pocket the commissions and the exchange on the immense trade carried on between New York and China, as well as South American and the West Indies; but New York would become, to America at least, what London is not to the rest of the world, namely, the place on which exchange is universally drawn. Millions of dollars would thereby be saved to our merchants annually, to say nothing of the difference of time, which is as precious as money.

We have heretofore spoken of the advantages to be obtained by the operation of the Pacific Railroad in developing the treasures of California and the Rocky Mountain region, and the easy access it afford to Asiatic trade. The gains, to be sure, are for the present purely speculative, but it is easy to conjecture the results from past experience. And we are to obtain all this by an estimated outlay of $45,000,000 currency for a road 1565 miles long … It will take time to overcome the commercial and financial derangement which the late war inflicted upon the court, and to stimulate the productive interests of the several sections to their full capacity; but by the time the Pacific Railroad is completed we hope to lie upon the top wave of prosperity, and to tax our new lines of intercommunication to their utmost limit.

* * *

[Alexander Topance on the Golden Spike ceremonies, Promontory Summit, Utah, May 10, 1869]

I saw the Golden Spike driven at Promontory, Utah, on May 10th, 1869. I had a beef contract to furnish meat to the construction camps of Benson and West. This West was my good friend. Bishop Chauncey W. West of Ogden. They had a grading contract with the Central Pacific and their camp was near Blue Creek. I also furnished beef for some of the Union Pacific contractors.

The Golden Spike could have been driven a couple of weeks earlier than it was. But the two companies had settled on Promontory as the meeting place some days prior to the actual meeting.

The Central Pacific had been planning to make the junction at Ogden as to be in touch with Salt Lake City and the settlements in Utah. But the Union Pacific planned to lay their iron as far west as Humboldt Wells, in Nevada, and had most of their grade completed that far west.

If the Union Pacific had crowded their work as hard as the Central Pacific did in the last two weeks the Golden Spike would have been driven a good many miles to the west. The Union Pacific employed white labor, largely Irish, and the Central Pacific had Chinese labor. The Irish and Chinese met on Promontory Hill.

The Union Pacific sold to the Central Pacific fifty-six miles of road, which brought the real junction back to a point five miles north of the Ogden depot, and then leased that five miles to the Central Pacific, making Ogden the junction.

On the last day only about 100 feet were laid and everybody tried to have a hand in the work. I took a shovel from an Irishman and threw a shovel full of dirt on the ties just to tell about it afterward.

A special train from the west brought Governor Leland Stanford of California and C. P. Huntington, Crocker, Hopkins and lots of California wine.

Another special train from the east brought Sidney Dillon, General Dodge, T. C. Durant, John R. Duff, S. A. Seymour, a lot of newspaper men, and plenty of the best brands of champagne.

Another train made up at Ogden carried the band from Fort Douglas, the leading men of Utah Territory, and a small, but efficient supply, of Valley Tan.

It was a very hilarious occasion, everybody had all they wanted to drink all the time. Some of the participants got "sloppy" and these were not all Irish and Chinese, by any means.

California furnished the Golden Spike. Governor Tuttle of Nevada furnished one of silver. General [i.e., Governor] Stanford presented one of gold, silver and iron from Arizona. The last tie was of California laurel.

When they came to drive the last spike. Governor Stanford, president of the Central Pacific, took the sledge and the first time he struck he missed the spike and hit the rail.

What a howl went up! Irish, Chinese, Mexicans, and everybody yelled with delight. Everybody slapped everybody else on the back and yelled "He missed it. Yee." The engineers blew the whistles and rang their bells. Then Stanford tried it again and tapped the spike and the telegraph operators had fixed their instruments so that the tap was reported in all the offices, east and west, and set bells to tapping in hundreds of towns and cities. W. N. Shilling was one of the telegraph operators.

Then Vice President T. C. Durant of the Union Pacific took up the sledge and he missed the spike the first time. Then everybody slapped everybody else again and yelled, "He missed it, [too], yow!"

It was a great occasion, everyone carried off souvenirs and there are enough splinters of the last tie in museums to make a good bonfire. When the connection was finally made the U. P. and the C. P. engineers ran their engines up until their pilots touched. Then the engineers shook hands and had their pictures taken and each broke a bottle of champagne on the pilot of the other's engine and had their pictures taken again.

The [C. P.] engine, the "Jupiter," was driven by my good friend, George Lashus, who still lives in Ogden.

Both before and after the spike driving ceremony there were speeches, which were cheered heartily. I do not remember what any of the speakers said now, but I do remember that there was a great abundance of champagne.

Document Analysis

These two excerpts clearly illustrate the excitement that surrounded the subject of the first railroad across the American West. Great things were expected to result from the completion of the first line, the combined Union Pacific and Central Pacific route from Omaha, Nebraska to Sacramento, California. The editorial in *Harper's Weekly*, written nearly two years before the line was completed, envisioned that all eastern railroads would become "tributary and subservient to it." The editors also predicted a merger or "combination" of all the leading roads in the East to form one "Western route under one management." While there have been many mergers in the history of American railroading, this prediction did not become true. Instead, the different railroads continued to operate independently, but interchanged traffic to create a national transportation network. The prediction that when the Pacific Railroad was completed, these tributary railroads "will converge toward the main stem, like the fingers of a hand," did come to pass in a sense. Eventually, five major railroad lines were built across the American West, and each of these companies built branches that reached north and south off of their trunk lines, and smaller regional railroads also interconnected with the transcontinental lines. Likewise, the prediction that New York would become a major world trade center was also fulfilled.

The second excerpt is from Alexander Toponce's memoirs of his days on the western frontier. Toponce had contracted with the railroads to provide beef for the camps of the construction crews. The Central Pacific Railroad had built 881 miles eastward from Sacramento, CA, and the Union Pacific had built 1,032 miles westward from Omaha, NE. Since the two companies received generous land grants and loans from the government for each mile of track built, they com-

peted to build the most track and refused to coordinate a meeting place until Congress dictated that the two lines would meet at Promontory, near Ogden in the Utah Territory. As Toponce notes, much of the Central Pacific's work force was immigrant Chinese labor, while the Union Pacific employed many Irish laborers. African Americans workers, many of them former slaves, also worked on the Union Pacific construction crews.

With his frequent references to the quantities and varieties of alcoholic beverages consumed, Toponce captures the celebratory mood of the day when the railroad was completed. Commemorative spikes of precious metals were temporarily installed, but the final spike was an iron one attached to telegraph lines. When Leland Stanford, former governor of California and president of the Central Pacific, hammered in the last spike, the message was to be instantly telegraphed across the nation. Stanford missed when he swung at the spike, but the telegraphers sent the message anyway. Nearly six years after Congress had authorized its construction, the Pacific Railroad was completed on May 10, 1869.

Essential Themes

These excerpts illustrate the sense of expectancy and promise that accompanied the building of the first transcontinental railroad. Although the railroad was built through regions that had very few non-Indian inhabitants, many political leaders, businessmen, editors and journalists believed the railroad would lead to widespread settlement and development throughout the region. Many of these predictions came true; farming and ranching in the Great Plains region, for example, boomed in the last decades of the nineteenth century. Little of this development would have been possible without the railroad to bring people and supplies to the frontier and to ship the commodities produced there to market. The railroad companies were heavily involved in "boosterism," extolling the virtues of the land they owned in the West in order to attract settlers. People who settled these lands sometimes charged that they were misled about the quality of the land and the climate. Eventually, four transcontinental lines were completed across the West, which all received government land grants. Besides the Union Pacific and Central Pacific, these included the Atchison, Topeka, and Santa Fe; the Southern Pacific; and the Northern Pacific—the latter three all being finished in 1883. A fifth transcontinental, the Great Northern, was completed in 1895, but did not receive a land grant from the federal government.

In time, the enthusiasm for the western railroads cooled. Farmers and businessmen who settled in the West realized the railroad made their commerce possible, but they also realized that, with few viable alternative forms of transportation, they were captive to the railroads' interests. The building of the transcontinental railroads also involved considerable mismanagement, waste, and outright fraud. When scandals such as the Crédit Mobilier affair became widely known, public opinion began to turn against the railroad companies. In the late nineteenth century, agrarian protest movements, such as the Grangers and the Populists, attacked the railroads and called for government ownership, or failing that, strict government regulation of railroad business practices. Many laws regulating the railroads were enacted during the Progressive Era in the early twentieth century.

—*Mark S. Joy, PhD*

Bibliography and Additional Reading

Ambrose, Stephen E. *Nothing Like It in the World: The Men Who Built the Transcontinental Railroad, 1863–1869*. New York: Simon and Schuster, 2000. Print.

Bain, David Hayward. *Empire Express: Building the First Transcontinental Railroad*. New York: Penguin Books, 1999. Print.

White, Richard. *Railroaded: The Transcontinentals and the Making of Modern America*. New York: W. W. Norton, 2011. Print.

Williams, John Hoyt. *A Great and Shining Road: The Epic Story of the Transcontinental Railway*. Lincoln: University of Nebraska Press, 1996. Print.

■ The Rush to Oklahoma

Date: May 18, 1889
Author: William Willard Howard
Genre: article

Summary Overview

In the 1830s, many American Indian tribes from the eastern part of the United States were relocated to the region known as Indian Territory, comprising present-day Oklahoma and Kansas as well as part of Nebraska, under the Indian Removal Act. After the Civil War, the federal government bought some land in the middle of present-day Oklahoma from the Creek, or Muskogee, tribe and the Seminole tribe, which became known as the Unassigned Lands. Early in 1889, Congress authorized opening these lands to settlement, and President Benjamin Harrison set April 22, 1889, as the opening date. Land seekers congregated around the Unassigned Lands, and when the deadline passed, they rushed into the area to stake their claims. Journalist William Willard Howard's firsthand account of the event, the first of several Oklahoma land runs, was published in the magazine *Harper's Weekly* in May of that year.

Defining Moment

In the thirty years after the Civil War, the last great expansion of agricultural settlement in the United States took place, largely in the lands west of the Mississippi River. Westward settlement across the United States initially skipped over the Great Plains region. The open, largely treeless plains, increasingly arid the farther west one went, seemed inhospitable to American farmers, and early settlers moved on to the mountain regions and the Pacific Coast. By the 1880s, however, many would-be settlers believed that the best available lands elsewhere had already been claimed, and they began to reconsider the Great Plains, and particularly the Unassigned Lands in the center of what is now Oklahoma. Prospective settlers called for this land to be opened for homesteading and settlement, as did the Atchison, Topeka, and Santa Fe Railroad, which had built a line through the area. Business owners and land speculators calling for settlement of these lands were often called "boomers."

Early in 1889, Representative William Springer of Illinois introduced an amendment to the Indian Appropriations Bill that would allow settlement in the Unassigned Lands. President Harrison signed the legislation, and set the official opening of the lands for noon on April 22, 1889. Immediately before that date, eager land seekers surrounded the Unassigned Lands, ready to rush in as soon as the deadline passed. People were seeking land not only for farms and ranches, but also for town sites and business locations. Howard's account captures the unbridled frenzy of the run into the land. But despite great enthusiasm among the land-hungry people who made the run, there was an unrealized irony to their eagerness. As farming was already at the dawn of a long-term transition from the small family farm to large-scale farming and agribusiness, the era of the family farmer was beginning to wane, and many of those who took out homesteads would never prosper. Nevertheless, this first land run was a significant step toward the formation of the Oklahoma Territory in May 1890.

Author Biography

William Willard Howard was born in Iowa on November 8, 1859. He had a long career as a popular journalist specializing in firsthand investigative reports, publishing widely in prominent magazines such as *Harper's Weekly*, *Scribner's*, and *The Century*. In addition to the Oklahoma land run, he covered the Detroit International Exposition and Fair of 1889 for *Harper's* and also made a trip to Colombia to report on platinum mining there. In the 1890s, Howard traveled abroad to distribute relief funds to Armenians and investigate the reports of massacres committed by the Ottoman Empire. He is perhaps best known for his book on the subject, *Horrors of Armenia: The Story of an Eyewitness*, published in 1896. Howard died in New York on December 6, 1933.

HISTORICAL DOCUMENT

The preparations for the settlement of Oklahoma had been complete, even to the slightest detail, for weeks before the opening day. The Santa Fe Railway, which runs through Oklahoma north and south, was prepared to take any number of people from its handsome station at Arkansas City, Kansas, and to deposit them in almost any part of Oklahoma as soon as the law allowed; thousands of covered wagons were gathered in camps on all sides of the new Territory waiting for the embargo to be lifted. In its picturesque aspects the rush across the border at noon on the opening day must go down in history as one of the most noteworthy events of Western civilization. At the time fixed, thousands of hungry home-seekers, who had gathered from all parts of the country, and particularly from Kansas and Missouri, were arranged in line along the border, ready to lash their horses into furious speed in the race for fertile spots in the beautiful land before them. The day was one of perfect peace. Overhead the sun shown down from a sky as fair and blue as the cloudless heights of Colorado. The whole expanse of space from zenith to horizon was spotless in its blue purity. The clear spring air, through which the rolling green billows of the promised land could be seen with unusual distinctness for many miles, was as sweet and fresh as the balmy atmosphere of June among New Hampshire's hills.

As the expectant home-seekers waited with restless patience, the clear, sweet notes of a cavalry bugle rose and hung a moment upon the startled air. It was noon. The last barrier of savagery in the United States was broken down. Moved by the same impulse, each driver lashed his horses furiously; each rider dug his spurs into his willing steed, and each man on foot caught his breath hard and darted forward. A cloud of dust rose where the home-seekers had stood in line, and when it had drifted away before the gentle breeze, the horses and wagons and men were tearing across the open country like fiends. The horsemen had the best of it from the start. It was a fine race for a few minutes, but soon the riders began to spread out like a fan, and by the time they had reached the horizon they were scattered about as far as eye could see. Even the fleetest of the horsemen found upon reaching their chosen localities that men in wagons and men on foot were there before them. As it was clearly

impossible for a man on foot to outrun a horseman, the inference is plain that Oklahoma had been entered hours before the appointed time. Notwithstanding the assertions of the soldiers that every boomer had been driven out of Oklahoma, the fact remains that the woods along the streams within Oklahoma were literally full of people Sunday night. Nine-tenths of these people made settlement upon the land illegally. The other tenth would have done so had there been any desirable land left to settle upon. This action on the part of the first claim-holders will cause a great deal of land litigation in the future, as it is not to be expected that the man who ran his horse at its utmost speed for ten miles only to find a settler with an ox team in quiet possession of his chosen farm will tamely submit to this plain infringement of the law.

Some of the men who started from the line on foot were quite as successful in securing desirable claims as many who rode fleet horses. They had the advantage of knowing just where their land was located. One man left the line with the others, carrying on his back a tent, a blanket, some camp dishes, an axe, and provisions for two days. He ran down the railway track for six miles, and reached his claim in just sixty minutes. Upon arriving on his land he fell down under a tree, unable to speak or see. I am glad to be able to say that his claim is one of the best in Oklahoma. The rush from the line was so impetuous that by the time the first railway train arrived from the north at twenty-five minutes past twelve o'clock, only a few of the hundreds of boomers were anywhere to be seen. The journey of this first train was well-nigh as interesting as the rush of the men in wagons. The train left Arkansas City at 8:45 o'clock in the forenoon. It consisted of an empty baggage car, which was set apart for the use of newspaper correspondents, eight passenger coaches, and the caboose of a freight train. The coaches were so densely packed with men that not another human being could get on board. So uncomfortably crowded were they that some of the younger boomers climbed to the roofs of the cars and clung perilously to the ventilators. An adventurous person secured at great risk a seat on the forward truck of the baggage car.

In this way the train was loaded to its utmost capacity. That no one was killed or injured was due as much to the careful management of the train as to the ability of the passengers to take care of themselves. Like their friends in the wagons, the boomers on the cars were exultant with joy at the thought of at last entering into possession of the promised land. At first appearances of the land through which the train ran seemed to justify all the virtues that had been claimed for it. The rolling, grassy uplands, and the wooded river-bottoms, the trees in which were just bursting into the most beautiful foliage of early spring, seemed to give a close reality of the distant charm of green and purple forest growths, which rose from the trough of some long swell and went having away to meet the brighter hues in the far-off sky. Throughout all the landscape were clumps of trees suggesting apple orchards set in fertile meadows, and here and there were dim patches of gray and white sand that might in a less barbarous region be mistaken for farmhouses surrounded by hedges and green fields. Truly the Indians have well-named Oklahoma the "beautiful land." The landless and home-hungry people on the train might be pardoned their mental exhilaration, when the effect of this wonderfully beautiful country upon the most prosaic mind is considered. It was an eager and an exuberantly joyful crowd that rode slowly into Guthrie at twenty minutes past one o'clock on that perfect April afternoon. Men who had expected to lay out the town site were grievously disappointed at the first glimpse of their proposed scene of operations. The slope east of the railway at Guthrie station was dotted white with tents and sprinkled thick with men running about in all directions.

"We're done for," said a town-site speculator, in dismay. "Someone has gone in ahead of us and laid out the town."

"Never mind that," shouted another town-site speculator, "but make a rush and get what you can."

Hardly had the train slackened its speed when the impatient boomers began to leap from the cars and run up the slope. Men jumped from the roofs of the moving cars at the risk of their lives. Some were so stunned by the fall that they could not get up for some minutes. The coaches were so crowded that many men were compelled to squeeze through the windows in order to get a fair start at the head of the crowd. Almost before the train had come to a standstill the cars were emptied. In their haste and eagerness, men fell over each other in heaps,

others stumbled and fell headlong, while many ran forward so blindly and impetuously that it was not until they had passed the best of the town lots that they came to a realization of their actions.

I ran with the first of the crowd to get a good point of view from which to see the rush. When I had time to look about me I found that I was standing beside a tent, near which a man was leisurely chopping holes in the sod with a new axe.

"Where did you come from, that you have already pitched your tent?" I asked.

"Oh, I was here," said he.

"How was that?"

"Why, I was a deputy United States marshal."

"Did you resign?"

"No; I'm a deputy still."

"But it is not legal for a deputy United States marshal, or any one in the employ of the government, to take up a town lot in this manner."

"That may all be, stranger; but I've got two lots here, just the same; and about fifty other deputies have got lots in the same way. In fact, the deputy-marshals laid out the town."

At intervals of fifteen minutes, other trains came from the north loaded down with home-seekers and town-site speculators. As each succeeding crowd rushed up the slope and found that government officers had taken possession of the best part of the town, indignation became hot and outspoken; yet the marshals held to their lots and refused to move. Bloodshed was prevented only by the belief of the home-seekers that the government would set the matter right.

This course of the deputy United States marshals was one of the most outrageous pieces of imposition upon honest home-seekers ever practiced in the settlement of a new country. That fifty men could, through influence, get themselves appointed as deputy United States marshals for the sole purpose of taking advantage of their positions in this way is creditable neither to them nor to the man who made their appointment possible. This illegal seizure thus became the first matter of public discussion in the city of Guthrie.

When the passengers from the first train reached the spot where the deputy-marshals had ceased laying out lots, they seized the line of the embryo street and ran it eastward as far as their numbers would permit. The second train load of people took it where the first left off, and ran it entirely out of sight behind a swell of ground at least two miles from the station. The following car of home-seekers went north and south, so that by the time that all were in for the day a city large enough in area to hold 100,000 inhabitants had been staked off, with more or less geometrical accuracy. A few women and children were in the rush, but they had to take their chances with the rest. Disputes over the ownership of lots grew incessant, for the reason that when a man went to the river for a drink of water, or tried to get his baggage at the railway station, another man would take possession of his lot, notwithstanding the obvious presence of the first man's stakes and sometimes part of his wearing apparel. Owing to the uncertainty concerning the lines of the streets, two and sometimes more lots were staked out on the same ground, each claimant hoping that the official survey would give him the preference. Contrary to all expectations, there was no bloodshed over the disputed lots. This may be accounted for by the fact that no intoxicating liquors of any kind were allowed to be sold in Oklahoma. It is a matter of common comment among the people that the peaceful way in which Oklahoma was settled was due entirely to its compulsory prohibition. Had whiskey been plentiful in Guthrie the disputed lots might have been watered in blood, for every man went armed with some sort of deadly weapon. If there could be a more striking temperance lesson than this, I certainly should like to see it.

When Congress gives Oklahoma some sort of government the prohibition of the sale of intoxicating liquor should be the first and foremost of her laws.

It is estimated that between six and seven thousand persons reached Guthrie by train from the north that first afternoon, and that fully three thousand came in by wagon from the north and east, and by train from Purcell on the south, thus making a total population for the first day of about ten thousand. By taking thought in the matter, three-fourths of these people had provided themselves with tents and blankets, so that even on the first night they had ample shelter from the weather. The rest of them slept the first night as best they could, with only the red earth for a pillow and the starry arch of heaven for a blanket. At dawn of Tuesday the unrefreshed home-seekers and town-site speculators arose, and began anew the location of disputed claims. The tents multiplied like mushrooms in a rain that day, and by night the building of frame houses had been begun in earnest in the new streets. The buildings were by no means elaborate, yet they were as good as the average frontier structure, and they served their purpose, which was all that was required.

On that day the trains going north were filled with returning boomers, disgusted beyond expression with the dismal outlook of the new country. Their places were taken by others who came in to see the fun, and perhaps to pick up a bargain in the way of town lots of commercial speculation.

By Wednesday the retreat from Guthrie was at its height. Two persons went home to each one that came in, yet the town seemed to be as lively and as populous as ever. The north-bound boomers asserted that there was nothing in or about Guthrie to support a city; that only a limited number of quarter sections of land on the river bottom were worth settling upon, and that the upland country was nothing but worthless red sand coated over with a film of green grass. To bear out their assertions, these disgusted men pointed to the city of Guthrie, where the red dust was ankle-deep in the main street. The red dust was an argument that could not be contradicted. It rose in clouds and hovered above the feverish city until the air was like fog at sunrise; it sifted through the provision boxes in the tents, it crept into blankets and clothing, and it stuck like wax to the faces and beards of the unhappy citizens. The heat and the dust and the phenomenal lack of food during the first three days created a burning thirst, which seemingly could not be quenched. This thirst was intensified tenfold by the knowledge that water was scarce, hard to get, and sometimes unfit to drink. The yellow Cimarron and the lukewarm Cottonwood were the only streams where water could be obtained, and on the third day he was very thirsty indeed who would drink from either. Boomers who were not engaged in holding down town lots peddled water in pails to their thirsty neighbors at five and ten cents a cupful. Once, when compelled to moisten my parched throat from one of these pails, I noticed that the water was unusually yellow and thick.

"See here," said I to the Frenchman who held the pail;

"you have washed your face in this water."

"No, monsieur," he said, with grotesque earnestness; "I do not wash my face for four days!"

I did not doubt it. His face had become so thickly encrusted with red dust and perspiration that he would not have recognized himself had he chanced to look in a mirror.

In this respect he was not worse off than his neighbors, most of whom had not thought of washing their faces since entering Oklahoma. This was not due to any personal negligence, but entirely to the scarcity of water. When men spent their whole time, night and day, in the work of keeping possession of town lots, they could not be expected to go half a mile or a mile for such a trifling diversion as washing their faces.

During the first three days food was nearly as hard to get as water. Dusty ham sandwiches sold on the streets as high as twenty-five cents each, while in the restaurants a plate of pork and beans was valued at seventy-five cents. Few men were well enough provided with funds to buy themselves a hearty meal. One disgusted home-seeker estimated that if he ate as much as he was accustomed to eat back in Missouri his board would cost him $7.75 per day. Not being able to spend that amount of money every day, he contented himself with such stray sandwiches as were within his means. In this manner he contrived to subsist until Wednesday afternoon, when he was forced to return to civilization in southern Kansas in order to keep from starving to death. A newspaper correspondent from Wichita, Kansas, who had never before known the feeling of hunger, was so far gone in the first stages of starvation that upon his return home on Friday he was hardly able to assimilate food. In appearance he was a walking spectre of famine. The only men in Guthrie who made money during the first week were the restaurant-keepers and the water-peddlers. After the first rush had subsided, however, there was no lack of food, and by the sinking of a number of wells there was a plentiful supply of water, so that the city of Guthrie in the matter of food and drink was no worse off than the ordinary frontier town. When the first well was dug, the home-seekers had an excellent opportunity of learning the exact character of the soil. The well-digger went through several feet of red sand after the sod had been cut through, and then found layers of gray and white sand so loose that the spade would sink

into it upon very slight downward pressure. Believing that all of the Oklahoma country consisted of this red, gray, and white sand, thousands of home-seekers took the earliest trains back into Kansas, more than ever contented with the fertile soil of the homes that they had left in the first rush to Oklahoma. By the end of the week the crowd of returning home-seekers had lessened, so that Guthrie had what might be called a permanent population with which to being the serious business of life. Just how long this population will remain, or what size Guthrie will be in another year, is a matter of some uncertainty, for the reason that nothing definite can be decided upon until a thorough test has been made of the farming country round about. Aside from its temporary importance as a land-office centre, the size of Guthrie will be determined, not by the speculative value of town lots, but by the agricultural capacity of the surrounding country. The city has already begun business upon a larger scale than the extent and fertility of the tributary country seems to justify. It has allowed itself the luxury of two mayors and two sets of municipal officers, one set being accredited to Guthrie proper and the other to the outlying district known as East Guthrie. I fancy that when business cools down to a substantial basis it will be found that one set of municipal officers will be enough for both towns.

The first Sunday in Guthrie showed that the new citizens had determined to begin life in the right way. Instead of spending the Sabbath in gambling, drinking, and other riotous ways of living, they held religious services in different parts of the town. If the present spirit of law and order and respectable conduct is continued, as it doubtless will be, the people of Guthrie need never be ashamed of the reputation of their town.

The rush of home-seekers into Oklahoma from the southern border was more picturesque than that from the north, although in numbers it was by no means as great. The intending settlers had been gathered at Purcell, in the Chickasaw Nation, for several months, waiting for the signal to cross the Canadian River and take possession of the coveted land. As the opening day drew near, many of the boomers provided themselves with fleet saddle-horses, and made careful observations of the half-dozen fords leading across the river, their intention being to dash into the river at noon on April 22d, and ride rapidly to their chosen claims. For this purpose the very best of horses were brought into use. Just before noon on the appointed day, hundreds of the horsemen gathered at the entrance to the fords waiting for the signal. Lieutenant Adair, of Troop "L," fifth Cavalry, was stationed on the sands on the opposite side of the river. He had arranged that at noon he should order his bugler to blow the recall, while riding a white horse around in a circle. By this means those who were too far away to hear the bugle could get the signal from the circling of the white horse. The lieutenant had caused all the boomers' watches to be set by his own, in order that there might be no false start. Just as the second hand of his watch touched the hour of twelve he gave the signal, and before the stirring notes of the bugle had found an echo against the walls of Purcell, the foremost horsemen had dashed into the fords. Spurred on by yelling and wildly excited riders, the horses made a furious dash through the water, throwing sand and spray on all sides like a sudden gust of rain and hail.

After the horsemen came the wagons, as thick as they could crowd together. The Canadian River is so treacherous, even at the fords, that horses and wagons must keep moving or run a great risk of being lost in the quicksands. The fear of the quicksands, added to the desire to reach the chosen lands, made the crossing on that quiet noonday particularly lively and stirring. The leaders ran a gallant race, but one by one they fell into deep holes in the river-bed, and for a time floundered about at imminent risk of drowning. A young woman, who pluckily held her place in the lead half-way across the river, went into a pool with a mighty splash. Even in the midst of his excitement the nearest boomer, who was racing with her, checked his horse and assisted her out to dry land, thus losing his place among the leaders. A big bay horse held the lead three-quarters of the way across the river, each furious jump giving him more and more of a lead over the others. In an unlucky moment he went into a deep pool head-first, and threw his rider half stunned upon the yellow sand. While the rider was gathering himself together in a half-dazed condition, the bit horse stood and looked at him a moment, and then started on again. He soon took his place at the lead of the race, and kept it there until the whole cavalcade had passed out of sight. Lieutenant Adair, who had watched this episode with quickening pulse, galloped up to the wet and discomfited rider.

"See here," said he, "I haven't much money about me, but if you'll take $250 for that horse, here's your money."

"No, lieutenant," said the man, with a weary smile; "you needn't make me an offer, because you haven't got money enough to buy him."

Most of the boomers who crossed the river at Purcell took up quarter sections of land that they had selected many weeks before; a few tried to organize a town on the flats opposite Purcell, while the others went on to Oklahoma City and Guthrie. Hundreds of boomers came into the southern part of Oklahoma from the Pottawotamie Indian country on the east and from the lands of the wild tribes on the west. As these portions of the border are not protected by soldiers, most of the boomers crossed the line long before the appointed time, and hid in the woods until Monday forenoon, when they emerged from their hiding-places and boldly took up their claims....

In this part of the country the poverty and wretched condition of some of the older boomers who have been waiting for years for the opening of Oklahoma were painfully apparent. Men with large families settled upon land with less than a dollar in money to keep them from starvation. How they expected to live until they could get a crop from their lands was a mystery which even they could not pretend to explain. Like unreasoning children, they thought that could they but once reach the beautiful green slopes of the promised land, their poverty and trouble would be at an end. They are now awakening to the bitter realization that their real hardships have just begun.

GLOSSARY

spectre: (or specter): a ghost or spirit

speculator: one who buys land in order to re-sell it at a profit

temperance: moderation or abstinence with respect to alcohol usage

Document Analysis

The April 1889 land run into the Unassigned Lands, which Howard describes in his article for *Harper's Weekly*, was the first of several such openings of what had been tribal lands in the Indian Territory. As such, it was an important step in the creation of the Oklahoma Territory, which occurred just one year later. All or parts of what are now Canadian, Cleveland, Kingfisher, Logan, Oklahoma, and Payne counties in the state of Oklahoma were opened for settlement and homesteading in this 1889 run.

Howard capably captures the spirit of frenzy, excitement, and optimism exhibited by the people making the run. He was impressed by what he saw, but was not taken in by the overly optimistic attitudes of the boomers and settlers he encountered. He makes note of many of the problems that arose, including the poor quality of some of the land, the scarcity of water in the area, and the fraud by which various marshals and others entered the area and laid out claims before it was legal to do so. He also notes that even during the brief time he was there, some speculative ventures, such as the sale of building lots in the newly settled towns, had already begun to fail.

Howard also describes the suffering that accompanied this opening of settlement. Many men came on their own, but if they brought their families, the children often had too little to eat due to the high price of food. Many people claimed land but had little cash to pay for supplies or to buy food until they could begin to produce their own. This was a common problem during the period of western settlement—even if settlers were given land at no cost, they still had to have some resources to live on while the land was being brought into production. Howard was realistic enough to see that the future potential of the Oklahoma region would depend on the agricultural productivity of the land. If the farms and ranches prospered, the towns and cities would as well. He predicted correctly that once some land in the heart of the Indian Territory had been opened for settlement, the rest of it would inevitably be opened as well.

Essential Themes

As the first of several runs into various parts of what would become the state of Oklahoma, the April 1889 rush into the Unassigned Lands reflects the great desire for land on the part of many would-be settlers and the frenzy with which they sought to stake their claims. This land hunger is one of the central themes of this document. Howard notes the rapidity with which claims were staked and communities were established. He reports that the town of Guthrie grew to a population of ten thousand virtually overnight. One might suspect an element of exaggeration in such a figure, but even discounting the possible overstatement, it is clear that thousands rushed into the region in a very brief period.

Fraud is also a theme illustrated in Howard's report. While the law barred entry before the official opening of the lands, there were many reports of "sooners," as they came to be called, who staked out claims earlier than the legally declared time. Howard also reports that some men serving as deputy US marshals had used their positions to stake out claims before ordinary settlers were allowed into the region. In addition, some of the new arrivals in Oklahoma realized that making money by selling supplies and services to the settlers might be a more certain business venture than starting a farm or ranch. At the end of a long supply line, settlers had to pay high and at times unreasonable prices for the supplies they needed.

Above all, Howard's account of the Oklahoma land run is characterized by the twin themes of hope and disappointment. Settlers rushed into the newly open territory, certain that owning land was an important stepping stone to individual autonomy and eventual prosperity. Some would-be settlers, however, found no land because of the many who had illegally made early claims. Others were disappointed in the quality of the land still available and ultimately returned to their original homes. After the initial excitement of the boom dissipated, those who had selected homesteads and sites for businesses realized that the real work was only just beginning.

—*Mark S. Joy, PhD*

Bibliography and Additional Reading

Gibson, Arrell M. Oklahoma: *A History of Five Centuries*. 2nd ed. Norman: U of Oklahoma P, 2010. Print.

Hoig, Stan. *The Oklahoma Land Rush of 1889*. Oklahoma City: Oklahoma Hist. Soc., 1989. Print.

Prucha, Francis Paul. *The Great Father: The United States Government and the American Indians*. 2 vols. Lincoln: U of Nebraska P, 1984. Print.

■ Mormon Disavowal of Plural Marriage

Date: September 24, 1890
Author: Wilford Woodruff, President of the Church of Jesus Christ of Latter-day Saints
Genre: manifesto

Summary Overview

This 1890 manifesto, written by Wilford Woodruff, the president of the Church of Jesus Christ of Latter-day Saints, denied that polygamy was being practiced by members of his church. He argued against accusations that the church was recognizing plural marriages. In this manifesto, Woodruff declares his intentions to lead his church's members to follow anti-polygamy laws and to refuse to teach church doctrine that may have subscribed to plural marriage. The practice of polygamy by members of the Mormon Church stood in the way of Utah's efforts to become a state. Woodruff's denunciation of plural marriage within the Mormon Church and his successor Lorenzo Snow's subsequent affirmation of the manifesto were crucial in the United States' decision to adopt Utah as a state in 1896.

Defining Moment

Prior to Woodruff's 1890 manifesto, many Mormons subscribed to the belief that men were divinely entitled to more than one wife. Woodruff himself had multiple wives. Despite not believing fully in the manifesto, Woodruff believed its issuance was necessary for the preservation of the church he represented. His manifesto effectively denounced and ended the open practice of plural marriages within the Church of Jesus Christ of Latter-day Saints (the LDS Church). Since 1847, Mormons had been increasingly populating the Salt Lake Valley. Brigham Young led the Mormons here, calling it the "promised land," to escape the hostile persecution they faced in Illinois, which resulted in the death of their president, Joseph Smith, and his brother, Hyrum. The Salt Lake Valley, which was under Mexican control upon their arrival in 1847, was ideal for their objectives, especially escaping the jurisdiction of the United States. In 1848, however, the United States obtained the territory through the Treaty of Hidalgo at the close of the Mexican War. The Mormons were no longer free from American interference. The Mormon settlers decided to seek statehood, led and represented entirely by Mormons. The proposed state was to include parts of surrounding states in addition to Utah, including parts of what are now California, Wyoming, Arizona, Nevada, New Mexico, Idaho, Oregon, and Colorado. Although Brigham Young was appointed the territorial governor in 1850, the president of the United States, Millard Fillmore, also appointed some officials who did not represent the Mormon Church. Members of the LDS Church wished to elect their own officials, which would require statehood. The announcement made by the authorities of the Mormon Church that they would follow the practice of plural marriage was not well received by US citizens generally. For the next forty-six years, the practice of polygamy stood in the way of statehood for Utah, until Wilford Woodruff's manifesto sought to distance the Mormon Church from this practice. This manifesto allowed for the Utah State Constitution to contain a ban on plural marriage, which fulfilled a Congressional Act requiring this in order for Utah to be considered for statehood.

Author Biography

Wilford Woodruff was born March 1 in 1807 in Farmington, Connecticut. His mother died during his infancy, and his father supported him and his eight siblings. He was baptized as a member of the Mormon Church in 1833. He met the Prophet Joseph Smith in 1834. Wilford Woodruff kept a diary documenting the Church of Jesus Christ of Latter-day Saints during his lifetime. He was ordained an apostle in 1839, one of the Church's Quorum of the Twelve Apostles. Woodruff practiced polygamy, having at one time five wives and thirty-three children. He divorced one of his wives. Woodruff was ordained as the fourth president of the Church of Jesus Christ of Latter-day Saints in 1889 and famously issued the 1890 manifesto disavowing plural marriage. He died in 1898 and was succeeded by Lorenzo Snow as church president.

HISTORICAL DOCUMENT

To Whom It May Concern:

Press dispatches having been sent for political purposes, from Salt Lake City, which have been widely published, to the effect that the Utah Commission, in their recent report to the Secretary of the Interior, allege that plural marriages are still being solemnized and that forty or more such marriages have been contracted in Utah since last June or during the past year, also that in public discourses the leaders of the Church have taught, encouraged and urged the continuance of the practice of polygamy—

I, therefore, as President of The Church of Jesus Christ of Latter-day Saints, do hereby, in the most solemn manner, declare that these charges are false. We are not teaching polygamy or plural marriage, nor permitting any person to enter into its practice, and I deny that either forty or any other number of plural marriages have during that period been solemnized in our Temples or in any other place in the Territory.

One case has been reported, in which the parties allege that the marriage was performed in the Endowment House, in Salt Lake City, in the Spring of 1889, but I have not been able to learn who performed the ceremony; whatever was done in this matter was without my knowledge. In consequence of this alleged occurrence the Endowment House was, by my instructions, taken down without delay.

Inasmuch as laws have been enacted by Congress forbidding plural marriages, which laws have been pronounced constitutional by the court of last resort, I hereby declare my intention to submit to those laws, and to use my influence with the members of the Church over which I preside to have them do likewise.

There is nothing in my teachings to the Church or in those of my associates, during the time specified, which can be reasonably construed to inculcate or encourage polygamy; and when any Elder of the Church has used language which appeared to convey any such teaching, he has been promptly reproved. And I now publicly declare that my advice to the Latter-day Saints is to refrain from contracting any marriage forbidden by the law of the land.

Wilford Woodruff
President of The Church of Jesus Christ of Latter-day Saints

Lorenzo Snow offered the following:

I move that, recognizing Wilford Woodruff as the President of The Church of Jesus Christ of Latter-day Saints, and the only man on the earth at the present time who holds the keys of the sealing ordinances, we consider him fully authorized by virtue of his position to issue the Manifesto which has been read in our hearing, and which is dated September 24th, 1890, and that as a Church in General Conference assembled, we accept his declaration concerning plural marriages as authoritative and binding.

Salt Lake City, Utah
October 6, 1890

GLOSSARY

Church of Jesus Christ of Latter-day Saints: a Christian religion founded by Joseph Smith in 1830; also known as LDS Church or Mormons

inculcate: to instill or impress through instruction

polygamy: the practice of having more than one spouse

sealing ordinance: a sacred covenant in the LDS Church whereby a husband and wife and their children are bound together for eternity

solemnize: to formally recognize or sanction under religious authority

Document Analysis

The Mormon Church came under much criticism for its members' practice of plural marriage, or polygamy. In 1843, the original leader of the Mormon Church, Joseph Smith, claimed to have received a divine revelation asserting that Mormon men were blessed by God with the right to have multiple wives. The Church of Jesus Christ of Latter-day Saints had existed for thirteen years prior to this claim by its leader. The practice of polygamy that is historically associated with Mormonism was not considered a part of the religion between its founding in 1830 and Smith's 1843 revelation.

The Mormon Church was split on the issue of polygamy, and a newspaper was started to publicly opine against the direction in which Smith was pushing the church. Smith and his brother, Hyrum, attempted to stop the newspaper presses, but were arrested and held on charges of violating the Constitution. The Smith brothers were lynched, shot, and killed by anti-Mormons. After the death of Smith, the next president, Brigham Young, took over. He led the Mormons from Illinois to what is now Salt Lake City, Utah, on what was called the Mormon Trek. Young selected this area because it was remote enough to insulate against persecution as well as for its placement within Mexican, rather than United States, jurisdiction. Young and his followers believed that they would be free to practice their religion as they chose, including the practice of plural marriage. The United States gained control of Utah in 1848, however, which threatened the religious freedom of the Mormons by once again subjecting them to US government interference.

Brigham Young was appointed territorial governor; however, some non-Mormons were also appointed by US President Millard Fillmore as territorial officials. Many Mormon residents of the Salt Lake Valley were unhappy with the appointments and wished to elect their own officials. This, however, would be possible only if Utah were granted status as a state (rather than a territory). Utah's quest for statehood began, only to be stymied by LDS officials' public acknowledgment of the common Mormon practice of plural marriage. Much of the general population of the United States were opposed to and offended by polygamy and its practice by Mormons in Utah territory. Indeed, the practice would continue to stand in the way of statehood for Utah until 1896.

Anti-polygamy laws were passed by Congress, including the Morrill Anti-Bigamy Act, which outlawed polygamy, and the Poland Act, which shifted the control of the Utah territory justice system from the LDS Church to US district courts, enabling successful prosecution of polygamists. The Edmunds Act of 1882 further restricted the rights of polygamists. As the United States took steps to eliminate polygamy, Utah continued to petition for statehood. Multiple petitions were rejected over the course of several decades, primarily owing to disagreements over plural marriage.

The 1890 manifesto by church president Woodruff demonstrated to Congress that members of the LDS Church were willing to abandon the practice of polygamy and that church leaders would neither condone nor recognize such unions. This was a significant step toward statehood for Utah. In 1894, Congress passed the Enabling Act, which outlined the terms under which Utah would be considered for statehood, including a ban on plural marriage. In 1895, a constitution for the state was drafted, and the following year, Utah was recognized as a state.

Essential Themes

Woodruff's manifesto addresses important themes, including First Amendment rights and the controversial practice of plural marriage. The Morrill Anti-Bigamy Act, which became law under President Abraham Lincoln, was viewed by many LDS Church members as a violation of their rights under the First Amendment to the United States Constitution, which protects the freedom to exercise religious practices. Followers of Joseph Smith, the founder of the Church of Jesus Christ of Latter-day Saints, believed in his prophecy that men were granted the divine right to marry multiple wives. For these believers, to interfere with their practice of plural marriage was to deny their right to practice their religion. For this reason, the Morrill Anti-Bigamy Act was largely ignored until further legislation enabled the prosecution of polygamists to a much greater extent than had been previously possible.

Plural marriage, bigamy, and infidelity continue to be common themes in the media in modern times. In United States history, polygamy within the LDS Church remains the most noteworthy example of an institutionally sanctioned form of the practice (at least in the past). Polygamy and polyamory—or having intimate relationships with more than one person—remain topics of debate among experts in the fields of anthropology and social psychology, as well as in the popular media. Some argue that polyamory is natural, and that males are biologically compelled to become intimately involved with multiple female partners. Others argue against it, often citing moral reasons why the practice is socially unacceptable. Polygamy, even when presented as a religious practice, was at the outset a topic of contention when Utah sought statehood. The initial refusal of the LDS Church to abandon polygamy prevented Utah from becoming a state for nearly fifty years from its first petition. The popularity of modern-day media accounts of polyamory suggests that although polygamy was once viewed as abhorrent and immoral, it is being revisited today in terms of its human, rather than its spiritual, possibilities.

—*Jennifer D. Henry, M.Ed.*

Bibliography and Additional Reading

Bachman, Daniel. "Plural Marriage." BYU *Harold B. Lee Library Digital Collections*, 2013. Web. 7 Nov. 2014.

Bowman, Matthew. *The Mormon People: The Making of an American Faith*. New York: Random House, 2012. Print.

Jessee, Dean C. "Woodruff, Wilford." *BYU Harold B. Lee Library Digital Collections*, 2013. Web. 7 Nov. 2014.

Van Wagoner, Richard S. *Mormon Polygamy: A History*. Salt Lake City, UT: Signature, 1989. Print.

Woodruff, Wilford. "Official Declaration I" (1890). *Scriptures, Doctrines, and Covenants*. The Church of Jesus Christ of Latter-day Saints, 18 Mar. 2014. Web. 7 Nov. 2014.

Yorgason, Ethan R. *Transformation of the Mormon Culture Region*. Champaign, IL: U of Illinois P, 2010. Print.

INDIAN WARS AND WOES

For almost a hundred years after its founding, the United States dealt with Indian tribes as it did with foreign nations. The lands and property of Native peoples was, theoretically, "never [to be] taken from them without their consent; and, in their property, rights, and liberty, they never shall be invaded or disturbed, unless in just and lawful wars authorized by Congress" (Northwest Ordinance of 1787). Treaties with Indians were negotiated with agents of the executive branch and ratified by the US Senate. By 1871, however, after many decades of broken promises, Congress had decided that it was no longer necessary to conduct relations in this way; a simple executive agreement was sufficient. And by 1887, under the Dawes Allotment Act, negotiations with Native nations became largely moot, as it was now the individual property owner rather than the collective entity that mattered most for legal purposes.

Over the course of those hundred years, many wars were fought between Indigenous groups and the United States. The idea of dealing with Indians justly and humanely, as one would in the case of members of a respected foreign nation, was quickly set aside amid the rush to expand white settlements and extend US control of western territories. Indians were removed to reservations, and then relocated yet again to more isolated reservations, in order to suit the needs of the white population. Most of these actions had some legal component to them; Indians signed treaties accepting compensation in the form of money, livestock, guns, and clothing. The overall effect, however, was to establish Native Americans as clearly subordinates in the pairing of powers on the continent. They were attacked militarily whenever it was deemed expedient to do so, leaving their numbers depleted and their spirits crushed.

By 1890, the only recourse among Indigenous peoples seemed to be the spiritist movement known as the Ghost Dance. This religion spread rapidly and led some to dream again of Native pride and independence. The movement's rise, however, also caused worry among white residents and leaders, who resorted, once again, to force in a move to quell it.

■ Accounts of the Sand Creek Massacre

Date: 1864–1865
Authors: various
Genre: articles; testimony

Summary Overview

Of all the dark events that occurred in the American West, of all the crimes perpetrated against Native peoples by the United States Army, few had as many far-reaching consequences as the Sand Creek Massacre. On November 29, 1864, 700 men of the Colorado Territory militia, led by Colonel John M. Chivington attacked a Cheyenne and Arapaho camp along the Big Sandy Creek. The action resulted in the death and mutilation of scores of Native Americans, many of them women and children, and several of the principal chiefs of the Cheyenne nation. The result of continued encroachment by settlers on Native land, racism, and the political ambitions of a bloody-minded commander, the massacre, sadly, was neither the first nor would it be the last incident of its kind. It marked just another chapter in the conquest of the West and the destruction of Native peoples. The massacre also set into motion a cycle of violence that would result in the deaths of many settlers, soldiers, and ultimately nearly cost the Cheyenne and Arapaho everything they had left.

Defining Moment

In the popular imagination, film, literature, and even standard history textbooks, the settling of the West is most often presented as a glorious victory over nature. In just a single generation, Americans were able to tame a vast wilderness stretching from the Atlantic to the Pacific Ocean. But the reality was much darker. At the time of first contact, North America was teeming with life. Thousands of independent cultures inhabited the vast territories across the whole of the continent. As Europeans moved in, they brought with them disease, notions of property, and feelings of racial superiority, born out of a sense of divine righteousness. Possessing superior technology and a grim determination to push ever further West, American settlers flooded the interior, clashing with Native peoples, whom they considered savage and inferior.

From the very beginning, the United States government seemed to adopt a split approach to Native Americans. On the one hand, the expansion of American power over the whole of the continent was seen as crucial not just to the economic stability of the young nation, but also to its safety. On the other hand, the United States was a democracy, founded on the principles of freedom and mutual respect. The Native peoples thus presented a quandary. How does one dispossess a population, while actively pursuing a policy of territorial annexation and consolidation?

Out of this murkiness came a double-edged policy. On the one hand, the government would attempt, usually in good faith, to sign treaties with Native tribes guaranteeing territorial rights and safety. On the other hand, the government would often encourage commanders in the field to respond forcefully to tribes threatening American settlers. These settlers, in turn, encroached on Native lands with the full support of local and federal policymakers.

In 1851, the Fort Laramie Treaty (not to be confused with the Fort Laramie treaty of 1868) gave several Native peoples, including the Cheyenne and Arapaho control over a vast stretch of territory across the northern plains. However, the discovery of gold in 1858 triggered a massive influx of settlers into the region. Clashes soon erupted between the tribes and the settlers, and therefore, the US government quickly amended the treaty, greatly reducing Native land holdings. Resentment grew among the tribes, creating pro-war and pro-peace factions within the Cheyenne, most notably the hawkish Dog Soldiers. With the outbreak of the Civil War, tension only grew between Native peoples and settlers, and the territory's governor encouraged military commanders to begin attacking Cheyenne settlements.

In 1864, the peaceful factions of the Cheyenne, led by chiefs Black Kettle and White Antelope, hoping to avoid bloodshed, negotiated with territorial authorities to settle their people north of Fort Lyon, on the eastern plains. Guaranteed rations and safe conduct by the military, the elements of Cheyenne and Arapaho, made camp. Then, in November, forces led by Colonel John Milton Chivington, a former Methodist minister turned rabid anti-Indian Army commander, attacked the encampment, slaughtering as many as 200 men, women, and children. At first, the pubic celebrated the event as a military victory against hostile bands of savage Indians; but as details emerged of what really happened, federal authorities had no choice but to launch an investigation into what would later be called the Sand Creek Massacre.

Author Biography

The primary sources in this case consist of two unsigned editorials featured in the *Rocky Mountain News*, followed by the testimony of John S. Smith. Not much is known about Smith. An Indian agent and an interpreter, he worked extensively with the Cheyenne and Arapaho, being personally acquainted with the tribes' chiefs, including Black Kettle, as well as the local Colorado militia commanders. He had a half-Cheyenne son named Jack, who was killed on the orders of Colonel Chivington.

HISTORICAL DOCUMENT

[Editorial I, *Rocky Mountain News* (1864)]

The Battle of Sand Creek

Among the brilliant feats of arms in Indian warfare, the recent campaign of our Colorado volunteers will stand in history with few rivals, and none to exceed it in final results. We are not prepared to write its history, which can only be done by some one who accompanied the expedition, but we have gathered from those who participated in it and from others who were in that part of the country, some facts which will doubtless interest many of our readers.

The people of Colorado are well aware of the situation occupied by the third regiment during the great snowstorm which set in the last of October. Their rendezvous was in Bijou Basin, about eighty miles southeast of this city, and close up under the foot of the Divide. That point had been selected as the base for an Indian campaign. Many of the companies reached it after the storm set in; marching for days through the driving, blinding clouds of snow and deep drifts. Once there, they were exposed for weeks to an Arctic climate, surrounded by a treeless plain covered three feet deep with snow. Their animals suffered for food and with cold, and the men fared but little better. They were insufficiently supplied with tents and blankets, and their sufferings were intense. At the end of a month the snow had settled to the depth of two fee, and the command set out upon its long contemplated march. The rear guard left the Basin on the 23rd of November. Their course was southeast, crossing the Divide and thence heading for Fort Lyon. For one hundred miles the snow was quite two feet in depth, and for the next hundred it ranged from six to twelve inches. Beyond that the ground was almost bare and the snow no longer impeded their march.

On the afternoon of the 28th the entire command reached Fort Lyon, a distance of two hundred and sixty miles, in less than six days, and so quietly and expeditiously had the march been made that the command at the fort was taken entirely by surprise. When the vanguard appeared in sight it was reported that a body of Indians were approaching, and precautions were taken for their reception. No one upon the route was permitted to go in advance of the column, and persons who it was suspected would spread the news of the advance were kept under surveillance until all danger from that source was past.

At Fort Lyon the force was strengthened by about two hundred and fifty men of the first regiment, and at nine o'clock in the evening the command set out for the Indian village. The course was due north, and their guide was the Polar star. As daylight dawned they came in sight of the Indian camp, after a forced midnight march of forty-two miles, in eight hours, across the rough, unbroken plain. But little time was required for preparation.

The forces had been divided and arranged for battle on the march, and just as the sun rose they dashed upon the enemy with yells that would put a Comanche army to blush. Although utterly surprised, the savages were not unprepared, and for a time their defense told terribly against our ranks. Their main force rallied and formed in line of battle on the bluffs beyond the creek, where they were protected by rudely constructed rifle-pits, from which they maintained a steady fire until the shells from company C's (third regiment) howitzers began dropping among them, when they scattered and fought each for himself in genuine Indian fashion. As the battle progressed the field of carriage widened until it extended over not less than twelve miles of territory. The Indians who could escaped or secreted themselves, and by three o'clock in the afternoon the carnage had ceased. It was estimated that between three and four hundred of the savages got away with their lives. Of the balance there were neither wounded nor prisoners. Their strength at the beginning of the action was estimated at nine hundred.

Their village consisted of one hundred and thirty Cheyenne and with Arapahoe lodges. These, with their contents, were totally destroyed. Among their effects were large supplies of flour, sugar, coffee, tea, &c. Women's and children's clothing were found; also books and many other articles which must have been taken from captured trains or houses. One white man's scalp was found which had evidently been taken but a few days before. The Chiefs fought with unparalleled bravery, falling in front of their men. One of them charged alone against a force of two or three hundred, and fell pierced with balls far in advance of his braves.

Our attack was made by five battalions. The first regiment, Colonel Chivington, part of companies C, D, E, G, H and K, numbering altogether about two hundred and fifty men, was divided into two battalions; the first under command of Major Anthony, and the second under Lieutenant Wilson, until the latter was disabled, when the command devolved upon Lieutenant Dunn. The three battalions of the third, Colonel Shoup, were led, respectively, by Lieutenant Colonel Bowen, Major Sayr, and Captain Cree. The action was begun by the battalion of Lieutenant Wilson, who occupied the right, and by a quick and bold movement cut off the enemy from their herd of stock. From this circumstance we gained our great advantage. A few Indians secured horses, but the great majority of them had to fight or fly on foot. Major Anthony was on the left, and the third in the centre.

Among the killed were all the Cheyenne chiefs, Black Kettle, White Antelope, Little Robe, Left Hand, Knock Knee, One Eye, and another, name unknown. Not a single prominent man of the tribe remains, and the tribe itself is almost annihilated. The Arapahoes probably suffered but little. It has been reported that the chief Left Hand, of that tribe, was killed, but Colonel Chivington is of the opinion that he was not. Among the stock captured were a number of government horses and mules, including the twenty or thirty stolen from the command of Lieutenant Chase at Jimmy's camp last summer.

The Indian camp was well supplied with defensive works. For half a mile along the creek there was an almost continuous chain of rifle-pits, and another similar line of works crowned the adjacent bluff. Pits had been dug at all the salient points for miles. After the battle twenty-tree dead Indians were taken from one of these pits and twenty-seven from another.

Whether viewed as a march or as a battle, the exploit has few, if any, parallels. A march of 260 miles in but a fraction more than five days, with deep snow, scanty forage, and no road, is a remarkable feat, whilst the utter surprise of a large Indian village is unprecedented. In no single battle in North America, we believe, have so many Indians been slain.

It is said that a short time before the command reached the scene of battle of an old squaw partially alarmed the village by reporting that a great herd of buffalo were coming. She heard the rumbling of the artillery and tramp of the moving squadrons, but her people doubted. In a little time the doubt was dispelled, but not by buffaloes.

A thousand incidents of individual daring and the passing events of the day might be told, but space forbids. We leave the task for eye-witnesses to chronicle. All acquitted themselves well, and Colorado soldiers have again covered themselves with glory.

* * *

[Editorial II, *Rocky Mountain News* (1864)]

The Fort Lyon Affair

The issue of yesterday's News, containing the following despatch, created considerable of a sensation in this city, particularly among the Thirdsters and others who participated in the recent campaign and the battle on Sand creek.

Washington, December 20, 1864 "The affair at Fort Lyon, Colorado, in which Colonel Chivington destroyed a large Indian village, and all its inhabitants, is to be made the subject of congressional investigation. Letters received from high officals in Colorado say that the Indians were killed after surrendering, and that a large proportion of them were women and children."

Indignation was loudly and unequivocally expressed, and some less considerate of the boys were very persistent in their inquiries as to who those "high officials" were, with a mild intimation that they had half a mind to "go for them." This talk about "friendly Indians" and a "surrendered" village will do to "tell to marines," but to us out here it is all bosh.

The confessed murderers of the Hungate family—a man and wife and their two little babes, whose scalped and mutilated remains were seen by all our citizens— were "friendly Indians," we suppose, in the eyes of these "high officials." They fell in the Sand creek battle.

The confessed participants in a score of other murders of peaceful settlers and inoffensive travelers upon our borders and along our roads in the past six months must have been friendly, or else the "high officials" wouldn't say so.

The band of marauders in whose possession were found scores of horses and mules stolen from government and from individuals; wagon loads of flour, coffee, sugar and tea, and rolls of broad cloth, calico, books, &c, robbed from freighters and emigrants on the plains; underclothes of white women and children, stripped from their murdered victims, were probably peaceably disposed toward some of those "high officials," but the mass of our people "can't see it."

Probably those scalps of white men, women and children, one of them fresh, not three days taken, found drying in their lodges, were taken in a friendly, playful manner; or possibly those Indian saddle-blankets trimmed with the scalp's of white women, and with braids and fringes of their hair, were kept simply as mementos of their owners' high affection for the pale face. At any rate, these delicate and tasteful ornaments could not have been taken from the heads of the wives, sisters or daughters of these "high officials."

That "surrendering" must have been the happy thought of an exceedingly vivid imagination, for we can hear of nothing of the kind from any of those who were engaged in the battle. On the contrary, the savages fought like devils to the end, and one of our pickets was killed and scalped by them the next day after the battle, and a number of others were fired upon. In one instance a party of the vidette pickets were compelled to beat a hasty retreat to save their lives, full twenty-four hours after the battle closed. This does not look much like the Indians had surrendered.

But we are not sure that an investigation may not be a good thing. It should go back of the "affair at Fort Lyon," as they are pleased to term it down east, however, and let the world know who were making money by keeping those Indians under the sheltering protection of Fort Lyon; learn who was interested in systematically representing that the Indians were friendly and wanted peace. It is unquestioned and undenied that the site of the Sand creek battle was the rendezvous of the thieving and marauding bands of savages who roamed over this country last summer and fall, and it is shrewdly suspected that somebody was all the time making a very good thing out of it. By all means let there be an investigation, but we advise the honorable congressional committee, who may be appointed to conduct it, to get their scalps insured before they pass Plum creek on their way out.

* * *

[Congressional Testimony of Mr. John S. Smith, March 14, 1865]

Mr. John S. Smith sworn and examined.

By Mr. Gooch:

Question. Where is your place of residence?

Answer. Fort Lyon, Colorado

Question. What is your occupation?

Answer. United States Indian interpreter and special Indian agent.

Question. Will you state to the committee all that you know in relation to the attack of Colonel Chivington upon the Cheyenne and Arapahoe Indians in November last?

Answer. Major Anthony was in command at Fort Lyon at the time. Those Indians had been induced to remain in the vicinity of Fort Lyon, and were promised protection by the commanding officer at Fort Lyon. The commanding officer saw proper to keep them some thirty or forty miles distant from the fort, for fear of some conflict between them and the soldiers or the traveling population, for Fort Lyon is on a great thoroughfare. He advised them to go out on what is called Sand creek, about forty miles, a little east of north from Fort Lyon. Some days after they had left Fort Lyon when I had just recovered from a long spell of sickness, I was called on by Major S.G. Colley, who asked me if I was able and willing to go out and pay a visit to these Indians, ascertain their numbers, their general disposition toward the whites, and the points where other bands might be located in the interior.

Question. What was the necessity for obtaining that information?

Answer. Because there were different bands which were supposed to be at war; in fact, we knew at the time that they were at war with the white population in that country; but this band had been in and left the post perfectly satisfied. I left to go to this village of Indians on the 26th of November last. I arrived there on the 27th and remained there the 28th. On the morning of the 29th, between daylight and sunrise—nearer sunrise than daybreak—a large number of troops were discovered from three-quarters of a mile to a mile below the village. The Indians, who discovered them, ran to my camp, called me out, and wanted to me to go and see what troops they were, and what they wanted. The head chief of the nation, Black Kettle, and head chief of the Cheyennes, was encamped there with us. Some years previous, he

had been presented with a fine American flag by Colonel Greenwood, a commissioner, who had been sent out there. Black Kettle ran this American flag up to the top of his lodge, with a small white flag tied right under it, as he had been advised to do in case he should meet with any troops out on the prairies. I then left my own camp and started for that portion of the troops that was nearest the village, supposing I could go up to the m. I did not know but they might be strange troops, and thought my presence and explanations could reconcile matters. Lieutenant Wilson was in command of the detachment to which I tried to make my approach; but they fired several volleys at me, and I returned back to my camp and entered my lodge.

Question. Did these troops know you to be a white man?

Answer. Yes, sir; and the troops that went there knew I was in the village.

Question. Did you see Lieutenant Wilson or were you seen by him?

Answer. I cannot say I was seen by him; but his troops were the first to fire at me.

Question. Did they know you to be a white man?

Answer. They could not help knowing it. I had on pants, a soldier's overcoat, and a hat such as I am wearing now. I was dressed differently from any Indian in the country. On my return I entered my lodge, not expecting to get out of it alive. I had two other men there with me: one was David Louderbach, a soldier, belonging to company G, lst Colorado cavalry; the other, a man by the name of Watson, who was a hired hand of Mr. DD Coolly, the son of Major Coolly, the agent.

After I had left my lodge to go out and see what was going on, Colonel Chivington rode up to within fifty or sixty yards of where I was camped; he recognized me at once. They all call me Uncle John in that country. He said, "Run here, Uncle John; you are all right." I went to him as fast as I could. He told me to get in between him and his troops, who were then coming up very fast; I did so; directly another officer who knew me—Lieutenant Baldwin, in command of a battery—tried to assist me to get a horse; but there was no loose horse there at the time. He said, "Catch hold of the caisson, and keep up with us."

By this time the Indians had fled; had scattered in every direction. The troops were some on one side of the river and some on the other, following up the Indians. We had been encamped on the north side of the river; I followed along, holding on the caisson, sometimes running, sometimes walking. Finally, about a mile above the village, the troops had got a parcel of the Indians hemmed in under the bank of the river; as soon as the troops overtook them, they commenced firing on them; some troops had got above them, so that they were completely surrounded. There were probably a hundred Indians hemmed in there, men, women, and children; the most of the men in the village escaped.

By the time I got up with the battery to the place where these Indians were surrounded there had been some considerable firing. Four or five soldiers had been killed, some with arrows and some with bullets. The soldiers continued firing on these Indians, who numbered about a hundred, until they had almost completely destroyed them. I think I saw altogether some seventy dead bodies lying there; the greater portion women and children. There may have been thirty warriors, old and young; the rest were women and small children of different ages and sizes.

The troops at that time were very much scattered. There were not over two hundred troops in the main fight, engaged in killing this body of Indians under the bank. The balance of the troops were scattered in different directions, running after small parties of Indians who were trying to make their escape. I did not go so see how many they might have killed outside of this party under the bank of the river. Being still quite weak from my last sickness, I returned with the first body of troops that went back to the camp.

The Indians had left their lodges and property; everything they owned. I do not think more than one-half of the Indians left their lodges with their arms. I think there were between 800 and 1,000 men in this command of United States troops. There was a part of three companies of the 1st Colorado, and the balance were what were called 100 days men of the 3rd regiment. I am not able to say which party did the most execution on the Indians, because it was very much mixed up at the time.

We remained there that day after the fight. By 11 o'clock, I think, the entire number of soldiers had returned back to the camp where Colonel Chivington had returned. On their return, he ordered the soldiers to destroy all the Indian property there, which they did, with the exception of what plunder they took away with them, which was considerable.

Question. How many Indians were there there?

Answer. There were 100 families of Cheyennes, and some six or eight lodges of Arapahoes.

Question. How many persons in all, should you say?

Answer. About 500 we estimate them at five to a lodge.

Question. 500 men, women and children?

Answer. Yes, sir.

Question. Do you know the reason for that attack on the Indians?

Answer. I do not know any exact reason. I have heard a great many reasons given. I have heard that that whole Indian war had been brought on for selfish purposes. Colonel Chivington was running for Congress in Colorado, and there were other things of that kind; and last spring a year ago he was looking for an order to go to the front, and I understand he had this Indian war in view to retain himself and his troops in that country, to carry out his electioneering purposes.

Question. In what way did this attack on the Indians further the purpose of Colonel Chivington?

Answer. It was said—I did not hear him say it myself, but it was said that he would do something; he had this regiment of three-months men, and did not want them to go out without doing some service. Now he had been told repeatedly by different persons—by myself, as well as others—where he could find the hostile bands.

The same chiefs who were killed in this village of Cheyennes had been up to see Colonel Chivington in Denver but a short time previous to this attack. He himself told them that he had no power to treat with them; that he had received telegrams from General Curtis directing him to fight all Indians he met with in that country. Still he would advise them, if they wanted any assistance from the whites, to go to their nearest military post in their country, give up their arms and the stolen property, if they had any, and then they would receive directions in what way to act. This was told them by Colonel Chivington and by Governor Evans, of Colorado. I myself interpreted for them and for the Indians.

Question. Did Colonel Chivington hold any communciation with these Indians, or any of them, before making the attack upon them?

Answer. No, sir, not then. He had some time previously held a council with them at Denver city. When we first recovered the white prisoners from the Indians, we invited some of the chiefs to go to Denver, inasmuch as they had sued for peace, and were willing to give up these white prisoners. We promised to take the chiefs to Denver, where they had an interview with men who had more power than Major Wynkoop had, who was the officer in command of the detachment that went out to recover these white prisoners. Governor Evans and Colonel Chivington were in Denver, and were present at this council. They told the Indians to return with Major Wynkoop, and whatever he agreed on doing with them would be recognized by them.

I returned with the Indians to Fort Lyon. There we let them go out to their villages to bring in their families, as they had been invited through the proclamation or circular of the governor during the month of June, I think. They were gone some twelve or fifteen days from Fort Lyon, and then they returned with their families. Major Wynkoop had made them one or two issues of provisions previous to the arrival of Major Anthony there to assume command. Then Major Wynkoop, who is now in command at Fort Lyon, was ordered to Fort Leavenworth on some business with General Curtis, I think.

Then Major Anthony, through me, told the Indians that he did not have it in his power to issue rations to them, as Major Wynkoop had done. He said that he had assumed command at Fort Lyon, and his orders were positive from headquarters to fight the Indians in the vicinity of Fort Lyon, or at any other point in the Territory where they could find them. He said that he had understood that they had been behaving very badly. But on seeing Major Wynkoop and others there at Fort Lyon, he was happy to say that things were not as had been presented, and he could not pursue any other course than that of Major Wynkoop except the issuing rations to them. He

then advised them to out to some near point, where there was buffalo, not too far from Fort Lyon or they might meet with troops from the Platte, who would not know them from the hostile bands. This was the southern band of Cheyennes; there is another band called the northern band. They had no apprehensions in the world of any trouble with the whites at the time this attack was made.

Question. Had there been, to your knowledge, any hostile act or demonstration on the part of these Indians or any of them?

Answer. Not in this band. But the northern band, the band known by the name of Dog soldiers of Cheyennes, had committed many depredations on the Platte.

Question. Do you know whether or not Colonel Chivington knew the friendly character of these Indians before he made the attack upon them?

Answer. It is my opinion that he did.

Question. On what is that opinion based?

Answer. On this fact, that he stopped all persons from going on ahead of him. He stopped the mail, and would not allow any person to go on ahead of him at the time he was on his way from Denver city to Fort Lyon. He placed a guard around old Colonel Bent, the former agent there; he stopped a Mr. Hagues and many men who were on their way to Fort Lyon. He took the fort by surprise, and as soon as he got there he posted pickets all around the fort, and then left at 8 o'clock that night for this Indian camp.

Question. Was that anything more than the exercise of ordinary precaution in following Indians?

Answer. Well, sir, he was told that there were no Indians in the vicinity of Fort Lyon, except Black Kettle's band of Cheyennes and Left Hand's band of Arapahoes.

Question. How do you know that?

Answer. I was told so.

By Mr. Buckalew:

Question. Do you know it of your own knowledge?

Answer. I cannot say I do.

Question. You did not talk with him about it before the attack?
Answer. No, sir.

By Mr. Gooch:

Question. When you went out to him, you had no opportunity to hold intercourse with him?
Answer. None whatever; he had just commenced his fire against the Indians.

Question. Did you have any communication with him at any time while there?
Answer. Yes, sir.

Question. What was it?
Answer. He asked me many questions about a son of mine, who was killed there afterwards. He asked me what Indians were there, what chiefs; and I told him as fully as I knew.

By Mr. Buckalew:

Question. When did you talk with him?
Answer. On the day of the attack. He asked me many questions about the chiefs who were there, and if I could recognize them if I saw them. I told him it was possible I might recollect the principal chiefs. They were terribly mutilated, lying there in the water and sand; most of them in the bed of the creek, dead and dying, making many struggles. They were so badly mutilated and covered with sand and water that it was very hard for me to tell one from another. However, I recognized some of them—among them the chief One Eye, who was employed by our government at $125 a month and rations to remain in the village as a spy. There was another called War Bonnet, who was here two years ago with me. There was another by the name of Standing-in-the-Water, and I supposed Black Kettle was among them, but it was not Black Kettle. There was one there of his size and dimensions in every way, but so tremendously mutilated that I was mistaken in him. I went out with Lieutenant Colonel Bowen, to see how many I could recognize.

By Mr. Gooch:

Question: Did you tell Colonel Chivington the character and disposition of these Indians at any time during your interviews on this day?
Answer. Yes, sir.

Question. What did he say in reply?
Answer. He said he could not help it; that his orders were positive to attack the Indians.

Question. From whom did he receive these orders?
Answer. I do not know; I presume from General Curtis.

Question. Did he tell you?
Answer. Not to my recollection.

Question. Were the women and children slaughtered indiscriminately, or only so far as they were with the warriors?
Answer. Indiscriminately.

Question. Were there any acts of barbarity perpetrated there that came under your own observation?
Answer. Yes, sir; I saw the bodies of those lying there cut all to pieces, worse mutilated than any I ever saw before; the women cut all to pieces.

By Mr. Buckalew:

Question. How cut?
Answer. With knives; scalped; their brains knocked out; children two or three months old; all ages lying there, from sucking infants up to warriors.

By Mr. Gooch:

Question. Did you see it done?
Answer. Yes, sir; I saw them fall.

Question. Fall when they were killed?
Answer. Yes, sir.

Question. Did you see them when they were mutilated?
Answer. Yes, sir.

Question. By whom were they mutilated?
Answer. By the United States troops.
Question. Do you know whether or not it was done by the direction or consent of any of the officers.
Answer. I do not; I hardly think it was.

By Mr. Buckalew:

Question. What was the date of that massacre?
Answer. On the 29th of November last.

Question. Did you speak of these barbarities to Colonel Chivington?
Answer. No sir; I had nothing at all to say about it, because at that time they were hostile towards me, from the fact of my being there. They probably supposed that I might be compromised with them in some way or other.

Question. Who called on you to designate the bodies of those who were killed?
Answer. Colonel Chivington himself asked me if I would ride out with Lieutenant Colonel Bowen, and see how many chiefs or principal men I could recognize.

Question. Can you state how many Indians were killed— how many women and how many children?
Answer. Perhaps one-half were men, and the balance were women and children. I do not think that I saw more than 70 lying dead then, as far as I went. But I saw parties of men scattered in every direction, pursuing little bands of Indians.

Question. What time of day or night was this attack made?
Answer. The attack commenced about sunrise, and lasted until between 10 and 11 o'clock.

Question. How large a body of troops?
Answer. I think that probably there may have been about 60 or 70 warriors who were armed and stood their ground and fought. Those that were unarmed got out of the way as they best could.

Question. How many of our troops were killed and how many wounded?
Answer. There were ten killed on the ground, and thirty-eight wounded; four of the wounded died at Fort Lyon before I came on east.

Question. Were there any other barbarities or atrocities committed there other than those you have mentioned, that you saw?
Answer. Yes, sir; I had a half-breed son there, who gave himself up. He started at the time the Indians fled; being a half-breed he had but little hope of being spared, and seeing them fire at me, he ran away with the Indians for the distance of about a mile. During the fight up there he walked back to my camp and went into the lodge. It was surrounded by soldiers at the time. He came in quietly and sat down; he remained there that day, that night, and the next day in the afternoon; about four o'clock in the evening, as I was sitting inside the camp, a soldier came up outside of the lodge and called me by name. I got up and went out; he took me by the arm and walked towards Colonel Chivington's camp, which was about sixty yards from my camp. Said he, "I am sorry to tell you, but they are going to kill your son Jack." I knew the feeling towards the whole camp of Indians, and that there was no use to make any resistance. I said, "I can't help it." I then walked on towards where Colonel Chivington was standing by his camp-fire; when I had got within a few feet of him I heard a gun fired, and saw a crowd run to my lodge, and they told me that Jack was dead.

Question. What action did Colonel Chivington take in regard to that matter?
Answer. Major Anthony, who was present, told Colonel Chivington that he had heard some remarks made, indicating that they were desirous of killing Jack; and that he (Colonel Chivington) had it in his power to save him, and that by saving him he might make him a very useful man, as he was well acquainted with all the Cheyenne and Arapahoe country, and he could be used as a guide or interpreter. Colonel Chivington replied to Major Anthony, as the Major himself told me, that he had no orders to receive and no advice to give. Major Anthony is now in this city.

By Mr. Buckalew:

Question. Did Chivington say anything to you, or you to him about the firing?
Answer. Nothing directly; there were a number of officers sitting around the fire, with the most of whom I was acquainted.

By Mr. Gooch:

Question. Were there any other Indians or half-breeds there at that time?
Answer. Yes, sir; Mr. Bent had three sons there; one employed as a guide for these troops at the time, and two others living there in the village with the Indians; and a Mr. Gerry had a son there.

Question. Were there any other murders after the first day's massacre?
Answer. There was none, except of my son.

Question. Were there any other atrocities which you have not mentioned?
Answer. None that I saw myself. There were two women that white men had families by; they were saved from the fact of being in my lodge at the time. One ran to my lodge; the other was taken prisoner by a soldier who knew her and brought her to my lodge for safety. They both had children. There were some small children, six or seven years old, who were taken prisoners near the camp. I think there were three of them taken to Denver with these troops.

Question. Were the women and children that were killed, killed during the fight with the Indians?
Answer. During the fight, or during the time of the attack.

Question. Did you see any women or children killed after the fight was over?
Answer. None….

Question. Have you spent any considerable portion of your life with the Indians?
Answer. The most of it.

Question. How many years have you been with the Indians?
Answer. I have been twenty-seven successive years with the Cheyennes and Arapahoes. Before that I was in the country as a trapper and hunter in the Rocky mountains.

Question. For how long time have you acted as Indian interpreter?
Answer. For some fifteen or eighteen years.

Question. By whom have you been so employed?
Answer. By Major Fitzpatrick, Colonel Bent, Major Colley, Colonel J.W. Whitfield, and a great deal of the time for the military as guide and interpreter.

By Mr. Buckalew:

Question. How many warriors were estimated in Colonel Chivington's report as having been in this Indian camp?
Answer. About nine hundred.

Question. How many were there?
Answer. About two hundred warriors; they average about two warriors to a lodge, and there were about one hundred lodges.

GLOSSARY

caisson: a chest or wagon for holding or conveying ammunition

howitzer: a short gun for firing shells on high trajectories at low velocities

rifle-pit: a short trench or excavation with a parapet of earth in front to shelter one or more riflemen

vidette: a mounted sentry positioned beyond an army's outposts to observe the movements of the enemy

Document Analysis

The first document in the series is an editorial featured in the *Rocky Mountain News*, shortly after the events at Sand Creek. Roaring with pride, the article is triumphant and celebratory, extolling the actions of Colonel Chivington and his soldiers in what it describes as being "among the brilliant feats of arms in Indian warfare." Setting the scene, the article describes the treacherous trek of the soldiers into hostile territory. Marching for days through heavy snows, the men were exposed to the elements and danger at every turn. They reached Fort Lyon and soon after made for the enemy, bravely and without the slightest hesitation. They fell upon the enemy, the Native warriors fighting back ferociously despite the surprise attack. And in the end, the brave Colorado militiamen triumphed. "It was estimated that between three and four hundred of the savages got away with their lives," laments the article, but of those killed, perhaps as many as five hundred, tellingly, there were no wounded or prisoners taken. According to the editorial the action was an unmatched triumph, and the Colorado soldiers "covered themselves with glory."

As we see by the second document, another editorial from the *Rocky Mountain News*, things unraveled quickly. We learn that a Congressional investigation is about to be launched into the events at Sand Creek. Colonel Chivington and his troops were suspected of perpetrating a massacre of men, women, and children. Immediately defensive, the editorial blasts the "high officials" in Washington who would make such unfounded accusations and slander Colorado's brave fighting men. "Probably those scalps of white men, women and children, one of them fresh, not three days taken, found drying in [Sand Creek], were taken in a friendly, playful manner" the editorial mocks. The Cheyenne and Arapaho were savages who "fought like devils" and deserve neither sympathy nor mourning—these marauders, thieves, and murderers. Case closed.

The third document consists entirely of the testimony of Indian agent and interpreter, John S. Smith, who was a first-hand witness to the events of November 29. Smith makes it clear that the Cheyenne and Arapaho at Sand Creek were ordered by the military to remain where they were and were peaceful. Unlike other bands, those at Sand Creek had not attacked settlers, and in fact, when Chivington's troops arrived that morning, Black Kettle, one of the chiefs of the Cheyenne immediately ran both an American flag and a white peace flag over the top of his lodge. It mattered not. According to

Smith, as the Cheyenne and Arapaho began to flee, the militia attacked. Many of those attempting to run were soon cornered and surrounded at the bank of the river and fired upon from all sides. After the smoke cleared it was obvious that many of those killed were women and children. Soon after, many of the bodies were mutilated by the American soldiers—torn apart, scalped, and sliced. Later that same evening, Smith's own son, a half Cheyenne who had surrendered, was shot, seemingly on the direct orders of Colonel Chivington.

Smith speculates that Chivington, who knew that the tribes gathered at Sand Creek were peaceful, attacked not only out of his hatred for Native peoples, but also in pursuit of his own political ambitions. Settlers in Colorado Territory were fervently hostile to the Cheyenne and Arapaho, and Chivington hoped to leverage the attack to win himself a state-wide office.

Essential Themes

The Sand Creek Massacre was a shocking, but sadly not uncommon occurrence in the history of the American West. Spurred on by racism, notions born out of imperialism, and an insatiable greed for land, settlers most often looked down on Native peoples with open hostility. Although some tribes certainly did attack pioneers and soldiers, many more simply desired to coexist peacefully. Whether out of deliberate malice or simple ignorance, officials and military commanders often didn't care or bother to try and tell tribes apart, and so all suffered.

After the close of the Congressional investigation, and despite several recommendations for punishment, no actions were taken against any of those responsible for the killing. Although Colonel Chivington was publically admonished, he lost nothing except perhaps his chances at being elected to Congress. In the years that followed, Chivington would gain the support of many who answered his call to "stand by Sand Creek." After the massacre the Treaty of the Little Arkansas was signed between the US government and representatives of the affected tribes, promising greater land rights and reparations, but within two years, the treaty was effectively cancelled and its provisions ignored. By the close of the decade, all Cheyenne and Arapaho were ordered to move onto reservations further west.

The survivors of Sandy Creek eventually made their way to join the Lakota. With most of the pro-peace chiefs having died in the massacre, the pro-war factions within the tribal hierarchy gained power, the Dog

Soldiers first among them. The Sioux, Cheyenne, and Arapaho, seeking vengeance, carried out several attacks against military forts and settlements. Many men, women, and children were killed in the attacks. Public outcries to tame the roaming savages led to the buildup of US military strength on the frontier and was one of the most important contributing factors in the escalation of the Indian Wars. As fighting raged, the US government continued to take an ever-harder line with Native peoples. Despite continued efforts by men like Black Kettle to sue for peace, many more massacres followed as officials demanded that tribes settle on ever shrinking reservations or face terrible consequences. In the end, much of the violence perpetrated against Native peoples was expunged from official history. The story of the American West, despite so much brutality, became instead a glorious tale about the taming of a savage wilderness.

—*KP Dawes, MA*

Bibliography and Additional Reading

Brown, Dee. *Bury My Heart at Wounded Knee*. 1970. New York: Holt, 2007. Print.

Dunbar-Ortiz, Roxanne. *An Indigenous Peoples' History of the United States*. Boston: Beacon P, 2014. Print.

Kelman, Ari. *A Misplaced Massacre: Struggling over the Memory of Sand Creek*. Cambridge: Harvard UP, 2013. Print.

Stannard, *David E. American Holocaust: The Conquest of the New World*. New York: Oxford UP, 1992. Print.

■ Status Report on the Condition of the Navajos

Date: May 30, 1868
Author: Theodore H. Dodd
Genre: report

Summary Overview

After four years in exile from their homelands at the Bosque Redondo reservation at Fort Sumner, New Mexico, the Navajos signed a treaty with the United States that allowed them to return home and regain sovereignty over their reservation that spans northeast Arizona, northwest New Mexico, and southeast Utah. Four years earlier, the US Army had force-marched the Navajos over 300 miles across the desert, resulting in hundreds of deaths over the eighteen-day-long march. Life once they arrived was not much easier. Farming was next to impossible in the alkali soil. Food and water were in short supply, as many more people were held there than the government had planned. About 9,000 Navajos reached Bosque Redondo in 1864, and this report, prepared for General William T. Sherman and Colonel Samuel F. Tappan, who were negotiating the peace treaty, profiles what remained of the Navajos on the eve of the signing of the treaty.

Defining Moment

The nineteenth century was a time of considerable change for the Navajos. During the early part of the century, spanning much of the time between the Mexican Revolution in 1821 to the conquest of the region by the United States in 1846, the Navajos maintained a sporadic raiding war against the Mexican and Pueblo settlements in New Mexico. Much of this unrest was aided by the sale of arms from Anglo-American traders to the Indians, thus making what was only a tenuous hold over the region by Mexican officials much more problematic. The situation was much the same during the 1850s–1860s. The Navajos maintained their raiding and hit-and-run tactics, effectively staying out of outnumbered conflicts with American military forces.

However, the 1863 campaign led by Kit Carson, with considerable assistance from the Hopis, Zunis, and Utes, resulted in two changes to Navajo life that would have immense ramifications. First, the sustained

military pressure finally forced the Navajos to the negotiating table, after Carson and his troops destroyed all means the Navajos had to feed and house themselves. However, perhaps the most demoralizing aspect of their defeat was the fact that it resulted in their expulsion from their homelands, and relocation to the reservation—in reality, an internment camp—at Bosque Redondo, New Mexico.

Federal Indian policy at the time held that Indian peoples were to be forced to remain on the reservations set out for them by the government, and were subject to military action and extermination if they resisted. On the reservations, such as Bosque Redondo, the Indians would be forced to assimilate to the American way of life, including farming, living in villages, non-Indian education for children, and forced instruction in Christianity. For the Navajos and the Mescalero Apache with whom they shared the camp, life at Bosque Redondo was dismal. They tried to grow crops, only to have them destroyed by insects. The Army provided rations, but not enough to support all of the people. The alkaline water of the Pecos River caused intestinal problems and many people died of a smallpox epidemic that swept through the camp. If the Navajos left, not only would the US Army pursue them, any women and children could be taken by Comanches and New Mexicans for the slave trade.

After four years, it was apparent that the Navajos were not assimilating and the United States no longer wanted to pay all of the costs to support the Navajos when they were self-sufficient on their homelands. Though some federal officials wanted to send the Navajos to Indian Territory in present-day Oklahoma, Navajo leader Barboncito and others were able to convince the treaty negotiators to send them home.

Author Biography

Theodore H. Dodd was, as most soldiers in the West

during the late 1860s, a veteran of the Civil War, having fought for the Union as a lieutenant colonel in the Second Colorado Infantry. After the Civil War, Dodd was assigned to Fort Sumner, and had the unenviable task of overseeing the Navajos and Mescalero Apaches there. Throughout 1867 and 1868, Dodd wrote about the problems faced by the Navajos with simple survival and the raids by the Comanches, who stole both horses and other Indians to be sold as slaves. Dodd noted in a June 1867 report to Congress that the Navajos were anxious to return to their homeland, and Dodd was a fervent supporter of the Navajos, seeing them as better behaved than other local tribes, such as the Comanches and the Apaches. With the negotiation of the 1868 treaty, Dodd's role as an advocate for the Navajo became even more vital.

HISTORICAL DOCUMENT

STATUS REPORT
Navajo Agency Fort Sumner N.M.
May 30th, 1868

Lieut. General W. T. Sherman
and Col. S. F. Tappan
Peace Commissioners

In pursuance to your request I have the honor to submit a report as to the condition of the Navajo Indians at the Bosque Redondo reservation under my charge and express my views in relation to their removal; their requirements and their present reservation.

On the 1st day of Nov. 1867, the Commanding Officer at Fort Sumner N. M. Maj. C. J. Whiting 3rd U. S. Cavalry transferred to my charge 7111 Navajo Indians, Viz.

2157 under 12 years of age
2693 Women
2060 Men
201   Age and Sex Unknown

During the month of November 193 who were absent of the day of the count came in making total number subsisted 7304. The cost of subsisting said Indians from the 1st of November 1867 to the 23rd day of May 1868 inclusive as per report herewith transmitted of Wm. Rosenthall Commissary for Navajos is Two Hundred and Eighty-Thousand Eight Hundred and Thirty 07/100 Dollars (280,830 07/100).

The number of acres of land cultivated at the Bosque Redondo reservation in the years 1865 & 1866 was about 3800 acres, 2800 of which was cultivated as a government farm & the balance 1000 acres was cultivated and worked in patches exclusively by the Indians.

The amount of produce raised on the Government farm during said years according to the books of the Indian Commissary Department at Fort Sumner N. M. is as follows,

1865

Corn	423682	pounds
Wheat	34113	"
Beans	2942	"
Pumpkins	30403	"

1866

Corn	201420	pounds
Beans	2942	"
Pumpkins	29152	"

In the year 1867 this crop proved a total failure.

The number of animals owned by the Navajos as counted by myself June 30th 1867 was as follows:

Horses   550
Mules   21
Sheep   940
Goats   1025

I estimate that since June 30th 1867 the Navajos

have captured from the Comanche Indians about 1000 horses making total number of horses in the possession of Navajos about 1500.

The number of families on the reservation is about 1850. Since I have been Agent (nearly three years) I have found that a majority of them living on the reservation are peaceable and well disposed. Some thieving ones have occasionally committed depredations by stealing stock from citizens. In many cases however the stock has been recovered and delivered to owners.

Their ideas upon agriculture are few and simple but in their way they manage to raise very fair crops.

They are acquainted with the principles of irrigation and are quite skillful in making acequias, adobes, blankets, bridles, bits and baskets and many other articles. Until this year they have always worked well on the government farm in plowing, hoeing corn, digging acequias, etc. Large numbers of them have been employed by the Military Dept., sutlers and ranchmen in making and laying adobes and other work. They usually get from 30 to 50 cents per day for their labor and also rations.

Nearly every family living in the Reservation have attempted to cultivate patches of their own, planting corn, pumpkins, melons, etc. but have never succeeded in raising very good crops. The Indians attribute their failure to the unproductiveness of the soil. I am of the opinion that about half of the land cultivated at the Bosque Redondo is productive with proper management and irrigation; the other half I consider unproductive in consequence of containing a large amount of alkaline matter. The most serious objection to the Bosque Redondo reservation is the scarcity of timber & fuel. Timber for building purposes is hauled a distance of about 100 miles from Fort Sumner and wood for the use of the Garrison is hauled from 25 to 35 miles. Mesquite roots is the principal wood used by the Indians which they dig and carry on their backs from 6 to 12 miles and it is not very abundant at that distance. There was much suffering among the Indians last winter for want of fuel.

For nearly two years the Navajos have been very much dissatisfied with their reservation at the Bosque Redondo, and they state that their discontent is in consequence of frequent raids being made upon them by Comanche and other Indians. The scarcity of fuel, unproductiveness of

the soil, bad water and unhealthyness. During the past year they have been constantly begging me to endeavor to have them removed to their old country where they say the soil is more productive, where there is an abundance of timber, where mescal, mesquite, beans, wild potatoes & fruits are found in abundance and where they would be far removed from their old enemies The Comanches, Kiowa and other Indians.

I am satisfied that the Navajos will never be contented to remain on this or any other reservation except one located west of the Rio Grande and I am also of the opinion that if they are not permitted to return to their old country that many will stealthily return and in doing so commit depredations upon the people of N.M. and thus keep up a state of insecurity.

I therefore believe that it would be better for the Indians and the people of N.M. and a saving to the Government & in the end more likely to succeed in civilizing and making them self-sustaining to locate them upon a good reservation west of the Rio Grande. With regard to the precise location proper for these Indians, I am not prepared to give an opinion but would respectfully suggest the appointment of a joint commission for that purpose to examine carefully the country and make the selection so as to include lands suitable with water, wood and other resources to insure a permanent reservation.

Not being acquainted with Southern N.M. and northern Arizona in the vicinity of Canon de Chelly & Tuni Cha mountains, I am not prepared to say whether a suitable reservation can be selected in that portion of the Country or not, but I am acquainted with a portion of the valley of the Rio San Juan and its northern tributaries and am satisfied that a good reservation can be selected in that locality with good lands and abundant timber, water and other resources.

In my judgement a reservation should be selected for these people where there is a sufficient arable land and other resources to enable them to settle as near each other as possible in order that their agent can keep an eye upon them and their acts and provide for their necessities. If they are scattered over a large tract of country it would be almost impossible to punish the thieves. In my judgement a military post and agency should be established near their settlement. It must be bourne in mind that about one third of the Navajos are a lazy, indolent &

thieving people who will have to be watched constantly and if they commit depredations, punished.

Wherever these people are located it will be necessary for the Government to subsist them until they can plant and gather their crops, otherwise they will depredate upon the flocks of the Inhabitants of the Rio Grande and other localities. It cannot be expected that 7000 Indians who have been comparatively nothing and have been fed by the Government for four years and who have subsisted partly by agriculture for several centuries can live without extreme suffering, when their only subsistence will be game and the wild fruit of the country.

It is now so late in the season that they will not be able to reach their country in time to plant this year. Therefore in my judgement the Government ought to feed them until they can gather their crops next year, say until Sept. 1869.

With this assistance and an annual appropriation of 100,000 dollars for a few years properly managed they will be able in my opinion to maintain themselves.

The Navajos is no doubt the best material in the country for rapid progress in agriculture as history proves that for several centuries they have been engaged in planting and they are far in advance of other tribes in manufacturing blankets, bridles, saddles and other articles, yet they are Savages and extremely superstitious.

The Utah Indians have been enemies of the Navajos for many years. It is very important that a treaty of peace be made between these tribes, otherwise the Utah Indians will constantly be making raids upon the settlements of the Navajos, stealing their children and stock.

At a Council I recently held with the head men of the Navajo tribe they stated they are willing and anxious to make peace with them. I would suggest that some of the principal men of the Navajos and Utahs meet at Santa Fe or some other point and arrange a treaty of peace at an early date.

I would recommend that the Navajos be furnished at least with 40,000 head of sheep and goats. I would also recommend that one physician, one blacksmith and one carpenter be employed at an early day and shops erected and provided with new tools, timbers, etc. All of which is respectfully submitted.

Very Respectfully
Your Obdt. Servant
(signed) *Theo. H. Dodd*
U. S. Indian Agent for Navajo Inds.

GLOSSARY

acequia: an irrigation channel or ditch

adobe: a brick of clay and straw; also, a structure built from these

mescal: a plant from which a liquor is made

mesquite: a small hardwood tree or shrub

sutler: a peddler or seller of wares to military field units

Document Analysis

Written on the eve of the 1868 treaty that would end the exile of the Navajos at Bosque Redondo, Theodore H. Dodd's report to Peace Commissioners General William T. Sherman and Colonel Samuel F. Tappan demonstrates both the fact that the Navajos had worked hard to survive in an inhospitable environment and their desire to return to their homelands. Dodd's text mixes facts and figures relating to the activities of the Navajos at the camp, along with his evaluations of the Navajos' state of mind.

Dodd begins by demonstrating that, although the soil is very poor and the water alkaline, the Navajos grew significant crops of corn, wheat, pumpkins, and beans during 1865 and 1866, though the 1867 crop failed due to an insect infestation. He then switches to talking about Navajo families, stating that "[s]ince I have been Agent (nearly three years) I have found that a majority of them living on the reservation are peaceable and well disposed." He notes that the Navajos do work hard, both as day laborers, and as cultivators of their own plots, though Dodd is clear that much of the land at Bosque Redondo is not very productive.

The second half of the report consists of Dodd's reflections on the Navajos' dissatisfaction with life at Bosque Redondo, and his thoughts on more suitable locations for the people. He notes that the Navajos, displeased with the scarcity of wood for fuel, the poor soil and water, and the bad weather, want more than anything to go back to their homelands, where they know where to obtain everything they need, and food and water are in abundance. He is so convinced of their desire to return home that he notes that "if they are not permitted to return to their old country that many will stealthily return and in doing so commit depredations upon the people of N.M. and thus keep up a state of insecurity."

Dodd recommends that the Navajos be placed on a reservation close to a fort, so that those Navajos who are idle (Dodd estimates this at one-third of the population) can be watched. He notes that they will need federal support to feed themselves until they can produce a crop, and importantly recommends that they be given at least 40,000 head of sheep and goats. Though he does not state this explicitly, sheep and goats were the basis of the Navajo economy and much of their identity, and any effort to resettle them—on their homelands or elsewhere—was likely to be easier with the provision of the animals that the Navajos traditionally kept.

Essential Themes

In 1868, Sherman and Tappan negotiated a new treaty with the Navajos and decided on their next move, as it was obvious that the Bosque Redondo experiment had failed. Sherman had hoped to move the Navajos to Indian Territory while Tappan wanted to move them back to their homeland. Once the Navajo delegates had expressed their trepidation at the prospect of going to Indian Territory, the tide turned toward Tappan's position. Once Sherman and Tappan had agreed to return the Navajo to their homelands, it was clear that the government was going to consider farming to be their main occupation, despite the fact that agriculture had largely failed at Bosque Redondo. On June 18, 1868, the Navajo began a second Long Walk—this time back home. They marched in an over ten-mile-long column. Once they arrived, many families were able to return to their former homes and live much as they had before the forced trip east.

As the Navajos already had a background in agriculture and federal policy was already leaning toward forcing Indians into farming as a means of civilizing them, this appeared to be the most practical solution. At the possibility of returning to their homelands, Navajo leader Barboncito expressed the hope that there the Navajos would be able to undertake a stable, agricultural existence. However, after their return from Bosque Redondo, the Navajos rebuilt their communities and economy around sheep and herding. Once settled on their homelands, both the number of Navajos and size of their herds grew steadily. The government even enlarged the Navajo reservation to accommodate the increase of human and animal population. By 1933, the Navajos numbered more than 40,000 and were self-sufficient sheepherders. Issued 14,000 sheep (far less than Dodd's recommendation of 40,000) with which to rebuild their herds in 1868, the Navajos had increased their stock to about 800,000 sheep and goats (21 per capita) by the eve of the Great Depression.

—*Steven L. Danver, PhD*

Bibliography and Additional Reading

Bailey, Lynn R. Bosque Redondo: *The Navajo Internment at Fort Sumner, New Mexico*, 1863–68. Tucson, AZ: Westernlore, 2000. Print.

Denetdale, Jennifer. *The Long Walk: The Forced Navajo Exile*. New York: Chelsea House, 2008. Print.

Iverson, Peter. Diné: *A History of the Navajos*. Albuquerque: U of New Mexico P, 2002. Print.

Kessell, John L. *"General Sherman and the Navajo Treaty of 1868: A Basic and Expedient Misunderstanding,"* Western Historical Quarterly 12 (1981). Print.

Lanehart, David. *"Regaining Dinetah: The Navajo and the Indian Peace Commission at Fort Sumner." Working the Range: Essays on the History of Western Land Management and the Environment*. Ed. John R. Wunder. Westport, CT, Praeger, 1985. Print.

Roessel, Ruth. *Navajo Stories of the Long Walk Period*. Tsaile, AZ: Navajo Community College Press, 1973. Print.

Sundberg, Lawrence D. *Dinétah: An Early History of the Navajo People*. Santa Fe, NM: Sunstone, 1995. Print.

White, Richard. *The Roots of Dependency: Subsistence, Environment, and Social Change among the Choctaws, Pawnees, and Navajos*. Lincoln: University of Nebraska P, 1988. Print.

■ Trouble on the Paiute Reservation

Date: 1888
Author: Sarah Winnemucca
Genre: memoir

Summary Overview

On March 14, 1865, elements of the First Nevada Volunteer Cavalry Battalion, under the command of Captain Almond B. Wells, descended on a Paiute encampment on Mud Lake in the territory's northwestern region while searching for suspected cattle thieves. Although it is unclear who fired the first shot, the action resulted in the death of twenty-nine Natives, most of them women and children. The incident was just one in a long chain of abuses suffered by the Paiute on their Nevada reservation. Corrupt Indian Agents, lack of support and infrastructure, hostile settlers, and an unsympathetic government eager to annex Native lands, made life on the Paiute reservation, and life across all reservations, miserable. The horrid conditions faced by Native peoples in the reservation system was the direct result of government policy, and despite the efforts of reformers and Native advocates, little changed for the better. Terrible conditions persisted throughout the nineteenth and twentieth centuries and, for many Native peoples, continue until this day.

Defining Moment

In the mid-nineteenth century, as settlers raced to conquer the vast continental interior, driven on by a belief in Manifest Destiny, the singular belief that God himself had bequeathed the West to Americans, they invariably came into contact with the Native peoples who already occupied the land. When clashes occurred, as they inevitably did, the US government could then justify sending in the Army to pacify Native peoples, whom they deemed savages, harassing innocent settlers. In this way, the US government could annex large swaths of territory, displacing Native inhabitants, without any obvious criminal or moral consequence. However, the big question was, what to do with Native peoples once they were moved off their lands?

The answer came in the form of reservations, a name derived ironically from the recognition that Na-

tive peoples were independent of US rule. Beginning in 1851, the first reservations were established in what is modern day Oklahoma, in the hopes of containing Native peoples and limiting the violence in the region. However, by the late 1860s, with the Indian Wars raging, inflamed by continued settler encroachment on Native lands, President Ulysses S. Grant established the "Peace Policy." Under this order, the Indian Bureau was reorganized, and new reservations were established, often on land deemed unsuitable for cultivation and usually far from tribal ancestral land. Tribes were ordered to relocate under threat of force and, once on the reservations, subject to reeducation and conversion at the hands of Christian missionaries.

Grant's policy was a complete disaster. Conditions on the reservations were horrible, and widespread corruption among the religious administrators reached epic proportions. Many tribes resisted relocation orders, leading to some of the bloodiest confrontations of the Indian Wars, including the Battle of Little Bighorn. Native American advocates, along with eastern reformers, pushed hard for a reorganization of the Indian Bureau, and in 1887, Congress passed the Dawes Act, which brought Indian affairs back under the supervision of government administrators and reallocated lands to individuals instead of whole tribes. The intent was to dismantle tribal affiliation, thereby speeding the process of "civilizing" Native peoples. The result was a further fragmentation of Native tribes and a further reduction in Native landholdings, sometimes by a significant amount. Life continued to be difficult on reservations for decades to come, and despite attempts at reform in the twentieth century, most Native peoples continue to live in some of the worst conditions in the country.

Author Biography

Sarah Winnemucca was born in what is Nevada in 1844. Shoshone by birth and Paiute by marriage, she was raised among her people but educated settlers. Fluent in English, she traveled extensively and even performed on the stage. After the massacre at Mud Lake, Sarah worked with both the Indian Bureau and the US Army, promoting cooperation and reform, this work then translated into a life of activism. By the 1880s, Winnemucca was travelling widely across the nation, lecturing and speaking on behalf of Native affairs. In 1883, she published the highly regarded book *Life Among the Paiutes*, which not only documented some aspects of tribal culture, but also addressed many of the injustices suffered by her people and shed light on the terrible conditions suffered by Native Americans on reservations. In her later years, Winnemucca returned to the reservation, where she opened a private Indian school. She died from tuberculosis in 1891.

HISTORICAL DOCUMENT

RESERVATION OF PYRAMID AND MUDDY LAKES.

This reservation, given in 1860, was at first sixty miles long and fifteen wide. The line is where the railroad now crosses the river, and it takes in two beautiful lakes, one called Pyramid Lake, and the one on the eastern side, Muddy Lake. No white people lived there at the time it was given us. We Piutes have always lived on the river, because out of those two lakes we caught beautiful mountain trout, weighing from two to twenty-five pounds each, which would give us a good income if we had it all, as at first. Since the railroad ran through in 1867, the white people have taken all the best part of the reservation from us, and one of the lakes also.

The first work that my people did on the reservation was to dig a ditch, to put up a grist-mill and saw-mill. Commencing where the railroad now crosses at Wadsworth, they dug about a mile; but the saw-mill and grist-mill were never seen or heard of by my people, though the printed report in the United States statutes, which my husband found lately in the Boston Athenæum, says twenty-five thousand dollars was appropriated to build them. Where did it go? The report says these mills were sold for the benefit of the Indians who were to be paid in lumber for houses, but no stick of lumber have they ever received. My people do not own any timber land now. The white people are using the ditch which my people made to irrigate their land. This is the way we are treated by our white brothers. Is it that the government is cheated by its own agents who make these reports?

In 1864–5 there was a governor by the name of Nye. There were no whites living on the reservation at that time, and there was not any agent as yet. My people were living there and fishing, as they had always done. Some white men came down from Virginia City to fish. My people went up to Carson City to tell Governor Nye that some white men were fishing on their reservation. He sent down some soldiers to drive them away. Mr. Nye is the only governor who ever helped my people,—I mean that protected them when they called on him in this way. In 1865 we had another trouble with our white brothers. It was early in the spring, and we were then living at Dayton, Nevada, when a company of soldiers came through the place and stopped and spoke to some of my people, and said, "You have been stealing cattle from the white people at Harney Lake." They said also that they would kill everything that came in their way, men, women, and children. The captain's name was Wells. The place where they were going to is about three hundred miles away. The days after they left were very sad hours, indeed. Oh, dear readers, these soldiers had gone only sixty miles away to Muddy Lake, where my people were then living and fishing, and doing nothing to any one. The soldiers rode up to their encampment and fired into it, and killed almost all the people that were there. Oh, it is a fearful thing to tell, but it must be told. Yes, it must be told by me. It was all old men, women and children that were killed; for my father had all the young men with him, at the sink of Carson on a hunting excursion, or they would have been killed too. After the soldiers had killed all but some little children and babies still tied up in their baskets, the soldiers took them also, and set the camp on fire and threw them into the flames to see them burn alive. I had one baby brother killed there. My sister jumped on father's best horse and ran away. As she ran, the soldiers ran after her; but, thanks be to the Good Father in the Spirit-land, my dear sister got away. This almost killed my poor papa. Yet my people kept peaceful.

That same summer another of my men was killed on the reservation. His name was Truckee John. He was an uncle of mine, and was killed by a man named Flamens, who claimed to have had a brother killed in the war of 1860, but of course that had nothing to do with my uncle. About two weeks after this, two white men were killed over at Walker Lake by some of my people, and of course soldiers were sent for from California, and a great many companies came. They went after my people all over Nevada. Reports were made everywhere throughout the whole country by the white settlers, that the red devils were killing their cattle, and by this lying of the white settlers the trail began which is marked by the blood of my people from hill to hill and from valley to valley. The soldiers followed after my people in this way for one year, and the Queen's River Piutes were brought into Fort Churchill, Nevada, and in that campaign poor General McDermit was killed. These reports were only made by those white settlers so that they could sell their grain, which they could not get rid of in any other way. The only way the cattle-men and farmers get to make money is to start an Indian war, so that the troops may come and buy their beef, cattle, horses, and grain. The settlers get fat by it....

Now, dear readers, this is the way all the Indian agents get rich. The first thing they do is to start a store; the next thing is to take in cattle men, and cattle men pay the agent one dollar a head. In this way they get rich very soon, so that they can have their gold-headed canes, with their names engraved on them. The one I am now speaking of is only a sub-agent. He told me the head agent was living in Carson City, and he paid him fifteen hundred dollars a year for the use of the reservation. Yet, he has fine horses and cattle and sheep, and is very rich. The sub-agent was a minister; his name was Balcom. He did not stay very long, because a man named Batemann hired some Indians to go and scare him away from the reservation, that he might take his place. The leader of these Indians was named Dave. He was interpreter at the Pyramid Lake Reservation. So Batemann got the minister away, and then he got rich in the same way....

Dear reader, I must tell a little more about my poor people, and what we suffer at the hands of our white brothers. Since the war of 1860 there have been one hundred and three (103) of my people murdered, and our reservations taken from us; and yet we, who are called blood-seeking savages, are keeping our promises to the government. Oh, my dear good Christian people, how long are you going to stand by and see us suffer at your hands? Oh, dear friends, you are wrong when you say it will take two or three generations to civilize my people. No! I say it will not take that long if you will only take interest in teaching us; and, on the other hand, we shall never be civilized in the way you wish us to be if you keep on sending us such agents as have been sent to us year after year, who do nothing but fill their pockets, and the pockets of their wives and sisters, who are always put in as teachers, and paid from fifty to sixty dollars per month, and yet they do not teach. The farmer is generally his cousin, his pay is nine hundred dollars ($900) a year, and his brother is a clerk. I do not know his name. The blacksmith and carpenter have from five hundred to eleven hundred dollars per year. I got this from their own statements. I saw a discharged agent while I was on my way here, who told me all the agents had to pay so much to the Secretary of the Interior, who had to make up what he paid to the agents. This I know to be a true confession, or the Secretary of the Interior and all the government officers would see into the doings of these Christian agents. Year after year they have been told of their wrong-doings by different tribes of Indians. Yet it goes on, just the same as if they did not know it.

Document Analysis

Sarah Winnemucca begins by detailing life on the reservation before the encroachment of white settlers. By her account life was very good. In fact, it should be noted that Winnemucca is not against the reservation system. On the contrary, she is a proponent of it, but the actions of settlers, Indian agents, and the US Army make things on the reservation less than idyllic.

Tension grows quickly in Winnemucca's account.

Corruption and theft quickly escalate into violence. Winnemucca recalls with obvious pain the events at Mud Lake in 1865, where a group of American soldiers massacred twenty-nine of her people, mainly women and children. She paints a horrific scene, in which those who weren't shot were thrown alive into bonfires. After the massacre, there is more violence against Native peoples. In all, over 100 are killed. The Paiute were relocated and put under the military supervision. Harsh treatment followed. Her account is typical of the experience of most Native peoples during the latter half of the nineteenth century. Dispossessed, constantly harassed by the Army and settlers driven both by racism and greed, Native peoples had to walk a fine line. To resist often meant violence and massacre, but to submit often meant an invitation for abuse and exploitation.

Winnemucca spends a good amount of time cataloguing the corruption of the Indian agents that administered the reservation. Money trades hands. Ranchers pay Indian agents to use reservation land for grazing. Farmers pay Indian agents money to use reservation land for cultivation. Deals are struck. The needs of Native people are ignored. It is interesting to consider what may occur when cattle grazing on reservation land stray too far or simply wander off. Would the Paiute then be accused of theft? If so, the Army would be called in to pacify the troublemakers, and if things escalated, the misunderstanding would likely become violent. Were these the circumstances that led to the massacre at Mud Lake?

Winnemucca is most skilled in the tact she uses to bring the abuses against her people to the attention of her white audience. She does not condemn the American people, the government, not even the Army or the reservation system, but instead focuses all her attention on just a handful of corrupt individuals. She tells her reader, who she addresses as "good Christian people," that only a few scheming, immoral officials are at fault. By framing her argument in this way, she is able to call for reform and stir sympathy, while also assuaging the guilt of her audience, thus eliminating the possibility of resentment. Furthermore, she appeals to Victorian notions of white superiority, by arguing that the real tragedy of the corruption that abounds in the Indian reservation system is not necessarily the violence and suffering, but the lack of civilizing progress. We could be like you, Winnemucca pleads, if you were just to teach us.

Essential Themes

The development and administration of the reservation system was a failure on the part of the United States government and a tragedy for Native peoples. The result of an unofficial policy of land acquisition and annexation, reservations were little more than holding pens for cultures deemed too savage to continue. Settlers, driving further west were often encouraged, even by the very officials who were tasked with protecting

Native interests, to encroach on reservation lands and help fuel the violence that would inevitably erupt. As a result, reformers and activists like Sarah Winnemucca had to walk a fine line, to openly advocate for their people, speaking out against the abuse of Native Americans, while also avoid assigning guilt on the system and society that made it happen. Specifically by appealing to notions of Social Darwinism, arguing that only through the gentle guidance of white civilization could Native peoples ever escape savagery, she and others pushed for sweeping changes to the reservations and the government agencies tasked with their administration. The immediate result of such efforts was the Dawes Act, which, although it did help eliminate some corruption by putting administrative control back in government hands, it also hastened the further destruction of Native cultures. By identifying tribal group affiliation as the primary hurdle in "civilizing" Native peoples, and encouraging greater individual autonomy through land redistribution and incentives toward assimilation into mainstream society, the Dawes Act had the effect of greatly diminishing Native landholdings and further reducing tribal populations. In 1934, as part of Franklin D. Roosevelt's New Deal, an attempt was made to address some of the largest issues in the reservation system. Millions of dollars in public aid were funneled into construction of schools, healthcare facilities, and infrastructure improvements on Native lands. However, this reform effort was short lived, and within a decade, policy shifted back to old attitudes, resulting in a new effort to eliminate tribal groups once and for all. Although some Native peoples are doing better today, thanks in large part to the legalization of gambling on reservation land, most Native Americans still suffer. In fact, rates of poverty, malnutrition, substance abuse, and infant mortality, are among the highest in the nation, not dissimilar to those in the developing world.

—KP Dawes, MA

Bibliography and Additional Reading

Brown, Dee. *Bury My Heart at Wounded Knee*. 1970. New York: Holt, 2007. Print.

Dunbar-Ortiz, Roxanne. *An Indigenous Peoples' History of the United States*. Boston: Beacon P, 2014. Print.

Greenwald, Emily. *Reconfiguring the Reservation: The Nez Perces, Jicarilla Apaches, and the Dawes Act*. Albuquerque: U of New Mexico P, 2002. Print.

Truer, David. *Rez Life*. New York: Atlantic Monthly P, 2012. Print.

■ Treaty of Fort Laramie

Date: April 29, 1868
Authors: William T. Sherman, et al.
Genre: law; legislation

Summary Overview

From the beginning of European colonization in the Americas, conflict with the American Indian tribes that inhabited the land was constant. As Americans spread into the western frontier in the nineteenth century, that conflict increased, especially when the trails that immigrants took to the West passed through territory inhabited by Indians. In 1868, the federal government sent out a peace commission, whose job it was to sign treaties with the tribes in order to facilitate their move onto reservations, out of the way of settlement. One of the groups that had proven most troublesome to settlers was the Lakota Sioux, led by Red Cloud. During the years 1866–68, Red Cloud had fought against the US Army because the government had blazed the Bozeman Trail through Lakota hunting grounds without permission. In spring 1868, a treaty conference was held at Fort Laramie, Wyoming Territory, to end the war and convince the Lakota to settle on the reservation in Dakota Territory.

Defining Moment

After the Civil War concluded in 1865, many Americans headed west, as the construction of railroads and the passage of the Homestead Act in 1863 had made establishing a farm an attractive option for many living in the East. At the same time, the discovery of gold in Montana started a rush of people looking to come west to find their fortunes. This influx of settlers meant that more and more Americans were passing through territory used by Indian tribes, such as the Sioux tribes and the Arapaho. From 1865 to 1867, a congressional committee studied the so-called Indian problem and recommended that a peace commission be sent out to negotiate treaties that would result in the Indian tribes being confined to reservations in order to allow non-Indian settlement to proceed unimpeded.

While this was happening, the Montana gold rush was beckoning settlers up the Bozeman Trail, through the Sioux and Arapaho hunting grounds near the Powder River in north-central Wyoming. During the 1850s, mountain man Jim Bridger had warned that a trail through the region was a bad idea, but in 1863, John Bozeman, acting with the approval of the federal government, blazed a trail directly through the Powder River Basin. The tensions heightened with the news that Colonel John M. Chivington's troops had massacred about 150 Arapaho and Cheyenne peacefully camped on Sand Creek in Colorado Territory in November 1864.

Warfare began in the region with the Sioux, Cheyenne, and Arapaho warriors attacking Platte Bridge Station in June 1865, killing twenty-six American troops. Three columns under the command of Brigadier General Patrick Connor were dispatched, but arrived at what they dubbed Fort Connor in poor condition and demoralized by their trip through the Dakota Territory's Badlands. In 1866, the federal government called for a peace conference at Fort Laramie, but at the same time sent Colonel Henry B. Carrington with 1,300 troops, which only angered Red Cloud and convinced him to continue fighting. In December, Red Cloud and war leader Crazy Horse defeated Captain William J. Fetterman and his eighty troops, but the following summer saw a change in the Sioux fortunes, as the US troops were outfitted with new quick-firing breech-loading rifles. After a number of poor showings, Red Cloud and his people agreed to meet with the peace commission, under the leadership of General William T. Sherman, at Fort Laramie.

For the Sioux tribes, the central point of the treaty would be that they would be allowed to settle in the Black Hills of the Dakota Territory. To the Sioux, there is no more sacred spot on earth than the Black Hills. For the federal government, the central point of the treaty would be that peace would be established and the Sioux and other tribes would not be able to leave their reservations, thus allowing western immigration to continue.

Author Biography

General William Tecumseh Sherman, the hero of the Civil War March to the Sea, was commander of the Missouri District, encompassing the region between the Mississippi River and the Rocky Mountains, after the war. He was convinced that the only practical policy of the United States toward Native American peoples was to confine them all to reservations and make war against any Indians that dared leave. As the highest pro-file member of the peace commission that had negotiated the Medicine Lodge Treaty of 1867 and was now sent to make peace with Red Cloud at Fort Laramie, the influence of Sherman's ideas is plainly visible in the treaty, with its strict conditions that the Sioux remain on their reservation in the Dakota Territory and no longer venture into their former hunting grounds or otherwise disrupt the continued immigration of easterners and that the Sioux be assimilated through education of children in boarding schools and conversion to Christianity.

HISTORICAL DOCUMENT

ARTICLES OF A TREATY MADE AND CONCLUDED BY AND BETWEEN

Lieutenant General William T. Sherman, General William S. Harney, General Alfred H. Terry, General O. O. Augur, J. B. Henderson, Nathaniel G. Taylor, John G. Sanborn, and Samuel F. Tappan, duly appointed commissioners on the part of the United States, and the different bands of the Sioux Nation of Indians, by their chiefs and headmen, whose names are hereto subscribed, they being duly authorized to act in the premises.

ARTICLE I.
From this day forward all war between the parties to this agreement shall for ever cease. The government of the United States desires peace, and its honor is hereby pledged to keep it. The Indians desire peace, and they now pledge their honor to maintain it.

If bad men among the whites, or among other people subject to the authority of the United States, shall commit any wrong upon the person or property of the Indians, the United States will, upon proof made to the agent, and forwarded to the Commissioner of Indian Affairs at Washington city, proceed at once to cause the offender to be arrested and punished according to the laws of the United States, and also reimburse the injured person for the loss sustained.

If bad men among the Indians shall commit a wrong or depredation upon the person or property of nay one, white, black, or Indian, subject to the authority of the United States, and at peace therewith, the Indians herein named solemnly agree that they will, upon proof made to their agent, and notice by him, deliver up the wrongdoer to the United States, to be tried and punished according to its laws, and, in case they willfully refuse so to do, the person injured shall be reimbursed for his loss from the annuities, or other moneys due or to become due to them under this or other treaties made with the United States; and the President, on advising with the Commissioner of Indian Affairs, shall prescribe such rules and regulations for ascertaining damages under the provisions of this article as in his judgment may be proper, but no one sustaining loss while violating the provisions of this treaty, or the laws of the United States, shall be reimbursed therefor.

ARTICLE II.
The United States agrees that the following district of country, to wit, viz: commencing on the east bank of the Missouri river where the 46th parallel of north latitude crosses the same, thence along low-water mark down said east bank to a point opposite where the northern line of the State of Nebraska strikes the river, thence west across said river, and along the northern line of Nebraska to the 104th degree of longitude west from Greenwich, thence north on said meridian to a point where the 46th parallel of north latitude intercepts the same, thence due east along said parallel to the place of beginning; and in addition thereto, all existing reservations of the east back of said river, shall be and the same is, set apart for

the absolute and undisturbed use and occupation of the Indians herein named, and for such other friendly tribes or individual Indians as from time to time they may be willing, with the consent of the United States, to admit amongst them; and the United States now solemnly agrees that no persons, except those herein designated and authorized so to do, and except such officers, agents, and employees of the government as may be authorized to enter upon Indian reservations in discharge of duties enjoined by law, shall ever be permitted to pass over, settle upon, or reside in the territory described in this article, or in such territory as may be added to this reservation for the use of said Indians, and henceforth they will and do hereby relinquish all claims or right in and to any portion of the United States or Territories, except such as is embraced within the limits aforesaid, and except as hereinafter provided.

ARTICLE III.

If it should appear from actual survey or other satisfactory examination of said tract of land that it contains less than 160 acres of tillable land for each person who, at the time, may be authorized to reside on it under the provisions of this treaty, and a very considerable number of such persons hsall be disposed to comence cultivating the soil as farmers, the United States agrees to set apart, for the use of said Indians, as herein provided, such additional quantity of arable land, adjoining to said reservation, or as near to the same as it can be obtained, as may be required to provide the necessary amount.

ARTICLE IV.

The United States agrees, at its own proper expense, to construct, at some place on the Missouri river, near the centre of said reservation where timber and water may be convenient, the following buildings, to wit, a warehouse, a store-room for the use of the agent in storing goods belonging to the Indians, to cost not less than $2,500; an agency building, for the residence of the agent, to cost not exceeding $3,000; a residence for the physician, to cost not more than $3,000; and five other buildings, for a carpenter, farmer, blacksmith, miller, and engineer-each to cost not exceeding $2,000; also, a school-house, or mission building, so soon as a sufficient number of children can be induced by the agent to attend school, which

shall not cost exceeding $5,000.

The United States agrees further to cause to be erected on said reservation, near the other buildings herein authorized, a good steam circular saw-mill, with a grist-mill and shingle machine attached to the same, to cost not exceeding $8,000.

ARTICLE V.

The United States agrees that the agent for said Indians shall in the future make his home at the agency building; that he shall reside among them, and keep an office open at all times for the purpose of prompt and diligent inquiry into such matters of complaint by and against the Indians as may be presented for investigation under the provisions of their treaty stipulations, as also for the faithful discharge of other duties enjoined on him by law. In all cases of depredation on person or property he shall cause the evidence to be taken in writing and forwarded, together with his findings, to the Commissioner of Indian Affairs, whose decision, subject to the revision of the Secretary of the Interior, shall be binding on the parties to this treaty.

ARTICLE VI.

If any individual belonging to said tribes of Indians, or legally incorporated with them, being the head of a family, shall desire to commence farming, he shall have the privilege to select, in the presence and with the assistance of the agent then in charge, a tract of land within said reservation, not exceeding three hundred and twenty acres in extent, which tract, when so selected, certified, and recorded in the "Land Book" as herein directed, shall cease to be held in common, but the same may be occupied and held in the exclusive possession of the person selecting it, and of his family, so long as he or they may continue to cultivate it.

Any person over eighteen years of age, not being the head of a family, may in like manner select and cause to be certified to him or her, for purposes of cultivation, a quantity of land, not exceeding eighty acres in extent, and thereupon be entitled to the exclusive possession of the same as above directed.

For each tract of land so selected a certificate, containing a description thereof and the name of the person selecting it, with a certificate endorsed thereon that the same has been recorded, shall be delivered to the party entitled to it, by the agent, after the same shall have been recorded by him in a book to be kept in his office, subject to inspection, which said book shall be known as the "Sioux Land Book."

The President may, at any time, order a survey of the reservation, and, when so surveyed, Congress shall provide for protecting the rights of said settlers in their improvements, and may fix the character of the title held by each. The United States may pass such laws on the subject of alienation and descent of property between the Indians and their descendants as may be thought proper. And it is further stipulated that any male Indians over eighteen years of age, of any band or tribe that is or shall hereafter become a party to this treaty, who now is or who shall hereafter become a resident or occupant of any reservation or territory not included in the tract of country designated and described in this treaty for the permanent home of the Indians, which is not mineral land, nor reserved by the United States for special purposes other than Indian occupation, and who shall have made improvements thereon of the value of two hundred dollars or more, and continuously occupied the same as a homestead for the term of three years, shall be entitled to receive from the United States a patent for one hundred and sixty acres of land including his said improvements, the same to be in the form of the legal subdivisions of the surveys of the public lands. Upon application in writing, sustained by the proof of two disinterested witnesses, made to the register of the local land office when the land sought to be entered is within a land district, and when the tract sought to be entered is not in any land district, then upon said application and proof being made to the Commissioner of the General Land Office, and the right of such Indian or Indians to enter such tract or tracts of land shall accrue and be perfect from the date of his first improvements thereon, and shall continue as long as be continues his residence and improvements and no longer. And any Indian or Indians receiving a patent for land under the foregoing provisions shall thereby and from thenceforth become and be a citizen of the United States and be entitled to all the privileges and immunities of such citizens, and shall, at the same time, retain all his rights to benefits accruing to Indians under this treaty.

ARTICLE VII.

In order to insure the civilization of the Indians entering into this treaty, the necessity of education is admitted, especially of such of them as are or may be settled on said agricultural reservations, and they, therefore, pledge themselves to compel their children, male and female, between the ages of six and sixteen years, to attend school, and it is hereby made the duty of the agent for said Indians to see that this stipulation is strictly complied with; and the United States agrees that for every thirty children between said ages, who can be induced or compelled to attend school, a house shall be provided, and a teacher competent to teach the elementary branches of an English education shall be furnished, who will reside among said Indians and faithfully discharge his or her duties as a teacher. The provisions of this article to continue for not less than twenty years.

ARTICLE VIII.

When the head of a family or lodge shall have selected lands and received his certificate as above directed, and the agent shall be satisfied that he intends in good faith to commence cultivating the soil for a living, he shall be entitled to receive seeds and agricultural implements for the first year, not exceeding in value one hundred dollars, and for each succeeding year he shall continue to farm, for a period of three years more, he shall be entitled to receive seeds and implements as aforesaid, not exceeding in value twenty-five dollars. And it is further stipulated that such persons as commence farming shall receive instruction from the farmer herein provided for, and whenever more than one hundred persons shall enter upon the cultivation of the soil, a second blacksmith shall be provided, with such iron, steel, and other material as may be needed.

ARTICLE IX.

At any time after ten years for the making of this treaty, the United States shall have the privilege of withdrawing the physician, farmer, blacksmith, carpenter, engineer, and miller herein provided for, but in case of such withdrawal, an additional sum thereafter of ten thousand dollars per annum shall be devoted to the education of said Indians, and the Commissioner of Indian Affairs shall, upon careful inquiry into their condition, make such rules and regulations for the expenditure of said sums as will best promote the education and moral improvement of said tribes.

ARTICLE X.

In lieu of all sums of money or other annuities provided to be paid to the Indians herein named under any treaty or treaties heretofore made, the United States agrees to deliver at the agency house on the reservation herein named, on or before the first day of August of each year, for thirty years, the following articles, to wit:

For each male person over 14 years of age, a suit of good substantial woollen clothing, consisting of coat, pantaloons, flannel shirt, hat, and a pair of home-made socks.

For each female over 12 years of age, a flannel shirt, or the goods necessary to make it, a pair of woollen hose, 12 yards of calico, and 12 yards of cotton domestics.

For the boys and girls under the ages named, such flannel and cotton goods as may be needed to make each a suit as aforesaid, together with a pair of woollen hose for each.

And in order that the Commissioner of Indian Affairs may be able to estimate properly for the articles herein named, it shall be the duty of the agent each year to forward to him a full and exact census of the Indians, on which the estimate from year to year can be based.

And in addition to the clothing herein named, the sum of $10 for each person entitled to the beneficial effects of this treaty shall be annually appropriated for a period of 30 years, while such persons roam and hunt, and $20 for each person who engages in farming, to be used by the Secretary of the Interior in the purchase of such articles as from time to time the condition and necessities of the Indians may indicate to be proper. And if within the 30 years, at any time, it shall appear that the amount of money needed for clothing, under this article, can be appropriated to better uses for the Indians named herein, Congress may, by law, change the appropriation to other purposes, but in no event shall the amount of the appropriation be withdrawn or discontinued for the period named. And the President shall annually detail an officer of the army to be present and attest the delivery of all the goods herein named, to the Indians, and he shall inspect and report on the quantity and quality of the goods and the manner of their delivery. And it is hereby expressly stipulated that each Indian over the age of four years, who shall have removed to and settled permanently upon said reservation, one pound of meat and one pound of flour per day, provided the Indians cannot furnish their own subsistence at an earlier date. And it is further stipulated that the United States will furnish and deliver to each lodge of Indians or family of persons legally incorporated with the, who shall remove to the reservation herein described and commence farming, one good American cow, and one good well-broken pair of American oxen within 60 days after such lodge or family shall have so settled upon said reservation.

ARTICLE XI.

In consideration of the advantages and benefits conferred by this treaty and the many pledges of friendship by the United States, the tribes who are parties to this agreement hereby stipulate that they will relinquish all right to occupy permanently the territory outside their reservations as herein defined, but yet reserve the right to hunt on any lands north of North Platte, and on the Republican Fork of the Smoky Hill river, so long as the buffalo may range thereon in such numbers as to justify the chase. And they, the said Indians, further expressly agree:

1st. That they will withdraw all opposition to the construction of the railroads now being built on the plains.

2d. That they will permit the peaceful construction of any railroad not passing over their reservation as herein defined.

3d. That they will not attack any persons at home, or travelling, nor molest or disturb any wagon trains, coaches, mules, or cattle belonging to the people of the United States, or to persons friendly therewith.

4th. They will never capture, or carry off from the settlements, white women or children.

5th. They will never kill or scalp white men, nor attempt to do them harm.

6th. They withdraw all pretence of opposition to the construction of the railroad now being built along the Platte river and westward to the Pacific ocean, and they will not in future object to the construction of railroads, wagon roads, mail stations, or other works of utility or necessity, which may be ordered or permitted by the laws of the United States. But should such roads or other works be constructed on the lands of their reservation, the government will pay the tribe whatever amount of damage may be assessed by three disinterested commissioners to be appointed by the President for that purpose, one of the said commissioners to be a chief or headman of the tribe.

7th. They agree to withdraw all opposition to the military posts or roads now established south of the North Platte river, or that may be established, not in violation of treaties heretofore made or hereafter to be made with any of the Indian tribes.

ARTICLE XII.

No treaty for the cession of any portion or part of the reservation herein described which may be held in common, shall be of any validity or force as against the said Indians unless executed and signed by at least three-fourths of all the adult male Indians occupying or interested in the same, and no cession by the tribe shall be understood or construed in such manner as to deprive, without his consent, any individual member of the tribe of his rights to any tract of land selected by him as provided in Article VI of this treaty.

ARTICLE XIII.

The United States hereby agrees to furnish annually to the Indians the physician, teachers, carpenter, miller, engineer, farmer, and blacksmiths, as herein contemplated, and that such appropriations shall be made from time to time, on the estimate of the Secretary of the Interior, as will be sufficient to employ such persons.

ARTICLE XIV.

It is agreed that the sum of five hundred dollars annually for three years from date shall be expended in presents to the ten persons of said tribe who in the judgment of the agent may grow the most valuable crops for the respective year.

ARTICLE XV.

The Indians herein named agree that when the agency house and other buildings shall be constructed on the reservation named, they will regard said reservation their permanent home, and they will make no permanent settlement elsewhere; but they shall have the right, subject to the conditions and modifications of this treaty, to hunt, as stipulated in Article XI hereof.

ARTICLE XVI.

The United States hereby agrees and stipulates that the country north of the North Platte river and east of the summits of the Big Horn mountains shall be held and considered to be unceded. Indian territory, and also stipulates and agrees that no white person or persons shall be permitted to settle upon or occupy any portion of the same; or without the consent of the Indians, first had and obtained, to pass through the same; and it is further agreed by the United States, that within ninety days after the conclusion of peace with all the bands of the Sioux nation, the military posts now established in the territory in this article named shall be abandoned, and that the road leading to them and by them to the settlements in the Territory of Montana shall be closed.

ARTICLE XVII.

It is hereby expressly understood and agreed by and between the respective parties to this treaty that the execution of this treaty and its ratification by the United States Senate shall have the effect, and shall be construed as abrogating and annulling all treaties and agreements heretofore entered into between the respective parties hereto, so far as such treaties and agreements obligate the United States to furnish and provide money, clothing, or other articles of property to such Indians and bands of Indians as become parties to this treaty, but no further.

In testimony of all which, we, the said commissioners, and we, the chiefs and headmen of the Brule band of the Sioux nation, have hereunto set our hands and seals at Fort Laramie, Dakota Territory, this twenty-ninth day of April, in the year one thousand eight hundred and sixty-eight.

Document Analysis

Written on April 29, 1868 and signed by the Ogallala Lakota on May 25, 1868, the Treaty of Fort Laramie, which ended Red Cloud's War and established the Great Sioux Reservation in Dakota Territory, set forth the terms under which the Ogallala Lakota Sioux, along with the Arapaho, Brulé Sioux, Miniconjou Sioux, Yanctonais Sioux, would settle on the reservation and promise not to leave nor make war against the US Army or settlers who were coming across into what had been their territory.

The treaty sought to guarantee peace between the United States and the tribes by setting forth the reservation's boundaries; encouraging the Indians to take up settled agriculture by guaranteeing individual Indians land; and promising the establishment of an agency to oversee the following: the reservation, a school and other facilities, distribution of the annual goods and cash annuity for the next thirty years, and the provision that Indian children be compelled to attend school and receive agricultural instruction. In return, the Indians agreed: not to oppose the construction of railroads across the Plains, so long as they did not cross their reservation; not to attack any settlers proceeding west; not to kidnap white women or children or scalp or otherwise harm white men; and not to oppose the presence of military forts south of the North Platte River.

The Great Sioux Reservation, which encompassed nearly the entire western half of present-day South Dakota and included the sacred Black Hills, was guaranteed to the Sioux tribes forever. The treaty gave the Sioux a degree of sovereignty, with the federal government promising that nobody "shall ever be permitted to pass over, settle upon, or reside in [this] country." Additionally, any lands in the Great Sioux Reservation could not be sold unless the sale was approved by three-fourths of the adult men of the tribes. Any Indians or non-Indians who violated the terms of the treaty were to be arrested and punished. However, it also took away much of the autonomy the Sioux had always prized, as they now could not leave the reservation without being subject to warfare at the hands of the US Army, and they now promised "to compel their children, male and female, between the ages of six and sixteen years, to attend school." Further, the treaty mandated that nearly all of the Sioux would engage in settled agriculture, which was nearly the antithesis of their prior semi-nomadic, hunting-based culture.

Essential Themes

The Fort Laramie Treaty of 1868 had an impact largely because of the events that followed. Though the Lakota and other tribes settled on the reservation, it only took until the discovery of gold in the Black Hills for the terms of the treaty to be ignored by the federal government. Six years after the treaty was signed, reports of gold in the Black Hills began to filter through to Washington, DC. In response, the US Army sent Lieutenant Colonel George Armstrong Custer with an expedition to find out for sure. When Custer's expedition verified the stories, a gold rush was on—into Sioux territory. The non-Indian miners demanded the protection of the Army from the people whose lands they were now invading.

As of January 1, 1876, the federal government declared any Sioux bands off of the reservation to be hostile, including the band headed by Sitting Bull and war leader Cr, and sent Custer and his Seventh Cavalry to intercept them. The resulting Battle of the Little Bighorn on June 25, 1876 saw the death of Custer and the vast majority of his men in one of the greatest Sioux victories over the US Army. However the resultant national outrage over the "massacre" of Custer and his men led to a resolve on the part of the Army to make sure all Sioux were confined to the reservation.

The federal government sent a treaty commission to attempt to negotiate for the sale of the Black Hills, but only 10 percent of Sioux adults—far short of the Treaty of Fort Laramie's stipulation of 75 percent—agreed. However, Congress took unilateral action and seized the Black Hills in 1877. It was not until nearly 100 years later that the US Supreme Court upheld the Sioux claim that the Black Hills were taken by the federal government in bad faith. Though the federal government has offered monetary reparation for the seizure of the Black Hills, the Sioux have declined, insisting upon their return. This seems unlikely, however, given the presence of Mount Rushmore National Memorial in their midst.

—*Steven L. Danver, PhD*

Bibliography and Additional Reading

Brown, Dee. Bury My Heart at Wounded Knee: An Indian History of the American West. New York: Bantam, 1970. Print.

Prucha, Francis Paul. American Indian Treaties: The History of a Political Anomaly. Berkeley: U of California P, 1994. Print.

_____. The Great Father: The United States Government and the American Indians. Lincoln: U of Nebraska P, 1984. Print.

Wilkinson, Charles F. American Indians, Time, and the Law: Native Societies in a Modern Constitutional Democracy. New Haven, CT: Yale UP, 1987. Print.

■ Accounts of the Battle of Little Bighorn

Date: July 4, 1876
Author: W. H. Norton; Chief Red Horse
Genre: articles; testimony

Summary Overview

On June 25, 1876, elements of the Seventh Cavalry led by the famed Civil War hero and Indian fighter George Armstrong Custer attacked a combined force of Lakota, Northern Cheyenne, and Arapaho near the Little Bighorn River in Montana Territory. As a result, and much to the shock of a nation just about to celebrate its centennial, five of twelve companies of the Seventh Cavalry were completely wiped out, while Custer himself, along with two of his brothers, a nephew, and a brother-in-law were killed. For the average American living East of the country, the Battle of Little Bighorn, or what soon became popularly known as Custer's Last Stand, hit like a thunderbolt. The event became a rallying cry, Custer a myth, a symbol of white America's brave resilience against dark savagery. For Native Americans, the Battle of Little Bighorn became one of the last in a series of long and bloody, but ultimately futile struggles against the encroachment of white settlers on their land.

Defining Moment

Since the purchase of the Louisiana Territory at the turn of the nineteenth century, white settlers had been moving onto the Great Plains, first in a trickle and soon in a flood. Encouraged by boosters, government officials, and land speculators, millions of Americans moved West in the hopes of making a new start. As white settlers moved in, they invariably came into direct conflict with Native peoples. These clashes culminated in a series of armed conflicts collectively known as the Sioux Wars. Fighting raged throughout the 1850s and 1860s as the Sioux and their allies tried desperately to defend themselves against an increasingly brutal campaign of displacement. Things did settle for a time in 1868, after the Treaty of Fort Laramie guaranteed to the Lakota a large portion of South Dakota Territory, but the discovery of gold in the sacred Black Hills, followed by an influx of miners eager to strike it rich, brought the tribes once again into open conflict with the United States government.

Enter George Armstrong Custer. Graduating at the bottom of his class from West Point just as the Civil War broke out, Custer quickly distinguished himself as a brave, flamboyant, but highly capable cavalry commander. Always at the front of his troops, leading charges through some of the bloodiest battles of the war, Custer was never once injured. As a result, the national press regarded him as a sort of sainted warrior. With the close of the Civil War, Custer was assigned to command the Seventh Cavalry and plunged right into the expanding conflict against the Native peoples of the Great Plains.

In 1868, Custer led a series of brutal attacks on the Cheyenne and Arapaho, including the massacre of a village full of unarmed women and children. Custer's brazen actions earned him accolades in the press, which depicted him as an Indian fighter, but this also had the unintended effect of unifying many of the Plains tribes under the leadership of Sitting Bull, a fearless Lakota chief determined to ignore the stipulations of any treaty. In direct response to Sitting Bull, President Ulysses S. Grant issued an ultimatum that any Native peoples who refused to settle on a reservation by 1876 would be considered hostile.

With orders to find Sitting Bull's band and force them onto the reservation, Custer and the Seventh Cavalry headed out west in the spring of 1876. Without waiting for the rest of his regiment, headstrong and eager to make headlines in time for the centennial, Custer launched a blind attack on what he thought was a small Lakota village on the bank of the Little Bighorn River, but this apparent village was in fact several large Lakota, Northern Cheyenne, and Arapaho encampments, home to thousands of armed Native warriors. The resulting battle quickly became a rout and, ultimately, a massacre, as Custer's outnumbered men tried desperately to fall back. Two hundred sixty-eight men, along with George Armstrong Custer were killed. Within days, newspaper headlines screamed about the loss of Custer and the Seventh Cavalry, painting Custer in the immediate aftermath with a hero's brush. The story became that of a great American warrior's last stand, as he fought off savage Indians, while the version of events told by the Native peoples—a story of survival—was almost completely ignored.

Author Biography

While we know nothing about the writer of the *Helena Daily Herald* article, W. H. Norton, we do know something about Chief Red Horse. Born in 1822 to a subdivision of the Sioux, he rose to become one of the chiefs under Sitting Bull. An eyewitness to the Battle of Little Bighorn, having taken part in fighting against both Custer and Marcus Reno, Custer's second in command, Red Horse recorded his recollections of the event in 1881. He died in 1907 on a reservation, having, like most of the Sitting Bull's Sioux, eventually surrendered to an aggressive US Army, eager to avenge their fallen hero.

HISTORICAL DOCUMENT

HELENA DAILY HERALD EXTRA
July 4, 1876
A TERRIBLE FIGHT

Gen. Custer and his Nephew KILLED
The Seventh Cavalry cut to pieces
The Whole Number Killed 315
From our Special Correspondent Mr. W. H. Norton
Stillwater, M. T., July 2nd, 1876.

Muggins Taylor, scout for Gen. Gibbons, got here last night, direct from Little Horn River with telegraphic despatches [dispatches]. General Custer found the Indian camp of about two thousand lodges on the Little Horn, and immediately attacked the camp. Custer took five companies and charged the thickest portion of the camp.

Nothing is Known of the Operation of this detachment, only as they trace it by the dead. Major Reno commanded the other seven companies and attacked the lower portion of the camp. The Indians poured in a murderous fire from all directions. Besides the greater portion fought on horseback. Custer, his two brothers, a nephew and a brother-in-law were All Killed and not one of his detachment escaped. 207 men were buried in one place and the killed are estimated at 300 with only 31 wounded. The Indians surrounded Reno's command and held them one day in the hills

Cut Off from Water until Gibbon's command came in sight, when they broke camp in the night and left.

The Seventh Fought Like Tigers and were overcome by mere brute force. The Indian loss cannot be estimated, as they bore off and cached most of their killed. The remnant of the Seventh Cavalry and Gibbon's command are returning to the mouth of the I Little Horn, where the steamboat lies. The Indians got all the arms of the killed soldiers. There were seventeen commissioned officers killed.

The Whole Custer Family died at the head of their column. The exact loss is not known as both Adjutants and the Sergeant Major were killed. The Indian camp was from three to four miles long and was twenty miles up the Little Horn from its mouth. The Indians actually pulled men off their horses in some instances. I give this as Taylor told me, as he was over the field after the battle.

The above is confirmed by other letters which say Custer met a fearful disaster.

* * *

[Chief Red Horse (Lakota)]
Five springs ago I, with many Sioux Indians, took down and packed up our tipis and moved from Cheyenne river to the Rosebud river, where we camped a few days; then took down and packed up our lodges and moved to the Little Bighorn river and pitched our lodges with the large camp of Sioux.

The Sioux were camped on the Little Bighorn river as follows: The lodges of the Uncpapas were pitched highest up the river under a bluff. The Santee lodges were pitched next. The Oglala's lodges were pitched next. The Brule lodges were pitched next. The Minneconjou lodges were pitched next. The Sans Arcs' lodges were pitched next. The Blackfeet lodges were pitched next. The Cheyenne lodges were pitched next. A few Arikara Indians were among the Sioux (being without lodges of their own). Two-Kettles, among the other Sioux (without lodges).

I was a Sioux chief in the council lodge. My lodge was pitched in the center of the camp. The day of the attack I and four women were a short distance from the camp digging wild turnips. Suddenly one of the women attracted my attention to a cloud of dust rising a short distance from camp. I soon saw that the soldiers were charging the camp. To the camp I and the women ran. When I arrived a person told me to hurry to the council lodge. The soldiers charged so quickly we could not talk (council). We came out of the council lodge and talked in all directions. The Sioux mount horses, take guns, and go fight the soldiers. Women and children mount horses and go, meaning to get out of the way.

Among the soldiers was an officer who rode a horse with four white feet. [This officer was evidently Capt. French, Seventh Cavalry.] The Sioux have for a long time fought many brave men of different people, but the Sioux say this officer was the bravest man they had ever fought. I don't know whether this was Gen. Custer or not. Many of the Sioux men that I hear talking tell me it was. I saw this officer in the fight many times, but did not see his body. It has been told me that he was killed by a Santee Indian, who took his horse. This officer wore a large-brimmed hat and a deerskin coat. This officer saved the lives of many soldiers by turning his horse and covering the retreat. Sioux say this officer was the bravest man they ever fought. I saw two officers looking alike, both having long yellowish hair.

Before the attack the Sioux were camped on the Rosebud river. Sioux moved down a river running into the Little Bighorn river, crossed the Little Bighorn river, and camped on its west bank.

This day [day of attack] a Sioux man started to go to Red Cloud agency, but when he had gone a short distance from camp he saw a cloud of dust rising and turned back and said he thought a herd of buffalo was coming near the village.

The day was hot. In a short time the soldiers charged the camp. [This was Maj. Reno's battalion of the Seventh Cavalry.] The soldiers came on the trail made by the Sioux camp in moving, and crossed the Little Bighorn river above where the Sioux crossed, and attacked the lodges of the Uncpapas, farthest up the river. The women and children ran down the Little Bighorn river a short distance into a ravine. The soldiers set fire to the lodges. All the Sioux now charged the soldiers and drove them in confusion across the Little Bighorn river, which was very rapid, and several soldiers were drowned in it. On a hill the soldiers stopped and the Sioux surrounded them. A Sioux man came and said that a different party of Soldiers had all the women and children prisoners. Like a whirlwind the word went around, and the Sioux all heard it and left the soldiers on the hill and went quickly to save the women and children.

From the hill that the soldiers were on to the place where the different soldiers [by this term, Red Horse always means the battalion immediately commanded by General Custer, his mode of distinction being that they were a different body from that first encountered] were seen was level ground with the exception of a creek. Sioux thought the soldiers on the hill [i.e., Reno's battalion] would charge them in rear, but when they did not the Sioux thought the soldiers on the hill were out of cartridges. As soon as we had killed all the different soldiers the Sioux all went back to kill the soldiers on the hill. All the Sioux watched around the hill on which were the soldiers until a Sioux man came and said many walking soldiers were coming near. The coming of the walking soldiers was the saving of the soldiers on the hill. Sioux can not fight the walking soldiers [infantry], being afraid of them, so the Sioux hurriedly left.

The soldiers charged the Sioux camp about noon. The soldiers were divided, one party charging right into the camp. After driving these soldiers across the river, the Sioux charged the different soldiers [i.e., Custer's] below, and drive them in confusion; these soldiers became foolish, many throwing away their guns and raising their hands, saying, "Sioux, pity us; take us prisoners." The Sioux did not take a single soldier prisoner, but killed all of them; none were left alive for even a few minutes. These different soldiers discharged their guns but little. I took a gun and two belts off two dead soldiers; out of one belt two cartridges were gone, out of the other five.

The Sioux took the guns and cartridges off the dead soldiers and went to the hill on which the soldiers were, surrounded and fought them with the guns and cartridges of the dead soldiers. Had the soldiers not divided I think they would have killed many Sioux. The different soldiers [i.e., Custer's battalion] that the Sioux killed made five brave stands. Once the Sioux charged right in the midst of the different soldiers and scattered them all, fighting among the soldiers hand to hand.

One band of soldiers was in rear of the Sioux. When this band of soldiers charged, the Sioux fell back, and the Sioux and the soldiers stood facing each other. Then all the Sioux became brave and charged the soldiers. The Sioux went but a short distance before they separated and surrounded the soldiers. I could see the officers riding in front of the soldiers and hear them shooting. Now the Sioux had many killed. The soldiers killed 136 and wounded 160 Sioux. The Sioux killed all these different soldiers in the ravine.

The soldiers charged the Sioux camp farthest up the river. A short time after the different soldiers charged the village below. While the different soldiers and Sioux were fighting together the Sioux chief said, "Sioux men, go watch soldiers on the hill and prevent their joining the different soldiers." The Sioux men took the clothing off the dead and dressed themselves in it. Among the soldiers were white men who were not soldiers. The Sioux dressed in the soldiers' and white men's clothing fought the soldiers on the hill.

The banks of the Little Bighorn river were high, and the Sioux killed many of the soldiers while crossing. The soldiers on the hill dug up the ground [i.e., made earthworks], and the soldiers and Sioux fought at long range, sometimes the Sioux charging close up. The fight continued at long range until a Sioux man saw the walking soldiers coming. When the walking soldiers came near the Sioux became afraid and ran away.

GLOSSARY

battalion: a large body of troops ready for battle

detachment: a dispatch of a military unit from a larger body for a special duty

infantry: soldiers armed and trained to fight on foot

telegraphic dispatches: a message transmitted by telegraph

tipi: variant of teepee, a Native American tent

Document Analysis

The document is broken up into two parts: the hero narrative, as presented by the press at the time, and the eyewitness testimony, as told by one of the Native peoples on the other side of the conflict. When seen together, they present not just an accounting of the Battle of Little Bighorn, but also the ways in which the history of the American West has been altered and mythologized.

The first part of the document features an article from the *Helena Daily Herald*, published July 4, 1876. Focusing on the tragic death of General Custer and the slaughter of his men, the article relays few, mainly inaccurate details of the battle. According to the article, Custer and Reno attacked an Indian camp, but were immediately overrun by the Indians' "murderous fire."

The article is clear to point out that the Seventh Cavalry fought bravely and tenaciously and were only defeated by "mere brute force." It serves as a good example of the narrative that would develop around the death of Custer, a shocking tragedy made possible only by superior numbers on the enemy's side. Disbelief mixed with a sense that perhaps the Seventh Cavalry might have even had a chance to win the fight. In this light, Custer is the fallen hero and the Native peoples mere savages.

The second part of the document is a transcript of Chief Red Horse's eyewitness testimony of the events surrounding the Battle of Little Bighorn. The collective tribes of the Sioux and their allies were set up along the bank of the river when the Seventh Cavalry suddenly attacked. There was no opportunity for talk or negotiation, but instead, the Native peoples were forced to immediately jump to their own defense. Here, we see corroboration not just of Custer's tendency to attack without deliberation, but of American military policy toward Native peoples. This was a deliberate act to remove the Sioux from their own land, as forcefully as possible. There was uncertainty from the side of the Sioux which of the officers was Custer, but Red Horse is quick to point out that the American soldiers fought bravely. In this telling there is no last stand. Custer is not the final man standing.

Red Horse goes on to document more of the events of those two days. The fight with Custer's men, followed by the engagement with Reno's battalion. He mentions that some of the soldiers attempted to surrender, that few managed to even fire their guns, then documents the Sioux's final departure from the Little Bighorn. When compared to the newspaper article, Red Horse's account conveys neither the tragedy or heroism of Custer's last stand. The myth comes unraveled. The American Army launched a foolhardy, unprovoked attack on superior numbers. They lost.

Essential Themes

Of the two accounts, the tragic hero narrative became the dominant account of the Battle of Little Bighorn—brave American soldiers standing firm against a tidal wave of brutality. Custer became not just a hero, but a symbol of right, power, and sacrifice: a mythological being, an American god torn down as blood sacrifice to the opening of the frontier. Testimony about that day from Red Horse and other Native peoples was largely ignored and forgotten. This was partly a deliberate choice to further justify the takeover of Native lands, as was done soon after the Battle of Little Bighorn, when the US government annexed all remaining Sioux land, including the Black Hills. The recasting of events was also partially driven by a lingering sense of disbelief that American soldiers, especially a war hero like Custer, could be so easily defeated by people whom many considered little more than primitives. But on some level, the battle's revised narrative was also driven by an intuitive human desire for a great story with a handsome, brave hero at its center. In the end, the victory of the Sioux at the Battle of Little Bighorn proved to be a disaster for Native Americans, as the US government intensified its anti-Native policies and, for the next century, the Sioux, along with all Native peoples, would be portrayed as the villains in books, films, and even children's backyard games.

—KP Dawes, MA

Bibliography and Additional Reading

Ambrose, Stephen E. *Crazy Horse and Custer: The Parallel Lives of Two American Warriors*. New York: Anchor Books, 1996. Print.

"Custer's Last Stand." American Experience. Dir. Stephen Ives. PBS, 2012. Film.

Donovan, James. *A Terrible Glory: Custer and the Little Bighorn—the Last Great Battle of the American West*. New York: Back Bay Books, 2008. Print.

Philbrick, Nathaniel. *The Last Stand: Custer, Sitting Bull, and the Battle of the Little Bighorn*. New York: Viking, 2010. Print.

■ Speech by Chief Joseph on a Visit to Washington, DC

Date: 1879
Author: Chief Joseph
Genre: speech

Summary Overview

Chief Joseph of the Nez Perce people came to Washington in 1879 to ask questions. His people had wanted to continue to live as they always had on their ancestral homeland. When white settlers desired the Nez Perces' land, however, the Nez Perce were forcibly removed. In 1877, fleeing a cavalry attack aimed at driving the Nez Perces from their home in Oregon's Wallowa Valley, Joseph led a group of 700 of his people (only 200 of whom were warriors) on a 1,400-mile tactical retreat, trying to reach safety in Canada. When he finally did surrender, he was promised that his people would be able to return to their homes in the Wallowa Valley, but they were instead forced to go to Kansas and then relocated to a reservation in Oklahoma. It was during this exile that Chief Joseph made his trip to Washington.

Defining Moment

Since the 1830s, Indian removal had been the official policy of the federal government in the East. In the Southeast, where white Americans were eager to plant cotton and other crops grown for profit on plantations worked by slaves, the federal government forced tribes like the Cherokee to move to Indian Territory, in present-day Oklahoma. By the 1850s and 1860s, the gaze of white settlers seeking more land turned to the West. In the Wallowa Valley of eastern Oregon and western Idaho, the Nez Perce people saw settlers coming down the Oregon Trail in large numbers. Chief Joseph's father, Old Joseph, worked with the territorial government to establish a reservation for his people, giving up some land in return for the hope of being able to remain in their territory. However, in 1863, the federal government reduced the size of the Nez Perce Reservation by some ninety percent—approximately six million acres—and Old Joseph was incensed.

When Chief Joseph took over leadership after his father's death in 1871, he continued his father's resistance to the small reservation in Idaho. An 1873 agreement reached with the federal government that allowed the Nez Perces to remain and prevented white settlement was revoked only two years later. By early 1877, however, Chief Joseph had seen the futility of resistance and began to lead his people to the reservation. After a number of young warriors in his group resisted by staging a raid that resulted in a number of white deaths, however, he was forced to continue resisting by trying to lead his people to safety in Canada while being pursued by the US Army. Fighting a number of defensive actions along the way, Joseph won almost universal praise not only for his skill as a military leader, but also for the "civilized" way in which he and his people fought, restraining themselves from scalping slain soldiers, releasing captive women, and not killing innocent families that lived near the battle sites. However influential Joseph was in the Nez Perce way of making war, later research has revealed that it was actually other leaders, such as one named Looking Glass, who deserve much of the credit for military strategy.

Although the popular press and stalwarts, such as General William Tecumseh Sherman praised Chief Joseph, such praise resulted in little benefit for his people. After being promised by General Nelson Miles, who led the pursuing forces, that he and his people would be allowed to return to the Idaho reservation if he surrendered, they were taken to Fort Leavenworth in Kansas, where poor conditions resulted in many deaths. The Nez Perces were eventually allowed to settle on a part of the Cherokee Reservation in Indian Territory, over a thousand miles from their homeland. It was then that Joseph began to do whatever he could to convince the federal government to allow his people to return to a reduced reservation close to their homelands.

Author Biography

Chief Joseph was named Hin-mah-too-lat-kekt (Thunder Rolling down the Mountain) upon his birth circa

1840, but also took the Christian name Joseph that his father had taken upon his conversion to Christianity. Chief Joseph became leader of his band of Nez Perces upon his father's death in 1871. His father had worked to maintain good relationships with the non-Indian settlers, so that his people would be able to stay in the Wallowa Valley. Their peaceful coexistence ended, however, after gold was discovered in the region in 1860 and the federal government reneged on its 1873 pledge of a permanent homeland for the Nez Perces in the valley a few years later. Subsequently, Chief Joseph led his people on a 1,400-mile trip, staying ahead of the Army when they could and fighting tactical battles when they could not. After his exhausted people submitted to the Army, Joseph delivered his iconic surrender speech, stating famously, "I will fight no more forever."

HISTORICAL DOCUMENT

At last I was granted permission to come to Washington and bring my friend Yellow Bull and our interpreter with me. I am glad I came. I have shaken hands with a good many friends, but there are some things I want to know which no one seems able to explain. I cannot understand how the Government sends a man out to fight us, as it did General Miles, and then breaks his word. Such a government has something wrong about it. I cannot understand why so many chiefs are allowed to talk so many different ways, and promise so many different things. I have seen the Great Father Chief [President Hayes]; the Next Great Chief [Secretary of the Interior]; the Commissioner Chief; the Law Chief; and many other law chiefs [Congressmen] and they all say they are my friends, and that I shall have justice, but while all their mouths talk right I do not understand why nothing is done for my people. I have heard talk and talk but nothing is done. Good words do not last long unless they amount to something. Words do not pay for my dead people. They do not pay for my country now overrun by white men. They do not protect my father's grave. They do not pay for my horses and cattle. Good words do not give me back my children. Good words will not make good the promise of your war chief, General Miles. Good words will not give my people a home where they can live in peace and take care of themselves. I am tired of talk that comes to nothing. It makes my heart sick when I remember all the good words and all the broken promises. There has been too much talking by men who had no right to talk. Too many misinterpretations have been made; too many misunderstandings have come up between the white men and the Indians. If the white man wants to live in peace with the Indian he can live in peace. There need be no trouble. Treat all men alike. Give them the same laws. Give them all an even chance to live and grow. All men were made by the same Great Spirit Chief. They are all brothers. The earth is the mother of all people, and all people should have equal rights upon it. You might as well expect all rivers to run backward as that any man who was born a free man should be contented penned up and denied liberty to go where he pleases. If you tie a horse to a stake, do you expect he will grow fat? If you pen an Indian up on a small spot of earth and compel him to stay there, he will not be contented nor will he grow and prosper. I have asked some of the Great White Chiefs where they get their authority to say to the Indian that he shall stay in one place, while he sees white men going where they please. They cannot tell me.

I only ask of the Government to be treated as all other men are treated. If I cannot go to my own home, let me have a home in a country where my people will not die so fast. I would like to go to Bitter Root Valley. There my people would be happy; where they are now they are dying. Three have died since I left my camp to come to Washington.

When I think of our condition, my heart is heavy. I see men of my own race treated as outlaws and driven from country to country, or shot down like animals.

I know that my race must change. We cannot hold our own with the white men as we are. We only ask an even chance to live as other men live. We ask to be recognized as men. We ask that the same law shall work alike on all men. If an Indian breaks the law, punish him by the law. If a white man breaks the law, punish him also.

Let me be a free man, free to travel, free to stop, free to work, free to trade where I choose, free to choose my own teachers, free to follow the religion of my fathers, free to talk, think and act for myself—and I will obey every law or submit to the penalty.

Whenever the white man treats the Indian as they treat each other then we shall have no more wars. We shall be all alike—brothers of one father and mother, with one sky above us and one country around us and one government for all. Then the Great Spirit Chief who rules above will smile upon this land and send rain to wash out the bloody spots made by brothers' hands upon the face of the earth. For this time the Indian race is waiting and praying. I hope no more groans of wounded men and women will ever go to the ear of the Great Spirit Chief above, and that all people may be one people.

Hin-mah-too-yah-lat-kekht has spoken for his people.

GLOSSARY

Bitter Root Valley: (or Bitterroot): an area in southwestern Montana

General Miles: Nelson Miles, US military commander in the Great Plains and Northern Plains regions

Hin-mah-too-lat-kekt: Nez Perce name of Chief Joseph

Document Analysis

Chief Joseph, who assumed the leadership of the Wallowa band of the Nez Perces in 1871, assumed a much wider leadership in 1877, when he led approximately seven hundred of his people on a quest to reach Canada in order to preserve their traditional way of life. However, when he and his people—worn out, tired, and hungry from the 1,400 mile trek—surrendered to General Nelson Miles in Montana, only forty miles short of the Canadian border, he became a symbol of what was perceived as the end of the traditional American Indian way of life. Some parts of that way of life could be maintained on reservations, but Joseph, like his father before him, was determined that the reservation should be on the homelands of his people in the Wallowa Valley.

After the surrender, however, Chief Joseph and his people were not returned home, but were taken first to Fort Leavenworth and then to Indian Territory in Oklahoma, which resulted in virulent disease outbreaks among his people. By June 1879, out of the 700 that started on the trek, only 370 remained alive. In January of that year, Chief Joseph had been allowed to go to Washington, DC, in order to meet with President Rutherford B. Hayes, but he was dissatisfied with the outcome. In his speech, Chief Joseph focuses on the dissonance between the words and the actions of the army and federal government. From Miles's promise of a return to Oregon to the promises of assistance in helping the Nez Perces start to farm, Chief Joseph concludes, "It makes my heart sick when I remember all the good words and all the broken promises."

The solution to the problem, according to Joseph, is as simple as it is American—that all people should be treated the same way under the law and that their freedom and self-determination should be respected. He has already accepted the inevitability of changing over to non-Indian ways of life, but the only way that he sees this being successful is by treating Indian people just as white people are before the law and allowing them the freedom of movement that is taken for granted by other Americans: "You might as well expect all rivers to run backward as that any man who was born a free man should be contented penned up and denied liberty to go where he pleases." Much of what Joseph says may seem like common sense in post–civil rights movement America, and may even echo earlier arguments, such as those made by Cherokee leader John Ross some forty years prior, but neither proved persuasive enough to slow, stop, or mediate white settlement and cultural domination of the United States or the government's corresponding maltreatment of American Indians.

Essential Themes

Chief Joseph's 1877 flight and his speeches both at the surrender and two years later in Washington, DC, enhanced his personal stature as a leader in the eyes of non-Indians, but unfortunately did very little for his people. Living in northeastern Oklahoma, in an unfamiliar land with no ties to Nez Perce spiritual life, near swamps that held diseases to which the Nez Perces had little immunity, and in a climate that was ill-suited to agriculture, the Nez Perces did not fare well. Chief Joseph's 1879 appearance in Washington, DC, did little to change that situation.

In 1885, however, Chief Joseph and his band were allowed to return to the Pacific Northwest, although nowhere near his beloved Wallowa Valley. They were settled on the Colville Indian Reservation in eastern Washington, approximately 300 miles away. After returning, Chief Joseph tried to live a traditional life and continued working to allow his people to return home. In 1899, he was allowed to visit the Wallowa Valley, only to find his father's grave ransacked and his bones taken as curios. He died in his home on the Colville Reservation on September 21, 1904.

Both in life and death, Chief Joseph became a symbol of a more noble vision of American Indian resistance. His surrender speech and his speech in Washington, DC, added to the transformation of many peoples' visions of American Indians as savages to a more benign or even positive view. His words and actions demonstrated his own morality at a time when some white Americans were just beginning to view federal Indian policy as immoral. Though late nineteenth-century white reform groups, such as Friends of the Indian, would push for what they saw as a more humane Indian policy and the end of warfare with Indian nations, their agenda—based on boarding school education, individual land ownership, and complete assimilation into mainstream American society—opposed the values and way of life that Chief Joseph took his principled stand to protect.

—*Steven L. Danver, PhD*

Bibliography and Additional Reading

Hampton, Bruce. *Children of Grace: The Nez Perce War of 1877. 1994.* Lincoln: U of Nebraska P, 2002. Print.

Josephy, Alvin M., Jr. *Nez Perce Country*. Lincoln: U of Nebraska P, 2007. Print.

_____. *The Nez Perce Indians and the Opening of the Northwest*. 1979. Boston: Houghton, 1997. Print.

West, Elliot. *The Last Indian War: The Nez Perce Story*. New York: Oxford UP, 2009. Print.

■ President Chester Arthur: Indian Policy Reform

Date: December 6, 1881
Author: Chester A. Arthur
Genre: speech; address

Summary Overview

In 1881, Republican president Chester A. Arthur, during his first annual address to Congress, presented a series of reform proposals designed to improve relations between white settlers and American Indians. The "Indian question" was one of the most divisive issues facing the federal government in the latter nineteenth century, as military and humanitarian policy proposals abounded; complicating the matter, the Bureau of Indian Affairs, the primary body tasked with addressing American Indian tribal issues, was hampered by corruption. Arthur's proposals to Congress included extending protections for reservations, promoting Indian agriculture, creating "Indian schools," and, most significantly, breaking up larger Indian-owned territories and reservations. The latter proposal, known as "severalty," would greatly enhance settlers' ability to negotiate land purchases as white frontiersmen continued their westward expansion.

Defining Moment

In the aftermath of the Civil War and Reconstruction, one of the most pressing security issues facing the federal government was the "Indian question." As settlers ventured westward and into Indian Territory, distrust, deceit, and violence between Indians and settlers were becoming more prevalent. Prior to the Civil War, the Bureau of Indian Affairs was transferred from the War Department to the Department of the Interior; after the Civil War, many in Congress called for the bureau's return to the War Department. Two clear factions existed: those who advocated for a peaceful solution to the Indian question and those who sought military action.

In 1869, a policy emerged to bring citizenship and cultural assimilation peaceably to the Indians. The Peace Policy, as it was known, established reservations on which Indians would reside as "wards" of the federal government as they worked toward economic independence and equal political rights with other Americans.

Two years later, Congress altered the Peace Policy by changing the manner by which treaties with the various warring tribes were negotiated. Instead of addressing each nation individually, the United States would establish agreements with Indians as a collective, although individual land deals and treaties would remain intact.

By the 1870s, however, the Peace Policy was largely undermined by both corruption in the Bureau of Indian Affairs and an inability of white settlers and nomadic Indians to peacefully coexist. With the Peace Policy faltering, the militaristic faction returned to the fore. President Rutherford B. Hayes seemed torn, publicly calling for reforms to the federal government's Indian relations program that would restore peaceful options to both sides, while at the same time suggesting that military action against aggressive Indian groups was also acceptable in certain situations.

In 1880, the unlikely pairing of Republicans James A. Garfield and Chester A. Arthur as presidential and vice presidential candidates, respectively, brought the two to Washington, DC. Garfield and Arthur were ardently anti-corruption, and Garfield focused some of that sentiment on the Bureau of Indian Affairs. Unfortunately, an assassin took Garfield's life before the end of his first year as president. Arthur also took aim at corruption in the bureau, but he also advocated reforms to the system itself. Arthur called for a humanitarian approach to the Indians, although he also agreed with the policy of severalty. In 1881, as one of his first acts as president, Arthur presented his ideas for Indian policy reform to Congress, calling upon legislators to enact laws that would strengthen Indians' rights, enhance Indians' education (particularly with regard to agriculture), and facilitate more peaceful land agreements.

Author Biography

Chester A. Arthur was born on October 5, 1829, in

Fairfield, Vermont. An 1848 graduate of Union College in New York, he taught school while studying for the bar. In 1854, Arthur, a strong abolitionist, began practicing law in New York City, taking on a number of civil rights cases. At the start of the Civil War, he was appointed quartermaster general of the state of New York. In 1871, he continued his political rise as collector of the port of New York.

In 1880, Arthur became Garfield's vice presidential candidate. Garfield's presidency was cut short when he was assassinated. Because of a kidney condition known as Bright's disease, Arthur served only one term as president. Leaving Washington, DC, in 1885, he moved back to New York and into private practice. A year later, in 1886, he succumbed to his illness.

HISTORICAL DOCUMENT

. . . Prominent among the matters which challenge the attention of Congress at its present session is the management of our Indian affairs. While this question has been a cause of trouble and embarrassment from the infancy of the Government, it is but recently that any effort has been made for its solution at once serious, determined, consistent, and promising success.

It has been easier to resort to convenient makeshifts for tiding over temporary difficulties than to grapple with the great permanent problem, and accordingly the easier course has almost invariably been pursued.

It was natural, at a time when the national territory seemed almost illimitable and contained many millions of acres far outside the bounds of civilized settlements, that a policy should have been initiated which more than aught else has been the fruitful source of our Indian complications.

I refer, of course, to the policy of dealing with the various Indian tribes as separate nationalities, of relegating them by treaty stipulations to the occupancy of immense reservations in the West, and of encouraging them to live a savage life, undisturbed by any earnest and well-directed efforts to bring them under the influences of civilization.

The unsatisfactory results which have sprung from this policy are becoming apparent to all.

As the white settlements have crowded the borders of the reservations, the Indians, sometimes contentedly and sometimes against their will, have been transferred to other hunting grounds, from which they have again been dislodged whenever their new-found homes have been desired by the adventurous settlers.

These removals and the frontier collisions by which they have often been preceded have led to frequent and disastrous conflicts between the races.

It is profitless to discuss here which of them has been chiefly responsible for the disturbances whose recital occupies so large a space upon the pages of our history.

We have to deal with the appalling fact that though thousands of lives have been sacrificed and hundreds of millions of dollars expended in the attempt to solve the Indian problem, it has until within the past few years seemed scarcely nearer a solution than it was half a century ago. But the Government has of late been cautiously but steadily feeling its way to the adoption of a policy which has already produced gratifying results, and which, in my judgment, is likely, if Congress and the Executive accord in its support, to relieve us ere long from the difficulties which have hitherto beset us.

For the success of the efforts now making to introduce among the Indians the customs and pursuits of civilized life and gradually to absorb them into the mass of our citizens, sharing their rights and holden to their responsibilities, there is imperative need for legislative action.

My suggestions in that regard will be chiefly such as have been already called to the attention of Congress and have received to some extent its consideration.

First. I recommend the passage of an act making the laws of the various States and Territories applicable to the Indian reservations within their borders and extending the laws of the State of Arkansas to the portion of the Indian Territory not occupied by the Five Civilized Tribes.

The Indian should receive the protection of the law. He should be allowed to maintain in court his rights of person and property. He has repeatedly begged for this privilege. Its exercise would be very valuable to him in his progress toward civilization.

Second. Of even greater importance is a measure which has been frequently recommended by my predecessors in office, and in furtherance of which several bills have been from time to time introduced in both Houses of Congress. The enactment of a general law permitting the allotment in severalty, to such Indians, at least, as desire it, of a reasonable quantity of land secured to them by patent, and for their own protection made inalienable for twenty or twenty-five years, is demanded for their present welfare and their permanent advancement.

In return for such considerate action on the part of the Government, there is reason to believe that the Indians in large numbers would be persuaded to sever their tribal relations and to engage at once in agricultural pursuits. Many of them realize the fact that their hunting days are over and that it is now for their best interests to conform their manner of life to the new order of things. By no greater inducement than the assurance of permanent title to the soil can they be led to engage in the occupation of tilling it.

The well-attested reports of their increasing interest in husbandry justify the hope and belief that the enactment of such a statute as I recommend would be at once attended with gratifying results. A resort to the allotment system would have a direct and powerful influence in dissolving the tribal bond, which is so prominent a feature of savage life, and which tends so strongly to perpetuate it.

Third. I advise a liberal appropriation for the support of Indian schools, because of my confident belief that such a course is consistent with the wisest economy. . .

GLOSSARY

aught else: anything else

ere long: before long

Five Civilized Tribes: a reference to those American Indian nations—the Cherokee, Choctow, Creek (Muscogee), Chicasaw, and Seminole—whom Anglo-European settlers thought to be the most congenial toward the settlers and their ways

holden: holding; beholden

Document Analysis

Arthur first references Indian policy to date, which, he argues, has been largely ineffective, marred by makeshift agreements, violence, and "unsatisfactory" results. The problems the US government has faced with regard to Indian relations date to the government's infancy, and yet, more than a century later, few solutions have been offered, Arthur states. The fundamental approach to the issue is flawed, he asserts. By dealing with each tribe as though it were a separate nation and, through treaties, assigning them to vast reservations, these tribes are left isolated from American civilization. As a result, he says, Indians are left to continue their own antiquated and "savage" way of life.

Arthur cites the fact that his recent predecessors have begun to see the folly of past Indian-relations policies. Too much money has been spent and too many lives have been lost over the last half century, he states, without improvement. However, the new approach—pursuing the assimilation of Indians into American civilization—offers great promise, he argues. It is, therefore, vital that the White House and Congress move collectively toward reform.

Having outlined the failings of the past and discussing the positive attributes of assimilation, Arthur presents his reform proposals. First, he states that the laws of the states and territories in which Indian reservations were located would apply to the people on those reservations as well (the only exception would be the territory of the so-called Five Civilized Tribes of what is modern-day Oklahoma—this territory comprised tribes that had largely adopted "civilized" practices and whose territory was by treaty left safe from additional white settlement). As a result of Arthur's proposal, Indians would enjoy the same protections under those laws as white settlers. Second—and, in his opinion, most important—Arthur called for passage of a law allowing for severalty. Indians, he believed, would benefit from such arrangements because severalty would provide them with opportunities to own land that is legally bound and free from additional (and disputable) settlement.

Arthur continues by suggesting that Indians could—in return for the government's "considerate action" of severalty and legal protection—take advantage of their new status as landowners and take a step away from an outdated nomadic hunting culture. Indeed, Arthur says, the fact that they would be entitled to a piece of property would almost certainly lead Indians to grow crops from it and live an agrarian lifestyle. Furthermore, passage of severalty and the adoption of agriculture would likely influence American Indians to disregard their tribal bonds and the "savage life" it promotes. Arthur states that many Indians have already expressed an interest in moving in such a direction, and the United States has an opportunity to educate American Indians on the benefits of American citizenship.

Essential Themes

Presidents Ulysses S. Grant, Rutherford B. Hayes, James A. Garfield, and Chester A. Arthur all served during a pivotal period of Indian relations. A lack of successful (and consistently peaceful) policy with regard to settlement in American Indian Territories meant that corruption, lawlessness, and violence would continue among settlers, Indians, and the government if the system were allowed to continue. Arthur acknowledged this persistent problem during his 1881 address to Congress and advocated for a more, in his view, humane approach of assimilating American Indians into American society and legal system.

The idea of severalty, in particular, was one that Arthur found compelling. By breaking reservations into smaller pieces that could be owned and operated by American Indians, Arthur believed, the new occupants would embark on an agrarian lifestyle that would create less tension with settlers on the open plains and bring Indians into modern society. Arthur also proposed educating Indians on the principles and practices of farming, leading them away from what he viewed as a "savage" hunting-oriented culture. Additionally, Arthur proposed extending to Indians the same protections under the law that other Americans enjoyed.

Arthur's address to Congress was an invitation as well as a challenge. To be sure, he said, Indian relations with the federal government had been a problem since the Constitution was ratified. Countless lives had been lost, innumerable crimes had been committed, and millions of dollars had been spent while trying to create stable relations with American Indians; each expenditure, he argued, was made in vain. In the late nineteenth century, however, Arthur hoped to steer away from the military option and toward a diplomatic, humanitarian approach to Indian relations.

In Arthur's opinion, the time had come to bring Indians into American society, providing them with legal protections and empowering them with the possibility of land ownership. Severalty and education, he told his congressional audience, would help foster an egalitarian relationship with Indians. In turn, American Indians would become "civilized" and gain a path to a better future.

—Michael P. Auerbach, MA

Bibliography and Additional Reading

Dehler, Gregory J. Chester Alan Arthur: *The Life of a Gilded Age Politician and President*. Hauppauge: Nova, 2007. Print.

Heidler, David Stephen, & Jeanne T. Heidler. *Daily Lives of Civilians in Wartime Modern America: From the Indian Wars to the Vietnam War*. Westport: Greenwood, 2007. Print.

Sturgis, Amy H. *Presidents from Hayes through McKinley: Debating the Issues in Pro and Con Primary Documents*. Westport: Greenwood, 2003. Print.

Wooster, Robert. *The Military and United States Indian Policy, 1865–1903*. Lincoln: U of Nebraska P, 1995. Print.

■ The Surrender of Geronimo

Date: 1886 (published 1906)
Author: Geronimo, with S. M. Barrett
Genre: autobiography

Summary Overview

Geronimo's autobiography, from which these passages are taken, was one of the few records that told of the Native American-white conflict from the Native American perspective. As such, it was and is of great value. Additionally, the fact that it was Geronimo, the last Apache leader to try to retain his freedom through the use of arms, made it even more significant. He was the last major American Indian leader to surrender to the US government, having fought on and off for three decades, and successfully evaded thousands of army troops. The inclusion of Geronimo's thoughts, in addition to his account of which events he deemed important, has made a substantial contribution to a full understanding of the conflict and its resolution. The surrender of Geronimo, and his followers, the focus of the text, brought to an end the last major deployment of army troops within the United States for a military purpose. For those settling in the American Southwest, Geronimo's surrender signified that this region was finally to be fully integrated into the United States.

Defining Moment

Although the Indian groups collectively known as the Apaches were not exceptionally large in number, they did make their presence known through their fierce interaction with their neighbors. When the Spanish, and later the Americans, came into contact with them, this pattern continued. However, these outside groups had not had historical interaction with the Apaches, and thus did not understand the Apache culture. The nineteenth-century transition from Spanish to Mexican to American claims for this territory, did not always go smoothly. The lack of understanding lingered, stirring up discontent and a series of wars between Apaches and the group currently claiming ownership of the region. During this transitional period, miscommunication and less than honorable negotiations, first with Mangus Coloradas (Central Apache), then with Cochise (Chiricahua Apache), and later with Geronimo (Bedonkohe Apache) stimulated the on-again, off-again fighting. Geronimo demonstrated an extraordinary ability to survive not only difficult living conditions, but also the battle with any number of opponents. By the end of the struggle there were more than 5,000 American Army troops, hundreds of Indian scouts, and hundreds more civilian volunteers arrayed against Geronimo and his fewer than forty Apache warriors. Special communication lines were established, in order to try to get any information about Geronimo quickly to these forces. Although he had evaded his opponents for years, it seems ultimately to have become clear to Geronimo that the Americans could not be stopped from taking over the region.

This was something that Native American tribes across North America had come to realize as American settlers came to find the region desirable. The Apache homeland just happened to be the last area, in what became the lower forty-eight states, where settlers arrived in large numbers. Thus, the surrender of Geronimo was the surrender of the last leader of a major tribe that had tried to use traditional warfare to preserve their freedom and way of life. While there were later battles and massacres, never again was there a Native American leader who systematically tried to defeat the deployed forces of the United States. This was the end of an era and part of what was known as the closing of the American frontier. Geronimo's autobiography was dictated two decades after the surrender, when the Apache leader sought to let Americans know his side of the story.

Author Biography

Geronimo (1829–1909) was born in what is now Arizona and became a leader of the Bedonkohe Apache people. His given name could be written as Goyathlay. His father had been tribal chief, but died before Geronimo reached maturity. Becoming a warrior at sixteen, he married the next year and had three children. In 1851, while he was peacefully trading in town, Mexican soldiers raided his camp, killing dozens, including all his family. From that day on he saw himself as a warrior, and attacked Mexicans whenever he had the chance. Trying to protect their traditional way of life, Geronimo joined with other Apaches to contest American intrusion, as well as in ongoing differences with Mexicans. From 1851 to 1886, Geronimo was a feared warrior, but he also tried several times to make peace with the Americans. In the 1880s, the American Army had more than 100 soldiers for each Apache warrior and finally ground down their resistance. Geronimo surrendered and lived the rest of his life as a prisoner of war, although relatively freely after the first few years. The last fifteen years of his life he lived in Oklahoma and became a national celebrity. His last words were that surrendering had been a mistake.

Geronimo was not literate, so he dictated his autobiography to S. M. Barrett, who had been superintendent of education in Lawton, Oklahoma. Barrett had previously helped Geronimo in another matter and was accepted as his friend by Geronimo when he discovered that Barrett had been wounded by a Mexican.

HISTORICAL DOCUMENT

CHAPTER XVI
IN PRISON AND ON THE WARPATH

Soon after we arrived in New Mexico two companies of scouts were sent from San Carlos. When they came to Hot Springs they sent word for me and Victoria to come to town. The messengers did not say what they wanted with us, but as they seemed friendly we thought they wanted a council, and rode in to meet the officers. As soon as we arrived in town soldiers met us, disarmed us, and took us both to headquarters, where we were tried by court-martial. They asked us only a few questions and then Victoria was released and I was sentenced to the guardhouse. Scouts conducted me to the guardhouse and put me in chains. When I asked them why they did this they said it was because I had left Apache Pass.

I do not think that I ever belonged to those soldiers at Apache Pass, or that I should have asked them where I might go. Our bands could no longer live in peace [32] together, and so we had quietly withdrawn, expecting to live with Victoria's band, where we thought we would not be molested. They also sentenced seven other Apaches to chains in the guardhouse.

I do not know why this was done, for these Indians had simply followed me from Apache Pass to Hot Springs. If it was wrong (and I do not think it was wrong) for us to go to Hot Springs, I alone was to blame. They asked the soldiers in charge why they were imprisoned and chained, but received no answer.

I was kept a prisoner for four months, during which time I was transferred to San Carlos. Then I think I had another trial, although I was not present. In fact I do not know that I had another trial, but I was told that I had, and at any rate I was released.

After this we had no more trouble with the soldiers, but I never felt at ease any longer at the Post. We were allowed to live above San Carlos at a place now called Geronimo. A man whom the Indians called "Nick Golee" was agent at this place. All went well here for a period of two years, but we were not satisfied.

In the summer of 1883 a rumor was current that the officers were again planning to imprison our leaders. This rumor served to revive the memory of all our past wrongs—the massacre in the tent at Apache Pass, the fate of Mangus-Colorado, and my own unjust imprisonment, which might easily have been death to me. Just at this time we were told that the officers wanted us to come up the river above Geronimo to a fort (Fort Thomas) to hold a council with them. We did not believe that any good could come of this conference, or that there was any need of it; so we held a council ourselves, and fearing treachery, decided to leave the reservation. We thought it more manly to die on the warpath than to be killed in prison.

There were in all about 250 Indians, chiefly the Bedonkohe and Nedni Apaches, led by myself and Whoa. We went through Apache Pass and just west of there had a fight with the United States troops. In this battle we killed three soldiers and lost none.

We went on toward Old Mexico, but on the second day after this United States soldiers overtook us about three o'clock in the afternoon and we fought until dark. The ground where we were attacked was very rough, which was to our advantage, for the troops were compelled to dismount in order to fight us. I do not know how many soldiers we killed, but we lost only one warrior and three children. We had plenty of guns and ammunition at this time. Many of the guns and much ammunition we had accumulated while living in the reservation, and the remainder we had obtained from the White Mountain Apaches when we left the reservation.

Troops did not follow us any longer, so we went south almost to Casa Grande and camped in the Sierra de Sahuaripa Mountains. We ranged in the mountains of Old Mexico for about a year, then returned to San Carlos, taking with us a herd of cattle and horses.

Soon after we arrived at San Carlos the officer in charge, General Crook, took the horses and cattle away from us. I told him that these were not white men's cattle, but belonged to us, for we had taken them from the Mexicans during our wars. I also told him that we did not intend to kill these animals, but that we wished to keep them and raise stock on our range. He would not listen to me, but took the stock. I went up near Fort Apache and General Crook ordered officers, soldiers, and scouts to see that I was arrested; if I offered resistance they were instructed to kill me.

This information was brought to me by the Indians. When I learned of this proposed action I left for Old Mexico, and about four hundred Indians went with me. They were the Bedonkohe, Chokonen, and Nedni Apaches. At this time Whoa was dead, and Naiche was the only chief with me. We went south into Sonora and camped in the mountains. Troops followed us, but did not attack us until we were camped in the mountains west of Casa Grande. Here we were attacked by Government Indian scouts. One boy was killed and nearly all of our women and children were captured. [33]

After this battle we went south of Casa Grande and made a camp, but within a few days this camp was attacked by Mexican soldiers. We skirmished with them all day, killing a few Mexicans, but sustaining no loss ourselves.

That night we went east into the foothills of the Sierra Madre Mountains and made another camp. Mexican troops trailed us, and after a few days attacked our camp again. This time the Mexicans had a very large army, and we avoided a general engagement. It is senseless to fight when you cannot hope to win.

That night we held a council of war; our scouts had reported bands of United States and Mexican troops at many points in the mountains. We estimated that about two thousand soldiers were ranging these mountains seeking to capture us.

General Crook had come down into Mexico with the United States troops. They were camped in the Sierra de Antunez Mountains. Scouts told me that General Crook wished to see me and I went to his camp. When I arrived General Crook said to me, "Why did you leave the reservation?" I said: "You told me that I might live in the reservation the same as white people lived. One year I raised a crop of corn, and gathered and stored it, and the next year I put in a crop of oats, and when the crop was almost ready to harvest, you told your soldiers to put me in prison, and if I resisted to kill me. If I had been let alone I would now have been in good circumstances, but instead of that you and the Mexicans are hunting me with soldiers." He said: "I never gave any such orders; the troops at Fort Apache, who spread this report, knew that it was untrue." Then I agreed to go back with him to San Carlos.

It was hard for me to believe him at that time. Now I know that what he said was untrue, [34] and I firmly believe that he did issue the orders for me to be put in prison, or to be killed in case I offered resistance.

FOOTNOTES [from original publication]:

[32] Victoria, chief of the Hot Spring Apaches, met his death in opposing the forcible removal of his band to a reservation, because having previously tried and failed he felt it impossible for separate bands of Apaches to live at peace under such arrangement.

[33] Geronimo's whole family, excepting his eldest son, a warrior, were captured.

[34] Geronimo's exact words, for which the Editor disclaims any responsibility.

CHAPTER XVII
THE FINAL STRUGGLE

We started with all our tribe to go with General Crook back to the United States, but I feared treachery and decided to remain in Mexico. We were not under any guard at this time. The United States troops marched in front and the Indians followed, and when we became suspicious, we turned back. I do not know how far the United States army went after myself, and some warriors turned back before we were missed, and I do not care.

I have suffered much from such unjust orders as those of General Crook. Such acts have caused much distress to my people. I think that General Crook's death [35] was sent by the Almighty as a punishment for the many evil deeds he committed.

Soon General Miles was made commander of all the western posts, and troops trailed us continually. They were led by Captain Lawton, who had good scouts. The Mexican [36] soldiers also became more active and more numerous. We had skirmishes almost every day, and so we finally decided to break up into small bands. With six men and four women I made for the range of mountains near Hot Springs, New Mexico. We passed many cattle ranches, but had no trouble with the cowboys. We killed cattle to eat whenever we were in need of food, but we frequently suffered greatly for water. At one time we had no water for two days and nights and our horses almost died from thirst. We ranged in the mountains of New Mexico for some time, then thinking that perhaps the troops had left Mexico, we returned. On our return through Old Mexico we attacked every Mexican found, even if for no other reason than to kill. We believed they had asked the United States troops to come down to Mexico to fight us.

South of Casa Grande, near a place called by the Indians Gosoda, there was a road leading out from the town. There was much freighting carried on by the Mexicans over this road. Where the road ran through a mountain pass we stayed in hiding, and whenever Mexican freighters passed we killed them, took what supplies we wanted, and destroyed the remainder. We were reckless of our lives, because we felt that every man's hand was against us. If we returned to the reservation we would be put in prison and killed; if we stayed in Mexico they would continue to send soldiers to fight us; so we gave no quarter to anyone and asked no favors.

After some time we left Gosoda and soon were reunited with our tribe in the Sierra de Antunez Mountains.

Contrary to our expectations the United States soldiers had not left the mountains in Mexico, and were soon trailing us and skirmishing with us almost every day. Four or five times they surprised our camp. One time they surprised us about nine o'clock in the morning, and captured all our horses [37] (nineteen in number) and secured our store of dried meats. We also lost three Indians in this encounter. About the middle of the afternoon of the same day we attacked them from the rear as they were passing through a prairie—killed one soldier, but lost none ourselves. In this skirmish we recovered all our horses except three that belonged to me. The three horses that we did not recover were the best riding horses we had.

Soon after this we made a treaty with the Mexican troops. They told us that the United States troops were the real cause of these wars, and agreed not to fight any more with us provided we would return to the United States. This we agreed to do, and resumed our march, expecting to try to make a treaty with the United States soldiers and return to Arizona. There seemed to be no other course to pursue.

Soon after this scouts from Captain Lawton's troops told us that he wished to make a treaty with us; but I knew that General Miles was the chief of the American troops, and I decided to treat with him.

We continued to move our camp northward, and the American troops also moved northward, [38] keeping at no great distance from us, but not attacking us.

I sent my brother Porico (White Horse) with Mr. George Wratton on to Fort Bowie to see General Miles, and to tell him that we wished to return to Arizona; but before these messengers returned I met two Indian scouts—Kayitah, a Chokonen Apache, and Marteen, a Nedni Apache. They were serving as scouts for Captain Lawton's troops. They told me that General Miles had come and had sent them to ask me to meet him. So I went to the camp of the United States troops to meet General Miles.

When I arrived at their camp I went directly to General Miles and told him how I had been wronged, and that I wanted to return to the United States with my people, as we wished to see our families, who had been captured [39] and taken away from us.

General Miles said to me: "The President of the United States has sent me to speak to you. He has heard of your trouble with the white men, and says that if you will agree to a few words of treaty we need have no more trouble. Geronimo, if you will agree to a few words of treaty all will be satisfactorily arranged."

So General Miles told me how we could be brothers to each other. We raised our hands to heaven and said that the treaty was not to be broken. We took an oath not to do any wrong to each other or to scheme against each other.

Then he talked with me for a long time and told me what he would do for me in the future if I would agree to the treaty. I did not greatly believe General Miles, but because the President of the United States had sent me word I agreed to make the treaty, and to keep it. Then I asked General Miles what the treaty would be. General Miles said to me: [40] "I will take you under Government protection; I will build you a house; I will fence you much land; I will give you cattle, horses, mules, and farming implements. You will be furnished with men to work the farm, for you yourself will not have to work. In the fall I will send you blankets and clothing so that you will not suffer from cold in the winter time.

"There is plenty of timber, water, and grass in the land to which I will send you. You will live with your tribe and with your family. If you agree to this treaty you shall see your family within five days."

I said to General Miles: "All the officers that have been in charge of the Indians have talked that way, and it sounds like a story to me; I hardly believe you."

He said: "This time it is the truth."

I said: "General Miles, I do not know the laws of the white man, nor of this new country where you are to send me, and I might break their laws."

He said: "While I live you will not be arrested."

Then I agreed to make the treaty. (Since I have been a prisoner of war I have been arrested and placed in the guardhouse twice for drinking whisky.)

We stood between his troopers and my warriors. We placed a large stone on the blanket before us. Our treaty was made by this stone, and it was to last until the stone should crumble to dust; so we made the treaty, and bound each other with an oath.

I do not believe that I have ever violated that treaty; but General Miles [41] never fulfilled his promises.

When we had made the treaty General Miles said to me: "My brother, you have in your mind how you are going to kill men, and other thoughts of war; I want you to put that out of your mind, and change your thoughts to peace."

Then I agreed and gave up my arms. I said: "I will quit the warpath and live at peace hereafter."

Then General Miles swept a spot of ground clear with his hand, and said: "Your past deeds shall be wiped out like this and you will start a new life."

FOOTNOTES [from original publication]:

[35] These are the exact words of Geronimo. The Editor is not responsible for this criticism of General Crook.

[36] Governor Torres of Sonora had agreed to coöperate with our troops in exterminating or capturing this tribe.

[37] Captain Lawton reports officially the same engagement, but makes no mention of the recapture (by the Apaches) of the horses.

[38] See note page 37.

[39] See page 33.

[40] For terms of treaty see page 154 [in original publication].

[41] The criticisms of General Miles in the foregoing chapter are from Geronimo, not from the Editor.

GLOSSARY

Apache Pass: a mountain pass in southeast Arizona, the location of a temporary reservation and Fort Bowie

Geronimo (location): The location of Fort Thomas in eastern Arizona, south of Safford; Geronimo and Fort Thomas are now abandoned, but the San Carlos Reservation remains

Mangus-Colorado: an Apache war leader from 1820–1862 who was tortured and murdered by Americans soldiers when he tried to negotiate a peace agreement

Document Analysis

Having spent two years on the San Carlos Reservation, Geronimo and his followers left the reservation in 1881. It was during this period off the reservation that Chapter XVI began. These two chapters of Geronimo's autobiography continue to document much of what had been contained in the previous fifteen, concerning the uncertainty of relations between the Apaches and the Army, or the Mexicans. When off the reservation, continual small skirmishes took a toll on both sides. Ultimately, Geronimo recognized that those who followed him could not continue to live a hard life on the run, and he decided to make peace. He did not believe anything promised him, having seen promises made to previous leaders disappear, as well as having personal experience with broken promises. However, at the time of the last chapter, about one-fourth of the US Army was trying to capture him, while he was supported by fewer than forty warriors, and accompanied by just over 100 others, who needed protection and were traveling with him. When Geronimo believed it was finally time to give up the fight, he arranged a meeting with General Miles, the commander in the region. They then reached an agreement to bring peace to the area, with the result that Geronimo and those with him were deported to military bases in Florida, and then Alabama, and finally ending up at Fort Sill, Oklahoma. As Geronimo stated, he did follow his end of the agreement for the remaining years of his life. With this peaceful surrender, at the end of the historical document, for the first time since the massacre of his family in 1951, he vowed to "quit the warpath and live at peace hereafter."

This autobiography was intended for the general public, in order that they might understand what the Apaches had faced. Because it was dictated, many scholars have said that it follows the form of oral histories that had been handed down as part of the Apache

heritage. Obviously told from Geronimo's perspective, it does seem to have followed the viewpoint of a traditional warrior. Because Geronimo was trying to avenge the loss of his family, or trying to help his people retain their way of life, he does not show any remorse for the fighting or the killing of so many people. The way his story unfolds, these were just events to be expected for someone in his position. When the tribe was attacked, it was the warrior's job to repel the attacker, whatever defensive or offensive efforts were necessary. While Geronimo adapted to the new way of life after his surrender, well into the 1900s when he was in Oklahoma, whenever the opportunity availed itself, he asked everyone—up to the president himself—to allow his people to return to Arizona. When he surrendered, the war had been lost and this request was never granted.

Essential Themes

Geronimo's recollection of the major events during the early 1880s are obviously one-sided, although if compared with army records, the central points are similar. However, what is not in the American or Mexican records are the feelings of mistrust felt by Geronimo and the other Apaches, and the belief that these outsiders could not be trusted. The Apaches did not live what would be viewed by Euroamericans as a "civilized" life, but they did have a way of life that was predictable. The lack of respect felt by Geronimo pushed him to the extreme. Thus, when he mentions that, toward the end of his time in Mexico, he killed every Mexican who crossed his path, reports made by the Mexican commander were that probably 600 people were killed in one to two years by Geronimo, with no appreciable losses among the Apaches. All of that killing was the result of Mexican soldiers thirty years earlier attacking an Apache encampment, while most of the men were peacefully trading with their neighbors. If that had not happened, Geronimo, the medicine man and warrior, might have remained the peaceful man that others had experienced in previous years.

It is clear that the American leaders did not understand the Apaches (or the various groupings within that designation). From the text, it is also clear that the Apaches did not fully understand the Americans, either. The hard life in this rather desolate region affected everyone. However, for decades, Geronimo was willing to live that hard life, scrambling from one place to another rather than face the uncertainties of living with and dealing with the Americans. For the Americans, this was unthinkable. This lack of understanding of the extremes to which Geronimo and the Apaches would go made the gulf between the two groups even wider. Fortunately, in the end, both General Miles and Geronimo were willing to look beyond the current situation and their personal preferences, to craft a solution that would end several decades of war, with Geronimo as the Apache leader for the last three. Calling upon the power of the unseen "President of the United States," Geronimo hoped that this agreement would be beneficial to everyone, even though he knew it meant the end of the traditional Apache way of life.

—*Donald A. Watt, PhD*

Bibliography and Additional Reading

Debo, Angie. *Geronimo*. Norman, Oklahoma: U of Oklahoma P, 1976, reprinted 2012. Print.

Geronimo & S.M. Barrett. Geronimo's Story of His Life. New York: Duffield & Co., 1906. *Project Gutenberg*, 2010. Web. 16 Oct. 2014.

"Obituary: Old Apache Chief Geronimo Is Dead." *The New York Times*, On this Day: February 18, 1909. *New York Times Company*, 18 Feb. 2010. Web. 16 Oct. 2014.

Utley, Robert M. *Geronimo*. New Haven: Yale UP, 2012. Print.

■ The Dawes Act

Date: February 8, 1887
Author: Henry Dawes
Genre: legislation

Summary Overview

The Dawes Act, officially the General Allotment Act, and sometimes referred to the as the Dawes Severalty Act, instituted the policy of "allotment in severalty." Under this policy, reservation lands that had been owned collectively by Native American tribes would be broken up into individual allotments or homesteads, with differing amounts of land being given to individuals based on their life situation—such as head of household, single adult, child, or orphan. The reformers who backed the allotment program hoped that individual land ownership would hasten the assimilation of Native peoples. While tribes as a whole generally opposed allotment, some highly-assimilated individual Indians did favor the policy, believing it would allow them to better manage their own affairs. On many reservations, some land would be declared surplus after all tribal citizens had received allotments, so land-hungry settlers and developers near the reservations favored the program.

Defining Moment

In the late 1800s, a group of reformers, mostly white Americans, but including a few highly-assimilated Native Americans, became known as the "Friends of the Indians." This was not an organized group, but simply a loose collection of men and women with similar interests and goals. Many of the Friends of the Indians did belong to groups promoting reform of government Indian policy, such as the Indian Protective Committee (founded in 1879), the Indian Rights Association (founded 1882), or the National Indian Defense Association (founded 1885). Likewise, many also attended the annual Lake Mohonk Conferences, held from 1883 to 1916 at a resort in upstate New York, where like-minded individuals met to discuss Indian affairs. The Friends of the Indians sought three major goals, all of which aimed at the eventual assimilation of the American Indians and their total absorption into the general American society.

Among the goals sought were the allotment of reservation lands as individually owned parcels, US citizenship for all Native Americans, and education for all Indian children. Passage of the Dawes Act in 1889 was considered one of their most important accomplishments, and Dawes was a prominent part of the Friends of the Indians movement. Allotment was considered a key idea because the reformers thought that individual land ownership would lead Native peoples to embrace the American values of thrift, hard work, and self-reliance. Under the original Dawes Act, an Indian who accepted an allotment became a US citizen, so the goal of citizenship was also obtained. The reformers also promoted the idea of schools where Indian children would learn the basic skills necessary to function in American society.

While the Friends of the Indians had a genuine concern for the Native Americans, they generally held condescending attitudes toward Indian culture and sought to erase the cultural traits of the Native people to facilitate assimilation. Because of the paternalistic, ethnocentric attitudes of the reformers, they promoted ideas that the Indians themselves cared little about, or in some cases—such as allotment—strenuously opposed. Indians generally cared little about the US citizenship issue, although in the long run, citizenship brought the Native Americans the constitutional protections of their civil and political rights. Many Indian families initially had some interest in education for their children, but when they saw that the schools aimed at breaking down their children's attachment to their own culture, this interest often turned to opposition. The allotment program proved to be a disastrous failure: promoted as a way to protect the individual Indian's right to his own land, it created a large class of landless Indians and caused a significant decrease in the total landholdings of the Native tribes.

Author Biography

Henry L. Dawes (1816–1903) was a Republican politician from western Massachusetts. He was born in Cummington, MA and graduated from Yale College in 1839. Before entering politics, he had been a school teacher and newspaper editor. He was elected to the US House of Representatives in 1852 and to the US Senate in 1875. Although he is best known for his sponsorship of the General Allotment Act, he was not extensively involved in Indian affairs until the late 1870s. In 1881, he became chairman of the Senate Committee on Indian Affairs. He became a leading figure in the loose coalition of reformers known as the "Friends of the Indians," who promoted highly ethnocentric, assimilationist reforms in government Indian policy. After retiring from the Senate in 1893, he led the Dawes Commission, which dealt with applying the Allotment Act among the Five Civilized Tribes in the Indian Territory. He died in Pittsfield, MA in 1903.

HISTORICAL DOCUMENT

An act to provide for the allotment of lands in severalty to Indians on the various reservations, and to extend the protection of the laws of the United States and the Territories over the Indians, and for other purposes.

Be it enacted, That in all cases where any tribe or band of Indians has been, or shall hereafter be, located upon any reservation created for their use, either by treaty stipulation or by virtue of an act of Congress or executive order setting apart the same for their use, the President of the United States be, and he hereby is, authorized, whenever in his opinion any reservation or any part thereof of such Indians is advantageous for agricultural and grazing purposes to cause said reservation, or any part thereof, to be surveyed, or resurveyed if necessary, and to allot the lands in said reservations in severalty to any Indian located thereon in quantities as follows:

To each head of a family, one-quarter of a section;

To each single person over eighteen years of age, one-eighth of a section;

To each orphan child under eighteen years of age, one-eighth of a section; and,

To each other single person under eighteen years now living, or who may be born prior to the date of the order of the President directing an allotment of the lands embraced in any , one-sixteenth of a section; . . .

...SEC. 5. That upon the approval of the allotments provided for in this act by the Secretary of the Interior, he shall . . . declare that the United States does and will hold the land thus allotted, for the period of twenty-five years, in trust for the sole use and benefit of the Indian to whom such allotment shall have been made, . . . and that at the expiration of said period the United States will convey the same by patent to said Indian, or his heirs as aforesaid, in fee, discharged of such trust and free of all charge or encumbrance whatsoever: . . .

SEC. 6. That upon the completion of said allotments and the patenting of the lands to said allottees, each and every member of the respective bands or tribes of Indians to whom allotments have been made shall have the benefit of and be subject to the laws, both civil and criminal, of the State or Territory in which they may reside; . . . And every Indian born within the territorial limits of the United States to whom allotments shall have been made under the provisions of this act, or under any law or treaty, and every Indian born within the territorial limits of the United States who has voluntarily taken up, within said limits, his residence separate and apart from any tribe of Indians therein, and has adopted the habits of civilized life, is hereby declared to be a citizen of the United States, and is entitled to all the rights, privileges, and immunities of such citizens, whether said Indian has been or not, by birth or otherwise, a member of any tribe of Indians within the territorial limits of the United States without in any manner impairing or otherwise affecting the right of any such Indian to tribal or other property. . . .

Document Analysis

The Dawes Act provided for distributing Indian reservation lands "in severalty" and to "extend the protection of the laws of the United States and the Territories over the Indians." The word severalty means the quality of being separate or individual, and the idea behind allotting reservation lands was to give each Indian family or individual their own privately held land. Those who accepted allotments, or those who had moved off of reservations and had "adopted the habits of civilized life," became US citizens. The bill also specified that US citizenship did not limit or impair the Indian's right to share in tribal property or other tribal benefits.

The act called for a survey of reservation lands, so that the precise acreage would be known before allotment was carried out. A head of a family would receive a quarter section of land—160 acres. This was also the amount of land that settlers could claim under the Homestead Act of 1862. However, a problem with both homesteading and the allotment policy is that while 160 acres was a good-sized farm in the eastern parts of the United States, in the arid West, much more land would be needed. Single people over eighteen years old or orphans under eighteen would receive a one-eighth section (eighty acres). Children living with a family would receive 40 acres. After all eligible tribal members had received their allotments, excess land could be sold to anyone, with the funds from these sales going into a trust fund for the tribe. For twenty-five years, the secretary of the interior would hold the title to each allottee's land in trust, so that the land could not be lost through mismanagement or failure to pay local property taxes (the land would not be taxable during this trust period). Initially, land could not be leased during the trust period, but later changes did allow the leasing of trust land. The Burke Act in 1906 also provided that an individual Indian allottee could petition to have their trust status ended earlier, if they were deemed competent to handle their own affairs. The Burke Act also amended the citizenship provisions, so that Indians would not become citizens until the end of the trust period. This change was made because many believed that citizenship was not consistent with an individual being held in a trustee or wardship status.

Allotment was intended to hasten the assimilation of the Native Americans by making them competent US citizens who farmed their own lands. Because of the sale of excess reservation lands and widespread fraud by whites gaining control of Indian lands, the policy proved a failure and led to many Indians living on greatly reduced reservations with no individual lands to call their own.

Essential Themes

A vast reduction in Native American landholdings was one of the long-term legacies of the Dawes Act. Those who promoted Allotment in Severalty hoped that the Indians would develop a strong attachment to owning their own land. However, for a variety of reasons, allotment resulted in much Indian land being transferred to non-Indian ownership. Many non-Indians fraudulently claimed Indian ethnicity in order to obtain an allotment. When the Dawes Act was later amended to allow leasing of land while it was still in the trust period, much land was ruined by mining operations, over-grazing, or clear-cutting of timber. When they received title to their land, many Indians sold it, having no interest in becoming farmers. Overall, the lands controlled by tribal peoples declined from roughly 150 million acres when the Dawes Act was passed in 1887 to approximately 48 million acres when allotment was formally ended in the legislation of the so-called Indian New Deal in 1934.

The debates over allotment also illustrate how mixed motives often drive major policy decisions. On many reservations, there would be excess land left over after allotments had been made, and this land would be sold to anyone who wished to purchase it. The reformers who promoted allotment appeared to be genuine in their belief that allotment would ultimately be beneficial to the Indians; the reformers saw owning private property as the gateway to becoming assimilated into American society. But many people with little sympathy for the Indians supported allotment because it would open up more land for white settlement. Senator Henry Teller from Colorado, who was not always supportive of Indian interests, condemned allotment and predicted that it would lead to much Indian land being lost and that the Indians then would be angered at those who had professed to help them. James Mooney and Lewis Henry Morgan, two pioneers in the field of anthropology, also condemned allotment as an attempt to force assimilation on the Native peoples too rapidly. Even President Grover Cleveland, who signed the Dawes Act, expressed little faith in the supposed benefits the law would have for the Indians.

—*Mark S. Joy, PhD*

Bibliography and Additional Reading

Genetin-Pilawa, C. Joseph. *Crooked Paths to Allotment: The Fight over Federal Indian Policy After the Civil War.* Chapel Hill: U of North Carolina P, 2014. Print.

Hoxie, Frederick E. *A Final Promise: The Campaign to Assimilate the Indians, 1880–1920.* Lincoln: U of Nebraska P, 1984. Print.

Prucha, Francis Paul. *The Great Father: The United States Government and the American Indian.* 2 vols. Lincoln: U of Nebraska P, 1995. Print.

■ Wovoka: The Messiah Letter

Date: c. January 1889 (recorded August 1891)
Author: Jack Wilson, a.k.a. Wovoka
Genre: letter; sermon

Summary Overview

The Messiah Letter, composed by Paiute medicine man Wovoka, also known as Jack Wilson, is a foundational document laying out the premise behind the Ghost Dance religious movement, which Wovoka claimed was revealed to him in a vision in January 1889. At the time of this revelation, American Indian tribes across the nation were in a period of difficult transition. Just over fifty years earlier, the federal government had begun to move all Indians to land west of the Mississippi River, then to smaller and smaller reservations as the demand for farmland for white Americans grew after the Civil War. Wovoka proposed a way for Indians to restore their idyllic past, but he did not call for warfare against the encroaching whites. Rather, he called for Indians to remain at peace, live ethically, abstain from drinking alcohol, work hard, and perform the sacred dance, which became known as the Ghost Dance.

Defining Moment

During the last thirty-five years of the nineteenth century, American Indian nations faced an increasingly hopeless situation. Many eastern tribes had already been forced off of their land and pushed across the country to settle in Oklahoma, while many western tribes were seeing more and more white Americans moving west in order to start farms and ranches. The lands granted to Native peoples were becoming progressively smaller, and the more fertile lands were being reserved for the new white immigrants. All the while, federal Indian policy held that they should be forced to give up their traditional religions, languages, and lifestyles in favor of American Christianity and farming.

By the 1880s, many tribes were becoming restless on reservations that held no opportunities or possibilities for them. About that time, a Northern Paiute prophet in western Nevada named Wovoka announced a new religious movement that would hasten the return of the dead (from which it got its name, the Ghost Dance), the elimination of the American settlers, and the restoration of the Indian way of life and all lands they had held before the arrival of European settlers. In order to achieve this, Indian people would have to perform the dance that God had revealed to Wovoka, strictly observe a moral code that had its roots in Christianity, and refuse to make war against or consume the alcohol brought by white people. As Indians in Wovoka's immediate vicinity began performing the dance, stories of the visions they received and healings that occurred began to spread across the West.

Wovoka had been influenced by a Northern Paiute mystic named Tävibo, whom Wovoka claimed was his father. Tävibo had started a similar movement some twenty years earlier, promising that all white people would be swallowed up by the earth if the Indians danced the circle dance he specified. Wovoka's message started from Tävibo's and incorporated aspects of a number of different Christian religious groups present in Nevada, including Presbyterians, Mormons, and the Indian Shaker Church. In January 1889, he claimed that he had received a vision in which God had revealed to him a new dance and a new message specifically for Indian people of all nations. This message combined all of the influences in Wovoka's life and offered hope to Indian people throughout the West, most of whom were facing the same difficult times.

Whereas Tävibo's 1870 movement had only spread to tribes in Nevada, California, and Oregon, Wovoka's Ghost Dance would travel across the West. Many tribes, notably the Arapaho and the Cheyenne, sent medicine men to receive his teachings. Tribes from the Canadian border to as far south as Texas and as far east as the Missouri River practiced the dance and religious acts described in the Messiah Letter.

Author Biography

Wovoka, or Jack Wilson, was born in western Nevada around 1856. Raised by a white rancher's family after his father died, he spoke English and was involved with a number of Christian groups during his early life. At the age of about thirty, Wovoka began to make prophecies about the end of white dominance of the region and a return to an idyllic past. These prophecies centered on the actions of the Indians themselves, whom Wovoka claimed must live a moral life and perform the Ghost Dance in order for his predictions to come true. His new religious movement was heavily Christian in many respects, including its espousal of pacifism and personal ethics as well as several explicit references to Jesus, but at the same time, it was influenced by the dances and mystical aspects of the religious beliefs of his own people. Wovoka's message only provided the basic outline of the Ghost Dance movement, allowing the tribes that embraced it to adapt its principles to meet their own circumstances.

HISTORICAL DOCUMENT

When you get home you must make a dance to continue five days. Dance four successive nights, and the last night keep up the dance until the morning of the fifth day, when all must bathe in the river and then disperse to their homes. You must all do in the same way.

I, Jack Wilson, love you all, and my heart is full of gladness for the gifts you have brought me. When you get home I shall give you a good cloud which will make you feel good. I give you a good spirit and give you all good paint. I want you to come again in three months, some from each tribe there [i.e., Indian Territory].

There will be a good deal of snow this year and some rain. In the fall there will be such a rain as I have never given you before.

Grandfather says, when your friends die you must not cry. You must not hurt anybody or do harm to anyone. You must not fight. Do right always. It will give you satisfaction in life. This young man has a good father and mother.

Do not tell the white people about this. Jesus is now upon the earth. He appears like a cloud. The dead are still alive again. I do not know when they will be here; maybe this fall or in the spring. When the time comes there will be no more sickness and everyone will be young again.

Do not refuse to work for the whites and do not make any trouble with them until you leave them. When the earth shakes do not be afraid. It will not hurt you.

I want you to dance every six weeks. Make a feast at the dance and have food that everybody may eat. Then bathe in the water. That is all. You will receive good words again from me some time. Do not tell lies.

GLOSSARY

earth shakes: a reference to the coming of the new world

good cloud: rain, perhaps

good paint: literally, face and body paint, but perhaps also presence or power

Grandfather: a universal title of reverence among Indians and here meaning the messiah

young man … father and mother: Possibly this refers to Casper Edson, the young Arapaho who wrote down this message of Wovoka

Document Analysis

Wovoka's Messiah Letter is a transcript of the message delivered to the Arapaho and Cheyenne delegates who had traveled to Nevada to meet with him and learn the Ghost Dance. It was written down by two attendees at the event, an Arapaho man named Casper Edson and the daughter of a Cheyenne delegate named Black Short Nose, and recorded by ethnographer James Mooney. The letter describes the basic tenets revealed in Wovoka's vision, leaving much room for interpretation and variation in how they were implemented.

The letter first says to perform the dance for five days. Although Wovoka does not specify the form of the dance, the actual dance performed, known as the circle dance, was common among western tribes. Then Wovoka begins to make prophecies. He says, "In the fall there will be such a rain as I have never given you before," clearly implying that he personally is responsible for bringing the rain and snow. Later in the letter, Wovoka claims, "Jesus is now upon the earth. He appears like a cloud," again referencing himself as the bringer of the weather.

His authority established, Wovoka moves into descriptions of how those who follow the Ghost Dance movement must live. He advises Indians not to cry when friends pass away, as they will all come back to life when the prophecy is fulfilled. He tells them to live in peace with all people, regardless of race, and to "do right always." While many tribes had been waging war against the white settlers encroaching on their lands, Wovoka calls for a different approach, asking his audience not to resist, since the fulfillment of the prophecies will make all things right. He also says that the Ghost Dance is for Indians alone and must not be shared or even discussed with whites.

Though religious beliefs often give hope of an eternal reward, Wovoka claims that the reward he is bringing is imminent and will come if people only perform the dance and live as he instructs. After referencing Jesus, and possibly identifying with him, Wovoka states that "the dead are still alive again" and that, though they have not yet arrived, they may be there by "this fall or in the spring."

At the end, Wovoka returns to the idea of keeping peace with white people, encouraging Indians to work for them and not to worry, as the coming changes that will remove the whites from their land will not affect them. His prophecy complete, he promises to return and give them another message, presumably about the imminent return of the dead and the new age that he intends to usher in. According to anthropologist Michael Hittman, Wovoka never lost faith in his prophecies or his own role as a supernatural being, acting as a medicine man almost until his death in 1932.

Essential Themes

It is unfortunate that the peaceful Ghost Dance movement came to be associated with the violence surrounding the death of the Lakota leader Sitting Bull and the tragedy of the Wounded Knee massacre in December 1890. The Lakota had adapted the Ghost Dance, as had many other tribes, to their own culture and situation, and one of those adaptations was the ghost shirts that the dancers wore, which they believed would stop white men's bullets. As the Lakota had been fighting white settlers and the US Army for more than twenty years, federal officials took the arrival of the Ghost Dance as a harbinger of more militant resistance. The Army arrived, and the ensuing tragedy at Wounded Knee ended both the widespread popularity of the Ghost Dance movement and, at least symbolically, open warfare between whites and Indians. Though local newspapers around Wovoka's home region raised concerns that the Paiutes, under Wovoka's influence, might follow the example of the Lakota, no violence ever came to pass, as it was antithetical to everything that Wovoka and the Ghost Dance stood for.

Despite the fact that his prophecies did not come true, Wovoka remained an influential religious leader among Indian people. The peaceful nature of his movement was not lost on Indian agents in his home region, who wanted him to remain there as a calming influence. In his later years, he made sporadic public appearances and was revered by Indian people from various tribes throughout the West. He was able to make a living by selling items that he had personally used, from clothing to the paint and feathers used in Indian religious ceremonies.

The movement Wovoka started may have faded into historical obscurity for most after the tragic events of 1890, but some tribes, especially on the Great Plains, still practiced the Ghost Dance for many years. During the Red Power movement of the 1960s, members of the American Indian Movement (AIM), specifically Oglala Lakota activist Leonard Crow Dog, performed the Ghost Dance. For them, the Ghost Dance was a perfect analogy for their own protest against US government policy and the loss of American Indian cultures.

—*Steven L. Danver, PhD*

Bibliography and Additional Reading

Hittman, Michael. *Wovoka and the Ghost Dance*. Ed. Don Lynch. Expanded ed. Lincoln: U of Nebraska P, 1997. Print.

Kehoe, Alice Beck. *The Ghost Dance: Ethnohistory and Revitalization*. New York: Holt, 1989. Print.

Mooney, James. *The Ghost-Dance Religion and the Sioux Outbreak of 1890*. 1892. Lincoln: U of Nebraska P, 1991. Print.

■ The Ghost Dance Among the Lakota

Date: June 20, 1890
Author: Z. A. Parker
Genre: report

Summary Overview

In January 1889, a Paiute medicine man named Wovoka had a vision that resulted in the birth of an American Indian religious revitalization movement called the Ghost Dance. A peaceful movement that called on Indians of all tribes to live peacefully and ethically, abstain from drinking alcohol, work hard, and perform the sacred dance, the Ghost Dance spread rapidly through many tribes in the western United States, as most tribes were facing difficult times and cultural upheaval due to being confined to reservations. By 1890, the Ghost Dance had reached the Lakota Sioux at the Pine Ridge Reservation in Dakota Territory. The Lakotas had been particularly hard hit by the realities of reservation life and had fought the US Army since 1866 for the right to continue their traditional way of life. This document gives an outside observer's perspective on the practice of the Ghost Dance at Pine Ridge.

Defining Moment

In late 1889, two Sioux medicine men, Short Bull and Kicking Bear, arrived in Nevada to visit Wovoka and learn the Ghost Dance, in order to bring it back to the Pine Ridge, Standing Rock, and Rosebud Reservations. When the Ghost Dance arrived at Pine Ridge in 1890, it gave hope to a people who had believed their future to be hopeless. It promised that if the Lakotas performed the dance with all of their hearts and abstained from violence and vice, the white people who were flooding into the Great Plains would be eradicated, and the idyllic lifestyle of the American Indians would be restored. A nomadic people who had once sustained themselves by following the bison, the Lakotas had been asked to practice agriculture on their reservations. Not only was this completely alien to their cultural background, but also the lands in the Dakota Territory, to which they had been assigned, were particularly poor for agriculture, especially without dependable irrigation methods, which were neither naturally occurring nor provided by the government.

Adding to the cultural crisis faced by the Lakotas, their holiest place, the Black Hills, which had been promised to them in perpetuity in the 1868 Treaty of Fort Laramie, had since been invaded by gold-seeking white Americans, resulting in the rebellion that led to the Lakotas' iconic victory over General George A. Custer at the Battle of the Little Bighorn in 1876. That victory, however, did not turn the tide of white expansion, and great Sioux leaders, such as Red Cloud, Crazy Horse, and Sitting Bull eventually settled on the reservations, dependent on government subsidies to help their people survive on a land that was not suited to agriculture and did not permit them to sustain themselves any other way.

Into this hopeless situation came the Ghost Dance, which promised a way back to the Lakotas' cultural past, and large numbers accepted its message and began participating in the dance. The most influential Lakota leader at the time, Sitting Bull, supported the practice among his people, though he did not participate in the dance itself. Agents of the US Bureau of Indian Affairs, including Standing Rock's James McLaughlin, opposed the movement, as they believed it presaged a renewed call for war against the United States.

Author Biography

Little is known about Mrs. Z. A. Parker, the woman who relayed this eyewitness account of the Ghost Dance. According to James Mooney, the ethnographer who took down her recounting of the dance, she was a teacher on the Pine Ridge Reservation who observed Lakotas performing a Ghost Dance near White Clay Creek on June 20, 1890. Much more is known about Mooney, as he was one of the foremost ethnographers of American Indian rituals and beliefs and the first scholar to do significant work on the Ghost Dance. Mooney worked for the Smithsonian Institution's Bureau of American Ethnology, where his job was to compile information on

American Indian tribes. His most significant work was among the Sioux and the Cherokees, and he was widely regarded as his generation's leading expert on American Indians.

HISTORICAL DOCUMENT

We drove to this spot about 10:30 o'clock on a delightful October day. We came upon tents scattered here and there in low, sheltered places long before reaching the dance ground. Presently we saw over three hundred tents placed in a circle, with a large pine tree in the center, which was covered with strips of cloth of various colors, eagle feathers, stuffed birds, claws, and horns—all offerings to the Great Spirit. The ceremonies had just begun. In the center, around the tree, were gathered their medicine-men; also those who had been so fortunate as to have had visions and in them had seen and talked with friends who had died. A company of fifteen had started a chant and were marching abreast, others coming in behind as they marched. After marching around the circle of tents they turned to the center, where many had gathered and were seated on the ground.

I think they wore the ghost shirt or ghost dress for the first time that day. I noticed that these were all new and were worn by about seventy men and forty women. The wife of a man called Return-from-scout had seen in a vision that her friends all wore a similar robe, and on reviving from her trance she called the women together and they made a great number of the sacred garments. They were of white cotton cloth. The women's dress was cut like their ordinary dress, a loose robe with wide, flowing sleeves, painted blue in the neck, in the shape of a three-cornered handkerchief, with moon, stars, birds, etc., interspersed with real feathers, painted on the waists, letting them fall to within 3 inches of the ground, the fringe at the bottom. In the hair, near the crown, a feather was tied. I noticed an absence of any manner of head ornaments, and, as I knew their vanity and fondness for them, wondered why it was. Upon making inquiries I found they discarded everything they could which was made by white men.

The ghost shirt for the men was made of the same material-shirts and leggings painted in red. Some of the leggings were painted in stripes running up and down, others running around. The shirt was painted blue around the neck, and the whole garment was fantasti-

cally sprinkled with figures of birds, bows and arrows, sun, moon, and stars, and everything they saw in nature. Down the outside of the sleeve were rows of feathers tied by the quill ends and left to fly in the breeze, and also a row around the neck and up and down the outside of the leggings. I noticed that a number had stuffed birds, squirrel heads, etc., tied in their long hair. The faces of all were painted red with a black half-moon on the forehead or on one cheek.

As the crowd gathered about the tree the high priest, or master of ceremonies, began his address, giving them directions as to the chant and other matters. After he had spoken for about fifteen minutes they arose and formed in a circle. As nearly as I could count, there were between three and four hundred persons. One stood directly behind another, each with his hands on his neighbor's shoulders. After walking about a few times, chanting, "Father, I come," they stopped marching, but remained in the circle, and set up the most fearful, heart-piercing wails I ever heard—crying, moaning, groaning, and shrieking out their grief, and naming over their departed friends and relatives, at the same time taking up handfuls of dust at their feet, washing their hands in it, and throwing it over their heads. Finally, they raised their eyes to heaven, their hands clasped high above their heads, and stood straight and perfectly still, invoking the power of the Great Spirit to allow them to see and talk with their people who had died. This ceremony lasted about fifteen minutes, when they all sat down where they were and listened to another address, which I did not understand, but which I afterwards learned were words of encouragement and assurance of the coming messiah.

When they arose again, they enlarged the circle by facing toward the center, taking hold of hands, and moving around in the manner of school children in their play of "needle's eye." And now the most intense excitement began. They would go as fast as they could, their hands moving from side to side, their bodies swaying, their arms, with hands gripped tightly in their neighbors', swinging back and forth with all their might. If one, more weak and frail, came near falling, he would be jerked up and into position until tired nature gave way. The ground had been worked and worn by many feet, until the fine, flour-like dust lay light and loose to the depth of two or three inches. The wind, which had increased, would sometimes take it up, enveloping the dancers and hiding them from view. In the ring were men, women, and children; the strong and the robust, the weak consumptive, and those near to death's door. They believed those who were sick would be cured by joining in the dance and losing consciousness. From the beginning they chanted, to a monotonous tune, the words

Father, I come;
Mother, I come;
Brother, I come;
Father, give us back our arrows.

All of which they would repeat over and over again until first one and then another would break from the ring and stagger away and fall down. One woman fell a few feet from me. She came toward us, her hair flying over her face, which was purple, looking as if the blood would burst through; her hands and arms moving wildly; every breath a pant and a groan; and she fell on her back, and went down like a log. I stepped up to her as she lay there motionless, but with every muscle twitching and quivering. She seemed to be perfectly unconscious.

Some of the men and a few of the women would run, stepping high and pawing the air in a frightful manner. Some told me afterwards that they had a sensation as if the ground were rising toward them and would strike them in the face. Others would drop where they stood. One woman fell directly into the ring, and her husband stepped out and stood over her to prevent them from trampling upon her. No one ever disturbed those who fell or took any notice of them except to keep the crowd away.

They kept up dancing until fully 100 persons were lying unconscious. Then they stopped and seated themselves in a circle, and as each recovered from his trance he was brought to the center of the ring to relate his experience. Each told his story to the medicine-man and he shouted it to the crowd. Not one in ten claimed that he saw anything. I asked one Indian—a tall, strong fellow, straight as an arrow—what his experience was. He said he saw an eagle coming toward him. It flew round and round, drawing nearer and nearer until he put out his hand to take it, when it was gone. I asked him what he thought of it. "Big lie," he replied. I found by talking to them that not one in twenty believed it. After resting for a time they would go through the same performance, perhaps three times a day. They practiced fasting, and every morning those who joined in the dance were obliged to immerse themselves in the creek.

GLOSSARY

consumptive: wasted of body; debilitated by illness, often pulmonary tuberculosis

medicine man: a traditional healer and spiritual leader

needle's eye: a chanting circle game in Victorian times

Document Analysis

Parker's account of the Ghost Dance demonstrates a number of differences between Wovoka's vision and the way the dance was practiced and thought about by the Lakotas. The account also conveys Parker's perception, common among white people at the time, that the practice of the Ghost Dance by the Lakotas was leading to resumed resistance to white expansionism.

One of Parker's most notable observations is her description of the Lakota ghost shirts, which were worn during the practice of the dance. Wovoka made no mention of such shirts; they were a purely Lakota addition to the dance. According to Parker, "The wife of a man called Return-from-scout had seen in a vision that her friends all wore a similar robe, and on reviving from her trance she called the women together and they made a great number of the sacred garments." There were different versions of the shirt for men and women to wear. Both versions were decorated by various painted symbols, including birds, stars, the sun, and the moon.

The ghost shirts were largely responsible for the perception of the Ghost Dance as a militant movement that could possibly lead to a renewal of warfare. While Wovoka had preached that Indians should coexist peacefully with white people, it has been argued that the Lakotas ignored this message of nonviolence and instead saw the Ghost Dance as a potential precursor to the elimination of the white race. They claimed that the ghost shirts would protect them against the bullets fired by the US Army. Additionally, part of the chant reported by Parker—"Father, I come; Mother, I come; Brother, I come; Father, give us back our arrows"—seems to imply both the resurrection of the Indians who had died before and the resumption of hostilities with the Americans. Parker's account demonstrates the fervor with which the Lakotas practiced the Ghost Dance, noting that at least one hundred of those participating danced until they fell unconscious.

Alarmed by accounts such as Parker's, McLaughlin called for the Lakotas to stop the dancing, but he was unable to control the spread of the movement. McLaughlin then asked the US Army to dispatch a unit to the reservation and also sent his own tribal police (Lakotas who worked directly for the reservation agent) to arrest Sitting Bull, whom he erroneously believed to be the leader of the movement. When the tribal police arrived at Sitting Bull's home on Standing Rock Reservation to bring him into custody, a firefight broke out that resulted in the death of the great Lakota spiritual leader.

Essential Themes

The Ghost Dance movement may have been short lived among the Lakotas, but it had a profound influence on their history and the history of American Indians as a whole, in both the short and the long term. Immediately after the killing of Sitting Bull, a Lakota chief named Spotted Elk, also known as Big Foot, took approximately 350 Lakotas, mostly women and children, and fled the nearby Cheyenne River Reservation for Pine Ridge. They were pursued by troops under the command of Major Samuel Whitside and were eventually intercept-

ed. Spotted Elk, who had contracted pneumonia during the journey, surrendered, and he and his band were escorted to Wounded Knee Creek. On December 29, 1890, soldiers were attempting to disarm the Lakotas when a shot was fired. The federal troops opened fire on the largely unarmed camp with Hotchkiss artillery, killing at least 150 Lakotas. The massacre at Wounded Knee is widely regarded as the symbolic end of the Sioux Wars, which had begun with the First Sioux War in 1854.

Despite the violent attempts at suppression, the Ghost Dance did not die out, and it was still being performed by a number of other tribes on the Great Plains into the 1960s. By the end of that decade, the American Indian Movement (AIM) had formed to advocate for Indian rights and welfare. Many of the movement's participants looked to the Ghost Dance as inspiration for their own conflict, as it symbolized American Indian resistance to US policy and the encroachment of American culture. Leonard Crow Dog, an Oglala Lakota holy man and AIM activist, revived the practice of the Ghost Dance in the 1970s.

In 1973, AIM activists and about 200 Lakota returned to Wounded Knee, seizing the town to protest the failed impeachment of Oglala tribal president Richard Wilson and the failure of the US government to honor its treaties with Indian nations. FBI agents and US marshals besieged the activists for seventy-one days, and one agent and two protesters were killed during the standoff. The event and the publicity given it by the press resulted in greater attention for the cause of American Indian rights throughout the United States.

—*Steven L. Danver, PhD*

Bibliography and Additional Reading

Brown, Dee. *Bury My Heart at Wounded Knee*: An Indian History of the American West. New York: Holt, 1970. Print.

Hittman, Michael. *Wovoka and the Ghost Dance*. Ed. Don Lynch. Expanded ed. Lincoln: U of Nebraska P, 1997. Print

Kehoe, Alice Beck. *The Ghost Dance: Ethnohistory and Revitalization*. New York: Holt, 1989. Print.

Niehardt, John G. *Black Elk Speaks: Being the Life of a Holy Man of the Oglala Sioux*. Premier ed. Albany: State U of New York P, 2008. Print.

■ Eyewitness to the Massacre at Wounded Knee

Date: December 29, 1890
Author: Philip Wells
Genre: report

Summary Overview

By December 1890, the Sioux Nation—which comprises the Lakota and Dakota groupings, among others—had largely been confined to reservations in the Plains States. The Ghost Dance movement, a religious movement that was quickly spreading throughout the reservations, was perceived as disruptive and potentially threatening to federal efforts to manage the American Indian population. In light of this perception, federal authorities planned to arrest the famous Lakota chief Sitting Bull in an effort to suppress the movement. Sitting Bull was killed during the arrest, and US authorities soon turned their attention to another Sioux leader, Spotted Elk, also known (derogatorily) as Big Foot. In December 1890, Spotted Elk and his followers were detained, and Spotted Elk was interrogated by Colonel James Forsyth, with the assistance of interpreter Philip Wells, while the other Sioux were searched for weapons. After a shot rang out in the crowd, Sioux fighters and American military personnel clashed, leaving as many as three hundred Sioux and twenty-five white soldiers dead. After the incident, Wells delivered his own account of the incident to his superiors.

Defining Moment

During the 1880s, American Indians suffered major setbacks, due in no small part to the United States government's efforts to control and assimilate the tribes into white society. As American Indians endured starvation, disease, and other hardships, an unusual movement began to spread among the tribes. The Ghost Dance, which had been first popularized by the Northern Paiute mystic Wodziwob during the early 1870s, saw a resurgence thanks to the efforts of another American Indian mystic, Wovoka, also known as Jack Wilson. Wovoka claimed that while suffering from a fever, he was taken to the spirit world and told that the dead would rise again and the plight of American Indians would soon end. If American Indians lived a good, up-

right life free of violence, the return to their traditional way of life would be hastened. Part of the commitment to this ideal involved wearing colorful garb and practicing a sacred dance that came to be known as the Ghost Dance.

As the Ghost Dance spread, however, an additional concept was added to the practice—one that gave white settlers and leaders pause. Some practitioners of the Ghost Dance believed that the dance would result in the ejection of white settlers from American Indian lands. White officials, seeing the movement's adherents as a hostile group, attempted to ban the Ghost Dance and prosecute those who practiced it.

Prominent Lakota shaman and chief Sitting Bull was accused of promoting the Ghost Dance movement, although he was not a follower of the practice, and US authorities attempted to arrest him at the Standing Rock Indian Reservation, which encompasses parts of North and South Dakota. During the ensuing confrontation, Sitting Bull was killed. Less than a month later, authorities attempted to arrest another Lakota leader, Spotted Elk, at a camp near Wounded Knee Creek in South Dakota. Spotted Elk and his 350 followers were detained by US troops. While American military forces, led by Colonel Joseph Forsyth, conducted their investigation and slowly disarmed Spotted Elk's followers, Forsyth's interpreter, Wells, spotted a medicine man, or shaman, throwing dirt into the air while praying. Wells reported that the man was attempting to incite an uprising.

Shortly thereafter, according to Wells's report, a shot fired from the crowd caused the military to open fire. Unarmed Sioux men, women, and children ran from the scene, but many were shot by the Army. Reports on the number of dead vary, but as many as three hundred Sioux may have died in the event, along with some twenty-five US soldiers. A few days later, the military launched an investigation of the incident. Wells, the only interpreter at the scene and, therefore, the only person with an understanding of what the Lakotas involved had said before the firefight, provided his own account.

Author Biography

Philip Faribault Wells was born in 1850 in Frontenac, Minnesota. The child of a white frontiersman and a woman of partial Sioux descent, Wells became conversant in a number of American Indian languages, including Sioux dialects. In 1865, Wells joined the Army as an interpreter and scout. During the 1880s, after leaving the Army, he held a number of positions on Sioux reservations, benefiting from his status as an American with Sioux blood. Wells was fiercely supportive of the US government, serving as its agent when dealing with the Sioux tribes. He later left the public service to become a rancher. Wells died in 1947.

Chief Spotted Elk, or "Big Foot," was born between 1820 and 1825 into the Miniconjou, a subgroup of the Teton Lakota (Sioux). His Lakota name was Unpan Gleška. The Miniconjou lived in northwestern South Dakota with the Hunkpapa, another band of the Teton Lakota led by Chief Sitting Bull. Spotted Elk was a cousin of the famous Crazy Horse through the latter's mother. In 1868, Spotted Elk signed the Ft. Laramie Treaty, which ceded lands to the Sioux, although the treaty was later violated by white gold prospectors and the US government, causing war. Spotted Elk was killed during the conflict at Wounded Knee. A photograph of him lying dead in the snow became an iconic image of the event.

HISTORICAL DOCUMENT

I was interpreting for General Forsyth [Forsyth was actually a colonel] just before the battle of Wounded Knee, December 29, 1890. The captured Indians had been ordered to give up their arms, but Big Foot [i.e., Spotted Elk] replied that his people had no arms. Forsyth said to me, "Tell Big Foot he says the Indians have no arms, yet yesterday they were well armed when they surrendered. He is deceiving me. Tell him he need have no fear in giving up his arms, as I wish to treat him kindly." Big Foot replied, "They have no guns, except such as you have found." Forsyth declared, "You are lying to me in return for my kindness."

During this time a medicine man, gaudily dressed and fantastically painted, executed the maneuvers of the ghost dance, raising and throwing dust into the air. He exclaimed "Ha! Ha!" as he did so, meaning he was about to do something terrible, and said, "I have lived long enough," meaning he would fight until he died. Turning to the young warriors who were squatted together, he said "Do not fear, but let your hearts be strong. Many soldiers are about us and have many bullets, but I am assured their bullets cannot penetrate us. The prairie is large, and their bullets will fly over the prairies and will not come toward us. If they do come toward us, they will float away like dust in the air." I turned to Major Whitside and said, "That man is making mischief," and repeated what he had said. Whitside replied, "Go direct to Colonel Forsyth and tell him about it," which I did.

Forsyth and I went to the circle of warriors where he told me to tell the medicine man to sit down and keep quiet, but he paid no attention to the order. Forsyth repeated the order. Big Foot's brother-in-law answered, "He will sit down when he gets around the circle." When the medicine man came to the end of the circle, he squatted down. A cavalry sergeant exclaimed, "There goes an Indian with a gun under his blanket!" Forsyth ordered him to take the gun from the Indian, which he did. Whitside then said to me, "Tell the Indians it is necessary that they be searched one at a time." The young warriors paid no attention to what I told them. I heard someone on my left exclaim, "Look out! Look out!" I saw five or six young warriors cast off their blankets and pull guns out from under them and brandish them in the air. One of the warriors shot into the soldiers, who were ordered to fire into the Indians. I looked in the direction of the medicine man. He or some other medicine man approached to within three or four feet of me with a long cheese knife, ground to a sharp point and raised to stab me. He stabbed me during the melee and nearly cut off my nose. I held him off until I could swing my rifle to hit him, which I did. I shot and killed him in self-defense.

Troop K was drawn up between the tents of the women

and children and the main body of the Indians, who had been summoned to deliver their arms. The Indians began firing into Troop K to gain the canyon of Wounded Knee creek. In doing so they exposed their women and children to their own fire. Captain Wallace was killed at this time while standing in front of his troops. A bullet,

striking him in the forehead, plowed away the top of his head. I started to pull off my nose, which was hung by the skin, but Lieutenant Guy Preston shouted, "My God Man! Don't do that! That can be saved." He then led me away from the scene of the trouble.

Document Analysis

Wells's account of the massacre at Wounded Knee identifies the Lakotas as the instigators of the outburst of violence. He claims that he and his military superiors showed patience and fairness toward Spotted Elk and the Lakotas, only to have that even-handedness challenged and returned with criminality and brutality. The Lakotas' actions, in Wells's view—and not the actions of Forsyth and his troops—resulted in the deaths of hundreds of Lakotas, including women and children, as well as more than two dozen US troops.

Wells's report begins by describing the deceptiveness of the captured chief, Spotted Elk. Forsyth, through Wells, told Spotted Elk that the Lakotas were to give up their arms. Spotted Elk, according to Wells, claimed that his followers had no weapons, even though the La-kotas who were captured the previous day were well armed. Wells argues that Forsyth insisted that the troops wished to treat the Lakotas well as long as they gave up their weapons, and that Spotted Elk returned this benevolence with lies.

At this point, Wells reports that he noticed a La-kota shaman throwing dirt in the air and practicing the Ghost Dance. According to Wells, the man next shouted out in a manner that Wells knew to be indica-tive of his intention to "do something terrible." The shaman then turned to his fellow Lakotas and invited them to join him, as the army's bullets would have no effect on them. Wells writes that he informed Forsyth, who joined him in confronting the shaman. Suddenly, a soldier noticed one of the Lakotas brandishing a gun, and as they attempted to disarm the man, several more Lakotas revealed that they were armed. One warrior, Wells recalls, fired into the line of troops. The soldiers fired back. During the ensuing battle, a Lakota man slashed Wells in the face, nearly severing his nose, and Wells killed him in self-defense. During the battle, Wells writes, the Lakotas endangered the many inno-cent women and children who were standing near the troops, injuring those innocents with their own fire.

Wells's account places the blame for the violence

squarely on the shaman, apparently an adherent of the Ghost Dance movement, as well as the intransigent Spotted Elk/Big Foot and his well-armed followers. The troops, whom Wells describes as calm and patient in the face of an unruly crowd, are presented as the victims of a surprise attack to which they were forced to respond. The resulting battle, Wells reports, ended with numerous dead Lakota, American troops, and in-nocent bystanders.

Essential Themes

Wells had spent his life living among American Indians and was a steadfast patriot, a combination of character-istics that made him a desirable intermediary between the US government and the Sioux. However, he was not fluent in the Lakota dialect and, according to observers and historians alike, likely misunderstood the shaman's actions, which in turn sparked the firefight. Certainly, the scene at the Wounded Knee camp was tense before the first shots, as hundreds of Lakotas were forced to wait to be searched for weapons. Although the accuracy of Wells's version of the story has been heavily debated by historians, his account is undeniably accurate in one important area: Once the first shot was fired, an already-tense situation exploded into a brutal battle.

In his account, Wells places the blame for the erup-tion of violence on the shoulders of the Lakotas. Spot-ted Elk, he claims in his account, angered the even-tempered Forsyth by lying about whether the Lakotas were still armed. The shaman, meanwhile, is portrayed in Wells's account as an instigator who attempted to inspire his fellow Lakotas to rise up against the troops. Wells even blames the Lakota men for the deaths of the Lakota women and children, arguing that the men po-sitioned themselves in such a way that these innocents would be fired upon. He describes the entire event as a Lakota attack on a nonaggressive military unit.

In addition to blaming the Lakotas for the massa-cre, Wells's account serves to elevate his own standing. Wells claims to have been the first person to alert For-syth of the imminent danger from the shaman. He was close at hand when the first weapons were allegedly pulled out from under the captured Lakotas' blankets. Finally, he was himself nearly a casualty of the violence, almost losing his nose to a Lakota attacker's knife. His account of this battle, however suspect, likely helped further his career as an agent of the government to which he steadfastly committed himself.

—*Michael P. Auerbach, MA*

Bibliography and Additional Reading

Beasley, Conger. *We Are a People in this World: The Lakota Sioux and the Massacre at Wounded Knee*. Fayetteville: U of Arkansas P, 1995. Print.

DiSilvestro, Roger L. *In the Shadow of Wounded Knee: The Untold Final Chapter of the Indian Wars*. New York: Walker, 2007. Print.

Flood, Reneé Sansom. *Lost Bird of Wounded Knee: Spirit of the Lakota*. Cambridge: Da Capo, 1998. Print.

Richardson, Heather Cox. *Wounded Knee: Party Politics and the Road to an American Massacre*. New York: Basic, 2010. Print.

■ Lakota Accounts of the Massacre at Wounded Knee

Date: February 11, 1891
Authors: Turning Hawk, Captain Sword, Spotted Horse, and American Horse
Genre: report; memoir

Summary Overview

The massacre at Wounded Knee Creek in South Dakota, which took place on December 29, 1890, is as infamous as it is iconic. The image of United States troops opening fire on a peaceful camp, mostly made up of women and children, is seared into the American conscience. It marked the end of the Sioux Wars, which had dragged on for over twenty years. But in a larger sense, it was also a symbolic end to the armed resistance of American Indian peoples to the forced reservation life. Though the American press lauded it as a victorious battle—revenge for the death of General George Custer at the Little Bighorn—American Indian peoples, not surprisingly, viewed these same events from a very different perspective.

These accounts, some by Lakotas who were actually present at the massacre, were taken down while the memories were still fresh—within forty-five days of the events taking place. They are remarkable not only because of the diversity of backgrounds of the Indian informants, but also because they present a uniformly horrific perspective on the actions of the United States Army.

Defining Moment

Various bands of the Lakota, Dakota, and Nakota Sioux were at war with the United States almost unceasingly from 1862 through 1890. From the Dakota War in Minnesota to the Wounded Knee Massacre, the bands of Sioux fought against the confiscation of their lands by the United States and the changes to their traditional lifeways that went along with it. As semi-nomadic peoples, the Lakotas, Dakotas, and Nakotas had well-established annual circuits that followed the buffalo herds across the Northern Plains. By the time of Wounded Knee, most of that lifestyle was gone. The Lakotas had been forced to sign the Treaty of Fort Laramie (1868), confining them to the Great Sioux Reservation, which was later broken up in the Black Hills gold

rush. Further, Hunkpapa Lakota spiritual leader Sitting Bull had ended his sojourn into Canada in 1881 and settled on the Standing Rock Agency in 1883.

However, the arrival in the fall of 1890 of the Ghost Dance, an intertribal religious movement that promised an end to the Native peoples' troubles, reignited the fears of white Indian agents, such as James McLaughlin, that another uprising was imminent. Sitting Bull's approval of the Ghost Dance led to his death on December 15, 1890, at the hands of tribal police. Upon Sitting Bull's death, about 350 Miniconjou and Hunkpapa Lakotas, of whom some 230 were women and children, left the reservation under the leadership of Spotted Elk (aka Big Foot); eventually they were forced by the US Seventh Cavalry to surrender and make camp on Wounded Knee Creek in southwestern South Dakota. On the morning of December 29, soldiers rode into the camp to disarm the men. Stories vary about what happened to spark the massacre (in the testimony, Spotted Horse claims that the Lakotas fired first, killing one of the soldiers), but, in any event, the surrounding army opened fire with their rifles and four artillery pieces. Estimates of the Lakota losses range from 128 to nearly 300 total dead, most of them women, children, and infants. Twenty-five to thirty-five of the roughly five hundred soldiers present were killed.

The Wounded Knee Massacre is considered a turning point in the history of the relationship between American Indians and the US government. It marked the end of armed resistance by the Sioux and is thought of as a symbolic end to most armed resistance by American Indian peoples across the nation. Reservation life, the breakup of tribal lands into individual parcels (with the larger portion of remaining land sold to white settlers), and the forced assimilation of Indian peoples were to be the fate of most tribal nations.

The testimony of Turning Hawk, Captain Sword, Spotted Horse, and American Horse stands as a rebuttal to the US interpretation of the events of the "battle." Though not all of them agreed with Big Foot's exodus from the reservation, they are all clear on the brutality of what occurred, as old men, adolescents, women, and children were all killed, seemingly indiscriminately.

Author Biography

In the aftermath of the Wounded Knee Massacre, four Lakotas—Turning Hawk, Captain Sword, Spotted Horse, and American Horse—traveled to Washington, DC, in order to testify to the events for the commissioner of Indian Affairs. Of the four who testified,

American Horse was the best known, as he had been an Oglala Lakota leader for some years. He had worked as a scout for the United States Army and had opposed the resistance to Anglo-American expansionism. He favored peace with the United States at any cost and assimilation to Anglo-American culture through Indian education at boarding schools, like Captain Richard Henry Pratt's Carlisle Indian Industrial School. It is clear in the testimony that, although none of the four Lakotas was in favor of the armed resistance advocated by leaders like Sitting Bull and Crazy Horse, they were all appalled by the carnage at Wounded Knee.

HISTORICAL DOCUMENT

TURNING HAWK, Pine Ridge (Mr. Cook, interpreter).

Mr. Commissioner, my purpose to-day is to tell you what I know of the condition of affairs at the agency where I live. A certain falsehood came to our agency from the west which had the effect of a fire upon the Indians, and when this certain fire came upon our people those who had farsightedness and could see into the matter made up their minds to stand up against it and fight it. The reason we took this hostile attitude to this fire was because we believed that you yourself would not be in favor of this particular mischief-making thing; but just as we expected, the people in authority did not like this thing and we were quietly told that we must give up or have nothing to do with this certain movement. Though this is the advice from our good friends in the east, there were, of course, many silly young men who were longing to become identified with the movement, although they knew that there was nothing absolutely bad, nor did they know there was anything absolutely good, in connection with the movement.

In the course of time we heard that the soldiers were moving toward the scene of trouble. After awhile some of the soldiers finally reached our place and we heard that a number of them also reached our friends at Rosebud. Of course, when a large body of soldiers is moving toward a certain direction they inspire a more or less amount of awe, and it is natural that the women and children who see this large moving mass are made afraid of it and be put in a condition to make them run away. At first

we thought the Pine Ridge and Rosebud were the only two agencies where soldiers were sent, but finally we heard that the other agencies fared likewise. We heard and saw that about half our friends at Rosebud agency, from fear at seeing the soldiers, began the move of running away from their agency toward ours (Pine Ridge), and when they had gotten inside of our reservation they there learned that right ahead of them at our agency was another large crowd of soldiers, and while the soldiers were there, there was constantly a great deal of false rumor flying back and forth. The special rumor I have in mind is the threat that the soldiers had come there to disarm the Indians entirely and to take away all their horses from them. That was the oft-repeated story.

So constantly repeated was this story that our friends from Rosebud, instead of going to Pine Ridge, the place of their destination, veered off and went to some other direction toward the "Bad Lands." We did not know definitely how many, but understood there were 300 lodges of them, about 1,700 people. Eagle Pipe, Turning Bear, High Hawk, Short Bull, Lance, No Flesh, Pine Bird, Crow Dog, Two Strike, and White Horse were the leaders.

Well, the people after veering off in this way, many of them who believe in peace and order at our agency, were very anxious that some influence should be brought upon these people. In addition to our love of peace we remembered that many of these people were related to us by blood. So we sent out peace commissioners to the people who were thus running away from their agency.

I understood at the time that they were simply going away from fear because of so many soldiers. So constant was the word of these good men from Pine Ridge agency that finally they succeeded in getting away half of the party from Rosebud, from the place where they took refuge, and finally were brought to the agency at Pine Ridge. Young-Man-Afraid-of-his-Horses, Little Wound, Fast Thunder, Louis Shangreau, John Grass, Jack Red Cloud, and myself were some of these peace-makers.

The remnant of the party from Rosebud not taken to the agency finally reached the wilds of the Bad Lands. Seeing that we had succeeded so well, once more we sent to the same party in the Bad Lands and succeeded in bringing these very Indians out of the depths of the Bad Lands and were being brought toward the agency. When we were about a day's journey from our agency we heard that a certain party of Indians (Big Foot's band) from the Cheyenne River agency was coming toward Pine Ridge in flight.

CAPTAIN SWORD.

Those who actually went off of the Cheyenne River agency probably number 303, and there were a few from the Standing Rock reserve with them, but as to their number I do not know. There were a number of Ogalallas, old men and several school boys, coming back with that very same party, and one of the very seriously wounded boys was a member of the Ogalalla boarding school at Pine Ridge agency. He was not on the warpath, but was simply returning home to his agency and to his school after a summer visit to relatives on the Cheyenne river.

TURNING HAWK.

When we heard that these people were coming toward our agency we also heard this. These people were coming toward Pine Ridge agency, and when they were almost on the agency they were met by the soldiers and surrounded and finally taken to the Wounded Knee creek, and there at a given time their guns were demanded. When they had delivered them up, the men were separated from their families, from the tipis, and taken to a certain spot. When the guns were thus taken and the men thus separated, there was a crazy man, a young man of very bad influence and in fact a nobody, among that bunch of Indians fired his gun, and of course the firing of a gun must have been the breaking of a military rule of some sort, because immediately the soldiers returned fire and indiscriminate killing followed.

SPOTTED HORSE.

This man shot an officer in the army; the first shot killed this officer. I was a voluntary scout at that encounter and I saw exactly what was done, and that was what I noticed; that the first shot killed an officer. As soon as this shot was fired the Indians immediately began drawing their knives, and they were exhorted from all sides to desist, but this was not obeyed. Consequently the firing began immediately on the part of the soldiers.

TURNING HAWK.

All the men who were in a bunch were killed right there, and those who escaped that first fire got into the ravine, and as they went along up the ravine for a long distance they were pursued on both sides by the soldiers and shot down, as the dead bodies showed afterwards. The women were standing off at a different place form where the men were stationed, and when the firing began, those of the men who escaped the first onslaught went in one direction up the ravine, and then the women, who were bunched together at another place, went entirely in a different direction through an open field, and the women fared the same fate as the men who went up the deep ravine.

AMERICAN HORSE.

The men were separated, as has already been said, from the women, and they were surrounded by the soldiers. Then came next the village of the Indians and that was entirely surrounded by the soldiers also. When the firing began, of course the people who were standing immediately around the young man who fired the first shot were killed right together, and then they turned their guns, Hotchkiss guns, etc., upon the women who were in the lodges standing there under a flag of truce, and of course as soon as they were fired upon they fled, the men fleeing in one direction and the women running in two different directions. So that there were three general directions in which they took flight.

There was a woman with an infant in her arms who

was killed as she almost touched the flag of truce, and the women and children of course were strewn all along the circular village until they were dispatched. Right near the flag of truce a mother was shot down with her infant; the child not knowing that its mother was dead was still nursing, and that especially was a very sad sight. The women as they were fleeing with their babes were killed together, shot right through, and the women who were very heavy with child were also killed. All the Indians fled in these three directions, and after most all of them had been killed a cry was made that all those who were not killed wounded should come forth and they would be safe. Little boys who were not wounded came out of their places of refuge, and as soon as they came in sight a number of soldiers surrounded them and butchered them there.

Of course we all feel very sad about this affair. I stood very loyal to the government all through those troublesome days, and believing so much in the government and being so loyal to it, my disappointment was very strong, and I have come to Washington with a very great blame on my heart. Of course it would have been all right if only the men were killed; we would feel almost grateful for it. But the fact of the killing of the women, and more especially the killing of the young boys and girls who are to go to make up the future strength of the Indian people, is the saddest part of the whole affair and we feel it very sorely.

I was not there at the time before the burial of the bodies, but I did go there with some of the police and the Indian doctor and a great many of the people, men from the agency, and we went through the battlefield and saw where the bodies were from the track of the blood.

TURNING HAWK.

I had just reached the point where I said that the women were killed. We heard, besides the killing of the men, of the onslaught also made upon the women and children, and they were treated as roughly and indiscriminately as the men and boys were.

Of course this affair brought a great deal of distress upon all the people, but especially upon the minds of those who stood loyal to the government and who did all that they were able to do in the matter of bringing about peace. They especially have suffered much distress and are very much hurt at heart. These peace-makers continued on in their good work, but there were a great many fickle young men who were ready to be moved by the change in the events there, and consequently, in spite of the great fire that was brought upon all, they were ready to assume any hostile attitude. These young men got themselves in readiness and went in the direction of the scene of battle so they might be of service there. They got there and finally exchanged shots with the soldiers. This party of young men was made up from Rosebud, Ogalalla (Pine Ridge), and members of any other agencies that happened to be there at the time. While this was going on in the neighborhood of Wounded Knee—the Indians and soldiers exchanging shots—the agency, our home, was also fired into by the Indians. Matters went on in this strain until the evening came on, and then the Indians went off down by White Clay creek. When the agency was fired upon by the Indians from the hillside, of course the shots were returned by the Indian police who were guarding the agency buildings.

Although fighting seemed to have been in the air, yet those who believed in peace were still constant at their work. Young-Man-Afraid-of-his-Horses, who had been on a visit to some other agency in the north or northwest, returned, and immediately went out to the people living about White Clay creek, on the border of the Bad Lands, and brought his people out. He succeeded in obtaining the consent of the people to come out of their place of refuge and return to the agency. Thus the remaining portion of the Indians who started from Rosebud were brought back into the agency. Mr. Commissioner, during the days of the great whirlwind out there, those good men tried to hold up a counteracting power, and that was "Peace." We have now come to realize that peace has prevailed and won the day. While we were engaged in bringing about peace our property was left behind, of course, and most of us have lost everything, even down to the matter of guns with which to kill ducks, rabbits, etc, shotguns, and guns of that order. When Young-Man-Afraid brought the people in and their guns were asked for, both men who were called hostile and men who stood loyal to the government delivered up their guns.

GLOSSARY

agency: Indian reservation

Hotchkiss gun: a large (42 mm) gun or canon

movement: a reference to the Ghost Dance, a religious movement that stirred hopes among Indian peoples and caused worries among white officials

Ogalalla: (or Oglala): one of the subgroups of the Lakota people

Document Analysis

During the final quarter of the nineteenth century, American Indians were divided in how they looked at the future. Some, such as Lakota leaders Sitting Bull and Crazy Horse, had favored attempts to engage the US Army in an effort to maintain their traditional semi-nomadic way of life. Others, such as American Horse and, later in his life, Red Cloud, became known as "reservation chiefs," who believed that resistance to American expansionism was pointless and reservation life and possibly assimilation into American society was the only future. In the aftermath of the Wounded Knee Massacre, the voices of the reservation chiefs were the only ones left to be heard by the government, and it would remain that way for at least until the Indian Reorganization Act of 1934. As the commissioner of Indian Affairs gathered testimony on the massacre, it was the pro-assimilation Lakotas who were allowed to speak. But even so, the brutality of the massacre comes through clearly.

Biases are revealed by all of the Lakota witnesses. Turning Hawk describes the Ghost Dance movement that sparked the conflict as a "certain falsehood [that] came . . . from the west which had the effect of a fire upon the Indians." The ensuing strife and death of Sitting Bull led Big Foot/Spotted Elk to leave the reservation with a few men and many women and children, eventually ending up camped out on Wounded Knee Creek. When the army came in to disarm the group, Spotted Horse states that it was one of the Lakotas who shot first, sparking the melee. American Horse agrees with him, but quickly points out that what ensued quickly became a massacre, stating, "Then they turned their guns, Hotchkiss guns, etc., upon the women who were in the lodges standing there under a flag of truce."

Finally, both American Horse and Turning Hawk note that the events of that day had caused many who had been loyal to the US government to question their decision, with some taking up arms against not only the soldiers, but also the reservation officials and the Indian police who protected them. Eventually, the peace chiefs prevailed upon the belligerents, and calm was eventually restored. This calm, however, was one of resignation by many Lakotas. The decades-long Sioux Wars were over, and most accepted the inevitability of reservation life. The four who testified to the commissioner of Indian Affairs were in favor of peace, but nevertheless were clearly horrified by the massacre and distressed at the loss of their own hunting rifles in its aftermath.

Essential Themes

The fact that conflict between American Indians and the US Army ended in a bloody massacre was not a surprise. Wounded Knee was not an isolated incident. Across Indian Country, from Prophetstown in Indiana to Sand Creek in Colorado to Camp Grant in Arizona, such massacres were all too common. Although groups, such as the Lake Mohonk Conference of Friends of the Indian and Other Dependent Peoples, were calling for a more humane way of forcing assimilation, the response afterward was typical. The commander of the US Army that day, James W. Forsyth, was initially discharged, but later exonerated of any wrongdoing and promoted, and some eighteen soldiers received Congressional Medals of Honor.

Within the Lakota Nation, the massacre brought about a less typical reaction. The ideological disagreement between the war chiefs and the reservation chiefs came to an end, as the reservation chiefs held sway. As Robert M. Utley demonstrates, American Horse himself became quite influential and was closely allied with the well-respected former war chief Red Cloud. In an interesting parallel, it was American Horse who replaced the deceased Sitting Bull as a headliner in Buffalo Bill's Wild West Show. Roger Di Silvestro points out that the aftermath of Wounded Knee led many to farm on the reservation, become soldiers themselves, or attend schools such as the Carlisle Indian Industrial School, where they would be forced to abandon their religions, languages, and cultures in favor of assimilation into white culture.

Eighty-three years later, the American Indian Movement (AIM) held a protest at the massacre site on the Pine Ridge Reservation. The reservation government had stood with the US government against the new Red Power movement, represented by AIM. After a seventy-one-day standoff, sporadic gunfire brought bloodshed, and again, Wounded Knee came to symbolize conflict between American Indians and the US government. However, the assimilation era had come to an end, and the move toward civil rights activism and cultural renewal for American Indian tribes was boosted by AIM's protests. Rather than symbolizing the end of resistance, during the 1970s, conflict at Wounded Knee signified the arrival of a new era for American Indians.

—*Steven L. Danver, PhD*

Bibliography and Additional Reading

Di Silvestro, Roger L. *In the Shadow of Wounded Knee: The Untold Final Story of the Indian Wars*. New York: Walker, 2007. Print.

Eastman, Charles Alexander (Ohiyesa). *From the Deep Woods to Civilization*. Rpt. Mineola: Dover, 2003. Print.

Mooney, James. *The Ghost-Dance Religion and Sioux Outbreak of 1890*: Fourteenth Annual Report of the Bureau of Ethnology. Washington: GPO, 1896. Print.

Neihardt, John G. *Black Elk Speaks: Being the Life Story of a Holy Man of the Oglala Sioux*. Lincoln: U of Nebraska P, 1932. Print.

Utley, Robert M. *Last Days of the Sioux Nation*. 2nd ed. New Haven: Yale UP, 2004. Print.

ASIAN AMERICAN AFFAIRS

Employed in the West as cheap labor for railroad construction, mining, agricultural work, and service industries, Chinese immigrants and, later, Japanese immigrants were described by European Americans as a "yellow peril" that threatened to overrun the region and destroy wages in the labor sector. Thus, even while they were exploited for their labor, immigrants from East Asia (or "Orientals," as they were called) were discriminated against on many fronts. They were excluded from unions, limited in the types of jobs they could work, and encouraged to live in urban ghettos in San Francisco and elsewhere. Ultimately, new Chinese immigrants were excluded altogether from the United States by an act of Congress in 1882, a ban that was not formally lifted until 1943.

■ A Chinese American Protest

Date: May 5, 1852
Author: Norman Asing
Genre: letter; editorial

Summary Overview

Norman Asing's pointed letter to Governor John Bigler reflects the concerns of many Chinese immigrants living in the United States in the 1850s. Initial welcome had turned to hostility, and as anti-Chinese sentiment grew, Chinese immigrants found themselves the target of racial violence and efforts to permanently drive them out of California. Anti-Chinese politicians and labor leaders depicted the Chinese as a threat to the life and livelihood of white Americans. The California legislature reacted by declaring the Chinese a menace to the well-being of the state's mining industry. In response to public demands for action, Governor Bigler gave a speech on April 25, 1852, echoing the arguments of anti-Chinese labor leaders and advocating for restrictions on Chinese immigration. The *San Francisco Daily Alta California* published Asing's letter to Bigler on May 5, 1852. The letter boldly attacks and counters anti-Chinese rhetoric at the same time that it represents the heroic efforts of the Chinese American community to directly combat racial prejudice.

Defining Moment

Following the discovery of gold in 1848, Chinese immigrants arrived in California seeking their share of America's wealth and an opportunity to provide for their families back home. They found employment in the mines and later in the shops, on the railroads, in the factories, and on the farms throughout the West. By 1852, Chinese immigrants numbered around twenty-five thousand and represented approximately 10 percent of California's population. At first welcomed as an industrious and cheap labor supply, the Chinese soon found themselves the targets of nativist efforts to oust them and prohibit their future immigration. Although the 1870s and 1880s marked the height of anti-Chinese sentiment, culminating in outright violence, demands for restrictions on Chinese immigration began as early as the 1850s. White workingmen who saw the presence of Chinese laborers as a threat to their own jobs and economic livelihood called on the governor and other elected officials to either act or risk losing office in the next election.

Anti-Chinese rhetoric presented the Chinese as members of a barbaric and inferior race and often attempted to associate the "heathen Chinese" with African and American Indian races. The Chinese were viewed not only as an economic drain on the economy but as moral threats to the sanctity and security of white families. The Chinese community as a whole was defined as lacking traditional domestic relations and middle-class family values. In 1852, when a committee of the California State Assembly issued a report declaring the Chinese a menace to the welfare and prosperity of the state, Governor John Bigler responded in a special message to the state legislature. In his address, Bigler outlined the potential moral, political, and economic dangers posed by the Chinese in California and called on legislators to act by passing legislation to restrict Chinese immigration.

The Chinese American community was understandably upset by these attacks. Community leaders responded by organizing to resist anti-Chinese rhetoric through letters, petitions, and legal challenges. Chinese American merchant Norman Asing, a San Francisco resident, penned a retort to the governor's claims, intending to make his objections public. The *San Francisco Daily Alta California* published Asing's open letter to the governor on May 5, 1852. Asing's letter represents a direct challenge to the authority of the governor and the power of the anti-Chinese movement.

Author Biography

Norman Asing, born Sang Yuen, was a merchant of significant influence in San Francisco's Chinatown. Asing was among the earliest Chinese immigrants who risked the long journey to come to the United States. He arrived in New York City in 1820 and later made Charleston, South Carolina, his home. There, he established a business and eventually attained United States citizenship. Asing considered himself a loyal American citizen and was proud of his Christian beliefs.

The California gold rush sparked a rapid rise in the number of immigrants to the United States from China. The large number of miners who flocked to the cities and gold fields of California needed supplies and sustenance. Enterprising individuals recognized that if money was to be made in the gold rush, it would not be in the mines. Besides laborers, Chinese merchants also migrated to California with the intention of making their fortune by providing for the miners who had journeyed so far from home.

Asing recognized the opportunities available in California. By 1850, he had moved to San Francisco, where he operated a restaurant in Chinatown. At that time, San Francisco's Chinatown was fairly small. Asing became a prominent member of the local community and helped to found and lead the Yeong Wo Association, an aid society that provided financial assistance and other support services for new Chinese immigrants. By 1854, he was serving as a foreign consul and had become well known in both the Chinese and European American communities.

Asing's letter to Bigler was published in one of San Francisco's leading newspapers. The letter would have elicited a wide range of responses from the people of San Francisco. Some resented the presence of the Chinese, viewing them in a light similar to that expressed by Bigler. Others, like the editors of the Daily Alta California, were less likely to see the Chinese question as an issue worthy of such hysteria. In fact, the editors had rebuked the governor and insisted that his claims of a "yellow peril" were overexaggerated. The newspaper defended the Chinese as industrious laborers and model citizens who contributed to the prosperity of the state. Those who were more ambivalent toward the Chinese and did not share the strong opinions of either Bigler or the newspaper editors may have nevertheless been swayed by the eloquence and persuasiveness of Asing's letter.

HISTORICAL DOCUMENT

To His Excellency Gov. Bigler,

Sir:—I am a Chinaman, a republican, and a lover of free institutions; am much attached to the principles of the Government of the United States, and therefore take the liberty of addressing you as the chief of the Government of this State. Your official position gives you a great opportunity of good or evil. Your opinions through a message to a legislative body have weight, and perhaps none more so with the people, for the effect of your late message has been thus far to prejudice the public mind against my people, to enable those who wait the opportunity to hunt them down, and rob them of the rewards of their toil. You may not have meant that this should be the case, but you can see what will be the result of your propositions.

I am not much acquainted with your logic, that by excluding population from this State you enhance its wealth. I have always considered that population was wealth; particularly a population of producers, of men who by the labor of their hands or intellect, enrich the warehouses or the granaries of the country with the products of nature and art. You are deeply convinced you say "that to enhance the prosperity and to preserve the tranquility of this State, Asiatic immigration must be checked." This, your Excellency, is but one step towards a retrograde movement of the Government, which, on reflection, you will discover; and which the citizens of this country ought never to tolerate. It was one of the principal causes of quarrel between you (when colonies) and England; when the latter pressed laws against emigration, you looked for immigration; it came, and immigration made you what you are—your nation what it is. It transferred you at once from childhood to manhood, and made you great and respectable throughout the nations of the earth. I am sure your Excellency cannot, if you would, prevent your being called the descendant of an immigrant, for I am sure you do not boast of being a descendant of the red men. But your further logic is more reprehensible. You argue that this is a republic of a particular race—that the constitution of the United States admits of no asylum to any other than the pale face. This proposition is false in the extreme; and you know it. The declaration of your independence, and all the acts of your government, your people, and your history, are against you.

It is true, you have degraded the negro because of your holding him in involuntary servitude, and because for the sake of union in some of your states such was tolerated, and amongst this class you would endeavor to place us; and no doubt it would be pleasing to some would-be freemen to mark the brand of servitude upon us. But we would beg to remind you that when your nation was a wilderness, and the nation from whom you sprung barbarous, we exercised most of the arts and virtues of civilized life; that we are possessed of a language and literature, and that men skilled in science and the arts are numerous among us; that the productions of our manufactories, our sail and work-shops, form no small share of the commerce of the world; and that for centuries colleges, schools, charitable institutions, asylums and hospitals, have been as common as in your own land. That our people cannot be reproved for their idleness, and that your historians have given them due credit for the variety and richness of their works of art, and for their simplicity of manners, and particularly their industry. And we beg to remark, that so far as the history of our race in California goes, it stamps with the test of truth the fact that we are not the degraded race you would make us. We came amongst you as mechanics or traders, and following every honorable business of life. You do not find us pursuing occupations of degrading character, except you consider labor degrading, which I am sure you do not; and if our countrymen save the proceeds of their industry from the tavern and the gambling house, to spend it in the purchase of farms or town lots or on their families, surely you will admit that even these are virtues. You say "you desire to see no change in the generous policy of this Government as far as regards Europeans." It is out of your power to say, however, in what way or to whom the doctrines of the Constitution shall apply. You have no more right to propose a measure for checking immigration, than you have to assume the right of sending a message to the Legislature on the subject. As far as regards the color and complexion of our race, we are perfectly aware that our population have been a little more tanned than yours.

Your Excellency will discover, however, that we are as much allied to the African race or the red man as you are yourself, and that as far as the aristocracy of skin is concerned, ours might compare with many of the European races; nor do we consider that your Excellency, as a Democrat, will make us believe that the framers of your declaration of rights ever suggested the propriety of establishing an aristocracy of skin. I am a naturalized citizen, your Excellency, of Charleston, South Carolina, and a Christian too; and so hope you will stand corrected in your assertion "that none of the Asiatic class," as you are pleased to term them, "have applied for benefits under our naturalization act." I could point out to you numbers of citizens, all over the whole continent, who have taken advantage of your hospitality and citizenship, and I defy you to say that our race have ever abused that hospitality or forfeited their claim on this or any of the governments of South America, by an infringement on the laws of the countries into which they pass. You find us peculiarly peaceable and orderly. It does not cost your State much for our criminal prosecution. We apply less to your courts for redress, and so far as I know, there are none that are a charge upon the State as paupers.

You say that "gold, with its talismanic power, has overcome those natural habits of non-intercourse we have exhibited." I ask you, has not gold had the same effect upon your people, and the people of other countries, who have migrated hither? Why it was gold that filled your country, (formerly a desert,) with people; filled your harbors with ships, and opened our much coveted trade to the enterprise of your merchants.

You cannot, in the face of facts that stare you in the face, assert that the cupidity of which you speak is ours alone; so that your Excellency will perceive that in this age a change of cupidity would not tell. Thousands of your own citizens come here to dig gold, with the idea of returning as speedily as they can.

We think you are in error, however, in this respect, as many of us, and many more, will acquire a domicil amongst you.

But, for the present, I shall take leave of your Excellency, and shall resume this question upon another occasion; which I hope you will take into consideration in a spirit of candor. Your predecessor pursued a different line of conduct towards us, as will appear by reference to his message.

I have the honor to be, your Excellency's very obedient servant,

NORMAN ASING.

GLOSSARY

acquainted with: familiar with

cupidity: greed, selfishness

degraded: ruined, humiliated, pushed to a lower position

domicil: home, family

endeavor: strive for, try

forfeited: gave up, surrendered

proposition: proposal, idea

redress: justice, reparation

reprehensible: unacceptable, shameful

reproved: criticized

talismanic: possessing magic power

Document Analysis

Asing's public condemnation of the governor's address to the legislature is an example of one of the ways in which the Chinese deflected criticism and fought back against racist policies in early California. By petitioning public officials and publishing letters in local newspapers, Chinese immigrants found an avenue for expressing their discontent. Asing's letter is clear and to the point. He starts by calling on Governor Bigler to fulfill his public duty as the chief representative of the state. In this case, that means acting as a representative and protector of all individuals living in the state, including the Chinese. Asing's letter then moves on to systematically deconstruct the arguments of the anti-Chinese movement. He counters the view of the Chinese as an economic deficit by focusing instead on the contributions of his people to the development of California. Asing also objects to the stereotype of the Chinese as an uncivilized, degraded race and offers evidence to the contrary. Finally, Asing takes the daring move of reproving the blatant racism in Bigler's arguments and insisting that Americans remember their commitment to liberty and equality.

Asing begins his argument by reminding the governor of the power of his position. He insists that the Governor's "opinions through a message to a legislative body have weight." Asing also encourages Bigler to carefully consider the effect that his words have on the people of California and the far-reaching implications for the Chinese living in the state. Although perhaps not the governor's intention, Asing argues that the impact of the governor's racialized rhetoric is to encourage those who would commit acts of violence against the Chinese: "the effect of your late message has been thus far to prejudice the public mind against my people, to enable those who wait the opportunity to hunt them down, and rob them of the rewards of their toil." Asing was clearly aware of the ever-present reality of hate crimes targeted at the Chinese. Racial violence in the gold fields was becoming more and more common. Disillusioned miners often took out their frustrations over their financial struggles on the Chinese, who unfortunately became scapegoats. Public hysteria created by the thoughtless words of politicians had the potential to fan the flames of racial tension. In reminding the governor of his duty as a defender of the rights of all Americans, citizens or otherwise, Asing is calling upon Bigler to exercise his public duty, especially as the leading public servant of California.

In the body of the letter, Asing directly and systematically targets each of the claims of the anti-Chinese movement, beginning with the argument that the Chinese are an economic drain on the people and the state. In response to the governor's calls for immigration restriction, Asing questions the logic of his argument "that by excluding population from this State you enhance its wealth." Instead, Asing makes a point that would become quite common in the arguments made by the Chinese community in their efforts to defend their presence in the state. He points to the ways in which Chinese laborers contribute to the economic growth and development of California, working not just in the mines but in the factories and on the farms. In fact, recruiters specifically sought out their labor, recognizing the value of Chinese immigrants as workers. Asing suggests that Chinese immigrants have contributed far more to California and its people than they have taken away.

Asing also objects to the common argument made by anti-Chinese politicians that the Chinese come to the United States as temporary sojourners with the sole intention of making money and returning home. The large number of Chinese bachelors immigrating to America and their tendency to save their money and send it home to their families in China was often presented as proof of this claim. This argument expands on the view of the Chinese as parasites who deplete the state of its resources. Governor Bigler took it one step further by claiming in his address to the legislature that the Chinese are unwilling and ultimately incapable of assimilation. Although Asing acknowledges that some Chinese laborers do intend to eventually return to their homes in China, he argues that an unacknowledged number of immigrants desire to make a permanent home in the United States and to apply for the right of citizenship. Asing uses himself as an example here, declaring that he is "attached to the principles of the Government of the United States" and "a lover of free institutions." As a naturalized citizen, he intends to correct the governor's false claim that the Chinese are incapable of assimilation. Nevertheless, it would be the United States government that would later declare the Chinese unable to apply for US citizenship, denying them the right to decide for themselves whether or not they wanted to do so. Lacking the rights and privileges of American citizens, many Chinese immigrants would eventually choose to return to China.

Asing rightfully takes offense to one of the most unpleasant stereotypes perpetuated by Bigler: the repre-

sentation of the Chinese as barbaric and uncivilized. Anti-Chinese rhetoric tended to paint the Chinese as animal-like heathens barely capable of governing themselves. Asing notes that many white Americans have assigned Chinese immigrants a place in the racial hierarchy ascribed to African Americans and American Indians. Chinese American community leaders often pointed to the advances of Chinese civilization in an attempt to counter the perception that the Chinese were a barbaric race. Historical fact itself stands as a strong testament to the achievements of the Chinese culture. The comparatively short history of the United States did little to help American racists validate their arguments of racial and cultural supremacy. Asing makes this point deliberately clear: "we would beg to remind you that when your nation was a wilderness, and the nation from which you sprung barbarous, we exercised most of the arts and virtues of civilized life." Asing argues that the Chinese developed language, literature, science, art, manufacturing, education, medicine, and charitable institutions long before the existence of the United States, thus invalidating American claims to superiority in advancement and civilization.

In direct response to the criticism that the Chinese who immigrated to California represent a "degraded race" of common laborers, Asing argues that the Chinese pursue "honorable" and respectable professions. This is especially important, since calls for immigration restriction often pointed to the imbalanced sex ratio, the lack of two-parent middle-class families, and the existence of crime and prostitution in Chinatowns as evidence of the alleged inherently degenerate nature of the Chinese race. Asing counters this assertion by insisting on the normalcy and propriety of the Chinese American community. He argues that the Chinese are not a class of criminals but are "peaceable and orderly" and that none have become dependent on the state as paupers. Asing even goes so far as to defend proprietors of saloons and gambling houses as pursuing respectable careers in the sense that their labor provides for the financial support of their families. Simply by referring to the many Chinese immigrants who have families to provide for, Asing is countering a common misconception of the Chinese as predominantly single men who failed to establish respectable domestic relations. The tactic of highlighting the numbers of Chinese American middle-class families living in America would prove important in the decades to come.

It is also significant that Asing does not refrain himself from declaring Bigler's statements racist. He argues that Bigler's logic is "reprehensible" and directly challenges the governor's authority when he states, "You argue that this is a republic of a particular race—that the constitution of the United States admits of no asylum to any other than the pale face. This proposition is false in the extreme; and you know it." Instead, Asing argues, the Declaration of Independence, the government, the American people, and American history all stand in opposition to Bigler's racist line of thinking. Asing denies that the governor has a right to determine "to whom the doctrines of the Constitution apply" any more than he does to propose immigration restrictions. This is especially true when such policy is determined on the basis of racism. Asing insists that "as far as regards the color and complexion of our race, we are perfectly aware that our population have been a little more tanned than yours." In this acerbic statement referencing skin tone, Asing is pointing to the overall irrational nature of Bigler's proposition and challenging the governor's and the nation's established racial hierarchy.

Although he is justified in denouncing the racism in the governor's statement, Asing's statements also ironically reflect a degree of racial prejudice themselves. In a tactical move, Asing seeks to distance himself and the Chinese community from association with so-called inferior races. Instead he allies the Chinese more closely with Caucasians, claiming that the Chinese race is more similar to Europeans than to Africans or American Indians. This tactic, although limited in effectiveness, reveals some of the racial attitudes that existed in the Chinese community at the time. Alliances with African Americans or American Indians in their battle for political, economic, and social equality seemed only to weaken the Chinese community's efforts. Instead, community leaders focused on emphasizing the ways in which the Chinese differed from these groups. Still, Asing condemns the extent of American racism, if not the reality of racism itself. He specifically decries African slavery and the degradation of African Americans through the very existence of slavery as an institution. Asing suggests to Bigler that the Founding Fathers never intended to create "an aristocracy of skin."

Perhaps one of the most persuasive arguments that Asing makes is his delineation of the hypocrisy in the American attitude toward immigrants, especially given the country's unique history. Asing appeals to Americans' sense of history and national pride when he argues

that England's attempt to restrict immigration in the colonies was one of the principal causes of tension that led to the American Revolution. He points to the irony of calls for immigration restriction by Americans who in the past saw such regulation by the English Crown as a sign of despotism. This is especially hypocritical, he argues, given that immigrants helped build the American nation into the powerful country it has become. This argument, more than perhaps any other, is intended to appeal directly to the heart of the readers who opened up the Daily Alta California and read the newspaper that day. By calling on Americans to stand by their commitment to the pursuit of liberty and justice for all, Asing is insisting on equal rights for his people.

Essential Themes

Norman Asing's public letter to Governor John Bigler represents the struggle of early Chinese immigrants to overcome racist and discriminatory laws and to ultimately establish a place for themselves in American society. Asing recognized the illogical and racialized rhetoric of the governor's arguments and found the courage to write in public protest. Especially given the hostile attitudes of many native-born white Americans toward foreigners, the Chinese had quite the battle before them. By the 1870s and 1880s, anti-Chinese hostilities would reach a boiling point. The demands of labor leaders and anti-Chinese politicians for an end to Chinese immigration would culminate in the passage of the Chinese Exclusion Act of 1882, which would succeed in severely restricting their numbers. By excluding Chinese laborers but allowing Chinese merchants, the exclusion act reflected both race- and class-based biases. Subsequent laws and regulations further restricted Chinese immigration, effectively halting it for sixty years. The United States immigration bureau would develop intensive procedures to ensure that Chinese laborers did not enter the country.

Anti-Chinese agitation did not end with the passage of Chinese exclusion. The act also deprived those who had been able to immigrate to the United States from becoming US citizens. This denial of the right to citizenship was reinforced in the Immigration Act of 1924 (National Origins Quote Act), in which the Chinese were among those declared "aliens ineligible for citizenship." Prejudice extended to other areas of daily life as well. Denied access to equal and integrated public education, segregated in public spaces, and prohibited from pursuing a range of job opportunities, the Chinese in San Francisco struggled for full access to the rights and privileges enjoyed by American citizens. The era of Chinese exclusion lasted from 1882 to 1943. During that period, many individual and collective efforts to resist discriminatory laws would rely on arguments similar to those espoused by Asing in his letter to Bigler. His efforts on behalf of the Chinese community were ultimately not in vain.

—*Wendy Rouse, PhD*

Bibliography and Additional Reading

Aarim-Heriot, Najia. *Chinese Immigrants, African Americans, and Racial Anxiety in the United States, 1848–82*. Urbana: U of Illinois P, 2006. Print.

Lai, Him Mark. *Becoming Chinese American: A History of Communities and Institutions*. Walnut Creek: AltaMira, 2004. Print.

McClain, Charles J. *In Search of Equality: The Chinese Struggle against Discrimination in Nineteenth-Century America*. Berkeley: U of California P, 1994. Print.

Rawls, James J., and Walton Bean. *California: An Interpretive History*. 9th ed. Boston: McGraw, 2008. Print.

Wong, K. Scott. *"Cultural Defenders and Brokers: Chinese Responses to the Anti-Chinese Movement."* Claiming America: Constructing Chinese American Identities during the Exclusion Era. Ed. Kevin Scott Wong and Sucheng Chan. Philadelphia: Temple UP, 1998. 3–40. Print.

Yung, Judy, Gordon H. Chang, and Him Mark Lai, eds. *Chinese American Voices: From the Gold Rush to the Present*. Berkeley: U of California P, 2006. Print.

Chan, Sucheng. *Asian Americans: An Interpretive History*. New York: Twayne, 1991. Print.

Lee, Erika. *At America's Gates: Chinese Immigration during the Exclusion Era, 1882–1943*. Chapel Hill: U of North Carolina P, 2007. Print.

Pfaelzer, Jean. *Driven Out: The Forgotten War against Chinese Americans*. New York: Random, 2007. Print.

Sandmeyer, Elmer Clarence. *The Anti-Chinese Movement in California*. Urbana: U of Illinois P, 1991. Print.

Takaki, Ronald. *Strangers from a Different Shore: A History of Asian Americans*. Boston: Little, 1998. Print.

◼ *People v. Hall*

Date: 1854
Author: Hugh Murray
Genre: court opinion

Summary Overview

George Hall was arrested and convicted for the 1853 murder of a Chinese immigrant miner in Nevada County, California. The Chinese immigrants who witnessed the murder provided the essential testimony that led to Hall's conviction. However, Hall appealed the court's decision, claiming that a Chinese immigrant should not be able to testify against a white man and citing a law that denied black individuals and Indians the right to testify. The case ultimately ended up in the California Supreme Court, where the justices were asked not only to consider the original intent of the law as it applied to Chinese immigrants but also, by default, to deliberate on the status of Chinese immigrants as members of American society. Chief Justice Hugh Murray delivered the majority opinion of the court, which concluded that Chinese immigrants were not entitled to the same rights and privileges as white people and therefore did not have the right to testify against a white man in court.

Defining Moment

After the discovery of gold in California, Chinese immigrants were among countless other immigrant groups who flocked to the gold mines seeking their fortune. Poverty, wars, and oppressive government policies pushed many Chinese families to send their sons looking for economic opportunities abroad. Chinese merchants and entrepreneurs recognized the lucrative potential of moving to California to establish businesses that provided goods and services for Chinese immigrants living and working in the goldfields. By 1852, approximately twenty-five thousand Chinese lived in the state. Initially they were welcomed by politicians and business owners, who saw their presence as a sign of the future wealth and prosperity of the state. Labor recruiters eagerly sought Chinese laborers to work in mining, manufacturing, and agricultural industries.

The initial welcome quickly faded, however. By the early 1850s, the placer deposits had dwindled, and mining became big business. Only those individuals with the capital to purchase heavy equipment and hire laborers to mine for gold were profiting. Companies employed Chinese immigrants partly because they were viewed as especially industrious workers and partly because they could pay them lower wages than white workers. Exasperated by limited job opportunities, white workingmen looked for scapegoats. Economic frustrations combined with rising racial tensions led to a backlash against foreign miners. This backlash manifested itself in the form of laws such as the Foreign Miner's Tax, which sought to force the Chinese from the mining camps by imposing a tax on them. Further oppressive laws followed. In some cases, tensions culminated in outright violence through efforts to forcibly remove Chinese immigrants from California towns and physical attacks on individual Chinese miners.

In 1853, George Hall and two other white men attempted to assault and rob a Chinese gold miner living and working along the Bear River in Nevada County, California. Ling Sing, another Chinese miner in the camp, was coming to the aid of his neighbor when Hall shot and killed him. Hall was promptly arrested and taken to court. The testimony of three Chinese witnesses led to Hall's conviction. The judge sentenced Hall to death by hanging. However, Hall challenged the conviction on the grounds that section 14 of California's Criminal Proceedings Act prohibited the testimony of "blacks, mulatto persons, or Indians" against a white person, insisting that the ban also extended to the Chinese. Hall appealed his case all the way to the California Supreme Court.

Author Biography

Chief Justice Hugh C. Murray, who delivered the majority opinion for the court in the case of *People v. Hall*, had a rather short but infamous career in law. Murray was born in Saint Louis, Missouri, in 1825. He was raised in Illinois and began to study law there in the 1840s. Murray served for a brief time as a second lieutenant in the United States infantry during the war with Mexico. Shortly after his admittance to the bar, he traveled to California to practice law. Murray reached San Francisco during the height of the gold rush in 1849 and found ample opportunities for personal and professional growth. The social connections he forged in San Francisco helped to build his career. Before long, he was serving as a justice of the Superior Court of San Francisco.

Murray continued his meteoric rise. In 1851, he was appointed to the State Supreme Court. The following year, he became chief justice after the resignation of H. A. Lyons. Murray was only twenty-seven years old when he became chief justice of the California Supreme Court and only twenty-nine years old when he rendered the decision in Hall, one of his most infamous decisions and the case for which he is perhaps most well known. Murray's career was cut short by consump-tion, which claimed his life in 1857.

Murray had a reputation for nativism as a member of the anti-immigrant, anti-Catholic American Party (also referred to as the Know-Nothing Party). This organization, composed primarily of Anglo-American Protestants, gained support and influence in the 1850s following a rapid increase in immigration to the United States. The gold rush only exacerbated the party's fears of an immigrant invasion. The party platform sought to limit immigration and naturalization, especially of Germans and Irish, who were perceived as more loyal to the Catholic Church and the Pope than to democratic values. The American Party further sought to inhibit the power and political influence of all foreigners already living in the United States, including the Chinese. Murray's American Party background and his nativist sentiments are clearly reflected in the Hall decision. His zeal for protecting white Americans from the potential harmful influences of inferior races is clear in the language of the majority opinion.

HISTORICAL DOCUMENT

Mr. Ch. J. MURRAY delivered the opinion of the Court, Mr. J. HEYDENFELDT concurred.

The appellant, a free white citizen of this State, was convicted of murder upon the testimony of Chinese witnesses.

The point involved in this case, is the admissibility of such evidence.

The 394th section of the Act Concerning Civil Cases, provides that no Indian or Negro shall be allowed to testify as a witness in any action or proceeding in which a White person is a party.

The 14th section of the Act of April 16th, 1850, regulating Criminal Proceedings, provides that "No Black or Mulatto person, or Indian, shall be allowed to give evidence in favor of, or against a white man."

The true point, at which we are anxious to arrive, is the legal signification of the words, "Black, Mulatto Indian and White person," and whether the Legislature adopted them as generic terms, or intended to limit their application to specific types of the human species.

Before considering this question, it is proper to remark the difference between the two sections of our Statute, already quoted, the latter being more broad and comprehensive in its exclusion, by use of the word "Black," instead of Negro.

Conceding, however, for the present, that the word "Black," as used in the 14th section, and "Negro," in 394th, are convertible terms, and that the former was intended to include the latter, let us proceed to inquire who are excluded from testifying as witnesses under the term "Indian."

When Columbus first landed upon the shores of this continent, in his attempt to discover a western passage to the Indies, he imagined that he had accomplished the object of his expedition, and that the Island of San Salvador was one of those Islands of the Chinese sea, lying near the extremity of India, which had been described by navigators

Acting upon this hypothesis, and also perhaps from the similarity of features and physical conformation, he gave to the Islanders the name of Indians, which appellation was universally adopted, and extended to the aboriginals of the New World, as well as of Asia.

From that time, down to a very recent period, the American Indians and the Mongolian, or Asiatic, were regarded as the same type of the human species.

In order to arrive at a correct understanding of the intention of our Legislature, it will be necessary to go back to the early history of legislation on this subject, our Statute being only a transcript of those of older States.

At the period from which this legislation dates, those portions of Asia which include India proper, the Eastern Archipelago, and the countries washed by the Chinese waters, as far as then known, were denominated the Indies, from which the inhabitants had derived the generic name of Indians.

Ethnology, at that time, was unknown as a distinct science, or if known, had not reached that high point of perfection which it has since attained by the scientific inquiries and discoveries of the master minds of the last half century. Few speculations had been made with regard to the moral or physical differences between the different races of mankind. These were general in their character, and limited to those visible and palpable variations which could not escape the attention of the most common observer.

The general, or perhaps universal opinion of that day was, that there were but three distinct types of the human species, which, in their turn, were subdivided into varieties or tribes. This opinion is still held by many scientific writers, and is supported by Cuvier, one of the most eminent naturalists of modern times.

Many ingenious speculations have been resorted to for the purpose of sustaining this opinion. It has been supposed, and not without plausibility, that this continent was first peopled by Asiatics, who crossed Behring's Straits, and from thence found their way down to the more fruitful climates of Mexico and South America. Almost every tribe has some tradition of coming from the North, and many of them, that their ancestors came from some remote country beyond the ocean.

From the eastern portions of Kamtschatka, the Aleutian Islands form a long and continuous group, extending eastward to that portion of the North American Continent inhabited by the Esquimaux. They appear to be a continuation of the lofty volcanic ranges which traverse the two continents, and are inhabited by a race who resemble, in a remarkable degree, in language and appearance, both the inhabitants of Kamtschatka (who are admitted to be of the Mongolian type,) and the Esquimaux, who again, in turn, resemble other tribes of American Indians. The similarity of the skull and pelvis, and the general configuration of the two races; the remarkable resemblance in eyes, beard, hair, and other peculiarities, together with the contiguity of the two Continents, might well have led to the belief that this country was first peopled by the Asiatics, and that the difference between the different tribes and the parent stock was such as would necessarily arise from the circumstances of climate, pursuits, and other physical causes, and was no greater than that existing between the Arab and the European, both of whom were supposed to belong to the Caucasian race.

Although the discoveries of eminent Archeologists, and the researches of modern Geologists, have given to this Continent an antiquity of thousands of years anterior to the evidence of man's existence, and the light of modern science may have shown conclusively that it was not peopled by the inhabitants of Asia, but that the Aborigines are a distinct type, and as such claim a distinct origin, still, this would not, in any degree, alter the meaning of the term, and render that specific which was before generic.

We have adverted to these speculations for the purpose of showing that the name of Indian, from the time of Columbus to the present day, has been used to designate, not alone the North American Indian, but the whole of the Mongolian race, and that the name, though first applied probably through mistake, was afterwards continued as appropriate on account of the supposed common origin.

That this was the common opinion in the early history of American legislation, cannot be disputed, and, therefore, all legislation upon the subject must have borne relation to that opinion.

Can, then, the use of the word "Indian," because at the present day it may be sometimes regarded as a specific, and not as a generic term, alter this conclusion? We think not; because at the origin of the legislation we are considering, it was used and admitted in its common and ordinary acceptation, as a generic term, distinguishing the great Mongolian race, and as such, its meaning then became fixed by law, and in construing Statutes the legal meaning of words must be preserved.

Again: the words of the Act must be construed in pari materia. It will not be disputed that "White" and "Negro," are generic terms, and refer to two of the great types of mankind. If these, as well as the word "Indian," are not to be regarded as generic terms, including the two great races which they were intended to designate, but only specific, and applying to those Whites and Negroes who were inhabitants of this Continent at the time of the passage of the Act, the most anomalous consequences would ensue. The European white man who comes here would not be shielded from the testimony of the degraded and demoralized caste, while the Negro, fresh from the coast of Africa, or the Indian of Patagonia, the Kanaka, South Sea Islander, or New Hollander, would be admitted, upon their arrival, to testify against white citizens in our courts of law.

To argue such a proposition would be an insult to the good sense of the Legislature.

The evident intention of the Act was to throw around the citizen a protection for life and property, which could only be secured by removing him above the corrupting influences of degraded castes.

It can hardly be supposed that any Legislature would attempt this by excluding domestic Negroes and Indians, who not unfrequently have correct notions of their obligations to society, and turning loose upon the community the more degraded tribes of the same species, who have nothing in common with us, in language, country or laws.

We have, thus far, considered this subject on the hypothesis that the 14th section of the Act Regulating Criminal Proceedings, and the 394th section of the Practice Act, were the same.

As before remarked, there is a wide difference between the two. The word "Black" may include all Negroes, but the term "Negro" does not include all Black persons.

By the use of this term in this connection, we understand it to mean the opposite of "White," and that it should be taken as contradistinguished from all White persons.

In using the words, "No Black, or Mulatto person, or Indian shall be allowed to give evidence for or against a White person," the Legislature, if any intention can be ascribed to it, adopted the most comprehensive terms to embrace every known class or shade of color, as the apparent design was to protect the White person from the influence of all testimony other than that of persons of the same caste. The use of these terms must, by every sound rule of construction, exclude every one who is not of white blood.

The Act of Congress in defining what description of aliens may become naturalized citizens, provides that every "free white citizen,". In speaking of this subject, Chancellor Kent says, that "the Act confines the description to "white" citizens, and that it is a matter of doubt, whether, under this provision, any of the tawny races of Asia can be admitted to the privileges of citizenship." 2 Kent's Com. 72.

We are not disposed to leave this question in any doubt. The word "White" has a distinct signification, which ex vi termini, excludes black, yellow, and all other colors. It will be observed, by reference to the first section of the second article of the Constitution of this State, that none but white males can become electors, except in the case of Indians, who may be admitted by special Act of the Legislature. On examination of the constitutional debates, it will be found that not a little difficulty existed in selecting these precise words, which were finally agreed upon as the most comprehensive that could be suggested to exclude all inferior races.

If the term "White," as used in the Constitution, was not understood in its generic sense as including the Caucasian race, and necessarily excluding all others, where was the necessity of providing for the admission of Indians to the privilege of voting, by special legislation?

We are of the opinion that the words "White," "Negro," "Mulatto," "Indian," and "Black person," wherever they occur in our Constitution and laws, must be taken in their generic sense, and that, even admitting the Indian of this Continent is not of the Mongolian type, that the words "Black person," in the 14th section must be taken as contradistinguished from White, and necessarily excludes all races other than the Caucasian.

We have carefully considered all the consequences resulting from a different rule of construction, and are satisfied that even in a doubtful case we would be impelled to this decision on grounds of public policy.

The same rule which would admit them to testify would admit them to all the equal rights of citizenship, and we might soon see them at the polls, in the jury box, upon the bench, and in our legislative halls.

This is not a speculation which exists in the excited and over-heated imagination of the patriot and statesman, but it is an actual and present danger.

The anomalous spectacle of a distinct people, living in our community, recognizing no laws of this State except through necessity, bringing with them their prejudices and national feuds, in which they indulge in open violation of law; whose mendacity is proverbial; a race of people whom nature has marked as inferior, and who are incapable of progress or intellectual development beyond a certain point, as their history has shown; differing in language, opinions, color, and physical conformation; between whom and ourselves nature has placed an impassable difference, is now presented, and for them is claimed, not only the right to swear away the life of a citizen, but the further privilege of participating with us in administering the affairs of our Government.

These facts were before the Legislature that framed this Act, and have been known as matters of public history to every subsequent Legislature.

There can be no doubt as to the intention of the Legislature, and that if it had ever been anticipated that this class of people were not embraced in the prohibition, then such specific words would have been employed as would have put the matter beyond any possible controversy.

For these reasons, we are of opinion that the testimony was inadmissible. The judgment is reversed and the cause remanded.

Mr. Justice WELLS dissented, as follows:

From the opinion of the Chief Justice, I must most respectfully dissent.

GLOSSARY

anomalous spectacle: strange sight

conformation: structure, appearance

convertible: interchangeable

degraded: inferior, pushed to a lower position

demoralized: morally corrupt

ex vi termini: by the force of the term

ingenious speculations: clever assumptions

mendacity: deceitfulness

Mongolian: an outdated term referring to all individuals of Asian descent, specifically Chinese

pari material: two laws analyzed together due to their similarity

signification: meaning, importance

Document Analysis

The majority opinion handed down by the California Supreme Court in the case of *People v. Hall* reflected not only the attempt of the court to provide a clear definition of racial categories in order to protect the interests of the white race but also reveals the racial anxieties and virulent anti-Chinese hostilities that existed in the United States at the time. The bulk of the testimony in the case against George Hall was provided by Chinese witnesses. The question before the court was whether or not such testimony should be admissible given that it was provided by nonwhite individuals. Section 14 of California's Criminal Proceedings Act, an 1850 act of the legislature that regulated criminal proceedings, had already established that "no Black or Mulatto person, or Indian," would be allowed to testify against a white man in a court of law. Since the law never specifically excluded the testimony of a Chinese individual, the justices sought to determine whether or not the law was intended to apply to the Chinese as well. Thus, they struggled first to define what the creators of the law intended by the terms black, white, and Indian. Second, they reflected on the implications of expanding rights and political power to nonwhite races. The text of the majority opinion clearly reflects the racial tensions and fears of the era and provides insight into the history of American race relations.

Defining Racial Categories

In the first section of the majority opinion, Murray turned to historical and scientific evidence to help deconstruct the meanings behind the racial categories defined by the 1850 law. Murray begins by making the argument that since the time of Columbus's first contact with the native people of San Salvador, the term Indian historically has been used to imply American Indians as well as Asians. Murray points out that Columbus, who was attempting to locate a passage to the Indies, assumed that the island was located in the Chinese sea near India and that its inhabitants were of Asian descent, and so he referred to the island's native people as Indians. Although Columbus's assumption was incorrect, the term Indian was henceforth applied generically to both Asians and American Indians.

Murray then moves to provide scientific evidence to buttress his argument. He claims that anthropological theories about the Asian origins of the ancestors of American Indians further seemed to validate the association between the two groups. Murray summarizes the ideas of ethnologists who had previously concluded that American Indian groups had originally migrated across the Bering Strait into North America. Although he admits that this theory had recently been challenged, Murray concludes that historical and scientific evidence confirms that "the name of Indian, from the time of Columbus to the present day, has been used to designate, not alone the North American Indian, but the whole of the Mongolian race."

Murray further defines the intent behind the use of the words black and white in the original 1850 legislation. The court argues the broadest definition of the terms. The word black is defined as "the opposite of 'white.'" Thus the court insists that the specific phras-

ing of the original legislation that denied any "Black or Mulatto person, or Indian," from testifying against a white person was intended "to embrace every known class or shade of color." Murray therefore concludes that the intent of the use of the term Indian in the law prohibiting Indians from testifying against white individuals was anticipated to apply to the Chinese as well. His intent here is to validate historically and scientifically the notion that white people have always viewed Chinese people as nonwhite and therefore not entitled to the same rights and privileges as white people.

Racial Anxieties

Clearly underlying the court's decision are the racial anxieties at play in American society at the time. An influx of immigrants from around the world contributed to heightened nativist sentiments. Heated discussions over the future of slavery and the question of the status of American Indians in American society raged in the political arena, and sectional tensions threatened to divide the nation. The case of *People v. Hall* reflected an overall concern about the future status of white people in the United States. The opinion clearly suggests that the court is concerned not only with protecting white people from the potentially damning testimony of untrustworthy "others" but also about the broader, potentially devastating implications of the decision to allow nonwhite individuals to testify in a court of law. Murray argues, for instance, that if the court allowed groups other than white people to testify in court, they might also be allowed the right to vote, serve on a jury, or gain positions of political power.

The potential of these groups to gain equal rights as citizens is imagined as a great threat to all of American society, in part because of the perception that these groups represented "inferior races." Murray argues,

The anomalous spectacle of a distinct people, living in our community . . . whom nature has marked as inferior, and who are incapable of progress or intellectual development . . . differing in language, opinions, color, and physical conformation: between whom and ourselves nature has placed an impassable difference . . . is now presented, and for them is claimed, not only the right to swear away the life of a citizen, but the further privilege of participating with us in administering the affairs of our Government.

Here, Murray clearly outlines the type of scientific racism implicit in his overarching argument, which justifies racist laws by suggesting that anthropology has delineated the distinctions between the races and ordered them hierarchically. He uses this pseudoscientific theory to legitimize his decision to deny these groups access to the exercise of full social and political equality, arguing that the "scientifically" proven racial inferiority of certain groups necessitates the interpretation of laws to shield the superior race from the potential harm of too much power in the hands of intellectually incapable races. Murray's fear was that allowing nonwhite groups to testify against white people would open the door to allowing these same groups to gain "equal rights of citizenship" and participate in the administration of "the affairs of our government."

The immediate implication of the court's decision was the reversal of Hall's conviction. Hall literally got away with murder because the testimony of the three Chinese witnesses had to be disregarded. The broader implication was effectively to make the Chinese a target. The ruling itself seemed to encourage acts of violence against the Chinese, with perpetrators fully aware that their actions would likely go unpunished. Denied equal protection under the law, the Chinese immigrant community responded with outrage at the court's decision. They objected to being categorized the same as other racial groups. Letters of protest sent to the governor pointed out the racism of the majority opinion and demanded equal protection of the law. A letter written by Lai Chun-Chuen representing the Chinese merchants in San Francisco countered anti-Chinese arguments that labeled the Chinese as primitive and barbaric. Lai argued that the history of Chinese civilization pointed to the superiority of the Chinese over less developed races such as black people and Indians. Although grounded in some of the same racialized rhetoric espoused by Murray and the court, the argument effectively countered stereotypes of the Chinese as less civilized then Caucasians. This attempt to distance themselves from black people and Indians and more closely associate themselves with white people would prove to be a common and somewhat successful tactic of the Chinese American community when challenging future racist laws. Similarly, the merchant class recognized an advantage in pointing out their class status and distancing themselves from common laborers as a means of arguing against discriminatory laws and for greater political power in the years to come.

Despite the ruling in *People v. Hall*, the Chinese immigrant community continued to take their cases before the court in hopes of obtaining justice. Their efforts sometimes proved successful, depending in large part on the judge, the jury, and the acumen of their lawyers. Calling upon an extensive transnational network of support, Chinese immigrants relied on family, friends, and kinship and district organizations to protect their rights and freedoms. They persisted in their protests and efforts to reverse discriminatory laws. White allies, including big business leaders and Christian missionaries who supported Chinese immigration, often came to the aid of the Chinese and spoke out publicly on their behalf. Reverend William Speer, a Presbyterian missionary, publicly insisted that the Hall decision violated principles of democracy, Christianity, and common humanity. The political influence of white community leaders like Speer helped gain some degree of public support for the Chinese cause.

Although *People v. Hall* would be effectively overturned by federal civil rights legislation in the 1870s, by that point the anti-Chinese movement on the Pacific coast was gaining significant political momentum. Anti-Chinese lobbyists would succeed in lobbying Congress to pass significant measures to curb Chinese immigration and ultimately exclude Chinese laborers, culminating in the passage of the Chinese Exclusion Act in 1882. Chinese people living in the United States suffered countless acts of violence in a concerted effort to drive them out of towns throughout the West Coast. Even large urban ethnic enclaves provided limited protection against anti-Chinese hostilities. San Francisco's Chinese community fought extensive legal battles against efforts to drive them from certain industries, segregate their children in the schools, and prevent their families from joining them in the United States. The era of anti-Chinese exclusion and hostility continued well into the twentieth century. It was not until China became a US ally in World War II that Chinese exclusion as an immigration policy was repealed. Even then, the institutionalized discrimination established substantial barriers to social, political, and economic progress that would require decades to overcome.

Essential Themes

The case of *People v. Hall* highlights not only the extent of the racial tensions between Chinese immigrants and white miners but also the ways in which the judicial branch established a racialized system of justice that privileged white persons above all other groups. Justice

Murray's opinion in *People v. Hall* echoed the racist rhetoric of the era and reflected larger tensions at play in the United States in the mid-nineteenth century as the nation struggled to come to terms with who would be allowed access to citizenship. Murray's writing reflects a common attitude held by white American nativists, who feared that the influx of large numbers of "inferior" classes of foreigners would lead to the ultimate downfall of the nation. Although it is clear that not all white Americans shared in this viewpoint, the political power exerted by individuals of Murray's status had far-reaching implications. The justices of the California Supreme Court had the power to validate discriminatory laws and extend the application of other laws, which ultimately codified racist sentiments into the US legal system, thus making the task of battling racism and injustice even more difficult for the generations of Chinese Americans that followed.

—*Wendy Rouse, PhD*

Bibliography and Additional Reading

Almaguer, Tomas. "'They Can Be Hired in Masses; They Can Be Managed and Controlled Like Unthinking Slaves.'" *Race and Racialization: Essential Readings*. Ed. Tania Das Gupta et al. Toronto: Canadian Scholars', 2007. 217–31. Print.

Camp, Edgar Whittlesey. "Hugh C. Murray: California's Youngest Chief Justice." *California Historical Society Quarterly* 20.4 (1941): 365–73. Print.

Daniels, Roger. *Asian America: Chinese and Japanese in the United States since 1850*. Seattle: U of Washington P, 1988. Print.

Limerick, Patricia Nelson. *The Legacy of Conquest: The Unbroken Past of the American West*. New York: Norton, 1987. Print.

McClain, Charles J. *In Search of Equality: The Chinese Struggle against Discrimination in Nineteenth-Century America*. Berkeley: U of California P, 1994. Print.

Pfaelzer, Jean. *Driven Out: The Forgotten War against Chinese Americans*. New York: Random, 2007. Print.

Rawls, James J., and Walton Bean. *California: An Interpretive History*. 9th ed. Boston: McGraw, 2008. Print.

Aarim-Heriot, N. *Chinese Immigrants, African Americans; Racial Anxiety in the United States, 1848-82*. Urbana: U of Illinois P, 2006. Print.

Chan, Sucheng. *Asian Americans: An Interpretive History*. New York: Twayne, 1991. Print.

Lee, Erika. *At America's Gates: Chinese Immigration during the Exclusion Era, 1882–1943*. Chapel Hill: U of North Carolina P, 2007. Print.

Sandmeyer, Elmer Clarence. *The Anti-Chinese Movement in California*. Urbana: U of Illinois P, 1991. Print.

Takaki, Ronald. *A History of Asian Americans: Strangers from a Different Shore*. Boston: Little, 1998. Print.

Yung, J., G. H. Chang, and H. M. Lai, eds. *Chinese American Voices: From the Gold Rush to the Present*. Berkeley: U of California P, 2006. Print.

■ Chinese Exclusion Act

Date: May 6, 1882
Author: Forty-Seventh US Congress
Genre: law

Summary Overview

In the spring of 1882, the Forty-Seventh Congress approved and President Chester A. Arthur signed the Chinese Exclusion Act, which strictly limited the ability of Chinese citizens to immigrate to the United States for a period of ten years. This law represented the first time the United States would restrict a particular ethnic group from immigrating to American shores. It also opened the door to other, similar acts targeting other ethnic groups. The act was seemingly a confluence of two major political forces. On one side were American- and European-born laborers, who lamented the influx of Chinese laborers that began during the California Gold Rush several decades prior. On the other side were leaders who wished to halt what they believed amounted to the importation of slave labor to work in the mines and in the manufacturing sector.

Defining Moment

During the late 1840s, after gold was discovered in the western United States, laborers flocked to the region to work in the mines. Among them were the Chinese, many of whom came overseas to escape the violence, poverty, and instability of the Taiping Rebellion (1850–64). Chinese laborers, however, came in two general groups: individual immigrants and "coolies" (unskilled or semiskilled laborers brought overseas on a contract).

After the Civil War, the United States began its Reconstruction efforts. The Republican-dominated Congress, wary of creating any environment in which slavery could return, pressed for civil rights for all races. In 1870, Senator William Stewart of Nevada, for example, offered legislation that guaranteed legal rights for all immigrants, including Chinese laborers who came to the United States voluntarily. His proposal was tabled at the time, largely because Republicans wavered on whether to regulate both importation and volun-

tary immigration. Ironically, wartime abolitionists were also divided on this issue, with some active opponents of slavery openly referring to the Chinese as "barbarians." Meanwhile, Chinese immigration and importation continued to increase in the western states. By 1870, even as the Gold Rush came to an end, Chinese workers comprised about a quarter of California's unskilled labor force, engendering animosity among the region's other laborers.

In 1870, the issue of Chinese importation and immigration reached the East Coast, where most of the nation's population (and political power) was based. In North Adams, Massachusetts, seventy-five Chinese laborers were brought in to break a strike at a large factory. The ensuing union protests against Chinese importation, though not immigration, were repeated across several eastern cities. The spotlight cast on the Chinese in the East only helped fan the flames of conflict in the West, where anti-Chinese violence and rhetoric surged as white laborers attacked Chinese workers. One of the chief voices against Chinese workers was labor leader Denis Kearney, himself an Irish immigrant, who raised the cry, "The Chinese must go!"

Kearney's Workingmen's Party of California began the push to ban Chinese labor in 1878, arguing that Chinese labor (which was cheaper than white labor) was forcing down wages in the country. At the same time, the "coolie trade" also remained under scrutiny, after the US consul general to Hong Kong, David Bailey, issued a report that claimed that coolies were frequently tricked or coerced into signing contracts to work in the United States for low wages and in inhumane conditions.

By 1880, anti-Chinese rhetoric had entered the national stage, as aspiring politicians sparred with one another in pursuit of support from the increasingly influential western states. That year, American diplomats successfully renegotiated a long-standing treaty with China regulating Chinese immigration to the United States. The Angell Treaty, as it was known, opened the door for Congress to pass a ten-year moratorium on Chinese laborers. The Chinese Exclusion Act, as the law was known, extended far beyond the decade, remaining in place until 1943.

HISTORICAL DOCUMENT

An Act to execute certain treaty stipulations relating to Chinese.

Whereas in the opinion of the Government of the United States the coming of Chinese laborers to this country endangers the good order of certain localities within the territory thereof: Therefore,

Be it enacted by the Senate and House of Representatives of the United States of America in Congress assembled, That from and after the expiration of ninety days next after the passage of this act, and until the expiration of ten years next after the passage of this act, the coming of Chinese laborers to the United States be, and the same is hereby, suspended; and during such suspension it shall not be lawful for any Chinese laborer to come, or having so come after the expiration of said ninety days to remain within the United States.

SEC. 2.

That the master of any vessel who shall knowingly bring within the United States on such vessel, and land or permit to be landed, any Chinese laborer, from any foreign port or place, shall be deemed guilty of a misdemeanor, and on conviction thereof shall be punished by a fine of not more than five hundred dollars for each and every such Chinese laborer so brought, and maybe also imprisoned for a term not exceeding one year.

SEC. 3.

That the two foregoing sections shall not apply to Chinese laborers who were in the United States on the seventeenth day of November, eighteen hundred and eighty, or who shall have come into the same before the expiration of ninety days next after the passage of this act, and who shall produce to such master before going on board such vessel, and shall produce to the collector of the port in the United States at which such vessel shall arrive, the evidence hereinafter in this act required of his being one of the laborers in this section mentioned; nor shall the two foregoing sections apply to the case of any master whose vessel, being bound to a port not within the United States, shall come within the jurisdiction of the United States by reason of being in distress or in stress of weather, or touching at any port of the United States on its voyage to any foreign port or place: Provided, That all Chinese laborers brought on such vessel shall depart with the vessel on leaving port.

SEC. 4.

That for the purpose of properly identifying Chinese laborers who were in the United States on the seventeenth day of November eighteen hundred and eighty, or who shall have come into the same before the expiration of ninety days next after the passage of this act, and in order to furnish them with the proper evidence of their right to go from and come to the United States of their free will and accord, as provided by the treaty between the United States and China dated November seventeenth, eighteen hundred and eighty, the collector of customs of the district from which any such Chinese laborer shall depart from the United States shall, in person or by deputy, go on board each vessel having on board any such Chinese laborers and cleared or about to sail from his district for a foreign port, and on such vessel make a list of all such Chinese laborers, which shall be entered in registry-books to be kept for that purpose, in which shall be stated the name, age, occupation, last place of residence, physical marks of peculiarities, and all facts necessary for the identification of each of such Chinese laborers, which books shall be safely kept in the custom-house.; and every such Chinese laborer so departing from the United States shall be entitled to, and shall receive, free of any charge or cost upon application therefor, from the collector or his deputy, at the time such list is taken, a certificate, signed by the collector or his deputy and attested by his seal of office, in such form as the Secretary of the Treasury shall prescribe, which certificate shall contain a statement of the name, age, occupation, last place of residence, persona description, and facts of identification of the Chinese laborer to whom the certificate is issued, corresponding with the said list and registry in all particulars. In case any Chinese laborer after having received such certificate shall leave such vessel before her departure he shall deliver his certificate to the master of the vessel, and if such Chinese laborer shall fail to return to such vessel before her departure from port the certificate shall be delivered by the master to the collector of customs for cancellation. The certificate herein provided for shall entitle the Chinese laborer to whom the same is issued to return to and re-enter the United States upon producing and delivering the same to the collector of customs of the district at which such Chinese laborer shall seek to re-enter; and upon delivery of such certificate by such Chinese laborer to the collector of customs at the time of re-entry in the United States said collector shall cause the same to be filed in the custom-house anti duly canceled.

SEC. 5.

That any Chinese laborer mentioned in section four of this act being in the United States, and desiring to depart from the United States by land, shall have the right to demand and receive, free of charge or cost, a certificate of identification similar to that provided for in section four of this act to be issued to such Chinese laborers as may desire to leave the United States by water; and it is hereby made the duty of the collector of customs of the district next adjoining the foreign country to which said Chinese laborer desires to go to issue such certificate, free of charge or cost, upon application by such Chinese laborer, and to enter the same upon registry-books to be kept by him for the purpose, as provided for in section four of this act.

SEC. 6.

That in order to the faithful execution of articles one and two of the treaty in this act before mentioned, every Chinese person other than a laborer who may be entitled by said treaty and this act to come within the United States, and who shall be about to come to the United States, shall be identified as so entitled by the Chinese

Government in each case, such identity to be evidenced by a certificate issued under the authority of said government, which certificate shall be in the English language or (if not in the English language) accompanied by a translation into English, stating such right to come, and which certificate shall state the name, title or official rank, if any, the age, height, and all physical peculiarities, former and present occupation or profession, and place of residence in China of the person to whom the certificate is issued and that such person is entitled, conformably to the treaty in this act mentioned to come within the United States. Such certificate shall be prima-facie evidence of the fact set forth therein, and shall be produced to the collector of customs, or his deputy, of the port in the district in the United States at which the person named therein shall arrive.

SEC.7.

That any person who shall knowingly and falsely alter or substitute any name for the name written in such certificate or forge any such certificate, or knowingly utter any forged or fraudulent certificate, or falsely personate any person named in any such certificate, shall be deemed guilty of a misdemeanor; and upon conviction thereof shall be fined in a sum not exceeding one thousand dollars, and imprisoned in a penitentiary for a term of not more than five years.

SEC.8.

That the master of any vessel arriving in the United States from any foreign port or place shall, at the same time he delivers a manifest of the cargo, and if there be no cargo, then at the time of making a report of the entry of the vessel pursuant to law, in addition to the other matter required to be reported, and before landing, or permitting to land, any Chinese passengers, deliver and report to the collector of customs of the district in which such vessels shall have arrived a separate list of all Chinese passengers taken on board his vessel at any foreign port or place, and all such passengers on board the vessel at that time. Such list shall show the names of such passengers (and if accredited officers of the Chinese Government traveling on the business of that government, or their servants, with a note of such facts), and the names and other particulars, as shown by their respective certificates; and such list shall be sworn to by the master in the manner required by law in relation to the manifest of the cargo. Any willful refusal or neglect of any such master to comply with the provisions of this section shall incur the same penalties and forfeiture as are provided for a refusal or neglect to report and deliver a manifest of the cargo.

SEC. 9.

That before any Chinese passengers are landed from any such line vessel, the collector, or his deputy, shall proceed to examine such passenger, comparing the certificate with the list and with the passengers; and no passenger shall be allowed to land in the United States from such vessel in violation of law.

SEC.10.

That every vessel whose master shall knowingly violate any of the provisions of this act shall be deemed forfeited to the United States, and shall be liable to seizure and condemnation in any district of the United States into which such vessel may enter or in which she may be found.

SEC. 11.

That any person who shall knowingly bring into or cause to be brought into the United States by land, or who shall knowingly aid or abet the same, or aid or abet the landing in the United States from any vessel of any Chinese person not lawfully entitled to enter the United States, shall be deemed guilty of a misdemeanor, and shall, on conviction thereof, be fined in a sum not exceeding one thousand dollars, and imprisoned for a term not exceeding one year.

SEC. 12.

That no Chinese person shall be permitted to enter the United States by land without producing to the proper officer of customs the certificate in this act required of Chinese persons seeking to land from a vessel. And any Chinese person found unlawfully within the United States shall be caused to be removed therefrom to the country from whence he came, by direction of the President of the United States, and at the cost of the United States, after being brought before some justice, judge, or commissioner of a court of the United States and found to be one not lawfully entitled to be or remain in the United States.

SEC.13.

That this act shall not apply to diplomatic and other officers of the Chinese Government traveling upon the business of that government, whose credentials shall be taken as equivalent to the certificate in this act mentioned, and shall exempt them and their body and household servants from the provisions of this act as to other Chinese persons.

SEC. 14.

That hereafter no State court or court of the United States shall admit Chinese to citizenship; and all laws in conflict with this act are hereby repealed.

SEC.15.

That the words "Chinese laborers", wherever used in this act shall be construed to mean both skilled and unskilled laborers and Chinese employed in mining.

Approved, May 6, 1882.

GLOSSARY

manifest (of cargo): a list of cargo or passengers

prima facie: (lit. at first view): true and authentic, self-evident

Document Analysis

The Chinese Exclusion Act establishes a broad set of strict regulations on Chinese laborers on two main fronts. First, it places strong restrictions on the Chinese government to prevent Chinese citizens from either immigrating to the United States or accepting contracts from would-be employers. Second, it places strong sanctions on the employers themselves (and/or the ship captains who carry the laborers to the United States), threatening prison and fines for bringing Chinese laborers to the United States. The Act does not clearly define who the laborers are in relation to other workers, however, leaving employers and relevant government officials to make the distinction themselves. The Chinese, the Act alleges, cause discord and disruption in the places in which they work. It is, therefore, deliberately short on such details, expecting workers' employers to take heed of the threat and altogether avoid exploring the use of Chinese workers.

The Act begins with a clear statement that Chinese laborers represent, in the view of the government, a threat to the order of the communities in which they work. The government does not state the basis for this assertion, although the protests (and violence associated with them), such as that which took place in North Adams, could be seen as examples of such disorder. Nevertheless, the Act clearly identifies Chinese laborers as a disruptive presence in the American economy.

In light of this perceived danger to the order of American society, Congress applies a ten-year moratorium on Chinese laborers. In an earlier draft of the bill, the ban actually extended to twenty years, although the president vetoed that version in light of the risks it posed to Sino-American relations. The moratorium would be enforced on two major fronts. The first of these fronts were the merchants who would recruit, contract, carry overseas, and put to work the laborers in question. The "master of any vessel" on which laborers would usually be delivered would receive a fine of up to five hundred dollars per illegal laborer found aboard their ships, for example. The merchants would also need to obtain proper paperwork to present to the customs officials from the ports from which they disembarked and the ports at which they unloaded their cargo. Merchants who brought Chinese laborers across the US border with either Canada or Mexico would receive a similar sanction.

On the second front were the government officials. In the United States, the responsibility of locating and capturing illegal laborers as well as examining the documentation of every merchant vessel would fall to the customs officials. China, too, would bear responsibility for ensuring that laborers would not emigrate or sign a contract that would take them to the United States. US negotiators spent a great deal of time working with Chinese officials on this point. Fourteen years earlier, the United States and China signed the Burlingame-Seward Treaty, which was designed to ease immigration restrictions between the two countries and mitigate perceived American interference in China. The Act references this treaty in section six, taking care to underscore the relationship between the two countries that was improved under that treaty. Additionally, although the Act does not clearly define the term "laborer" (except in section fifteen, where it identifies both "skilled" and "unskilled" laborers and those involved in mining), section thirteen ensures that the term would not apply to any Chinese diplomat or government official.

The Act does not attempt to reconcile the differences between immigration and importation of Chinese laborers. Rather, it strongly regulates both immigrants and workers, threatening illegal Chinese laborers with jail sentences and fines if caught approaching or on American territory. Furthermore, the Act does not attempt to define groups that might be exempted from the law (except the aforementioned diplomats). Instead, the Act requires that any individual who would be exempted from the law be able to produce comprehensive documentation, sanctioned by Chinese authorities, that clearly states in English the lawfulness of his or her presence. Under the Act, any exemption certificate must be approved by both the US and Chinese governments before the Chinese individual in question could enter the United States. Such bureaucracy is deliberate—most potential Chinese immigrants who might be worthy of exemption would undoubtedly be deterred by the certification process.

Terms for Chinese laborers already residing in the United States became harsher as well. Their travel in and out of the country was likewise restricted and monitored with the use of certificates issued by the US government. Under the Act, they were also deemed ineligible for US citizenship.

Essential Themes

The Chinese Exclusion Act of 1882 represents the first government policy designed to prevent certain racial or ethnic groups from entering the United States. Born of pressure from organized labor groups in the western states (where Asian laborers, particularly those of Chinese origin, were rapidly becoming the largest group of minority laborers) and specific incidents of violence, the Act took a bold step that would be repeated with regard to other racial and ethnic groups in the decades leading up to World War II.

The Act, extended repeatedly in the late nineteenth century and repealed in 1943, worked to prevent Chinese laborers from entering the United States, as such laborers allegedly posed a threat to local economies. However, the Act deliberately avoids providing a clear definition of "laborers" and, with the threat of imprisonment and/or fines, provided enough of a deterrent for any possible candidates for exemption to proceed with immigrating to America.

Additionally, the Act does not wade into the immigration-versus-importation issue that vexed previous attempts to curtail the influx of Chinese laborers. Rather, it simply halts both immigration and commercial importation of Chinese nationals, empowering American customs officials and relevant law enforcement entities to investigate and capture Chinese laborers. Those who were found in the United States ninety days or more after the law's implementation would need to produce a certificate, officially issued by the Chinese government and validated by American customs, proving that the holders were exempt from the law. With the amount of bureaucracy involved in obtaining such documents, few Chinese seeking to enter the United States would carry such certificates. Lacking such information, any persons of Asian origin—a race that Reconstruction-era Americans still found alien even in comparison to recently freed blacks—would be considered criminals and subject to prosecution.

—*Michael P. Auerbach, MA*

Bibliography and Additional Reading

Gyory, Andrew. *Closing the Gate: Race, Politics, and the Chinese Exclusion Act*. Chapel Hill: U of North Carolina P, 1998. Print.

Lee, Erika. *At America's Gates: Chinese Immigration During the Exclusion Era, 1882–1943*. Chapel Hill: U of North Carolina P, 2007. Print.

Mills, Charles. *The Chinese Exclusion Act and American Labor*. Alexandria: Apple Cheeks, 2009. Print.

Soennichsen, John. *The Chinese Exclusion Act of 1882*. Westport: Greenwood, 2011. Print.

Tian, Kelly. *"The Chinese Exclusion Act of 1882 and Its Impact on North American Society."* Undergraduate Research Journal for the Human Sciences 9 (2010): n. pag. Web. 16 Jan. 2014.

COWBOYS AND OUTLAWS

The American cowboy played a relatively short-lived but important role in the creation of the West and in its perseverance in modern times. Texas cowboys are perhaps the best known, partly because of the importance of Texas as a source for cattle, but there were cowboys throughout the West. Their work consisted of branding, grazing, rounding up, and driving cattle along established trails in order to bring them to market and satisfy the demand for beef in the East. The cowboy became known for his courage, fairness, and folk philosophy, and also, to a lesser extent, for having included in his number persons of Hispanic and African American heritage. Above all, cowboy culture was a culture of manliness. Yet, in the domestic life of cattlemen, women played a key role, too.

Similarly representative of the American West is the outlaw or renegade. Given the lack of formal legal institutions in the frontier region, communities were left to devise systems of their own to handle crime and public safety. For every dozen or more outlaws in an area, there were, at best, one community-designated lawman and a few earnest deputies who were charged with maintaining law and order. The matchup between outlaw and sheriff/deputy became the stuff of legend, endlessly recounted in tall tales, dime novels, and folk songs throughout the region—and beyond. The theme eventually made its way into motion pictures and television series. Today, of course, a more critical perspective is used to separate fact from fiction, history from folklore.

■ On Being a Pony Express Rider

Dates: c. 1860–1861 (published 1879)
Author/s: William F. Cody (with Glenn D. Bradley)
Genre: biography; memoir

Summary Overview

The document excerpted here is a personal account of "Buffalo Bill" Cody's experiences while working as a Pony Express delivery rider, including his recollections of another noted rider at the time, Wild Bill Hickok. Besides offering a glimpse into the life of the famous character Buffalo Bill, the excerpt shows how the Pony Express riders faced the difficult conditions of the Old West, while remaining dedicated to their task, thus guaranteeing that communications between the eastern and westerns portions of the developing nation could continued. Although there is some dispute about the validity of Buffalo Bill's claim that he was a Pony Express rider, the only evidence being Cody's personal account, there is little argument about the general outlines of his description. His use of Express riders in his famous Wild West show in later decades did much to create a place for the Pony Express in the legend of the American West.

Defining Moment

This excerpt illustrates a part of American history that has contributed as much to the legend as to the history of the Old West. The Pony Express ran only from April 1860 until October 1861, yet the riders' place in history looms much larger than that short time span would suggest. Much of this is owing to their incredible dedication—having lost only one mail satchel in the entire run of the Express (and that was because the rider had been killed and his horse not recovered). Playing an important part of communication before the invention of the telegraph and the completion of the transcontinental railroad, the Pony Express was the only way to get messages from the East to the West; coast-to-coast communication took under twelve days. But this was not a settled time, geographically or politically, and incidents with western Indian tribes, as described in the article, result in military escorts being needed for the riders and the loss of many lives on both sides of the conflict. Nevertheless, the Pony Express continued to run with few breaks until it was made redundant by the telegraph line and finally shut down with the expansion of the railroads.

Despite its quick demise, the Pony Express lives on in the collective memory of this time period because of the riders' amazing skill and dedication. Moreover, Buffalo Bill ensured that these men were not forgotten by using their experiences and skills in his Wild West show, which was formed about ten years after he left the Pony Express. Traveling as quickly as possible, through both hostile environments and virtually any type of weather, the Pony Express riders faced the very real possibility of death each time they headed out. In that respect, they embodied the character and spirit that inspired easterners to push into the "Wild West" in order to seek their fortune and a new life for themselves and their families. Riding around ninety miles distance at a time, sometimes changing horses on the fly, and dodging outlaws and hostile Indians, the riders kept their oath to serve the people and carry out their duties with dignity and honor, even though a few, like Buffalo Bill, were barely more than children at the time.

Author Biography

William Cody, better known as Buffalo Bill, was born in Iowa in 1846, but grew up primarily in Kansas. By age fifteen, he had already been away from home for several years, working various jobs before becoming a Pony Express rider in 1860. He earned his nickname "Buffalo Bill" in the years following this, while working as a hunter in the West and was soon something of a sensation, appearing in several newspapers. Then in 1872, he began his career in entertainment, with a series of shows, the most popular of which was his Wild West show. This prelude to modern-day rodeos showcased cowboys and cowgirls doing tricks, as well as many types of animals common to the West. Cody became so famous that he was invited to perform his show in England for Queen Victoria's Golden Jubilee celebration and before a crowd of 18,000 at the 1893 Chicago World's Fair. Cody died in 1917 in Denver.

HISTORICAL DOCUMENT

[Mr. Slade, the manager of a Pony Express station] assigned me to duty on the road from Red Buttes on the North Platte, to the Three Crossings of the Sweetwater—a distance of seventy-six miles—and I began riding at once.

One day when I galloped into Three Crossings, my home station, I found that the rider who was expected to take the trip out on my arrival had got into a drunken row the night before and had been killed; and that there was no one to fill his place. I did not hesitate for a moment to undertake an extra ride of eighty-five miles to Rocky Ridge, and I arrived at the latter place on time. I then turned back and rode to Red Buttes, my starting place, accomplishing on the round trip a distance of 322 miles.

Slade heard of this feat of mine, and one day as he was passing on a coach he sang out to me, "My boy, you're a brick, and no mistake. That was a good run you made when you rode your own and Miller's routes, and I'll see that you get extra pay for it."

Slade, although rough at times and always a dangerous character—having killed many a man—was always kind to me. During the two years that I worked for him as pony-express-rider and stage-driver, he never spoke an angry word to me.

As I was leaving Horse Creek one day, a party of fifteen Indians jumped me in a sand ravine about a mile west of the station. They fired at me repeatedly, but missed their mark. I was mounted on a roan California horse—the fleetest steed I had. Putting spurs and whip to him, and lying flat on his back, I kept straight on for Sweetwater Bridge—eleven miles distant—instead of trying to turn back to Horse Creek. The Indians came on in hot pursuit, but my horse soon got away from them, and ran into the station two miles ahead of them. The stock-tender had been killed there that morning, and all the stock had been driven off by the Indians, and as I was therefore unable to change horses, I continued on to Ploutz's Station—twelve miles further—thus making twenty-four miles straight run with one horse. I told the people at Ploutz's what had happened at Sweetwater

Bridge, and with a fresh horse went on and finished the trip without any further adventure.

About the middle of September the Indians became very troublesome on the line of the stage road along the Sweetwater. Between Split Rock and Three Crossings they robbed a stage, killed the driver and two passengers, and badly wounded Lieut. Flowers, the assistant division agent. The red-skinned thieves also drove off the stock from the different stations, and were continually lying in wait for the passing stages and pony express-riders, so that we had to take many desperate chances in running the gauntlet.

The Indians had now become so bad and had stolen so much stock that it was decided to stop the pony express for at least six weeks, and to run the stages but occasionally during that period; in fact, it would have been almost impossible to have run the enterprise much longer without restocking the line.

[Buffalo Bill on Wild Bill Hickok, western Kansas]
The custom with the express riders, when within half a mile of a station, was either to begin shouting or blowing a horn in order to notify the stock tender of his approach, and to have a fresh horse already saddled for him on his arrival, so that he could go right on without a moment's delay.

One day, as Wild Bill neared Rock Creek station, where he was to change horses, he began shouting as usual at the proper distance; but the stock-tender, who had been married only a short time and had his wife living with him at the station, did not make his accustomed appearance. Wild Bill galloped up and instead of finding the stock-tender ready for him with a fresh horse, he discovered him lying across the stable door with the blood oozing from a bullet-hole in his head. The man was dead, and it was evident that he had been killed only a few moments before.

In a second Wild Bill jumped from his horse, and looking in the direction of the house he saw a man coming towards him. The approaching man fired on him at once, but missed his aim. Quick as lightning Wild Bill pulled his revolver and returned the fire. The stranger fell dead, shot through the brain.

"Bill, Bill! Help! Help! save me!" Such was the cry that Bill now heard. It was the shrill and pitiful voice of the dead stock tender's wife, and it came from a window of the house. She had heard the exchange of shots, and knew that Wild Bill had arrived.

He dashed over the dead body of the villain whom he had killed, and just as he sprang into the door of the house, he saw two powerful men assaulting the woman.

One of the desperadoes was in the act of striking her with the butt end of a revolver, and while his arm was still raised, Bill sent a ball crashing through his skull, killing him instantly. Two other men now came rushing from an adjoining room, and Bill, seeing that the odds were three to one against him, jumped into a corner, and then firing, he killed another of the villains.

Before he could shoot again the remaining two men closed in upon him, one of whom had drawn a large bowie knife. Bill wrenched the knife from his grasp and drove it through the heart of the outlaw.

The fifth and last man now grabbed Bill by the throat, and held him at arm's length, but it was only for a moment, as Bill raised his own powerful right arm and struck his antagonist's left arm such a terrible blow that he broke it. The disabled desperado, seeing that he was no longer a match for Bill, jumped through the door, and mounting a horse he succeeded in making his escape— being the sole survivor of the Jake McCandless gang.

Wild Bill remained at the station with the terrified woman until the stage came along, and he then consigned her to the care of the driver. Mounting his horse he at once galloped off, and soon disappeared in the distance, making up for lost time.

GLOSSARY

bowie knife: a large knife with a single-edged blade; named after James Bowie

"brick": a good or generous person; informal usage

desperadoes: a bold, reckless criminal or outlaw, especially in the American West

roan: a horse with a chestnut, bay, or sorrel coat and with a sprinkling of gray or white

"running the gauntlet": enduring a series of problems or threats

stage-driver: the driver of a stagecoach

stock-tender: one who takes care of livestock (horses, etc.)

Document Analysis

Much of this document describes the dangerous conditions that the Pony Express riders faced on the trips they took. Between Indians and outlaws, many riders, tenders, and stable workers were injured or killed, often for their animals, but also simply because they were easy targets, being alone in the vast and empty miles between towns. Additionally, a close reading reveals the personal commitment to their jobs that the riders had and their intent to see things through to the end. These stories show a certain insensitivity toward violence and mortal peril, which the riders faced on a regular basis.

The possibility of being hurt or killed while on a delivery was just part of daily life.

This document shows the clear problems that existed in the American West, namely, violent conflicts between the Indians and the rest of the area's inhabitants, as well as the lack of law-enforcement to protect individuals from outlaws and "desperadoes." In his account, Buffalo Bill focuses mostly on how he made his trips between towns; the Indians who "fired at me repeatedly" or were "in hot pursuit" are not the main point of the story. Such confrontations are simply facts of the journey; the main point is that he completed his rides. The only time this attitude changes is when the attacks become so bad that the Pony Express was actually halted for a short time. In this last section, Cody explains that the normal amount of danger had become so increased that it now a kind of "gauntlet." But even this section ends with a mention that this break came at a good time, since the riders needed more horses anyway if they were to continue on. Cody always spoke very highly of Native Americans, even protecting them and their culture; but in this instance he is very clear, yet still respectful, about the fact that they posed a great risk to himself and his fellow riders. Even so, the matter does not seem to bother him overmuch.

In the second story, another rider, Wild Bill Hickok, also faces a clear danger—in this case, the presence of violent outlaws. As is apparent from this story, Wild Bill was no stranger to inflicting his own violence on someone; but the most interesting part is the very last paragraph. Wild Bill, after driving away the attackers, simply stays with the woman until he knows she is safely in someone else's care; he then continues on his way, riding for the next town. The Pony Express riders' dedication to their job made it much more than a job; it was more of a calling, and one that they pursued no matter what the circumstances or personal dangers were. While it may seem odd that Wild Bill simply carried on with his route, this was part of the ethic of the Old West: life continued on, even with violence all around.

Essential Themes

This is not simply a document about the technical details of a Pony Express ride between two towns, although Buffalo Bill includes quite a few of these details as well. Rather, this is more a document providing evidence of the character and internal strength of the men and the rough world of the Old West (or "Wild West"). For just over a year, these men risked their lives to deliver mail in order to ensure that prompt communication could occur over the vast and ever-growing land that eventually became the lower forty-eight states. The Old West

was a violent and dangerous place in which to live, but these men show the brighter side of that world as well, doing their jobs with integrity and determination.

As for Buffalo Bill Cody's involvement in the Pony Express, there are some doubts as to the legitimacy of his claims. That is, not much material evidence exists that includes him as one of the riders. In any case, his inclusion of former riders in his troupe of entertainers, and his use of the Pony Express in his Wild West shows for the next few decades, achieved something that the Pony Express would not have been able to accomplish on its own. Cody put on display the spirit of the Pony Express, illustrating the riders' ingenuity and dedication to the task. The Express riders were a small and select group and operated for a short time. They might well have fallen between the cracks of historical memory but for Buffalo Bill's influence. As numerous children's books, movies, and television shows attest, the Pony Express and its renowned riders live on, noted for their riding tricks and for being the first links between the eastern and western halves of the country.

—*Anna Accettola, MA*

Bibliography and Additional Reading

"*A Brief History of William F. 'Buffalo Bill' Cody.*" Buffalo Bill Museum & Grave, n.d. Web. 17 Oct. 2014.

Driggs, Howard R., & William Henry Jackson. *The Pony Express Goes Through; an American Saga Told by Its Heroes.* New York: Frederick A. Stokes, 1935. Print.

Gunn, J. M. "*The Pony Express.*" Annual Publication of the Historical Society of Southern California and Pioneer Register, Los Angeles 5.2 (1901): 168–75. Web. 17 Oct. 2014.

"*The Pony Express.*" Pony Express National Museum. Pony Express National Museum, 2014. Web. 15 Oct. 2014.

Settle, Raymond W., & Mary Lund Settle. *Saddles and Spurs: The Pony Express Saga.* Lincoln: U of Nebraska P, 1972. Print.

■ Jesse James in His Own Defense

Date: 1870–1872
Author: Jesse James
Genre: letter

Summary Overview

Of all the outsized outlaws to stir the public imagination, none has ever equaled the stature of Jesse James. A one-time Confederate guerilla who never gave up the fight, Jesse, with the help of his brother Frank and an ever evolving gang of likeminded bandits and killers, became a sort of living myth throughout the American South and West during the 1870s. Portrayed as an American Robin Hood, stealing from the rich to give to the poor, he was made the symbol for Southern resentment against the victorious North, and later, after his own violent end, the nation's most enduring folk hero—a bulwark against the forces of modernity, which only a few decades later swelled to unmake the agrarian nation that was. But Jesse was none of these things. Underneath the layers of lies, myths, and tall tales, he was just a murderer and a thief. He was an outlaw who found brief success in the chaos of the postwar frontier.

Defining Moment

In the aftermath of the Civil War, tensions ran high throughout the old Confederacy. Anger over the South's defeat, the emancipation of the slaves, and the imposition of Northern Republican rule on state governments, swirled to create a storm of resentment. Violence flared against carpetbaggers, Union sympathizers, and recently freed blacks. As the old Southern Democratic establishment fought to regain power, millions of men who had served in the Rebel armies found little work and little opportunity in the towns and cities they called home. Some turned to vigilante groups, like the Ku Klux Klan, as a means to exact revenge for their perceived wrongs, while others decided to leverage the experience they gained in the war to seek a more lucrative form of vengeance.

Jesse James was no stranger to violence. Having been too young to enlist in the regular army when the Civil War broke out, and taught by his mother to despise the Union, he instead became a bushwhacker—a Confed-erate guerilla fighter—in a Missouri band led by the infamous William "Bloody Bill" Anderson. Free from the rules and conventions of war, Bloody Bill's bushwhackers instigated chaos across the state, butchering Northerners by the hundreds and spreading terror wherever they went. James, who had lost his father at an early age, admired the psychotic Bloody Bill and was deeply affected when Union forces finally gunned him down in 1864.

After the surrender of Robert E. Lee, James and his brother Frank, possessing little in the way of non-lethal skill, decided to keep fighting. Reinventing themselves as outlaws, they started robbing banks and stagecoaches. Jesse James might have been no one of consequence, just another criminal operating on the edge of the frontier, but in 1870, upon learning that Bloody Bill's killer now operated a bank in the town of Gallatin, Missouri, James murdered a bank teller in hopes of exacting revenge. Despite having botched the assassination by killing the wrong man and stealing nothing of consequence, Jesse James was suddenly thrust into the national spotlight. Hungry for a sympathetic former Rebel to frame as a freedom fighter, Southern newspapers, following the lead of the respected editor John Newman, painted James as a victim of Northern exploitation. While the James brothers robbed the banks and the railroads, murdering dozens of innocent people, Newman crafted an image of Jesse as a sort of American Robin Hood and personally edited letters written by Jesse for publication across the South. In the eyes of many, Jesse James had taken on the mantle of the Confederate cause, a "bold robber," as he wrote himself.

For over ten years, the James gang, pursued by lawmen and even the famed Pinkerton Detective Agency, evaded capture while wreaking havoc across the American South and West. It wasn't until the 1880s that the popularity of the mythic outlaw finally began to wane. As Southern Democrats regained control of the old

Confederacy, Jesse James became their problem to deal with. Out of favor, and grown increasingly paranoid and violent, James was finally gunned down in April 1882 by one of his own men on the promise of a pardon.

Author Biography

Jesse Woodson James was born in Clay County, Missouri in 1847. The son of a rabidly pro-slavery Baptist preacher, Jesse and his brother, Frank, were brought up to despise what their mother, Zerelda, considered a hostile and intrusive North. After the death of their father, and the start of the Civil War, the James boys joined the violent Confederate guerilla factions operating within the state. Jesse came under the mentorship of William "Bloody Bill" Anderson, an infamous bushwhacker, known for scalping his Union victims. After the loss of the Confederacy, Jesse and Frank became outlaws, specifically robbing stagecoaches, banks, and trains. In 1870, Jesse James gained notoriety for the murder of a bank clerk in the town of Gallatin. With help from Confederate loyalists and a sympathetic Southern press, Jesse James quickly rose to become the most famous outlaw in America. Ultimately, he was killed by Robert Ford, a member of his own gang in 1882.

HISTORICAL DOCUMENT

The Liberty Tribune, **June 24, 1870**
June, 1870

Governor McClurg:

DEAR SIR: I and my brother Frank are charged with the crime of killing the cashier and robbing the bank at Gallatin, Mo., Dec. 7th, 1869. I can prove, by some of the best men in Missouri, where I was the day of the robbery and the day previous to it, but I well know if I was to submit to an arrest, that I would be mobbed and hanged without a trial. The past is sufficient to show that bushwhackers have been arrested in Missouri since the war, charged with bank robbery, and they most all have been mobbed without trials. I will cite you the case of Thomas Little, of Lafayette county, Mo. A few days after the bank was robbed at Richmond, in 1867, Mr. Little was charged with being one of the party who perpetrated the deed. He was sent from St. Louis to Warrensburg under a heavy guard. As soon as the parties arrived there, they found out that he (Mr. Little) could prove, by the citizens of Dover, that he was innocent of the charge—as soon as these scoundrels found out that he was innocent—a mob was raised, broke in the jail, took him out and hanged him.

Governor, when I think I can get a fair trial, I will surrender myself to the civil authorities of Missouri. But I never will surrender to be mobbed by a set of bloodthirsty poltroons. It is true that during the war I was a Confederate soldier, and fought under the black flag, but since then I have lived a peaceable citizen, and obeyed the laws of the United States to the best of my knowledge. The authorities of Gallatin say the reason that led them to suspect me was that the mare left at Gallatin, by the robbers, was identified as belonging to me. That is false. I can prove that I sold the mare previous to the robbery. It is true that I fought Deputy Sheriff Thomason, of Clay county, but was not my brother with me when we had the fight. I do not think that I violated the law when I fought Thomason as his posse refused to tell me who they were.

Three different statements have been published in reference to the fight that I had with Thomason, but they are all a pack of falsehoods. Deputy Sheriff Thomason has never yet given any report of the fight, that I have seen. I am personally acquainted with Oscar Thomason, the Deputy's son, but when the shooting began, his face was so muffled up with furs that I did not recognize him. But if I did violate the law when I fought Thomason I am perfectly willing to abide by it.

But as to them mobbing me for a crime that I am innocent of, that is played out. As soon as I think I can get a just trial I will surrender myself to the civil authorities of Missouri, and prove to the world that I am innocent of the crime charged against me.

Respectfully,
Jesse W. James

The *Kansas City Times*, October 15, 1872
[This letter was not signed "Jesse James," but historians believe he wrote it.]

As a great deal has been said in regard to the robbery which occurred at the Kansas City Exposition grounds, I will give a few lines to the public, as I am one of the party who perpetrated the deed. A great many say that we, the robbers, deserve hanging. What have we done to be hung for? It is true that I shot a little girl, though it was not intentional, and I am very sorry that the child was shot; and if the parents will give me their address through the columns of the *Kansas City Weekly Times*, I will send them money to pay her doctor's bill. And as to Mr. Wallace, I never tried to kill him. I only shot to make him let go my friend. If I had been so disposed, I could have shot him dead. Just let a party of men commit a bold robbery, and the cry is hang them, but [President Ulysses] Grant and his party can steal millions, and it is all right. It is true, we are robbers, but we always rob in the glare of the day and in the teeth of the multitude; and we never kill only in self defense, without men refuse to open their vaults and safes to us, and when they refuse to unlock to us we kill. But a man who is [expletive] enough fool to refuse to open a safe or a vault when he is covered with a pistol ought to die. There is no use for a man to try to do anything when an experienced robber gets the go on him. If he gives the alarm, or resists, or refuses to unlock, he gets killed, and if he obeys, he is not hurt in the flesh but he is in the purse.

Some editors call us thieves. We are not thieves—we are bold robbers. It hurts me very much to be called a thief. It makes me feel like they were trying to put me on a par with Grant and his party. We are bold robbers, and I am proud of the name, for Alexander the Great was a bold robber, and Julius Caesar, and Napoleon Bonaparte, and Sir William Wallace—not old Ben Wallace—and Robert Emmet. Please rank me with these, and not with the Grantites. Grant's party has no respect for anyone. They rob the poor and rich, and we rob the rich and give to the poor. As to the author of the letter, the public will never know. I will close by hoping that Horace Greeley will defeat Grant, and then I can make an honest living, and then I will not have to rob, as taxes will not be so heavy.

GLOSSARY

bushwhacker: a guerilla fighter from the American Civil War

poltroon: an utter coward

posse: a body of men, typically armed, summoned by a sheriff to enforce the law

Document Analysis

The first document, written by Jesse James in 1870 and edited by John Newman, is a complete denial of charges in the robbery of the bank in Gallatin, Missouri some time earlier, which resulted in the death of the bank's clerk. Although James had indeed committed the crimes of which he was accused, even boasting of it as he escaped, the letter, addressed to the Governor of the state, claims that James can produce evidence of his innocence, while also asserting that if he were to try and surrender to authorities, as he'd like to do, he'd be mobbed and lynched. In fact, the letter was a carefully crafted narrative, masterminded by Newman, to paint Jesse James as the victim of Northern persecution. A Southern man, the letter claimed, could no longer find justice in the South. James wasn't a saint by any stretch, but under a cloud of danger, he'd have to take action. The second letter, also written by Jesse James and edited by John Newman, was a more direct attack on the Republican-dominated federal government. Yes, the letter stated, James had robbed the Kansas City Exposition and had killed people in the process, but his crimes were nothing compared to those of President Ulysses S. Grant and his government. James was a "bold robber," a man of conviction fighting for the common man, while Grant and his Northern cronies were nothing more than simple thieves. In terms that any person with common sense can understand, James had committed murder only when he had to. He was a bold robber, in the company of other bold robbers, such as Julius Caesar, Napoleon Bonaparte, and William Wallace. All at once, he was a conqueror, a liberator, and a freedom fighter. A great man destined to remake the world, but also the embodiment of all Southerners.

Together these letters represent the split duality of the former Confederacy. Victim on the one hand, exploited and mistreated by a criminal government, and champion on the other, still fighting the War of Northern Aggression. Put together, they are the story of Robin Hood: victim and savior both. Forced by injustice into a life of crime, to steal from the rich to give to the poor, Jesse James would ultimately liberate those enslaved by villainy. In fact, James himself makes the connection when he writes: "Grant's party has no respect for anyone. They rob the poor and rich, and we rob the rich and give to the poor."

Essential Themes

Jesse James was a cold-blooded killer. Shaped by the hands of a ruthless pro-slavery guerilla fighter amidst the bloodiest conflict in American history, he murdered innocent people, most often without provocation, while stealing from banks, stagecoaches, and trains. No evidence exists that any of his ill-gotten gains made their way into the hands of the needy or the poor. And yet, thanks to a concerted effort on the part of Confederate loyalists and the winds of political opportunity, Jesse James was made into an American folk hero, the young nation's very own Robin Hood—a brave, moral man forced to fight against the juggernaut of tyranny. In life,

Jesse James was a common criminal, who, for a brief time, managed to capture the imagination of millions and become the instrument for their frustrated salvation. In death, he became even bigger. Immediately following his assassination in 1882, thousands of people flocked to see his final resting place, to buy pieces of his house, even to buy pebbles from his grave. His wife, his mother, and his brother all cashed in. They sold their stories, and they told their tales. Frank James even became a regular player in Buffalo Bill's Wild West show. The acts of brutality, Jesse's violence, his instability, his crimes even, were all washed away and eventually forgotten. The outlaw became a legend. The legend became myth. As North and South reconciled and became one, as industry increasingly became the enemy, the story of the Missouri outlaw increasingly resonated with people. In the end, Jesse James became what he always wanted himself to be, a savior, a hero, a martyr for the cause.

—*KP Dawes, MA*

Bibliography and Additional Reading

Jackson, Cathy M. *"The Making of an American Outlaw Hero: Jesse James, Folklore and Late Nineteenth-Century Print Media."* PhD dissertation, University of Missouri-Columbia, 2004. Print.

"Jesse James." American Experience. Dir. Mark Zwonitzer. PBS, 2006. Film.

Stiles, T. J. *Jesse James: Last Rebel of the Civil War.* New York: Random House, 2002. Print.

Yeatman, Ted P. *Frank and Jesse James: The Story Behind the Legend.* Nashville, TN: Cumberland House Publishing, 2000. Print.

■ On Billy the Kid

Dates: c. 1879–1881 (published 1937)
Authors: Francisco Trujillo (with Edith Crawford)
Genre: biography; autobiography; memoir

Summary Overview

In the text reproduced here, one Francisco Trujillo, with occasional interjections by his interviewer (Edith Crawford), tells of his experiences with the American outlaw and Wild West folk hero William H. Bonney, otherwise known as Billy the Kid. Trujillo was not directly involved in every aspect of the story he tells, which takes place sometime after the so-called Lincoln Country War in New Mexico Territory in 1878 (an event that first brought Billy the Kid to public notice). Yet the escapades of Billy the Kid were soon to become well known, and his death in 1881 at the hand of Sherriff Pat Garret was big news, both at the time and in the folklore of the region for decades afterward. Trujillo's interactions with the Kid and his gang reveal elements of the sort of interpersonal dynamics and race relations that reigned in the Old West, as well as the lawlessness that was common to the era.

Defining Moment

Trujillo's memoir provides a glimpse, if not always first-hand, into the life and death of a legendary American character. Although it is not clear at first from the narrative, the events that Trujillo recounts in the beginning concern the Lincoln County War, which took place in the late 1870s in Lincoln County, New Mexico Territory. The conflict was between, on one side, a rancher named John Chisum and his two partners, Alexander McSween and John Tunstall, and, on the other side, a competing faction led by Lawrence Murphy and his partner James Dolan. The conflict was over commercial trade in the area, particularly the dry goods trade. Each faction wanted a lock on the business. Billy the Kid was a member of Chisum's faction, working as a ranch hand at Tunstall's cattle operation and as part of an armed "protection" group known as the Regulators. As Trujillo states, several characters in the story, beginning with Tunstall, were killed during the on-again, off-again fighting that unfolded. The final phase of the Lincoln County War was a multi-day shootout during which John Chisum was killed and Billy the Kid and the Regulators were forced to disband and flee.

This memoir, or oral history, by Francisco Trujillo comes from the Federal Writers' Project, a government program during the 1930s that was concerned with the collection and preservation of autobiographical narratives by people who lived in the United States during the previous century. (There was also another, contemporary component to the Writers' Project, but Trujillo's narrative falls into the oral history category.) People's recollections of their experiences often reveal the realities of the times in which they lived. In this case, Trujillo's story illustrates tensions and alliances among several different ethnic groups in the Southwest during the late 1800s. It also shows that Billy the Kid and his gang, although involved in a very bloody conflict, were not always overtly violent: they allow Trujillo and his brother Juan to pass by without much incident. Without the contributions from such witnesses as Trujillo, information about figures and events from the past are often sketchy or lost completely. While newspapers from the era published accounts of the Lincoln County War and seemed fascinated by Billy the Kid, their reports were often cursory or wrong because of the limited access they had to the participants and/or any corroborating facts or witnesses. Early newspapers were also prone to exaggeration and the filling of gaps in the story with fabrications. Oral memoirs like Trujillo's can help bring a sharper focus to the historical picture.

Author Biography

Unfortunately, there appears to be little or no substantive information available about Francisco "Kiko" Trujillo (or for his interviewer, Edith Crawford). We know only that at the time of the recording of his narrative, in May 1937, Trujillo was eighty-five years old and living in the small town of San Patricio, Lincoln County, New

going to Lincoln, the Mexicans to San Patricio whence they arrived on Sunday afternoon.

Billy the Kid then said to Jose Chaves, "Let us draw to see who has to wait for Macky Swin tomorrow at Lincoln. The lots fell to Charley Barber, John Milton and Jim French White, whereupon the leader decided that all nine Anglos should go. Bill thought that it was best for none of the Mexican boys to go and when Chaves protested saying that the Anglos were no braver than he, Bill explained that Brady was married to a Mexican and that it was a matter of policy, all Mexicans being sentimental about their own. Chaves, being appeased, urged the rest to go on promising to render assistance should a call come for help. A Texan name Doke said that since his family was Mexican too, he would remain with the others. Stock then gave orders to proceed. The horses were saddled and they left for Lincoln. Doke, Fernando Herrera, Jesus Sais and Candelario Hidalgo left for Ruidoso. The next morning dom Pancho Sanches left for Lincoln to make some purchases at the store.

Being in the store about eleven, the mail arrived and with it Macky Swin. There also arrived Brady and a Texan name George Hamilton. At this juncture Brady also arrived where he found Billy the Kid, Jim French, Charley Barber and John Melton. They were in the corral from whence two of the gang shot at one, and two others at the other, where they fell.

Billy the Kid then jumped to snatch Brady's rifle and as he was leaning over someone shot at him from a house they used to call "El Chorro."

Macky Swin then reached the house where the nine Macky Swins were congregated—the four who were in the corral and five who had been at the river. There they remained all day until nightfall and then proceeded to San Patricio.

The next morning they proposed going to the hills should there be a war and so that it could be waged at the edge of town in order not to endanger the lives of the families living there. The same day, toward evening, six Mexicans came to arrest Macky Swin. They did not arrive at the Plaza but camped a little further down between the acequia and the river at a place where there were thick brambles. Shortly after the Mexicans arrived Macky Swin came with his people to eat supper at the house of Juan Trujillo—that being their headquarters, that also being

their mess hall, having hired a negro to prepare the meals. After supper they scattered among the different houses, two or three in each house.

In one of these at the edge of town Macky Swin and an American boy whose name was Tome locked themselves in. Next day early in the morning the six Mexicans who had been looking for Macky Swin showed up. When they arrived at the house where Macky Swin was Tome came out and shot at the bunch of Mexicans and hit Julian, about forty Marfes came down to San Patricio killing horses and chickens. At this point there arrived two Marfes, an American and a Mexican. The American's name was Ale Cu, and the Mexican's Lucio Montoya. When the Macky Swins became aware of them, they began to fire and killed all the horses. The two Marfes ran away to San Patricio where the rest of the Marfes were tearing down a house and taking out of the store everything that they could get hold of. From there all the Marfes went to Lincoln and for about a month nothing of interest occurred.

I don't recall exactly when Macky Swin, who was being hounded down by the Marfes, was killed but I do remember that he gathered together all his friends and went back home to Lincoln accompanied by eight Mexicans and two Americans, also his wife. When the Marfes found out that he was in the house they surrounded him but seeing that they were unable to hurt him they caused to be brought over a company of soldiers and a cannon from the nearby Fort. Notwithstanding this Macky Swin instructed his people not to fire. For this reason the soldiers had to sit until it was dark. The Marfes then set fire to the house and the soldiers returned to the fort. When the first room burned down, Ginio Salazar and Ignacio Gonzales came out to the door but the Marfes knocked them down and left them there, dazed. When the flames reached the middle room, an American proposed to go out through the doors of the kitchen on the north side. No sooner did he jump than the Marfes knocked him down. Francisco Samora jumped also and he too was shot. Vincente Romero was next and there the three remained in a heap. It was then proposed by Billy the Kid and Jose Chaves y Chaves to take aim at the same time and shoot, first to one side then to the other. Chaves took Macky Swin by the arm and told him to go out to which Macky Swin answered by taking a chair and placing it in the corner stating that he would die right there. Billy and Jose Chaves then jumped to the middle door, one on one side, and the other on the other.

Then Robert Bakers and a Texan jumped and said, "Here is Macky Swin". Drawing out his revolver he shot him three times in the breast.

When the last shot was fired Billy the Kid said "Here is Robert," and thrust a revolver in his mouth while Jose Chaves shot at the Texan and hit him in the eye. Billy and Chaves then went along the river headed for San Patricio where they both remained for some time.

In October the Governor accompanied by seven soldiers and other persons came to Sam Patricio camping. Having heard about the exploits of Billy, the Governor expressed a desire to meet him and sent a messenger to fetch him. The interview was in the nature of a heart to heart talk wherein the Governor advised Billy to give up his perilous career. At this point occurred the General Election and George Kimbrall was elected sheriff of the county.

Obeying the Governor's orders he called out the militia having commissioned Sr. Patron as captain and Billy the Kid as first lieutenant. During that year—that of '79— things were comparatively quiet and Billy led a very uneventful life.

About the last part of October of the same year, the Governor issued an order that the militia should make an effort to round all bandits in Chaves county, a task which the militia was not able to accomplish hence it disbanded. Billy the Kid received an honorable discharge and would probably have gone straight from them had it not been that at this juncture the District Court met and the Marfes swore a complaint against him and ordered Sheriff Kimbrall [Kimbrell] to arrest him. Billy stubbornly refused to accompany the sheriff and threatened to take away his life rather than to be apprehended.

Again nothing was heard for a time and then Pat Garrett offered to bring in the desperado for a reward. The Governor having been made aware of the situation himself offered a reward of $500. Immediately Pat Garrett, accompanied by four other men, got ready to go after Billy and found him and three other boys, whom they surrounded. One morning, during the siege, one of Billy's companions went out to fetch a pail of water whereupon Pat Garrett shot at him, as well as the others, hitting him in the neck and thereby causing him to drop the pail and to run into the house. With a piece of cloth, Billy was able to dress the wound of the injured man and at least stop the hemorrhage. He then advised the wounded man to go out and to pretend to give himself up, hiding his firearm but using it at the first opportune moment to kill Pat. Charley did as he was told but when he went to take aim, dropped dead.

Bill and the other three companions were kept prisoners [under the siege] for three days, but finally hunger and thirst drove them out and caused them to venture forth and to give themselves up. Billy was arrested, there being no warrant for the others.

Then followed the trial which resulted in a sentence to hang within thirty days. News of the execution having spread about, people began to come in for miles around to be present on the fatal day, but Billy was not to afford them much pleasure having escaped three days before the hanging. A deputy and jailer had been commissioned to stand guard over him. On the day of the escape at noon the jailer told the deputy to go and eat his dinner and that he would then go himself and fetch the prisoner's. It was while the jailer and Billy remained alone that the prisoner stepped to the window to fetch a paper. He had somehow gotten rid of his hand-cuffs and only his shackles remained. With the paper in his hand he approached the officer and before the latter knew what his charge was up to, yanked his revolver away from him—and the next instant he was dead. Billy lost no time in removing his keeper's cartridge belt as well as a rifle and a "44 W.C.F." which were in the room.

When the deputy heard the shots he thought that the jailer must have shot Billy who was trying to escape and ran from the hotel to the jail, on the steps of which he met Billy who said "hello" as he brushed past him, firing at him as he dashed by. Billy's next move was to rush to the hotel and to have Ben Eale remove his shackles. He also provided for him a horse and saddled it for Billy upon the promise that he was to leave it at San Patricio. True to his word Billy secured another horse at San Patricio from his friend Juan Trujillo, promising in turn to return the same as soon as he could locate his own.

Billy now left San Patricio and headed for John Chisum's cattle ranch. Among the cowboys there was a friend of Billy Mote who had sworn to kill the Kid whenever he found him in order to avenge his friend. But Billy did not give him time to carry out his plan, killing him on the spot.

From there Billy left for Berendo where he remained a few days. Here he found his own horse and immediate sent back Juan Trujillo's. From Berendo, Billy left for Puerto de Luna where he visited Juan Patron, his former capitan. Patron did everything to make his and his companion's stay there a pleasant as possible. On the third evening of their stay there was to have been a dance and Billy sent his companion to make a report of what he saw and heard.

While on his way there, and while he was passing in front of some abandoned shacks, Tome was fired upon by one of Pat Garrett's men and killed. No sooner had Billy heard the distressing news than he set out for the house of his friend Pedro Macky at Bosque Grande where he remained in hiding until a Texan named Charley Wilson, and who was supposed to be after Billy, arrived.

The two exchanged greetings in a friendly fashion and then the stranger asked Billy to accompany him to the saloon, which invitation Billy accepted. There were six or seven persons in the saloon when the two entered. Drinks were imbibed in a general spirit of conviviality prevailed when someone suggested that the first one to commit a murder that day was to set the others up. "In that case the drinks are on me," said Charley who commanded all to drink to their heart's content.

Billy then ordered another round of drinks, and by this time Charley who was feeling quite reckless began to shoot at the glasses, not missing a single one until he came to Billy's. This he pretended to miss, aiming his shot at Bill instead. This gave Billy time to draw out his own revolver and before Charley could take aim again, Billy had shot the other in the breast twice. When he was breathing his last Billy said, "Do not whisper; you were too eager to buy those drinks." It was Billy's turn now to treat the company.

Quiet again reigned for a few days. In the meantime Pat Garrett was negotiating with Pedro Macky for the deliverance of Billy. When all details were arranged for, Pat left for Bosque Grande secretly. At the ranch house, Pedro hid Pat in a room close beside the one Billy was occupying.

Becoming hungry during the night, Billy got up and started to prepare a lunch. First he built a fire, then he took his hunting knife and was starting to cut off a hunk of meat from a large piece that hung from one of the rafters when he heard voices in the adjoining room. Stepping to the door he partially opened it and thrusting his head in asked Pedro who was with him.

Pedro replied that it was only his wife and asked him to come in. Seeing no harm in this, Billy decided to accept the invitation—only to be shot in the pit of the stomach as he stood in the door. Staggering back to his own room, it was not definitely known that the shot had been fatal until a cleaning woman stumbled over the dead body upon entering the room, the following morning.

GLOSSARY

44 W.C.F.: a .44 caliber Winchester Center Rifle

acequia: a Spanish word meaning a ditch

compadre: a Spanish word meaning a friend or companion

deputize: to appoint a deputy, a sheriff's second-in-command

fandango: a Spanish style dance, performed in triple time with a male and female dancer playing castanets

hemorrhage: a large loss of blood

Macky Swin: a transcriptional error of McSween, a key player in the Lincoln County War

Marfe: a transcriptional error of Murphy, a key player in the Lincoln County War

shackles: rings or other fastenings, usually of iron, to prevent movement of the wrists and ankles

Document Analysis

This memoir helps to shed light on the history and legend of Billy the Kid, including his death at the hands of Sheriff Pat Garrett. Yet, Trujillo's narrative gives us more than a retelling of parts of one man's life. Also apparent in his account are the social dynamics, including underlying tensions, at work among the different ethnic groups—Mexicans, Mexican-Americans, white Euroamericans (Anglo-Americans), and Indians (Juan Armijo).

Even fifty years after the time when these events took place, Trujillo recalls the various ethnic groups and how they related to one another and played into the story. He describes how a posse was put together with eight Mexicans and an unknown number of Americans. The posse was then broken up into a guard for McSween. Trujillo states, "Of the original eight Mexicans in the party, four were left to join the Americans, not having admitted the other four to do so." While this could be attributed simply to not needing additional men, the way in which Trujillo says that the remaining Mexicans were not "admitted … to do so" seems to suggest some cultural boundaries or limitations at play in interactions between the Americans and Mexicans.

One of the Regulators, Chaves, was Mexican, and he too was occasionally discriminated against by his own gang on the basis of his ethnicity. Although the tensions within the Regulators do not seem to be as prominent, the American perception of Mexicans would have sometimes bled over into their relationship with Chaves. The leader of the Regulators states that "all Mexicans [are] sentimental about their own." This was the reason that Chaves was left out of a rendezvous with McSween. But unlike the rest of the characters in the story, one man is left completely without any identifiers, not even a name. Trujillo makes a point to tell most everyone's name, even if they play only a minor role in the story. In one case, however, Trujillo makes mention of the "negro" who cooked their meals; the man has no name or homeland. In a rather different way, Trujillo highlights the presence of a lone Indian, almost always identifying him as "the Indian, Juan Armijo" (instead of simply Juan Armijo). Elsewhere, Trujillo distinguishes between Mexicans, Americans, and even a Texan. In any case, his account brings out the nature of social relations then obtaining in the relatively lawless Southwest.

The last few pages of the document explain the circumstances that led to the end of Billy the Kid, when he was shot and killed by Sheriff Pat Garrett (as assisted by a friend of the Kid's). At this point in his life, Billy had already killed several men, although the exact number remains disputed. He had also escaped jail after being sentenced to death for these killings and his role in the Lincoln County War. After the confrontation between them, Sheriff Pat Garrett was pardoned for the death of Billy the Kid; the act was considered to be carried out in the line of duty and legally justified. Garrett later wrote a memoir of his own, partly to burnish his reputation.

Essential Themes

Narratives such as this one capture a period in history during which people spread across North America at such a rapid pace and to such a great extent that the laws, customs, and traditions of past generations had begun to break down, creating a world in which outlaws and heroes, gunslingers and defenders of honor could thrive. Much of the information regarding the life and death of Billy the Kid comes from newspaper articles, selected eye-witness accounts, and second- and third-hand accounts by those who never interacted with him. From these and similar sources, there soon arose legends about the man and his actions, fueled by a pulp fiction industry consisting of dime novels, popular serials, and, much later, movies. Even the legend itself was subject to transformation over time. Over the years, Billy the Kid has variously been portrayed as a gunslinging psychopath, a romantic Robin Hood figure, a tragic, corrupted youth, and a mercurial hero of the Old West. Perhaps for this reason, the great western novelist Larry McMurtry begins his book *Anything for Billy* with the lines, "The first time I met Billy he came walking out of a cloud. He had a pistol in each hand and a scared look on his rough young face. The cloud drifted in from the plains earlier in the morning and stopped over the Hidden Mountains…"

From questions about his name and place of birth, his travels and activities, the number of people he killed, and whether he shot with his left hand or his right, Billy the Kid is interesting historically because he, along with a few others of his ilk, seems to stand at the intersection of the hero and the villain. Such characters as Billy highlight the fact that rarely are there simply "good" or "bad" people in life—despite the popularity of recounting stories in precisely these stark terms. In Billy the Kid's case, the fact that he lived his life during a time of great change and instability, amid the rise of a prominent gun culture, helps us to understand how the contents of his life could end up being distorted. Also playing into the "mythologizing" of the Kid is the fact that he seemed to move between Mexican (Mexican-American) and American cultures, remembered by many Hispanic residents of the Southwest as a noble young man, who was kind to their people (some of whom he lived with at various times); yet to most Americans, he was a crude gangster. His legendary status is augmented by the fact that he escaped custody so often, serving, in that respect, as a sort of classic "trickster" figure. Such anomalies and contradictions are the stuff of which myths and legends are made.

—*Michael Shally-Jensen, PhD; Anna Accettola, MA*

Bibliography and Additional Reading

"Billy the Kid." American Experience. Dir. Joe Maggio. PBS, 2011. Web. 21 Oct. 2014.

Gardner, Mark Lee. *To Hell on a Fast Horse: Billy the Kid, Pat Garrett, and the Epic Chase to Justice in the Old West.* New York: HarperCollins, 2010. Print.

Lacy, Ann, & Anne Valley-Fox, eds. *Stories from Hispano New Mexico: A New Mexico Federal Writers' Project Book.* Santa Fe: Sunstone P, 2012.

McMurtry, Larry. *Anything for Billy: A Novel.* New York: Simon & Schuster, 2001. Print.

Meyer, Richard E. "The Outlaw: A Distinctive American Folktype." Journal of the Folklore Institute 17.2/3 (1980): 94–124. Web. 30 Sept. 2014.

Wallis, Michael. *Billy the Kid: The Endless Ride.* New York: W.W. Norton, 2007. Print.

■ Shootout at the O.K. Corral

Date: November 16, 1881
Author: Wyatt S. Earp
Genre: testimony

Summary Overview

At 3:00 p.m. on Wednesday, October 26, 1881, in the sleepy frontier town of Tombstone in Arizona Territory, a gunfight broke out between the Earp brothers and a group of ranchers tied to an outlaw gang called the Cowboys. The entire event lasted only about thirty seconds, but almost immediately after, it became the stuff of legend and grew to define the lives of the participants, especially that of Wyatt Earp, for the remainder of their days. For Americans more generally, the shootout eventually came to define law and justice on the frontier, with the deputy marshal at the center of events playing both hero and villain. In popular imagination, Wyatt Earp became somewhat of an avenging angel, the lone gunslinger, taking the law into his own hands, having gone up against an armed band of desperados. This archetype would come to define heroism in not just the American West, but throughout the world.

Defining Moment

Tombstone, in southeastern Arizona Territory was not that different from the hundreds of frontier boomtowns that began to appear in the region in the late 1800s. Initially established thanks to the railroads and expanding in response to the prospect of mining riches, such dusty backwaters were known to appear suddenly and vanish just as quickly once all available resources were picked clean. If someone were smart enough and quick enough, they could make a small fortune in the interim. It was for this reason that Wyatt Earp and his brothers, Virgil and Morgan, arrived in Tombstone in the winter of 1879, just a few months after the town's founding.

The Earps, long-time ramblers seeking their fortune, hoping to join western high society, quickly, albeit reluctantly, took on jobs in law enforcement. Having worked as lawmen in frontier towns before, including the raucous Dodge City, the Earps understood that they were expected to walk a fine line. They were charged with keeping the peace, but also, more importantly, in pro-

tecting the interests of the wealthy ranchers and miners who were the real power in the region. As long as business wasn't disrupted, trivial things like the law did not really matter. It was in this environment that the Earps came into direct conflict with "the Cowboys"—a loose confederacy of outlaws and cattle smugglers, who made their living by robbing the territory's ranchers and miners.

In the Spring of 1881, after a band of Cowboys attacked a stage coach, murdering the driver, Wyatt Earp, hoping to use the publicity of a successful capture to boost his chances of getting elected sheriff, made a secret deal with Ike Clanton, a corrupt local rancher with ties to the Cowboys, in which Clanton would turn over the fugitives in exchange for cash. The deal came to nothing, but Clanton began to grow increasingly nervous that Earp would reveal their secret deal to the Cowboys.

On the night of October 25, 1881, a drunk, nerved-up Ike Clanton started publically threatening the lives of the Earp brothers, telling anyone who would listen that he planned to gun all three down the next morning. Acting on rumors of an imminent ambush, and bowing to pressure from wealthy interests eager to see the Cowboys disbanded, Wyatt, Virgil, Morgan, and Wyatt's good friend, Doc Holiday, a mysterious, hot-tempered gunslinger from the deep South, went to confront Ike Clanton and his brother Billy, who had gathered along with fellow ranchers, Tom and Frank McLaury, at a small enclosure known as the O.K. Corral. Immediately upon approaching the ranchers, after Wyatt told Ike Clanton he was under arrest, gunfire erupted from both sides. The shootout lasted thirty seconds. Virgil, Morgan, and Doc had all been wounded, Frank and Tom McLaury, along with Billy Clanton were killed, Ike Clanton ran, only to be arrested later. Wyatt Earp came through unscathed.

The gunfight at the O.K. Corral became an immediate sensation, and the Earps were largely celebrated for their actions. However, the event soon set off a long chain of violence and reprisals, from both Ike Clanton and his Cowboy allies, and, after the murder of Morgan and the attempted assassination of Virgil, from Wyatt Earp as well. In the end, Wyatt, backed and encouraged by the territorial business interests, would track down and kill many of the men whom he thought responsible for the attack on his family. Only Ike Clanton escaped Wyatt's retribution, only to be killed in an unrelated incident six years later.

Author Biography

Wyatt Earp was born in 1848, the third of five boys, sons to a father who moved the family farther and farther west, partly in search of opportunity, and partly to escape paying off the family's extensive debts. Growing up on the frontier, never staying in one place long enough to plant any roots, the Earp brothers learned to rely on each other, with Wyatt standing in as their silent, steady center. Wyatt set out to make his own destiny at the age of seventeen. He worked as a laborer on the railroads and briefly as a brothel operator, but eventually found his way into law work. In 1879, Wyatt and his brothers moved to Tombstone, with dreams of easy riches, but his famous clashes with the Cowboys soon derailed those plans. Somewhat of a pariah after his well-publicized vendetta and hounded by both the public and media over his infamous gun battle, Wyatt eventually settled in San Francisco. There, with his partner Josephine, he attempted various business ventures, including mining, real estate speculation, fight promotion, and prospecting. Wyatt eventually died in 1929 at the ripe old age of eighty, never quite having found his fortune and haunted always by the shootout at the O.K. Corral.

HISTORICAL DOCUMENT

Statement of Wyatt S. Earp
in the Preliminary Hearing in the Earp-Holliday Case,
Heard before Judge Wells Spicer

November 16, 1881
[On this sixteenth day of November, 1881, upon the hearing of the above entitled action, on the examination of Wyatt Earp and J. H. Holliday, the prosecution having closed their evidence in chief, and the defendants, Wyatt Earp and J. H. Holliday, having first been informed of his rights to make a statement as provided in Section 133, page 22 of the laws of Arizona, approved February 12, 1881, and the said Wyatt Earp having chosen to make a statement under oath and having been personally sworn, makes such statement under oath in answer to interrogatories as follows:]

(Q) Give any explanations you may think proper of the circumstances appearing in the testimony against you, and state any facts which you think will tend to your exculpation.
(A) The difficulty which resulted in the death of William Clanton and Frank McLaury originated last spring, and at a little over a year ago, I followed Tom and Frank McLaury and two other parties who had stolen six government mules from Camp Rucker. Myself, Virgil Earp, and Morgan Earp, and Marshall Williams, Captain Hurst and four soldiers; we traced those mules to McLaury's ranch.

While at Charleston I met a man by the name of Dave Estes. He told me I would find the mules at McLaury's ranch. He said he had seen them there the day before. He said they were branding the mules "D S," making the "D. S." out [of] "D. S." We tracked the mules right up to the ranch. Also found the branding iron "D. S." Afterwards, some of those mules were found with the same brand.

After we arrived at McLaury's ranch, there was a man by the name of Frank Patterson. He made some kind of a compromise with Captain Hurst. Captain Hurst come to us boys and told us he had made this compromise, and by so doing, he would get his mules back. We insisted on following them up. Hurst prevailed on us to go back to Tombstone, and so we came back. Hurst told us two or three weeks afterwards, that they would not give up the mules to him after we left, saying that they only wanted to get us away, that they could stand the soldiers off. Captain Hurst cautioned me and my brothers, Virgil and Morgan, to look out for those men, as they had made some threats against our lives.

About one month after we had followed up those mules. I met Frank and Tom McLaury in Charleston. They tried to pick a fuss out of me down there, and told me if I ever followed them up again as close as I did before, they would kill me. Shortly after the time Bud Philpot was killed by the men who tried to rob the Benson stage, as a detective [working for Wells, Fargo & Co.] I helped trace the matter up, and I was satisfied that three men, named Billy Leonard, Harry Head, and James Crane were in that robbery. I knew that Leonard, Head and Crane were friends and associates of the Clantons and McLaurys and often stopped at their ranches.

It was generally understood among officers and those who have information about criminals, that Ike Clanton was sort of chief among the cowboys that the Clantons and McLaurys were cattle thieves and generally in the secret of the stage robbery, and that the Clanton and McLaury ranches were meeting places and places of shelter for the gang.

I had an ambition to be Sheriff of this County at the next election, and I thought it would be a great help to me with the people and businessmen if I could capture the men who killed Philpot. There were rewards offered of about $1,200 each for the capture of the robbers. Altogether there was about $3,600 offered for their capture. I thought this sum might tempt Ike Clanton and Frank McLaury to give away Leonard, Head, and Crane, so I went to Ike Clanton, Frank McLaury, and Joe Hill when they came to town. I had an interview with them in the back yard of the Oriental Saloon. I told them what I wanted. I told them I wanted the glory of capturing Leonard, Head, and Crane and if I could do it, it would help me make the race for Sheriff at the next election. I told them if they would put me on the track of Leonard, Head, and Crane, and tell me where those men were hid; I would give them all the reward and would never let anyone know where I got the information.

Ike Clanton said he would like to see them captured. He said that Leonard claimed a ranch that he claimed, and that if he could get him out of the way, he would have no opposition in regard to the ranch. Clanton said that Leonard, Head, and Crane would make a fight, that they would never be taken alive, and that I must find out

if the reward would be paid for the capture of the robbers dead or alive. I then went to Marshall Williams, the agent of Wells, Fargo & Co., in this town and at my request, he telegraphed to the agent, or superintendent, in San Francisco to find out if the reward would be paid for the robbers dead or alive. He received, in June, 1881, a telegram, which he showed me, promising the reward would be paid dead or alive.

The next day I met Ike Clanton and Joe Hill on Allen Street in front of a little cigar store next to the Alhambra. I told them that the dispatch had come. I went to Marshall Williams and told him I wanted to see the dispatch for a few minutes. He went to look for it and could not find it, but went over to the telegraph office and got a copy of it, and he came back and gave it to me. I went and showed it to Ike Clanton and Joe Hill and returned it to Marshall Williams, and afterwards told Frank McLaury of its contents.

It was then agreed between us that they were to have all the $3,600 reward, outside of necessary expenses for horse hire in going after them, and that Joe Hill should go to where Leonard, Head, and Crane were hid, over near Yreka, in New Mexico, and lure them in near Frank and Tom McLaury's ranch near Soldier's Holes, 30 miles from here, and I would be on hand with a posse and capture them.

I asked Joe Hill, Ike Clanton, and Frank McLaury what tale they would make them to get them over here. They said they had agreed upon a plan to tell them there would be a paymaster going from Tombstone to Bisbee, to payoff the miners, and they wanted them to come in and take him in. Ike Clanton then sent Joe Hill to bring them 'in. Before starting, Joe Hill took off his watch and chain and between two and three hundred dollars in money, and gave it to Virgil Earp to keep for him until he got back. He was gone about ten days and returned with the word that he got there a day too late; that Leonard and Harry Head had been killed the day before he got there by horse thieves. I learned afterward that the thieves had been killed subsequently by members of the Clanton and McLaury gang.

After that, Ike Clanton and Frank McLaury claimed that I had given them away to Marshall Williams and Doc Holliday, and when they came in town, they shunned us, and Morgan, Virgil Earp, Doc Holliday and myself began to hear their threats against us.

I am a friend of Doc Holliday because when I was city marshal of Dodge City, Kansas, he came to my rescue and saved my life when I was surrounded by desperadoes.

About a month or more ago [October 1881], Morgan Earp and myself assisted to arrest Stilwell and Spence on the charge of robbing the Bisbee stage. The McLaurys and Clantons were always friendly with Spence and Stilwell, and they laid the whole blame of their arrest on us, though the fact is, we only went as a sheriff's posse. After we got in town with Spence and Stilwell, Ike Clanton and Frank McLaury came in.

Frank McLaury took Morgan Earp into the street in front of the Alhambra, where John Ringo, Ike Clanton, and the two Hicks boys were also standing. Frank McLaury commenced to abuse Morgan Earp for going after Spence and Stilwell. Frank McLaury said he would never speak to Spence again for being arrested by us.

He said to Morgan, "If you ever come after me, you will never take me." Morgan replied that if he ever had occasion to go after him, he would arrest him. Frank McLaury then said to Morgan Earp, "I have threatened you boys' lives, and a few days later I had taken it back, but since this arrest, it now goes." Morgan made no reply and walked off.

Before this and after this, Marshall Williams, Farmer Daly, Ed Barnes, Old Man Urrides, Charley Smith and three or four others had told us at different times of threats to kill us, by Ike Clanton, Frank McLaury, Tom McLaury, Joe Hill, and John Ringo. I knew all these men were desperate and dangerous men, that they were connected with outlaws, cattle thieves, robbers and murderers. I knew of the McLaurys stealing six government mules, and also cattle, and when the owners went after them finding his stock on the McLaury's ranch; that he was drove off and told that if he ever said anything about it, he would be killed, and he kept his mouth shut until several days ago, for fear of being killed.

I heard of John Ringo shooting a man down in cold blood near Camp Thomas. I was satisfied that Frank and Tom McLaury killed and robbed Mexicans in Skeleton Canyon, about three or four months ago, and I naturally kept my eyes open and did not intend that any of the gang should get the drop on me if I could help it.

Ike Clanton met me at the Alhambra five or six weeks ago and told me I had told Holliday about this transaction, concerning the capture of Head, Leonard, and Crane. I told him I had never told Holliday anything. I told him when Holliday came up from Tucson I would prove it. Ike said that Holliday had told him so. When Holliday came back I asked him if he said so.

On the night of the 25th of October, Holliday met Ike Clanton in the Alhambra Saloon and asked him about it. Clanton denied it. They quarreled for three or four minutes. Holliday told Clanton he was a damned liar, if he said so. I was sitting eating lunch at the lunch counter. Morgan Earp was standing at the Alhambra bar talking with the bartender. I called him over to where I was sitting, knowing that he was an officer and told him that Holliday and Clanton were quarreling in the lunch room and for him to go in and stop it. He climbed over the lunch room counter from the Alhambra bar and went into the room, took Holliday by the arm and led him into the street. Ike Clanton in a few seconds followed them out. I got through eating and walked out of the bar. As I stopped at the door of the bar, they were still quarreling.

Just then Virgil Earp came up, I think out of the Occidental, and told them, Holliday and Clanton, if they didn't stop their quarreling he would have to arrest them. They all separated at that time, Morgan Earp going down the street to the Oriental Saloon, Ike going across the street to the Grand Hotel. I walked in the Eagle Brewery where I had a faro game which I had not closed. I stayed in there for a few minutes and walked out to the street and there met Ike Clanton. He asked me if I would take a walk with him, that he wanted to talk to me. I told him I would if he did not go too far, as I was waiting for my game in the Brewery to close, and I would have to take care of the money. We walked about halfway down the brewery building, going down Fifth Street and stopped.

He told me when Holliday approached him in the Alhambra that he wasn't fixed just right. He said that in the morning he would have man-for-man, that this fighting talk had been going on for a long time, and he guessed it was about time to fetch it to a close. I told him I would not fight no one if I could get away from it, because there was no money in it. He walked off and left me saying, "I will be ready for you in the morning."

I walked over to the Oriental. He followed me in

and took a drink, having his six-shooter in plain sight. He says, "You must not think I won't be after you all in the morning." He said he would like to make a fight with Holliday now. I told him Holliday did not want to fight, but only to satisfy him that this talk had not been made. About that time the man that is dealing my game closed it and brought the money to me. I locked it in the safe and started home. I met Holliday on the street between the Oriental and Alhambra. Myself and Holliday walked down Allen Street, he going to his room, and I to my house, going to bed.

I got up the next day, October 26, about noon. Before I got up, Ned Boyle came to me and told me that he met Ike Clanton on Allen Street near the telegraph office, that Ike was armed, that he said, "as soon as those damned Earps make their appearance on the street today the ball will open, we are here to make a fight. We are looking for the sons-of-bitches!" I laid in bed some little time after that, and got up and went down to the Oriental Saloon.

Harry Jones came to me after I got up and said, "What does all this mean?" I asked him what he meant. He says, "Ike Clanton is hunting you boys with a Winchester rifle and six-shooter." I said, "I will go down and find him and see what he wants." I went out and on the corner of Fifth and Allen I met Virgil Earp, the marshal. He told me how he heard Ike Clanton was hunting us. I went down Allen Street and Virgil went down Fifth Street and then Fremont Street. Virgil found Ike Clanton on Fourth Street near Fremont Street, in the mouth of an alleyway.

I walked up to him and said, "I hear you are hunting for some of us." I was coming down Fourth Street at the time. Ike Clanton then threw his Winchester rifle around toward Virgil. Virgil grabbed it and hit Ike Clanton with his six-shooter and knocked him down. Clanton had his rifle and his six-shooter was in his pants. By that time I came up. Virgil and Morgan Earp took his rifle and six-shooter and took them to the Grand Hotel after examination, and I took Ike Clanton before Justice Wallace.

Before the investigation, Morgan Earp had Ike Clanton in charge, as Virgil Earp was out at the time. After I went into Wallace's Court and sat down on a bench, Ike Clanton looked over to me and said, "I will get even with all of you for this. If I had a six-shooter now I would make a fight with all of you." Morgan Earp then said to him, "If you want to make a fight right bad, I will give you

this one!" at the same time offering Ike Clanton his own six-shooter.

Ike Clanton started to get up and take it, when Campbell, the deputy sheriff, pushed him back in his seat, saying he would not allow any fuss. I never had Ike Clanton's arms at any time, as he stated.

I would like to describe the positions we occupied in the courtroom. Ike Clanton sat on a bench with his face fronting to the north wall of the building. I myself sat down on a bench that ran against and along the north wall in front of where Ike sat. Morgan Earp stood up on his feet with his back against the wall and to the right of where I sat, and two or three feet from me.

Morgan Earp had Ike Clanton's Winchester in his hand, like this, with one end on the floor, with Clanton's six-shooter in his right hand. We had them all the time. Virgil Earp was not in the courtroom during any of this time and came there after I had walked out. He was out, he told me, hunting for Judge Wallace.

I was tired of being threatened by Ike Clanton and his gang and believe from what he said to me and others, and from their movements that they intended to assassinate me the first chance they had, and I thought that if I had to fight for my life with them I had better make them face me in an open fight. So I said to Ike Clanton, who was then sitting about eight feet away from me. "You damned dirty cow thief, you have been threatening our lives and I know it. I think I would be justified in shooting you down any place I should meet you, but if you are anxious to make a fight, I will go anywhere on earth to make a fight with you, even over to the San Simon among your crowd!" He replied, "I will see you after I get through here. I only want four feet of ground to fight on!"

I walked out and then just outside of the courtroom near the Justice's Office, I met Tom McLaury. He came up to me and said to me, "If you want to make a fight I will make a fight with you anywhere." I supposed at the time that he had heard what had just transpired between Ike Clanton and myself. I knew of his having threatened me, and I felt just as I did about Ike Clanton and if the fight had to come, I had better have it come when I had an even show to defend myself. So I said to him, "All right, make a fight right here!" And at the same time slapped him in the face with my left hand and drew my pistol with my right. He had a pistol in plain sight on his right hip in his pants, but made no move to draw it. I said to him, "Jerk your gun and use it!" He made no reply and I hit him on the head with my six-shooter and walked away, down to Hafford's Corner. I went into Hafford's and got a cigar and came out and stood by the door.

Pretty soon after I saw Tom McLaury, Frank McLaury, and William Clanton pass me and went down Fourth Street to the gunsmith shop. I followed them to see what they were going to do. When I got there, Frank McLaury's horse was standing on the sidewalk with his head in the door of the gun shop. I took the horse by the bit, as I was deputy city marshal, and commenced to back him off the sidewalk. Tom and Frank and Billy Clanton came to the door. Billy Clanton laid his hand on his six-shooter. Frank McLaury took hold of the horse's bridle and I said, "You will have to get this horse off the sidewalk." He backed him off into the street. Ike Clanton came up about this time and they all walked into the gun shop. I saw them in the gun shop changing cartridges into their belts. They came out of the shop and walked along Fourth Street to the corner of Allen Street. I followed them as far as the corner of Fourth and Allen Streets. They went down Allen Street and over to Dunbar's Corral. [Dunbar and Behan.]

Virgil Earp was then city marshal; Morgan Earp was a special policeman for six weeks or two months, wore a badge and drew pay. I had been sworn in Virgil's place, to act for him while Virgil was gone to Tucson on Spence's and Stilwell's trial. Virgil had been back several days but I was still acting and I knew it was Virgil's duty to disarm those men. I expected he would have trouble in doing so, and I followed up to give assistance if necessary, especially as they had been threatening us, as I have already stated.

About ten minutes afterwards, and while Virgil, Morgan, Doc Holliday and myself were standing on the corner of Fourth and Allen Streets, several people said, "There is going to be trouble with those fellows," and one man named Coleman said to Virgil Earp, "They mean trouble. They have just gone from Dunbar's Corral into the O.K. Corral, all armed, and I think you had better go and disarm them." Virgil turned around to Doc Holliday, Morgan Earp and myself and told us to come and assist him in disarming them.

Morgan Earp said to me, "They have horses, had we not better get some horses ourselves, so that if they make a running fight we can catch them?" I said, "No, if they try to make a running fight we can kill their horses and then capture them."

We four started through Fourth to Fremont Street. When we turned the corner of Fourth and Fremont we could see them standing near or about the vacant space between Fly's photograph gallery and the next building west. I first saw Frank McLaury, Tom McLaury, Billy Clanton and Sheriff Behan standing there. We went down the left-hand side of Fremont Street.

When we got within about 150 feet of them I saw Ike Clanton and Billy Clanton and another party. We had walked a few steps further and I saw Behan leave the party and come toward us. Every few steps he would look back as if he apprehended danger. I heard him say to Virgil Earp, "For God's sake, don't go down there, you will get murdered!" Virgil Earp replied, "I am going to disarm them." he, Virgil, being in the lead. When I and Morgan came up to Behan he said, "I have disarmed them." When he said this, I took my pistol, which I had in my hand, under my coat, and put it in my overcoat pocket. Behan then passed up the street, and we walked on down.

We came up on them close; Frank McLaury, Tom McLaury, and Billy Clanton standing in a row against the east side of the building on the opposite side of the vacant space west of Fly's photograph gallery. Ike Clanton and Billy Claiborne and a man I don't knows were standing in the vacant space about halfway between the photograph gallery and the next building west.

I saw that Billy Clanton and Frank and Tom McLaury had their hands by their sides, Frank McLaury and Billy Clanton's six-shooters were in plain sight. Virgil said, "Throw up your hands; I have come to disarm you!" Billy Clanton and Frank McLaury laid their hands on their six-shooters. Virgil said, "Hold, I don't mean that!" I have come to disarm you!" Then Billy Clanton and Frank McLaury commenced to draw their pistols. At the same time, Tom McLaury threw his hand to his right hip, throwing his coat open like this, [showing how] and jumped behind his horse. [Actually it was Billy Clanton's horse.]

I had my pistol in my overcoat pocket, where I had put it when Behan told us he had disarmed the other parties. When I saw Billy Clanton and Frank McLaury draw their pistols, I drew my pistol. Billy Clanton leveled his pistol at me, but I did not aim at him. I knew that Frank McLaury had the reputation of being a good shot and a dangerous man, and I aimed at Frank McLaury. The first two shots were fired by Billy Clanton and myself, he shooting at me, and I shooting at Frank McLaury. I don't know which was fired first. We fired almost together. The fight then became general. After about four shots were fired, Ike Clanton ran up and grabbed my left arm. I could see no weapon in his hand, and thought at the time he had none, and so I said to him, "The fight had commenced. Go to fighting or get away," at the same time pushing him off with my left hand, like this. He started and ran down the side of the building and disappeared between the lodging house and photograph gallery.

My first shot struck Frank McLaury in the belly. He staggered off on the sidewalk but fired one shot at me. When we told them to throw up their hands Claiborne threw up his left hand and broke and ran. I never saw him afterwards until late in the afternoon, after the fight. I never drew my pistol or made a motion to shoot until after Billy Clanton and Frank McLaury drew their pistols. If Tom McLaury was unarmed, I did not know it, I believe he was armed and fired two shots at our party before Holliday, who had the shotgun, fired and killed him. If he was unarmed, there was nothing in the circumstances or in what had been communicated to me, or in his acts or threats, that would have led me even to suspect his being unarmed.

I never fired at Ike Clanton, even after the shooting commenced, because I thought he was unarmed. I believed then, and believe now, from the acts I have stated and the threats I have related and the other threats communicated to me by other persons as having been made by Tom McLaury, Frank McLaury, and Ike Clanton, that these men last named had formed a conspiracy to murder my brothers, Morgan and Virgil, Doc Holliday and myself. I believe I would have been legally and morally justified in shooting any of them on sight, but I did not do so, nor attempt to do so. I sought no advantage when I went as deputy marshal [city marshal] to help disarm them and arrest them. I went as a part of my duty and under the direction of my brother, the marshal; I did not intend to fight unless it became necessary in self-defense and in the performance of official duty. When

Billy Clanton and Frank McLaury drew their pistols, I knew it was a fight for life, and I drew in defense of my own life and the lives of my brothers and Doc Holliday.

I have been in Tombstone since December 1, 1879. I came here directly from Dodge City, Kansas. Against the protest of businessmen and officials, I resigned the office of city marshal, which I held from 1876. I came to Dodge City from Wichita, Kansas. I was on the police force in Wichita from 1874 until I went to Dodge City.

The testimony of Isaac Clanton that I ever said to him that I had anything to do with any stage robbery or giving information to Morgan Earp going on the stage, or any improper communication whatever with any criminal enterprise is a tissue of lies from beginning to end.

Sheriff Behan made me an offer in his office on Allen Street in the back room of a cigar store, where he, Behan, had his office, that if I would withdraw and not try to get appointed sheriff of Cochise County, that he would hire a clerk and divide the profits. I done so, and he never said an¬other word about it afterwards, but claimed in his statement and gave his reason for not complying with his contract, which is false in every particular.

Myself and Doc Holliday happened to go to Charleston the night that Behan went down there to subpoena Ike Clanton. We went there for the purpose to get a horse that I had had stolen from me a few days after I came to Tombstone. I had heard several times that the Clantons had him. When I got there that night, I was told by a friend of mine that the man that carried the dispatch from Charleston to Ike Clanton's ranch had rode my horse. At this time I did not know where Ike Clanton's ranch was.

A short time afterwards I was in the Huachucas locating some water rights. I had started home to Tombstone. I had got within 12 or 15 miles of Charleston when I met a man named McMasters. He told me if I would hurry up, I would find my horse in Charleston. I drove into Charleston and saw my horse going through the streets toward the corral. I put up for the night in another corral. I went to Burnett's office to get papers for the recovery of the horse. He was not at home having gone down to Sonora to some coal fields that had been discovered. I telegraphed to Tombstone to James Earp and told him to have papers made out and sent to me. He went to Judge Wallace and Mr. Street. They made the papers out and sent them to Charleston by my youngest brother, Warren Earp, that night. While I was waiting for the papers, Billy Clanton found out that I was in town and went and tried to take the horse out of the corral. I told him that he could not take him out, that it was my horse. After the papers came, he gave the horse up without the papers being served, and asked me if I had any more horses to lose. I told him I would keep them in the stable after this, and give him no chance to steal them.

I give here, as part of the statement, a document sent me from Dodge City since my arrest on this charge, which I wish attached to this statement and marked "Exhibit A."

In relation to the conversation that I had with Ike Clanton, Frank McLaury, and Joe Hill was four or five different times, and they were all held in the backyard of the Oriental Saloon.

I told Ike Clanton in one of those conversations that there were some parties here in town that were trying to give Doc Holliday the worst of it by their talk, that there was some suspicion that he knew something about the attempted robbery and killing of Bud Philpot, and if I could catch Leonard, Head, and Crane, I could prove to the citizens that he knew nothing of it.

In following the trail of Leonard, Head, and Crane, we struck it at the scene of the attempted robbery, and never lost the trail or hardly a footprint from the time we started from Drew's ranch on the San Pedro, until we got to Helm's ranch in the Dragoons. After following about 80 miles down the San Pedro River and capturing one of the men named King that was supposed to be with them, we then crossed the Catalina Mountains within 15 miles of Tucson following their trail around the foot of the mountain to Tres Alamos on the San Pedro River, thence to the Dragoons to Helm's ranch.

We then started out from Helm's ranch and got on their trail. They had stolen 15 or 20 head of stock, so as to cover their trail. Virgil Earp and Morgan Earp, Robert H. Paul, Breakenridge the deputy sheriff, Johnny Behan the sheriff and one or two others still followed their trail to New Mexico.

Their trail never led south from Helm's ranch as Ike Clanton has stated. We used every effort we could to capture those men or robbers. I was out ten days. Virgil and Morgan Earp were out sixteen days, and [we] all done all we could to catch those men, and I safely say if it had not been for myself and Morgan Earp they would not have got King as he started to run when we rose up to his hiding place and was making for a big patch of brush on the river and would have got in it, if [it] had not been for us two.

[Signed] *Wyatt S. Earp*

GLOSSARY

corral: a pen for livestock

faro: a gambling card game

stage: slang for stagecoach

Document Analysis

The document represents the firsthand testimony of Wyatt Earp about the events leading up to, and including the shootout at the O.K. Corral. Earp goes into great detail, trying to explain the complicated web of tensions that connected the Earps to the Clantons, McLaurys, and the Cowboys. Establishing the corrupt, illegal practices of Ike Clanton and Frank McLaury long before the shootout, then addressing the deal brokered for the capture of the fugitive Cowboys, Wyatt Earp carefully lays out every piece of the sordid drama. By the time he finally comes to the events of October 26, 1881, the entire affair appears to be spiraling toward an unavoidable confrontation. Despite this buildup, even at the last moment, Wyatt Earp appeared to hope for a resolution. His intention, he says, was to arrest the men, not shoot them.

It is important to remember that this is Wyatt Earp's court testimony. We have only his version of events. As a lawman, Earp understood that, in order to avoid legal troubles of his own, he had to lay a foundation of criminality at the feet of Ike Clanton and establish that he had no other option but the use of force. At the same time, there's little reason to doubt Earp's testimony. Ike Clanton and the Cowboys were not innocent bystanders. The threats against the Earp brothers, Ike Clanton's erratic, aggressive behavior was not in question, and tensions, in fact, had been boiling for months. The tone of Wyatt Earp's testimony is steady, there's little in way of exaggeration or sensationalism. His version of events, though clearly one-sided, has the air of authenticity. The fact that he could have shot Ike Clanton but spared him, speaks volumes to his credibility.

After the events in Tombstone, Wyatt Earp was never the same again. Not for the loss of his brother Morgan, although that too had a profound effect, but more so for the shootout at the Corral. Up until the end of his life, he never made peace with that had happened. He carried that burden always. In reading his testimony, it is difficult not to get a sense of the weight on Wyatt Earp's shoulders. He did what he had to; there was no other choice.

Essential Themes

After the dust settled in Tombstone, the shootout at the O.K. Corral became an instant legend. Immediately, it became the basis for dime novels and stage plays from coast to coast. Wyatt Earp's testimony was widely circulated. It was published in newspapers and books, reprinted millions of times over, and read by people across the globe. And although he was generally celebrated for his swift justice and eventually exonerated of any wrong doing, many loud voices in both the press and in the public derided Earp for his lack of restraint, calling him little more than a thug and a killer. As a result he was shunned by polite society, left to exist as a sort of curiosity. For the rest of his life, Earp tried desperately to set the record straight, to further justify his actions and expand on his testimony. He hoped more than anything

that motion pictures might serve as a vehicle to aid his rehabilitation. But it wasn't until the twentieth century, after Earp passed away, that a public in desperate need of heroes, began to reevaluate the events of October 26, 1881. Many of the details that Earp so laboriously catalogued were edited out and the story greatly simplified. The primary focus became that of a righteous frontier lawman, going toe-to-toe against a band of nefarious outlaws. And so in this document, we have the birth of the modern protagonist—the archetypal lone hero. Wyatt Earp's story, the shootout and the quest for vengeance that followed, was popularized in film and literature. It was the story of a good man wronged and taking the law into his own hands. It became a popular narrative, one that still influences storytelling today. As for Wyatt Earp, he became the quintessential frontier lawman. His brand of justice came to define all discussion of law and order in the chaotic American West.

—*KP Dawes, MA*

Bibliography and Additional Reading

Barra, Allen. *Inventing Wyatt Earp: His Life and Many Legends*. New York: Carol & Graf, 1998. Print.

Guin, Jeff. *The Last Gunfight: The Real Story of the Shootout at the O.K. Corral and How It Changed the American West*. New York: Simon & Schuster, 2011. Print.

Marks, Paula Mitchell. *And Die in the West: The Story of the O.K. Corral Gunfight*. Norman, OK: U of Oklahoma P, 1989. Print.

Slotkin, Richard. *Gunfighter Nation: The Myth of the Frontier in Twentieth-Century America*. Norman: U of Oklahoma P, 1998. Print.

Tefertiller, Casey. *Wyatt Earp: The Life Behind the Legend*. New York: John Wiley & Sons, 1997. Print.

■ Theodore Roosevelt in Cowboy-Land

Date: 1896
Author: Theodore Roosevelt
Genre: autobiography

Summary Overview

As president of the United States, Theodore Roosevelt had a reputation for being a strong, brave, and rugged figure. T. R., as he was later known, is often credited with defining what it was to be a man at the turn of the century. In this view, masculinity was tough, adventurous, and uncompromising. But Roosevelt, born and raised in New York, did not learn the art of manliness among the East Coast's high society or even in the tumultuous world of politics. He learned it, as many Americans did, on the western frontier. Lured by the promise of adventure after a personal tragedy, T. R. got his most important education from cowboys and ranchers, from lawmen and outlaws whom he encountered amidst the wilds. Afterward, he was able to utilize the symbols of the American West to his political advantage. Roosevelt would become the first cowboy president, influencing not just how the public viewed the presidency, but also the men who held the office.

Defining Moment

After the death of his wife and mother on the same night in 1884, a young Theodore Roosevelt, heir to a wealthy and powerful New York family, fled west to the Badlands in Dakota Territory. As it did for so many countless other Americans in the mid- to late nineteenth century, the frontier, wild and untamed, held the promise of reinvention. Through hunting, killing, taming nature, facing danger, a man might truly become a man. It was there, amid the cowboys and Indians, that Roosevelt could escape his pain, and perhaps find new meaning. Equipping himself richly, with expensive clothes and western accessories, T. R. settled on a ranch on the banks of the Little Missouri. At first, the cowhands and ranchers he met and worked with had little respect for the New York dandy come to pretend he was a cowboy, but it wasn't long before this changed.

Roosevelt threw himself into his new life with fierce determination, and soon, he earned the respect of the frontiersmen and settlers he met. In a famous episode, which he would retell often in later years, he knocked out cold a cattlehand who dared make fun of his glasses. Roosevelt came to embody the essence of what it was to be an American cowboy. Never giving up, facing nature under even the most brutal conditions, relying solely on himself, T. R. would be reborn or die trying. Roosevelt did everything one can do in the West. He rode, drove cattle, drank, gambled, even pursued and captured outlaws. At one point, he met and befriended the famous sheriff of Deadwood, South Dakota, Seth Bullock, with whom he would maintain a friendship his whole life. The West did for T. R. exactly what he wanted. Life on the range reinvigorated the once sickly youth. He grew stronger, more confident, and more determined.

Upon his return east, Roosevelt wrote of his experiences in a book titled, *Ranch Life and the Hunting Trail*. Published in 1888, the book was a great success. It stirred the imagination of an American public already fascinated by the frontier. It also enlarged Roosevelt's stature, giving him the credentials of a strong and powerful man. Most importantly the book helped build, in the eyes of millions of Americans, the myth of the West—a magical place where men are men.

Author Biography

Theodore "T. R." Roosevelt was born in New York City on October 27, 1858 to a noted upper class family. Suffering from poor health throughout his youth, T. R. sought strength in his father, a businessman and philanthropist, whom he idealized as a model of strength and courage. After his father's death in 1878, Roosevelt threw himself into his studies, eventually publishing a highly influential book on naval warfare. After the death of his first wife, T. R. travelled out West, where he reinvented himself as a rugged frontiersman and naturalist. Upon his return to New York he quickly remarried and pursued a career in politics, becoming assistant secretary of the Navy in 1897, only to resign a year later to join the fight during the Spanish-American War. After leading a company of cavalrymen famously called the Rough Riders, T. R. was celebrated as a war hero and leveraged his fame to win the governorship of New York, becoming Vice President a short time later. After the assassination of McKinley, T. R. became the twenty-sixth president of the United States, overseeing the breaking of the trusts and the building of the Panama Canal. After a failed bid for a third term (though technically only his second) in 1912, under the Progressive ticket, T. R. spent the remainder of his life exploring, writing, and loudly denouncing the policies of both Republican and Democratic presidents. He died in 1919.

HISTORICAL DOCUMENT

RANCH LIFE AND THE HUNTING TRAIL
by Theodore Roosevelt
CHAPTER 1
THE CATTLE COUNTRY OF THE FAR WEST

Cattle-ranching can only be carried on in its present form while the population is scanty; and so in stack-raising regions, pure and simple, there are usually few towns, and these are almost always at the shipping points for cattle. But, on the other hand, wealthy cattlemen, like miners who have done well, always spend their money freely; and accordingly towns like Denver, Cheyenne, and Helena, where these two classes are the most influential in the community, are far pleasanter places of residence than cities of five times their population in the exclusively agricultural States to the eastward.

A true "cow town" is worth seeing,—such a one as Miles City, for instance, especially at the time of the annual meeting of the great Montana Stock-raisers' Association. Then the whole place is full to overflowing, the importance of the meeting and the fun of the attendant frolics, especially the horse-races, drawing from the surrounding ranch country many hundreds of men of every degree, from the rich stock owner worth his millions to the ordinary cowboy who works for forty dollars a month. It would be impossible to imagine a more typically American assemblage, for although there are always a certain number of foreigners, usually English, Irish, or German, yet they have become completely Americanized; and on the whole it would be difficult to gather a finer body of men, in spite of their numerous shortcomings. The ranch-owners differ more from each other than do the cowboys; and the former certainly compare very favorably with similar classes of capitalists in the East.

Anything more foolish than the demagogic outcry against "cattle kings" it would be difficult to imagine. Indeed, there are very few businesses so absolutely legitimate as stock-raising and so beneficial to the nation at large; and a successful stock-grower must not only be shrewd, thrifty, patient, and enterprising, but he must also possess qualities of personal bravery, hardihood, and self-reliance to a degree not demanded in the least by any mercantile occupation in a community long settled. Stockmen are in the West the pioneers of civilisation, and their daring and adventurousness make the after settlement of the region possible. The whole country owes them a great debt.

The most successful ranchmen are those, usually South-westerners, who have been bred to the business and have grown up with it; but many Eastern men, including not a few college graduates, have also done excellently by devoting their whole time and energy to their work,—although Easterners who invest their money in cattle without knowing anything of the business, or who trust all to their subordinates, are naturally enough likely to incur heavy losses. Stockmen are learning more and more to act together; and certainly the meetings of their associations are conducted with a dignity and good sense that would do credit to any parliamentary body.

But the cowboys resemble one another much more and outsiders much less than is the case even with their employers, the ranchmen. A town in the cattle country, when for some cause it is thronged with men from the neighborhood, always presents a picturesque sight. On the wooden sidewalks of the broad, dusty streets the men who ply the various industries known only to frontier existence jostle one another as they saunter to and fro or lounge lazily in front of the straggling, cheap looking board houses. Hunters come in from the plains and the mountains, clad in buckskin shirts and fur caps, greasy and unkempt, but with resolute faces and sullen, watchful eyes, that are ever on the alert. The teamsters, surly and self-contained, wear slouch hats and great cowhide boots; while the stage-drivers, their faces seamed by the hardship and exposure of their long drives with every kind of team, through every kind of country, and in every kind of weather, proud of their really wonderful skill as reinsmen and conscious of their high standing in any frontier community, look down on and sneer at the "skin hunters" and the plodding drivers of the white-topped prairie schooners. Besides these there are trappers, and wolfers, whose business is to poison wolves, with shaggy, knock-kneed ponies to carry their small bales and bundles of furs—beaver, wolf, fox, and occasionally otter; and silent sheep-herders, with cast-down faces, never able to forget the absolute solitude and monotony of their dreary lives, nor to rid their minds of the thought of the woolly idiots they pass all their days in tending. Such are the men who have come to town, either on business or else to frequent the flaunting saloons and gaudy hells of all kinds in search of the coarse, vicious excitement that in the minds of many of them does duty as pleasure-the only form of pleasure they have ever had a chance to know. Indians too, wrapped in blankets, with stolid, emotionless faces, stalk silently round among the whites, or join in the gambling and horseracing. If the town is on the borders of the mountain country, there will also be sinewy lumbermen, rough-looking miners, and packers, whose business it is to guide the long mule and pony trains that go where wagons can not and whose work in packing needs special and peculiar skill; and mingled with and drawn from all these classes are desperadoes of every grade, from the gambler up through the horse-thief to the murderous professional bully, or, as he is locally called, "bad man"—now, however, a much less conspicuous object than formerly.

But everywhere among these plainsmen and mountain-men, and more important than any, are the cowboys,—the men who follow the calling that has brought such towns into being. Singly, or in twos or threes, they gallop their wiry little horses down the street, their lithe, supple figures erect or swaying slightly as they sit loosely in the saddle; while their stirrups are so long that their knees are hardly bent, the bridles not taut enough to keep the chains from clanking. They are smaller and less muscular than the wielders of ax and pick; but they are as hardy and self-reliant as any men who ever breathed—with bronzed, set faces, and keen eyes that look all the world straight in the face without flinching as they flash out from under the broad-brimmed hats. Peril and hardship, and years of long toil broken by weeks of brutal dissipation, draw haggard lines across their eager faces, but never dim their reckless eyes nor break their bearing of defiant self-confidence. They do not walk well, partly because they so rarely do any work out of the saddle, partly because their chaperajos or leather overalls hamper them when on the ground; but their appearance is striking for all that, and picturesque too, with their jingling spurs, the big revolvers stuck in their belts, and bright silk handkerchiefs knotted loosely round their necks over the open collars of the flannel shirts. When drunk on the villainous whisky of the frontier towns, they cut mad antics, riding their horses into the saloons, firing their pistols right and left, from boisterous light heartedness rather than from any viciousness, and indulging too often in deadly shooting affrays, brought on either by the accidental contact of the moment or on account of some long-standing grudge, or perhaps because of bad blood between two ranches or localities; but except while on such sprees they are quiet, rather self-contained men, perfectly frank and simple, and on their own ground treat a stranger with the most whole-souled hospitality, doing all in their power for him and scorning to take any reward in return. Although prompt to resent an injury, they are not at all apt to be rude to outsiders, treating them with what can almost be called a grave courtesy. They are much better fellows and pleasanter companions than small farmers or agricultural laborers; nor are the mechanics and workmen of a great city to be mentioned in the same breath.

The bulk of the cowboys themselves are South-westerners; but there are also many from the Eastern and the Northern States, who, if they begin young, do quite as well as the Southerners. The best hands are fairly bred to the work and follow it from their youth up. Nothing can be more foolish than for an Easterner to think he can become a cowboy in a few months' time. Many a young fellow comes out hot with enthusiasm for life on the plains, only to learn that his clumsiness is greater than he could have believed possible; that the cowboy business is like any other and has to be learned by serving a painful apprenticeship; and that this apprenticeship implies the endurance of rough fares hard living, dirt, exposure of every kind, no little toil, and month after month of the dullest monotony. For cowboy work there is need of special traits and special training, and young Easterners should be sure of themselves before trying it: the struggle for existence is very keen in the far West, and it is no place for men who lack the ruder, coarser virtues and physical qualities, no matter how intellectual or how refined and delicate their sensibilities. Such are more likely to fail there than in older communities. Probably during the past few years more than half of the young Easterners who have come West with a little money to learn the cattle business have failed signally and lost what they had in the beginning. The West, especially the far West, needs men who have been bred on the farm or in the workshop far more than it does clerks or college graduates.

Some of the cowboys are Mexicans, who generally do the actual work well enough, but are not trustworthy; moreover, they are always regarded with extreme disfavor by the Texans in an outfit, among whom the intolerant caste spirit is very strong. Southern-born whites will never work under them, and look down upon all colored or half-caste races. One spring I had with my wagon a Pueblo Indian, an excellent rider and roper, but a drunken, worthless, lazy devil; and in the summer of 1886 there were with us a Sioux half-breed, a quiet, hard-working, faithful fellow, and a mulatto, who was one of the best cow-hands in the whole round-up.

Cowboys, like most Westerners, occasionally show remarkable versatility in their tastes and pursuits. One whom I know has abandoned his regular occupation for the past nine months, during which time he has been in succession a bartender, a school-teacher, and a probate judge! Another, whom I once employed for a short while, had passed through even more varied experiences, including those of a barber, a sailor, an apothecary, and a buffalo-hunter.

As a rule the cowboys are known to each other only by their first names, with, perhaps, as a prefix, the title of the brand for which they are working. Thus I remember once overhearing a casual remark to the effect that "Bar Y Harry" had married "the Seven Open A girl," the latter being the daughter of a neighboring ranchman. Often they receive nicknames, as, for instance, Dutch Wannigan, Windy Jack, and Kid Williams, all of whom are on the list of my personal acquaintances.

No man traveling through or living in the country need fear molestation from the cowboys unless he himself accompanies them on their drinking-bouts, or in other ways plays the fool, for they are, with us at any rate, very good fellows, and the most determined and effective foes of real law-breakers, such as horse and cattle thieves, murderers, etc. Few of the outrages quoted in Eastern papers as their handiwork are such in reality, the average Easterner apparently considering every individual who wears a broad hat and carries a six-shooter a cowboy. These outrages are, as a rule, the work of the roughs and criminals who always gather on the outskirts of civilisation, and who infest every frontier town until the decent citizens become sufficiently numerous and determined to take the law into their own hands and drive them out. The old buffalo-hunters, who formed a distinct class, became powerful forces for evil once they had destroyed the vast herds of mighty beasts the pursuit of which had been their means of livelihood. They were absolutely shiftless and improvident; they had no settled habits; they were inured to peril and hardship, but entirely unaccustomed to steady work; and so they afforded just the materials from which to make the bolder and more desperate kinds of criminals. When the game was gone they hung round the settlements for some little time, and then many of them naturally took to horse-stealing, cattle-killing, and highway robbery, although others, of course, went into honest pursuits. They were men who died off rapidly, however; for it is curious to see how many of these plainsmen, in spite of their iron nerves and thews, have their constitutions completely undermined, as much by the terrible hardships they have endured as by the fits of prolonged and bestial revelry with which they have varied them.

The "bad men," or professional fighters and man-killers, are of a different stamp, quite a number of them being, according to their light, perfectly honest. These are the men who do most of the killing in frontier communities; yet it is a noteworthy fact that the men who are killed generally deserve their fate. These men are, of course, used to brawling, and are not only sure shots, but, what is equally important, able to "draw" their weapons with marvelous quickness. They think nothing whatever of murder, and are the dread and terror of their associates; yet they are very chary of taking the life of a man of good standing, and will often weaken and back down at once if confronted fearlessly. With many of them their courage arises from confidence in their own powers and knowledge of the fear in which they are held; and men of this type often show the white feather when they get in a tight place. Others, however, will face any odds without flinching; and I have known of these men fighting, when mortally wounded, with a cool, ferocious despair that was terrible. As elsewhere, so here, very quiet men are often those who in an emergency show themselves best able to hold their own. These desperadoes always try to "get the drop" on a foe—that is, to take him at a disadvantage before he can use his own weapon. I have known more men killed in this way, when the affair was wholly one-sided, than I have known to be shot in fair fight; and I have known fully as many who were shot by accident. It is wonderful, in the event of a street fight, how few bullets seem to hit the men they are aimed at.

During the last two or three years the stockmen have united to put down all these dangerous characters, often by the most summary exercise of lynch law. Notorious bullies and murderers have been taken out and hung, while the bands of horse and cattle thieves have been regularly hunted down and destroyed in pitched fights by parties of armed cowboys; and as a consequence most of our territory is now perfectly law-abiding. One such fight occurred north of me early last spring. The horse-thieves were overtaken on the banks of the Missouri; two of their number were slain, and the others were driven on the ices which broke, and two more were drowned. A few months previously another gang, whose headquarters were near the Canadian line, were surprised in their hut; two or three were shot down by the cowboys as they tried to come out, while the rest barricaded themselves in and fought until the great log-hut was set on fire, when they broke forth in a body, and nearly all were killed at once, only one or two making their escape. A little over two years ago one committee of vigilantes in eastern Montana shot or hung nearly sixty—not, however, with the best judgment in all cases.

GLOSSARY

apothecary: a person who prepared and sold medicines and drugs

teamster: a driver of a team of animals

Document Analysis

Theodore Roosevelt paints for the reader a portrait of life on the frontier. Life on the prairie revolves around cattle-ranching. People of all shapes and sizes, from all corners of the United States can be found in the "cow towns" that dot the region. These are strong men, rugged men, and, Roosevelt says, "it would be difficult to gather a finer body of men, in spite of their numerous shortcomings." Roosevelt writes time and time again about which men are suited for which professions, and he describes the various interdependencies at play. Mostly however, his account is full of romanticism. Hunters, mountain men, settlers, ranchers all together, lounging under wooden awnings or galloping through town—these are true Americans, the rough core of the nation. They are men doing manly things in pursuit of business and progress. And among them, the cowboy is king.

The cowboy in T. R.'s writing is the hero of the West. Not as big or as strong as some of the other frontiersmen, the cowboy is lean, quiet, stoic, and duty-bound. He wears a hat, a scarf, and boots. He is the sentinel of the West. The perfect expression of Americanism, the cowboy embodies all the traits that make the nation great—courage, restraint, civility, and knowhow. Only when he's drunk does the cowboy let loose with "mad antics," firing off his pistols in boisterous fun, but real men are allowed to let off steam. Real men are allowed to sometimes run wild. For Roosevelt, there is no comparison, the cowboy is everything a man should be, far greater than farmers, laborers, or factory workers. And more to the point, the ideal cowboy is white because, for the Victorian T. R., nothing else could do.

Roosevelt warns his readers that the best cowboys are from the nation's Southwest. Easterners are not suited and not necessary for this type of work. Only in rare, exceptional cases—such as his own—can an Easterner hope to replicate a cowboy's skill and silent grace, for a cowboy is skill incarnate, an artist as much as a cowhand. And yes, T. R. admits that there are bad elements on the frontier, but these are not cowboys. Yes, they may wear the same costumes, but horse thieves and outlaws are not of the same class. They are corrupted, foul, often former buffalo hunters made evil by the destruction of the bison. The cowboy, however, is pure and perfect and good. In the end, the forces of darkness will be eliminated. It's happening even now.

Essential Themes

Roosevelt's account of life on the frontier and specifically his descriptions of the cowboy, served both to romanticize the West, but also the image of a sort of perfect manliness. For T. R., a nineteenth-century Victorian, raised on notions of American exceptionalism and the superiority of the white race, cowboys were the embodiment of perfection—stoic, silent, courageous men. In this narrative, cowboys were the leaders of American progress. It's no coincidence, then, that Roosevelt strongly linked himself to the image he so greatly admired. The cowboy was the perfect man, and through his experience, T.R. just happened to be a one. Although not a calculated political move to better position himself for a future in the public sphere, as T.R. was generally very self-centered, the link between himself and the frontier strongly resonated with voters across the nation. Roosevelt became the embodiment of the West, and in turn, the West helped shape Roosevelt. The notion of a white America, strong and resolute, standing firm against a sea of savagery would inform most of T.R.'s foreign policy and that of many presidents to follow. But perhaps more importantly, the image of the cowboy president, the rugged loner, the ultimate decision maker, forever transformed the office of the presidency itself. Before Roosevelt, the presidency was a relatively weak office, but after T.R.'s brand of frontier leadership, the office would grow increasingly more powerful. As the balance shifted towards the executive branch, the men elected to that position in the decades to follow were expected to have the same grace, the same stoic perfection as those men of the frontier, the lone warrior, never afraid to do what had to be done in order to guarantee success. This notion of the cowboy-in-chief is still very much alive in American politics, as is the cowboy as hero, evident in popular culture, and the cowboy as ultimate expression of masculinity. No matter how far removed we are from the period when Americans settled the West, some aspects of that history still paint our national character today.

—*KP Dawes, MA*

Bibliography and Additional Reading

Bederman, Gail. *Manliness and Civilization: A Cultural History of Gender and Race in the United States, 1880–1917.* Chicago: U of Chicago P, 1995. Print.

Di Silvestro, Roger L. *Theodore Roosevelt in the Badlands: A Young Politician's Quest for Recovery in the American West.* New York: Walker Publishing, 2011. Print.

Morris, Edmund. *The Rise of Theodore Roosevelt.* New York: Random House, 1979. Print.

■ A Scout with the Buffalo Soldiers

Date: April 1889
Author: Frederic Remington
Genre: article; journal

Summary Overview

Frederic Remington was an emerging artist, who at one time aspired to be a magazine correspondent. Thus, his abilities in both areas were put to use in an 1886 assignment to travel to Arizona to observe the Tenth Cavalry. This African American unit, created by Congress after the Civil War, patrolled what was then a federal territory to enforce peace between the Native American tribes and the settlers, as well as to generally keep order. In this article, Remington described his experience as he joined a small detachment for a two-week scouting expedition. His illustrations, as well as the article, accurately portrayed the events of this trip. In this article and throughout his career, Remington presented a positive picture of the soldiers, rather than the negative racial stereotype of the unit, which prevailed in this era. His willingness to personally join them on this journey, and his respect for their dedication and ability, made the article stand out from others that were written by correspondents who stayed in the relative comfort of the forts.

Defining Moment

By the mid-1880s, the American West was becoming tame. The last of the major conflicts with Native Americans had ended, with the surviving leaders surrendering. Buffalo Bill's Wild West show started performing throughout the East. There was a growing interest both in the West as it was and for a nostalgic West of the past, as imagined by people who had never lived there. Thus, magazines such as *The Century* commissioned writers and artists to travel to the West to describe what they encountered. Frederic Remington, an emerging artist who already had a number of published illustrations to his credit, was sent to the Southwest as a part of the magazine's attempt to communicate its vision of America to its readers. (The magazine's editorial policy at that time was strongly conservative, with a pro-American, pro-Christian, pro-white, agenda.) Rem-

ington had traveled to that region several years earlier, for another publication, in a vain attempt to cover the struggle with Geronimo. Thus, he was familiar with the climate and the people of the region.

Writing for the magazine's readers, who were middle and upper class members of the general public, Remington used a descriptive literary style, as well as his illustrations, to communicate the hardships that soldiers faced in the Arizona Territory. Using common terminology of the day, Remington let the reader know that the Tenth Calvary was composed of African Americans, but he did not focus on this aspect of their lives. The term "Buffalo Soldier" had been given to the African American soldiers by Comanche and Apache warriors to describe the men they had fought. Different quotes from that time refer to the willingness of the soldiers to fight like a wounded buffalo and to their hair being like that of a buffalo. In either event, it was not created as derogatory designation, and the African American soldiers accepted it as a term for themselves and their units. While this article was well received in general, to African Americans back East, it represented a source of pride that even in that era of segregation and persecution, one could witness an African American unit serving the nation in the same manner as white army units did.

Author Biography

Frederic Remington was born in Canton, New York, to Seth and Clara Remington on October 4, 1861. He was a very active, non-academic child, who rode horses and drew from an early age. He had some formal training in art, although he did not apply himself to it. His father died when he was eighteen, and the next year, he traveled west, to invest his inheritance in something that would make more money without much effort. Over the next several years, he went through his money as he tried several jobs. None allowed him to make money without hard work. Eventually, in 1885, he fell back on his drawing, illustrating articles for magazines and newspapers. When *The Century* magazine hired him to illustrate articles by Theodore Roosevelt, it led to a contract to write and illustrate his own articles. From that time forward, Remington was able focus on the West, with more than 2,000 illustrations published in various magazines, as well as his more formal paintings and, eventually, bronze sculptures. Beginning in the early 1890s, in addition to his art, he became a regular on the lecture circuit, for which he adopted a western persona. Having had a full life as a correspondent, author, illustrator, painter, and sculptor, he died of appendicitis in 1909.

HISTORICAL DOCUMENT

A Scout with the Buffalo Soldiers
written and illustrated by Frederic Remington

I sat smoking in the quarters of an army friend at Fort Grant, and through a green lattice-work was watching the dusty parade and congratulating myself on the possession of this spot of comfort in such a disagreeably hot climate as Arizona Territory offers in the summer, when in strode my friend the lieutenant, who threw his cap on the table and began to roll a cigarette.

Marching in the Desert with the Buffalo Soldiers

"Well," he said, "the K.O. has ordered me out for a two-week's scouting up the San Carlos way, and I'm off in the morning. Would you like to go with me?" He lighted the cigarette and paused for my reply.

I was very comfortable at that moment, and knew from some past experiences that marching under the summer sun of Arizona was real suffering and not to be considered by one on pleasure bent; and I was also aware that my friend the lieutenant had a reputation as a hard rider, and would in this case select a few picked and seasoned cavalrymen and rush over the worst possible country in the least possible time. I had no reputation as a hard rider to sustain, and, moreover, had not backed a horse for the year past. I knew too that Uncle Sam's beans, black coffee, and the bacon which every old soldier will tell you about would fall to the lot of any one who scouted with the 10th Dragoons. Still, I very much desired to travel through the country to the north, and in a rash moment said, "I'll go."

"You understand that you are amenable to discipline," continued the lieutenant with mock seriousness, as he regarded me with that soldier's contempt for a citizen which is not openly expressed but is tacitly felt.

"I do," I answered meekly.

"Put you afoot, citizen; put you afoot, sir, at the slightest provocation, understand," pursued the officer in his sharp manner of giving commands.

I suggested that after I had chafed a Government saddle for a day or two I should undoubtedly beg to be put afoot, and, far from being a punishment, it might be a real mercy.

"That being settled, will you go down to stable-call and pick out a mount? You are one of the heavies, but I think we can outfit you," he said; and together we strolled down to where the bugle was blaring.

At the adobe corral the faded coats of the horses were being groomed by black troopers in white frocks; for the 10th United States Cavalry is composed of colored men. The fine alkaline dust of that country is continually sifting over all exposed objects, so that grooming becomes almost as hopeless a task as sweeping back the sea with a housebroom. A fine old veteran cavalry-horse detailed for a sergeant of the troop, was selected to bear me on the trip. He was a large horse of a pony build, both strong and sound except that he bore a healed-up saddle-gore, gotten, probably, during some old march upon an endless Apache trail. Well satisfied with my mount, I departed.

On the following morning I was awakened and got up to array myself in my field costume. My old troop-horse was at the door, and he eyed his citizen rider with malevolent gaze. Even the dumb beasts of the army share that quiet contempt for the citizen which is one manifestation of the military spirit, born of strength, and as old as when the first man went forth with purpose to conquer his neighbor man.

Down in front of the post-trader's was gathered the scouting party. A tall sergeant, grown old in the service, scarred on battlefield, hardened by long marches,—in short, a product of the camp—stood by his horse's head. Four enlisted men, picturesquely clad in the cavalry soldier's field costume, and two packers, mounted on diminutive bronco mules, were in charge of four pack-mules loaded with apperajos and packs. This was our party. Presently the lieutenant issued from the headquarters' office and joined us. An orderly led up his horse. "Mount," said the lieutenant; and swinging himself into his saddle he started off up the road. Out past the groups of adobe houses which constitute a frontier military village or post we rode, stopping to water our horses at the little creek, now nearly dry—the last water for many miles on our trail,—and presently emerged upon the great desert. Together at the head of the little cavalcade rode the lieutenant and I, while behind, in single file, came the five troopers, sitting loosely in their saddles with the long stirrup of the United States cavalry seat, forage-hats set well over the eyes, and carbines, slickers, canteens, saddle-pockets, and lariats rattling at their sides. Strung out behind were the four pack mules, now trotting demurely along, now stopping to feed, and occa-

sionally making a solemn and evidently well-considered attempt to get out of line and regain the post which we were leaving behind. The packers brought up the rear, swinging their "blinds" and shouting at the lagging mules in a manner which evinced a close acquaintance with the character and peculiarities of each beast.

The sun was getting higher in the heavens and began to assert its full strength. The yellow dust rose about our horses' hoofs and settled again over the dry grass and mesquite bush. Stretching away on our right was the purple line of the Sierra Bonitas, growing bluer and bluer until lost in the hot scintillating atmosphere of the desert horizon. Overhead stretched the deep blue of the cloudless sky.

A Halt to Tighten the Packs

Presently we halted and dismounted to tighten the packs, which work loose after the first hour. One by one the packers caught the little mules, threw a blind over their eyes, and "Now, Whitey! Ready! eve-e-e-e—gimme that loop," came from the men as they heaved and tossed the circling ropes in the mystic movements of the diamond hitch. "All fast, Lieutenant," cries a packer, and mounting we move on up the long slope of the mesa towards the Sierras. We enter a break in the foothills, and the grade becomes steeper and steeper, until at last it rises at an astonishing angle. The slopes of the Sierra Bonitas are very steep, and as the air became more rarified as we toiled upward I found that I was panting for breath. My horse—a veteran mountaineer—grunted in his efforts and drew his breath in long and labored blowing; consequently I felt as though I was not doing anything unusual in puffing and blowing myself.

On the trail ahead I saw the lieutenant throw himself on the ground. I followed his example, for I was nearly "done for." I never had felt a rock as soft as the one I sat on. It was literally downy. The old troop-horse heaved a great sigh, and dropping his head went fast asleep, as every good soldier should do when he finds the opportunity. The negro troopers sat about, their black skins shining with perspiration, and took no interest in the matter in hand. They occupied such time in joking and merriment as seemed fitted for growling. They may be tired and they may be hungry, but they do not see fit to augment their misery by finding fault with everybody and everything. In this particular they are charming men with whom to serve.

After a most frugal lunch we resumed our journey towards the clouds. Climbing many weary hours, we at last stood on the sharp ridge of the Sierra. Behind us we could see the great yellow plain of the Sulphur Spring Valley, and in front, stretching away, was that of the Gila, looking like a bed of a sea with the water gone.

Here we had a needed rest, and then began the descent on the other side. This was a new experience. The prospect of being suddenly overwhelmed by an avalanche of horseflesh as the result of some unlucky stumble makes the recruit constantly apprehensive. But the trained horses are sure of foot, understand the business, and seldom stumble except when the treacherous ground gives way. On the crest the prospect was very pleasant, as the pines there obscured the hot sun; but we suddenly left them for the scrub mesquite which bars your passage and reaches forth for you with its thorns when you attempt to go around.

We wound downward among the masses of rock for some time, when we suddenly found ourselves on a shelf of rock. We sought to avoid it by going up and around, but after a tiresome march we were still confronted by a drop of about a hundred feet. I gave up in despair; but the lieutenant after gazing at the unknown depths which were masked at the bottom by a thick growth of brush, said, "This is a good place to go down." I agreed that it was if you once got started; but personally I did not care to take the tumble.

Taking his horse by the bits, the young officer began the descent. The slope was at an angle of at least sixty degrees, and was covered with loose dirt and boulders, with the mask of brush at the bottom concealing the awful possibilities of what might be beneath. The horse

hesitated a moment, then cautiously put his head down and his leg forward and started. The loose earth crumbled, a great stone was precipitated to the bottom with a crash, the horse slid and floundered along. Had the situation not been so serious it would have been funny, because the angle of the incline was so great that the horse actually sat on his haunches like a dog. "Come on!" shouted the redoubtable man of war and I started. My old horse took it unconcernedly, and we came down all right, bringing our share of dirt and stones and plunging through the wall of brush at the bottom to find our friend safe on the lower side. The men came along without so much as a look of interest in the proceeding. Down came the mules, without turning an ear, and then followed the packers, who, to my astonishment, rode down.

Our camp was pitched by a little mountain stream near a grassy hillside. The saddles, packs, and apperajos were laid on the ground and the horses and mules herded on the side of the hill by a trooper, who sat perched on a rock above them, carbine in hand. I was thoroughly tired and hungry, and did my share in creating the famine which it was clearly seen would reign in that camp ere long. We sat about the fire and talked. The genial glow seems to possess an occult quality: it warms the self-confidence of a man; it lulls his moral nature; and the stories which circulate about a campfire are always more interesting than authentic. Soldiers have no tents in that country, and we rolled ourselves in our blankets and, gazing up, saw the weird figure of the sentinel against the last red gleam of the sunset, and beyond that the great dome of the sky. Then we fell asleep.

A Campfire Sketch

When I awoke the next morning the hill across the canyon wall was flooded with a golden light, while the gray tints of our camp were steadily warming up. The soldiers had the two black camp-pails over the fire and were grooming the horses. Everyone was good-natured, as befits the beginning of the day. The tall sergeant was meditatively combing his hair with a currycomb; such delightful little unconventionalities are constantly observed about the camp. The coffee steamed up in our nostrils, and after a rub in the brook I pulled myself together and declared to my comrade that I felt as good as new. This was a palpable falsehood, as my labored movements revealed to the hard-sided cavalryman the sad effeminacy of the studio. But our respite was brief, for almost before I knew it I was again on my horse, following down the canyon after the black charger bestrided by the junior lieutenant of K troop. Over piles of rocks fit only for the touch and go of a goat, through the thick mesquite which threatened to wipe our hats off or to swish us from the saddle, with the air warming up and growing denser, we rode along. A great stretch of sandy desert could be seen, and I foresaw hot work.

In about an hour we were clear of the descent and could ride along together, so that conversation made the way more interesting. We dismounted to go down a steep drop from the high mesa into the valley of the Gila, and then began a day warmer even than imagination had anticipated. The awful glare of the sun on the desert, the clouds of white alkaline dust which drifted up until lost above, seemingly too fine to settle again, and the great heat cooking the ambition out of us, made the conversation lag and finally drop altogether. The water in my canteen was hot and tasteless, and the barrel of my carbine, which I touched with my ungloved hand, was so heated that I quickly withdrew it. Across the hot-air waves which made the horizon rise and fall like the bosom of the ocean we could see a whirlwind or sand-storm winding up in a tall spiral until it was lost in the deep blue of the sky above.

Lizards started here and there; a snake hissed a moment beside the trail, then sought the cover of a dry bush; the horses moved along with downcast heads and drooping ears. The men wore a solemn look as they rode along, and now and then one would nod as though giving over to sleep. The pack-mules no longer sought fresh feed along the way, but attended strictly to business. A short halt was made, and I alighted. Upon remounting I threw myself violently from the saddle, and upon examination found that I had brushed up against a cactus and gotten my corduroys filled with thorns. The soldiers were overcome with glee at this episode, but they volunteered to help me pick them from my clothes. Thus we marched all day, and with canteens empty we "pulled into" Fort Thomas that afternoon.

At the fort we enjoyed that hospitality which is a kind of freemasonry among army officers. But for all that Fort Thomas is an awful spot, hotter than any other place on the crust of the earth. The siroccos continually chase each other over the desert, the convalescent wait upon the sick, and the thermometer persistently reposes at the figures 125 degrees Fahrenheit. Soldiers are kept in the Gila Valley posts for only six months at a time before they are relieved, and they count the days.

TROOPER IN TOW.

On the following morning at an early hour we waved adieus to our kind friends and took our way down the valley. If the impression is abroad that a cavalry soldier's life in the Southwest has any of the lawn-party element in it, I think the impression could be effaced by doing a march like that. The great clouds of dust choke you and settle over horse, soldier, and accouterments until all local color is lost and black man and white man wear a common hue. The "chug, chug, chug" of your tired horse as he marches along becomes infinitely tiresome, and cavalry soldiers never ease themselves in the saddle. No pains are spared to prolong the usefulness of an army horse, and every old soldier knows that his good care will tell when the long forced march comes some day, and when to be put afoot by a poor mount means great danger in Indian warfare. The soldier will steal for his horse, will share his camp bread, and will moisten the horse's nostrils and lips with the precious water in the canteen.

Through a little opening in the trees we see a camp and stop in front of it. A few mesquite trees, two tents, and some sheds made of boughs beside an acequia make up the background. By the cooking-fire lounge two or three rough frontiersmen, veritable pirates in appearance, with rough flannel shirts, slouch hats, brown canvas overalls, and an unkempt air; but suddenly, to my intense astonishment, they rise, stand in their tracks as immovable as graven images, and salute the lieutenant; then these men were soldiers! It was a camp of instruction for Indians and a post of observation. They were nice fellows and did everything in their power to entertain the cavalry. We were given a tent, and one man cooked the army rations in such strange shapes and mysterious ways that we marveled as we ate. After dinner we lay on our blankets watched the groups of San Carlos Apaches who came to look at us. Some of them knew the lieutenant, with whom they had served and whom they now addressed as "Young Chief." They would point him out to others with great zest. Great excitement prevailed when it was discovered that I was using a sketch-book, and I was forced to disclose the half-finished visage of one villainous face to their gaze. It was straightway torn up, and I was requested with many scowls and grunts, to discontinue that pastime, for Apaches more than any other Indians dislike to have their portraits made.

All along the Gila Valley can be seen the courses of stone which were the foundations of the houses of a dense population long since passed away. The lines of old irrigating ditches were easily traced, and one is forced to wonder at the changes in Nature, for at the present time there is not water sufficient to irrigate land necessary for the support of as large a population as probably existed at some remote period. We "raised" some foothills, and could see in the far distance the great flat plain, the buildings of the San Carlos agency, and the white canvas of the cantonment. Nearer and nearer shone the white lines of tents until we drew rein in the square where officers crowded around to greet us. The jolly post-commander, the senior captain of the 10th, insisted upon my accepting the hospitalities of his "large hotel," as he called his field tent, on the ground that I too was a New Yorker. Right glad have I been ever since that I accepted his courtesy, for he entertained me in the true frontier style.

Being now out of the range of country known to our command, a lieutenant in the same regiment was detailed to accompany us beyond. This gentleman was a character. The best part of his life had been spent in this rough country, and he had so long associated with Apache scouts that his habits while on a trail were exactly those of an Indian. I jocosely insisted that Lieutenant Jim only needed a breech-clout and long hair in order to draw rations at the agency. In the morning, as we started under his guidance, he was a spectacle. He wore shoes and a white shirt, and carried absolutely nothing in the shape of canteens and other "plunder" which usually constitute a cavalryman's kit. He was mounted on a little runt of a pony so thin and woebegone as to be remarkable among his kind. It was insufferably hot as we followed our queer guide up a dry canyon, which cut off the breeze from all sides and was a veritable human frying-pan. I marched next to our leader, and all day long the patter, patter of that Indian pony, bearing his tireless rider, made an aggravating display of insensibility to fatigue, heat, dust, and climbing. On we marched over the rolling hills, dry, parched, desolate, covered with cactus and loose stones. When we reached water and camp that night our ascetic leader had his first drink. It was a long one and a strong one, but at last he arose from the pool and with a smile remarked his "canteens were full." Officers in the regiment say that no one will give Lieutenant Jim a drink from his canteen, but this does not change his habit of not carrying one; nevertheless, by the exercise of self-denial, which is at times heroic, he manages to pull through. They say that he sometimes fills an old meat-tin with water in anticipation of a long march, and stories which try credulity are told of the amount of water he has drunk at times.

Yuma Apaches come into camp, shake hands gravely with everyone, and then in their Indian way begin the inevitable inquiries as to how the coffee and flour are holding out. The campfire darts and crackles, the soldiers gather round it, eat, joke, and bring out the greasy pack of cards. The officers gossip of army affairs, while I lie on my blankets, smoking and trying to establish relations with a very small and very dirty little Yuma Apache, who sits near me and gazes with sparkling eyes at the strange object which I undoubtedly seem to him.

It seems but an instant before a glare of sun strikes my eyes and I am awake for another day. I am mentally quarreling with that insane desire to march which I know possesses Lieutenant Jim; but it is useless to expostulate, and before many hours the little pony constantly moving along ahead of me becomes a part of my life. There he goes. I can see him now—always moving briskly along, pattering over the level, trotting up the dry bed of a stream, disappearing into the dense chapparal thicket that covers a steep hillside, jumping rocks, and doing everything but "halt."

We are now in the high hills, and the air is cooler. The chapparal is thicker, the ground is broken into a succession of ridges, and the volcanic boulders pile up in formidable shapes. My girth loosens and I dismount to fix it. The command moves on and is lost to sight in a deep ravine. Presently I resume my journey, and in the meshwork of ravines I find that I no longer see the trail of the column. I retrace and climb and slide down hill, forcing my way through chapparal, and after a long time I see the pack-mules go out of sight far away on a mountain slope. The blue peaks of the Pinals tower away on my left, and I begin to indulge in mean thoughts concerning the indomitable spirit of Lieutenant Jim, for I know he will take us clear over the top of that pale blue line of far-distant mountains.

In course of time I came up with the command, which had stopped at a ledge so steep that it had daunted even these mountaineers. It was only a hundred foot drop, and they presently found a place to go down, where, as one soldier suggested, "there isn't footing for a lizard." On we go, when suddenly with a great crash some sandy ground gives way, and a collection of hoofs, troop-boots, ropes, canteens, and flying stirrups goes rolling over in a cloud of dust and finds lodgment in the bottom of a dry watercourse. The dust settles and discloses a soldier and his horse. They rise to their feet and appear astonished, but as the soldier mounts and follows on we know he is unhurt. Now a coyote, surprised by our cavalcade and unable to get up the ledge, runs along the opposite side of the canyon wall. "Pop, pop, pop, pop" go the six-shooters, and then follow explanations by each marksman of the particular thing which made him miss.

That night we were forced to make a "dry camp"; that is, one where no water is to be found. There is such an amount of misery locked up in the thought of a dry camp that I refuse to dwell upon it.

We were glad enough to get upon the trail in the morning, and in time found a nice running mountain-brook. The command wallowed in it. We drank as much as we could hold and then sat down. We arose and drank some more, and yet we drank again, and still once more, until we were literally water-logged. Lieutenant Jim became uneasy, so we took up our march. We were always resuming the march when all nature called aloud for rest. We climbed straight up impossible places. The air grew chill, and in a gorge a cold wind blew briskly down to supply the hot air rising from sands of the mesa far below. That night we made a camp, and the only place where I could make my bed was on a great flat rock. We were

now among the pines, which towered above us. The horses were constantly losing one another in the timber in their search for grass, in consequence of which they whinnied, while the mules brayed, and made the mountain hideous with sound.

By another long climb we reached the extreme peaks of the Pinal range, and there before us was spread a view which was grand enough to compensate us for the labor. Beginning in "gray reds," range after range of mountains, overlapping each other, grow purple and finally lose themselves in pale blues. We sat on a ledge and gazed. The soldiers were interested, though their remarks about the scenery somehow did not seem to express an appreciation of the grandeur of the view which impressed itself strongly upon us. Finally one fellow, less aesthetic than his mates, broke the spell by a request for chewing-tobacco, so we left off dreaming and started on.

That day Lieutenant Jim lost his bearings, and called upon that instinct which he had acquired in his life among the Indians. He "cut the signs" of old Indian trails and felt the course to be in a certain direction—which was undoubtedly correct, but it took us over the highest points of the Mescal range. My shoes were beginning to give out, and the troop-boots of several soldiers threatened to disintegrate. One soldier, more ingenious than the rest, took out some horse-shoe nails and cleverly mended his boot-gear. At times we wound around great slopes where a loose stone or the giving way of bad ground would have precipitated horse and rider a thousand feet below. Only the courage of the horses brings one safely through. The mules suffered badly.

At last we reached the Gila, and nearly drowned a pack-mule and two troopers in the quicksand. We began to pass Indian huts, and saw them gathering wheat in the river bottoms, while they paused to gaze at us and doubtless wondered for what purpose the buffalo-soldiers were abroad in the land. The cantonment appeared, and I was duly gratified when we reached it. I hobbled up to the "Grand Hotel" of my host the captain, who laughed heartily at my floundering movements and observed my nose and cheeks, from which the sun had peeled the skin, with evident relish at the thought of how I had been used by his lieutenant. At his suggestion I was made an honorary member of the cavalry, and duly admonished "not to trifle again with the 10th Nubian Horse if I expected any mercy."

In due time the march continued without particular incident, and at last the scout "pulled in" to the home post, and I again sat in my easy-chair behind the lattice-work, firm in the conviction that soldiers, like other men, find more hard work than glory in their calling.

GLOSSARY

apperajos: rigs

colored: in the nineteenth century, a non-derogatory term for African Americans

dust devil: a strong, but small whirlwind

Nubian: archaic romanticized term for people of African descent who were believed to be above average

Sierra Bonitas Mountains: archaic name for the mountains in southeastern Arizona

Document Analysis

With a flowing style and excellent illustrations, Frederic Remington described highlights of a two-week trip through rugged Arizona terrain with members of the Tenth Cavalry as his companions. Although Remington occasionally made reference to their race and accurately depicted them in his illustrations, he did not make an issue of the fact that they were African Americans. The unit endured the hardships of service in the Southwest's desert climate, just as members of other units did. Although the territory would become a state in less than twenty-five years, it was a very remote and undeveloped area. Remington came to understand that to survive in this environment, people had to work together, and that race made no difference on the trail. In addition to his description of the people and scenery, the readers of his account could gain further insight into the difficult lifestyle of the soldiers, by Remington's comments on his physical discomfort as compared to the lack of complaints by his companions. Due to his excellent reporting, Remington's readers could vicariously join with him in his travels.

The dual focus of environment and people made this a well-balanced article. Foreshadowing the trials that were to follow, Remington began by mentioning how comfortable he was at Fort Grant. However, once he accepted the challenge to join the expedition, this all changed. On a horse selected because of Remington's size (weight), he ventured into the wilderness. The dust, harsh sunlight, and unfriendly vegetation wore him down. Thus, he was glad to find a "soft" rock upon which to briefly rest. The transition from desert valleys to more temperate mountains was helpful, but getting up and down was not always easy, as Remington described the journey. As he recorded events, he made it clear that even though the major Indian wars had stopped, it was not a "lawn-party" for the Tenth Cavalry.

While Remington may have been sent to report on the West, the other focus of this journal was the people. The variety of those with whom Remington came into contact was clearly indicated in the article, and yet at the same time, the essential sameness of them came through strongly. In reference to the difficult conditions, Remington mentioned the dust, which resulted in a situation in which the "black man and white man wear a common hue." In the 1880s, throughout American society, there was a strong inclination toward white supremacy resulting in segregation and discrimination. As Remington viewed the work being done by the Army on the frontier, he saw that the Buffalo Soldiers were as solid and dedicated as the white soldiers in other units. In fact, it seemed that he thought they were more content as they did not "see fit to augment their misery by finding fault." While Remington went down steep mountainsides with great trepidation, the soldiers went down the same slopes unconcerned with the danger. Whatever his previous views of African Americans might have been, on this journey through the wilderness, his writing indicated that he accepted them as equals.

The illustrations that Remington created for this article were based on sketches he made during the trip. Some art historians believe that this trip was a turning point in Remington's ability to accurately transfer images from his sketchpad to print. These also illustrated what would become his trademark style. Using a style opposite to previous artists depicting the West, Remington made the people the focus of his work, not the scenery.

Essential Themes

As Remington described the situation and his expedition with members of the Tenth Cavalry, the hardship of their service and the men's strength of character were at the forefront. The land and climatic conditions to which they had been sent were worthy opponents in the struggle to survive. Members of the Tenth Cavalry had adapted well, as Remington described their attitude during the trip and their ability to cope with the harsh surroundings. As he came to know them better, and as he described them in his writings, one can understand his opinion that the Buffalo Soldiers were no different from other soldiers in similar circumstances. They had the skills, insights, and ability to adapt which served them well in the wilderness, as well as in skirmishes with enemy combatants. The reputation that this unit acquired was well-deserved. It was one reason why a decade later Theodore Roosevelt requested that they be assigned to his force in the invasion of Cuba during the Spanish-American War. Although this article did not transform society's view of African Americans, Remington did make a contribution toward helping all Americans understand the innate equality of people whatever their ancestry. The unit remained segregated until it was disbanded during World War II. In the early twentieth century, members of the unit had such pride in the period when their military predecessors were called Buffalo Soldiers that they adopted the buffalo as part of the insignia for the Tenth Cavalry.

At the same time as Remington was illustrating the common humanity of all on the expedition, he was also recording the beauty of nature in the harsh terrain. His ability to communicate both the "grandeur of the view" and the dangerous conditions that it contained was remarkable. The struggle to get through each new obstacle was set in opposition to the friendship offered by each group they encountered along the way. While Remington might be said to have had a romantic vision of the world, which made his writing quite enjoyable to read, he was also enough of a realist to help the reader understand the basics of surviving in what was left of the frontier West.

—*Donald A. Watt, PhD*

Bibliography and Additional Reading

Buckland, Roscoe L. *Frederic Remington: The Writer.* New York: Twayne, 2000. Print.

Glasrud, Bruce A., & Michael N. Searles, eds. *Buffalo Soldiers in the West: A Black Soldiers Anthology.* College Station: Texas A&M UP, 2007. Print.

Thayer, Tolles. *"Frederic Remington (1861–1909)" Heilbrunn Timeline of Art History.* The Metropolitan Museum of Art, 2014. Web. 13 Oct. 2014.

Utley, Robert M. *"Buffalo Soldiers"* Fort Davis National Historic Site. National Park Service, 2002. Web. 13 Oct. 2014.

ENVIRONMENTAL ACTIONS

Conservation was a wholly new concept at the end of the nineteenth century and would not gain widespread attention until well into the twentieth century. It began with a few early adopters, such as John Muir and John Wesley Powell, and took off too among sport hunters, like Theodore Roosevelt and George Bird Grinnell. Muir, who traveled up and down the country on foot, came to appreciate the splendors of untainted natural areas and wanted to preserve them whole. Powell, who trained as a geologist but later went on to head the Bureau of American Ethnology, felt that land settlement in the West should be suited to its arid conditions—small and concentrated in irrigated areas. Meanwhile, Roosevelt and other hunting enthusiasts wanted to preserve areas for wildlife, while also allowing selective access to developers of natural resources. The latter perspective is close to that of Roosevelt's friend and fellow conservation leader, Gifford Pinchot, who did as much as anyone to launch the conservation movement.

These environmental perspectives are sampled in the section that follows. They are combined here with material relating to the purchase of Alaska by the United States in 1867; the founding of two of the first US National Parks (Yellowstone and Yosemite); and a look at the virtual extinction of the bison through wanton hunting and the earliest effort to save the species.

■ The Alaska Purchase

Date: March 30, 1867; and 1916 (memoir)
Author: US Congress; Frederick Seward
Genre: treaty; memoir

Summary Overview

The treaty covering the sale of Alaska to the United States has been a document of interest to more than just those residents of what is now the forty-ninth state. It was and is, rather, the second largest purchase of territory by the United States; only the Louisiana Purchase is larger. The Alaska Purchase represented one of the high points in diplomatic relations between the Unites States and Russia. The treaty outlined the peaceful transfer of ownership from Russia to the United States and recognized the rights of the Russians who were living in the territory. At the same time, no rights were given to the Native peoples.

The second document examined here—a brief memoir by the son of US Senator and Secretary of State William Seward—who was principally responsible for the treaty, adds a human dimension to the story. It illustrates the degree of trust existing at the time between the two nations and their leaders. The anecdotes that make up this narrative help one to understand the difference between diplomacy in 1867 and diplomacy in later years.

Defining Moment

With the Civil War having ended in 1865, the vision of many once again turned to the expansion of the nation and the development of the West. Although much still needed to be done to reincorporate the South into the Union, the West represented the hopes of many, even before the war ended. Thus, the administration of President Andrew Johnson sought to move forward on an issue on which the nation was relatively unified. Having given then Secretary of State William Seward full control of American diplomacy, the Johnson administration followed Seward's lead with respect to the acquisition of Alaska. From the Russian perspective, Alaska had come to be seen as a rather precarious asset. Russia was now determined to gain some benefit from its territory, and the Americans seemed to be the only

nation interested in it. Additionally, great changes that had occurred in Russia during the early 1860s meant that the Russian Empire was now in need of money. The sale of Alaska satisfied the desires of both nations and their leaders.

Although Congress was skeptical of anything that President Johnson proposed, Secretary Seward was a consummate politician, and he enlisted leaders in the Senate to get the treaty ratified. Thus, the proposal that he had set forth was not altered by the Senate. The technical descriptions of the territory, and the manner in which private and governmental property was to be treated, served both nations well, and no further problems arose regarding the change in nationality. The exchange was also accepted by the other nations of the world as a valid exercise.

The reflections by Frederick Seward on the Alaska Purchase were included in his autobiography, published a year after his death. The passage included here was, it seems, written in the previous decade and intended as a speech. While it was principally written to strengthen the Sewards' legacy, it was also used to create continued public support for the expansion of American territorial interests. The younger Seward's ability to supply details not normally included in history books and his understanding of how Alaska had contributed far more than the pessimists at the time had assumed turned his account into something that supported the continued presence of the United States in Alaska (and other territories acquired at the end of the nineteenth century).

Author Biography

The Treaty with Russia (Alaska Purchase) was negotiated by William H. Seward (1801–1872) for the United States and Edward de Stoeckl (1804–1892) for the Russian Empire. It was ratified by the US Senate in a special session that opened the Fortieth Congress. Seward served as secretary of state under both presidents Lincoln and Johnson; previously, he had served as governor of New York and as a US senator from that state. His counterpart, de Stoeckl, was a career diplomat and served Russia in Washington from 1850 to 1869. The Senate that ratified the treaty was overwhelmingly (85 percent) Republican in composition—at a time when Republicans were the more liberal and progressive of the two major political parties.

Frederick Seward (1830–1915) was the son of William Seward and served as assistant secretary of state in the 1860s, when his father was secretary of state, and then again in the late 1870s. His reflections on the events surrounding the purchase of Alaska were included in the book *Reminiscences of a War-Time Statesman and Diplomat, 1840–1915*. In between stints in the State Department, he served in the New York State Assembly.

HISTORICAL DOCUMENT

CONVENTION between the United States of America and His Majesty the Emperor of Russia, for the Cession of the Russian Possessions in North America to the United States, Concluded at Washington, March 30, 1867; Ratification Advised by Senate, April 9, 1867; Ratified by President, May 28, 1867; Ratification Exchanged at Washington, June 20, 1867; Proclaimed, June 20, 1867.

The United States of America and His Majesty the Emperor of all the Russias, being desirous of strengthening, if possible, the good understanding which exists between them, have, for that purpose, appointed as their Plenipotentiaries, the President of the United States, William H. Seward, Secretary of State; and His Majesty the Emperor of all the Russias, the Privy Counsellor Edward de Stoeckl, his Envoy Extraordinary and Minister Plenipotentiary to the United States;

And the said Plenipotentiaries, having exchanged their full powers, which were found to be in due form, have agreed upon and signed the following articles:

Article I

His Majesty the Emperor of all the Russias, agrees to cede to the United States, by this convention, immediately upon the exchange of the ratifications thereof, all the territory and dominion now possessed by his said Majesty on the continent of America and in adjacent islands, the same being contained within the geographical limits herein set forth, to wit: The eastern limit is the line of demarcation between the Russian and the British possessions in North America, as established by the convention between Russia and Great Britain, of February 28—16, 1825, and described in Articles III and IV of said convention, in the following terms:

"III Commencing from the southernmost point of the island called Prince of Wales Island, which point lies in the parallel of 54 degrees 40 minutes north latitude, and between the 131st and 133d degree of west longitude (meridian of Greenwich), the said line shall ascend to the north along the channel called Portland Channel, as far as the point of the continent where it strikes the 56th degree of north latitude; from this last-mentioned point, the line of demarcation shall follow the summit of the mountains situated parallel to the coast, as far as the point of intersection of the 141st degree of west longitude (of the same meridian); and finally, from the said point of intersection, the said meridian line of the 141st degree, in its prolongation as far as the Frozen Ocean.

"IV With reference to the line of demarcation laid down in the preceding article, it is understood—

"1st That the island called Prince of Wales Island shall belong wholly to Russia" (now, by this cession to the United States).

"2d That whenever the summit of the mountains which extend in a direction parallel to the coast, from the 56th degree of north latitude to the point of intersection of the 141st degree of west longitude, shall prove to be at the distance of more than ten marine leagues from the ocean, the limit between the British possessions and the line of coast which is to belong to Russia as above mentioned (that is to say, the limit to the possessions ceded by this convention), shall be formed by a line parallel to the winding of the coast, and which shall never exceed the distance of ten marine leagues therefrom."

The western limit within which the territories and dominion conveyed are contained passes through a point in Behring's Straits on the parallel of sixty-five degrees thirty minutes north latitude, at its intersection by the meridian which passes midway between the islands of Krusenstern of Ignalook, and the island of Ratmanoff, or Noonarbook, and proceeds due north without limitation, into the same Frozen Ocean. The same western limit, beginning at the same initial point, proceeds thence in a course nearly southwest, through Behring's Straits and Behring's Sea, so as to pass midway between the northwest point of the island of St. Lawrence and the southeast point of Cape Choukotski, to the meridian of one hundred and seventy-two west longitude; thence, from the intersection of that meridian, in a southwesterly direction, so as to pass midway between the island of Attou and the Copper Island of the Kormandorski couplet or group, in the North Pacific Ocean, to the meridian of one hundred and ninety-three degrees west longitude, so as to include in the territory conveyed the whole of the Aleutian Islands east of that meridian.

Article II

In the cession of territory and dominion made by the preceding article, are included the right of property in all public lots and squares, vacant lands, and all public buildings, fortifications, barracks, and other edifies which are not private individual property. It is, however, understood and agreed, that the churches which have been built in the ceded territory by the Russian Government, shall remain the property of such members of the Greek Oriental Church resident in the territory as may choose to worship therein. Any Government archives, papers, and documents relative to the territory and dominion aforesaid, which may now be existing there, will be left in the possession of the agent of the United States; but an authenticated copy of such of them as may be required, will be, at all times, given by the United States to the Russian Government, or to such Russian officers or subjects as they may apply for.

Article III

The inhabitants of the ceded territory, according to their choice, reserving their natural allegiance, may return to Russia within three years; but if they should prefer to remain in the ceded territory, they, with the exception of uncivilized native tribes, shall be admitted to the enjoyment of all the rights, advantages, and immunities of citizens of the United States, and shall be maintained and protected in the free enjoyment of their liberty, property, and religion. The uncivilized tribes will be subject to such laws and regulations as the United States may from time to time adopt in regard to aboriginal tribes of that country.

Article IV

His Majesty, the Emperor of all the Russias, shall appoint, with convenient despatch, an agent or agents for the purpose of formally delivering to a similar agent or agents, appointed on behalf of the United States, the territory, dominion, property, dependencies, and appurtenances which are ceded as above, and for doing any other act which may be necessary in regard thereto. But the cession, with the right of immediate possession, is nevertheless to be deemed complete and absolute on the exchange of ratifications, without waiting for such formal delivery.

Article V

Immediately after the exchange of the ratifications of this convention, any fortifications or military posts which may be in the ceded territory shall be delivered to the agent of the United States, and any Russian troops which may be in the territory shall be withdrawn as soon as may be reasonably and conveniently practicable.

Article VI

In consideration of the cession aforesaid, the United States agree to pay at the Treasury in Washington, within ten months after the exchange of the ratifications of this convention, to the diplomatic representative or other agent of His Majesty the Emperor of all the Russias, duly authorized to receive the same, seven million two hundred thousand dollars in gold. The cession of territory and dominion herein made is hereby declared to be free and unincumbered by any reservations, privileges, franchises, grants, or possessions, by any associated companies, whether corporate or incorporate, Russian or any other; or by any parties, except merely private individual property-holders; and the cession hereby made conveys all the rights, franchises, and privileges now belonging to Russia in the said territory or dominion, and appurtenances thereto.

Article VII

When this convention shall have been duly ratified by the President, of the United States, by and with the advice and consent of the Senate, on the one part, and, on the other, by His Majesty the Emperor of all the Russias, the ratifications shall be exchanged at Washington within three months from the date thereof, or sooner if possible.

In faith whereof the respective Plenipotentiaries have signed this convention, and thereto affixed the seals of their arms.

Done at Washington, the thirtieth day of March, in the year of our Lord one thousand eight hundred and sixty-seven.

William H. Seward [L. S.]
Edward de Stoeckl [L. S.]

* * *

[Frederick Seward, son of Senator William Seward, reflects on the Alaska Purchase, circa 1916]

It was during this period [c. 1860], that Senator William Henry Seward, in a speech at St. Paul, Minnesota, made his memorable prediction:

"Standing here and looking far off into the Northwest, I see the Russian, as he busily occupies himself in establishing sea-ports and towns and fortifications, on the verge of this continent as the outposts of St Petersburg: and I can say…Go on, and build up your outposts all along the coast, up even to the Arctic Ocean, they will yet become the outposts of my own country, —monuments of the civilization of the United States in the Northwest."

Soon after came our great Civil War. There were many evidences of unfriendly feeling on the part of foreign powers. But Russia remained a constant friend. Unequivocal good wishes for the maintenance and restoration of the Union were expressed by the Emperor Alexander II, and his prime minister, Prince Gortschakoff, and their diplomatic agents. As a manifestation of national amity two fleets were sent over, one anchoring at San Francisco, and the other visiting Washington and New York, where exchange of hospitalities marked the entente cordiale, between the governments.

Senator Seward had now become Secretary of State.

One of the lessons which the war had forcibly impressed upon him was our lack of naval outposts in the Caribbean Sea and the North Pacific Ocean. The cordial relations existing with Russia enabled him to at once open informal discussion of the subject with Mr. Stoecki, the Russian Minister. He found that Russia would in no case allow her American possessions to pass into the hands of any European power. But the United States always had been, and probably always would be a friend. Russian America was a remote province, not easily defensible, and not likely to be soon developed. Under American control it would develop more rapidly and be more easily defended. To Russia, instead of a source of danger, it might become a safeguard. To the United States it would give a foothold for commercial and naval operations, accessible from the Pacific States.

Seward and Gortschakoff were not long in arriving at an agreement upon a subject which instead of embarrassing with conflicting interests, presented some mutual advantages. After the graver question of national ownership came the minor one of pecuniary cost. The measure of the value of land to an individual owner, is the amount of yearly income it can be made to produce. But national domain gives prestige, power and safety to the state, and so is not easily to be measured by dollars and cents. Millions cannot purchase these, nor compensate for their loss. However, it was necessary to fix upon a definite sum, to be named in the treaty,—not so small as to belittle the transaction in the public eye, nor so large as to deprive it of its real character as an act of friendship on the part of Russia toward the United States. Neither side was especially tenacious about the amount. The previous treaties for the acquisition of territory from France, Spain and Mexico seemed to afford an index for valuation. The Russians thought $10,000,000 would be a reasonable amount. Seward proposed $5,000,000. Dividing the difference made it $7,500,000. Then at Seward's suggestion, the half million was thrown off, but the territory was still subject to some franchises and privileges of the Russian Fur Company. Seward insisted that these should be extinguished by the Russian Government before the transfer, and was willing that $200,000 should be added on that account to the $7,000,000. At this valuation of $7,200,000 the bargain could be deemed satisfactory, even from the stand point of an individual fisherman, miner, or woodcutter, for the timber, mines, furs and fisheries would easily yield the annual interest on that sum.

On the evening of Friday, March 29th, Seward was playing whist in his parlor with some of his family, when the Russian Minister was announced.

"I have a dispatch, Mr. Seward, from my government, by cable. The Emperor gives his consent to the cession. Tomorrow, if you like, I will come to the Department and we can enter upon the treaty."

Seward, with a smile of satisfaction pushed away the whist table, saying:

"Why wait till tomorrow, Mr. Stoeckl? Let us make the treaty tonight."

"But your Department is closed. You have no clerks, and my secretaries are scattered about the town," said Stoeckl.

"Never mind that," responded Seward. "If you can muster your legation together before midnight, you will find me awaiting you at the Department, which will be open and ready for business."

In less than two hours afterward light was streaming out of the windows of the Department of State and apparently business was going on as at midday. By four o'clock on Saturday morning, the treaty was engrossed, signed, sealed and ready for transmission by the President to the Senate. There was need of this haste, in order that it might be acted upon before the end of the session, now near at hand.

I was then the Assistant Secretary of State. To me had been assigned the duty of finding Mr. [Charles] Sumner, the Chairman of the Committee of the Senate Committee on Foreign Relations, to inform him of the negotiations in progress, and to urge his advocacy of the treaty in the Senate…

On the following morning, while the Senate was considering its favorite theme of administrative delinquencies the Sergeant-at-Arms announced: "A message from the President of the United States." Glances were significantly exchanged, with the muttered remark, "Another veto!"—Great was the surprise in the Chamber, when the Secretary read, "A Treaty for the cession of Russian America."—Nor was the surprise lessened, when the Chairman of Foreign Relations, a leading opponent of the President, rose, to move favorable action.

His remarks showed easy familiarity with the subject, and that he was prepared to give reasons for the speedy approval of the treaty.

The debate which followed in the Senate was animated and earnest, but in the end the treaty was confirmed. But the purchase was not consummated without a storm of raillery in conversation and ridicule in the press. Russian America was declared to be, "a barren, worthless, God-forsaken region, whose only products were ice bergs and polar bears." It was said that the ground was frozen six feet deep and the streams were glaciers. "Walrussia" was suggested as a name for it, if it deserved to have any. Vegetation was said to be limited to mosses, and no useful animals could live there. There might be some few wretched fish, only fit for wretched Esquimaux to eat. But nothing could be raised there. Seven millions of good money were going to be wasted in buying it. Many more millions would have to be spent in holding and defending it,—for it was remote, inhospitable, and inaccessible. It was "Seward's Folly." It was "Johnson's Polar Bear Garden." It was "an egregious blunder, a bad bargain, palmed off on a silly Administration by the shrewd Russians"…

Most of these jeers and flings were from those who disliked the President and blamed Seward for remaining in his Cabinet. Perhaps unwillingness to believe that anything wise or right could be done by "Andy Johnson's Administration," was the real reason for the wrath visited upon the unoffending Territory. The feeling of hostility to the purchase was so strong that the House of Representatives would not take action toward accepting the territory or appropriate any money to pay for it.

The Russian Government courteously waived any demand for immediate payment, and signified readiness to make the final transfer whenever the United States might desire. Accordingly, commissioners were appointed, who proceeded to Sitka. On a bright day in August, 1867, with brief but impressive ceremonies, amid salutes from the Russian and American naval vessels, the American flag was raised over the new territory to be thenceforth known as "Alaska."

It was not until the 27th of July in the following year that the act making appropriation to pay for Alaska was finally passed and approved—the Chairman of the Foreign Affairs Committee of the House, Gen. Banks, being its effective advocate. On the next day the Secretary of State made his requisition upon the Treasury for $7,200,000 to be paid to the Russian Government.

The United States, at first, merely garrisoned the forts at Wrangell, Tongass and Sitka, with small detachments of troops. The Russian inhabitants generally remained, but they were few. The Indians were peaceable and friendly in the neighborhood of the forts, though sometimes warlike in the remoter regions. A shrewd old Indian chief was one day watching the soldiers drilling. He said to the commander: "What for you work your men on land with guns? Why you no work them on water with canoes?" It was a valuable suggestion. As the Indians lived principally on fish and marine animals, their villages were all on the shores of bays, sounds and rivers. Armed vessels, patrolling the waters could easily control them, while soldiers cooped up in garrison or struggling through forests would be useless. When this became understood at Washington, naval vessels and revenue cutters were ordered to Alaskan waters, and rendered good service there…

Alaska was left for some years under the supervision of the military and naval and revenue officers of the government—their chief duties being, to keep the peace, arrest criminals, collect the revenue and prevent smuggling, especially of illicit liquors and firearms.—Meanwhile, fur traders and explorers continued to go there in increasing numbers, but emigrants generally were deterred from going to a region where the settler could not get a title to house or land, and could not feel assured of adequate protection or redress at law. Congress was engrossed by other matters, and so neglected the remote province, which the general public seemed to regard with indifference,—for the old notion of its being all bleak and barren still had hold of the popular imagination.

Yet there were sagacious and enterprising business men, especially on the Pacific Coast, who perceived that there were potentialities of wealth in Alaska. They availed themselves of the opportunities and organized companies for seal fishing, fur trading, salmon canning and quartz mining, —most of which succeeded beyond expectation.

But most important and most beneficent of all was the work done by the missionaries and school teachers. Various denominations established missions, churches and schools at widely separated points. The Presbyterians took the lead, but were soon followed by others. Wisely devoting their chief attention to the education of the native children, they soon wrought a marvellous transformation. Laying aside the habits and ideas of savage life, these pupils began to acquire those of educated American citizens. The government at Washington next took part in the good work, and Congress made an appropriation for schools, that were placed under the supervision of the Bureau of Education. Under the judicious direction of Dr. Sheldon Jackson and others, instruction was given not merely in school books but in useful trades and handicrafts, enabling the pupils to become at once civilized and self supporting.

It was a surprise to the Eastern public, when they were informed, a few years since, that the neglected territory was already paying into the national treasury more than it had cost, and that its productions and revenue were yearly increasing. Within another decade, the explorers, miners and prospectors began to report their discoveries of gold, silver, copper and coal in apparently inexhaustible supply. Alaska commenced repaying its cost price over and over again, each year,—so that now, in return for our seven millions, we are likely to have seventy times seven.

During the last year of Seward's life [1872] he was visited at Auburn by Frank Carpenter, who painted the historic picture of "The Emancipation Proclamation." The artist asked him:

"Governor Seward, which of your public acts do you think will live longest in the memory of the American People?" Seward replied, "The purchase of Alaska. But," he added, "it will take another generation to find it out."

GLOSSARY

entente cordiale: friendship between nations, but not a formal treaty

Frozen Ocean: the Arctic Ocean

plenipotentiary: a diplomat with power to represent all aspects of a government

Document Analysis

The acquisition of Alaska by the United States, was an important step in the development of the nation and in its relations with European powers. The official treaty outlined a clear process for the transition of power and illustrated the ease of friendly nations working together. The treaty, as well as the memoir, demonstrate some of the differences in nineteenth-century diplomacy versus that of the twenty-first century. Two men in 1867 could sit in an office and draw up a major agreement without outside interference or assistance. The memoir also demonstrates the vision that William Seward had for the nation, as well as his understanding of the American political system. From the time of the Klondike gold rush (1896–99), most have accepted the purchase as having been a good economic investment, quite beside the military and other civilian values the territory has had for the United States down through the decades.

While the memoir only mentions the highpoints in the process of negotiations, it can easily be seen that the talks flowed very smoothly. Although not formal allies, Russia and the United States had been on good terms since America's independence. With the common goal of limiting the power of Western European nations, the two had worked peacefully together, even when there had been territorial competition between the nations over the West Coast of North America. The terms used to describe the boundaries of Alaska were taken from previous treaties, to clearly show that Russia would have no territorial claims in North America. The ease of arriving at a common figure of $7 million for the territory was facilitated by the fact that, while asking for $10 million, the Russian minister had actually been instructed to get no less than $5 million for the sale. Seward's decision to work through the night to prepare the final text suggests a somewhat unusual way of doing business, but it reflects his understanding regarding the Congressional schedule and the need to get the treaty completed and ratified quickly.

Although Russia might have been seen as a second-tier European nation, having lost the Crimean War ten years earlier, the fact that the United States and Russia could negotiate as equals helped reestablish America's position in Europe. The American Civil War had caused many in Europe to question America's viability, but this latest diplomatic undertaking, two years after the end of the war, put the European nations on notice that things in the Western Hemisphere were back to normal. Thus, the purchase of Alaska not only helped solidify American's position in the Pacific, it also indicated that the United States was once again looking outward.

Much of the memoir has to do with American politics. The fact that the secretary of state was given a free hand to negotiate with Russia was unusual. Placing the document before the Senate less than twelve hours after its completion is something that is unheard of in the present era. The Sewards' understanding of who needed to be convinced prior to taking it to the Senate and their ability to do so quickly was a key to the treaty's ratification. Also, although appropriating the money that was required represented a longer process, the Sewards' ability to get that done under an unpopular president indicates their prowess regarding the political system in which they worked. They seem to have understood the significance of the Alaska acquisition to a much greater degree than most, not just in economic terms but in terms of the possibilities it offered to the United States.

Essential Themes

The treaty transferring Alaska to the United States was clear in its intent, and the eastern border of Alaska was the same as that outlined in the 1825 Anglo-Russian Convention. Exactly how to measure the line determined by the "summit of the mountains" parallel to the coast, however, was somewhat ambiguous, and the exact line was only clarified by arbitration between the Americans and British in 1903. The southernmost point in Alaska had been settled by the 1825 Anglo-Russian Convention, and the 1824 Russo-American Treaty. The exclusion of the "uncivilized native tribes" from any protections regarding their civil liberties and their exclusion from automatic American citizenship reflects the era in which the treaty was written. Just as Russia had not included native peoples as citizens in its empire, so too in this case would they be turned over to the mercies of the American government. They were included in the sale, rather, as part of the "appurtenances" conveyed to the United States. The work to "civilize" the Native inhabitants was seen by Frederick Seward as a major accomplishment of the early decades, although many today might see things differently. As the territory increasingly became a military district, the movement of people into Alaska from the states and territories south of Canada was very slow. The types of military conflicts experienced elsewhere in the West—i.e., wars between Native Americans and Euroamerican settlers—did not occur in the case of Alaska.

The fact that William Seward so eagerly entered into negotiations for the purchase of Alaska illustrates that he regarded the territory as important not only militarily but economically and in other respects as well. His observation that this act was his greatest accomplishment says much, particularly since he had worked hard during the Civil War to keep the British and French from aligning themselves with the Confederates and, after the war, had pressured Napoleon III into leaving Mexico. If any of these other endeavors had turned out differently, the United States might have had to forge a different path to achieve its goals. Seward's willingness to work with an unpopular president and with a sluggish Congress showed his determination to help the nation move toward the goals he had set for it: to become the preeminent nation in the world. For him and for others, the purchase of Alaska was a major step toward that goal.

—*Donald A. Watt, PhD*

Bibliography and Additional Reading

Office of the Historian. *"Biographies of the Secretaries of State: William Henry Seward."* U.S. Department of State, n.d. Web. 13 Oct. 2014.

Manaev, Georgy. *"Why Did Russia Sell Alaska to the United States?"* Russia Beyond the Headlines. Rossiyskaya Gazeta, 20 Apr. 2014. Web. 13 Oct. 2014.

Seward, Frederick W. *Reminiscences of a War-Time Statesman and Diplomat 1830–1915.* New York: Putnam's Sons, 1916. Print.

Stahr, Walter. Seward: *Lincoln's Indispensable Man.* Boston: Simon & Schuster, 2012. Print.

"Treaty with Russia for the Purchase of Alaska." Web Guides: Primary Documents in American History. Library of Congress, 2012. Web. 13 Oct. 2014.

■ From *Canyons of the Colorado*

Date: 1869 (published 1895)
Author: John Wesley Powell
Genre: journal

Summary Overview

John Wesley Powell, a professor of geology, was fascinated by the system of rivers that flow into the Colorado River, as well as the Colorado itself. Just two years into his teaching career, he traveled to Wyoming to begin the first in a series of exploratory river trips, with the most famous being the second one in which he and his team successfully floated through the Grand Canyon. This document, published more than twenty-years after that famous second journey, contained excerpts from the journals he kept during the first two expeditions. These passages from *Canyons of the Colorado* are from the book's preface and fifth chapter, which focused on the first leg of the journey, from the city of Green River, Wyoming, to the Flaming Gorge canyon. As can be seen from the introductory passage, there had been many misconceptions about Powell's explorations, so he published material from his journals to provide an accurate account of the expedition and its scientific findings.

Defining Moment

When the 1890 census was compiled, the Census Bureau declared that the American frontier no longer existed. The settlement of the West, while not as dense as settlement east of the Mississippi River, had created a region throughout which people of Euroamerican descent could now be found. While the doctrine of Manifest Destiny and overly optimistic reports about the resources of the West had lured people across the continent to bring "order" to the wilderness (or so it was thought), many people felt a sense of loss as the wilderness areas continued to shrink. The western forests were the focus of much of the work to conserve wilderness areas, including the creation of Yosemite and Sequoia National Parks and the passing of the Forest Reserve Act (the predecessor to the creation of the National Forests). Under this act, the Grand Canyon was designated a forest reserve in 1893, reigniting interest

in the land and the river. Other pivotal leaders of the conservation movement were publishing well-received books on their earlier expeditions into the wilderness. Having recently retired from the United States Geological Survey, John Wesley Powell had the time to create a new edition of his travel journals, in what he called "popular form," with the addition of illustrations based on photographs, as well as some photographs from the 1871–72 trip.

Accounts of this trip had previously been published in 1875, as alluded to in the text, in the form of four magazine articles and then a book. However, Powell had never taken the time to create a full picture of not just what he and his associates had experienced, but also of the Native American peoples they encountered and the geological formations that had created these scenic wonders. The general public was eager to vicariously experience what was seen as the heroic actions of those who had challenged the wilderness in previous decades. Powell's journey into the unknown reaches of the Colorado River and the Grand Canyon more than fulfilled the general population's desires. In addition, over the prior few years, several individuals had begun developing tourist facilities on the south rim of the canyon, increasing the desire to learn about it for those considering travel to what was then a remote area. Thus, the time was right both for Powell to share his experiences and views, and for the public to receive them.

Author Biography

John Wesley Powell (1834–1902) was born in New York and died in Maine. However, the work for which he was best known was in the western United States on the Colorado River and its tributaries. His family ended up in Illinois, from where he undertook several trips on the Mississippi and its tributaries. After studying the natural sciences in college, he served in the Civil War, where he lost his right arm. Afterwards, he served as a geology professor at Illinois Wesleyan, the Illinois Normal School, and became the head of the US Geological Survey (USGS) from 1881 to 1894. He was the director of the Bureau of American Ethnology (BAE) at the Smithsonian Institution until his death. While he made great contributions to science and general knowledge by his transformation of the USGS and as founder of the BAE, his best known exploits were his exploratory trips down the Green and Colorado Rivers between 1867 and 1872.

HISTORICAL DOCUMENT

PREFACE.

On my return from the first exploration of the canyons of the Colorado, I found that our journey had been the theme of much newspaper writing. A story of disaster had been circulated, with many particulars of hardship and tragedy, so that it was currently believed throughout the United States that all the members of the party were lost save one. A good friend of mine had gathered a great number of obituary notices, and it was interesting and rather flattering to me to discover the high esteem in which I had been held by the people of the United States. In my supposed death I had attained to a glory which I fear my continued life has not fully vindicated.

The exploration was not made for adventure, but purely for scientific purposes, geographic and geologic, and I had no intention of writing an account of it, but only of recording the scientific results. Immediately on my return I was interviewed a number of times, and these interviews were published in the daily press; and here I supposed all interest in the exploration ended. But in 1874 the editors of *Scribner's Monthly* requested me to publish a popular account of the Colorado exploration in that journal. To this I acceded and prepared four short articles, which were elaborately illustrated from photographs in my possession.

In the same year—1874—at the instance of Professor Henry of the Smithsonian Institution, I was called before an appropriations committee of the House of Representatives to explain certain estimates made by the Professor for funds to continue scientific work which had been in progress from the date of the original exploration. Mr. Garfield was chairman of the committee, and after listening to my account of the progress of the geographic and geologic work, he asked me why no history of the original exploration of the canyons had been published. I informed him that I had no interest in that work

as an adventure, but was interested only in the scientific results, and that these results had in part been published and in part were in course of publication.

Thereupon Mr. Garfield, in a pleasant manner, insisted that the history of the exploration should be published by the government, and that I must understand that my scientific work would be continued by additional appropriations only upon my promise that I would publish an account of the exploration. I made the promise, and the task was immediately undertaken.

My daily journal had been kept on long and narrow strips of brown paper, which were gathered into little volumes that were bound in sole leather in camp as they were completed. After some deliberation I decided to publish this journal, with only such emendations and corrections as its hasty writing in camp necessitated. It chanced that the journal was written in the present tense, so that the first account of my trip appeared in that tense. The journal thus published was not a lengthy paper, constituting but a part of a report entitled "*Exploration of the Colorado River of the West and its Tributaries. Explored in 1869, 1870, 1871, and 1872, under the direction of the Secretary of the Smithsonian Institution.*" The other papers published with it relate to the geography, geology, and natural history of the country. And here again I supposed all account of the exploration ended. But from that time until the present I have received many letters urging that a popular account of the exploration and a description of that wonderful land should be published by me. This call has been voiced occasionally in the daily press and sometimes in the magazines, until at last I have concluded to publish a fuller account in popular form. In doing this I have revised and enlarged the original journal of exploration, and have added several new chapters descriptive of the region and of the people who inhabit it.

Realizing the difficulty of painting in word colors a land so strange, so wonderful, and so vast in its features, in the weakness of my descriptive powers I have sought refuge in graphic illustration, and for this purpose have gathered from the magazines and from various scientific reports an abundance of material. All of this illustrative material originated in my work, but it has already been used elsewhere.

Many years have passed since the exploration, and those who were boys with me in the enterprise are—ah, most of them are dead, and the living are gray with age. Their bronzed, hardy, brave faces come before me as they appeared in the vigor of life; their lithe but powerful forms seem to move around me; and the memory of the men and their heroic deeds, the men and their generous acts, overwhelms me with a joy that seems almost a grief, for it starts a fountain of tears. I was a maimed man; my right arm was gone; and these brave men, these good men, never forgot it. In every danger my safety was their first care, and in every waking hour some kind service was rendered me, and they transfigured my misfortune into a boon....

CHAPTER V.
FROM GREEN RIVER CITY TO FLAMING GORGE.

In the summer of 1867, with a small party of naturalists, students, and amateurs like myself, I visited the mountain region of Colorado Territory. While in Middle Park I explored a little canyon through which the Grand River runs, immediately below the now well-known watering place, Middle Park Hot Springs. Later in the fall I passed through Cedar Canyon, the gorge by which the Grand leaves the park. A result of the summer's study was to kindle a desire to explore the canyons of the Grand, Green, and Colorado rivers, and the next summer I organized an expedition with the intention of penetrating still farther into that canyon country.

As soon as the snows were melted, so that the main range could be crossed, I went over into Middle Park, and proceeded thence down the Grand to the head of Cedar Canyon, then across the Park Range by Gore's Pass, and in October found myself and party encamped on the White River, about 120 miles above its mouth. At that point I built cabins and established winter quarters, intending to occupy the cold season, as far as possible, in exploring the adjacent country. The winter of 1868–69

proved favorable to my purposes, and several excursions were made, southward to the Grand, down the White to the Green, northward to the Yampa, and around the Uinta Mountains. During these several excursions I seized every opportunity to study the canyons through which these upper streams run, and while thus engaged formed plans for the exploration of the canyons of the Colorado. Since that time I have been engaged in executing these plans, sometimes employed in the field, sometimes in the office. Begun originally as an exploration, the work was finally developed into a survey, embracing the geography, geology, ethnography, and natural history of the country, and a number of gentlemen have, from time to time, assisted me in the work.

Early in the spring of 1869 a party was organized for the exploration of the canyons. Boats were built in Chicago and transported by rail to the point where the Union Pacific Railroad crosses the Green River. With these we were to descend the Green to the Colorado, and the Colorado down to the foot of the Grand Canyon.

May 24, 1869.
—The good people of Green River City turn out to see us start. We raise our little flag, push the boats from shore, and the swift current carries us down.

Our boats are four in number. Three are built of oak; stanch and firm; double-ribbed, with double stem and stern posts, and further strengthened by bulkheads, dividing each into three compartments. Two of these, the fore and aft, are decked, forming water-tight cabins. It is expected these will buoy the boats should the waves roll over them in rough water. The fourth boat is made of pine, very light, but 16 feet in length, with a sharp cutwater, and every way built for fast rowing, and divided into compartments as the others. The little vessels are 21 feet long, and, taking out the cargoes, can be carried by four men.

We take with us rations deemed sufficient to last ten months, for we expect, when winter comes on and the river is filled with ice, to lie over at some point until spring arrives; and so we take with us abundant supplies of clothing, likewise. We have also a large quantity of ammunition and two or three dozen traps. For the purpose of building cabins, repairing boats, and meeting other exigencies, we are supplied with axes, hammers, saws, augers, and other tools, and a quantity of nails and screws. For scientific work, we have two sextants, four chronometers, a number of barometers, thermometers, compasses, and other instruments.

The flour is divided into three equal parts; the meat, and all other articles of our rations, in the same way. Each of the larger boats has an axe, hammer, saw, auger, and other tools, so that all are loaded alike. We distribute the cargoes in this way that we may not be entirely destitute of some important article should any one of the boats be lost. In the small boat we pack a part of the scientific instruments, three guns, and three small bundles of clothing, only; and in this I proceed in advance to explore the channel....

Our boats are heavily loaded, and only with the utmost care is it possible to float in the rough river without shipping water. A mile or two below town we run on a sandbar. The men jump into the stream and thus lighten the vessels, so that they drift over, and on we go.

In trying to avoid a rock an oar is broken on one of the boats, and, thus crippled, she strikes. The current is swift and she is sent reeling and rocking into the eddy. In the confusion two other oars are lost overboard, and the men seem quite discomfited, much to the amusement of the other members of the party. Catching the oars and starting again, the boats are once more borne down the stream, until we land at a small cottonwood grove on the bank and camp for noon.

During the afternoon we run down to a point where the river sweeps the foot of an overhanging cliff, and here we camp for the night. The sun is yet two hours high, so I climb the cliffs and walk back among the strangely carved rocks of the Green River bad lands. These are sandstones and shales, gray and buff, red and brown, blue and black strata in many alternations, lying nearly horizontal, and almost without soil and vegetation. They are very friable, and the rain and streams have carved them into quaint shapes. Barren desolation is stretched before me; and yet there is a beauty in the scene. The fantastic carvings, imitating architectural forms and suggesting rude but weird statuary, with the bright and varied colors of the rocks, conspire to make a scene such as the dweller in verdure-clad hills can scarcely appreciate.

Standing on a high point, I can look off in every direction over a vast landscape, with salient rocks and cliffs glittering in the evening sun. Dark shadows are settling in the valleys and gulches, and the heights are made higher and the depths deeper by the glamour and witchery of light and shade. Away to the south the Uinta Mountains stretch in a long line,—high peaks thrust into the sky, and snow fields glittering like lakes of molten silver, and pine forests in somber green, and rosy clouds playing around the borders of huge, black masses; and heights and clouds and mountains and snow fields and forests and rock-lands are blended into one grand view. Now the sun goes down, and I return to camp.

May 25.
—We start early this morning and run along at a good rate until about nine o'clock, when we are brought up on a gravelly bar. All jump out and help the boats over by main strength. Then a rain comes on, and river and clouds conspire to give us a thorough drenching. Wet, chilled, and tired to exhaustion, we stop at a cottonwood grove on the bank, build a huge fire, make a cup of coffee, and are soon refreshed and quite merry. When the clouds "get out of our sunshine" we start again. A few miles farther down a flock of mountain sheep are seen on a cliff to the right. The boats are quietly tied up and three or four men go after them. In the course of two or three hours they return. The cook has been successful in bringing down a fat lamb. The unsuccessful hunters taunt him with finding it dead; but it is soon dressed, cooked, and eaten, and makes a fine four o'clock dinner.

"All aboard," and down the river for another dozen miles. On the way we pass the mouth of Black's Fork, a dirty little stream that seems somewhat swollen. Just below its mouth we land and camp.

May 26.
—To-day we pass several curiously shaped buttes, standing between the west bank of the river and the high bluffs beyond. These buttes are outliers of the same beds of rocks as are exposed on the faces of the bluffs,—thinly laminated shales and sandstones of many colors, standing above in vertical cliffs and buttressed below with a water-carved talus; some of them attain an altitude of nearly a thousand feet above the level of the river.

We glide quietly down the placid stream past the carved cliffs of the "mauvaises terres," now and then obtaining glimpses of distant mountains. Occasionally, deer are started from the glades among the willows; and several wild geese, after a chase through the water, are shot. After dinner we pass through a short and narrow canyon into a broad valley; from this, long, lateral valleys stretch back on either side as far as the eye can reach.

Two or three miles below, Henry's Fork enters from the right. We land a short distance above the junction, where a "cache" of instruments and rations was made several months ago in a cave at the foot of the cliff, a distance back from the river. Here they were safe from the elements and wild beasts, but not from man. Some anxiety is felt, as we have learned that a party of Indians have been camped near the place for several weeks. Our fears are soon allayed, for we find the "cache" undisturbed. Our chronometer wheels have not been taken for hair ornaments, our barometer tubes for beads, or the sextant thrown into the river as "bad medicine," as had been predicted. Taking up our "cache," we pass down to the foot of the Uinta Mountains and in a cold storm go into camp.

The river is running to the south; the mountains have an easterly and westerly trend directly athwart its course, yet it glides on in a quiet way as if it thought a mountain range no formidable obstruction. It enters the range by a flaring, brilliant red gorge, that may be seen from the north a score of miles away. The great mass of the mountain ridge through which the gorge is cut is composed of bright vermilion rocks; but they are surmounted by broad bands of mottled buff and gray, and these bands come down with a gentle curve to the water's edge on the nearer slope of the mountain.

This is the head of the first of the canyons we are about to explore—an introductory one to a series made by the river through this range. We name it Flaming Gorge. The cliffs, or walls, we find on measurement to be about 1,200 feet high.

GLOSSARY

Grand River: the name used at that time for the section of the Colorado River north (upstream), from where it joins with the Green River in Utah

mauvaises terres: badlands

talus: loose rocks at the base of a cliff

Document Analysis

Powell's preface is basically an explanation of why the journey had been made and why previous editions of his journal had been published in the forms in which they were. Powell also gives thanks to those who had gone with him and for the experience. In the passage from the fifth chapter, he records the initial days of the journey. This gives an indication of the difficulty of river travel as well as the concerns that might have affected his careful planning. In this passage, he also demonstrates his emphasis on keeping scientifically accurate records. However, in reading the full text, it can be seen that these first few days were tame compared with some that were yet to come.

Dedicating his book to the other nine on the 1869 expedition, Powell closes the preface by indicating the high esteem in which he held the others. Although not all of them completed the journey, Powell knew that each was important. Although his focus on scientific inquiry, rather than completing the journey as quickly as possible, did cause conflict with many of the others, it was the scientific aspect of the expedition which made such a valuable contribution to filling in one of the last gaps on the maps of the western United States. The preface also indicates why the book needed to be changed from past editions, since those were done quickly to recoup the finances he had put toward the effort or to assure funding for future research. By adding the illustrations and photographs, Powell hoped to make up for the "weakness" of his "descriptive powers." In the full text, there are more than 225 illustrations, making this a luxurious book for its day.

The material from the fifth chapter describes the preparations he had made, a shorter expedition on the

Green River two years previously, some land exploration he had done in the months prior to May 1869, and the placement of supplies. The specially ordered boats, fully described in the opening section of the first day, suggest the care with which Powell prepared for the expedition. In his later years, Powell was known as a consummate administrator, and this was reflected in his preparations. Many of the supplies, enumerated in this section, would not have been taken by other explorers, but Powell wanted to ensure success. However, also differing from other expedition leaders, Powell did not carry a gun.

The sturdiness of the boats is illustrated by the accident the first day out, when one of them struck a rock and sustained no damage except a broken oar. As implied by his previous description of the boats, this type of incident was something he expected to happen quite often. Stopping early the first evening not only assured their safety, but also allowed time for his research. Even though he had previously had been on this part of the river, for Powell there was always more to learn and new things to see and experience. The richness of his language belies his claim that he did not have the literary skill to do the terrain justice.

The unpleasantness of the second day, followed by the beauty of the third, set the pattern of what was to follow. Over the length of the journey, the weather could not be depended upon to be beautiful every day, but the beauty and unique formation of the rocks were always present. This was especially true as they entered what they named "Flaming Gorge," at the approach toward the northern border of Utah. Even someone as well traveled as Powell is awestruck at the sight of the beautiful cliffs. They were only three days and sixty-two miles into their journey, and already, the wonders of nature were overwhelming them.

Essential Themes

From the time he had to take charge of his family farm at age twelve, John Wesley Powell understood the need not only to plan, but also to have a vision of what direction he needed to move. Throughout this excerpt from his book, it is clear that Powell has the administrative skills necessary to be successful, and he knows how to implement them. This did not mean that everything worked perfectly, but having the proper plans helped make things work. Thus, he quickly published his journals in the 1870s, in order to secure funding for future research. (His skills also included the ability to navigate Washington politics.) He did preparatory explorations

for his major expedition, had boats constructed that could withstand the many barriers the river would present, and put equipment along the river. Planning was clearly one of his strengths.

Although he modestly said otherwise, Powell's ability to communicate through the written word was a great asset. This was necessary for him to help the reader understand the beauty and ruggedness of the area around the Green and Colorado Rivers. From the first day out, the difference between what eastern readers knew of the world and the terrain through which the Green and Colorado Rivers flowed, was clearly illustrated. In a dramatic fashion, Powell depicted the flow of the river, the rocks, and the cliffs between which they floated. His explorations after they stopped for the evening added to the scientific knowledge and also to the richness of Powell's description of the region. The entry into Flaming Gorge was the first major point of exploration for the team. The manner in which he introduces it seems to intentionally give a hint of what would lie ahead for the expedition crew and the reader.

The power of the river on which he and the others were traveling was neatly summarized by his description that "it glides on it a quiet way as if it thought a mountain range no formidable obstruction." Thus, the beauty and peacefulness of nature is set in opposition to the almost absolute power which had cut these canyons through the rocks. These first few days on the Green River reflect what would be found when they entered the main channel of the Colorado.

—*Donald A. Watt, PhD*

Bibliography and Additional Reading

deBuys, William, ed. *Seeing Things Whole: The Essential John Wesley Powell*. Washington: Island P, 2001. Print.

"Lost in the Grand Canyon," The American Experience. PBS/WGBH, 1996–2009. Web. 16 Oct. 2014.

Powell, John Wesley. *Canyons of the Colorado*. Washington, D.C.: Smithsonian Institution, 1895. Project Gutenberg, 2012. Web. 16 Oct. 2014.

Rabbitt, Mary C. *"John Wesley Powell's Exploration of the Colorado River,"* Geological Survey. Washington, D.C.: US Geological Survey, 1978 – 2006. Web. Accessed 16 October 2014.

US Geological Survey. *"John Wesley Powell: Soldier, Explorer, Scientist."* Geological Survey Information 74–24. US Geological Survey, 1976–2006. Web. 16 Oct. 2014.

■ The Establishment of Yellowstone National Park

Date: March 1, 1872
Authors: US Congress; President Ulysses S. Grant
Genre: legislation; law

Summary Overview

The document shown here is a piece of legislation that defines and explains how Yellowstone National Park, which covers nearly 3,500 square miles of northwestern Wyoming and adjacent areas of Montana and Idaho, was formed by the United States Senate and the House of Representatives. Although the text does not reveal the importance of this event, Yellowstone was the first national park in the United States, designed to protect numerous wild animal and plant species. The first paragraph, Section 1, lays out the boundaries of the park. The second paragraph, or Section 2, explains the role of the secretary of the interior and the Interior Department's control over the activities that occur inside the park boundaries. This document was signed into law by Ulysses S. Grant, the eighteenth president of the United States, on March 1, 1872. The action came to fruition thanks to the work of Ferdinand V. Hayden and the Hayden Geological Survey of 1871, which explored the area and made detailed reports of its natural wonders.

Defining Moment

Before the creation of Yellowstone National Park, the idea of a nationally protected piece of land, open for the public to enjoy at their leisure, seemed a foreign concept. While many people appreciated the beauty of many different areas, the idea that the government would pay to keep such areas pristine struck some as a waste of resources. Because of the tenacity of advocates like Ferdinand V. Hayden, however, the importance of preserving national treasures, such as Yellowstone and other parks, like California's Yosemite, became a government priority and was placed under the purview of the Department and the Interior, a governmental entity that continues to oversee national parks today. While the creation of Yellowstone as a national site was not without its problems, including a lack of funding and proper management, the importance of it and other such sites continued to grow. Sites such as Old Faith-

ful, Yellowstone's most famous geyser, continue to draw visitors from around the country and the world, showing that while problems may have existed in the beginning, the push for governmental support of national parks was an idea with lasting benefits.

On the other side, however, there was at the time local resistance to the idea of restricting development within such a large expanse. As Section 2 of the legislation states, the types of buildings that can be erected and their placement within protected lands are subject to regulation—a matter that lawmakers, Interior Department officials, and local residents had to wrestle with as the park came into being. Overall, however, the formation of this first national park set a precedent, allowing and even encouraging the formation of fifty-eight other parks in the decades to come. Many of these parks were originally protected national monuments, but Congress has increased their status over the years and extended their protection, while also allowing closely regulated access and limited resource use in some cases. While there are many beautiful areas in the United States, national parks are set apart, owing to their unique attributes. These attributes, which include natural beauty as well as geological formations of rare or exceptional character and unusual ecosystems, provide park visitors with a unique experience and encourage the public's enjoyment of these areas. Without the push to protect them, it is entirely possible that many of these areas would have ceased to exist in their natural state a long time ago.

Author Biography

The United States Congress, made up of the Senate and the House of Representatives, passed this piece of legislation, allowing it to then go to the Executive Office, where it was signed into law by President Ulysses S. Grant. Grant was the eighteenth president and the former commanding general who led the Union to victory against the Confederacy in the Civil War. Born on April 27, 1822, Grant attended the US Military Academy at West Point, fought in several wars, and played a major role in Reconstruction after the Civil War. He then served two terms as president, having been elected in 1868 and 1872.

Although not technically an author of the legislation, Ferdinand V. Hayden led scientific explorations of the region that contributed to Yellowstone's being created as the first US national park. Hayden was born in 1887 and studied natural history and medicine—serving as a surgeon in the Civil War—before taking up geological field research. He was appointed head of a US geological survey of western territories in 1867, landing at Yellowstone in 1871. With him on the Yellowstone expedition were, among others, the photographer William Henry Jackson and the painter Thomas Moran. Hayden's report on the region, along with Jackson's large-format prints and Moran's artwork, proved instrumental in convincing Congress to preserve the area for public enjoyment.

HISTORICAL DOCUMENT

AN ACT to set apart a certain tract of land lying near the headwaters of the Yellowstone River as a public park.

Be it enacted by the Senate and House of Representatives of the United States of America in Congress assembled, That the tract of land in the Territories of Montana and Wyoming, lying near the headwaters of the Yellowstone River, and described as follows, to wit, commencing at the junction of Gardiner's river with the Yellowstone river, and running east to the meridian passing ten miles to the eastward of the most eastern point of Yellowstone lake; thence south along said meridian to the parallel of latitude passing ten miles south of the most southern point of Yellowstone lake; thence west along said parallel to the meridian passing fifteen miles west of the most western point of Madison lake; thence north along said meridian to the latitude of the junction of Yellowstone and Gardiner's rivers; thence east to the place of beginning, is hereby reserved and withdrawn from settlement, occupancy, or sale under the laws of the United States, and dedicated and set apart as a public park or pleasuring-ground for the benefit and enjoyment of the people; and all persons who shall locate or settle upon or occupy the same, or any part thereof, except as hereinafter provided, shall be considered trespassers and removed therefrom.

SEC 2. That said public park shall be under the exclusive control of the Secretary of the Interior, whose duty it shall be, as soon as practicable, to make and publish such rules and regulations as he may deem necessary or proper for the care and management of the same. Such regulations shall provide for the preservation, from injury or spoliation, of all timber, mineral deposits, natural curiosities, or wonders within said park, and their retention in their natural condition. The Secretary may in his discretion, grant leases for building purposes for terms not exceeding ten years, of small parcels of ground, at such places in said park as shall require the erection of buildings for the accommodation of visitors; all of the proceeds of said leases, and all other revenues that may be derived from any source connected with said park, to be expended under his direction in the management of the same, and the construction of roads and bridle-paths therein. He shall provide against the wanton destruction of the fish and game found within said park, and against their capture or destruction for the purposes of merchandise or profit. He shall also cause all persons trespassing upon the same after the passage of this act to be removed therefrom, and generally shall be authorized to take all such measures as shall be necessary or proper to fully carry out the objects and purposes of this act.

GLOSSARY

bridle-path: a wide pathway for riding horses; a bridle is the harness placed on a horse's head

GLOSSARY CONTINUED

meridian: a circle of the earth passing through the poles and any given point on the earth's surface

pleasuring-ground: an early term for a public or national park

thence: from that place

to wit: that is to say; namely

tract: an expanse of land

wanton: deliberate and without motive or provocation

Document Analysis

The first part of the document and its second section are quite different in their purposes, although their styles both reflect the official tone and nature of government legislation. While the first section details the expanse of the park and the uses for which it is designed, the second section deals exclusively with who holds the responsibility for protecting and managing the space. An understanding of both parts is necessary to appreciate the way in which an official government charter is arranged and the language that is used in its construction.

While it might seem easier simply to state that Yellowstone National Park would cover a certain amount of miles, starting in one place and ending at another, considerable detail is needed to identify official boundaries. Because the government funds the protection and upkeep of this land, officials need specific lines of demarcation to show where responsibility starts and ends. Also, public and private lands are subject to different laws, so the specifics laid out in the first section (which is, in fact, a single sentence), are necessary. The description might seem excessively wordy, or even confusing, but for someone working with a map, this type of explanation provides a clear outline of the park.

Such dense factual and legal wording continues in the second section, but here are laid out the duties of the secretary of the interior. Basically this section gives this secretary, one of fourteen in US Cabinet members, complete control over how Yellowstone is preserved—from care of the trees and wildlife to actions taken against trespassers (including what constitutes trespassing on the land). Because national parks were created to maintain the natural beauty of the United States, as well as to make these rarities open for the public to enjoy, every aspect of their care falls to the secretary of the interior and those who work in this area in the Interior Department. The document empowers the secretary of the interior, but it is then up to those in his or her department to conserve the lands on behalf of the American public.

Essential Themes

The most important short-term effect of this legislation was, of course, the creation of the Yellowstone National Park. The bill managed to pass through the House of Representative and the Senate and be signed into law by the president. This was, moreover, a ground-breaking piece of legislation, one that also had considerable long-term impact. The longer-term result was, by means of the precedent it set, the eventual creation of numerous other national parks. If a push had not been made to find an official way to preserve lands, it is possible that some of the most beautiful places in the nation would have been destroyed in the course of accessing the natural resources they possessed. Eighteen years after the creation of Yellowstone, two other parks (Yosemite; Sequoia) were created, and then two more (Mt. Rainier; Crater Lake) after that, and so on down the line. Over the subsequent century and a half, a total of fifty-eight additional parks would follow in the footsteps of Yellowstone as places in which the public could experience the joy and the beauty of nature. Such areas are protected from mining, deforestation, overhunting, and other uses that threaten local ecology and wildlife populations.

—Anna Accettola, MA

Bibliography and Additional Reading

Magoc, Chris J. *Yellowstone: The Creation and Selling of an American Landscape, 1870–1903.* Albuquerque, NM: U of New Mexico P, 1999. Print.

Meringolo, Denise D. *Museums, Monuments, and National Parks: Toward a New Genealogy of Public History.* Amherst, MA: U of Massachusetts P, 2012. Print.

Schullery, Paul, & Lee Whittlesey. *Myth and History in the Creation of Yellowstone National Park.* Lincoln, NE: U of Nebraska P, 2003. Print.

US National Park Service. *"Yellowstone National Park." National Parks Service.* US Department of the Interior, 15 Sept. 2014. Web. 26 Sept. 2014.

■ The Extermination of the American Bison

Date: 1889
Author: William T. Hornady
Genre: article; report

Summary Overview

William Hornady was the director of the newly established National Zoological Gardens in Washington when this article was published. As a staff member of what is now the Smithsonian Institution, Hornady was assigned the task of making certain it had enough buffalo specimens. Having ascertained that there were not enough, he traveled to the western United States to secure more. There, he discovered that the tens of millions of wild buffalo had been reduced to about one thousand. The following report is an impassioned plea for the conservation of the species. In this document, the author briefly outlines parts of the known history of the buffalo, the cause of the decrease in numbers, and some initial plans for keeping the species from going extinct. This is the first formal plea for saving the North American Bison, and it was instrumental in their preservation.

Defining Moment

The wilderness of the American West had been rapidly disappearing since the end of the Civil War. The movement of people seeking new opportunities through mining, faming, or ranching; the completion of the transcontinental railroad; and the push to force the Native Americans to adopt a new way of life, all meant that much of the wilderness was being transformed to meet the needs of people in the East. While the first national park had preserved one unique location almost two decades prior to the publishing of Hornady's call to action, most of the land had been open to development. Where there were expanses of grass, people saw the opportunity for cattle to graze as well as the possibility of tilling the soil. The buffalo that roamed there were a nuisance for travelers and could be killed for their meat and hides. Thus, just as trees had been cleared for fields when people settled east of the Mississippi River, most non-Native Americans believed the buffalo needed to be cleared from the Great Plains in order that the land

could be used. A second benefit, as perceived by the American government, was that the Native Americans would lose their traditional source of food and hides, forcing them to move to the reservations and follow a more "civilized" way of life.

Thus, while the decrease in the number of North American bison had begun when the first people arrived with guns, it had rapidly declined during the 1830s and then at a much faster rate in the two decades since the Civil War. When Hornady researched the situation, he was astounded and appalled. His resulting work was the first major effort in North America, and probably the world, to save what had become a highly endangered species. Unlike some who have become interested in an environmental cause, Hornady had the position and resources to make a substantial contribution to saving the buffalo. He was able to raise public awareness regarding the issue, and he was able to use zoological resources for a captive breeding program, to help the species survive. The reprinting for the general public of what had originally been part of a much longer internal government report, meant that people were made aware that their vision of the past, with millions of buffalo roaming the plains, was not an accurate picture of the world in 1889. Although there are other more famous conservationists from this era, for the North American bison, Hornady was the person who should be credited with the survival of the species.

Author Biography

Dr. William Temple Hornady (1854–1937) was born to William Hornady, Sr. and Martha Varner Hornady in Indiana. However, his education in zoology was obtained at two schools in Iowa. He became a taxidermist, creating scientific displays for Wards National Science Foundation. After visiting Florida and the Caribbean, and then South and Southeast Asia, collecting museum specimens, he became the head taxidermist at the

United States National Museum, a part of the Smithsonian Institution. It was during this time that he traveled through the territory previously inhabited by buffalo and then wrote this document as part of the museum report. He then helped to create, within the National Museum section of the Smithsonian, what became the National Zoological Park. He was its first director in 1888, but resigned in 1890 in a dispute with his superiors. In 1896, he became the director of the Bronx Zoo, for the New York Zoological Society, where he stayed until retiring in 1926. During that time he helped form the American Bison Society and served as its president.

HISTORICAL DOCUMENT

Of all the quadrupeds that have lived upon the earth, probably no other species has ever marshaled such innumerable hosts as those of the American bison. It would have been as easy to count or to estimate the number of laves in a forest as to calculate the number of buffaloes living at any given time during the history of the species previous to 1870. Even in South Central Africa, which has always been exceedingly prolific in great herds of game, it is probable that all its quadrupeds taken together on an equal area would never have more than equaled the total number of buffalo in this country forty years ago....

Between the Rocky Mountains and the States lying along the Mississippi River on the west, from Minnesota to Louisiana, the whole country was one vast buffalo range, inhabited by millions of buffaloes. One could fill a volume with the records of plainsmen and pioneers who penetrated or crossed that vast region between 1800 and 1870, and were in turn surprised, astounded, and frequently dismayed by the tens of thousands of buffaloes they observed, avoided, or escaped from. They lived and moved as no other quadrupeds ever have, in great multitudes, like grand armies in review, covering scores of square miles at once. They were so numerous they frequently stopped boats in the rivers, threatened to overwhelm travelers on the plains, and in later years derailed locomotives and cars, until railway engineers learned by experience the wisdom of stopping their trains whenever there were buffaloes crossing the track....

No wonder that the men of the West of those days, both white and red, thought it would be impossible to exterminate such a mighty multitude. The Indians of some tribes believed that the buffaloes issued from the earth continually, and that the supply was necessarily inexhaustible. And yet, in four short years the southern herd was almost totally annihilated....

Causes of Extermination

The causes which led to the practical extinction (in a wild state, at least) of the most economically valuable wild animal that ever inhabited the American continent, are by no means obscure. It is well that we should know precisely what they were, and by the sad fate of the buffalo be warned in time against allowing similar causes to produce the same results with our elk, antelope, deer, moose, caribou, mountain sheep, mountain goat, walrus, and other animals. It will be doubly deplorable if the remorseless slaughter we have witnessed during the last twenty years carries with it no lessons for the future. A continuation of the record we have lately made as wholesome game butchers will justify posterity in dating us back with the mound-builders and cave-dwellers, when man's only known function was to slay and eat.

The primary cause of the buffalo's extermination, and the one which embraced all others, was the descent of civilization, with all its elements of destructiveness, upon the whole of the country inhabited by that animal. From the Great Slave Lake to the Rio Grande the home of the buffalo was everywhere overrun by the man with a gun; and, as has ever been the case, the wild creatures were gradually swept away, the largest and most conspicuous forms being the first to go.

The secondary causes of the extermination of the buffalo may be catalogued as follows:

(1) Man's reckless greed, his wanton destructiveness, and improvidence in not husbanding such resources as come to him from the hand of nature ready made.

(2) The total and utterly inexcusable absence of protective measures and agencies on the part of the National Government and of the Western States and Territories.

(3) The fatal preference on the part of hunters generally, both white and red, for the robe and flesh of the cow over that furnished by the bull.

(4) The phenomenal stupidity of the animals themselves, and their indifference to man.

(5) The perfection of modern breech-loading rifles and other sporting fire-arms in general. . . .

Effects of the Extermination

The buffalo supplied the Indian with food, clothing, shelter, bedding, saddles, ropes, shields, and innumerable smaller articles of use and ornament. In the United States a paternal government takes the place of the buffalo in supplying all these wants of the red man, and it costs several millions of dollars annually to accomplish the task. . . .

The Indians of what was once the buffalo country are not starving and freezing, for the reason that the United States Government supplies them regularly with beef and blankets in lieu of buffalo. Does any one imagine that the Government could not have regulated the killing of buffaloes, and thus maintained the supply, for far less money than it now costs to feed and clothe those 54,758 Indians? . . .

Preservation of the Species from Absolute Extinction

There is reason to fear that unless the United States Government takes the matter in hand and makes a special effort to prevent it, the pure-blood bison will be lost irretrievably . . .

At least eight or ten buffaloes of pure breed should be secured very soon by the Zoological Park Commission, by gift if possible, and cared for with special reference to keeping the breed absolutely pure, and keeping the herd from deteriorating and dying out through in-and-in breeding.

The total expense would be trifling in comparison with the importance of the end to be gained, and in that way we might, in a small measure, atone for our neglect of the means which would have protected the great herds from extinction. In this way, by proper management, it will be not only possible but easy to preserve fine living representatives of this important species for centuries to come...

GLOSSARY

pure-blood bison: an reference to the fact that bison can breed with cattle, resulting in animals whose genes derive from both species, making some buffalo non-pure-blood

red man: a commonly used term in the nineteenth century for Native Americans

Document Analysis

Originally written as part of the 1886–87 Annual Report of the United States National Museum, the full 178-page document was encyclopedic in its description of the history, social and economic value, extermination, and present state of the North American bison. The historical document in this article was extracted from several sections of this extensive report, and contained key facts regarding the then current status of the buffalo and proposals for public policy that would keep the species alive. Hornady's ability to have this section of the annual report made it much more widely available to the general public resulted in his ideas having a greatly increased impact. Although he understood that history could not be undone, Hornady did believe that the poor policy choices of the past should be pointed out and that better ones (for the buffalo) should be adopted for the future.

As can be seen from the various subtitles in the document, Hornady discusses the interaction between people and buffalo from the time the first European observed one in 1521. As a zoologist, he then discusses the biological aspects of the animal. Moving on to the extermination of the great herds, he writes not only about the economic reasons, but also the social. People's desire to kill hundreds of thousands of buffalo each year made Americans, in his view, no more advanced than "cave-dwellers" whose "function was to slay and eat." Obviously, as Hornady points out, the introduction of the rifle made this a much more efficient proposition. Secondarily, he blames the local and national governments for not protecting at least part of the herds. Hornady points to the facts that people's greed, in conjunction with the buffalo's lack of fear, meant that, with modern weapons, they were easy to kill.

While Hornady was aware of the desire by the American government and the western settlers to move the Native Americans onto reservations, and to transform them into copies of white Americans, he also knew the tremendous cost of this effort. In the section of the document reprinted here, Hornady mentions the millions of dollars that would be needed to support those who had previously lived off hunting buffalo. He had done a survey of the number of Native Americans living on reservations, but hailing from tribes that had once extensively hunted buffalo, to come up with the exact number of 54,758. While the conservation movement was growing at that time, yet not totally accepted, Hornady focuses on the economic costs of having almost wiped out the buffalo, rather than appealing to people's social conscience.

Toward the end of the report, Hornady does put forward proposals to help secure a future for pure-bred buffalo. His proposal for the National Zoo to acquire a small number of buffalo was only a start. To prevent inbreeding, other zoos would have to acquire buffalo as well, in addition to whatever pure-bred animals might be found elsewhere. (In the full text, he estimates that 541 buffalo existed in the United States, with about the same number in Canada.) One of the missions of the National Zoo was to help preserve animals that were on the verge of extinction, so that his proposal was not out of line. Hornady was opinionated on a number of topics, as can be seen in his report, and one of them was that the North American bison should be saved from extinction.

Essential Themes

Looking back on the interaction between people and buffalo, Hornady sees that people took the animals—and all parts of nature—for granted. While hunters knew that they were decreasing the number of buffalo in the immediate area, neither they nor the general population understood the dramatic change that had been occurring across North America. As people expanded the area they needed, or desired, to provide a living, the buffalo herds had continually shrunk. His view that people in general had "reckless greed" was the foundation for his understanding of why the buffalo had been pushed out of the way. However, Hornady strongly objected to this philosophy. He warned that this approach

to nature would lead to the disappearance not only of the buffalo, but of other large wild mammals as well. Although he was not the first conservationist, he was focused on the issue and had the means to take action to help buffalo survive. For him, the growing conservation movement was following the correct path, and his writing and his work assisted and strengthened this movement.

While supporting conservation, versus the more normal "wanton destructiveness" of humanity, Hornady had a vision for the future of the buffalo. While, obviously, this was expounded upon in greater length in the full report, the closing paragraph of what is reprinted here gives the essence of what was possible. By using human understanding to preserve nature rather than destroy it, Hornady believes, it would be "easy to preserve fine living representatives of this important species for centuries to come." Since being assigned the task of gathering buffalo specimens for the National Museum, this had become Hornady's focus in life. And in this, he was successful. In the century since his report was written, there has been a large amount of discussion regarding how best to preserve buffalo and even how to expand the species' range. The question as to whether the buffalo should be preserved has not been a part of the conversations. While not all other animal species have been as fortunate, Hornady's view, that civilization must take the needs of non-human inhabitants into consideration, has become far more mainstream than it was at the time he was writing.

—*Donald A. Watt, PhD*

Bibliography and Additional Reading

Branch, E. Douglas, J. Frank Dobie (introduction), & Andrew C. Isenberg (introduction). *The Hunting of the Buffalo.* 1929. Lincoln: U of Nebraska P, 1997. Print.

Czajka, Christopher W. *"The Descent of Civilization: The Extermination of the American Buffalo."* Frontier House. PBS, 2014. Web. 13 Oct. 2014.

Hornaday, William T. *The Extermination of the American Bison.* Washington, D.C.: Smithsonian Institution, 1889. Project Gutenberg, 2006. Web. 13 Oct. 2014.

Patent, Dorothy Hinshaw, & William Munoz. *The Buffalo and the Indians: A Shared Destiny.* Boston: Houghton Mifflin Harcourt, 2006. Print.

Features of the Proposed Yosemite National Park

Date: September, 1890
Author: John Muir
Genre: article

Summary Overview

By the end of the nineteenth century, John Muir had become a major figure in American society, representing, to many, the conservation movement. Having spent many years living in and visiting the Yosemite area, in east central California, he was convinced that it was a special area in need of preservation. With pressure increasing to open this area for widespread use, in the late 1880s Muir began pushing hard for its incorporation as a national park, as Yellowstone, in northwestern Wyoming, had previously been. After convincing the editor of *The Century* magazine to visit Yosemite, the editor understood the need for this to happen. Muir was invited to write an article for the magazine advocating the protection of Yosemite. Thus, this article was written and published in early 1890, and by the end of the year, the highlands area around the Yosemite Valley had been designated a national park. It would take another sixteen years of pressure by Muir for the federal government to take control of the valley and of the Mariposa Grove, thereby incorporating what later became the major tourist destinations into the park.

Defining Moment

With the movement of more and more people into the western part of the United States, less and less land was being left in its natural state. While most land was still undeveloped, this did not mean that logging, mining, and grazing were not extending into what had once been remote wilderness. Although the first attempt at conservation had been in 1864, when President Lincoln signed a bill giving the state of California control of the Yosemite Valley and Mariposa Grove for the preservation of these areas, in the following decades, the pressure to exploit natural resources had far surpassed the movement to conserve or preserve natural areas. However, conservation steps were taken, such as the establishment of the first national park in 1872, administered by the Army. John Muir's sojourn into the Yosemite wilderness in 1869 transformed his life and eventually the nation. He came to experience the wilderness as a religious experience. For him, it was not to be conserved; rather, it should be preserved.

Ranchers' desires for more land upon which to graze their animals resulted in their unrestricted movement onto federal land. If at any time they did violate any federal statute, enforcement was a low priority for the government. Thus, domestic sheep were grazing on the highlands around the Yosemite Valley, causing great harm to the native plants. Witnessing what was occurring, Muir felt compelled to protect this beautiful wilderness area from harm. For several years he advocated for federal protection of the region just outside what had been granted to California. Finally, in 1889, he was able to get the editor of *The Century* magazine to join the cause, resulting in this article and the creation of the national park the next year.

Once he had an appropriate forum through which to communicate his ideas to the nation, Muir was able to get quick results—as he had become a leading figure in the conservation movement. In 1871, Muir published his first article about the region. From that time forward, Muir wrote numerous articles, and by 1876, he began giving public lectures, advocating for the protection of forests, especially in and around Yosemite. His articles about the wilderness and his travels were so popular that some were used in school textbooks. With no strong opposition to the incorporation of the land into a park, Muir's push succeeded with virtually no opposition. This accomplishment, along with his writings and other accomplishments, have made Muir virtually the patron saint of the wilderness preservation movement in the United States.

Author Biography

John Muir (1838–1914) was born in Scotland, but his family moved to Wisconsin in 1849. His father was a strict conservative Christian who disapproved of Muir's interest in the world around him. He was mechanically inclined, attended the University of Wisconsin, and took science classes before moving to Canada during the Civil War. After the war, he returned to Indiana, where an accident in a saw mill injured one eye. After recovery, he walked to the Florida Keys, traveled to Cuba, then back to New York, studying the plants all along the way. In 1868, he sailed to California, and then visited what would become Yosemite National Park. He took up residence there, working as a shepherd, and studied all aspects of the area. He would later travel as far north as Alaska, but his focus was upon the Sierra Nevada Mountains, and especially the Yosemite area. From 1878 until his death, he split his time between the wilderness and Martinez, California, where he married Louisa Strentzel in 1880. His later years included writing numerous books and articles, co-founding the Sierra Club, and lobbying for the preservation of wilderness areas and the creation of national parks.

HISTORICAL DOCUMENT

The cañon begins near the lower end of the meadows and extends to the Hetch Hetchy Valley, a distance of about eighteen miles, though it will seem much longer to any one who scrambles through it. It is from 1200 to about 5000 feet deep, and is comparatively narrow, but there are several fine, roomy, park-like openings in it, and throughout its whole extent Yosemite features are displayed on a grand scale—domes, El Capitan rocks, gables, Sentinels, Royal Arches, glacier points, Cathedral Spires, etc. There is even a Half Dome among its wealth of rock forms, though less sublime and beautiful than the Yosemite Half Dome. It also contains falls and cascades innumerable. The sheer falls, except when the snow is melting in early spring, are quite small in volume as compared with those of Yosemite and Hetch Hetchy, but many of them are very beautiful, and in any other country would be regarded as great wonders. But it is the cascades or sloping falls on the main river that are the crowning glory of the cañon, and these in volume, extent, and variety surpass those of any other cañon in the Sierra. The most showy and interesting of the cascades are mostly in the upper part of the cañon, above the point where Cathedral Creek; and Hoffman Creek enter. For miles the river is one wild, exulting, on-rushing mass of snowy purple bloom, spreading over glacial waves of granite without any definite channel, and through avalanche taluses, gliding in silver plumes, dashing and foaming through huge boulder-dams, leaping high into the air in glorious wheel-like whirls, tossing from side to side, doubling, glinting, singing in glorious exuberance of mountain energy. Every one who is anything of a mountaineer should go on through the entire length of the cañon, coming out by Hetch Hetchy. There is not a dull step all the way. With wide variations it is a Yosemite Valley from end to end.

THE HETCH HETCHY VALLEY.

Most people who visit Yosemite are apt to regard it as an exceptional creation, the only valley of its kind in the world. But nothing in Nature stands alone. She is not so poor as to have only one of anything. The explorer in the Sierra and elsewhere finds many Yosemites that differ not more than one tree differs from another of the same species. They occupy the same relative positions on the mountain flanks, were formed by the same forces in the same kind of granite, and have similar sculpture, waterfalls, and vegetation. The Hetch Hetchy Valley has long been known as the Tuolumne Yosemite. It is said to have been discovered by Joseph Screech, a hunter, in 1850, a year before the discovery of the great Merced Yosemite. It lies in a northwesterly direction from Yosemite, at a distance of about twenty miles, and is easily accessible to mounted travelers by a trail that leaves the Big Oak Flat road at Bronson's Meadows, a few miles below Crane Flat. But by far the best way to it for those who have useful limbs is across the divide direct from Yosemite. Leaving the valley by Indian Cañon or Fall Cañon, you cross the dome-paved basin of Yosemite Creek, then bear to the left around the head fountains of the South Fork of the Tuolumne to the summit of the Big Tuolumne Cañon, a few miles above the head of Hetch Hetchy. Here you will find a glorious view. Immediately beneath you, at a depth of more than 4000 feet, you see a beautiful ribbon of level a ground, with a silver thread in the middle of it, and green or yellow according to the time of year. That ribbon is a strip of meadow, and the silver thread is the main Tuolumne River. The opposite wall of the cañon rises in precipices, steep and angular, or with rounded brows like those of Yosemite, and from this wall as a base extends a fine wilderness of mountains, rising dome above dome, ridge above ridge, to a group of snowy peaks on the summit of the range. Of all this sublime congregation of mountains Castle Peak is king: robed with snow and light, dipping unnumbered points and spires into the thin blue sky, it maintains amid noble companions a perfect and commanding individuality.

You will not encounter much difficulty in getting down into the cañon, for bear trails may readily be found leading from the upper feeding-grounds to the berry gardens and acorn orchards of Hetch Hetchy, and when you reach the river you have only to saunter by its side a mile or two down the cañon before you find yourself in the open valley. Looking about you, you cannot fail to discover that you are in a Yosemite valley. As the Merced flows through Yosemite, so does the Tuolumne through Hetch Hetchy. The bottom of Yosemite is about 4000 feet above sea level, the bottom of Hetch Hetchy is about 3800 feet, and in both the walls are of gray granite and rise abruptly in precipices from a level bottom, with but little debris along their bases. Furthermore it was a home and stronghold of the Tuolumne Indians, as Ahwahne was of the grizzlies. Standing boldly forward from the south wall near the lower end of the valley is the rock Kolána, the outermost of a picturesque group corresponding to the Cathedral Rocks of Yosemite, and about the same height. Facing Kolána on the north side of the valley is a rock about 1800 feet in height, which presents a bare, sheer front like El Capitan, and over its massive brow flows a stream that makes the most graceful fall I have ever seen. Its Indian name is Tu-ee-u-la-la, and no other, so far as I have heard, has yet been given it. From the brow of the cliff it makes a free descent of a thousand feet and then breaks up into ragged, foaming web of cascades among the boulders of an earthquake talus. Towards the end of summer it vanishes, because its head streams do not reach back to the lasting snows of the summits of the range, but in May and June it is indescribably lovely. The only fall that I know with which it may fairly be compared is the Bridal Veil, but it excels even that fall in peaceful, floating, swaying gracefulness. For when we attentively observe the Bridal Veil, even towards the middle of summer when its waters begin to fail, we may discover, when the winds blow aside the outer folds of spray dense comet-shaped masses shooting through the air with terrible energy; but from the top of the cliff, where the Hetch Hetchy veil first floats free, all the way to the bottom it is in perfect repose. Again, the Bridal Veil is in a shadow-haunted nook inaccessible to the main wind currents of the valley, and has to depend for many of its gestures on irregular, teasing side currents and whirls, while Tu-ee-u-la-la, being fully exposed on the open cliff, is sun drenched all day, and is ever ready to yield graceful compliance to every wind that blows. Most people unacquainted with the behavior of mountain streams fancy that when they escape the bounds of their rocky channels and launch into the air they at once lose all self-control and tumble in confusion. On the contrary, on no part of their travels do they manifest more calm self-possession. Imagine yourself in Hetch Hetchy. It is a sunny day in June, the pines sway dreamily, and you are shoulder-deep in grass and flowers. Looking across the valley through beautiful open groves you see a bare granite wall 1800 feet high rising abruptly out of the green and yellow vegetation and glowing with sunshine, and in front of it the fall, waving like a downy scarf, silver bright, burning with white sun-fire in every fiber. In coming forward to the edge of the tremendous precipice and taking flight a little hasty eagerness appears, but this is speedily hushed in divine repose. Now observe the marvelous distinctness and delicacy of the various kinds of sun-filled tissue into which the waters are woven. They fly and float and drowse down the face of that grand gray rock in so leisurely and unconfused a manner that you may examine their texture and patterns as you would a piece of embroidery held in the hand. It is a flood of singing air, water, and sunlight woven into cloth that spirits might wear.

The great Hetch Hetchy Fall, called Wa-páma by the Tuolumnes, is on the same side of the valley as the Veil, and so near it that both may be seen in one view. It is about 1800 feet in height, and seems to be nearly vertical when one is standing in front of it, though it is considerably inclined. Its location is similar to that of the Yosemite Fall, but the volume of water is much greater. No two falls could be more unlike than Wa-páma and Tu-ee-u-la-la, the one thundering and beating in a shadowy gorge, the other chanting in deep, low tones and with no other shadows about it than those of its own waters, pale-gray mostly, and violet and pink delicately graded. One whispers, "He dwells in peace," the other is the thunder of his chariot wheels in power. This noble pair are the main falls of the valley, though there are many small ones essential to the perfection of the general harmony.

The wall above Wa-páma corresponds, both in outlines and in details of sculpture, with the same relative portion of the Yosemite wall. Near the Yosemite Fall the cliff has two conspicuous benches extending in a horizontal direction 500 and 1500 feet above the valley. Two benches similarly situated, and timbered in the same way, occur on the same relative position on the Hetch Hetchy wall, and on no other portion. The upper end of Yosemite is closed by the great Half Dome, and the upper end of Hetch Hetchy is closed in the same way by a mountain rock. Both occupy angles formed by the confluence of two large glaciers that have long since vanished. In front of this head rock the river forks like the Merced in Yosemite. The right fork as you ascend is the main Tuolumne, which takes its rise in a glacier on the north side of Mount Lyell and flows through the Big Cañon. I have not traced the left fork to its highest source, but, judging from the general trend of the ridges, it must be near Castle Peak. Upon this left or North Fork there is a remarkably interesting series of cascades, five in number, ranged along a picturesque gorge, on the edges of which we may saunter safely and gain fine views of the dancing spray below. The first is a wide-spreading fan of white, crystal-covered water, half leaping half sliding over a steep polished pavement, at the foot of which it rests and sets forth clear and shining on its final flow to the main river. A short distance above the head of this cascade you discover the second, which is as impressively wild and beautiful as the first, and makes you sing with it as though you were a part of it. It is framed in deep rock walls that are colored yellow and red with lichens, and fringed on the jagged edges by live-oaks and sabine pines, and at the bottom in damp nooks you may see ferns, lilies, and azaleas.

Three or four hundred yards higher you come to the third of the choir, the largest of the five. It is formed of three smaller ones inseparably combined, which sing divinely, and make spray of the best quality for rainbows. A short distance beyond this the gorge comes to an end, and the bare stream, without any definite channel, spreads out in a thin, silvery sheet about 150 feet wide. Its waters are, throughout almost its whole extent, drawn out in overlapping folds of lace, thick sown with diamond jets and sparks that give an exceedingly rich appearance. Still advancing, you hear a deep muffled booming, and you push eagerly on through flowery thickets until the last of the five appears through the foliage. The precipice down which it thunders is fretted with projecting knobs, forming polished keys upon which the wild waters play.

The bottom of the valley is divided by a low, glacier-polished bar of granite, the lower portion being mostly meadow land, the upper dry and sandy, and planted with fine Kellogg oaks, which frequently attain a diameter of six or seven feet. On the talus slopes the pines give place to the mountain live-oak, which forms the shadiest groves in the valley and the greatest in extent. Their glossy foliage, warm yellow-green and closely pressed, makes a kind of ceiling, supported by bare gray trunks and branches gnarled and picturesque. A few specimens of the sugar pine and tamarack pine are found in the valley, also the two silver firs. The Douglas spruce and the libocedrus attain noble dimensions in certain favorable spots, and a few specimens of the interesting Torreya Californica may be found on the south side. The brier-rose occurs in large patches, with tall, spiky mints and arching grasses. On the meadows lilies, larkspurs and lupines of several species are abundant, and in some places reach above one's head. Rock-ferns of rare beauty fringe and rosette the walls from top to bottom—Pellaea densa, P. mucronata and P. Bridgesii, Cheilanthes gracillima, Allosorus, etc. Adiantum pedatum occurs in a few mossy corners that get spray from the falls. Woodwardia radicans and Asplenium felix-faemina are the tallest ferns of the valley—six feet high, some of them. The whole valley was a charming garden when I last saw it, and the huts of the Indians and a lone cabin were the only improvements.

GLOSSARY

cañon: canyon, using Spanish punctuation

Merced Yosemite: what is now known as Yosemite Valley, through which the Merced River flows

taluses: plural of talus, loose rock at the bottom of rock walls

Document Analysis

The text reprinted here is virtually the whole second half of the article written by John Muir in his proposal for the creation of a national park consisting of the region around Yosemite Valley. The proposed park would contain about 15,000 square miles, with two major valleys, the Hetch Hetchy Valley and the Yosemite Valley, sometimes referred to by Muir as the Merced Yosemite Valley. This half of the article focused on the Hetch Hetchy Valley, which was flooded by the completion of a reservoir in 1923. The two valleys paralleled each other not only in orientation, but in their physical characteristics and beauty. Thus, there are many references comparing the two valleys: their rock formations and their waterways. While there was and is a wide variety of flora and fauna within the region, Muir understood that what would draw people to a national park in Yosemite were the panoramic views of water and rock.

Beginning upstream from Hetch Hetchy, Muir describes the beauty of what is now known as the Grand Canyon of the Tuolumne River. As in Muir's day, this area is today not accessible by vehicle. The description of the formations that border the river is a virtual catalog of the formations found in Yosemite. El Capitan, Cathedral Spires, Half Dome, and others are compared to what could be found in this canyon. Having traveled extensively in the Sierra Nevada Mountains, Muir's statement that the cascades in the river in this canyon "surpass those of any other cañon in the Sierra" has great meaning.

Moving into the broader, now flooded, Hetch Hetchy Valley, Muir continues to describe the wonders of the region. The directions he gives for traveling from Yosemite to Hetch Hetchy are where the roads and trails are still located. The gray rock that created the walls along both canyons is described as the same. Standing out in both valleys were the waterfalls which poured water hundreds of feet from the hills and mountains into the valleys. Describing them in great detail, Muir hoped that the unique waterways would help gain support by those who might want to see them in the future, undisturbed by people. His poetic language regarding how he saw an ethereal quality in the Tueeulala Falls demonstrates the spiritual quality that the wilderness had for Muir. Having referred to the "divine repose" of the flowing stream, Muir ends his description by proclaiming the wonders of the falls he saw as a "flood of singing air, water, and sunlight woven into cloth that spirits might wear." For Muir—and, he hoped, for those considering the creation of the park—this was the essence of wondrous beauty. Unlike most lobbying efforts, Muir's article says nothing about the proposed legislation until the last paragraph of the full text. Having tried to share a vision of the unique features of the Yosemite and Hetch Hetchy Valleys, he hopes that they can be preserved.

Essential Themes

John Muir wanted all people to have the opportunity to experience nature as he had experienced it. This meant that the wilderness must be preserved, not just conserved. It also meant that he tried to help others experience it with the same mindset which guided him, a mindset which saw the natural world as an ethereal experience. He believed that if he were able to help others view the world as he did, then preserving the wilderness and, in this case, establishing a national park at Yosemite could be accomplished. In terms of the creation of the national park, Muir was totally successful. In terms of saving all the wilderness, especially Hetch Hetchy Valley, he was not as successful. However, Muir and others demonstrated that there was popular support for the creation of national parks and for preserving wilderness areas.

In this article, Muir spends more time describing the Tuolumne River canyons and valleys than he did the

Merced/Yosemite Valleys. Because fewer people had visited Hetch Hetchy, and thus it was less disturbed, Muir hoped that by focusing on it, a truer picture of the wilderness might be given to the readers. Even though later in the 1890s, there would be a split in the movement between those who sought to conserve (i.e., carefully manage) the wilderness areas and those, like Muir, who sought to preserve the wilderness areas, in the twentieth-century Muir became an iconic figure for people in both movements. His dedication to the wilderness, his travels throughout western North America, and his ability to communicate what he experienced has made his writings timeless for those seeking to continue his legacy. The Sierra Club is a good example of how his influence has continued to play a major role in American society. John Muir was a man who lived at a pivotal time in American history, the period when a decision had to be made whether or not to preserve what remained of the wilderness. He was not totally against the use of forest resources or ranching, but he did recognize that the unique beauty of certain areas was worth more than devastating them for a relatively small economic gain. Muir helped convince the general public, and political leaders that the wilderness was worth saving. This has inspired many people to continue his mission.

—*Donald A. Watt, PhD*

Bibliography and Additional Reading

Fox, Stephen. *American Conservation Movement: John Muir and his Legacy*. Madison: U of Wisconsin P, 1986. Print.

"The John Muir Exhibit." Sierra Club. Sierra Club, 2014. Web. 13 Oct. 2014.

Muir, John. *The Yosemite*. 1912. The Sierra Club, 2003 Web. 13 Oct. 2014.

Perrottet, Tony. *"John Muir's Yosemite,"* Smithsonian. com. Smithsonian Institution, Jul. 2008. Web. 13 Oct. 2014.

Worster, Donald. *A Passion for Nature: The Life of John Muir*. Oxford: Oxford UP, 2008. Print.

■ Letters to John Muir

Dates: April 8, 1894; May 23, 1894; October 21, 1896; December 9, 1896; December 15, 1897; February 2, 1900
Author: Gifford Pinchot
Genre: letter

Summary Overview

These letters represent some of the communications between one of the leading conservationists at the end of the nineteenth century, Gifford Pinchot, and one of the leading preservationists, John Muir. While, initially, the two worked together to protect forests from wanton destruction, they parted ways in 1897 over the policies advocated by Pinchot in his December 1897 letter: the management of forests as resources versus their preservation in a natural state. Pinchot was from the East, with social and political connections that allowed him to be a part of the nation's power structure. As such, his views were important in the development of policies for the use of federal lands. Thus, throughout these letters are references to individuals and groups with whom Pinchot interacted and through whom he was able to directly shape the emerging policy for federally-owned forests.

Defining Moment

The 1890s represent a key period in the administration of the forests owned by the United States government. American economic growth during the previous decades had been built on virtually open access to government-owned natural resources, resulting in the shrinkage of the forests. There was growing concern regarding National Forest lands. It was also a time when there was a split between those who wanted to focus on managing forests (Pinchot) and those whose focus was on preserving wilderness areas (Muir). These letters, from Pinchot to Muir, were the primary means of communication between these two environmental leaders. Although there had been a Division of Forestry within the Department of Agriculture since 1881, it was not until 1891 that protected forest reserves were authorized by Congress. Even though the forest reserves were under the Department of the Interior, it was the Division of Forestry that was charged with drawing up plans for the use of all federally owned forests.

Although virtually all of these letters were written prior to Pinchot becoming Chief of the Division of Forestry, they do contain indications of not only Pinchot's appreciation of the forest and wilderness areas, but his philosophy toward managing these resources. Thus, while he was not against using federally-owned forests to provide lumber needed by society, Pinchot did believe that there was a science to forest management. In part, it was because of his scientific approach to the forests that, in 1896–1897, Muir and Pinchot came to a parting of ways. The 1897 letter reprinted here indicates this difference, Pinchot seeking a politically expedient way to conserve some of the forests as against Muir's desire to preserve entire areas. Thus, the curt 1900 letter, when Pinchot held the title of Forester, shows a very different relationship than the friendly correspondence of six years earlier. The split between the conservation movement and the preservation movement was, by then, clear. In Pinchot's case, achieving some conservation measures through means that were virtually a politically sure thing was a far better path than gambling everything on a high-risk approach requiring the preservation of large tracts through the building of a broader political consensus. For whatever reason, the enthusiasm of the early letters faded when Pinchot had an opportunity to make real changes within the political system.

Author Biography

Gifford Pinchot (1865–1946) was born into a wealthy family in Connecticut. He graduated from Yale University, and then studied forestry in France, because no forestry program existed in the United States. (He later had his family endow a forestry program at Yale.) In 1891, he started full-time work, quickly becoming forester at the Biltmore Estate, in North Carolina, and then moving on to become Chief of the Division of Forestry in 1898. He served in this agency, working closely with President Theodore Roosevelt, as it evolved into the US Forest Service, until resigning after arguing with President William H. Taft. He continued to work in the conservation movement through the National Conservation Association. He was governor in Pennsylvania for two terms, during which he focused on the needs of the rural population and on regulating utilities. He married Cornelia Bryce later in life and had one son.

HISTORICAL DOCUMENT

New York City, April 8, 1894.

Dear Mr. Muir:

I have felt for a long time that I owed you a report of progress, and I have very often meant to write, and as often felt uncomfortable because I had not done so. It is not because I have in any degree forgotten your kindness and interest in my work, or the advice you gave me to take time to get rich. I have kept that phrase pretty constantly in mind, and have been trying to live up to it. Not with any conspicuous success, as yet, but the chances seem to be that I shall have better luck in that line in the future.

Since your letter came, a long time back, I have been going on more or less steadily with my regular work at Biltmore, a short account of which has been printed, so far as the first year is concerned. I send you a copy by this mail. Beyond that, a good deal of my time has been given to getting my old papers in order and opening an office. One new branch of work has arisen in the large arboretum which is to be made at Biltmore. The enclosed type-written circular, prepared to send to foresters in Europe, but which I hope you will accept as an urgent request for help, will give you a rough idea of what is in prospect. This is, unfortunately, one of the times when there was no chance to get rich at all, and so I had to take up the work on my very meagre preparation. It seemed likely that it would not be done unless I did it.

I had hoped to begin this summer putting your advice into practical operation by taking several months in the Sierras, studying the forest, and to follow that up with several months each year in the different government reservations, until I had an idea of what treatment each of them was best suited to. But reasons which are based on the interest of others have prevented that, and so I am to stay home and try to get a short primer of forestry ready to print. This is, I think, a useful piece of work, but not that which I would have chosen first. However, the other is only put off.

I am just starting for a month in camp in the southern Alleghenies, to study the treatment of a tract of about 150 square miles, part of it well timbered. As I must take others with me I am not going very light. It seems likely to be a pleasant trip, especially as I shall spend a good deal of time studying the reproduction of the Liriodendron, which seems likely to turn out in the end the most important timber tree of that region, as it certainly is just now. I think I am going to be able to start a friend of mine, who has been studying forestry for the last year, at work studying the reproduction and growth otherwise of the white Pine in Pa. and Mich, and the Adirondacks. He will keep at it for at least six months, and then I am to put his results into shape and get them published. I shall also make his scheme of study.

We have been having rather a curious time with the N. Y. State Forest Commission, the members of which have been desirous of letting the lumbermen into the state woods, with a merely nominal restriction, but at market prices for all logs cut. I hope the plan may be killed in the Comptroller's office.

Is there any chance of your coming East again in the near future? If so, I hope you will not fail to let me know. All my people have spoken so often of the pleasure you gave them that we do not want to miss you. And for myself, I have more than ever to talk over with you, and much advice to ask.

Very sincerely yours,
Gifford Pinchot

My father sends his best regards.

***

GIFFORD PINCHOT,
CONSULTING FORESTER,
NEW YORK.
UNITED CHARITIES BUILDING,
FOURTH AVE. AND 22D ST.

May 23rd, 1894.

Mr. John Muir,
Martinez, California.

Dear Mr. Muir:

I hope you do not mind typewritten letters. If you do please let me know and I will send you no more of them. But as it is so such easier to write this way I fall into it on all occasions. I am just up from the south, where your letter reached me, and have been in the woods for something over three weeks. In a very small way I have tried your plan of going alone, and was off for four days by myself. Except that I happened to be a little under the weather at the time, they were as pleasant days as I have ever passed in the woods, and I am only waiting for the chance to do more of the same thing. I am perfectly satisfied that I can learn more and get more out of the woods than is possible when there is any one else along, or at least any one who has not the same feeling about them that I have. While I am afraid that I shall never be able to do the amount of hard work that you have done, or get along on such slender rations, still I am going to put together a camp kit this summer that will weight not over 20 lbs. and will keep me in working order for a week or two, and then I hope to be able to get more into the life of the forest than I have ever done before.

I sent you the other day a pamphlet about the Adirondacks in the hope that you might be interested in looking it over.

Mr. Alvord has been kind enough to send me certain publications of the Sierra Club. These are Bulletins of January and June, 1893, and January, 1894, and "Articles of Association, etc.", 1892. Could you help me to get the others? I have been greatly interested in them, although I have had almost no time to look them over.

My people would all send their best regards if they knew I was writing. We have all said very often how greatly we missed your visit last fall.

Very sincerely yours,
Gifford Pinchot

* * *

N.L.W.
GIFFORD PINCHOT,
CONSULTING FORESTER,
NEW YORK.

UNITED CHARITIES BUILDING,
FOURTH AVE. AND 22D ST.

Oct. 21st, 1896

Mr. John Muir,
Martinez, Cal.

Dear Mr. Muir:

I am sending you this hasty note (typewritten at that) just to say that I find a copy of *The White Pine* was sent to you as President of the Sierra Club in San Francisco. If it does not turn up speedily please let me know and I will be very glad indeed to send you another copy. I hope your opinion of it may be somewhat more favorable than that expressed by Mr. Fernow. In spite of the kindness of your interpretation I find his letter full of rather severe things, and since I read it to-day I have been considering how to answer it most effectively. I rather think it will be necessary to do so.

All our people are well and happy and much delighted that I was fortunate enough to spend so much time with you. I have told them the story of our day and night on the edge of the Canyon, much to their interest and pleasure, and I greatly wish that I could repeat to them the stories you told me that night. The next dog I get will be named after the one in your story.

We have a meeting of the Commission on Saturday of this week, at which I suppose the policy to be pursued will be decided. I am getting ready for it now and am somewhat anxious to know just how the eat will jump. It is a rather critical time.

I must ask you to excuse this hasty letter, dictated because in the immediate rush of business this is the only way I could write you. With many thanks for all your kindness, believe me,

Very sincerely yours,

***

GIFFORD PINCHOT,
CONSULTING FORESTER,
NEW YORK.

UNITED CHARITIES BUILDING,
FOURTH AVE. AND 22D ST.

Dec. 9th, 1896

John Muir, Esq.,
Martinez, Cal.

My Dear Mr. Muir:
I am going to take the liberty of sending you another copy of my little book on the White Pine, because I want very much to have you see it, and because I am fearful else the copy which I sent you last Spring may have been lost. If the two reach you safely perhaps you can find someone else upon whom the burden of one of them may be thrown.

As Prof. Sargent may have written you, the report of the Commission will not be presented to the coming Congress but to its successor. While I had been strongly in favor of immediate action, still my own personal convenience is very materially served by this delay for it has given me a chance to get at certain work which would otherwise have been still longer delayed. I am going ahead with it now full steam.

In accordance with your advice, and also I must say, with my own inclination in the matter, I have made no answer to Mr. Fernow; After going over his article very carefully I found that an adequate answer would be so vigorous an attack on his whole conception of Forestry in this country that I did not think the result would be worth the quarrel. On the other hand, I am trying to get "square" with him by laying the foundations for two more

books, so that he will eventually have considerable new material upon which to exercise himself.

My hope for getting into the West this winter is completely gone. In fact, I am beginning to figure rather anxiously on the time which will see the end of the office work which confronts me now. I am laying plans for another trip to the West, beginning, if it is in any way possible, about the middle of May. But whether any such luck will befall me is, I am afraid, very doubtful, for a good many reasons. If it does I will, of course, write you as soon as I know myself, and this time I shall most earnestly hope to be able to accompany you on some longer trip than was my fortune last summer. You know that my appetite for being in the woods with you has grown vastly by what it fed on.

Both my father and mother would send their best regards if they knew I was writing. They were both extremely pleased at your remembrance of them.

Very sincerely yours,

***

DEPARTMENT OF THE INTERIOR,
WASHINGTON, D.C.

Dec. 15, 1897

Mr. John Muir,
Martinez, California.

Dear Mr. Muir:
The work in the field is at an end for the present season, and I am now busy preparing my report. Two alternatives present themselves for the treatment of the reserved public timber lands. One is to reserve all such lands at one blow by refusing to allow any forest lands of the United States to be disposed of hereafter. This course would probably require Congressional action, and it is by no means certain that such action could be obtained. The other course is to secure the reservation of considerable bodies not now reserved, so as to include, as far as possible, all mountain ranges and any other considerable bodies of government timber land which may exist.

The President has the necessary authority, and Congress would not require to be directly consulted. I shall recommend the general withdrawal of all lands as the best plan, but if it is out of reach, I wish to be in a position to describe accurately such large bodies of government forests, that with good will on the part of the President, we could secure essentially the same result. Of course, we can be said to have secured nothing so far except the chance to fight, but even that is a great thing.

***

[Feb. 2, 1900]

Mr. John Muir.
Martinez, Calif.

Dear Mr. Muir:
Many thanks for your telegram, which gives us exactly the information I was after. We are going to try to interest Congress in the preservation of the Calaveras Groves. I will keep you posted from time to time as the matter progresses.

Very sincerely yours,

[illegible]

Forester.

GLOSSARY

Biltmore: an estate built by the Vanderbilt family in western North Carolina

Calaveras Groves: two groves of giant sequoia trees, now in a California state park

Liriodendron: commonly known as the tulip tree

Southern Alleghenies: a section of the Appalachian Mountains, the north part of the west side

Document Analysis

Gifford Pinchot and John Muir were worlds apart in every way except for their concern for forests. Pinchot was born into a supportive, wealthy New England family, an Ivy League graduate, formally trained in the methods of European forestry, and a part of the Eastern establishment, who used a scientific approach to implement his interest in conserving natural resources, especially the forests. Muir, a generation older, was born in Scotland as part of a working-class immigrant family, attended a few years of college, trained himself regarding forests, lived on the fringes of the American West, and approached many forests and wilderness areas in an almost spiritual way, seeking to preserve them, untouched. When the men first met, their common interest in experiencing forests and making this experience available to others, brought them together. However, as they developed different sociopolitical bases for their efforts to control the development of the federally-owned forests, their ways began to diverge. In the end, while they could both seek the same goals, the friendship had

disappeared; they were only professional allies.

The two letters that Pinchot sent to Muir in 1894 were letters of friendship. They two men had met in 1893, when Muir was in New York. Assuming that they each discussed their work, Pinchot's April 1894 letter basically summarizes the work he had recently completed at the Biltmore Estate, along with related documents. Demands upon Pinchot to publish a book on forestry, and his willingness to do that rather than travel through the western United States, was an indication of the differences between Pinchot and Muir. Muir would have done just the opposite. It also indicates the fact that Pinchot was interested in applying science to forestry and using this to develop the means for conservation. The May 1894 letter indicates that Pinchot had been introduced to Muir's new advocacy group, the Sierra Club.

The 1896 letters were sent after the National Forest Commission, composed of leading scientists with ties to the federal government, had been established, giving Pinchot a means to directly influence federal policy.

This differed greatly from the Sierra Club, which did not have the connections in Washington that the commission had. Muir wanted things to change immediately, while Pinchot was willing to work through the system. This was reflected in the second letter, where Pinchot passively accepted a delay in the National Forest Commission report. The trip to which Pinchot refers was a fact-finding tour for the commission, for which Pinchot was the secretary and which Muir joined unofficially. Mr. Fernow, the Chief of the Forest Division and the immediate predecessor to Pinchot, was not a member of the commission. Thus, his disagreements with Pinchot were not only based on the differences between his Prussian training and Pinchot's French training, but also on professional rivalry. Pinchot did not want to lose possible support from the Forest Division, so he let things slide. Thus, even in these friendly letters to Muir, Pinchot comes through clearly as concerned with political realities, not just nature conservation.

The 1897 and 1900 letters were from a period when Pinchot was a part of the Forest Division, initially as a special agent, then as its head. Here, the division with Muir is clear. In the 1897 letter, Pinchot makes it clear that he was willing to take small steps and preserve some land while losing other areas. The land disposal, to which Pinchot refers, was states seeking land in order to allow more economic development on it than the federal government would allow. Pinchot believed that preserving some by presidential declaration would "secure essentially the same result" as the more ambitious proposal from Muir. In the 1900 letter, Pinchot acknowledged receiving the "information I was after," and gave a standard affirmation of keeping in touch, perhaps without meaning it. While even Muir accepted the idea that some of the National Forests would be harvested to supply lumber to the country, he differed with Pinchot as to the extent to which this should happen. Thus, with the 1900 letter, it was clear that the two men, who once had been close associates, were going their separate ways.

Essential Themes

Although John Muir is much better known than Gifford Pinchot, Pinchot had almost as much influence, but in a different manner. Muir, and the Sierra Club, were, and are, internationally known for their advocacy of the preservation of wilderness and other areas of special significance. While Pinchot was also interested in preserving areas of special significance, his contribution was much broader. By helping to bring the applied science of forestry to the United States, he made a major contribution to the preservation of forests, as well as to the sustainable use of this natural resource. While he and his family helped found what is now the oldest school of forestry in the United States (at Yale), this was only part of his contribution. His work in using his studies and his skills in the development of the National Forest Service demonstrated to politicians and the public that having professionally trained foresters was something desirable.

Pinchot was also one of the individuals who helped make efforts to conserve forests, and other unique natural entities, a widely acceptable goal. Although working with President Theodore Roosevelt obviously greatly contributed to the cause, Pinchot's ability to work with him, and with other politicians, brought conservation to the forefront. Some people credit Pinchot and Roosevelt jointly with coining the word "conservation," as a description of what they hoped to do. As one who was seen by many as part of the Eastern establishment, Pinchot had the connections to excel in this effort. Pinchot's willingness to compromise was much greater than was Muir's, allowing him to accomplish more politically. However, his principles of conservation and the "wise use" of forest resources were not always followed in practice. Pinchot was outraged when he saw the widespread clear-cutting in the Pacific Northwest, as this was not his conception of how to make use of the National Forests. Yet, even though his ideas and example were not always followed by his successors in the National Forest Service, Pinchot offered to many a more practical view of how to save America's natural resources than did the more radical preservationists, such as John Muir.

—*Donald A. Watt, PhD*

Bibliography and Additional Reading

Forest History Society. *"Gifford Pinchot (1865–1946)."* U.S. Forest Service History. Durham, North Carolina: Forest History Society, 2014. Web. 15 Oct. 2014.

Miller, Char. *Gifford Pinchot and the Making of Modern Environmentalism.* Washington, DC: Island P, 2004. Print.

Pennsylvania Historical & Museum Commission. *"Governor Gifford Pinchot,"* Pennsylvania Historical & Museum Commission. Harrisburg: Pennsylvania Historical & Museum Commission, 2014. Web. 15 Oct. 2014.

Pinchot, Gifford. *Breaking New Ground.* 1947. Washington, DC: Island P, 1998. Print.

Walsh, Barry, Edward Barnard, & John Nesbitt. *"The Pinchot-Muir Split Revisited,"* Society of American Foresters. Bethesda, Maryland: Society of American Foresters, 2014. Web. 15 Oct. 2014.

BEYOND THE WEST

The West has been mythologized in many forms of media: tales, songs, novels, film, and television. One of the first, and perhaps most influential, means by which the culture and history of the West was exploited and turned into a media fanfare was the traveling Wild West show. The Wild West show is, as a genre, virtually synonymous with Buffalo Bill's Wild West show, but following Buffalo Bill's success in the late nineteenth century, there came a few less well known imitators, such as Pawnee Bill's Wild West show. All of these shows sought to reenact western history (or, rather, reinvent it) for popular audiences in the East and elsewhere (including Europe). The central theme was the "taming" of the West by forthright white cowboys and soldiers as they vanquished unruly Indians and harnessed beasts and other of nature's gifts. We look at such performances today, of course, through a critical lens.

Also near the end of the nineteenth century, it was said that the frontier era had come to a close. That, at least, was the thesis advanced by historian Frederick Jackson Turner in his seminal 1893 essay "The Significance of the Frontier in American History." Turner noted that US social and political development repeated itself with each new extension of the frontier, as people and institutions advanced toward addressing the problems before them. Through this process, moreover, the American character came to be what it is. We examine Turner's "frontier thesis" in the present section.

Finally, we look at a nationalistic call by another historian (and politician), Albert Beveridge, for the spread of American democracy into the far reaches of the globe. Beveridge's call was issued in the context of the nation's presumed success in having developed the western frontier and the need, therefore, to continue the mission in other parts of the world. Beveridge's message is one of imperialism and Manifest Destiny, announced at a time (1898) when the United States was engaged in the Spanish-American War involving Cuba and Puerto Rico and looking to annex the Philippines, as well.

■ Buffalo Bill's Wild West Show

Date: 1880s and 1890s
Author: William F. "Buffalo Bill" Cody
Genre: memoir

Summary Overview

Of all the big personalities to come out of the American West, none was perhaps bigger than William F. Cody, popularly known as Buffalo Bill. An Army scout, Indian fighter, Pony Express rider, and gold miner all by the time he was fourteen, Cody made a name for himself as first a buffalo hunter and, later, as one of the greatest showmen of the nineteenth century. His travelling circus, Buffalo Bill's Wild West, not only gave audiences across the United States and Europe a taste of life on the vanishing frontier, but also became the template for how popular culture would forever after depict life in the West—the enduring story of savagery conquered by civilization. In the process of the show's nearly three-decade run, Cody became a living legend, and his actors and performers, both cowboys and Native peoples, became the icons of a much romanticized and often exaggerated, uniquely American era.

Defining Moment

The latter half of the nineteenth century in the American West is arguably the most romanticized era in United States history. A great amount of sentimentalized art, literature, and film has depicted the "Old West" as a place of villainous bandits, wild savage Natives, and heroic cowboys. Few have helped shape this image more than William F. "Buffalo Bill" Cody.

A prodigious showman and self-promoter, Cody lived and worked a myriad of jobs throughout the western United States during the 1860s and 1870s, at the very height of the settlement expansion. Thanks in part to his many, often exaggerated experiences, Cody was able to touch on nearly every aspect of life in the American West. Theatrical by nature, and having tasted the interest of eastern audiences for tales of life on the frontier, in 1883, Cody packaged his exploits (making some up as he went along) and founded Buffalo Bill's Wild West. The show, a traveling circus of western attractions, featured performances by both cowboys and Native peo-

ples. Among the large, shifting troupe were such notables as sharp-shooters Annie Oakley and Lillian Smith; cowboys Will Rogers and Wild Bill Hickok; and Native Americans, including Chief Sitting Bull (Lakota), Chief Joseph (Nez Perce), and Geronimo (Apache).

Each show would follow a somewhat standard format, beginning with a parade on horseback, followed by "historical reenactments," such as a bison hunt or train robbery. In some shows, Cody would stage a reenactment of the Battle of Little Bighorn, in which General Custer dies the last man standing, gloriously fighting his Sioux attackers to the bitter end, after which Cody himself would appear to take revenge for the fallen hero. Shooting demonstrations, cowboy tricks, rodeo events, and races were all featured throughout. Finally, every show would then conclude with an Indian attack on a "burning cabin," a scene in which, again, Buffalo Bill would emerge as the savior.

Buffalo Bill's Wild West toured throughout the New and Old World, with special performances even given to many of the crown heads of Europe, most notably the British royal family, including Queen Victoria herself. The show was a spectacular success, drawing large crowds wherever it went. It also struck a nerve with a public fascinated by a place and a time that was quickly disappearing. By the time the last of Buffalo Bill's performances closed in 1908, his story of the West became the story of the West.

Author Biography

William F. Cody was born in Iowa in 1846. Following the death of his father, Cody, barely a teenager, struck out to support his family, finding odd jobs as a freight carrier, unofficial scout during the Utah War, gold miner, and even as a rider in the famed, albeit short-lived, Pony Express. In 1863, Cody joined the Union Army and, following the defeat of the Confederacy became a scout for the reconstituted United States Army. In short order, Cody made a reputation for himself as not just a talented scout and tracker, but also as famed buffalo hunter, having shot as many as 4,282 bison in a period of eighteen months for the Kansas Pacific Railroad, thus earning for himself the nickname, "Buffalo Bill." In 1872, Cody began to perform in Wild West shows and, in 1883, established his own, Buffalo Bill's Wild West. In addition to his travelling circus, Cody was a tireless self-promoter, writing multiple autobiographies and self-aggrandizing histories. He was also a land speculator and sometime investor. Cody died in 1917, one of the most famous men in America, if not the world.

HISTORICAL DOCUMENT

[from Buffalo Bill's Life Story]

It was because of my great interest in the West, and my belief that its development would be assisted by the interest I could awaken in others, that I decided to bring the West to the East through the medium of the Wild West Show. How greatly I was to succeed in this venture I had no idea when it first occurred to me. As I have told you, I had already appeared in a small Western show, and was the first man to bring Indians to the East and exhibit them. But the theater was too small to give any real impression of what Western life was like. Only in an arena where horses could be ridden at full gallop, where lassos could be thrown, and pistols and guns fired without frightening the audience half to death, could such a thing be attempted.

After getting together a remarkable collection of Indians, cowboys, Indian ponies, stage-coach drivers, and other typical denizens of my own country under canvas I found myself almost immediately prosperous.

We showed in the principal cities of the country, and everywhere the novelty of the exhibition drew great crowds. As owner and principal actor in the enterprise I met the leading citizens of the United States socially, and never lost an opportunity to "talk up" the Western country, which I believed to have a wonderful future. I worked hard on the program of the entertainment, taking care to make it realistic in every detail. The wigwam village, the Indian war-dance, the chant of the Great Spirit as it was sung on the Plains, the rise and fall of the famous tribes, were all pictured accurately.

It was not an easy thing to do. Sometimes I had to send men on journeys of more than a hundred miles to get the right kind of war-bonnets, or to make correct copies of the tepees peculiar to a particular tribe. It was my effort, in depicting the West, to depict it as it was. I was much gratified in after years to find that scientists who had carefully studied the Indians, their traditions and habits, gave me credit for making very valuable contributions to the sum of human knowledge of the American native.

The first presentation of my show was given in May, 1883, at Omaha, which I had then chosen as my home. From there we made our first summer tour, visiting practically every important city in the country.

For my grand entrance I made a spectacle which comprised the most picturesque features of Western life. Sioux, Arapahoes, Brulés, and Cheyennes in war-paint and feathers led the van, shrieking their war-whoops and waving the weapons with which they were armed in a manner to inspire both terror and admiration in the tenderfoot audience.

Next came cowboys and soldiers, all clad exactly as they were when engaged in their campaigns against the Indians, and lumbering along in the rear were the old stage-coaches which carried the settlers to the West in the days before the railroad made the journey easy and pleasant.

I am sure the people enjoyed this spectacle, for they flocked in crowds to see it. I know I enjoyed it. There was never a day when, looking back over the red and white men in my cavalcade, I did not know the thrill of the trail, and feel a little sorry that my Western adventures would thereafter have to be lived in spectacles.

Without desiring to dim the glory of any individual I can truthfully state that the expression "rough riders," which afterward became so famous, was my own coinage. As I rode out at the front of my parade I would bow to the audience, circled about on the circus benches, and shout at the top of my voice:

"Ladies and gentlemen, permit me to introduce you to the rough riders of the world!"

For three years we toured the United States with great success. One day an Englishman, whose name I never learned, came to see me after the show.

"That is a wonderful performance," he told me. "Here in America it meets with great appreciation, but you have no idea what a sensation it would be in the Old World, where such things are unheard of."

That set me to thinking. In a few days, after spending hours together considering the matter, I had made up my mind that Europe should have an opportunity to study America as nearly at first-hand as possible through the medium of my entertainment.

Details were soon arranged. In March, 1886, I chartered the steamer State of Nebraska, loaded my Indians, cowboys, horses, and stage-coaches on board, and set sail for another continent.

It was a strange voyage. The Indians had never been to sea before, and had never dreamed that such an expanse of water existed on the planet. They would stand at the rail, after the first days of seasickness were over, gazing out across the waves, and trying to descry something that looked like land, or a tree, or anything that seemed familiar and like home. Then they would shake their heads disconsolately and go below, to brood and muse and be an extremely unhappy and forlorn lot of savages. The joy that seized them when at last they came in sight of land, and were assured that we did not intend to keep on sailing till we fell over the edge of the earth, was something worth looking at.

At Gravesend we sighted a tug flying the American colors, and when the band on board responded to our cheers with "The Star-Spangled Banner" even the Indians tried to sing. Our band replied with "Yankee Doodle," and as we moved toward port there was more noise on board than I had ever heard in any battle on the Plains.

When the landing was made the members of the party were sent in special coaches to London. Crowds stared at us from every station. The guards on the train were a little afraid of the solemn and surly-looking Indians, but they were a friendly and jovial crowd, and when they had recovered from their own fright at the strange surround-

ings they were soon on good terms with the Britishers.

Major John M. Burke, who was my lifetime associate in the show business, had made all arrangements for housing the big troupe. We went to work at our leisure with our preparations to astonish the British public, and succeeded beyond our wildest dreams. The big London amphitheater, a third of a mile in circumference, was just the place for such an exhibition. The artist's brush was employed on lavish scale to reproduce the scenery of the Western Plains. I was busy for many days with preparations, and when our spectacle was finally given it was received with such a burst of enthusiasm as I had never witnessed anywhere.

The show began, after the grand entry, with the hour of dawn on the Plains. Wild animals were scattered about. Within their tents were the Indians sleeping. As the dawn deepened the Indians came out of their tents and went through one of their solemn and impressive war-dances. While this was going on the British audience held its breath. You could have heard a whisper in almost any part of the arena.

Then in came a courier to announce the neighborhood of a hostile tribe. Instantly there was a wild scramble for mounts and weapons. The enemy rushed in, and for ten minutes there was a sham battle which filled the place with noise and confusion. This battle was copied as exactly as it could be copied from one of the scrimmages in which I had taken part in my first days as a scout. Then we gave them a buffalo hunt, in which I had a hand, and did a little fancy shooting. As a finish there was a Wild Western cyclone, and a whole Indian village was blown out of existence for the delectation of the English audience.

The initial performance was given before the Prince and Princess of Wales, afterward King Edward and his Queen, and their suite. At the close of the program the Prince and Princess, at their own request, were introduced to all the leading members of the company, including many of the Indians. When the cowgirls of the show were presented to the Princess they stepped forward and offered their hands, which were taken and well shaken in true democratic fashion.

Red Shirt, the most important chief in the outfit, was highly pleased when he learned that a princess was to visit him in his camp. He had the Indian gift of oratory, and he replied to her greeting with a long and eloquent speech, in which his gestures, if not his words, expressed plainly the honor he felt in receiving so distinguished a lady. The fact that he referred to Alexandria as a squaw did not seem to mar her enjoyment.

That the Prince was really pleased with the exhibition was shown by the fact that he made an immediate report of it to his mother. Shortly thereafter I received a command from Queen Victoria to appear before her.

This troubled me a good deal—not that I was not more than eager to obey this flattering command, but that I was totally at a loss how to take my show to any of the great residences occupied by Her Majesty.

Finally, after many cautious inquiries, I discovered that she would be willing to visit the show if a special box was prepared for her. This we did to the best of our ability. The box was placed upon a dais covered with crimson velvet and handsomely decorated. When the Queen arrived I met her at the door of the box, with my sombrero in my hand and welcomed her to "the Wild West of America."

One of the first acts in the performance was to carry the flag to the front. This was done by a soldier. Walking around the arena, he offered the Stars and Stripes as an emblem of the friendship of America to all the world. On this occasion he carried the flag directly to the royal box, and dipped it three times before the Queen.

Absolute silence fell over the great throng. Then the Queen rose and saluted the flag with a bow, her suite following her example. There was a wild cheer from everyone in the show, Indians included, and soon all the audience was on its feet, cheering and waving flags and handkerchiefs.

This gave us a fine start and we never put on a better performance. When it was all over Her Majesty sent for me, and paid me many compliments as well as to my country and the West. I found her a most gracious and charming woman, with none of the haughtiness which I had supposed was inseparable from a person of such exalted rank. My subsequent experiences with royalty convinced me that there is more real democracy among the rulers of the countries of Europe than you will find among the petty officials of a village.

It was interesting to watch old Red Shirt when he was presented to the Queen. He clearly felt that this was a ceremony between one ruler and another, and the dignity with which he went through the introduction was wonderful to behold. One would have thought to watch him that most of his life was spent in introductions to kings and queens, and that he was really a little bored with the effort required to go through with them. A second command from the Queen resulted in an exhibition before a number of her royal guests, including the Kings of Saxony, Denmark, and Greece, the Queen of the Belgians, and the Crown Prince of Austria.

The Deadwood coach, one of the features of the show, was of particular interest to my royal guests. This was a coach with a history. It was built in Concord, N.H., and sent by water to San Francisco to run over a route infested with road-agents. A number of times it was held up and robbed. Finally, both driver and passengers were killed and the coach abandoned on the trail. It remained for a long time a derelict, but was afterward brought into San Francisco by an old stage-driver and placed on the Overland trail.

As it worked its way East over the Overland route its old luck held steadily. Again were driver and passengers massacred; again it was abandoned. At last, when it was "hoodooed" all over the West and no independent driver or company would have anything to do with it I discovered it, bought it, and used it for my show.

One of the incidents of my program, as all who have seen it will remember, was an Indian attack on this coach. The royal visitors wanted a real taste of Western life—insisted on it, in fact, and the Kings of Denmark, Greece, Saxony, and the Crown Prince of Austria climbed to the box with me.

I had secretly instructed the Indians to throw a little real energy into their pursuit of the coach, and they followed my instructions rather more completely than I expected. The coach was surrounded by a demoniac band of shooting and shouting Indians. Blank cartridges were discharged at perilously close proximity to the rulers of four great nations. Looking around to quiet my followers, I saw that the guests of the occasion were a trifle pale, but they were all of them game, and came out of the affair far less scared than were the absolutely terrified members of the royal suites, who sat in their boxes and wrung their hands in wild alarm.

In recognition of this performance the Prince of

Wales sent me a souvenir consisting of a feathered crest, outlined in diamonds, with the words "Ich dien" worked in jewels underneath. A note in the Prince's own hand expressed the pleasure of his guests in the entertainment I had provided for them.

After a tour of the principal cities we returned to America, proud of our success, and well rewarded in purse for our effort.

The welcome to America was almost as elaborate as that from England. I quote from the description of it printed in the New York World:

> The harbor probably has never witnessed a more picturesque scene than that of yesterday, when the Persian Monarch steamed up from Quarantine. Buffalo Bill stood on the captain's bridge, his tall and striking figure clearly outlined, and his long hair waving in the wind; the gaily painted and blanketed Indians leaned over the ship's rail; the flags of all nations fluttered from the masts and connecting cables. The cowboy band played "Yankee Doodle" with a vim and enthusiasm which faintly indicated the joy felt by everybody connected with the "Wild West" over the sight of home.

Shortly after my arrival I was much pleased by the receipt of the following letter:

FIFTH AVENUE HOTEL, NEW YORK.
COLONEL WM. F. CODY:

Dear Sir—In common with all your countrymen, I want to let you know that I am not only gratified but proud of your management and success. So far as I can make out, you have been modest, graceful, and dignified in all you have done to illustrate the history of civilization on this continent during the past century. I am especially pleased with the compliment paid you by the Prince of Wales, who rode with you in the Deadwood coach while it was attacked by Indians and rescued by cowboys. Such things did occur in our days, but they never will again.

As nearly as I can estimate, there were in 1865 about nine and one-half million of buffaloes on the Plains between the Missouri River and the Rocky Mountains; all are now gone, killed for their meat, their skins, and their bones. This seems like desecration, cruelty, and murder, yet they have been replaced by twice as many cattle. At that date there were about 165,000 Pawnees, Sioux, Cheyennes, and Arapahoes, who depended upon these buffaloes for their yearly food. They, too, have gone, but they have been replaced by twice or thrice as many white men and women, who have made the earth to blossom as the rose, and who can be counted, taxed, and governed by the laws of Nature and civilization. This change has been salutary, and will go on to the end. You have caught one epoch of this country's history, and have illustrated it in the very heart of the modern world—London—and I want you to feel that on this side of the water we appreciate it.

This drama must end; days, years, and centuries follow fast; even the drama of civilization must have an end. All I aim to accomplish on this sheet of paper is to assure you that I fully recognize your work. The presence of the Queen, the beautiful Princess of Wales, the Prince, and the British public are marks of favor which reflect back on America sparks of light which illuminate many a house and cabin in the land where once you guided me honestly and faithfully, in 1865–66, from Fort Riley to Kearney, in Kansas and Nebraska.

Sincerely your friend,
W.T. SHERMAN.

Our next descent on Europe was made in the steamer Persian Monarch, which was again chartered. This time our destination was France. The Parisians received the show with as much favor as had the Londoners.

Everything American became the fad during our stay. Fashionable young men bought American and Mexican saddles for their rides in the Bois. Cowboy hats appeared everywhere on the street. There was a great cry for stories of the Plains and all the books that could be found that dealt with the West were translated into the French language. Relics from the Plains and mountains, bows, moccasins, and Indian baskets, sold like hot cakes in the souvenir stores....

I have now come to the end of my story. It is a story of "The Great West that Was," a West that is gone forever.

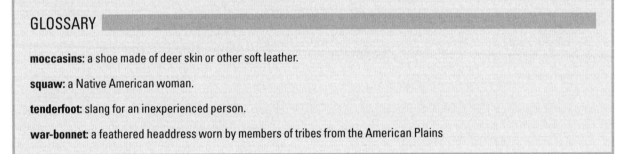

All my interests are still with the West—the modern West. I have a number of homes there, the one I love best being in the wonderful Big Horn Valley, which I hope one day to see one of the garden spots of the world.

In concluding, I want to express the hope that the dealings of this Government of ours with the Indians will always be just and fair. They were the inheritors of the land that we live in. They were not capable of developing it, or of really appreciating its possibilities, but they owned it when the White Man came, and the White Man took it away from them. It was natural that they should resist. It was natural that they employed the only means of warfare known to them against those whom they regarded as usurpers. It was our business, as scouts, to be continually on the warpath against them when they committed depredations. But no scout ever hated the Indians in general.

There have been times when the Government policy toward the Indians has been unwise and unjust. That time, I trust, has passed forever. There are still many thousand Indians in the country, most of them engaged in agricultural pursuits. Indian blood has added a certain rugged strength to the characters of many of our Western citizens. At least two United States Senators are part Indian, and proud of it.

The Indian makes a good citizen, a good farmer, a good soldier. He is a real American, and all those of us who have come to share with him the great land that was his heritage should do their share toward seeing that he is dealt with justly and fairly, and that his rights and liberties are never infringed by the scheming politician or the short-sighted administration of law.

GLOSSARY

moccasins: a shoe made of deer skin or other soft leather.

squaw: a Native American woman.

tenderfoot: slang for an inexperienced person.

war-bonnet: a feathered headdress worn by members of tribes from the American Plains

Document Analysis

This selection from William F. Cody's autobiography details the European tours of Buffalo Bill's Wild West, with special emphasis given to the many prestigious guests who attended the performances. We get a sense of Cody's boastful nature and his real pride over the success of his shows in Europe, but we also glimpse some sadness at the loss of the frontier and his inherent contradictions about Native peoples. Most importantly, we witness his role in crafting the narrative of the American West.

Cody believes that he's offering audiences an authentic experience. Whether it be in the form of a war-bonnet from the Great Plains or a stagecoach from the Black Hills, Cody spares no expense in securing artifacts from the West to use in his show. At the same time, he has an obvious flare for showmanship, crafting spectacle with grand entrances and fake gunfire. He wants to dazzle audiences, while also giving them something of what they already expect. His aim is to make real what they've imagined the West to be. He takes special delight in entertaining royalty, who shower him with gifts and praise and, according to Cody, often seem more "democratic" than many of the elected officials he's met. In fact, Cody loves his tours of Britain, where his show finds bigger success than in the United States—not surprising considering that, at the time, Victorian Britain controlled the largest empire in the world.

Throughout Cody's account his depiction of his Native American performers is most interesting. While he professes his respect for his Native American performers, going so far as to say that Native peoples had every right to defend themselves against "the white man," and that the policies of the US Government were "unwise and unjust," he's still not above using his Native American performers to play on the stereotypes of the audience. The Native peoples in this Wild West show are the aggressors, whooping and screaming, the savage hordes come down on an unsuspecting wagon train or log cabin. Cody often seems amused when his Native performers seem out of their element. Respect them though he might, Cody obviously considers Native peoples quite primitive.

Overall one gets the sense from the document that Cody is very conscious of the frontier's imminent demise. The West is fading from memory, and never again will there be anything like it. The best that Cody can do is to try and recreate something of it through his over-the-top, larger than life performances. Through his shows in Europe, all things of the American West have become trendy. Cody might argue that what he's created is authentic and realistic, but in truth, it's just it's just a caricature, and he knows it. As he laments several times throughout his account, and indirectly through the inclusion of a letter from W. T. Sherman, all that was is gone, and only spectacle remains.

Essential Themes

William F. Cody was an adventurer, a performer, and an imperialist, and it was all three of these traits that shaped the way we remember the American West. A rough and tumble character, full of the kind of get-rich-quick zeal that defined western expansion, Cody spent his young life pursuing one western dream after another. What he didn't experience himself, he borrowed from others. The fact and fiction of the frontier coalesced in his mind to produce Buffalo Bill's Wild West, a loud, gaudy, boisterous, spectacle full of savage Indians and heroic cowboys. A show tailor-made for the sensibilities of a Victorian world that thought itself as the pin-nacle of civilization, in which Native peoples, whether they be in the American West, South America, Asia, or Africa, were primitives in need of protection. For all the pomp and ceremony, the central theme throughout Buffalo Bill's Wild West was that of savagery tamed by the forces of white civilization. It was a celebration of conquest, in which the conqueror was also the victim, forced to defend himself at every turn. And it was this story more than any other that became the standard narrative about the American West: civilization versus savagery, conquest without guilt. As the show traveled the nation, and crisscrossed Europe, this message was broadcast and appropriated by the heads of state who came to watch. Today we still see this theme in art, literature, and film. It pervades our culture. But whatever the American West really was, it was not as Cody presented it because, in the end, Buffalo Bill did not care about celebrating the story of the settlement of the frontier as much as he cared about celebrating himself.

—KP Dawes, MA

Bibliography and Additional Reading

Blackstone, Sarah J. *The Business of Being Buffalo Bill*. New York: Praeger, 1988. Print.

Bridger, Bobby. *Buffalo Bill and Sitting Bull: Inventing the Wild West*. Austin: U of Texas P, 2002. Print.

Carter, Robert A. *Buffalo Bill Cody: The Man Behind the Legend*. New York: John Wiley & Sons, 2000. Print.

Warren, Lois S. *Buffalo Bill's America: William Cody and the Wild West Show*. New York: Random House, 2005. Print.

■ The Significance of the Frontier in American History

Date: July 12, 1893
Author: Frederick Jackson Turner
Genre: essay; speech

Summary Overview

In his seminal 1893 essay "The Significance of the Frontier in American History," Frederick Jackson Turner presents his frontier thesis, a framework through which many historians would study and understand the American West and its effect on American democracy and national character for the next century. In this essay, Turner argues that the availability of free, unsettled land beyond the western edge of settlement in the United States and the accommodations that settlers needed to make once they arrived on that frontier were the factors that have made the United States distinct from Europe. This unique frontier heritage explained not only the American love of freedom, but also the freedom that characterized American political, economic, and social structures. The challenges of settling the frontier fostered a strong sense of individualism and practicality that were not found in the same form under European hierarchical class structures or traditional customs. Turner's thesis gave the identification of Americans with the West a degree of intellectual legitimacy. There were, however, historians in Turner's day—most notably Charles Beard—who disputed the idea that the frontier was the formative factor in the development of the American national character and political culture. However, even today, popular historians still reference Turner's moving frontier, where free, unsettled land acts as the principal Americanizing force.

Defining Moment

The United States was undergoing a number of significant transformations at the time that Frederick Jackson Turner presented "The Significance of the Frontier in American History" at a meeting of the American Historical Association at the World's Columbian Exposition in Chicago in 1893. The Industrial Revolution was rapidly changing the ratio of rural to urban dwellers, as well as the nature of the work that the average American performed. Large waves of immigration, mostly from southern and eastern Europe, were changing many people's perceptions of what it meant to be an American. The large-scale migration to the American West that began in earnest after the Civil War had been changing the nation in many important ways over three decades.

When Turner stepped to the podium on July 12, 1893, at the world fair held in Chicago to mark the four hundredth anniversary of Christopher Columbus's voyage to the New World, it is doubtful that many in the audience expected him to deliver an address that would become a defining paradigm for the study of US history. His was the last of five lengthy presentations given that evening, mostly on rather mundane topics. Up to that point, the so-called germ theory of politics was one common hypothesis used to explain the historical and cultural development of the United States, positing antecedents for American institutions in the ancient Teutonic tribes of central Europe. But what the germ theory could not explain was the changes that were reshaping American society in the late nineteenth century. What had made the United States unique, and why was it now becoming more like Europe (urban, industrial, and ethnically diverse)?

The answer, to Turner, lay in the 1890 US Census Bureau report. In 1890, for the first time, settlements in the West were so numerous and widely distributed that there was no "frontier line"—a line on the map to the east of which there was a population of more than two people per square mile, and to the west of which there were fewer than two people per square mile. Now that the United States no longer had an open and unsettled frontier, Turner took the opportunity to examine the role the frontier had played in US history up until that point. It was a simple idea and a simple framework for examining an entire era of American history, but Turner's frontier thesis had a profound effect, both on how historians talked about the nation and on how Americans thought of themselves, the vibrancy of American democracy, and what was going to come next for the nation.

Author Biography

Frederick Jackson Turner was born in Portage, Wisconsin, on November 14, 1861. His father was a journalist and amateur local historian, who sparked Turner's interest in history. Turner attended the University of Wisconsin, graduating in 1884, and went on to graduate school under the mentorship of the well-known historian Herbert Baxter Adams at Johns Hopkins University, where Turner received his PhD in history in 1890. At that time, he was teaching at his alma mater, the University of Wisconsin.

Although the response to Turner's 1893 address was less than enthusiastic both inside and outside of the historical profession, Turner's perseverance gradually won acceptance of his ideas. His notoriety was so great that in 1910 he left the University of Wisconsin for a position at Harvard University, where he remained until 1924. He then worked as a research associate at the Huntington Library in San Marino, California, until his death on March 14, 1932.

HISTORICAL DOCUMENT

This brief official statement marks the closing of a great historic movement. Up to our own day American history has been in a large degree the history of the colonization of the Great West. The existence of an area of free land, its continuous recession, and the advance of American settlement westward explain American development. Behind institutions, behind constitutional forms and modifications lie the vital forces that call these organs into life and shape them to meet changing conditions. Now the peculiarity of American institutions is the fact that they have been compelled to adapt themselves to the changes of an expanding people—to the changes involved in crossing a continent, in winning a wilderness, and in developing at each area of this progress out of the primitive economic and political conditions of the frontier into the complexity of city life.

Said Calhoun in 1817, "We are great, and rapidly—I was about to say fearfully—growing!" So saying, he touched the distinguishing feature of American life. All peoples show development: the germ theory of politics has been sufficiently emphasized. In the case of most nations, however, the development has occurred in a limited area; and if the nation has expanded, it has met other growing peoples whom it has conquered. But in the case of the United States we have a different phenomenon.

Limiting our attention to the Atlantic Coast, we have the familiar phenomenon of the evolution of institutions in a limited area, such as the rise of representative government; the differentiation of simple colonial governments into complex organs; the progress from primitive industrial society, without division of labor, up to manufacturing civilization. But we have in addition to this a recurrence of the process of evolution in each western area reached in the process of expansion. Thus American development has exhibited not merely advance along a single line but a return to primitive conditions on a continually advancing frontier line, and a new development for that area.

American social development has been continually beginning over again on the frontier. This perennial rebirth, this fluidity of American life, this expansion westward with its new opportunities, its continuous touch with the simplicity of primitive society, furnish the forces dominating American character. The true point of view in the history of this nation is not the Atlantic Coast, it is the Great West. Even the slavery struggle, which is made so exclusive an object of attention by writers like Professor von Holst, occupies its important place in American history because of its relation to westward expansion.

In this advance, the frontier is the outer edge of the wave—the meeting point between savagery and civilization. Much has been written about the frontier from the point of view of border warfare and the chase, but as a field for the serious study of the economist and the historian it has been neglected.

What is the frontier? It is not the European frontier—a fortified boundary line running through dense populations. The most significant thing about it is that it lies at the hither edge of free land. In the census reports it is treated as the margin of that settlement which has a density of two or more to the square mile. The term is an elastic one, and for our purposes does not need sharp definition. We shall consider the whole frontier belt, including the Indian country and the outer margin of the "settled area" of the census reports. This paper will make no attempt to treat the subject exhaustively; its aim is simply to call attention to the frontier as a fertile field for investigation, and to suggest some of the problems which arise in connection with it.

But with all these similarities there are essential differences, due to the place element and the time element. It is evident that the farming frontier of the Mississippi Valley presents different conditions from the mining frontier of the Rocky Mountains. The frontier reached by the Pacific Railroad, surveyed into rectangles, guarded by the United States Army, and recruited by the daily immigrant ship, moves forward at a swifter pace and in a different way than the frontier reached by the birch canoe or the pack horse. The geologist traces patiently the shores of ancient seas, maps their areas, and compares the older and the newer. It would be a work worth the historian's labors to mark these various frontiers and in detail compare one with another. Not only would there result a more adequate conception of American development and characteristics, but invaluable additions would be made to the history of society.

Loria, the Italian economist, has urged the study of colonial life as an aid in understanding the stages of European development, affirming that colonial settlement is for economic science what the mountain is for geology, bringing to light primitive stratifications. "America," he says, "has the key to the historical enigma which Europe has sought for centuries in vain, and the land which has no history reveals luminously the course of universal history." He is right. The United States lies like a huge page in the history of society. Line by line as we read from west to east we find the record of social evolution.

It would not be possible in the limits of this paper to trace the other frontiers across the continent. Travelers of the eighteenth century found the "cowpens" among the canebrakes and pea-vine pastures of the South, and the "cow drivers" took their droves to Charleston, Philadelphia, and New York. Travelers at the close of the War of 1812 met droves of more than a thousand cattle and

swine from the interior of Ohio going to Pennsylvania to fatten for the Philadelphia market. The ranges of the Great Plains, with ranch and cowboy and nomadic life, are things of yesterday and of to-day. The experience of the Carolina cowpens guided the ranchers of Texas. One element favoring the rapid extension of the rancher's frontier is the fact that in a remote country lacking transportation facilities the product must be in small bulk, or must be able to transport itself, and the cattle raiser could easily drive his product to market. The effect of these great ranches on the subsequent agrarian history of the localities in which they existed should be studied.

The maps of the census reports show an uneven advance of the farmer's frontier, with tongues of settlement pushed forward and with indentations of wilderness. In part this is due to Indian resistance, in part to the location of river valleys and passes, in part to the unequal force of the centers of frontier attraction. Among the important centers of attraction may be mentioned the following: fertile and favorably situated soils, salt springs, mines, and army posts.

The frontier army post, serving to protect the settlers from the Indians, has also acted as a wedge to open the Indian country, and has been a nucleus for settlement. In this connection, mention should also be made of the government military and exploring expeditions in determining the lines of settlement. But all the more important expeditions were greatly indebted to the earliest pathmakers, the Indian guides, the traders and trappers, and the French voyageurs, who were inevitable parts of governmental expeditions from the days of Lewis and Clark. Each expedition was an epitome of the previous factors in western advance.

In an interesting monograph, Victor Hehn has traced the effect of salt upon early European development, and has pointed out how it affected the lines of settlement and the form of administration. A similar study might be made for the salt springs of the United States. The early settlers were tied to the coast by the need of salt, without which they could not preserve their meats or live in comfort. Writing in 1752, Bishop Spangenburg says of a colony for which he was seeking lands in North Carolina,

They will require salt & other necessaries which they can neither manufacture nor raise. Either they must go to Charleston, which is 300 miles distant ...Or else they must go to Boling's Point in Va on a branch of the James & is also 300 miles from here...Or else they must go down the Roanoke—I know not how many miles— where salt is brought up from the Cape Fear. This may serve as a typical illustration.

An annual pilgrimage to the coast for salt thus became essential. Taking flocks or furs and ginseng root, the early settlers sent their pack trains after seeding time each year to the coast. This proved to be an important educational influence, since it was almost the only way in which the pioneer learned what was going on in the East. But when discovery was made of the salt springs of the Kanawha, and the Holston, and Kentucky, and central New York, the West began to be freed from dependence on the coast. It was in part the effect of finding these salt springs that enabled settlement to cross the mountains.

From the time the mountains rose between the pioneer and the seaboard, a new order of Americanism arose. The West and the East began to get out of touch of each other. The settlements from the sea to the mountains kept connection with the rear and had a certain solidarity. But the over-mountain men grew more and more independent. The East took a narrow view of American advance, and nearly lost these men. Kentucky and Tennessee history bears abundant witness to the truth of this statement. The East began to try to hedge and limit westward expansion. Though Webster could declare that there were no Alleghenies in his politics, yet in politics in general they were a very solid factor.

Good soils have been the most continuous attraction to the farmer's frontier. The land hunger of the Virginians drew them down the rivers into Carolina, in early colonial days; the search for soils took the Massachusetts men to Pennsylvania and to New York. The exploitation of the beasts took hunter and trader to the West, the exploitation of the grasses took the rancher west, and the exploitation of the virgin soil of the river valleys and prairies attracted the farmer. As the eastern lands were taken up, migration flowed across them to the west. Daniel Boone, the great backwoodsman, who combined the occupations of hunter, trader, cattle-raiser, farmer, and surveyor—learning, probably from the traders, of the fertility of the lands of the upper Yadkin, where the traders were wont to rest as they took their way to the Indians, left his Pennsylvania home with his father, and passed down the Great Valley road to that stream.

Learning from a trader whose posts were on the Red River in Kentucky of its game and rich pastures, he pioneered the way for the farmers to that region. Thence he passed to the frontier of Missouri, where his settlement was long a landmark on the frontier. Here again he helped to open the way for civilization, finding salt licks, and trails, and land. His son was among the earliest trappers in the passes of the Rocky Mountains, and his party are said to have been the first to camp on the present site of Denver. His grandson, Col. A. J. Boone, of Colorado, was a power among the Indians of the Rocky Mountains, and was appointed an agent by the government. "Kit" Carson's mother was a Boone. Thus this family epitomizes the backwoodsman's advance across the continent.

The farmer's advance came in a distinct series of waves. In Peck's *New Guide to the West*, published in Cincinnati in 1848, occurs this suggestive passage:

Generally, in all the western settlements, three classes, like the waves of the ocean, have rolled one after the other. First comes the pioneer, who depends for the subsistence of his family chiefly upon the natural growth of vegetation, called the "range," and the proceeds of hunting. His implements of agriculture are rude, chiefly of his own make, and his efforts directed mainly to a crop of corn and a "truck patch." The last is a rude garden for growing cabbage, beans, corn for roasting ears, cucumbers, and potatoes. A log cabin, and, occasionally, a stable and corn-crib, and a field of a dozen acres, the timber girdled or "deadened," and fenced, are enough for his occupancy. It is quite immaterial whether he ever becomes the owner of the soil. He is the occupant for the time being, pays no rent, and feels as independent as the "lord of the manor."

With a horse, cow, and one or two breeders of swine, he strikes into the woods with his family, and becomes the founder of a new county, or perhaps state. He builds his cabin, gathers around him a few other families of similar tastes and habits, and occupies till range is somewhat subdued, and hunting a little precarious, or, which is more frequently the case, till the neighbors crowd around, roads, bridges, and fields annoy him, and he lacks elbow room. The Preemption Law enables him to dispose of his cabin and cornfield to the next class of emigrants; and, to employ his own figures, he "breaks for the high timber, clears out for the New Purchase," or migrates to Arkansas or Texas to work the same process over.

The next class of emigrants purchase the lands, add field to field, clear out the roads, throw rough bridges over the streams, put up hewn log houses, with glass windows and brick or stone chimneys, occasionally plant orchards, build mills, school-houses, courthouses, etc., and exhibit the picture and forms of plain, frugal, civilized life.

Another wave rolls on. The men of capital and enterprise come. The settler is ready to sell out and take the advantage of the rise in property, push farther into the interior and become, himself, a man of capital and enterprise in turn. The small village rises to a spacious town or city; substantial edifices of brick, extensive fields, orchards, gardens, colleges, and churches are seen. Broad-cloths, silks, leghorns, crepes, and all the refinements, luxuries, elegancies, frivolities, and fashions are in vogue. Thus wave after wave is rolling westward—the real Eldorado is still farther on.

A portion of the two first classes remain stationary amidst the general movement, improve their habits and condition, and rise in the scale of society.

The writer has traveled much amongst the first class—the real pioneers. He has lived many years in connection with the second grade; and now the third wave is sweeping over large districts of Indiana, Illinois, and Missouri. Migration has become almost a habit in the West. Hundreds of men can be found, not over 50 years of age, who have settled for the fourth, fifth, or sixth time on a new spot. To sell out and remove only a few hundred miles makes up a portion of the variety of backwoods life and manners.

Omitting the pioneer farmer who moves from the love of adventure, the advance of the more steady farmer is easy to understand. Obviously the immigrant was attracted by the cheap lands of the frontier, and even the native farmer felt their influence strongly. Year by year the farmers who lived on soil, whose returns were diminished by unrotated crops were offered the virgin soil of the frontier at nominal prices. Their growing families demanded more lands, and these were dear. The competition of the unexhausted, cheap, and easily tilled prairie lands compelled the farmer either to go west and continue the exhaustion of the soil on a new frontier, or to adopt intensive culture. Thus the census of 1890 shows, in the Northwest, many counties in which there is an absolute or a relative decrease of population. These States have been sending farmers to advance the frontier on the Plains, and have themselves begun to turn to intensive farming and to manufacture. A decade before this, Ohio had shown the same transition stage. Thus the demand for land and the love of wilderness freedom drew the frontier ever onward.

Having now roughly outlined the various kinds of frontiers and their modes of advance, chiefly from the point of view of the frontier itself, we may next inquire what were the influences on the East and on the Old World. A rapid enumeration of some of the more noteworthy effects is all that I have time for.

First, we note that the frontier promoted the formation of a composite nationality for the American people. The coast was preponderantly English, but the later tides of continental immigration flowed across to the free lands. This was the case from the early colonial days. The Scotch-Irish and the Palatine Germans, or "Pennsylvania Dutch," furnished the dominant element in the stock of the colonial frontier. With these peoples were also the freed indented servants, or redemptioners, who at the expiration of their time of service passed to the frontier. Governor Spotswood of Virginia writes in 1717, "The inhabitants of our frontiers are composed generally of such as have been transported hither as servants, and, being out of their time, settle themselves where land is to be taken up and that will produce the necessaries of life with little labor." Very generally these redemptioners were of non-English stock.

In the crucible of the frontier the immigrants were Americanized, liberated, and fused into a mixed race, English in neither nationality nor characteristics. The process has gone on from the early days to our own. Burke and other writers in the middle of the eighteenth century believed that Pennsylvania was "threatened with the danger of being wholly foreign in language, manners, and perhaps even inclinations." The German and Scotch-Irish elements in the frontier of the South were only less great. In the middle of the present century the German element in Wisconsin was already so considerable that leading publicists looked to the creation of a German state out of the commonwealth by concentrating their colonization. Such examples teach us to beware of misinterpreting the fact that there is a common English speech in America into a belief that the stock is also English.

In another way the advance of the frontier decreased our dependence on England. The coast, particularly of the South, lacked diversified industries, and was dependent on England for the bulk of its supplies. In the South there was even a dependence on the Northern colonies for articles of food. Governor Glenn of South Carolina writes in the middle of the eighteenth century:

Our trade with New York and Philadelphia was of this sort, draining us of all the little money and bills we could gather from other places for their bread, flour, beer, hams, bacon, and other things of their produce; all which, except beer, our new townships begin to supply us with, which are settled with very industrious and thriving Germans. This no doubt diminishes the number of shipping and the appearance of our trade, but it is far from being a detriment to us.

Before long the frontier created a demand for merchants. As it retreated from the coast it became less and less possible for England to bring her supplies directly to the consumer's wharfs and carry away staple crops, and staple crops began to give way to diversified agriculture for a time. The effect of this phase of the frontier action upon the northern section is perceived when we realize how the advance of the frontier aroused seaboard cities like Boston, New York, and Baltimore, to engage in rivalry for what Washington called "the extensive and valuable trade of a rising empire."

The legislation which most developed the powers of the national government, and played the largest part in its activity, was conditioned on the frontier....

So long as free land exists, the opportunity for a competency exists, and economic power secures political power. But the democracy born of free land, strong in selfishness and individualism, intolerant of administrative experience and education, and pressing individual liberty beyond its proper bounds, has its dangers as well

as its benefits. Individualism in America has allowed a laxity in regard to governmental affairs which has rendered possible the spoils system and all the manifest evils that follow from the lack of a highly developed civic spirit....

From the conditions of frontier life came intellectual traits of profound importance. The works of travelers along each frontier from colonial days onward describe certain common traits, and these traits have, while softening down, still persisted as survivals in the place of their origin, even when a higher social organization succeeded. The result is that, to the frontier, the American intellect owes its striking characteristics. That coarseness and strength combined with acuteness and inquisitiveness, that practical, inventive turn of mind, quick to find expedients, that masterful grasp of material things, lacking in the artistic but powerful to effect great ends, that restless, nervous energy, that dominant individualism, working for good and for evil, and withal that buoyancy and exuberance which comes with freedom—these are traits of the frontier, or traits called out elsewhere because of the existence of the frontier. ...

For a moment, at the frontier, the bonds of custom are broken and unrestraint is triumphant. There is not tabula rasa. The stubborn American environment is there with its imperious summons to accept its conditions; the inherited ways of doing things are also there; and yet, in spite of environment, and in spite of custom, each frontier did indeed furnish a new field of opportunity, a gate of escape from the bondage of the past; and freshness, and confidence, and scorn of older society, impatience of its restraints and its ideas, and indifference to its lessons, have accompanied the frontier.

What the Mediterranean Sea was to the Greeks, breaking the bond of custom, offering new experiences, calling out new institutions and activities, that, and more, the ever retreating frontier has been to the United States directly, and to the nations of Europe more remotely. And now, four centuries from the discovery of America, at the end of a hundred years of life under the Constitution, the frontier has gone, and with its going has closed the first period of American history.

GLOSSARY

girdled or "deadened": a process by which a tree's circumference is cut into or "ringed" in order to kill and dry the tree, thus improving its flotation qualities for river transport

salt lick: a natural surface deposit of salt or other minerals, used by animals for nutritional purposes

Webster: Daniel Webster (1782—1852), US senator from Massachusetts; the quote about "no Alleghenies" refers to Webster's view that state concerns are often national concerns—there are no barriers in that regard

Document Analysis

Frederick Jackson Turner's thesis begins with a simple statement of fact: the frontier, the line between densely populated and sparsely populated land, was gone as of 1890, according to the US Census report. In this essay, Turner seizes upon that simple fact to reflect upon and argue a whole host of points about the development and unique aspects of American society. Whereas many historians have criticized Turner's thesis, arguing against his assertions about American exceptionalism in regard to egalitarianism, many others have used Turner's thesis as the basis for their fundamental views on what defines and distinguishes the United States and Americans. In the most sweeping of statements, Turner asserted that "the existence of an area of free land, its continuous recession, and the advance of American settlement westward explain American development. . . . Now, the peculiarity of American institutions is the fact that they have been compelled to adapt themselves to the changes of an expanding people—to the changes involved in crossing a continent, in winning a wilderness, and in developing at each area of this progress out of the primitive economic and political conditions of the frontier into the complexity of city life." Turner clearly saw the frontier's influence as foundational to the development of a distinct American national character, as well American political and social institutions and customs. He contrasts the United States with most other countries, where "development has occurred in a limited area; and if the nation has expanded, it has met other growing people whom it has conquered."

What Turner describes as the frontier line was less a specific location than a process that was repeated time after time as Americans pushed ever further west.

Americans, entering a new territory, had to create new institutions out of a raw, unsettled, and primitive setting. These institutions had to serve the needs of a population made up of people who typically did not own the property they tilled and were roughly equal with one another. Turner believed that the availability of free land to be tamed by American settlers was what ensured the independence of thought that many foreign commentators, such as Alexis de Tocqueville and J. Hector St. John Crèvecoeur, had written about as a distinguishing feature of the American people. That independence filtered up to the national government, and Turner argues that the central ideas about the role of the government in the United States were first created on the frontier.

In terms of the development of American society, Turner argued that "this perennial rebirth, this fluidity of American life, this expansion westward with its new opportunities, its continuous touch with the simplicity of primitive society, furnish the forces dominating American character." Whereas the East Coast was the great commercial and cultural center of the nation at the time, Turner asserts that the forces that created American society were not furnished by immigrants from Europe but from the harsh experiences of settlers in the West. Turner argues that the West was where savagery met civilization, and the interaction between the two provided continual vitality to the progress of American society.

Turner's thesis asserts that the frontier process explains what he calls the "the first period of American history," but the unspoken corollary of Turner's thesis was that there was uncertainty at best as to what would happen during the next century, now that the availability of unsettled land in the West had been exhausted. His implicit conclusion is that, with the disappearance of the frontier, the United States could become more susceptible to the class tensions and social ills that he associated with Europe.

Essential Themes

Turner had his critics, even among his contemporaries. Another prominent historian of the time, Charles Beard, asserted that while the availability of free land was an important factor, that alone could not explain American development, but needed to be combined with the spread of agriculture and the presence of slavery, common labor, and capitalism. However, throughout the early twentieth century, it seemed that Turner's disciples outnumbered his critics. Some of Turner's most prominent adherents were Ray Allen Billington, whose book *Westward Expansion: A History of the American Frontier* (1949) relied heavily on the Turner thesis, and Walter Prescott Webb, who used the Turner thesis to explain the development of white American populations in various locations from the Great Plains to the Southwest.

Beginning in the 1960s, many historians began to turn away from Turner's triumphalist celebration of western individualism and egalitarianism. With the emergence of the field of new western history in the 1980s, Turner's frontier thesis fell further out of favor. The work of new western historians concentrate on aspects of America's frontier past that Turner and his disciples had never considered adequately in their work, arguing that factors other than the process of settling the frontier make the history of the American West distinctive. Further, new western historians have sought to illuminate the experiences of those not included in Turner's West, namely women, American Indians, and other minority groups. New western historian Patricia Nelson Limerick challenges many elements of the Turner thesis in her 1987 book *The Legacy of Conquest:*

The Unbroken Past of the American West; for example, Limerick highlights the cultural diversity of the West and the competition for resources among various ethnic groups as critical to the historical development of the region.

However, Turner's ideas have not been done away with completely. Contemporary adherents of the Turner thesis have accepted the fact that the new western historians added the experiences of previously overlooked groups to the historical study of the American West but assert that the Turner thesis is still useful as a tool to explain the progressive development of the United States through the advance of the frontier line. Furthermore, Turner's ideas have had a significant influence on the field of environmental history, which emerged in the 1980s and examines the influence of the regional environment on societal development in cultures worldwide. Well over a century after its initial presentation, Frederick Jackson Turner's frontier thesis still looms large in both historical discussions as well as dialogues over whether there is an exceptional nature to the American character.

—*Steven L. Danver, PhD*

Bibliography and Additional Reading

Cronon, William. *"Turner's First Stand: The Significance of Significance in American History."* Writing Western History: Essays on Major Western Historians. Ed. R. W. Etulain. Albuquerque: U of New Mexico P, 1991. 73–101. Print.

Gressley, Gene M. *"The Turner Thesis: A Problem in Historiography."* Agricultural History 32.4 (1958): 227–49. Print.

Limerick, Patricia Nelson, Clyde A. Milner II, and Charles E. Rankin, eds. *Trails: Toward a New Western History.* Lawrence: UP of Kansas, 1991. Print.

Turner, Frederick Jackson. *The Frontier in American History.* Rev. ed. Tucson: U of Arizona P, 1994. Print.

■ The March of the Flag

Date: September 16, 1898
Author: Albert J. Beveridge
Genre: speech

Summary Overview

By the close of the nineteenth century, Americans had done the impossible: they had occupied and settled an entire continent, and they had done it in a single generation. Beginning in the 1840s and completed by the 1890s, settlers and pioneers, mainly coming from the East, had rushed toward the Pacific in a mad orgy of construction, cultivation, and violence. Wherever they went they built towns and cities, laid track, and dispossessed what they considered to be a primitive native population. The force that drove them, beyond the promises of easy riches and the allure of fresh beginnings, was an absolute conviction that they were agents of God himself, tasked by holy writ to bring civilization to savagery. As the frontier finally closed and a new uncertain century loomed ahead, this sense of divine exceptionalism turned outward, toward places like Cuba, Puerto Rico, and the Philippines, culminating in the birth of American imperialism.

Defining Moment

Americans have always been fascinated by the West. The promises of opportunity, prosperity, and reinvention, along with the naturally fertile landscape of the Pacific coast, all coalesce to create an idea often too powerful to resist. Adventure, mystery, and danger, all serve to only sweeten the pot. In the mid-nineteenth century, a generation of Americans and newly-arrived immigrants took it upon themselves to follow the trails, or ride the rails, to a new, undiscovered country. Most of the pioneers who set off from places like Chicago and Independence, Missouri, went in the hopes of claiming a plot of land: a homestead that they could then pass on to future generations. Others followed news of gold and silver strikes, or promises of work in building the vast tracks meant to finally connect the two distant coasts.

All the while, as the government fanned the flames of expansion, as boosters drummed up excitement, a new philosophy was forming in the minds of many Americans, which aimed to explain what was fast becoming one of the largest migrations in human history. It was called Manifest Destiny, the singular belief that the United States generally, and Westward expansion specifically, were consecrated by the divine. Although the view was not universally accepted, most notably by many in the Republican party, the notion that God favored the growth of the United States over other nations, appealed strongly to those struggling to start over on the frontier. America was exceptional. Americans were exceptional, blessed by the Almighty in their deeds, whether that be building homesteads or driving Native peoples off their lands. Such notions of divine authority helped justify the annexation of Oregon Territory and the war with Mexico.

As the frontier finally closed in the 1890s, the notion of Manifest Destiny began to change. In this new version, America had a responsibility to spread its brand of exceptionalism beyond its shores. It was for the United States to civilize and pacify the savage world, to spread democracy, and further national interests. The argument made was that if America was destined to forever change the world, it needed to pursue a policy of perpetual expansion. In April 1898, bolstered by this new imperialist philosophy, the United States went to war against Spain. Officially sanctioned to liberate Cuba, Puerto Rico, and the Philippines from Spanish rule, the move was really made to gain those territories in order expand American interests. Immediately afterward, debate erupted between those for and against annexation. The arguments used would set American foreign policy for the next hundred years.

Author Biography

Albert Jeremiah Beveridge was born in Ohio in 1862. Hailing from an English background, Beveridge was raised with the same frontier attitudes as millions of Americans. To gain success and achieve God's will, one had to work hard and take rather than wait for something to be given. Growing in prominence as a pro-expansionist orator, often speaking on behalf of political candidates for major office, Beveridge was elected to the US Senate under the Republican ticket in 1899. A loyal Roosevelt progressive, Beveridge followed his former commander-in-chief to the Progressive Party in 1912, effectively ending his own political career. Eventually,

Beveridge became a historian, writing several highly influential works, including a biography of Justice John Marshall, which earned him a Pulitzer Prize. By the end of his life, the former firebrand imperialist began to regret many of his former expansionist leanings, and before his death in 1927, he gave many speeches warning about the unchecked growth of American power.

HISTORICAL DOCUMENT

It is a noble land that God has given us; a land that can feed and clothe the world; a land whose coastlines would inclose half the countries of Europe; a land set like a sentinel between the two imperial oceans of the globe, a greater England with a nobler destiny.

It is a mighty people that He has planted on this soil; a people sprung from the most masterful blood of history; a people perpetually revitalized by the virile, man ¬producing working ¬folk of all the earth; a people imperial by virtue of their power, by right of their institutions, by authority of their Heaven-directed purposes-the propagandists and not the misers of liberty.

It is a glorious history our God has bestowed upon His chosen people; a history heroic with faith in our mission and our future; a history of statesmen who flung the boundaries of the Republic out into unexplored lands and savage wilderness; a history of soldiers who carried the flag across blazing deserts and through the ranks of hostile mountains, even to the gates of sunset; a history of a multiplying people who overran a continent in half a century; a history of prophets who saw the consequences of evils inherited from the past and of martyrs who died to save us from them; a history divinely logical, in the process of whose tremendous reasoning we find ourselves today.

Therefore, in this campaign, the question is larger than a party question. It is an American question. It is a world question. Shall the American people continue their march toward the commercial supremacy of the world? Shall free institutions broaden their blessed reign as the children of liberty wax in strength, until the empire of our principles is established over the hearts of all mankind?

Have we no mission to perform no duty to discharge to our fellow man? Has God endowed us with gifts beyond our deserts and marked us as the people of His peculiar favor, merely to rot in our own selfishness, as men and nations must, who take cowardice for their companion and self for their deity—as China has, as India has, as Egypt has?

Shall we be as the man who had one talent and hid it, or as he who had ten talents and used them until they grew to riches? And shall we reap the reward that waits on our discharge of our high duty; shall we occupy new markets for what our farmers raise, our factories make, our merchants sell-aye, and please God, new markets for what our ships shall carry?

Hawaii is ours; Porto Rico is to be ours; at the prayer of her people Cuba finally will be ours; in the islands of the East, even to the gates of Asia, coaling stations are to be ours at the very least; the flag of a liberal government is to float over the Philippines, and may it be the banner that Taylor unfurled in Texas and Fremont carried to the coast.

The Opposition tells us that we ought not to govern a people without their consent. I answer, The rule of liberty that all just government derives its authority from the consent of the governed, applies only to those who are capable of self¬-government We govern the Indians without their consent, we govern our territories without their consent, we govern our children without their consent. How do they know what our government would be without their consent? Would not the people of the Philippines prefer the just, humane, civilizing government of this Republic to the savage, bloody rule of pillage and extortion from which we have rescued them?

And, regardless of this formula of words made only for enlightened, self-governing people, do we owe no duty to the world? Shall we turn these peoples back to the reeking hands from which we have taken them? Shall we abandon them, with Germany, England, Japan, hungering for them? Shall we save them from those nations, to give them a self¬ rule of tragedy?

They ask us how we shall govern these new possessions. I answer: Out of local conditions and the necessities of the case methods of government will grow. If England can govern foreign lands, so can America. If Germany can govern foreign lands, so can America. If they can supervise protectorates, so can America. Why is it more difficult to administer Hawaii than Nevs Mexico or California? Both had a savage and an alien population: both were more remote from the seat of government when they came under our dominion than the Philippines are to¬day.

Will you say by your vote that American ability to govern has decayed, that a century s experience in self¬rule has failed of a result? Will you affirm by your vote that you are an infidel to American power and practical sense? Or will you say that ours is the blood of government; ours the heart of dominion; ours the brain and genius of administration? Will you remember that we do but what our fathers did-we but pitch the tents of liberty farther westward, farther southward-we only continue the march of the flag?

The march of the flag! In 1789 the flag of the Republic waved over 4,000,000 souls in thirteen states, and their savage territory which stretched to the Mississippi, to Canada, to the Floridas. The timid minds of that day said that no new territory was needed, and, for the hour, they were right. But Jefferson, through whose intellect the centuries marched; Jefferson, who dreamed of Cuba as an American state, Jefferson, the first Imperialist of the Republic-Jefferson acquired that imperial territory which swept from the Mississippi to the mountains, from Texas to the British possessions, and the march of the flag began!

The infidels to the gospel of liberty raved, but the flag swept on! The title to that noble land out of which Oregon, Washington, Idaho and Montana have been carved was uncertain: Jefferson, strict constructionist of constitutional power though he was, obeyed the Anglo¬Saxon impulse within him, whose watchword is, "Forward!": another empire was added to the Republic, and the march of the flag went on!

Those who deny the power of free institutions to expand urged every argument, and more, that we hear, to¬day; but the people's judgment approved the command of their blood, and the march of the flag went on!

A screen of land from New Orleans to Florida shut us from the Gulf, and over this and the Everglade Peninsula waved the saffron flag of Spain; Andrew Jackson seized both, the American people stood at his back, and, under Monroe, the Floridas came under the dominion of the Republic, and the march of the flag went on! The Cassandras prophesied every prophecy of despair we hear, to¬day, but the march of the flag went on!

Then Texas responded to the bugle calls of liberty, and the march of the flag went on! And, at last, we waged war with Mexico, and the flag swept over the southwest, over peerless California, past the Gate of Gold to Oregon on the north, and from ocean to ocean its folds of glory blazed.

And, now, obeying the same voice that Jefferson heard and obeyed, that Jackson heard and obeyed, that Monroe heard and obeyed, that Seward heard and obeyed, that Grant heard and obeyed, that Harrison heard and obeyed, our President today plants the flag over the islands of the seas, outposts of commerce, citadels of national security, and the march of the flag goes on!

Distance and oceans are no arguments. The fact that all the territory our fathers bought and seized is contiguous, is no argument. In 1819 Florida was farther from New York than Porto Rico is from Chicago today; Texas, farther from Washington in 1845 than Hawaii is from Boston in 1898; California, more inaccessible in 1847 than the Philippines are now. Gibraltar is farther from London than Havana is from Washington; Melbourne is farther from Liverpool than Manila is from San Francisco.

The ocean does not separate us from lands of our duty and desire—the oceans join us, rivers never to be dredged, canals never to be re paired. Steam joins us; electricity joins us—the very elements are in league with our destiny. Cuba not contiguous? Porto Rico not contiguous! Hawaii and the Philippines not contiguous! The oceans make them contiguous. And our navy will make them contiguous.

But the Opposition is right—there is a difference.

We did not need the western Mississippi Valley when we acquired it, nor Florida! nor Texas, nor California, nor the royal provinces of the far northwest We had no emigrants to people this imperial wilderness, no money to develop it, even no highways to cover it. No trade awaited us in its savage fastnesses. Our productions were not greater than our trade There was not one reason for the land¬lust of our statesmen from Jefferson to Grant, other than the prophet and the Saxon within them But, to¬day, we are raising more than we can consume, making more than we can use. Therefore we must find new markets for our produce.

And so, while we did not need the territory taken during the past century at the time it was acquired, we do need what we have taken irl 18981 and we need it now. The resource and the commerce of the immensely rich dominions will be increased as much as American energy is greater than Spanish sloth.

In Cuba, alone, there are 15,000,000 acres of forest unacquainted with the ax, exhaustless mines of iron, priceless deposits of manganese, millions 0f dollars' worth of which we must buy, to¬day, from the Black Sea districts There are millions of acres yet unexplored.

The resources of Porto Rico have only been trifled with. The riches of the Philippines have hardly been touched by the finger¬tips of modern methods. And they produce what we consume, and consume what we produce—the very predestination of reciprocity—a reciprocity "not made with hands, eternal in the heavens." They sell hemp, sugar, cocoanuts, fruits of the tropics, timber of price like mahogany; they buy flour, clothing, tools, implements, machinery and all that we can raise and make. Their trade will be ours in time. Do you indorse that policy with your vote?

Cuba is as large as Pennsylvania, and is the richest spot on the globe. Hawaii is as large as New Jersey; Porto Rico half as large as Hawaii; the Philippines larger than all New England, New York, New Jersey and Delaware combined. Together they are larger than the British Isles, larger than France, larger than Germany, larger than Japan.

If any man tells you that trade depends on cheapness and not on government influence, ask him why England does not abandon South Africa, Egypt, India. Why does France seize South China, Germany the vast region whose port is Kaou-chou?

Our trade with Porto Rico, Hawaii and the Philippines must be as free as between the states of the Union, because they are American territory, while every other nation on earth must pay our tariff before they can compete with us. Until Cuba shall ask for annexation, our trade with her will, at the very least, be like the preferential trade of Canada with England. That, and the excellence of our goods and products; that, and the convenience of traffic; that, and the kinship of interests and destiny, will give the monopoly of these markets to the American people.

The commercial supremacy of the Republic means that this Nation is to be the sovereign factor in the peace of the world. For the conflicts of the future are to be conflicts of trade, struggles for markets, commercial wars for existence. And the golden rule of peace is impregnability of position and invincibility of preparedness. So, we see England, the greatest strategist of history, plant her flag and her cannon on Gibraltar, at Quebec, in the Bermudas, at Vancouver, everywhere.

So Hawaii furnishes us a naval base in the heart of the Pacific; the Ladrones another, a voyage further on; Manila another, at the gates of Asia—Asia, to the trade of whose hundreds of millions American merchants, manufacturers, farmers, have as good right as those of Germany or France or Russia or England; Asia, whose commerce with the United Kingdom alone amounts to hundreds of millions of dollars every year; Asia, to whom Germany looks to take her surplus products; Asia, whose doors must not be shut against American trade. Within five decades the bulk of Oriental commerce will be ours.

No wonder that, in the shadows of coming events so great, free-silver is already a memory. The current of history has swept past that episode. Men understand, today, the greatest commerce of the world must be conducted with the steadiest standard of value and most convenient medium of exchange human ingenuity can devise. Time, that unerring reasoner, has settled the silver question. The American people are tired of talking about money—they want to make it.

. . . .

There are so many real things to be done-canals to be dug, railways to be laid, forests to be felled, cities to be builded, fields to be tilled, markets to be won, ships to be launched, peoples to be saved, civilization to be proclaimed and the Rag of liberty Hung to the eager air of every sea. Is this an hour to waste upon triflers with nature's laws? Is this a season to give our destiny over to word¬mongers and prosperity-wreckers? No! It is an hour to remember our duty to our homes. It is a moment to realize the opportunities fate has opened to us. And so is all hour for us to stand by the Government.

Wonderfully has God guided us Yonder at Bunker Hill and Yorktown. His providence was above us At New Orleans and on ensanguined seas His hand sustained us. Abraham Lincoln was His minister and His was the altar of freedom the Nation's soldiers set up on a hundred battle¬fields. His power directed Dewey in the East and delivered the Spanish fleet into our hands, as He delivered the elder Armada into the hands of our English sires two centuries ago [Note—actually in 1588]. The American people can not use a dishonest medium of exchange; it is ours to set the world its example of right and honor. We can not fly from our world duties; it is ours to execute the purpose of a fate that has driven us to be greater than our small intentions. We can not retreat from any soil where Providence has unfurled our banner; it is ours to save that soil for liberty and civilization.

GLOSSARY

constructionist: one who adheres to a conservative legal philosophy which limits interpretation to a strict reading of the applicable text

contiguous: sharing a common border

protectorate: a state that is controlled and protected by another

Document Analysis

In a campaign speech given in late 1898, Albert Beveridge is arguing for annexation of the former Spanish colonies won during the Spanish-American War, but generally, he is also pushing for a policy of unrestrained imperialism. In his opinion, the United States has only to gain by expanding outward beyond its borders—new resources, new markets, and most importantly, a new progression in American authority.

The speech begins with the language of Manifest Destiny. God is invoked several times to describe the special place that America holds in the world. Americans are the chosen people, placed on Earth, on this continent to transform it into a new Eden and, from there, strike out to build God's kingdom across the whole of the world. Over the nineteenth century, Beveridge argues, thanks to the will of great thinking men such as Thomas Jefferson, the United States was transformed from a savage wilderness into a glorious new republic. But if the nation were to stop there, if expansion were to stop with the conquering of the West, Beveridge warns, America will slide backward, becoming something more closely resembling China, or India, or Egypt—a once great empire, now only a shadow of itself.

For Beveridge, the projection of American power is not governance of others without consent, it is the right and responsibility of the American people. How are the populations of places like Cuba and the Philippines to govern themselves when they are incapable of self-rule? Much like the civilized European imperial powers, America must serve as a shepherd, a parent caring for undeveloped children. In the process, the United States stands to gain wealth and resources, which it can then use to better rule over those inferior nations. This imperialist credo, Beveridge continues, is nothing new in American history. It has been a driving force since the nation's founding and must continue to be. Not only out of duty to God, but to the world as a whole. Because America is the driving force for good and freedom throughout the globe. Without the leadership of the United States, Beveridge hints, conflict may be unavoidable in the future.

Beyond Beveridge's arguments for God, for destiny,

and markets, is the persistent use of the march as a rhetorical device: marching westward, marching forward, marching always toward progress. In this way, Beveridge is able to make an argument for imperialism based not just in a sense of Manifest Destiny, linked to the work of the Founding Fathers, but also as biological inevitability. To resist expansion is to resist the very course of social evolution. It is tantamount to reverting to a more primitive state.

Essential Themes

Drawing on the ideas comprising Manifest Destiny, but also Social Darwinism, evangelism, and patriotism, Albert Beveridge tried to pull together past, present, and future, to make a case for a new, aggressive American imperialism. Built on the foundation of America's breathtaking westward expansion, his speech made a case for a new world order, in which the somewhat isolationist United States would play the role of global leader. The benefits, according to Beveridge were clear: resources; new markets; safety; and, above all, progress. It was a vision of unrelenting, limitless progress, toward a sort of new American utopia. This new imperialism wasn't a choice. It had to happen. It would happen. The very forces of history demanded it.

This speech and others, given by the leading politicians of the time, served to slowly turn American foreign policy increasingly outward. Despite the inherent racism and militarism of such policies, defenders of American expansionism argued that it was a sort of benevolent imperialism. As the United States was a just and democratic nation, it would rule others in a just and democratic fashion. Not strictly for the benefit of the United States, but for that of all nations. Besides, the form of American rule would not be the type practiced by other nations. It would be less direct, more directorial.

After the Spanish-American War, which the expansionists upheld as a bright example of the righteousness of their ideology, America followed a course of increased internationalism, colored by imperialism. Cuba, Puerto Rico, and the Philippines all fell under the sphere of American influence, a state of affairs which served to create long standing resentments and, at times, even open conflict. Although official policy shifted over the course of the twentieth century from one of annexation to intervention, many of the same arguments made by the likes of Albert Beveridge—ideas that America was the sole champion of democracy and freedom, that American exceptionalism demanded that the United States serve as a global leader—remain central to American foreign policy to this day. Recent conflicts in the Middle East, interventions in Central and South America, even the War in Vietnam, are all legacies of America's imperial past, born out of the religious fervor of the settling of the West.

—KP Dawes, MA

Bibliography and Additional Reading

Braeman, John. *Albert J. Beveridge: American Nationalist*. Chicago: U of Chicago P, 1971. Print.

Howe, Daniel Walker. *What Hath God Wrought: The Transformation of America, 1815–1848*. New York: Oxford UP, 2007. Print.

Kinzer, Stephen. *Overthrow: America's Century of Regime Change from Hawaii to Iraq*. New York: Time Books, 2006. Print.

Morgan, Robert. *Lions of the West*. Chapel Hill: Algonquin Books, 2012. Print.

Appendixes

Chronological List

Web Resources

pbs.org/weta/thewest

Offers an array of source materials linked to the PBS/WETA documentary film series The West, including lesson plans and additional resources.

lcweb2/loc.gov/ammem/amrvhtml/conshome.html

From the Library of Congress's American Memory project, a useful collection of materials relating to the emergence of the conservation movement in the United States.

csvivc.csi.cuny.edu/westweb/files/

WestWeb is a topically-organized website about the study of the American West created and maintained by born-and-bred Westerner Catherine Lavender of the Department of History, College of Staten Island, City University of New York.

digital.denverlibrary.org/cdm/photographs/

30,000 photographs pertaining to the West from the Denver Public Library.

publications.newberry.org/frontiertoheartland/

Based on the world-renowned collections of the Newberry Library in Chicago, "Frontier to Heartland" offers access to historical primary sources, scholarly perspectives on the past, and more.

theautry.org/research/women-of-the-west

From the Autry National Center, "Women of the West" provides resources for understanding women's contribution to western history and culture.

kmorrissey.faculty.arizona.edu/web_resources

From Professor Katherine Morrissey of the University of Arizona, a list of web resources featuring academic centers devoted to the study of the West.

Bibliography

Aarim-Heriot, Najia. *Chinese Immigrants, African Americans, and Racial Anxiety in the United States, 1848–82.* Urbana: U of Illinois P, 2006. Print.

"A Brief History of William F. 'Buffalo Bill' Cody." *Buffalo Bill Museum & Grave,* n.d. Web. 17 Oct. 2014.

Almaguer, Tomas. "'They Can Be Hired in Masses; They Can Be Managed and Controlled Like Unthinking Slaves.'" *Race and Racialization: Essential Readings.* Ed. Tania Das Gupta et al. Toronto: Canadian Scholars', 2007. 217–31. Print.

Ambrose, Stephen E. *Crazy Horse and Custer: The Parallel Lives of Two American Warriors.* New York: Anchor Books, 1996. Print.

Ambrose, Stephen E. *Nothing Like It in the World: The Men Who Built the Transcontinental Railroad, 1863–1869.* New York: Simon and Schuster, 2000. Print.

Bagley, Will. *So Rugged and Mountainous: Blazing the Trails to Oregon and California, 1812–1848.* Norman: U of Oklahoma P, 2010. Print.

Bailey, Lynn R. *Bosque Redondo: The Navajo Internment at Fort Sumner, New Mexico, 1863–68.* Tucson, AZ: Westernlore, 2000. Print.

Bain, David Hayward. *Empire Express: Building the First Transcontinental Railroad.* New York: Penguin Books, 1999. Print.

Barra, Allen. *Inventing Wyatt Earp: His Life and Many Legends.* New York: Carol & Graf, 1998. Print.

Beasley, Conger. *We Are a People in this World: The Lakota Sioux and the Massacre at Wounded Knee.* Fayetteville: U of Arkansas P, 1995. Print.

Bederman, Gail. *Manliness and Civilization: A Cultural History of Gender and Race in the United States, 1880–1917.* Chicago: U of Chicago P, 1995. Print.

"Biographies of the Secretaries of State: William Henry Seward." U.S. Department of State, n.d. Web. 13 Oct. 2014.

Billington, Ray Allen. *Westward Expansion: A History of the American Frontier,* 5th ed. New York: Macmillan, 1982. Print.

"Billy the Kid." *American Experience.* Dir. Joe Maggio. PBS, 2011. Web. 21 Oct. 2014.

Blackstone, Sarah J. *The Business of Being Buffalo Bill.* New York: Praeger, 1988. Print.

Blake, David Haven, & Michael Robertson. *Walt Whitman, Where the Future becomes Present.* Iowa City: U of Iowa P, 2008. Print.

Bloom, John Porter, ed. *The Treaty of Guadalupe Hidalgo, 1848.* Las Cruces: Yucca Tree, 1999. Print.

Braeman, John. Albert J. *Beveridge: American Nationalist.* Chicago: U of Chicago P, 1971. Print.

Branch, E. Douglas, J. Frank Dobie (introduction), & Andrew C. Isenberg (introduction). *The Hunting of the Buffalo.* 1929. Lincoln: U of Nebraska P, 1997. Print.

Brands, H. W. *The Age of Gold: The California Gold Rush and the New American Dream. Rev. ed.* New York: Random, 2002. Print.

Bridger, Bobby. *Buffalo Bill and Sitting Bull: Inventing the Wild West.* Austin: U of Texas P, 2002. Print.

Brooks, N.C. *A Complete History of the Mexican War.* Philadelphia: Grigg, Elliot & Co., 1849. Internet Archive, 2009. Web. 17 Oct. 2014.

Brown, Dee. *Bury My Heart at Wounded Knee.* 1970. New York: Holt, 2007. Print.

Brown, Dee. *Bury My Heart at Wounded Knee: An Indian History of the American West.* New York: Bantam, 1970. Print.

Brown, Sharon. "Women on the Overland Trails—A Historical Perspective." *Overland Journal* 2.1 (1984): 35–39. Print.

Buckland, Roscoe L. *Frederic Remington: The Writer.* New York: Twayne, 2000. Print.

Camp, Edgar Whittlesey. "Hugh C. Murray: California's Youngest Chief Justice." *California Historical Society Quarterly* 20.4 (1941): 365–73. Print.

Carter, Robert A. *Buffalo Bill Cody: The Man Behind the Legend.* New York: John Wiley & Sons, 2000. Print.

Chaffin, Tom. *Pathfinder: John Charles Fremont and the Course of American Empire.* 2002. Norman: U of Oklahoma P, 2014. Print.

Chan, Sucheng. *Asian Americans: An Interpretive History.* New York: Twayne, 1991. Print.

Chemerka, William R. *Juan Seguín: Tejano Leader.* Houston: Bright Sky, 2012. Print.

Cronon, William. "Turner's First Stand: The Significance of Significance in American History." *Writing Western History: Essays on Major Western Historians.* Ed. R. W. Etulain. Albuquerque: U of New Mexico P, 1991. 73–101. Print.

"Custer's Last Stand." *American Experience.* Dir. Stephen Ives. PBS, 2012. Film.

Czajka, Christopher W. "The Descent of Civilization: The Extermination of the American Buffalo." *Fron-*

tier House. PBS, 2014. Web. 13 Oct. 2014.

Daniels, Roger. *Asian America: Chinese and Japanese in the United States since 1850.* Seattle: U of Washington P, 1988. Print.

Debo, Angie. *Geronimo.* Norman, Oklahoma: U of Oklahoma P, 1976, reprinted 2012. Print.

Dehler, Gregory J. *Chester Alan Arthur: The Life of a Gilded Age Politician and President.* Hauppauge: Nova, 2007. Print.

Denetdale, Jennifer. *The Long Walk: The Forced Navajo Exile.* New York: Chelsea House, 2008. Print.

"Diaries, Memoirs, Letters, and Reports along the Trails West." *The Overland Trail.* Elizabeth Larson, n.d. Web. 25 Mar. 2013.

Dillon, Richard. *Fool's Gold: The Decline and Fall of Captain John Sutter of California.* Sanger, CA: Write Thought, 2012. Print.

DiSilvestro, Roger L. *In the Shadow of Wounded Knee: The Untold Final Chapter of the Indian Wars.* New York: Walker, 2007. Print.

Di Silvestro, Roger L. *Theodore Roosevelt in the Badlands: A Young Politician's Quest for Recovery in the American West.* New York: Walker Publishing, 2011. Print.

Donovan, James. *A Terrible Glory: Custer and the Little Bighorn—the Last Great Battle of the American West.* New York: Back Bay Books, 2008. Print.

Driggs, Howard R., & William Henry Jackson. *The Pony Express Goes Through; an American Saga Told by Its Heroes.* New York: Frederick A. Stokes, 1935. Print.

Dunbar-Ortiz, Roxanne. *An Indigenous People's History of the United States.* Boston: Beacon Press, 2014. Print.

Eastman, Charles Alexander (Ohiyesa). *From the Deep Woods to Civilization.* Rpt. Mineola: Dover, 2003. Print.

Espiritu, Yen Le. *Home Bound: Filipino American Lives across Cultures, Communities, and Countries.* Berkeley: U of California P, 2009. Print.

Flood, Renee Sansom. *Lost Bird of Wounded Knee: Spirit of the Lakota.* Cambridge: Da Capo, 1998. Print.

Folsom, Ed, & Kenneth M. Price, eds. *Walt Whitman Archive.* Center for Digital Research in the Humanities at the University of Nebraska–Lincoln, 2014. Web. 20 Feb. 2014.

Fox, Stephen. *American Conservation Movement: John Muir and his Legacy.* Madison: U of Wisconsin P, 1986. Print.

Fremont, John C., Donald Jackson, & Mary Lee Spen-

ce, eds. *The Expeditions of John Charles Fremont.* Vol. 1 "Travels from 1838 to 1844." Urbana: U of Illinois P, 1970. Web. 13 Oct. 2014.

Fremont, John C., with Anne F. Hyde (introduction). *Fremont's First Impressions: The Original Report of his Exploring Expeditions of 1842–1844.* Lincoln: U of Nebraska P, 2012. Print.

Frizzell, Lodisa. *Across the Plains to California in 1852: Journal of Mrs. Lodisa Frizzell.* Ed. Victor Hugo Paltsits. 1915. Project Gutenberg, 2010. E-book. Web. 25 Mar. 2013.

Fryer, Judith. *"The Anti-Mythical Journey: Westering Women's Diaries and Letters."* Old Northwest 9.1 (1983): 77–90. Print.

Galdeano, Daniel. *"Juan Seguín: A Paradox in the Annals of Texas History."* Seguín Family Historical Society. Seguín Family Historical Society, n.d. Web. 14 Mar. 2013.

Garcia y Griego, Manuel. "Persistence and Disintegration: New Mexico's Community Land Grants in Historical Perspective." *Natural Resources Journal* 48.4 (2008): 847–56. Academic Search Premier. Web. 12 Aug. 2012.

Gardner, Mark Lee. *To Hell on a Fast Horse: Billy the Kid, Pat Garrett, and the Epic Chase to Justice in the Old West.* New York: HarperCollins, 2010. Print.

Genetin-Pilawa, C. Joseph. *Crooked Paths to Allotment: The Fight over Federal Indian Policy After the Civil War.* Chapel Hill: U of North Carolina P, 2014. Print.

Geronimo & S.M. Barrett. *Geronimo's Story of His Life.* New York: Duffield & Co., 1906. Project Gutenberg, 2010. Web. 16 Oct. 2014.

Gibson, Arrell M. *Oklahoma: A History of Five Centuries.* 2nd ed. Norman: U of Oklahoma P, 2010. Print.

Glasrud, Bruce A., & Michael N. Searles, eds. *Buffalo Soldiers in the West: A Black Soldiers Anthology.* College Station: Texas A&M UP, 2007. Print.

Greenwald, Emily. *Reconfiguring the Reservation: The Nez Perces, Jicarilla Apaches, and the Dawes Act.* Albuquerque: U of New Mexico P, 2002. Print.

Gressley, Gene M. "The Turner Thesis: A Problem in Historiography." *Agricultural History* 32.4 (1958): 227–49. Print.

Griswold del Castillo, Richard. "Appendix 1: The Original Text of Articles IX and X of the Treaty of Guadalupe Hidalgo and the Protocol of Querétaro." *The Treaty of Guadalupe Hidalgo: A Legacy of Conflict.* Norman: U of Oklahoma P, 1990. 179–82. Print.

Guin, Jeff. *The Last Gunfight: The Real Story of the*

Shootout at the O.K. Corral and How It Changed the American West. New York: Simon & Schuster, 2011. Print.

Gunn, J. M. "The Pony Express." *Annual Publication of the Historical Society of Southern California and Pioneer Register,* Los Angeles 5.2 (1901): 168–75. Web. 17 Oct. 2014.

Gwartney, Debra. "Plucked from the Grave: The First Female Missionary to Cross the Continental Divide Came to a Gruesome End Partly Caused by Her Own Zeal. What Can Learn from Her?" *American Scholar* 80.3 (2011), 71–81. Print.

Gyory, Andrew. *Closing the Gate: Race, Politics, and the Chinese Exclusion Act.* Chapel Hill: U of North Carolina P, 1998. Print.

Hampton, Bruce. *Children of Grace: The Nez Perce War of 1877. 1994. Lincoln:* U of Nebraska P, 2002. Print.

Heidler, David Stephen, & Jeanne T. Heidler. *Daily Lives of Civilians in Wartime Modern America: From the Indian Wars to the Vietnam War.* Westport: Greenwood, 2007. Print.

Henderson, Timothy J. *A Glorious Defeat: Mexico and Its War with the United States.* New York: Farrar, 2007. Print.

Henderson, Timothy J. *A Glorious Defeat: Mexico and Its War with the United States.* New York: Hill and Wang, 2008. Print.

Hernández, Sonia. *"The Legacy of the Treatyof GuadalupeHidalgo on Tejanos' Land."* Journal of Popular Culture 35.2 (2001): 101. Print.

Hittman, Michael. *Wovoka and the Ghost Dance.* Ed. Don Lynch. Expanded ed. Lincoln: U of Nebraska P, 1997. Print

Hoig, Stan. *The Oklahoma Land Rush of 1889.* Oklahoma City: Oklahoma Hist. Soc., 1989. Print.

Holliday, J. S. *The World Rushed In: The California Gold Rush Experience.* New York: Simon, 1981. Print.

Hornaday, William T. *The Extermination of the American Bison.* Washington, D.C.: Smithsonian Institution, 1889. Project Gutenberg, 2006. Web. 13 Oct. 2014.

Howe, Daniel Walker. *What Hath God Wrought: The Transformation of America, 1815–1848.* New York: Oxford UP, 2007. Print.

Hoxie, Frederick E. *A Final Promise: The Campaign to Assimilate the Indians, 1880–1920.*

Hurtado, Albert L. *John Sutter: A Life on the North American Frontier.* Norman: U of Oklahoma P, 2006.

Print.

Iverson, Peter. *Diné: A History of the Navajos.* Albuquerque: U of New Mexico P, 2002. Print.

Jackson, Cathy M. "The Making of an American Outlaw Hero: Jesse James, Folklore and Late Nineteenth-Century Print Media." PhD dissertation, University of Missouri-Columbia, 2004. Print.

Jaksic, Ivan. *The Hispanic World and American Intellectual Life, 1820–1880.* Hampshire: Palgrave, 2012. Print.

"Jesse James." *American Experience.* Dir. Mark Zwonitzer. PBS, 2006. Film.

Johnson, Kevin R. *Immigration, Citizenship, and U.S./ Mexico Relations. Bilingual Review* 25.1 (2000): 23–39. Print.

Jones, Karen. "'My Winchester Spoke to Her': Crafting the Northern Rockies as a Hunter's Paradise, c.1870–1910." *American Nineteenth Century History* 11.2 (2010), p. 183–203. Print.

Josephy, Alvin M., Jr. *Nez Perce Country.* Lincoln: U of Nebraska P, 2007. Print.

Kehoe, Alice Beck. *The Ghost Dance: Ethnohistory and Revitalization.* New York: Holt, 1989. Print.

Kelman, Ari. *A Misplaced Massacre: Struggling over the Memory of Sand Creek.* Cambridge: Harvard UP, 2013. Print.

Kessell, John L. "General Sherman and the Navajo Treaty of 1868: A Basic and Expedient Misunderstanding," *Western Historical Quarterly* 12 (1981). Print.

Keyes, Sarah. "'Like a Roaring Lion': The Overland Trail as a Sonic Conquest." *Journal of American History* 96.1 (2009), 19–43. Print.

Kinzer, Stephen. *Overthrow: America's Century of Regime Change from Hawaii to Iraq.* New York: Time Books, 2006. Print.

Lacy, Ann, & Anne Valley-Fox, eds. *Stories from Hispano New Mexico: A New Mexico Federal Writers' Project Book.* Santa Fe: Sunstone P, 2012.

Lai, Him Mark. *Becoming Chinese American: A History of Communities and Institutions.* Walnut Creek: AltaMira, 2004. Print.

Lamar, Howard R., ed. *The New Encyclopedia of the American West.* New Haven: Yale UP, 1998. Print.

Lanehart, David. "Regaining Dinetah: The Navajo and the Indian Peace Commission at Fort Sumner." *Working the Range: Essays on the History of Western Land Management and the Environment.* Ed. John R. Wunder. Westport, CT, Praeger, 1985. Print.

Lee, Erika. *At America's Gates: Chinese Immigration during the Exclusion Era, 1882–1943.* Chapel Hill: U of North Carolina P, 2007. Print.

Limerick, Patricia Nelson, Clyde A. Milner II, and Charles E. Rankin, eds. *Trails: Toward a New Western History.* Lawrence: UP of Kansas, 1991. Print.

Limerick, Patricia Nelson. *The Legacy of Conquest: The Unbroken Past of the American West.* New York: Norton, 1987. Print.

Magoc, Chris J. *Yellowstone: The Creation and Selling of an American Landscape, 1870–1903.* Albuquerque, NM: U of New Mexico P, 1999. Print.

Mahin, Dean B. *Olive Branch and Sword: the United States and Mexico, 1845–1848.* Jefferson: McFarland, 1997. Print.

Manaev, Georgy. "Why Did Russia Sell Alaska to the United States?" *Russia Beyond the Headlines. Rossiyskaya Gazeta,* 20 Apr. 2014. Web. 13 Oct. 2014.

Marks, Paula Mitchell. *And Die in the West: The Story of the O.K. Corral Gunfight.* Norman, OK: U of Oklahoma P, 1989. Print.

McClain, Charles J. *In Search of Equality: The Chinese Struggle against Discrimination in Nineteenth-Century America.* Berkeley: U of California P, 1994. Print.

McGlashan, C. F. *History of the Donner Party. 1881.* Palo Alto, California: Stanford UP, 1940. Print.

McLynn, Frank. *Wagons West: The Epic Story of America's Overland Trails.* London: Cape, 2002. Print.

McMurtry, Larry. *Anything for Billy: A Novel.* New York: Simon & Schuster, 2001. Print.

Menard, Andrew. "Down the Santa Fe Trail to the City upon a Hill." *Western American Literature* 45.2 (2010): 162–188. Print.

Menchaca, Martha. *Recovering History, Constructing Race: The Indian, Black, and White Roots of Mexican Americans.* Austin: U of Texas P, 2001. Print.

Meringolo, Denise D. *Museums, Monuments, and National Parks: Toward a New Genealogy of Public History.* Amherst, MA: U of Massachusetts P, 2012. Print.

Merry, Robert W. *A Country of Vast Designs: James K. Polk, the Mexican War, and the Conquest of the American Continent.* New York: Simon, 2009. Print.

Meyer, Richard E. "The Outlaw: A Distinctive American Folktype." *Journal of the Folklore Institute* 17.2/3 (1980): 94–124. Web. 30 Sept. 2014.

"Milestones: 1830–1860." *Office of the Historian.* Bureau of Public Affairs, United States Department of State, 2010. Web. 15 Mar. 2013.

Mills, Charles. *The Chinese Exclusion Act and American Labor. Alexandria:* Apple Cheeks, 2009. Print.

Montejano, David. *Anglos and Mexicans in the Making of Texas, 1836–1986.* Austin: U of Texas P, 1994. Print.

Mooney, James. *The Ghost-Dance Religion and Sioux Outbreak of 1890: Fourteenth Annual Report of the Bureau of Ethnology.* Washington: GPO, 1896. Print.

Mooney, James. *The Ghost-Dance Religion and the Sioux Outbreak of 1890. 1892.* Lincoln: U of Nebraska P, 1991. Print.

Morgan, Robert. *Lions of the West.* Chapel Hill: Algonquin Books, 2012. Print.

Morris, Edmund. *The Rise of Theodore Roosevelt.* New York: Random House, 1979. Print.

Muir, John. *The Yosemite.* 1912. The Sierra Club, 2003 Web. 13 Oct. 2014.

Murphy, Virginia Reed. *Across the Plains in the Donner Party.* Silverthorne, CO: Vistabooks, 1995. Print.

Neihardt, John G. *Black Elk Speaks: Being the Life Story of a Holy Man of the Oglala Sioux.* Lincoln: U of Nebraska P, 1932. Print.

Ngai, Mae M. *Impossible Subjects: Illegal Aliens and the Making of Modern America.* Princeton: Princeton UP, 2004. Print.

Niehardt, John G. *Black Elk Speaks: Being the Life of a Holy Man of the Oglala Sioux.* Premier ed. Albany: State U of New York P, 2008. Print.

"Obituary: Old Apache Chief Geronimo Is Dead." *The New York Times, On this Day: February 18, 1909. New York Times* Company, 18 Feb. 2010. Web. 16 Oct. 2014.

Ohrt, Wallace. *Defiant Peacemaker: Nicholas Trist in the Mexican War.* College Station: Texas A; M UP, 1997. Print.

Osborne, Thomas J. *Pacific Eldorado: A History of Greater California.* New York: Wiley-Blackwell, 2013. Print.

Owens, Kenneth N., ed. *John Sutter and a Wider West.* Rev. ed. Lincoln: U of Nebraska P, 2002. Print.

"Pablo de la Guerra Speaks Out against Injustice." *Santa Barbara Independent. Santa Barbara Independent,* 2 Aug. 2007. Web. 12 Aug. 2012.

Paredes, Américo. *George Washington Gómez: A Mexicotexan Novel.* Houston: Arte Publico, 1990. Print.

Patent, Dorothy Hinshaw, & William Munoz. *The Buffalo and the Indians: A Shared Destiny.* Boston: Houghton Mifflin Harcourt, 2006. Print.

Perrottet, Tony. "John Muir's Yosemite," *Smithsonian.com.* Smithsonian Institution, Jul. 2008. Web. 13

Oct. 2014.

Pfaelzer, Jean. *Driven Out: The Forgotten War against Chinese Americans.* New York: Random, 2007. Print.

Philbrick, Nathaniel. *The Last Stand: Custer, Sitting Bull, and the Battle of the Little Bighorn.* New York: Viking, 2010. Print.

"Prelude to War." *The U.S.-Mexican War (1846-1848).* PBS/KERA, 1995–2006. Web. 17 Oct. 20014.

Pringle, Catherine Sager. *Across the Plains in 1844.* c.1860. Archives of the West. West Film Project and WETA (PBS), 2001. Web. 25 Mar. 2013.

Prucha, Francis Paul. *American Indian Treaties: The History of a Political Anomaly.* Berkeley: U of California P, 1994. Print.

Prucha, Francis Paul. *The Great Father: The United States Government and the American Indian.* 2 vols. Lincoln: U of Nebraska P, 1995. Print.

Rarick, Ethan. *Desperate Passage: The Donner Party's Perilous Journey West.* New York: Oxford UP, 2008. Print.

Rawls, James J., and Walton Bean. *California: An Interpretive History.* 9th ed. Boston: McGraw, 2008. Print.

Reynolds, David S. *Walt Whitman's America: A Cultural Biography.* London: Vintage, 1996. Print.

Richardson, Heather Cox. *Wounded Knee: Party Politics and the Road to an American Massacre.* New York: Basic, 2010. Print.

Riches for All: The California Gold Rush and the World. Lincoln: U of Nebraska P, 2002. Print.

Roberts, David. *A New World: Kit Carson, John C. Fremont, and the Claiming of the American West.* New York: Simon & Schuster, 2001. Print.

Robinson, Forrest G. "Introduction: Rethinking California." *Rethinking History* 11.1 (2007): 1–9. Print.

Roessel, Ruth. *Navajo Stories of the Long Walk Period.* Tsaile, AZ: Navajo Community College Press, 1973. Print.

Royce, Sarah. *Across the Plains: Sarah Royce's Western Narrative.* Ed. Jennifer Dawes Adkison. Tucson: U of Arizona P, 2009. Print.

Rush for Riches: Gold Fever and the Making of California. Berkeley: U of California P, 1999. Print.

Sandmeyer, Elmer Clarence. *The Anti-Chinese Movement in California.* Urbana: U of Illinois P, 1991. Print.

Schlissel, Lillian. "Mothers and Daughters on the Western Frontier." *Frontiers: A Journal of Women Studies* 3.2 (1978): 29–33. Print.

Schroeder, John H. *Mr. Polk's War: American Opposition and Dissent, 1846–1848.* Madison: U of Wisconsin P, 1973. Print.

Schullery, Paul, & Lee Whittlesey. *Myth and History in the Creation of Yellowstone National Park.* Lincoln, NE: U of Nebraska P, 2003. Print.

Seguín, Juan N. "The Fate of the Tejanos, 1858." *American History* 135, Primary Documents. U. of South Alabama, 2009. Web. 14 Mar. 2013.

Settle, Raymond W., & Mary Lund Settle. *Saddles and Spurs: The Pony Express Saga.* Lincoln: U of Nebraska P, 1972. Print.

Seward, Frederick W. *Reminiscences of a War-Time Statesman and Diplomat 1830–1915.* New York: Putnam's Sons, 1916. Print.

Shetler, Douglas. "Monetary Aggregates Prior to the Civil War: A Closer Look." *Journal of Money, Credit; Banking* 5.4 (1973): 1000–1006. Print.

Slotkin, Richard. *Gunfighter Nation: The Myth of the Frontier in Twentieth-Century America.* Norman: U of Oklahoma P, 1998. Print.

Smith, Andrea. *Conquest: Sexual Violence and American Indian Genocide.* Cambridge, MA: South End, 2005.

Soennichsen, John. *The Chinese Exclusion Act of 1882.* Westport: Greenwood, 2011. Print.

Spence, Mary Lee. "John Charles Fremont" *Utah History to Go.* State of Utah, 2014. Web. 13 Oct. 2014.

Stahr, Walter. *Seward: Lincoln's Indispensable Man.* Boston: Simon & Schuster, 2012. Print.

Stannard, David E. *American Holocaust: The Conquest of the New World.* New York: Oxford UP, 1992. Print.

Starr, Kevin. *Americans and the California Dream, 1850–1915.* New York: Oxford UP, 1986. Print.

Stiles, T. J. *Jesse James: Last Rebel of the Civil War.* New York: Random House, 2002. Print.

Sturgis, Amy H. *Presidents from Hayes through McKinley: Debating the Issues in Pro and Con Primary Documents.* Westport: Greenwood, 2003. Print.

Sundberg, Lawrence D. *Dinétah: An Early History of the Navajo People.* Santa Fe, NM: Sunstone, 1995. Print.

Takaki, Ronald. *A History of Asian Americans: Strangers from a Different Shore.* Boston: Little, 1998. Print.

Tate, Michael L. *Indians and Immigrants: Encounters on the Overland Trails.* Norman: U of Oklahoma P, 2006. Print.

Tefertiller, Casey. *Wyatt Earp: The Life Behind the Legend.* New York: John Wiley & Sons, 1997. Print.

Thayer, Tolles. "Frederic Remington (1861–1909)"

Heilbrunn Timeline of Art History. The Metropolitan Museum of Art, 2014. Web. 13 Oct. 2014.

"The Donner Party." *American Experience.* Dir. Ric Burns. PBS. 1992. Film.

————. *The Great Father: The United States Government and the American Indians.* Lincoln: U of Nebraska P, 1984. Print.

"The John Muir Exhibit." *Sierra Club.* Sierra Club, 2014. Web. 13 Oct. 2014.

————. *The Nez Perce Indians and the Opening of the Northwest.* 1979. Boston: Houghton, 1997. Print.

"The Pony Express." Pony Express National Museum. Pony Express National Museum, 2014. Web. 15 Oct. 2014.

The West. Dir. Stephen Ives. PBS/WETA, 1996. Film.

Thompson, Erwin N. *Shallow Grave at Waiilatpu: The Sagers' West.* Portland: Western Imprints, 1985. Print.

Tian, Kelly. "The Chinese Exclusion Act of 1882 and Its Impact on North American Society." *Undergraduate Research Journal for the Human Sciences* 9 (2010): n. pag. Web. 16 Jan. 2014.

Trafzer, Clifford E. and Joel R. Hyer, eds. *Exterminate Them! Written Accounts of the Murder, Rape, and Slavery of Native Americans during the California Gold Rush, 1848–1868.* East Lansing: Michigan State UP, 1999. Print.

"Treaty of Guadalupe Hidalgo; February 2, 1848." *Treaties and Conventions between the United States of America and Other Powers since July 4, 1776.* Washington: GPO, 1871. Avalon Project. Web. 15 Mar. 2013.

"Treaty with Russia for the Purchase of Alaska." *Web Guides: Primary Documents in American History.* Library of Congress, 2012. Web. 13 Oct. 2014.

Truer, David. *Rez Life.* New York: Atlantic Monthly P, 2012. Print.

Turner, Frederick Jackson. *The Frontier in American History.* Rev. ed. Tucson: U of Arizona P, 1994. Print.

Unruh, John David. *The Plains Across: Emigrants, Wagon Trains, and the American West.* London Pimlico, 1992. Print.

U.S.-Mexican War: 1846–1848. KERA, 14 Mar. 2006. Web. 15 Mar. 2013.

US National Park Service. "Yellowstone National Park." *National Parks Service.* US Department of the Interior, 15 Sept. 2014. Web. 26 Sept. 2014.

Utley, Robert M. "Buffalo Soldiers" Fort Davis National Historic Site. *National Park Service,* 2002. Web. 13 Oct. 2014.

Utley, Robert M. *Geronimo.* New Haven: Yale UP, 2012. Print.

Utley, Robert M. *Last Days of the Sioux Nation.* 2nd ed. New Haven: Yale UP, 2004. Print.

Vaught, David. *After the Gold Rush: Tarnished Dreams in the Sacramento Valley.* Baltimore: Johns Hopkins UP, 2007. Print.

Vazquel, Josefina Zoraida. "War and Peace with the United States." *The Oxford History of Mexico.* Eds. Michael C. Meyer & William H. Beezley. Oxford: Oxford UP, 2000. Print.

Vehik, Susan C. "Conflict, Trade, and Political Development on the Southern Plains." *American Antiquity* 67.1 (2002): 37–64. Print.

Wadsworth, Ginger. *Words West: Voices of Young Pioneers.* New York: Clarion, 2003. Print.

Wallis, Michael. *Billy the Kid: The Endless Ride.* New York: W.W. Norton, 2007. Print.

Warren, Lois S. *Buffalo Bill's America: William Cody and the Wild West Show.* New York: Random House, 2005. Print.

Weber, David J., ed. *Foreigners in Their Native Land: Historical Roots of the Mexican Americans.* Albuquerque: U of New Mexico P, 1973. Print.

Weber, David J. *Spanish Frontier in North America.* New Haven: Yale UP, 2009. Print.

Wellman, Paul I. *A Dynasty of Western Outlaws.* Lincoln: U of Nebraska P, 1986. Print.

Werner, Emmy E. *Pioneer Children on the Journey West.* Boulder: Westview P, 1995. Print.

West, Elliot. *The Essential West: Collected Essays.* Norman: U of Oklahoma P, 2012. Print.

West, Elliot. *The Last Indian War: The Nez Perce Story.* New York: Oxford UP, 2009. Print.

White, Richard. *Railroaded: The Transcontinentals and the Making of Modern America.* New York: W. W. Norton, 2011. Print.

White, Richard. *The Roots of Dependency: Subsistence, Environment, and Social Change among the Choctaws, Pawnees, and Navajos.* Lincoln: University of Nebraska P, 1988. Print.

Whitman, Walt. *November Boughs.* Philadelphia: McKay, 1888. Print.

Wilkinson, Charles F. *American Indians, Time, and the Law: Native Societies in a Modern Constitutional Democracy.* New Haven, CT: Yale UP, 1987. Print.

Williams, John Hoyt. *A Great and Shining Road: The Epic Story of the Transcontinental Railway.* Lincoln: University of Nebraska Press, 1996. Print.

With Golden Visions Bright before Them: Trails to the Mining West, 1849–1852. Norman: U of Oklahoma P, 2012. Print.

Women's Diaries of the Westward Journey. New York: Schocken, 1992. Print.

Wong, K. Scott. "Cultural Defenders and Brokers: Chinese Responses to the Anti-Chinese Movement." *Claiming America: Constructing Chinese American Identities during the Exclusion Era.* Ed. Kevin Scott Wong and Sucheng Chan. Philadelphia: Temple UP, 1998. 3–40. Print.

Wooster, Robert. *The American Military Frontiers: The United States Army in the West, 1783–1900.* Albuquerque: U of New Mexico P, 2009. Print.

Wooster, Robert. *The Military and United States Indian Policy, 1865–1903.* Lincoln: U of Nebraska P, 1995. Print.

Worster, Donald. *A Passion for Nature: The Life of John Muir.* Oxford: Oxford UP, 2008. Print.

Yeatman, Ted P. *Frank and Jesse James: The Story Behind the Legend.* Nashville, TN: Cumberland House Publishing, 2000. Print.

Yung, J., G. H. Chang, and H. M. Lai, eds. *Chinese American Voices: From the Gold Rush to the Present.* Berkeley: U of California P, 2006. Print.

Index